Ethics in Research Practice and Innovation

Antonio Sandu
Stefan cel Mare University of Suceava, Romania

Ana Frunza
LUMEN Research Center in Social and Humanistic Sciences, Romania

Elena Unguru
University of Oradea, Romania

A volume in the Advances in Library and
Information Science (ALIS) Book Series

Published in the United States of America by
IGI Global
Information Science Reference (an imprint of IGI Global)
701 E. Chocolate Avenue
Hershey PA, USA 17033
Tel: 717-533-8845
Fax: 717-533-8661
E-mail: cust@igi-global.com
Web site: http://www.igi-global.com

Library of Congress Cataloging-in-Publication Data

Names: Sandu, Antonio, editor.
Title: Ethics in research practice and innovation / Antonio Sandu, Ana Frunza, and Elena Unguru, editors.
Description: Hersey, PA : Information Science Reference, [2019] | Includes bibliographical references.
Identifiers: LCCN 2018008110| ISBN 9781522563105 (hardcover) | ISBN 9781522563112 (ebook)
Subjects: LCSH: Research--Moral and ethical aspects.
Classification: LCC Q180.55.M67 E83716 2019 | DDC 174/.90014--dc23 LC record available at https://lccn.loc.gov/2018008110

This book is published in the IGI Global book series Advances in Library and Information Science (ALIS) (ISSN: 2326-4136; eISSN: 2326-4144)

British Cataloguing in Publication Data
A Cataloguing in Publication record for this book is available from the British Library.

For electronic access to this publication, please contact: eresources@igi-global.com.

Advances in Library and Information Science (ALIS) Book Series

Alfonso Ippolito
Sapienza University-Rome, Italy
Carlo Inglese
Sapienza University-Rome, Italy

ISSN:2326-4136
EISSN:2326-4144

Mission

The **Advances in Library and Information Science (ALIS) Book Series** is comprised of high quality, research-oriented publications on the continuing developments and trends affecting the public, school, and academic fields, as well as specialized libraries and librarians globally. These discussions on professional and organizational considerations in library and information resource development and management assist in showcasing the latest methodologies and tools in the field.

The **ALIS Book Series** aims to expand the body of library science literature by covering a wide range of topics affecting the profession and field at large. The series also seeks to provide readers with an essential resource for uncovering the latest research in library and information science management, development, and technologies.

Coverage

- Intellectual Freedom
- Recruitment of Library Professionals
- Conservation
- University Libraries in Developing Countries
- User Surveys and Focus Groups
- Library Budget Allocation
- Digital Library Economics
- Service Learning in Libraries
- Staffing and Salaries in the Library Field
- Librarian Education

IGI Global is currently accepting manuscripts for publication within this series. To submit a proposal for a volume in this series, please contact our Acquisition Editors at Acquisitions@igi-global.com or visit: http://www.igi-global.com/publish/.

The Advances in Library and Information Science (ALIS) Book Series (ISSN 2326-4136) is published by IGI Global, 701 E. Chocolate Avenue, Hershey, PA 17033-1240, USA, www.igi-global.com. This series is composed of titles available for purchase individually; each title is edited to be contextually exclusive from any other title within the series. For pricing and ordering information please visit http://www.igi-global.com/book-series/advances-library-information-science/73002. Postmaster: Send all address changes to above address.

Titles in this Series

For a list of additional titles in this series, please visit: www.igi-global.com/book-series

Literacy Skill Development for Library Science Professionals
S. Thanuskodi (Alagappa University, India)
Information Science Reference • copyright 2019 • 295pp • H/C (ISBN: 9781522571254) • US $175.00 (our price)

Innovative Applications of Knowledge Discovery and Information Resources Management
Susan Swayze (The George Washington University, USA) and Valerie Ford (ISP Global Communications LLC, USA)
Information Science Reference • copyright 2018 • 325pp • H/C (ISBN: 9781522558293) • US $195.00 (our price)

Library and Information Science in the Age of MOOCs
Anna Kaushik (University of Kota, India)
Information Science Reference • copyright 2018 • 309pp • H/C (ISBN: 9781522551461) • US $185.00 (our price)

Changing the Scope of Library Instruction in the Digital Age
Swati Bhattacharyya (University of California – Riverside, USA) and K Rama Patnaik (Indian Institute of Management Bangalore, India)
Information Science Reference • copyright 2018 • 286pp • H/C (ISBN: 9781522528029) • US $175.00 (our price)

Handbook of Research on Innovative Techniques, Trends, and Analysis for Optimized Research Methods
Victor X. Wang (Grand Canyon University, USA) and Thomas G. Reio Jr. (Florida International University, USA)
Information Science Reference • copyright 2018 • 445pp • H/C (ISBN: 9781522551645) • US $275.00 (our price)

Measuring the Validity of Usage Reports Provided by E-Book Vendors Emerging Research and Opportunities
Aiping Chen-Gaffey (Slippery Rock University of Pennsylvania, USA) and Heather Getsay (Slippery Rock University of Pennsylvania, USA)
Information Science Reference • copyright 2018 • 130pp • H/C (ISBN: 9781522532385) • US $135.00 (our price)

Examining the Emotional Dimensions of Academic Librarianship Emerging Research and Opportunities
Megan Lowe (University of Louisiana – Monroe, USA) and Lindsey M. Reno (University of New Orleans, USA)
Information Science Reference • copyright 2018 • 168pp • H/C (ISBN: 9781522537618) • US $145.00 (our price)

Handbook of Research on Managing Intellectual Property in Digital Libraries
Adeyinka Tella (University of Ilorin, Nigeria) and Tom Kwanya (The Technical University of Kenya, Kenya)
Information Science Reference • copyright 2018 • 461pp • H/C (ISBN: 9781522530930) • US $245.00 (our price)

IGI Global
DISSEMINATOR OF KNOWLEDGE

701 East Chocolate Avenue, Hershey, PA 17033, USA
Tel: 717-533-8845 x100 • Fax: 717-533-8661
E-Mail: cust@igi-global.com • www.igi-global.com

Editorial Advisory Board

Table of Contents

Section 2
Ethics of Research With Human Subjects

Section 3
Ethical Evaluation of Technologies and Responsibility Toward Their Implications for Humankind

Detailed Table of Contents

Ethics in research is a very important consideration that researchers and scientists all over the world should be aware and consciously recognize its importance. Ethics in research did not gloriously appear one day; it advanced and was perfected over time. It took the Nuremberg Code (1951), The Declaration of Helsinki (1964), The Belmont Report (1979), the APA Ethical guidelines (1947, 1953, 2002), and government regulations to assist in setting a guide to research ethics involving key principles to protect respondents. The focal point of ethics in research is to protect the respondents from harm and safeguard their dignity, anonymity, and confidentially. If the test subject is human, plant, or animal, there should be a humane way of handling test subjects. This chapter looks at research ethics and its relevance to post-grad students conducting research at a university. It is pivotal that students are aware of their ethical responsibility towards their test subjects/respondents whilst conducting their study.

The chapter aims to decipher some aspects (of form and content) of the codes of ethics that are present and in force within the representative academic communities in Romania. The main thesis is that in the Romanian university system there is still no unitary practice in respecting the norms of academic conduct, on the background of implicit university autonomy, which can explain some negative consequences recorded throughout the social life, from the pre-university education system to the decision-making structures.

The pressure to publish rapidly and constantly is a phenomenon engulfing academia in all countries of the globe. It has, over the years, affected research and innovation in a mostly negative way. In Nigerian universities in particular, this culture has mainly been a syndrome, manifested by (1) the urge among faculty members to publish more for promotions and positions than for genuine research production, (2) publishing for purely capitalistic motivations, (3) the use of unorthodox methodologies to boost citation index, and (4) fictive authorship of research works among others. All these objectionable practices have been responsible for various forms of decay in research and teaching in the Nigerian university system. They have, for instance, made plagiarism, data mining, predatory journals, duplicate publications, among other challenges, pervade research in Nigerian universities, causing innovation to remain more an ideal than a reality in these tertiary institutions. Using empirical understandings and critical observations, this chapter illustrates all these issues.

Section 2
Ethics of Research With Human Subjects

The second section brings to the reader's attention a series of specific aspects of the research involving the human participant, the imperative of respect for the autonomy of the participants in the research, and hence, the need to obtain information of informed consent from them, the protection of the rights of the participants in the research, risks and benefits of research for the participant and for the society, care for participants belonging to vulnerable populations, etc. This section, although starting from biomedical research, is intended to extend the ethical principles of research on human beings for research in the psycho-social and economic fields.

The concept of vulnerability and the attendant responsibility of researchers to provide special protections for research participants deemed to be vulnerable are considered to be foundational concepts in bioethics. However, not only do international and national guidelines differ in their definition of vulnerability, but they also vary with respect to who is to be considered vulnerable in research. This chapter describes the ways in which vulnerability has been defined by international and national guidelines, discusses the considerations deemed relevant by international and national guidance and writers on the topic, and concludes with thoughts on how the meaning of vulnerability might be communicated in teaching.

This chapter considers the problematic of ethics in clinical research in the countries that are new in terms of implementation or building an adequate structure. The chapter intends to assess the extent to which the clinical trials performed in four former communist East-European countries considered the ethical norms into their research procedures. A framework of existing literature on ethics in clinical research, along with the regional context, is discussed in the next section. The methods section includes the instruments, sources, and procedures for data collection. The data analysis procedures and structure are further explained and grounded relative to the study main purpose. The next section includes the facts and figures on the presence of ethical requirements in clinical trials in the specific political and cultural background in a number of former European communist countries. Finally, a number of suggestions and recommendation are also discussed.

A core element in protecting human participants in clinical research is the assurance of a favorable risk-benefit balance, in accordance with the ethical principle of beneficence. However, the assessment of risks and benefits may sometimes be challenging. In this chapter, the authors review the concepts, ethical principles, and applicability of those terms. The assessment approaches used by regulators and research reviewers who are working in clinical practice are then discussed, together with a highlight of the new trends in risk-benefit analysis and their impact on drug development and approval. Analysis of some research situations which pose particular challenges are presented at the end of the chapter.

Informed consent (IC) in research is a key element in ensuring the ethical character of any research involving human subjects, either bio-medical or psychosocial. IC involves three elements: validity, communication of information, and deliberation. Obtaining IC is a dynamic process of ethical reflection in order to facilitate the expression of autonomy of the subject involved in research. The process of obtaining the IC must be accompanied by the administrative procedure for completing a consent form signed by both the participant and the researcher. If the participant cannot sign—either because he is a minor or because of the medical condition—a delegated consent signed by the legal representatives of the subject is required.

This chapter rides on the premise that the concept of personhood, as embedded in research ethics principles, needs re-examining. As the base upon which the principles were developed and falsely universalized, it needs pointing out that personhood in the Euro-American sense differs markedly from what it is in non-Western cultures. A careful delineation of this understanding should be a teaching moment for researchers, clinicians, bioethicists, students and academics as they confront multicultural perspectives in health research. Hence, it helps to properly inform and effectively erase presumptive tendencies, so people can avoid any voluntary or involuntary unethical behavior, which may arise from ignorance particularly in multicultural settings.

Foreword

The term *ethics* originates in the Greek word *ethos*, which translates as tradition, custom, but also someone's way of being. Understood as moral philosophy, ethics aims to guide the conduct of individuals and groups towards what is good, beautiful, desirable. A series of ethics have imposed over time, the most important being the normative one, based on guiding the conduct of the individual or the community based on certain principles and norms generally accepted by the community, and of prohibitions regarding the attitudes and behaviours considered socially unacceptable. The descriptive ethics analyses the moral conducts of the moral subjects, in their quality of either individual or collective actors.

As a branch of philosophy, theoretical ethics follows the desirable behaviour of the generic moral actor, in abstracto, while the applied ethics tackles the human behaviour in social and professional particular contexts, being situated in a transdisciplinary perspective where the knowledge of the particular area of expertise, being either particular science, profession or social practice, is the one underlying the theories derived from the great theories of moral philosophy, such as the Kantian or the utilitarist ones, contextualized in order to be able to guide particular behaviours in real situations and contexts, encountered in the everyday social and professional life.

The today society is self-defined as the society of knowledge. The knowledge-based society is a concept meant to explain the civilization-related and social-cultural particularities of our time. This is based on a new economic paradigm, the equivalent of a new way of production, based on the intellectual capital and on knowledge management, with the purpose of ensuring prosperity. This new way of production, called the economy of knowledge, emphasizes the implementation of innovation, that radically changes the relation to the Alterity, either because it concerns the colleague that is a researcher in the same field, or in completely different areas of knowledge, or the participants in the research, other stakeholders involved in the activity of research/innovation, as well as, in the first place, the public as a beneficiary of the research results. The knowledge-based society calls for a unique moral charge, the *responsibility*, either directed to the individual, social group or the society as a whole, or even towards the future generations.

The knowledge-based society and economy requires the development of a new form of ethics, that drifts apart from the horizon of the speculative theoretical approach, being oriented towards offering practical and punctual solutions where the direct ethical reflection appears to be necessary. Thus it constitutes particular domains of ethics, of which, in this paper, the ethics of research, bioethics, techno-ethics and the ethical evaluation of the technologies are privileged. The technology as power of action requires moral evaluation. The responsibility represents, firstly, the acceptance and solidarity of the individual with his own actions. The manner in which this solidarity effectively works in the area of research and innovation is the focal point of this volume.

The volume Ethics in Research Practice and Innovation aims at an ambitious task of reuniting the different ethical perspectives, such as the ethics of the research project, of scientific publication, with the issue of research on human subjects, the ethical evaluation of medical technologies—research on stem cells and the genetic engineering—but also those coming from the area of the development of artificial intelligence. What unites all these separate fields is the researcher's need for responsibility in any of the above-mentioned fields, both to the results of own research, and for the impact—positive or negative—that those results can have when they will be developed and integrated into technologies and public policies, meant to improve the humans' life, but which can, in certain cases, prove to be threats to the health and life of the individuals, the functioning of different ecosystems, or even the humanity in general.

The volume aims to overcome the limited and limiting vision on the ethics of research and innovation, that most of the time places this branch of applied ethics in the role of guarantor of fairness of the researcher, and instance of control of the integrity and honesty of the researchers. The volume wishes to bring a contribution to an affirmative ethics of responsibility and the avatars of this value in different particular areas of research and innovation.

Principles such as benevolence, non-maleficence, respect for autonomy, justice are somehow subsumed to the central value of responsibility. Assuming these values by the researcher, as well as the institutions involved in the area of research and/or communicating knowledge, is the most direct way towards gaining the public's trust in science achieved with honesty, good intentions, respect for the research subjects and, not least, based on the values of the research, the impact and risks involved by it.

Diana Bulgaru-Iliescu
Grigore T. Popa University of Medicine and Pharmacy, Romania

Preface

Ethics of research and innovation has become a particularly important field in recent years, a particularly important component of any research project, ethical dimensions refer to very varied categories of practice, from the protection of human subjects involved in medical and social research to ethical standards for the publication of results research. The destructive capacity of the current technology requires an ethical approach, balancing the value of the results with the risks involved by the research - on the one hand, but more recently with the estimation of the possible consequences that the implementation of the technologies resulting from the innovation research can have for the subjects of the research, respectively for the local or the global human community, going to radical mutations in the existence and becoming of the human species.

Ethics is a term derived from the Greek "ethos" – manner, habit, character, and it designates a philosophical discipline that studies the theoretical and practical aspects of morality. In current language, the term ethics is used synonymously with that of moral.

The applied ethics aims to discuss the ethical specific features of some controversial and difficult aspects of contemporary life, whose management cannot be achieved exclusively through the theories of classical philosophical ethics.

Ethics of research and innovation, as a particular dimension of applied ethics, is a transdisciplinary approach par excellence, requiring knowledge both from the general sphere of ethical theories, as well as from the particular field of science in which it is exercised. Among the specific themes considered in the approaching of the ethics of research and innovation, which we find in this volume, we mention:

- Ethical value of knowledge;
- Ethical limits of knowledge;
- Responsibility towards the Other;
- Research on human subjects, limits and ethical risks;
- Normative perspectives in research on human subjects: Oviedo Convention, Belmont Report, Helsinki Declaration, Council of Europe Directives etc.;
- Principles of research on human subjects (principle of non-maleficence, principle of beneficence, principle of justice, principle of promoting the autonomy);
- Ethics of science publication and communication;
- Ethical principles in conducting research;
- Ethical perspectives in the design of the research project; Ethical approval for research; Standards and procedures for obtaining informed consent; Protection of research participants; Data management; Conflict of interests; The responsibility of the researcher and the research institution;

- Ethical misconduct in research: plagiarism, forgery of data, ghost writing;
- Research involving vulnerable populations;
- Consent in research;
- Research Ethics Committees;
- Ethical perspectives on the use of medical technologies;
- Medically assisted human reproduction;
- Experiments on human embryos;
- Ethics of technologies with a major impact on lifestyle;
- Ethics of Artificial Intelligence development;
- Ethics in research in the natural and life sciences: genetically modified organisms.

THE CHALLENGES

Abusing ethics and turning it into a coercive system turns ethics into its opposite, a witch hunt, ineffective in promoting good practice in research.

The establishment of ethics of scientific research and of innovation is predominantly happening with the purpose of avoiding malpractice and derived sanctions, and not from truly instituting social responsibility. Social responsibility is a legitimate structure used for image purposes, and less a true adherence to ethical values.

In our opinion, the integrity is narrowly understood by many researchers and even by some institutions involved in the ethical regulation of research and innovation, and it is predominantly reduced to its negative latitude, which prohibits the obtaining of undue results from the exercise of various activities in the field of production and communication of knowledge, creating a partial confusion with the ethical compliance dimension, as it develops tools for controlling non-conforming behaviours, called integrity control. Incorrect conduct in research may be based on deliberate fraud, but also on honest errors that the researcher was unaware of, or questionable practices in research, among which the most frequent are the publication of poor works, negligence and superficiality in contouring and developing the research, in using the research procedures, in developing the critical apparatus and in citing sources, uncorrected errors, etc.

Unfortunately the ethical discourse in the sphere of research and innovation is of a reactive nature, being generally concerned with the increasing reported number of cases of unethical conduct and with an attempt to universalize the retributive character of ethics. We are in favour of an ethics of research based on a clear and effective normative construction that facilitates the voluntary adherence of members of the academic community to the values underpinning ethics in research and innovation, among which we consider that the dignity - of human being a swell as of humanity in general -, the honesty, the trust, the respect for the person, the autonomy of the participants in research, the transparency, the equity, the equal opportunities, all these hold the place of honour.

SEARCHING FOR SOLUTION

Epistemological perspectives gain an ethical sense in the context of *trusting* the results of the research. The principles of research ethics: benevolence, non-maleficence, respect for the autonomy of research participants, justice, should be the basis of the conduct of any person engaged in research or innovation, adhering to these principles and to others alike, generally valid or specific to each particular field of research being the guarantee of honesty and proper demeanour.

The truth, in the context of new epistemologies of post-positivist nature, acquires ethical significance in correlation with the methodology of science and research. Scientific research is considered to be burdened by the subjectivity of the researcher, but in the same time this will impose on him the ethical responsibility for the social significance of the research, the correctness of the use of methodology, the honesty, the presentation of the limits of research, including the epistemic and methodological ones, and for the needs of the subjects involved in the investigation. Collaborative creativity and peer review are both elements of ethical valence. Collaboration and collegiality imply an affirmative ethics, an assumption that the Other - the colleague, the financier, the reader - is not only equal to me, but also a resource without which my own research would become impossible and useless.

Deontological norms should have as basis an ethical value, to translate it into a moral maxim. The Kantian model provides such value, namely the human dignity, which is transposed into the moral principle in the form of that second formulation of the categorical imperative, which claims to treat a human being as an aim in itself and never as a means. The fulfilment of this imperative requires the individual's ability to rationalize his behaviour in such a way that his own moral norm can stand as a moral maxim for others.

In the Kantian vision, the moral subject must have the capacity to build its own moral norms, and to act in such a way that they can be considered universal maxims, integrity is the consistency in the implementation of these own moral norms, while autonomy is the capacity of the subject to establish such rules. Integrity - in general, in research and innovation in this work - is synonymous with honesty and fairness, being a conduct opposite to hypocrisy, falsity, inconsistency. Integrity aims to express personal virtues in research, especially compliance with standards, that governs a certain area of research and innovation. Integrity is usually analysed from the negative perspective, insisting on the need to control unethical conduct. In the framework of affirmative ethics policies in the field of research and innovation, the emphasis is on integrity as a virtue, and on the promotion of integrity in the organizational environment and its internalization.

The affirmative perspective of integrity refers to the individual's efforts to maintain consistency with himself and his own authenticity. Lack of integrity leads to a non-authentic behaviour in the sense that the individual can no longer be coherent with himself from a moral point of view. In order to properly assess the integrity of a person or organization, it must be taken into account the system of values and principles that govern ethical behaviour. In the absence of a research ethics policy at the researching organization level, or of a specialized in technology for the transfer and implementation of innovation one, as well as an ethics management system at the Organization level, we cannot speak of integrity because we cannot relate the behaviour of the individual with a pre-existing normativity.

We believe that applied ethics, the ethics of research and innovation in the particular case of this written work, should avoid its perpetual positioning within the purview of legitimizing the social action through values such as *moral responsibility, social justice or equality*. Ethics of research and innovation should represent the horizon of *excellence* reconfiguring the idea of *professional virtue*. We make a distinction between minimal ethics (minimum acceptable standards for socio-professional activity) that act negatively, in a prohibiting way and affirmative (appreciative) ethics that aims the professional excellence by codifying successful experiences in professional standards.

The work brings together some of the main themes of ethics in research and innovation, which will allow readers - researchers, but especially researchers in training, to acquire the standards of their own type of practice and thus avoid any voluntarily, but especially involuntarily unethical behaviour, which may arise from ignorance of the ethical meaning of the type of research the researcher is involved in.

The volume could be used as a research ethics manual in doctoral schools, research masters in fields such as biomedicine, technology, and social sciences. We hope that the volume will contribute to the unification of ethical practices in the field of science and technology through the mutual transfer of know-how between relatively separate research areas through the unitary understanding of the ethical significance of research and good practice, especially in terms of publication, avoiding misconduct and assessing the possible impact that research can have on the results. The handbook can help ethicists, members of the ethics committees, counsellors of ethics and ethics consultants as well as PhD adviser - generally the principal investigators and, ultimately, any researcher interested in ethical reflection on their own practice.

THE STRUCTURE OF THE VOLUME

Section 1: Integrity and Trust – Core Values in Research Ethics

Section 1 brings to the attention of readers the issue of academic integrity and trust that should happen at the scientific community level.

Chapter 1: From the Ethics of the Research Project to the Ethical Communication of Science – Particularities in the Social and Humanistic Fields

Dr. Antonio Sandu (Ştefan cel Mare University of Suceava, Romania) aims to familiarize readers with the ethical dimensions of the research project from the stage of writing the project proposal through the peer review, obtaining the opinion of a Research Ethics Commission - if the research involves the participation of human subjects - the implementation of the research project, collecting and processing data until the results are communicated and published.

Chapter 2: Research Integrity Dissemination System – "Science RIDS of Misconduct"

Dr. Artem Artyukhov (Sumy State University, Ukraine) and Dr. Tetyana Vasilyeva (Sumy State University, Ukraine review a series of unethical behaviours in research, suggesting a perspective Eastern Europe on the dissemination of ethical practices and the fight against inappropriate conduct. The authors present a case study on the existence and functioning of the Research Integrity Dissemination System at their university of origin.

Chapter 3: Relevance and Importance of Ethics in Post-Grad Research at South African Universities

Dr. Vannie Naidoo (University of KwaZulu-Natal, South Africa) proposes a review of the emergence and stages of the development of research ethics. The perspective addressed by the author aims, through a case study, for the relevance of research ethics as perceived by post-graduate students in South African Universities for their own research.

Chapter 4: Comparative Analysis of the Codes of Ethics in Top Universities in Romania

Tomiţă Ciulei (Valahia University from Targoviste, Romania) analyses the ethical framework of the research included in the ethics codes of the Romanian universities. The lack of unity in approaching ethical standards between the different universities analysed explains a number of negative consequences that these unethical behaviours can have at university level by diminishing the perceived value of academic integrity and academic autonomy, but also of society in general.

Chapter 5: The Effects of the "Publish or Perish Syndrome" on Research and Innovation in Nigerian Universities – Insights From Recent Research and Case Studies

Dr. Floribert Patrick C. Endong (University of Calabar, Nigeria) makes a critique, from an ethical perspective, upon the practice of conditioning the academic status by the volume of publications and not necessarily by their scientific quality. The unethical elements reviewed are about publishing for purely capitalistic motives, the use of unorthodox methodologies to boost citation index, and fictive authorship of research works among others.

Section 2: Ethics of Research With Human Subjects

The second section brings to the reader's attention a series of specific aspects of the research involving the human participant, the imperative of respect for the autonomy of the participants in the research, and hence the need to obtain information of informed consent from them, the protection of the rights of the participants in the research, risks and benefits of research for the participant and for the society, care for participants belonging to vulnerable populations, etc. Within this section, although starting from bio-medical research, it is intended to extend the ethical principles of research on human beings also for research in the psycho-social and economic field.

Chapter 6: Vulnerability in Research – Defining, Applying, and Teaching the Concept

Dr. Sana Loue (Case Western Reserve University School of Medicine, USA) and Dr. Bebe Loff (Monash University School of Public Health and Preventive Medicine, Australia) conduct an extensive review of literature on the research on people belonging to different minorities, but also on other categories of vulnerable persons.

Chapter 7: Addressing Research Ethics in Clinical Trials in 4 of the Former Communist European Countries – A Shared Responsibility

Dr. George Florian Macarie (University of Medicine and Pharmacy "Carol Davila" Bucharest, Romania) and Ana Voichita Tebeanu (University Politehnica of Bucharest, Romania) analyse the compliance with clinical research ethics in the countries that are new in terms of implementation or building an adequate structure. The study intends to assess the extent to which the clinical trials performed in four former communist East-European countries considered the ethical norms into their research procedures.

Chapter 8: Risk-Benefit Evaluation in Clinical Research Practice

Dr. Samia Hassan Rizk (Cairo University, Egypt) makes a literature review over some key concepts in the field of ethics regarding research on human subjects, where these terms are reviewed from the perspective of ethical principles and their applicability in order to ensure a favourable risk-benefit balance, according to the ethical principle of beneficence.

Chapter 9: Informed Consent in Research Involving Human Subjects

Dr. Antonio Sandu (University of Suceava, Romania) and Ana Frunză (LUMEN Research Center in Social and Humanistic Sciences) present Informed Consent (IC) in research as a key element in ensuring the ethical character of any research involving human subjects, either bio-medical or psychosocial. IC involves three elements: validity, communication of information and deliberation.

Chapter 10: Personhood, Cultural Ethics, and Biomedical Research – African vs. Euro-American Perspectives

Dr. Ike Valentine Iyioke (University of Michigan-Flint, USA) develops a multicultural perspective of redefining the concept of personhood as it is used in research ethics principles.

Chapter 11: The Ethics of Risk in Psychiatry – The Interplay Between Risk and Probability

Dr. Jean Pierre Clero (Universite de Rouen, France) identifies a series of ethical issues relating to the particularity of the illnesses and also of the patients in the research and therapy of psychiatric patients.

Chapter 12: Ethical Issues in Couple and Family Research and Therapy

Dr. Maria Nicoleta Turliuc (Alexandru Ioan Cuza University, Romania) and Octav Sorin Candel (Alexandru Ioan Cuza University, Romania) show that in couple and family research and therapy, the perspective changes from the individual to the dyad or group. The chapter presents an overview of current research topics in family research and therapy, such as intimate partner violence, illness or multiculturalism, insisting on their ethical implications for the family itself and for society. The chapter proposes a series of possible approaches to ethical dilemmas emerging in the psycho-social research of the family.

Section 3: Ethical Evaluation of Technologies and Responsibility Toward Their Implications for Humankind

Section 3 addresses the issue of the ethical responsibility of research organizations from the perspective of the social, ecological, cultural and even anthropological impact that technologies such as bio-medical (cloning, genetic engineering, human embryo research) may have, those who aim at developing computing technologies and constructing artificial intelligence, human enhancement technologies etc.

Chapter 13: The Ethics of Embryonic Stem Cells Research – The Human Being in the Early Stages of Development: A "Medicine" or an End in Itself?

Alexandra Huidu (Researcher at LUMEN Research Center in Social and Humanistic Sciences, Iasi, Romania) raises a number of controversies of an ethical nature related to Embryonic stem cell research.

Chapter 14: Tailoring Humans – The Ethics of Genetic Engineering

Alexandra Huidu (Researcher at LUMEN Research Center in Social and Humanistic Sciences, Iasi, Romania) analyses the ethical perspectives of genetic research and human genome decryption. The author asserts that what began as an attempt to eradicate serious illnesses seems to have become, in some cases, under the impetus of human imagination and technological evolution, an exercise by which scientists come to compete with the attributes of divinity: augmenting human beings at a basic level, that affects the identity of the species. Hybrid embryos and chimeric embryos, although still in the experimental stage, can become a reality in relatively short time. The ethical analysis proposed by the author aims at answering questions like What are the limits and who or what sets the standards?

Chapter 15: AIRSE – The Ethics of Artificial Intelligent Robots and Systems

Dr. Bogdan Popoveniuc (Ştefan cel Mare University of Suceava, Romania) formulates a series of ethical reflections involved in the development of Artificial Intelligence technology and the possibility of Technological Singularity, a machine that uses learning algorithms to overcome human intelligence, not only in terms of computing power but also of general intelligence.

Chapter 16: White-Collar Criminals and Organizational Criminology – Theoretical Perspectives

Dr. Seçil Taştan (Marmara University, Turkey) presents a conceptualization of white-collar criminality and enables to understand the psychological, organizational and situational motives behind white-collar crimes. The presented perspective aims to facilitate the creation of an ethical organizational climate that avoids unethical behaviour or even the various forms of fraud.

Antonio Sandu
Stefan cel Mare University of Suceava, Romania

Ana Frunză
LUMEN Research Center in Social and Humanistic Sciences, Romania

Elena Unguru
University of Oradea, Romania

Section 1

Integrity and Trust:
Core Values in Research Ethics

Section 1 brings to the attention of readers the issue of academic integrity and trust that should happen at the scientific community level.

Chapter 1
From the Ethics of the Research Project to the Ethical Communication of Science:
Particularities in the Social and Humanistic Fields

Antonio Sandu
University of Suceava, Romania & LUMEN Research Center in Social and Humanistic Sciences, Romaina

ABSTRACT

A postmodern interference between bioethics, epistemology, and philosophy of science arises from the field of ethics of research on human subjects. Being a research with a high level of subjectivity, it will also load the researcher with the responsibility towards the social meaning of the results, the correctness of using the methodology, honesty, presenting the limits of research, including the epistemic and methodological ones, as well as the needs of the subjects participating in the investigation. The ethics of research is based on a series of principles, of which the most significant are the honesty of obtaining and presenting results, the non-harm of human subjects, the respect for the autonomy of the subjects, and the principle of beneficence.

INTRODUCTION

A postmodern interference between bioethics, epistemology and philosophy of science arises from the field of ethics of research on human subjects. Being a research with a high level of subjectivity, it will also load the researcher with the responsibility towards the social meaning of the results (Vicol, Bulgaru-Iliescu & Astărăstoae, 2009), the correctness of using the methodology, the honesty, the presenting of the limits of research, including the epistemic and methodological ones, as well as the needs of the subjects participating in the investigation.

DOI: 10.4018/978-1-5225-6310-5.ch001

The incorrect conduct in research may be based on deliberate fraud, but also on honest error, of which the researcher was not aware, or questionable practices in research, among which the most frequent are the publication of low-quality papers, negligence and superficiality in designing and conducting the research, in using the research procedures, in establishing the critical apparatus and the citation of resources, uncorrected errors, etc.

The ethics of research is based on a series of principles, among which the most significant are the honesty of achieving and presenting the results, the non-harm of human subjects, the respect of the autonomy of subjects and the principle of beneficence. The principle of autonomy is, however, defining for the whole liberal modernity, being placed at the foundation of the western cultural model.

Scientific research – especially in the field of social sciences -, in its postmodern acception, is considered to be loaded with the researcher's subjectivity, which will at the same time burden him with the ethical responsibility towards the social meaning of the research, the correctness of using the methodology, honesty, presenting the limits of the research, including the epistemic and methodological ones, and towards the needs of the subjects participating in the investigation.

THE MAINSTREAM AND THE SCIENTIFIC NATURE OF A RESEARCH

The deviation from mainstream, when the reseacher finds it necessary in order to completly revolutionize the area of research, must in turn be governed by laws or norms of research accepted or acceptable in that academic community. Precisely this epistemological nucleus makes a research be declared as scientific. In reality, the scientific mainstream is much more than the current of thought that is majoritary in that branch of science. The concept is thereof a cultural construct, rather than a scientific current. We present a series of acceptions of the concept:

- Elements of knowledge accesible to the public (in case of scientific mainstream accesible to the targeted audience, members of the scientific community);
- Elements of knowledge related to the institutional environment (Sandu, 2009a).

In the cultural sense, the term *mainstream* can be understood as an opinion current, in the sense of majoritary culture, opposed to what we call counter-cultures or minoritary cultures. The affiliation to the majoritary opinion generates social conformism, being thus an instrument of social control. Within the scientific framework, the existing theories that have an increased number of followers will tend to be established as a mainstream and then, using the instrument of „peer control" or peer review, to dictate over the results, not only the method. The methodology itself is part of the theoretical corpus of a paradigm, as such the methodological approach establishes a control over the topics of the research and, implicitly, on the results, rationalizing what is scientific and what is not. The scientific truth becomes a social construct. Being a mediation of interpretations, the scientific truth must be subject to an ethical control. But what is the recommended ethical attitude, in a scientific univers that is more and more constructed of „meanings" rather than „systematic knowledge"? The same ethical dilemma co-exists in all fields in which the Alterity no longer works as a limitation. The elements of affirmative ethics emphasize on the value of „intersubjectivity" (Sandu, 2009a). The collaborative creativity emphasizes both the social nature of the product of the creating process, as well as that of the process in itself. The collaborative creativity and the peer evaluation are both elements with ethical valence. Collaboration and collegiality imply an affirmative ethics, an assumption of „the other is not only my equal, but also a resource without which my approach would become impossible and useless".

THE ETHCAL DIMENSION OF TRUTH IN SCIENCE

The idea of scientific truth is based on the ontological assumption of the existence of a unique reality that can be known. The concept of truth is necessary in the framework of the theoretical models, in order for progress to exist. In this regard, truth only appears as a non-fake. Truth as certainty, however, is no longer fully suited to sciences. The concept of truth suffers from an epistemic mutation within the constructionist epistemologies. The social-constructionist epistemologies abandon the idea according to which the mind of the individual is the mirror of reality. The constructonism is based on relationships and supports the role of the individual in the construction of significant realities. Concepts such as that of verosimilitude become more adequate to describe the nature of the new laws formulated within sciences, which are increasingly drifting away from what can literally be experimented or even directly observed. The top sciences talk about models of Univers having the value of mathematical truth, and not correspondence – truth. Even the mathematical modeling of cosmology starts from an axiomatic universe that best describes the results of the observations (Sandu, 2012a).

Truth, in the context of new epistemologies of post-positivist nature, gain an ethical meaning in correlation with the methodology of science and research. The construction of science being an endless series of explanatory models of reality, we can ultimately accept them as being social constructs that facilitate the consensual understanding of reality. The distinction between explanation – understanding becomes limited to the way of applying the methodological instruments of research, without being fully operational regarding the validity of the research results.

The epistemological perspectives gain an ethical meaning in the context in which we discuss about *trust* in the results of the researchers. In order to justify the trust of the academic community in the results of the research, a series of ethical rules target the honesty of the researcher (Charlton, 2009):

- Honesty and fairness in elaborating research proposals, in the process of research and reporting the results obtained;
- Accuracy and fairness in presenting the contributions of each author to the research proposal and the research reports – including obtaining data, where this contribution is really significant;
- Spirit of collegiality, accompanied by the availability towards communication and sharing results, but where appropriate, also in cases specific to the research institution and the resources destined for research;
- Disclosure and avoidance of potential conflicts of interest;
- The protection of the participants in the research;
- The care for the animals used in the research;
- Assuming the mutual responsibility of the research team coordinator and researchers, but also of the coordinator and the researcher in training – MA, PhD student, etc. (ORI, n.d.)

Developing a research within large teams, with inter and transdisciplinary nature where each researcher is chosen for his area of expertise, most of the time being the only one in the team, being thus impossible to cross-check the results, makes it necessary that between the members of the team there is a mutual trust when a potential error from a member of team may affect the entire team, including from the point of view of the honesty perceived within the academic community (Hardwig, 1985, 1988; Longino, 2016). Both scientific and common knowledge are based on a series of pre-existing knowledge – in the process of research, in the case of science -, whose fairness we do not challenge precisely due to the trust in the validity of that knowledge, based on the *trust* (Longino, 2016) we have in the results already obtained by other researchers before us, or who act in concert with us in our own research team.

It is precisely this *trust* that works as an assumption of the possibility of full knowledge, that will not always question the corpus of knowledge existing and recorded in what is called *scientific literature*, which is a fundamental element of *social construction of the scientific truth*. We can thus consider that the entire science is the result of a process of social construction (Sandu & Unguru, 2017). The value of the *confession* (Longino, 2016) of other researchers, exposed as published articles or reported results, is based on the assumption of the honesty of participants in different scientific communities. Hence the need *for honesty and correctness of citing all sources* used in the documentation of the research proposal or own publication. The value of a research is dependent on the credibility of the sources that were used in documenting the research, hence the need for citation of reliable sources, usually considered to be those in scientific journals and monographs or collective volumes, validated by the scientific community in the field through the process of peer-review.

An axiological aspect, implicated by the scientific knowledge and correlated with the foundations of this form of knowledge subsume the assumption of a science voided of axiological and exclusively oriented towards objectivity, is that the objectivity itself is a value. The very awareness of the axiological dimensions of knowledge, considering the implied discourse of power in the scientific knowledge (Foucoult, 1991, 1998), generates the need for a new ethical approach of producing knowledge – research – and implementing knowledge in everyday life – innovation. This ethics of knowledge is increasingly imperative as the risks involved by the very process of research, - the use of human subjects in research that involves risks for their health state or even life, risks of nuclear accidents or such in the research of physics of high energies, etc. – but also of implementing results as technologies – polluting technologies, technologies that involve major risks in exploition, military technologies that allow the existence of mass-distruction weapons, either chemical, biological or nuclear, etc. – or of public policies, become more and more obvious. Presumptions such as the one on the rationality and cognoscibility of the world, which becomes a founding myth of modernity (Zhang, 2013), have as dominant speech the scientific discourse, and as a result, the *re-enchantment* - in the meaning used by Ioan Petru Culianu, who attributes technology a magical function, that of creating connections between apparently disparate parts of the reality, but connected through forces and unseen influences – of the world through technology.

The distinction between the knower and the object to be known (Sandu, 2011a, 2012b) fundament the classic epistemology based on the concept of objectivity and the axioma that *The Universe is objective, cognizable and independent from the knower*. Anne Harrington states that a cultural substrate of the evolution of science in Europe is the Christian vision of the person created after the image and likeness of God (Zajonc, 2006). The human mind – similar to that of God – is rational and fully capable of understanding and mastering nature. Nature is external to the human being, thus it can and must be seen from the outside. This premise made science possible, as a form of specifically western knowledge, oriented towards the exteriority of nature, which it examines through observation and aims to explain through mathematic models. We consider that there is, generally, a positive correlation between the involvement of the researcher in the environment studied, and the quality of the knowledge obtained. In direct accordance with the ontological assumptions on the nature of reality, the researcher will reflect upon the possibility of knowledge and the way in which this knowledge can be formulated (Sandu, 2011b).

The researcher that assumes a realist assumption will consider knowledge to be possible and the reality to be measurable. The causal explanation will be preffered, the measurements tending to be considered valid if and only if they have statistical relevance, offer a causal explanation of the phenomenon, and eventually have predictive power over the course of social events. The researcher who starts from a constructionist assumption according to which the – social – reality is multiple and the result of a negotiation of interpretations will priviledge from an epistemological point of view the understanding of the phenomena. Validity rather refers to the completness of the sources of knowledge and the „voices" that are made to be heard. Knowledge is contextual, the theories generated being eventually extrapolated, but without assuming the claim of universality. The universality is „suspected" of not taking into account the subjective particularities specific for the world of human (Creswell, 2007). The epistomological concept of validity, which has become, through an interpretative drift, a constitutive ethical value of science as predominant discourse of modernity – which makes it necessary for the emergence of a certain social institution (Frunza, 2016; Frunza & Sandu, 2017) -, is the one who also manages the ethical perspectives on research, since it – the scientific discourse – can have *effect of power*, through technologies or derived policies, only if the *research is valid*. Ensuring the validity of research and the credibility of the results obtained is the purpose of the ethical concerns about the elimination of certain intellectual frauds, among which data falsifying or eliminating data that contradict the initial hypotheses.

Archie Bahm (1971) draw the attention to the *myth of knowledge free of values*. On the contrary, Bahm shows that the entire knowledge is saturated with values in all its levels, both in the stage of producing knowledge, and in that of dissemination. The author shows that the very idea of benefit of knowledge is based on a valuable decision, reason for which the value added by a research to the corpus of knowledge in the field, the theoretical and practical importance, as well as the social importance of a research are elements in the analysis of the ethical acceptability of a research project. Knowledge generates a certain type of material and spiritual benefits, which we appreciate as being good, desirable or, on the contrary, generally inadequate, through the risks that may emerge in case of inappropriate use of resulted technologies, or inadequate to the involved human cost – in case of researchers who involve human subjects that would be subject to disproportionate risks for life or health, against the potential value of the results that will be obtained.

GENERAL ETHICAL PRINCIPLES IN RESEARCH

In the majority of codes of ethics on research and innovation there are a series of principles with universal value, that should underlie any research project, both in the stage of creation, as well as in development and communicating results. We will continue to present a series of ethical principles of responsible research and innovation, synthesized and adapted by us after Resnik (2015) and Shamoo and Resnik (2015).

- Honesty includes a series of desirable behaviours – affirmative -, the correct reporting of results and methods, techniques and procedures used in obtaining results, but also limitating – which eliminate the undesirable behaviours -, such as the refusal to manufacture or falsify the data or the insufficient prezentation of those or some of them, the lack of a deceptive behaviour towards the colleagues, financers and sponsors, participants in the research – except for the case in which this behaviour is necessary for research, when the approval of a research ethics committee – and of the audience – is required.

- Objectivity, obtained by avoiding – intentional – errors in the design of the research, analysis and/or data interpretation, planning and elaboration of the research project, peer-review, avoding situations of self-disappointment in the process of research, sincerity in the analysis and disclosure of potential inclusive particular interest of financial nature that could affect the research. Another violation, most times involuntary, of objectivity is the ideological, reigious, political or any other kind of partisanship, within the research. A series of early-stage researchers formulate, for example, objectives such as:
    - We wish to demonstrate the importance of a certain social practice, for example in increasing the quality of life of a category of subjects, when, through research, it would be better to aim to evaluate the importance of that practice;
    - The difference is that when we aim to demonstrate something, we don't approach the subject with epistemic neutrality, but with partisanship;
    - It is possible, if the researcher is honest, to even have results contrary to what we expect, that would fairly be made public, the research remaining honest;
    - But from the perspective of objectivity, the idea of epistemic neutrality, although impossible to be complete, as we have previously developed, leads to a more careful behaviour in research, which has the chance to capture more sides of the social phenomenon and, implicitly, to include them in the resulting theory; when the purpose of a research is obviously the partisanship, the chance of an unethical conduct is increased, the social value of the idea that aims to be scientifically proven being able to overcome, for the (pseudo)researcher, the value of scientific objectivity of the research.
- The academic integrity, expressed through sincerity and consistency in good practices, respecting promises and commitments made, including the terms and the project of research development, the abstinence from dishonest behaviours even when they might bring material, social and professional benefits. Systematically avoiding to publish in journal well-known for their exigent peer-review process and the preference for journals with a low rate of rejection – eventually in the so-called *predatory journals*, which partly or totally falsify the result of the peer-review process – may be a lack of integrity when the purpose of this action is to obtain undeserved academic credits. This is true even when those articles prove to be scientifically valuable. The phenomenon occurs due to the will to publish fast, or the lack of trust in own research. However, in general, the lack of integrity is correlated with the publication of articles pretending to be scientific, but which do not present the results of an actual research or documented syntheses of the scientific literature in the field. Most times, those publications are simply replications of certain theories, more or less documented, with no theoretical or practical relevance.
- The exigence in research is manifested through the attention to own errors, the critical examination of own papers, as well as those of colleagues'. In this same requirement of a good research we also notice the need for a good management of research, the highlighting and careful recording of the research activities, of the data collected, of the correspondence with the financer, with the editors, etc.
- The openness to sharing ideas and results, including by accepting to publish in *open access*, accepting criticisms and different opinions.

- The respect for intellectual property, including but not limited to abstaining from plagiarism or self-plagiarism, using a ghost author that would write the paper on the behalf of the declared authors (*ghost writing*), unjustified inclusion or exclusion of an author from the authorship, abstaining from using unpublished resources, or even quoting them within possibilities, abstaining from using other researchers' unpublished data or methods which would lead to confusion regarding the scientific priority of those data and methods, including in the acknowledgment contributors that do not qualify to be authors.
- Maintaining the confidentiality of the research data concerning the identity of te participants or institutions until the moment of publication. Confidentiality should be kept in a manner that doesn't contravene the public order.
- Respecting the rights of the research participants, including the withdrawal from research at any Time, and the researcher's obligation to obtain informed consent from all research participants.
- Responsible publication, by avoiding unjustified multiple publishing, of self-plagiarism and exclusive publication for the purpose of obtaining the academic credit, of works that do nothing to contribute to the advance the knowledge in the field;
- The responsible mentoring of students and young researchers, including their guidance in order to develop own scientific creativity. The coordinator, as a mentor, has the obligation to explain to the young researchers and teach them to respect the ethical principles of research and the epistemological requirements in the field.

The respect towards colleagues is the result of understanding science as a collaborative practice, the respect and correctness towards colleagues being an inclusive obligation – but not only – at the time of elaborating peer-reviews or other forms of evaluation, when involved in a competition, etc.

The social responsibility of the researcher and the institution of research is the orientation of research towards purposes that are beneficial to the society, that will promote public good and avoid that through research, it would harm persons or categories of persons through their participation in the research or transposing the results of the research into technology. The ethical evaluation of technologies, developed with the help of research ethics committees, has the role to limit the research in the fields in which the emergence of certain technologies could generate negative results for the society. The social responsibility of the researcher and the research institution is expressed through projecting and developing certain research that could have – at least theoretically – practical applicability, and the abstain from spending resources destined for research on research projects whose social utility is questionable. The lack of social utility of the researches, when they are not transfered to production through innovative technologies, may generate a low responsibility of the researcher towards the results of his work, which he sees as being useful only to his own academic benefit, fact which could determine him to reach to unethical scientific practices. At least in the social and humanistic field, many of the researches conducted remain unenforceable, even if the results of the research itself have a transforming potential for the society. This situation arises from the inefficiency of promoting science and the incoherence of the policies of technological transfer, the lack of concern from the authors for the applicative value of the research and its use in practice, the exclusive interest in publishing in journals with high impact factor which is important for the scientific community, but is less accesible to the community of practitioners, the lack of interest of the researcher towards the social value of his work, being exclusivelt preoccupied by his scientific value or his academic promotion.

Non-discrimination refers both to the level of the academic community, and the participants in the research. At the level of the academic community, the discrimnating practices can be based on gender, race, ethnicity, as well as any other criteria that doesn't concern the competence and integrity of the person. In the editorial practice, for example, there could be situations of rejection to publication of a paper even without going through the process of peer-review for the only reason that the authors come from cultural and scientific spaces where the scientific productivity is perceived – most time based on a preconception – as being of a lower quality. Such rejections may correctly occur when are based on the existence of methodological or theoretical errors in the paper, independent from the ethnic origin of the researcher, but also when the author's communication skills in the language of publication of the journal are insufficient, the text containing grammar or expression errors. The rejection of the paper on ground of English language errors cannot be considered as discriminating, since the publication has ensure equal chances, the quality of the text being the reason for the decision, and not the author's ethnic background. Likewise, the refusal to publish a work with different regional specific than the majority of the readers of that journal is also not considered discriminating.

The professional competence as an ethical standard requires the researchers to have continuous professional training and improvement of own expertise in that field, but also in related scientific fields, when this aspect is necessary for the good development of the research. The principle of professional competence also requires the researcher to be interested in developing the scientific field in which he is active, promoting it nationally and internationally, including by manifesting special interest in the quality of the didactic and training act of future specialists and researchers.

The principle of legality requires the researcher to know and apply the normative framework in act for that field of research. We discuss here about the legislation specific for education and research, as well as the particular legislation in different social, economic fields, etc. The interdiction of conducting research in a specific field, such as human cloning, mustn't be violated in researches on the ground of scientific or social importance of the research topic. In our opinion, the results of research conducted illegaly or with disobedience of ethical rules of research on human subjects should not be accepted by the scientific community and refused for publication by journals, even if the research has been conducted in geographic areas where that research is allowed, especially belonging to developing countries or countries with dictatorial regime which manifests a major lack of respect towards the human rights. The Nazi experiments on concentration camp detinees have generated data that could be valid and lead to the development of important therapeutic measures, in fields such as the resistance to pain, to hypothermia, etc. The scientific literature (Cohen, n.d.) discusses about the ethical acceptability of data publication by Nazi doctors, and their use in contemporary biomedical research. The opinions expressed vary from absolute rejection of publishing these data, due to the completly inhuman way in which they were obtained, to the publication of data precisely in honor of the victims of the Holocaust. In our opinion, the refusal to publish illegally obtained data, regardless of their alleged value, shows the consistency of the academic community to respect legality and unconditional adherence to humanist ethical values that underlie science, along with the respect for human dignity, beneficence and nonmaleficence.

The protection of human subjects in research involves maximizing the benefits of research, by making the research project more efficient, the absolute respect for the dignity of the human being and its autonomy, equity in obtaining research benefits, including by promoting free access to articles presenting research results, the reduction of risks to human subjects involved in research, the inclusion of participants in research only on the basis of explicit and voluntary informed consent, and the expression of care when research involves the participation of vulnerable populations.

Care for animals in the case of research involving laboratory animal experiments requires that they be carried out only to the extent necessary, avoiding those experiments whose outcome can be obtained in another way, even if more costly, and rejecting research whose design is mistakenly built or unclear, which does not justify legitimate interest and outstanding scientific and practical value. In the case of animal experiments, cruelty towards them should be avoided (Resnik, 2015).

RESEARCH PROJECT. ETHICAL PERSPECTIVES

The ethical nature of the purpose of research (Vicol & Astărăstoae, 2009) should result since the research proposal, until the final moment of presenting the results. The social research should generate a practice either at the level of policies and institutions, or at the level of individuals, such as the researches in the field of sciences of life or nature should be capable of being used in elaborating a technology. In general, modern science is considered to be free of axiological value, meaning that knowledge is the main purpose of research, and not necessarily the practical use of results. However, when the research involves human subjects, it can no longer be free of any practical value, because neither people nor animals can be subject to life endangering experiments, without the practical value expressed to be considered superior to the risks that can be determined. The ethical character is intended to justify possible practices that will result from the perspective of individual or public good. Research itself may have a non-ethical purpose, ranging from manipulation of voting intentions, for example through surveys, to the establishment of another social order, based, for example, on distributive justice instead of retributive justice. The purpose of social research can not be limited to the mere knowledge of a social phenomenon, as the knowledge exerted on this phenomenon changes it in the very process of knowledge. The path that the research will follow, but also the line on which the social phenomenon will develop after the completion of the research - especially in the research-intervention situations - is a potential of the ethical construction of the research that should be taken into account when designing the research (Cojocaru, Sandu, 2011). The value of the research is an ethical dimension (Vicol & Astărăstoae, 2009) which is analyzed both by the proposer of the research and by the ethics commission called to assess its ethical acceptability from the perspective of the social significance of the results and the potential for social progress after the completion of the research. As far as research design is concerned, it must be plausible, honesty being an important ethical value in social research. Validity also raises an ethical problem correlated with the potential manipulator of social research. Respect for the autonomy of individuals participating in research as unanimously accepted value is correlated with the use of informed consent (John & Left, 2009).

The general principles of research ethics are:

- The principle of beneficence, namely: research must deliver real benefits for both research participants - as far as possible - and for the society, reflecting the ethical obligation to maximize benefits and minimize risks (Vicol & Astărăstoae, 2009);
- The principle of non-harm: is the obligation not to harm through the practice of research, either to the subjects involved, or to other categories that could be harmed by possible implementations of the research results (Vicol & Astărăstoae, 2009);
- The principle of distributive justice, in the form of equitable distribution of the risks and benefits of research (Ioan & Left, 2009);

- The principle of subjects' confidentiality and data protection: it does not provide information about the participants in research and the anonymity of information in data processing (Ioan & Stanga, 2009).

THE ELEMENTS OF THE RESEARCH PROJECT AND THE ETHICAL IMPLICATIONS OF THE RESEARCH

The research project is based on a central idea that is the purpose of the project and can be transposed into a research question, whose answer is unknown. The purpose should be legitimate, the knowledge should lead to a specific social value and could be conducted with minimum risks for potential participants. There are researches whose purpose doesn't involve a valuable knowledge, or at least useful from a social point of view, situation in which, from an ethical point of view, it is discussed the fair use of resources – especially in the case of public financed research – from other projects, whose purpose involves a higher social utility. This principle, however, should not be universal, research whose utility is not evident from the beginning, such as those in the field of philosophy, humankind in general, bringing considerable advantages to humanity, for example by developing the axiological side, ethics of knowledge. Starting from the above-mentioned principle of the immediate utility of science, the Trump Administration has reduced the human resources research budget (Mervis, 2017; Trump's Budget Plan, 2017), which in our opinion produces an imbalance of knowledge between the humanist- axiological and pragmatic-technological ones. When formulating the purpose of the research, there should usually be a presumption of what might be the answer to the research question. The assumption substantiates the thesis of research and, if it can be formulated in the form of relations between variables, the research hypothesis.

The research can be very narrow, object oriented or extended, involving correlations between different research subjects. The topic of the research should be clear and obvious. Although the clarity and evidence of the research subject expresses an epistemological request, we can attribute it an ethical value, the clarity of the subject and the way in which it was expressed leading to a correct reception from the interested audience, thus bringing an added value to the research field, but also to saving resources that would be necessary in developing the research.

The need for clarity is correlated with the emphasis on the empirical content of the research goal, which guides both the researcher's and the research project evaluators and the final beneficiary of the research, respectively.

Novelty and Foundation

For a research project to be scientifically accepted, the proposed research must have a certain degree of novelty and, at the same time, be based on previous scientific knowledge in the field. From an ethical point of view, we must notice the inflation of research and articles proposed to different journals, but whose results don't bring any novelty and don't enrich the knowledge in the field. Although the articles could be well written from a technical point of view and be based on valid methodological research, they could be insufficient for bringing value to the field since they don't explore or solve a real theoretical or practical issue, but resume, under different experimental or field conditions, other researches whose previous results are known or obvious. This informational redundancy is ethically criticised, since introducing the article into the scientific circuit by publishing and indexing it in databases brings an informational ballast that makes it harder to document the honest researchers in the field.

The purpose of a fundamental research, such as a PhD thesis, would be to include primarily theoretical objectives that improve the corpus of the field and, in the subsidiary, by applying the theoretical innovations, to open the way for changes at the level of public policies. Applied research, though very important, has a much diminished international visibility, unlike the one that aims to achieve theoretical goals, to be applied globally and not just locally. Considering the manner of formulating the objectives, many research papers that present specific situations in certain geographic areas self-limitate the potential audience to national decision-makers and, eventually, to professionals in that region. The research with regional impact is far from being worthless in itself, leading to effective policies, adapted to the local specificity, but should be communicated by publishing it or presenting it in local conferences and, preferably, in the language in which the research was conducted. Only when the results are extrapolable to other socio-cultural spaces, it would be useful to be published in an international language in journals with global access.

The delineation of the purpose of the research, by clearly specifying fundamental or applicable contributions, makes the interested researcher able to easily and quickly select the useful sources, making it easy to distinguish between regional impact research and pseudo-research conducted solely for the purpose of publishing, and thus obtaining an academic credit, knowing that publishing is absolutely necessary in the career of a researcher or academic teacher. Publishing exclusively for the purpose of increading the academic value of the person, without producing any value in a certain research field, could be considered scientific fraud through the illegitimate access to academic positions. We distinguish two categories of scientific publication, the first one being the one that publishes the results of the research and has the purpose to improve the corpus of knowledge, and the second one, with a pronounced didactic nature, which makes the knowledge of future specialists or training researchers accesible. Although both categories of publication are legitimate in the career of a researcher, they should be clearly delineated considering the purpose of the publication, both for facilitating the search of those who wish to document themselves in a specific field, and for facilitating the activity of the committees that analyse the quality of the scientific or didactic act of the authors. Science includes two fundamental dimensions, namely discovery and exposure. The discovery is a laborious task of building new concepts, ways of thinking, paradigms, constructive or interpretative solutions, etc. This dimension involves generating the new one and is often called *fundamental research.*

Another important dimension of research is the application of the results from fundamental research in concrete situations, in solving problems, in building technologies. It does not necessarily bring a novelty in the knowledge plan, but a plus-value in the one of action.

Michael Kirton (1976) makes a distinction between the types of creativity. This is defined as being adaptive or innovative. From our point of view, we could extend this distinction as an analysis of the types of dominant intelligence, the theoretical one or the social one. In the economic jargon, innovation could be understood as an „out of the box thinking".

The innovative is described by Kirton as producing transparadigmatic solutions. The innovative researcher will, thus, rather undertake a fundamental research, which involves creating new models of understanding the reality of new visions, new paradigms.

The adaptive researcher will rather have the tendency to apply fundamental theories to specific cases, in solving certain problems, in conceiving technologies that would apply the discoveries produced by the fundamental research. Both types of research, we would say, are significant, since the first one advances knowledge, and the second one transforms it into a social field. By analysing the two forms of knowledge from a constructionist point of view, we could appreciate that the fundamental research, which is meant to produce new theories that would adapt the understanding of phenomena to experimental results, is a form of priviledged negotiation of reality, conducted within an extremely small group of experts, whose main feature is to be able to represent their new paradigm and the openness to „negotiate" it.

A scientific theory doesn't have a pragmatic value as long as the result cannot be used for a „reframing" of reality. Naturally, such theories should, at first, be accessible to that group of experts, who would recapitalize it based on the dominant theories, or have the capacity of establish it as a dominant theory. In the current science, especially the fundamental one, we talk more about the plausible theoretical models, rather than the accepted anonymous hypotheses. Theoretical models are even more "productive" as new theories and models can be developed. Further development, even if it is part of the corpus of fundamental research, has a higher degree of adaptability than the original theory. A prime example of science is the theory of relativity, which is a breaking of the Newtonian paradigm, which includes it as a particular case. Albert Einstein will overcome his own theory, proposing the theory of generalized relativity which, although takes into account the results of the narrow theory of relativity, includes it as a case at the limit. These are examples of innovative approaches of science.

The construction of an engine that would facilitate travelling at a speed close to that of light would be an example of innovative transfer of a research into technology. A special situation would be inventing a superluminal engine that would contradict the theory of relativity and would require a theoretical construction that would justify the technological reality. In fact, in the history of science and technology it has happened many times that technological inventions have preceded the theoretical explanation. Turning to the two ways to make science, adaptive and innovative, we consider specific tools to marketize these results.

The justification of the novelty and the scientific foundation of a research proposal will be made on the basis of the literature review, which helps in the selection of the subject of the research and in its suitability to the existing knowledge, previously doubled by maintaining the novelty level.

Feasibility and Challenge

The research is recommended to be planned in such a way that it would be completed in the given time and with the project resources. The feasibility of the reseach proposal is correlated both with its justification in the context of the results already existing in the scientific literature, and in correlation with the limit of time and finances imposed by the size and experience of the research team. Also, the extent of the research should be correlated with the financial and time budget available to the research team (Chapin, 2004). The ethics of research resources targets the analysis of the feasibility of the research from the stage of research proposal, in order not to leave place for ambiguity that would negatively affect the research and its feasibility. The research is recommended to not only be feasible, but also provocative from an intellectual point of view, in other words its results would spark the interest of the scientific community. The provocative nature of knowledge shouldn't be confused with the exceptionalism in chosing the research themes. For example, a criticism of the first draft of Horizon-Europe 2020-2024 was that in the medical field, research funds are invested for rare diseases, with almost zero incidence in the majority of European countries and, basically, inaccessible to researchers for study – for example, those in Eastern Europe – while the diseases that are serious health hazard in those countries – in our example, the cardiovascular diseases – are ignored, no budget being proposed in the project for this type of research (Radu Iliescu, intervention in the conference – Program Horizon-Europe conducted at the Romanian Parliament, June 15, 2018)

Theoretical or Empirical

A series of researchers, among which Paul Chapin (2004, p. 8) consider that for a research to be accepted from a scientific point of view, it should explain the regularities encountered in the data collected, based on a theoretic model, that would lead to a logical foundation of the research. This vision is an objectivist one, the constructionist epistemic models (Sandu, 2012c) will target the local particularities of the universe of research, insisting on the limitations of the specificity of the human group in which the study was conducted. The local or universal relevance of the research is important from the perspective of the possible theoretical construction and the generalization of data. The non-generalizable data can be used in projects, targeting the alteration of public policies with focus on the community studied, which is why they are not pragmatically irrelevant, but are less visible in the international scientific community.

Chapin (2004) insists on the importance of the theoretical model in generating hypotheses and research questions. In the absence of a theoretical model, research questions and / or assumptions may be irrelevant, research not having explanatory power but merely descriptive. But there is an exploratory dimension in social research, which aims to identify and describe a social phenomenon, by constructing the theoretical explanatory case based on the data obtained on the field, compared to others, and their generalization until the emergence of an explanatory model with increasing degree of generalization and applicable to different contexts, but similar to the one directly studied. Such a model of research is that achieved through the Grounded Theory (Sandu, 2018).

Project Planning

The project's organizing phase involves identifying the relevant specialist literature, research objectives and the methodology to respond to those objectives. The research objectives detail the purpose of the research, being thought together to respond as fully as possible to the purpose of the research. When the goal is very vast, the objectives specify how the goal will be achieved, showing what the goal will be achieved in the present research, and that the rest will be the subject of further research. Research objectives can be formulated in an affirmative or interrogative way, where research questions are. An appropriately planned project will naturally and logically generate the research proposal. Designing research aims to guide research and give evaluators a clear idea of what is to be researched and how research will actually take place. Planning is the construction of a road between what is already known and what is meant to be known.

The research proposal should include a more detailed description of the methodology, in order for the evaluators to decide whether the methods used could lead to obtaining the results planned during the project development and with the resources available for the project team. In case the research involves the participation of human subjects, it is preferable that the summary of the research project would include an ethical reflection on the risks the participants take, the risk-benefit balance brought by the research and the methods of diminishing or eliminating the risks. Prior to implementation, the research project, together with a broader description of the effects mentioned, the risks and benefits of how to get the informed sentiment, will be subject to a separate evaluation by an ethics committee (Research etics commitee) who will have to decide on the usefulness of the research and the benefits it brings to the risks to which the beneficiaries might be subjected. In order to be able to evaluate the project correctly, at least from the perspective of the ethics committee, the methodology should be clearly highlighted, including research tools, not just the methods and techniques to be used.

The research tools, such as the interview guide, questionnaire guide, etc., customize for this research the standard methodology presented in the original project. The project proposal, when assessed for possible funding, must comply with the sponsor's instructions, including the size and format of the funding research, which is why a number of elements of the research project could be partially omitted or briefly presented. However, these will need to be explained separately in the application submitted to the ethics committee and will have to be in the project documents.

The research project should include a concise and comprehensive presentation of the researches in the field, including own researches. It is necessary to present different approaches to the subject, such as the way in which the project will relate to it. Where they exist, presentations of their own results and expertise in the studied field are necessary. The design of the project will include information regarding: the materials necessary for the research, the subjects who will be involved in the research (the sample), the places where the research will be conducted, the methodologies of collecting data, the research control (validity), limits, consistency, coherence, methods of data analysis and interpretation. It is important to describe the meaning and limitations of the project. From the point of view of significance, how to develop scientific knowledge in the research area and how to extend the boundaries of knowledge through the research will be presented (Chapin, 2004: 64). The description of the project should include elements for disseminating the research results and also argue the qualification of the researchers to achieve the project.

Developing a timetable for project activities guides the researchers in establishing the limits of the research and formulating a specific plan to run it. Planning is a process of establishing the priorities and customizing them for the research questions.

The inclusion of a research proposal must take into account its addressability (Chapin, 2004: 61) from an institutional point of view, whether it is a financing body, the evaluation committee of a doctoral proposal, etc. The research proposal will be forwarded to evaluators, grouped into a panel of consultants, or program coordinators.

The scientific research is, by definition, a process of continuous perfecting under mutual peer-supervision. Subjecting the results of a scientific approach to the attention of colleagues in the field of research that come from a wider academic area, maximizez the chances to have, on one hand, scientific impact, and on the other hand, to diminish the risks of a methodological error. Peer-review evaluation is in no way a form of censorship to the scientific text, since it doesn't directly target the validity of the results, but the validity of the scientific approach which lead to achieving those results. Creativity and scientific and technological innovation should not be limited to submitting own opinions to the attention of the peers, but on the contrary, the opinions of the reviewers, in the case of really valuable papers, could contribute to the increase of scientific value for the paper. Submitting the paper to peer-review should never be conditioned by the belonging to the scientific mainstream in the field, the innovation and inventiveness being the strenghts of the scientific research.

The evaluators can act in the *double-work* (double-blind peer-review) mode - when evaluators do not know the origin of the research project, and the authors of the proposal will not find out who did the evaluation - or in the *blind peer-review manner* - you know who did the research proposal's evaluation. If in the evaluation of publication proposals, the most used system is double work, this is more rarely encountered in the evaluation of research projects, because the composition of the research team is important for estimating the success of the project. The previous experience of the project manager and the research project members is an important element that is taken into account in the proposed evaluation, because an experienced team has a higher academic credibility, the evaluators more easily accepting that the team can implement it more easily the research proposal. In the case of some of the funding institutions, the importance of the previous experience of the department manager, possibly of the entire team, can go up to 60% of the total score that can be given to the research proposal. This is the case, for example, of the program *Ideas*, supported by the Ministry of Research and Innovation in Romania (UEFISCDI, n.d.). In this program, in some components the previous experience is justified by the existence of a number of publications in the main scientific circuit (Web of Science), in journals classified in qvartils 1 and 2. We express our reservations about this interpretation on the international visibility of the researchers who form the project team, at least for the Social and Humanistic Sciences fields, for the following reasons:

- The scientometric indicators such as impact factors, *article influence score*, etc., although it measures the visibility of a publication and it can be considered that a publication with large impact factor will have a more strict selection of articles to be published, are not entirely relevant for the quality of the articles, especially those of young researchers; the scientometric indicators varies from one year to another for many journals in the field of Social Sciences, and the researcher cannot specifically estimate, at the time of proposing an article, what impact factor will it have and in what qvartile will the journal be at the time of publication – knowing the fact that for most journal in the main circuit, the publication process takes more than a year.
- Estimating the visibility of the research team should not exceed 35-40% of the potential project score, for the novice researchers to be able to access funding that would result in articles publishable in the main circuit.
- An excessive emphasis on the importance of researchers' experience and visibility introduces imbalances of power within the academic community, stimulating unethical behaviors such as ghost writing, especially in the form of co-opting authors who do not necessarily have a real contribution to writing articles / projects, but they have good academic positioning and broad scientific visibility, their co-opment in the team increasing the chances of accepting the project.

The panel of consultants consists of 5 to 20 researchers with expertise and visibility, that periodically get together to evaluate projects with continuous or ad-hoc deposit, in order to evaluate the proposals within a certain call (Chapin, 2004). Evaluators are selected in a database at the disposal of the funder, based on a match between the field (s) of interest and the areas of expertise of the evaluators. From the ethical point of view, the selection of the panel of assessors should assess the potential conflicts of interest between evaluators and project members, including significant previous collaborations, especially having a financial impact on the evaluator, as well as animosities or hostilities among them, or research projects in a very close area - which could lead to rejection of the project for reasons of competition and not of scientific value or even theft of ideas.

Project Financing

Project financing is usually done through research grants, offered nationally or internationally or through research contracts concluded with public or private beneficiaries. Cost projections are conducted in order to establish the viability of the project and the financing sources. The technical costs, equipment, consultancy, use of research infrastructure will be planned, along with the costs necessary for human resources, such as salary, daily allowances, participation in congresses and conferences, publication fees. As far as the publishing fees are concerned, they appear especially when it is aimed for *open access* publication, the article being available for free online, for any person interested. In this situation, the *open-access* fee covers the publishing expenses involved in producing and maintaining the article online. The open-access policy is very important from an ethical point of view because it ensures the equity of access to knowledge and equal chances for researchers. The European Union, in the Horizon Europe project, has the objective of publishing all results in open-access, ensuring the cover of the open-access fee among eligible costs. Depending on these budgets, the dimension of the research will be projected, maintaining its main objectives.

From an ethical point of view, when a funded research is carried out, it is very important to know the possible political, cultural, religious or scientific views that various private donors can have. Custom research may be vitiated by the financier's intention to manipulate public opinion through research that shows its favorable outcomes and ignores the opposite. In biomedical research, for example, a number of pharmaceutical companies fund studies that highlight the results of using a particular drug therapy. Clinical research should shows both the potential beneficial effects, as well as the adverse effects of using that therapy. When the researchers – at the suggestion of the financer, or just considering that is what the financer would wish – avoids publishing the adverse reactions or establishes the targeting of an experiment in such way that the favourable results would be minimal, the study being thus considered a scientific fraud by falsifying the results. An important rule regarding the development and financing of research is the respect for the independence of the researcher, the research institution and the financer. This independence should be affirmed against any potential groups of economic, political-ideological or religious interests.

COMPONENTS OF THE RESEARCH PROJECT: LITERATURE REVIEW

Presenting the scientific literature (*the literature review*) has the purpose of configuring the scientific context in which the whole research falls. Within this presentation, it must be highlighted the area in which knowledge needs to be deepened, presenting information on the way in which the issue approaches is being regarded in the scientific literature. A good literature review doesn't exhaustively approach the topic of the research, but formulates a scientific literature reading grid. This is selected and interpreted in correlation with the purpose of the current research, in order to later analyze whether the empirical results or theoretical proposals are consistent with the literature or propose a change of paradigm, contrasting with other previously published results. Levy and Ellis (2006) show that a literature review should use the information in the literature to justify a particular approach to the research topic, how to select the methodology, the areas where novelties are brought, etc. A good literature review builds the framework for new scientific achievements in the field. Levy and Ellis (2006) present the following features of the literature review: the methodological analysis, the selection and synthesis of the quality literature in the field, the construction of a solid analysis base leading to the achievement of the research objectives, and a clear demonstration of the place of the current research in the totality of the researches in the field.

The literature review is a process of gradual application of methodical steps of collecting, analyzing, understanding, evaluating the applicability, analysis and synthesis of convergent quality literature for the purposes of research, without being exhaustive, for the purpose of identifying the place of research in the whole of the knowledge in the field and the possibility of own contribution to the development of knowledge.

It is especially important to include in the literature review the papers underlying the research proposal. In case the project develops a theory, an own point of view, different from other researchers previously published, those papers should be presented in the literature review and credited accordingly, with citation. The way in which the articles mentioned influece that research should also be mentioned. A research can be placed further or in opposition to one or several of the results published in the scientific literature papers. In the case of theoretical articles, which critically refer to the scientific literature, the stage of literature review will be followed by wide theoretical analyses (Baumeister & Leary, 1997), including the papers cited in the literature review which can be revised, criticized, contradicted or, on the contrary, used in own argumentation. The stage of literature review is itself a critical analysis, because by the very synthesis we are making, we express our theoretical positioning towards the consulted work (Journal of Young Investigators, 2005). A good literature review should refer both to the literature that supports one's own point of view, and to one that contradicts it. In the stage of proposing a research project, its own point of view, taking into account the prerequisites of research, a methodological reserve to them should be emphasized and expressed. If their own opinions can be validated in the research, they should be validated as research assumptions.

From an ethical point of view, the lack of transparency with regard to assumptions that influence research, either through the particular design of the research, or by the prior selection of favorable congenial results - which will lead to falsification of the results - can be interpreted as an attempt of fraud in research results. This may be the case for some research on gay communities, starting from the implicit but not explicitly assumed premise that the development of these communities and the rights granted to these minorities are harmful to the society. The research will - as assumptions that it will attempt to demonstrate -, base a series of considerations on that community, which it will not treat with axiological impartiality and neutrality.

That vice of many social research starts from the intention of highlighting the supremacy of a position through pseudo-surveys lacking axiological neutrality. Although apparently such research can follow the rules of good research, it is in itself unethical, unbiased, or discriminatory. Proper ethical research should analyze the phenomenon from all points of view, including those that contradict the research hypothesis. A particular mention must be made of a series of constructional research (Gergen, 2001) which assumes that neutrality and objectivity can not be absolute and that the views of researchers can influence the results, in which case these views and how could they influence the results are clearly expressed in the research project and, respectively, in the publications that will result from them. The same ideological partisanship can influence not only the researcher, but also the evaluator, who may be inclined to accept a project that is convergent with its own choices and to reject another that seems to contradict them.

In our opinion, the ideological-neutral attitude should be maintained by including all predictable directions in the project, where significant results may appear, such as: the methodological option for narrative research should be completed with semi-structured interviews, in case the first ones will not generate a saturation of the model, that will include all constitutive elements of the phenomenon, at least how they are predictable for the researcher, including following the scientific literature.

The literature review will not widely present the existing data in the literature, but will only make mentions on taking them into consideration when developing the research, the way the proponents forsee that the positions expressed in the literature will influence the research approach, as well as the position of the researcher or research team towards the researched subject. It is advisable to present a more detailed theory when the whole research, or fragments thereof, are based on that particular theory or methodology, and it has a certain degree of novelty for readers or for evaluators who, although familiar with the research area, may not know all the particular theories in their subdomains. This is particularly true in trans-and interdisciplinary research.

It is possible that a current theory in a certain area of research may require explanations when used as a theoretical support in an area where it has not been, or has been poorly developed. By reading the literature review, a medium-level reader of the field must be able to understand the project without having to resort to additional reading, which he most probably would not do. Levy and Ellis (2006) assert that it is preferable to review the literature focusing on key concepts and exploring their relevance and recession, the meanings in which key concepts are used, rather than focusing on the chronological aspect or the contribution of one or a small group of authors. The scientific literature should be interrogated about its relevance to the research team.

The presence of an article in a journal in the main flow log should not be considered as a guarantee of its quality, nor does the occurrence of an article in a journal outside the main circuit automatically classify it as less scientifically. However, an article in the main stream or in journals indexed in databases is more likely to influence the advance of science in a particular field. The selection of the literature to be quoted should take into account not only the adequacy and relevance to the theme, but also the relative validity and veracity of the research results.

Randolph (2009) draws the attention that the failure in writing the literature review usually brings the failure of the entire research. Boote and Beile show that a good literature review is based on a conceptualization of the relevant literature, and that this conceptualization increases the chances of the evaluators to appreciate the value of the research project (Randolph, 2009). The quoted author points out that a good literature review can itself be a publishable work. Other purposes for which the literature review is carried out may be the creation of new research lines, the avoidance of approaches that will be doomed to failure, the theoretical support for the data obtained, the methodological clarifications, etc.

Cooper carries out a taxonomy of literature reviews, which he classifies according to the following characteristics (Randolph, 2009):

- **Focusing:** Following this criterion, the literature review aims at: the synthesis of the results in a field, the methodological synthesis, the theoretical approaches and the practical applications of researches in a field;
- **After Purpose:** Aims to theoretically integrate through generalization, to develop certain linguistic compatibilites between different fields of science, theoretical compatibility, critical approach in a field;
- **Approach Perspectives:** A literature review can be elaborated as a neutral presentation or presenting own position towarde the cited authors;
- **Covering the Literature in the Field:** Exhaustive, especially in treaties and university courses; selectively exhaustive, in theoretical papers and literature review published as such, or focused on topics and key concepts;
- From the point of view of organizing the review – it can be approached historically, conceptually or methodologically;
- From the perspective of the audience – a review can address an academic audience strictly specialized and narrow, a general academic audience, an audience generally constituted of practitioners and decision factors in the field, or a general audience.

If, in the case of a thesis or dissertation, the literature review spans a whole chapter, in a journal article the dimensions are much smaller, only the most significant references will be commented, usually using the paraphrase, avoiding quoting the source entirely (Cochrane, 2005).

From the perspective of the evaluation of the research project, it is analyzed how the researcher is familiar with, and is aware of the researches carried out in the respective field. A good position towards the literature allows avoiding the repetition of already existing and documented research in the literature, but also the carrying out of some early research. The analysis of the scientific literature is part of the research proposal, which shows the correct positioning of the research compared to the rest of the scientific literature in the field.

RATIONALITY OF RESEARCH

From the point of view of the rationality of the research, it is considered the logic that links the hypotheses or research questions with the specifics of the research plan:

- The selection of subjects and research materials: it is considered the number of persons the research will be conducted on, how will the access to the investigated population will occur, and how;
- Methods of data collection: here we consider the observational or experimental nature, the working protocols, data collection control, what data will be collected and where;
- The way of interpreting the data: this should be logical and clearly stated in the research proposal, more precisely it should highlight the quantitative (statistical) or qualitative (inductive or deductive) data analysis method.

ETHICAL PERSPECTIVES ON SOCIO-HUMAN RESEARCH METHODOLOGY

The methodology chapter describes the main methods and techniques used to achieve the results. Study design, data collection, etc. are presented. The methodological chapter is mainly used in empirical research based on direct field investigation. For the fields of theoretical research, including philosophy, law, literature, the argumentative approach, it is even the methodological dimension of the research, and therefore some publications call for methodological references in articles with a theoretical character, even if they will not necessarily be included in a chapter of methodology (Epstein & King, 2002; Stolker, 2005).

The methodologies used in the theoretical research can be: critical analysis, comparative method, case study, hermeneutical method, phenomenological methodology, semiotics method, historical methodology, discourse analysis etc.

The empirical methodologies used in the case of articles that value the field research can be, for example, experiments, quantitative research through survey, qualitative research through interview etc. (Wy, 2009). As far as the methodological dimension of research is concerned, it includes a series of implications of ethical nature regarding its scientific nature and the potential risks for participants.

In the experimental design, the limitations, the way of obtaining informed consent from participants, the risk and benefits etc. will be expresly presented.

Also in the methodology, when the articles are based on collecting and interpreting field data, will be considered the way of sampling and its validity (Wy, 2009), the data representativity for the researched population, the establishment of the experimental group, where working with the experimental method. In the case of qualitative, content analysis, aside from the brief presentation of the interpretation method, presenting the limitations of the research is considered, corelated with the ontological and epistemological approach to which the research is subsumed. This is about the realistic, positivist, constructivist etc. paradigm. In the methodological part it can be discussed about the validity of the instruments and their translation and the permission to use the instrument. The practical way of applying the field instruments is also recommended to be included in the methodology.

When the research on human subjects, and especially on vulnerable groups is being discussed, the article should discuss the way of obtaining the informed consent (Wy, 2009) and the ethical perspectives considered in elaborating the research.

The most important role of the part of methodology is that it allows to duplicate the results in future research or deepen them and obtain different local results. This is why, when particular data collection or interpretation techniques, that are less known to the usual readers of the journal, are being used, they should be explained in detail.

The concrete and explicit elaboration of a research design that would include methods and techniques of collecting data, the instruments used, the data collecting phases, sampling and including participants in the research, allows to estimate the possibilities of reaching the objectives of the research, feasibility and credibility of the research, limitation of risks of presenting unrealistic data, the level of involvement of human subjects, the risks that the participation in the research may involve for the subjects, the existence or inexistence of alternative strategies of data collecting, etc. Not respecting the research project, when this affects the credibility and validity of the results and making the participants face undue risks is an unethical behaviour in research. For example, the lack of reflection on the representative sample in a sociological quantitative research makes it invalid, and the presentation of the data as being complete can, in a way, be considered as falsifying the research results. The development of chaotic research, that doesn't respect or is not based on a research project, does not have a scientific nature, the data obtained not being considered valid, thus the research is unethical from the perspective of trust of the scientific community.

METHODS OF DATA ANALYSIS

There are considered, for example, mathematic or statistic instruments used for analysing data and extracting meaning in data analysis, which consider correlating data with research hypotheses and whether they are supported by data or not.

The mere exposure of qualitative or quantitative data is not sufficient in lack of correlations with other or data, or with similar or contradictory data in the scientific literature. The data interpretation should be done in terms of answering to the research questions and validating or invalidating the hypotheses. When the research is presented, by publishing or presenting it to conferences, it is necessary to present the meanings of data in the chapter of results, other than those consistent with the objectives of the research, that either contradict the hypotheses, or open the way for future research, not foreseen initially. The scientific literature recommends avoiding the presentation of the same data under several forms: graphic, tabel, narration etc. (Vintan, 2006).

The presentation of data is done from particular to general, emphasizing on the meaning of data and not numbers obtained, which will, however, not be ommited where the research has lead to numerical data. In the case of statistics, it is necessary to specify the existing correlations, but also the direct meaning of the results. The results of the test of meaning and validity should also be presented (Bem, 2003). Statistics have the purpose of serving the analysis, not substituting it. In the case of mixed studies, the quantitative and qualitative results will be presented separately, insisting on the way in which they support each other.

The qualitative interpretation of data, obtained through interviews, focus groups, press analysis etc. will contain significant expressions from the original data material, followed closely by their interpretations, categorizations, theoretical and metatheoretical constructions (Bem, 2003). In the case of qualitative data, they must go through processes of inductive-deductive selection, the reader having access to a series of exemples of intermediary procedures and raw data only where the editorial space allow it.

An ethical issue related to the presentation of data is that of the multiple presentation. Especially in the wide-ranging social research, the data chosen exceeds the size of an article, and as such, the data should be published in a number of articles that show the data according to the size of the research.

Excessive fragmentation of data is considered an unethical practice, since artificially increases the number of publications of research team members and implicitly their academic credit. When it is necessary to repeat a part of the data in several articles, either for a secondary analysis of them or to make intelligible other data to which the data is centered, the previously published data is quoted appropriately, either by an aknowledgement, or simply by mentioning the previous articles in the literature review chapters. It is necessary to avoid repeated publication of the same content in the same scientific context. Repeated publication is legitimate when it is done in scientific contexts, for example in different language publications, in different forms of publications, such as in the proceedings of a conference, followed by the extenso publication of a journal article, the resumption for didactic purposes in courses and textbooks of the results of a research, etc. In either of these situations, it is necessary to quote the first source and possibly to include an aknowledgement certifying that it is a work that has been republished with the consent of the holders of the publishing rights.

Another element considered for a research proposal is how the results will be disseminated: journal articles, monographs, CDs, websites, conference presentations, a combination of the above, or other possibilities.

The social-constructionist paradigm on social research (Sandu, 2016) discusses even the renunciation of the idea of the validity of research, especially in the qualitative one, and its replacement with the verosimilitude, credibility. Validity is a construct belonging to the objective, realistic science paradigm that postulates the cognoscibility of the world and the net distinction between the researched reality and the researcher. In the practice of social research, such a distinction is not always operative, the very fact that a community is questioned about a certain social phenomenon is elemental that forces it to reflect upon it and, implicitly, modifies the interpretations of that social phenomenon. Social research changes the social reality through the investigative approach. As such, ethical reflection on the impact that certain social research - such as those in the field of *policy research*, social assistance, micro-sociology of groups and organizations, etc. - has on the population under investigation is necessary, at least there is a need for a response on non-maleficence, non-discrimination, social justice and respect for the autonomy and dignity of the members of the *investigated community*, not just the direct participants in research, of these researches.

A research-intervention can not be axiologically irrelevant, and ultimately there is an ideological - theoretical foundation behind the research project. On the other hand, the subjectivity of the researcher inevitably puts its mark on the process of designing research, analyzing data, especially qualitative ones, where the hermeneutical freedom the researcher has is significant. These influences of the researcher's subjectivity must be presented in a subchapter of discussions and limits, which should exist both in the research proposal and in the publications resulting from the research project.

Another possible violation of objectivity is the excessive predilection for a research method that is being taken by the researcher, despite its obvious limits of providing the full or partial results required to achieve the purpose of the research. The predilection for a certain qualitative methodology, for example, when it fails to capture all the facets of a social phenomenon, can generate a lack of objectivity of research, the researcher tends to censure that part of the social phenomenon that could not be captured, precisely by expressing this impossibility as a limit of research. Correct expression of research boundaries is a tool for exercising the fairness and honesty of the researcher and should aim at real limitation given by the objective and subjective research and limitations of the methodology itself, but these limits should be objectively overcome, including by calling on other methodologies of a quantitative nature in our case, that would make it possible to capture other aspects of the studied phenomenon.

ELEMENTS OF ETHICS OF SCIENCE COMMUNICATION

Scientific publishing implies laborious work, which has in time shaped its own communication methodology, different from other article forms, such as journalism. The elaboration of the article in accordance with the rules in the field increases the chances that it attracts the attention of the reviewers and editors of the scientific journals and, implicitly, the acceptance of the article for publication. Once published, the article will attract interested readers from the field and then quotes in specialized publications. For specialized journals, compliance with these rules is usually a sign of scientific maturity and editorial experience, waking up the authors' trust in the field in which the journal aims to perform (Sandu, 2011c).

Ethical Elements in the Process of Publication and Communication of Science

If the excellency research addresses a high-profile audience, it should be promoted in notorious publication, which are rather accepted by reference researchers in a certain field. It is the case of ISI indexed publications, included in the first two quartiles – the so-called „red zone" of the ranking made by Clarivate Analytics – former ISI, Thomson Reuters -, as being journals with the highest notoriety in the field.

David Hull (1988) argues that the system of research is configured so that it is based on rewarding the results – in the form of academic credit obtained by the researchers – and the punishment of behaviours that lack scientific honesty, so that it should be enough to ensure the credibility of the results of the published results (Longino, 2016), even in lack of repeated verification – in the manner proposed by Popper (1972, 2008). The need for trust in the results previously obtained or, more precisely, in the honesty with which they were obtained – since a characteristic of the scientific research is the frequent change of explicative paradigms -, brings the emergence of an increased demand for the credibility of the results from the perspective of their honesty, but also from that of their basic evaluation through the peer-review process. On the other hand, the need to publish, in order to obtain those academic credits, may cause some scholars to appeal to journals that do not make peer-review, or whose peer review quality is questionable (Kelly, Sadeghieh & Adeli, 2014). Although publishing in questionable quality journals is not really an academic fraud, this may diminish the academic credibility of a researcher who publishes exclusively or largely only in this category of journals.

The peer-review process – along with the reproducibility of the results – is represented by methods of ensuring credibility of a scientific production, both at the level of the research project, and of publication of results (Longino, 2016). As regards the peer-review process, this ensures an evaluation of the quality of research from the perspective of the methodology used, the originality and its meaning for the research field, and for science in general. A series of researches (Lee, 2012) suggests the existence of serious bias in the process of peer-review, even in well ranked journals, especially in the field of social and humanistic sciences, related to the conservatorism of the reviewers on the methodology used, the trans-paradigmatic researches that question the theoretical perspectives which constitute the scientific mainstream of the field etc. In some situations, there were cases of discrimination related to the gender or nationality of the researchers - probably due to journal publishers rather than peer reviewers, during the blind peer review process (Kelly et al., 2014). These results, with regard to the limits of peer review as the sole mechanism for the selection of scientific projects and publications, add another series of criticisms related to the inconsistency of reviews for the same work (Lee, 2012) when a reviewer suggests rejection from publication on the basis of methodologies or outcomes considered to be mistaken, and another one recommends publication on the basis of the same methodologies and outcomes. Moreover, in the social and humanistic field it is possible to reject an article or research project based on the inconsistency between the ideological perspective of the reviewer and the ideological background, or even the empirical results obtained by the researcher.

The most radical criticisms of the peer review process state that it is useless in ensuring the scientific quality of the publications, due to the subjectivity of the reviewers (Harris, 2009). Fiona Godlee, editor for the British Medical Journal, one of the most respected journals in the medical field, has conducted an experiment, introducing 8 intended errors in an article that was already accepted for publication, and then sending it to 420 reviewers. 221 of them have identified 2 of the errors, while 16% of the reviewers identified none (Harris, 2009).

A number of limits of using the peer-review system in evaluating the contemporary scientific production, are:

- Subjectivity of the reviewers can put its mark on the quality of the peer-review process; in general, the important journals require the opinion of several reviewers to fundament their decision of accepting or rejecting from publication, in many situations, but the opinion of a single reviewer is used to justify the decision of rejection from publication, without the reviewers' views being discussed by the authors; in some cases, for example, in evaluating a proposal of research project (Popa, 2016) there is a stage of *rebutle*, where the proponents of the project express their opinion towards the position of the evaluators, contradicting it; also reffering to the subjectivity of the reviewers, this is manifested in the availability of giving advice for improving the articles worth being published, but which doesn't meet all the requirements for publication in the proposed form;
- The long time for the peer-review process, in the case of certain journals who have a large number of articles proposed for publication, may last up to 2 years between the moment of sending the article in its initial form and the time of publication, after a few rounds of successive re-sending and re-evaluation, the process of peer-review basically slows down the editorial process, making a series of data irrelevant, or in case of similar theories, making a researcher lose priority over it to

another researcher who published in a faster-publishing journal; a partially used sollution used by journals is to publish within the article the date it was proposed at, and the date it was accepted.

- The peer-review system is difficult to use in detecting fraudulent publications based on falsifying data, because the reviewer doesn't have direct access to the data underlying the article (Harris, 2009), but only to those mentioned, that can be true or falsified, including by truncating them and presenting only those that support the hypotheses of the researchers;
- the limited number of researchers accepting to be peer-reviewers for different financing bodies or scientific journals, especially under the conditions in which this activity, at least in the case of the majority of journals, is voluntary (Kelly et. al., 2014); under these circumstances, certain journals accept researchers with a smaller experience in the field to be reviewers, and who despite their best intentions and honesty, may produce incorrect or incomplete peer-reviews, either by too quickly rejecting the article, without giving improvement suggestions, or by accepting them with very little or no suggestions at all;
- The possible ethical frauds in elaborating the review, when personalities in the field reject research projects or articles that could question their own previous results (Harris, 2009) – or would simply be a competition for them – or, on the contrary, accept with maximum ease projects or articles comming from members of the formal networks, but especially the informal ones, of researchers that help each other;
- A lack of clarity concerning the copyright on the suggestions made by the reviewer within the process of peer-review raises a series of questions, as follows: if the suggestions offered by the reviewer become the intellectual property of the author of the article, in the hypotheses in which the article includes the suggestions but is published in a journal other than the one for which the peer review was done, brings the issue whether using them without mentioning the source is or is not considered plagiarism (Poff, 2017); if the reviewer holds the copyright, then the dilemma is whether this should be mentioned at least in acknowledgment or bibliography (but in that case, the anonymous character of the review disappears), and if the copyright is automatically transferred to the author of the article, it brings the question of whether the reviewers are motivated to offer valuable suggestions to the authors, knowing that their ideas will be incorporated into the article without any credit; At present, Clarivate Analythics's initiative facilitates the recognition of reviewer quality through the Publons website, but this is done in a general manner, without mentioning reviewers' contributions to each article;
- The possibility of false reviews, though fictitious reviewer accounts belonging, in fact, to the author of the article or his/her collaborators (Poff, 2017); this possibility emerges in the case of journals, but also of research funding lines that require the author to indicate a possible list of reviewers in the field of the article, from which the journal or financer would chose some of them as reviewers.

Despite these limits of peer review use in the editorial process, this remains the current form of assessment of the scientific quality of research projects and the results of research proposed for publication in articles or books.

On the other hand, the results of the transfer of research into technology should be published in journals or publications that are accesible to the manager that could use them in practice. Publication in ISI journals with very high ranking either obliges the managers to cite those journals, which are not actually destined for them, or condemns the results of the transfer of researches in technology to remaining sterile (Sandu, 2011c).

The journals considered significant in a certain field have a rejection rate of articles that varies between 30% and 70%, based on the positioning of the journal in the national and international hierarchy or the impact factor, elements that materialize in the number of articles available for publication. Many of the important journals in different fields will prefer to publish a smaller number of articles, with the greatest chance of being cited, eliminating scientifically correct articles, but presumed by the editors to attract fewer citations. The international classifications, especially the ones given by Thomson Reuters (former ISI Thomson) and Scopus, consider the number of citations the articles in a journal receive in a given period of time.

As such, journals wishing to enter these classifications, to maintain and obtain a best position, will admit predominantly or even exclusively articles validated from the point of view of scientific correctness, which the editors of the journal appreciate would bring citations. From this point of view, a selection criterion, unethical from our perspective, but frequently used in practice, even outside of the peer-review process, is the analysis of previous citations of the author's publications in databases, a process that the chief editor performs. Even if an article receives favorable references from reviewers, it may be rejected because it is considered unattractive for the positioning of the publication on the scientific market.

The existence of platforms such as ORCID and the calculation of some scientometric indicators, such as the hirch factor, may encourage this behavior of journal editors in the legitimate desire to position themselves in the rankings that take as a reference the number of citations, such as those related to impact factor or score influence articles, which may be inclined to reject more easily articles from early career researchers who have a limited capacity to attract citations by means other than the intrinsic value of the article, and more easily admits senior researchers who are part of formal or informal research networks and thus attract quotes from within the network. Research networks are legitimate and encouraged to form, precisely to encourage the development of a particular field of research.

The researchers that study within the same field know each other directly, by participating in congresses or research stages, or indirectly, only by constantly reading the articles published by other members of the network. Thus, mutual influences occur within the research networks, translated also by cross-citations of members of the network.

An ethical error associated with the existence of networks of researchers is the manipulation of the impact factor of journals and, in general, of scientometric indicators by reciprocal citation of members of such a network, especially of an informal nature, whether the article has been used or not as a source of documentation for that project or article. Another practice is the direct or indirect obligation, including by the existence of a common sense at the level of the research institution, of doctoral students to quote the publications of their tutors and / or the members of the theses evaluation committee. This practice, legitimate in itself, when the PhD student works in a joint research project with his coordinator or a project based on previous coordinator results becomes fraudulent when the quoted sources have nothing to do with the doctoral work, but they only come in order to increase the scientific visibility of the coordinator. Another informal practice is the coordinator's suggestion for the PhD student or the members of the research team to avoid citing a researcher with whom the coordinator is in conflict or competition.

Publication of research results is considered part of the author's marketing of science and personal branding, and not as the simple fulfillment of the ethical or contractual obligations of disseminating the research's own results. In the case of articles of equal scientific quality, some of the journals that question the problem of the editorial space insufficiency might first prefer an author with a higher citation index, an author who also published in that journal, thus quoting him, and only in the last place an author who has not previously been published. The existence of a significant number of articles published by an author, but subsequently undetected, may result in a reduction in the chances of publishing in important journals.

Nevertheless, it is necessary to take into account the editorial offices of significant publications in terms of positioning in the scientific journals market, given that in the social and human domain the number of citations is much lower than in other fields of science. In the field of sociology, for example, the average impact factor of an ISI publication is around 1, with a peak around the figure of 3 and the median at 0.5, while in other areas of the sciences the average impact factors on the field are often around the number 3.

Appreciating the work of a researcher exclusively after the criteria of publishing in journals with high scientific prestige condemns the research to be separated from the production or the social practice in general. Rethinking the research marketing based on the addressability of a research doesn't exclude the need for scientific rigor and peer-review (Sandu, 2011c).

We consider that the publication with role of promoting the research results should be differentiated from those with role of disseminating the research results inside the scientific community.

We do not consider that a real hierarchy between fundamental and applied research can be established, since they both participate to the progress of knowledge. The stimulation of the valorification of research results by promoting them outside the narrow frameworks of the projects in which they were conducted, could attract a more rapid insertion of scientific knowledge into the social practice, and thus, a more rapid transition to the „knowledge-based society".

Another dimension of the promotion of science is the fast exposure of ideas, models and theories towards the scientific and academic audience. This is achieved through means of scientific books and university courses. We can formulate the question whether the making of such scientific books and courses is indeed a work of research, or is it another field of the scientific authorship (Sandu, 2009).

From our point of view, the development of a specialized book is an effective research, in terms of selecting the most significant theories and with the greatest chances of impact in professional practice. All research is the development of points of view on exposed theories, which will eventually lead to the opening of new areas of research. On one hand, we could state that the fundamental research by writing books can be done, since too few scientific theories or absolutely original points of view require such an extensive treatment. On the other hand, the wide exposure space offered by a volume allows the researcher to expose his ideas in a more clear and argumented way, but *in extenso*, outlining the possible collateral openings, unique methodological approaches, typologies of understanding the scientific reality etc. Therefore the ideas presented in a book with scientific value should widely present at least one original point of view of the author and focus around it.

The role of promoter of science that the scientific book has, creates a new applicative opening of the theories or ideas contained in the volume or is a scientific pseudolithology.

The scientific paper also has two levels of addressability, to the experts and researchers in a given field, to provide them with new ideas and research directions, and professionals, to whom they have to present models, techniques or technologies that can be applied in the activity practice. Books targeting experts and researchers should have a higher level of abstraction and, as such, a more limited audience.

The volumes addressed to professionals should be built in such a way as to be accessible to at least medium-level professionals to assist in their professional practice.

University courses and textbooks have the mission to disseminate the results of science to future professionals and / or researchers. Their construction should be based on the principle of opening the students' horizon to the exposed issues and providing them with the main tools for exercising the profession and / or carrying out the research. Exposing scientific or practical, professional theories should not focus on their excellence, but rather the know-how of their application in practice. Thus, we ask ourselves the question: what are the dimensions of scientific authoring in the development of professional manuals? These should be analyzed according to the criterion of the practical efficiency of the information provided and, at the same time, of the conceptual openings, rather than the scientific and novelty value (Sandu, 2009).

All these types of scientific writing generate, in their own way, the general advance of knowledge. The editing of scientific literature raises the issue of the need for scientific qualification of publishers and ample professional representation in the editorial board. If for fundamental science, the role of the reviewer is to methodologically analyze the approach proposed by the author, in the case of a scientific publishing, the role of the reviewers and editors of the scientific book is to appreciate the existence of elements of originality within the volume, the premises of future scientific exploitation. In textbooks and university courses, they should stop at the pragmatic dimension of the paper and the way in which prospective professionals can extract competences from the study.

Scientific Authorship: Who Are the Authors of the Articles and How to Establish the Order of the Authorship of a Scientific Article

The authors of the scientific articles are generally those who participate in the elaboration of the research and the writing of the article itself. In theoretical research, such as philosophical, legal or political, one or at most a few people participate in all stages of the research.

In exact sciences and in sciences of nature, and partly in social sciences where the research is wider, there are a large number of people involved in research, both in preliminary phases, in collecting experimental data, and in drawing conclusions and writing the article.

Aside from them, a number of specialists can provide meaningful feedback in writing the article, especially from the coordinators of the research group or the scientific coordinators of the dissertation or doctoral thesis, which are often involved in the research and the drafting of the theses. Karl Swedberg (2008) shows that the definition of scientific authority and a clear interpretation of which individuals are entitled to sign an article, are far from being clarified in the literature.

The journals in different areas of science apply different rules regarding the inclusion of a leader in the list of authors and the order of the authors. Swedberg (2008) shows that for a person to be on the list of authors, it should have significant intellectual contributions in at least one of the domains: conceiving and design of the paper, data acquisition, data analysis and interpretation, analysis statistics, scientific supervision of the research, elaboration of a draft of the article, formulation of substantial reviews with important intellectual content.

All authors must agree on publication and be able to support research by answering questions about this research. Contributors who do not meet the criteria to be authors should be included in the acknowledgments. It is not very usual in the Romanian scientific literature that, together with the doctoral or master student who publishes an article, the coordinating professor should also sign, although in many situations this should be taken into account both because of the increased volume of the coordinator's scientific contribution, and the credibility that a scientific personality with weight brings to the work. The contact between young researchers and highly experienced researchers will be responsible for both sides, reducing the risk of plagiarism or misrepresentation of data (Sandu, 2011c).

As regards the authors' order, this should respect the volume of work submitted and the importance of the scientific contribution of each author. Presenting in alphabetical order, mentioning the equal contribution of each author in acknowledgment, draws attention to the equal quoting of author in each signatory. Thomson Reuters identifies, together with the lead author, co-authors, and the *reprint author* as the correspondent with potential readers. In some journals, the last author is past the coordinator of the paper, when appropriate.

Affiliations

Affiliations are usually referred to as footnotes on the first page of the article, even when no footnotes are used for the critical apparatus (Sandu, 2011c). The CNCS-UEFISCDI recommendations for Romanian scientific journals require, according to international practice, that at least the scientific title of the author (required) be included in the affiliation, the name of the university under which the article is to be published (required), the department (optional) author's address (optional - personal or institutional), author's phone number (required), author's e-mail address (required). This data is requested to all authors (Bala, 2010).

Acknowledgments

Acknowledgments usually include the recognition of the contribution of third parties to the research, that led to creating the article, or the actual writing of the article, but whose contribution is not so significant as to be considered authors. Also, the acknowledgments include information on the source of research funding (Bala, 2010), the research organization in which the authors carried out the research activity or research project in which the data was obtained (Sandu, 2011c).

Citation and Critical Apparatus

From an ethical perspective, correct and complete quoting of all sources used in the documentation process avoids plagiarism. Plagiarism is the taking of ideas or scientific, artistic, literary, or other kinds of creation, in whole or in part, and their presentation as the creation of the author who takes them. Plagiarism takes different forms, from the full take up of broad contents of certain materials exactly in the form in which it appears in original, to the taking of one or some ideas, even processed by storytelling, paraphrasing etc., without mentioning the original source. Plagiarism can be involuntary, when previously heard or read ideas are presented unintentionally as their own, especially when a significant period has passed since they were received and were reconceptualized with the author's own ideas.

Voluntary plagiarism occurs when the ideological content is taken voluntarily, the author being aware that this content does not belong to him. Voluntary plagiarism is a form of intellectual theft (Shashabuddin, 2009). The discovery of plagiarism leads to serious consequences, reaching to the exclusion of the plagiarist from the academic community, the withdrawal of scientific and professional titles obtained fraudulently, etc. To detect plagiarism, academic institutions and publishers use a number of anti-plagiarism software, the most well-known of which is Turnitin. Anti-plagiarism software highlights the similarity between the text being analyzed and other texts existing in the database, made available by the software and the Internet. The existence of similarities does not necessarily mean plagiarism - the software highlighting, for example, the name of the research institution or references as similar to others already existing. Plagiarism by paraphrasing or translating from one language into another is usually not detected through the software, and the academic community has the final role to play in the plagiarism detection. Clear plagiarism situations, in which significant fragments are taken identically, without the distinctive citation signs and without mentioning the source, are added to situations in which plagiarism is not obvious, the idea taken up being enriched and transformed by the author. Plagiarism can be made from unpublished sources, private discussions, presentations at unpublished conferences, etc., impossible to detect with the help of the software or even by members of the academic community.

Self-plagiarism is taking the author's own ideas and repeatedly publishing them in the same form, without mentioning the republication and without proper citation.

Honest quoting can be of several ways:

- The simple quote through which a fragment of a work is taken, given in quotation marks or other forms of clear citation, followed by a bibliographic reference by footnote or note in the text;
- Continuous quote, when several fragments are taken identically and quoted, interleaved with the comments of the author quoting and accompanied by a single bibliographic reference;
- The bibliographic reference, which indicates the source of an idea without taking fragments from the work (Stoenescu, 2017).

A series of discussions arise when many ideas are taken from a work that is quoted, but not after every idea taken and not in a manner in which it is obvious it was take from the same source of all ideas, especially when between them, downloads from other sources intervene.

A rule in the realization of the bibliographic apparatus is that the existing bibliography would be found in the text and reciprocally, and all citations in the text are presented in the bibliography. It is not correct to mention in the bibliography some works to which there are no references in the text, motivated by the fact that those sources were generally used as an ideological framework. It is necessary to specify which of the ideas expressed in the text have as its source the material mentioned in the bibliography.

Another plagiarism situation is the use of the ideas of one of the participants in the research, but for some reasons it has not been included or withdrawn from the authorship of the article.

The current scientific literature uses several citation styles, either with footnotes or with notes in the text: APA Style, Vancouver style, Chicago style, Turabian style, etc.

Some Considerations Regarding the Elements of a Successful Article

The article's convergence with the purpose of the journal and the topic of the issue, if it is presented, increases the chances of an article to be published. Regarding the research objective of the article, it will usually be analyzed from the point of view of the scientific importance and potential beneficiaries of the results (Sandu, 2011c).

The results of a research can be used as a starting point or background for other research, or can be used directly by practitioners. Strictly academic journals tend to prefer articles that will be developed in subsequent research by the same author or other authors. This option is partly justified by the fact that these articles will attract citations faster, including self-citations, if, based on the results published in an article, at least one of the authors will make further developments. The self-citation of a previous article, which was the basis of a new research, is justified and even mandatory to avoid self-plagiarism.

Although in the Romanian system of evaluation of research performance self-assessments are not taken into account, they are considered acceptable in the ISI system, contributing to the impact factor and the Hirsch index. Thomson Reuters considers a 35% self-citation rate of an article or publication to be acceptable. In the impact factor for 2010 of most of the Romanian scientific publications, self-citations entered at a rate higher than 50%, which shows the tendency of grouping Romanian research around publications that make nuclei of researchers publishing on the same topic and who appreciate each other (Sandu, 2011c).

Self-citation is mandatory when a scientific text previously published in a journal is resumed later and developed in an article published in the same or another journal. Our analyzes of Romanian ISI publications show a low rate of citation of Romanian authors by other Romanian authors, and even a low rate of self-citation of a researcher's articles in articles published in other journals than those in which the article was published originally. This fact leads us to the lack of trust of Romanian authors in the research of their colleagues or the fear of provincialization.

Another observation made following the analysis of the Romanian ISI publications shows a small interest of the Romanian authors to quote articles from the main scientific flow (Thomson Reuters). Since Thomson Reuters analyzes the number of readers of ISI indexed journals in ISI published articles, many journals are rejecting articles with a small number of citations from other ISI articles. Rejection is justified by the argument that publications in the main scientific flow are generally topical and contain reliable results (Sandu, 2011c).

The lack of citations in this field may indicate a provincialization of the Romanian research. Obviously, in some areas, including Romanian law, Romanian language and literature and other specific Romanian studies, they are fully justified to address research based on local interest and less of global relevance.

REFLECTIONS ON THE ETHICAL NATURE OF THE RESEARCH PROPOSAL

When submitting the application for obtaining the ethical approval for a research project, a series of ethical aspects must be considered, which are necessary to be explicitly presented in the request addressed to the ethics committee.

First of all, when the research project responds to the fundamental principles of research ethics: the principle of benefit, the principle of respect for the person, the principle of non-harm, the confidentiality of subjects and the protection of personal data, should be reflected upon and considered when necessary.

The analysis should consider:

- The ethical character of the purpose of the research,
- The value of the research,
- The ethical issues,
- The benefits brought by the research,
- The clear and ethically and legally accepted scientific objectives,
- The scientific validity of data and results in general,
- The plausible research design,
- What will the participation of the persons involved in the research consist of,
- The duration,
- The anonymous character and the protection of data of participants in the research,
- The direct benefits, including material and financial incentives for the participants in the research,
- The need for using strategies of misleading the participants on the real purposes of the research,
- Estimating the risks of the participants in the research,
- Strategies of minimizing the risk,

- The limitations of the participation of human subjects in the research and their possibility to withdraw at any given time,
- The selection of subjects participating in the research, including the methods of sampling or of chosing the sample of participants,
- The existence or non-existence of the control group,
- The criteria of selection and inclusion or exclusion from the sample,
- The use of the placebo effect in case of control group,
- The use of informed consent, the care for the participants, especially to those from vulnerable categories,
- The approach of potential injuries, the protection of subjects,
- The lack of alternative methods of research, that would not involve the participation of human subjects,
- Possible conflicts of interest, both at the level of the implementation team and the involved institutions: implementors, partners, funders,
- The ethical aspects emerging in the research (for example: the use of the genetic material and other human biological products, of human embryos, of human fetal tissues/cells, of human embryonic stem cells, genetic information processing, animal studies),
- Other ethical aspects that may occur.

PROPOSAL MODEL FOR ETHICAL EVALUATION OF THE RESEARCH PROJECT "THE SOCIAL CONSTRUCTION OF THE AUTONOMY AND RESPONSIBILITY OF PERSONS UNDER THE SUPERVISION OF PROBATION SERVICES"

We will continue to present a model of proposal to the Ethics Committee of Research, which requests the evaluation of the ethical acceptability of a project on the social construction of autonomy and responsibility of people placed under the supervision of probation services.

To the attention of the Research Ethics Commission,

Summary of the Research

The project is based on a constructionist option, according to which the social reality is the results of an interpretative, (re)negotiated agreement between the communicational actors, and based on which the social consensus is traded (Sandu & Unguru, 2014). The purpose of the research is to identify the particularities of the social construction and the responsibility of the minor who committed criminal acts. The context of the research targets the particularities of the communicative action carried out within the probation services in the N.-E. area of Romania and the Republic of Moldova.

The research aims to identify the ethical frameworks in which the process of obtaining informed consent is developed, in medical institutions (in the N.-E. region of Romania) authorized to conduct medical research on human subjects, and the meaning of the ethical practice according to the specialists. The research is developed within the LUMEN Research Center in Social and Humanistic Sciences, as part of the project „Informed Consent between Theory and Practice in North-Eastern Region of Romania Medical Research Field".

Objectives of the research:

O1: The development of a study that aims to diagnose the institutional context of functioning of probation services in Romania and the Republic of Moldova, through the reform in the field of justice;
O2: The elaboration of a theory concerning the contexts and processes of social construction of the autonomy and responsibilities of delinquent minors;
O3: The construction and piloting of an institutional model of implementing the restorative justice – through probation -, that would consider the particularities of the mechanisms of social construction of autonomy and responsibility of young delinquents.

The research will be based on a mixed, qualitative (content analysis and Grounded Theory) and quantitative (online surveys) methodology.

Introduction

The social balance in a community is disturbed by the commitment of a crime, and can be best restored by all parts assuming the responsibility, including the community and the victim and not only the offender. Assuming the responsibility of each part should be based on an autonomous decision of the subjects involved – criminals, victim and the community. We consider that the probation services responsible for the process of social construction of autonomy and responsibility of the offender placed under supervision, as a strategy based on communicative action and not only on social action, as it is now. The *responsibility* as ethical value means a characteristic of the agent to act knowingly, having competence, maturity and training, as well as the conditions of liberty, so as to recognize himself in the actions and take responsibility for them (Cozma & Magureanu, 2008). The term *autonomy* knows, in turn, several meanings:

- *Autonomy as self-determination* (individual autonomy) belongs to the individual who is capable of establishing his own options, for the general unfolding of his life, and for a decision he must take in a particular situation (O'Neill, 2006);
- *Autonomy as authenticity* (Sandu, 2012d) is the individual's capacity to be consistent with his own decisions, this being the ethical decision in act – a direct manifestation of the individual's capacity of agent as social actor;
- *Relational autonomy* is correlated with the fact that the current ethical decision is the result of the process of socialization and internalization of moral norms of the community in which the individual operates (Sandu, 2014).

The social acceptability of the individual, even in the context of committing a criminal act, can be correlated with the phenomena of social control for the management of relational autonomy.

For details, see the project attached to this request.

Objectives of the Project

O1: The development of a study that would target the diagnose of the institutional context of functioning of the probation services in Romania and the Republic of Moldova, through the reform in the field of justice;

O2: The development of a theory regarding the contexts and processes of social construction of autonomy and responsibility in case of delinquent minors;

O3: The development and piloting of an institutional model of implementing restorative justice – through probation -, that would consider the particularities of the mechanisms of social construction of autonomy and responsibility of the young delinquents.

Expected Results

The results obtained in this research will be used to achieve an implementation of a model of *appreciative-affirmative ethics* in the area of fighting criminality, through highlighting the impact of the social construction of ethical values on the social change, both at the level of the individuals who committed criminal acts, as well as the institutions. It is expected that, following the deployment of the project, there will be an operational model for the implementation of restorative justice through the development of the social and relational autonomy of the individuals who have committed criminal offenses and, consequently, the responsibility of these individuals for their own prosocial behavior and for the consequences of the deeds antisocial actions they have committed.

Preventing the Expected Risks and Benefits

Risks

- Please describe the risks (including risks associated with the use of personal information) as well as risk minimization methods. Determine potential injury (stress, physical, psychological, social or economic damage) that can be borne by the participants in this study:

No harm caused by stress, physical, psychological, social or economic harm will be borne by the participants in this study. However, the subjects under the supervision of probation services have committed a series of offenses for which they have been punished with a non-custodial or non-custodial educational measure, so counseling provided by probation services is therefore required. We are not talking about unvoluntary participation in these services because they expressed their agreement to the way of inforcing non-custodial sanctions, but the alternative would have been the execution of the sentence in detention. Participation in research, beyond the specific counseling program provided by probation services, is voluntary, participants under supervision signing a consent form for participation in the research. In the process of obtaining informed consent from these participants, we will, in particular, ensure the voluntary nature of the participation, the fact that no particular benefits are expected from the participation, and also that the subject does not consider participation to be an obligation in the process of enforcement of non-custodial measures. Other categories of research participants, probation advisers, service managers and other specialists are volunteering to research, signing the informed consent form after being explained the nature of their participation in the research.

Subjects may be dissatisfied with the fact that they should spend time answering questions and we will make sure that this does not happen by ensuring the subjects can withdraw at any time of the interview.

- Do the collected data reffer to illegal activities? (If so, explain)
- The collected data may refer to illegal activities, both in interviews with persons in the care of probation services, which briefly or broadly expose their own criminal offenses, as well as probation counselors who can give examples to the types of offenses for which the subjects are under surveillance. In principle, none of the accounts of criminal offenses should refer to facts that are not brought to the attention of the authorities, however, because during interviews with persons placed under supervision, they could bring to light facts that they did, but have not been made known to the authorities, but in the process of obtaining informed consent they will be informed of the confidentiality limits and the obligation to inform the authorities of those facts.
- Methods to ensure anonymity or confidentiality:

The transcripts of interviews will not contain any identification data for the subjects. Subjects will be informed about the confidentiality of their data. If the subject mentions data that may lead to its identification or affiliation, it will be anonymized when transcribing the data.

- The plan for destroying private and identifiable data, at the end of the research project:
- The recordings will be deleted at the end of the project. In the case of applied questionnaires, these will be non-nominative and will be kept in separate places from the informed consent forms.

Benefits

- Benefits for improving knowledge in the field:
- The main theoretical benefit is the elaboration of a model for the analysis of the functioning of restorative justice as the background of the development of ethical behaviors based on responsibility and autonomy in persons who have committed criminal offenses.
- Benefits for public policies:
- To formulate suggestions for institutional and public ethics policies aimed at the development of restorative justice through probation practice centered on empowering and developing the social and relational autonomy of persons who have committed criminal offenses.
- The institutional diagnosis will be completed with public policy proposals to develop probation practice, which will allow competent authorities to make appropriate decisions on criminal policies and social policies on non-custodial sanctions.
- Benefits for participants in the research:
- There are no direct benefits for participants other than those related to the possible therapeutic value of the narrative approach to interviews with supervised persons.

Participants

- Number | Average age | Gender
- *To the interview:* 30 (minimum), to the saturation of the sample | between 28 and 60 years old | male and female

- *To the focus group:* between 8 and 12 in each focus group | between 28 and 60 years old | male and female
- Recruitment population, including criteria of inclusion/exclusion:

For the qualitative analysis we will proceed to identifying, for each interview, minimum 2 representatives from each institution, by using the „snowball method", starting from the contacts obtained by phone. The specific criteria for inclusion will be for people placed under surveillance, the type of crime committed, and for the probation services staff, their initial specialization, as well as their experience in the system. If we identify other categories of personnel, we will also include them in the sample. We will include at least two heads of probation services in the sample.

The final sample list will contain names, phone numbers of the respondents and the date of the first 30 scheduled interviews. In case the sample is saturated (there are no new data obtained through analysing data collected in every interview), no other interview will be conducted. If not, we will continue the process of selection in the same way, until saturation. See the selection process specific for Grounded Theory sampling:

- Recruitment procedures:
- A sampling using the „snowball method" will be conducted (for interviews).
- Incentives and compensations:
- There are no incentives or compensations.
- The method of establishing the research group:
- There is no control group. There is no randomized clinical study.

Informed Consent

The procedure of obtaining informed consent from all participants (or parents or legal guardian): describe the method of obtaining informed consent (attach the informed consent form).

Obtaining the informed consent will be done based on a process of information and deliberation. The persons placed under surveillance being a vulnerable group, it will be paid a special consideration that by participating in the research, the vulnerability linked to re-living the committed crimes is not amplified, even if talking about the committed deed and the eventual regret is part of the normal process of probation counselling. The aim of this research is not to have the nature of a research-intervention and, as such, the questions will be formulated and addressed in a way that doesn't involve emotional stress, doesn't denote a behaviour of condemning the committed deeds etc. Within the process of obtaining the IC a special attention will be paid to the voluntary nature of the participation and the fact that the subjects have understood that the participation to the interviews in the research is not an integrated part of the process of surveillance through probation. The participants will be informed on their rights, including that of withdrawing from the research at any given time.

In case of minors or other participants that are unable to provide legal informed consent, please describe the procedures used in obtaining the consent to participate, in addition to the agreement of the parent or legal guardian.

If interviews with minors are conducted, the informed consent will be obtained from their parents, and from the minors, because they are at least 14 years of age – the age at which they are criminally liable – an *assent* will be requested. In case the minors are in foster care, the legal representative from the guardianship authority will be the one signing the informed consent.

Design and Study Methods

For the detailed design of the project, see the research project that accompanies the present request.

- *Methods of collecting data and intervention, including the duration of subjects' involvement:*
- Interviews (between 40 minutes and 1 hour) – the interview guide is attached.
- *Measuring instrument (the survey and questionnaire guides are attached as annexes).*
- *Equipment for meeting with the subjects:*
- Recorders.
- If misleading is necessary, justify the motivation and how to do it. Describe the analysis procedures (Attach the annex)
- No deception is required.
- Analysis of the results:

Grounded Theory for the qualitative analysis, and statistical analysis for the study.

Statement of the Conflict of Interest

There was no conflict of interest identified.

References

See the project proposal attached to this request[1].

Annexes

- Interview guide;
- Informed consent form for the interview;
- Informed consent for applying online surveys;

Protection of human subjects' information – GDPR specific forms.
Signature of the proponant:
Date:

Instead of Conclusions

The ethical dimension of the research project targets a series of aspects such as the social utility and its scientific value, its correct design and implementation, credibility and validity of the results, the research development financing, the publication of the results and the participants' way of involvement. In turn, the ethical communication of science through the participation in conferences and publication involves a series of ethical aspects referring to the structure of the paper itself, the authorship, including the order of the authors, the correctness and the verifiability of the published results, the peer review process, the avoidance of plagiarism. The principles of the research ethics, of which the most well-known are that of beneficence, non-maleficence, promotion of autonomy for participants in the research, justice and equity, is completed with principles such as the responsibility of the researcher and the research organization towards the subjects of the research, the results and implications of technological transfer and implementation of results etc.

Although the ethics of research is generally seen as being prohibitive, due to promoting the means of combating academic fraud, plagiarism, falsification of results, data fabrication etc., the ethics of research should be considered in an affirmative manner, as a framework of the development of science and the assumption of the researcher's and research institutions' responsibility.

ACKNOWLEDGMENT

Chapter developed within the project „Etică şi integritate academică de excepţie în cercetarea ştiinţifică şi actul didactic" [Ethics and academic integrity exceptional in scientific research and didactic act]; Implementor: Stefan cel Mare University in Suceava with financial support from FDI2018, Domain 5, Improving the quality of didactic activity, including respecting academic deontology and ethics. Project code: CNFIS-FDI-2018-0545.

The reproduction of ideas previously expressed by the authors of the chapter was appropriately signaled by citation, and the reproduction of some short fragments of the original articles was done with the editor's agreement.

REFERENCES

Astărăstoae, V., Loue, S., & Ioan, B. (Eds.). (2009). Etica cercetării pe subiecţi umani [Ethics of research on human subjects]. Iaşi, România: "Gr. T. Popa" U.M.F. Iaşi Publishing House.

Bahm, A. (1971). Science is not value free. *Policy Sciences*, *2*(4), 391–396. doi:10.1007/BF01406139

Bala, C. (2010). *Redactarea lucrărilor ştiinţifice* [Writing scientific papers]. Bucharest, Romania: Programul Doctoratul în şcoli de excelenţă.

Baumeister, R. F., & Leary, M. K. (1997). Writing narrative literature reviews. *Review of General Psychology*, *1*(3), 311–320. doi:10.1037/1089-2680.1.3.311

Bem, D. J. (2003). Writing the empirical journal article. In J. M. Darley, M. P. Yanna, & H. L. Roediger III, (Eds.), *The Complete Academic: A Practical Guide for the Beginning Social Scientist* (2nd ed.). Washington, DC: American Psychological Association.

Chapin, P. G. (2004). *Research projects and research proposals. A guide for scientists seeking funding*. New York: Cambridge University Press.

Charlton, B. G. (2009). Are you an honest scientist? Truthfulness in science should be an iron law, not a vague aspiration. *Medical Hypotheses*, *73*(5), 633–635. doi:10.1016/j.mehy.2009.05.009 PMID:19501471

Cochrane, J. H. (2005). *Writing tips for Ph. D. students*. Chicago: Graduate School of Business University of Chicago. Retrieved from http://gsbwww.uchicago.edu/fac/john./cochrane/research/papers

Cohen, B. C. (n.d.). Nazi medical experimentation: The ethics of using medical data from Nazi experiments. *Jewish Virtual Library*. Retrieved from https://www.jewishvirtuallibrary.org/the-ethics-of-using-medical-data-from-nazi-experiments

Cojocaru, D., & Sandu, A. (2011). (Bio)ethical and social reconstructions in transmodernity. *Journal for the Study of Religions and Ideologies*, *10*(30), 258–276.

Cozma, C., & Măgureanu, L. (2008). Valori etice fundamentale, între constanţă şi metamorfoză [Fundamental ethical values, between constancy and metamorphosis]. In M. M. Pivniceru & C. Luca (Eds.), *Deontologia profesiei de magistrat. Repere contemporane* [Deontology of the Profession of Magistrate. Contemporary Landmarks]. Bucharest, Romania: Hamangiu.

Creswell, J. W. (2007). *Qualitative inquiry and research design: Choosing among five traditions* (2nd ed.). Thousand Oaks, CA: Sage Publication Inc.

Culianu, I. P. (2003). *Eros şi magie în Renaştere. 1484* [Eros and magic in the Renaissance. 1484]. Iaşi, Romania: Polirom.

Epstein, L., & King, G. (2002). The rules of inference. *The University of Chicago Law Review. University of Chicago. Law School*, *69*(1), e1. doi:10.2307/1600349

Foucault, M. (1991). *Discipline and punish: The birth of a prison*. London, UK: Penguin.

Foucault, M. (1998). *The History of sexuality: The Will to knowledge*. London, UK: Penguin.

Frunză, A. (2016). *Către o nouă expertiză etică. Deconstruind valorile etice* [Towards a new ethical expertise. Deconstructing ethical values]. Iaşi, Romania: Lumen.

Frunză, A., & Sandu, A. (2017). Supervision of ethics in social work practice: A reconstruction of ethics expertise. In *Ethical Issues in Social Work Practice* (pp. 175–209). Hershey, PA: IGI Global.

Gergen, K. (2005). *Social construction in context*. London, UK: Penguin.

Hardwig, J. (1985). Epistemic dependence. *The Journal of Philosophy*, *82*(7), 335–349. doi:10.2307/2026523

Hardwig, J. (1988). Evidence, testimony, and the problem of individualism. *Social Epistemology*, *2*(4), 309–321. doi:10.1080/02691728808578498

Harris, W. (2009). *How scientific peer review works*. Retrieved from: https://science.howstuffworks.com/innovation/scientific-experiments/scientific-peer-review.htm

Hull, D. (1988). *Science as a process: An evolutionary account of the social and conceptual development of science*. Chicago: University of Chicago Press. doi:10.7208/chicago/9780226360492.001.0001

Ioan, B., & Stângă, O. (2009). Respectul pentru persoană, [Respect for the person]. In V. Astărăstoae, S. Loue & B. Ioan (Eds.), Etica cercetării pe subiecţi umani [Ethics of Research on Human Subjects]. Iaşi, Romania: "Gr. T. Popa" U.M.F. Iaşi Publishing House.

Journal of Young Investigators. (2005). Writing scientific manuscripts. A guide for undergraduates. *Journal of Young Investigators*. Retrived from http://www.jyi.org/

Kelly, J., Sadeghieh, T., & Adeli, K. (2014). Peer review in scientific publications: Benefits, critiques and a survival guide. *The Journal of the International Federation of Clinical Chemistry and Laboratory Medicine*, *25*(3), 227–243. PMID:27683470

Kirton, M. (1976). Adaptors and innovators: A description and measure. *The Journal of Applied Psychology*, *61*(5), 622–629. doi:10.1037/0021-9010.61.5.622

Lee, C. J. (2012). A Kuhnian critique of psychometric research on peer review. *Philosophy of Science*, *79*(5), 859–870. doi:10.1086/667841

Levy, Y., & Elis, J. T. (2006). A systems approach to conduct an effective literature review. *Support of Information Systemy Research Informing Science Journal*, *9*, 181–212. doi:10.28945/479

Longino, H. (2016). The social dimensions of scientific knowledge. In N. Zalta (Ed.), *The Stanford Encyclopedia of Philosophy*. Retrieved from: https://plato.stanford.edu/archives/spr2016/entries/scientific-knowledge-social/

Maddux, J. (2011). *Publishing in English language journals in psychology; tips for increasing the odds.* Paper presented at "A. I. Cuza" University from Iaşi during the Doctoral Program in Schools of Excellence.

Mervis, J. (2017). Research is an afterthought in first Trump budget. *Science*. Retrieved from http://www.sciencemag.org/news/2017/03/research-afterthought-first-trump-budget

O'Neill, O. (2006). Etica lui Kant [Kant's ethics]. In P. Singer (Ed.), *Tratat de etică* [Ethics Treaty] (pp. 205–215). Iaşi, Romania: Polirom.

Poff, D. C. (2017). *Peer review: Strengths, limitations and emerging issues*. Committee of Publication Ethics (COPE). Retrieved from https://publicationethics.org/files/Deborah_Poff_PRESENTATION_final_ENGLISH.pdf

Popa, M. (2016). Evaluarea raportului de cercetare şi etica cercetării ştiinţifice [Evaluation of the research report and scientific research ethics]. In M. Popa (Ed.), *Metodologia cercetării (note de curs)* [Methodology of Research (Course Notes)]. Bucharest, Romania: Asociaţia de Psihologie Industrială şi Organizaţională. Retrieved from http://www.apio.ro/upload/mc12_eval_etica_cercet.pdf

Popper, K. (1972). *Objective knowledge*. Oxford, UK: Oxford University Press.

Popper, K. (2008). *Conjectures and refutations: The growth of scientific knowledge* (2nd ed.). London, UK: Routledge.

Randolph, J. (2009). Guide to writing the dissertation literature review. *Practical Assessment, Research & Evaluation, 14*(13).

Resnik, D. B. (2015). *What is ethics in research and why is it important?* National Institute of Environmental Health Sciences. Retrieved from https://www.niehs.nih.gov/research/resources/bioethics/whatis/index.cfm

Sandu, A. (2009). *Dimensiuni etice ale comunicării în postmodernitate* [Ethical dimensions of postmodern communication]. Iaşi, Romania: Lumen.

Sandu, A. (2011a, December). Proiectul de cercetare în ştiinţele sociale [The research project in social sciences]. *Jurnalul de studii juridice.*

Sandu, A. (2011b). *Perspective semiologice asupra transmodernităţii* [Semiological perspectives on transmodernity] (2nd ed.). Iaşi, Romania: Lumen.

Sandu, A. (2011c). Scientific writting. Epistemological and methodological considerations regarding research articles' elaboration. *Jurnalul de studii juridice*, (S1), 23-29.

Sandu, A. (2012a). *Filosofia socială construcţionistă. Direcţii epistemice, etice şi pragmatice* [Social constructive philosophy. Epistemic, ethical and pragmatic directions]. Cluj-Napoca, Romania: Presa Universitară Clujeană.

Sandu, A. (2012b). Metode de cercetare în ştiinţa comunicării [Methods of research in communication science]. Curs universitar. Iaşi, Romania: Lumen.

Sandu, A. (2012c). *Social constructionist epistemology. A transmodern overview*. Saarbrucken, Germany: LAP LAMBERT Academic Publishing, GmbH & Co. KG.

Sandu, A. (2012d). *Etică şi deontologie profesională* [Ethics and professional deontology]. Iaşi, Romania: Lumen.

Sandu, A. (2014). *Etică profesională şi transparenţă în administraţia publică* [Professional ethics and transparency in public administration]. Bucharest, Romania: Didactică şi Pedagogică.

Sandu, A. (2016). *Social construction of reality as communicative action*. Cambridge, UK: Cambridge Scholars Publishing.

Sandu, A. (2018). Constructionist Grounded Theory - GT. conceptual and methodological clarifications. *Revista Românească pentru Educaţie Multidimensională, 10*(1), 183-209. doi:10.18662/rrem/28

Sandu, A., & Unguru, E. (2014). *Acţiune comunicativă, justiţie deliberativă şi restaurativă. Perspective socio-juridice asupra medierii şi probaţiunii* [Communicative action, deliberative and restorative justice. Socio-legal perspectives on mediation and probation]. Bucharest, Romania: Tritonic.

Sandu, A., & Unguru, E. (2017). Several conceptual clarifications on the distinction between constructivism and social constructivism. *Postmodern Openings*, *8*(2), 51–61. doi:10.18662/po/2017.0802.04

Shamoo, A., & Resnik, D. (2015). *Responsible Conduct of Research* (3rd ed.). New York: Oxford University Press.

Shashabuddin, S. (2009). Plagiarism in academia. *International Journal on Teaching and Learning in Higher Education*, *21*(3), 353–359.

Stoenescu, A. M. (2017). *Citarea şi infracţiunea de plagiat* [Citation and the offense of plagiarism]. Retrieved from https://www.cotidianul.ro/citarea-si-infractiunea-de-plagiat/

Stolker, M. (2005). Legal journals: In pursuit of a more scientific approach. *European Journal of Legal Education*, *2*(2), 77–79. doi:10.1080/16841360600844796

Swedberg, K. (2008). Who is an author? *European Journal of Heart Failure*, *10*(6), 523–524. doi:10.1016/j.ejheart.2008.05.002 PMID:18502171

Trump's budget plan cuts funding for arts, humanities and public media. (2017, March 16). Retrieved from https://www.npr.org/2017/03/16/520401246/trumps-budget-plan-cuts-funding-for-arts-humanities-and-public-media?t=1532423598874

Unitatea Executivă pentru Finanţarea Învăţământului Superior, a Cercetării, Dezvoltării şi Inovării (Ue-Fiscadi). (n.d.). [Executive Unit for Financing Higher Education, Research, Development and Innovation]. *Programul Idei. Arhivă*. Retrieved from http://old.uefiscdi.ro/Public/cat/70/Program-IDEI--arhiva.html

US Department of Health and Human Services, The Office of Research Integrity (ORI). (n.d.). *Chapter 1: The Ethical Basis of RCRH*. Retrieved from https://ori.hhs.gov/education/products/ucla/chapter1/Chapter1.pdf

Vicol, M. C., & Astărăstoae, V. (2009). Principiul beneficiului [The beneficence principle]. In V. Astărăstoae, S. Loue & B. G. Ioan (Eds.), Etica cercetării pe subiecţi umani [Ethics of Research on Human Subjects]. Iaşi, Romania: "Gr. T. Popa" U.M.F. Iaşi Publishing House.

Vintan, L. (2006). Calitatea cercetării prin abordări scientometrice [Quality of research through scientometric approaches]. *Euroeconomia, 21*(53).

Wy, L. (2009). Knowledge in writing a good scientific paper. *Malaysian Journal of Psychiatry*, *18*(2).

Zajonc, A. (2006). *Noua fizică şi cosmologie. Dialoguri cu Dalai Lama* [The new physics and cosmology. Dialogues with the Dalai Lama]. Bucharest, Romania: Tehnică.

Zhang, C. (2013). The evolution of rationality and modernity crisis. *Sociology Mind*, *3*(2), 179–184. doi:10.4236m.2013.32024

KEY TERMS AND DEFINITIONS

Ethical Approval: A component of the research process, whose purpose is to protect both the researcher and the participants in the research, which should have their dignity, rights, safety, and welfare respected. The existence of ethical approval is mandatory in all biomedical research and also in all research on human subjects that include vulnerable populations, or in situations that could bring, in any way, harm to the participant.

Ghost Writing: The action of writing a paper or research project on behalf of another person, who will assume the credit of authorship. Although this practice is usual in domains such as politics, business, law etc., it is an unethical behavior in scientific writing.

Open Access: Type of publication available online for free, that can or cannot allow the author(s) to retain the copyright of their article(s). Some of the open-access journals charge the author(s) or their institution of affiliation with a fee for maintaining the article online and available for free.

Peer Review: The process of evaluating the research projects or papers proposed to be published, by experts in the field of the paper. Usually the process of peer-review is blind (most commonly in evaluating research proposals)—the author not being informed of who is the reviewer for his paper—or double-blind (usually used for scientific papers in journals or books)—the authors has no idea who is the reviewer, and the reviewer has no knowledge of the identity of the author(s).

Predatory Journal: A scientific journal that apparently has a legitimate business model, and usually charges for publication, but has a very poor, or none at all, peer-review process.

Research on Demand: A research developed upon request. This kind of research could be legit, the authors fulfilling all epistemological or methodological criteria, but could also present falsified or incomplete results in order to prove and support the financer's point of view. The companies or free-lancers who write scientific papers upon request (for example doctoral theses), aside from falsifying the authorship (ghost writing), justify their activity as being research on demand, thus transferring the entire responsibility of using data and texts to the client.

ENDNOTE

1 The bibliographic references in this model of application to the Research Ethics Committee have been unified with the bibliographic references of this paper.

Chapter 2
Research Integrity Dissemination System:
"Science RIDS of Misconduct"

Artem Artyukhov
Sumy State University, Ukraine

Tetyana Vasilyeva
Sumy State University, Ukraine

ABSTRACT

The chapter deals with the description of the author's university research integrity dissemination system. The scientific infrastructure of the classical university is shown (by the example of Sumy State University); SWOT-analysis of scientific activity in terms of observing the principles of research integrity is carried out. Some cases of violation of the principles of research integrity (Ukraine as a case study) are presented. The blocks of the research integrity dissemination system in various sectors of research activity are described. The activity of the university center for technology transfer and coordination of research integrity in the scientific activity of the university is presented.

INTRODUCTION

The ancient wisemen said: in order to protect oneself from evil, one must renounce it – "If I do not see evil, do not hear about evil, and do not say anything about it, then I am protected from it". A similar phrase is in the book of Confucius "Lun Yu": "Do not look at what is wrong; do not listen to what is wrong; do not say what is wrong". Among the Slavs, the most popular version is "I do not see anything, I do not hear anything, I will not tell anyone", which actually characterizes detachment from the problem and unwillingness to solve it. It is here that a parallel is drawn between ancient philosophy and the modern state of the scientific world, which is subject to constant attacks by pseudo-scientists and hunters for quantitative indicators and easy scientific prey. The distorted expression of the ancient wisemen is the best description of the state, which ever wider areas of scientific research were "infected" with. These areas are subject to the influence of fraudsters who are ready for any scientific "crimes" for the sake of

DOI: 10.4018/978-1-5225-6310-5.ch002

their vanity. The consequence of this "infection" is an increase in cases of violation of the principles of research integrity and impunity for committing these violations.

However, the words of the ancient wisemen have a continuation: "do not do what is wrong", "if I do not commit evil, then I am protected from it". Compliance with this rule is the basis of the system of research integrity and the ethics of academic relationships.

It is crucial that researchers acquire knowledge, methodology of research and ethical practices in their field of activity. Failure to follow best research practices leads to violations in the performance of one's own professional duties. All this harms the research processes, worsens the relationship between researchers, undermines the credibility of the research and its authority, spends resources and can damage research subjects, users, society or the environment.

The scientist is at the crossroads: to achieve quantitative indicators (while sacrificing quality) or to achieve a qualitative breakthrough in a scientific research with the prospect of its commercialization (Aryukhov, 2015; Artyukhov & Liuta, 2017).

The answer in this case is unambiguous (although it is very difficult for someone): the quality of scientific research is not for the sake of quantitative indicators, but for the sake of successful implementation in industry. Otherwise – see Figure 2.

As we see, the observance of the principles of research integrity is important not only in the process of carrying out research (and, of course, promulgating them), but also in the transition from a scientific idea to its practical implementation. These are two interrelated problems, and the control function in this case should be carried by one university scientific unit. The effectiveness of innovation activity is associated with a balanced process of transferring the results of research work in production. In the structure

Figure 1. "If I do not see evil, do not hear about evil, do not say anything about it, and do not do what is wrong then I am protected from it" - basis of the system of research integrity and the ethics of academic relationships
(Source: authors' own image)

Figure 2. Scientific research and research integrity: quantitative indicators or real implementation of useful innovations?
(Source: authors' own image)

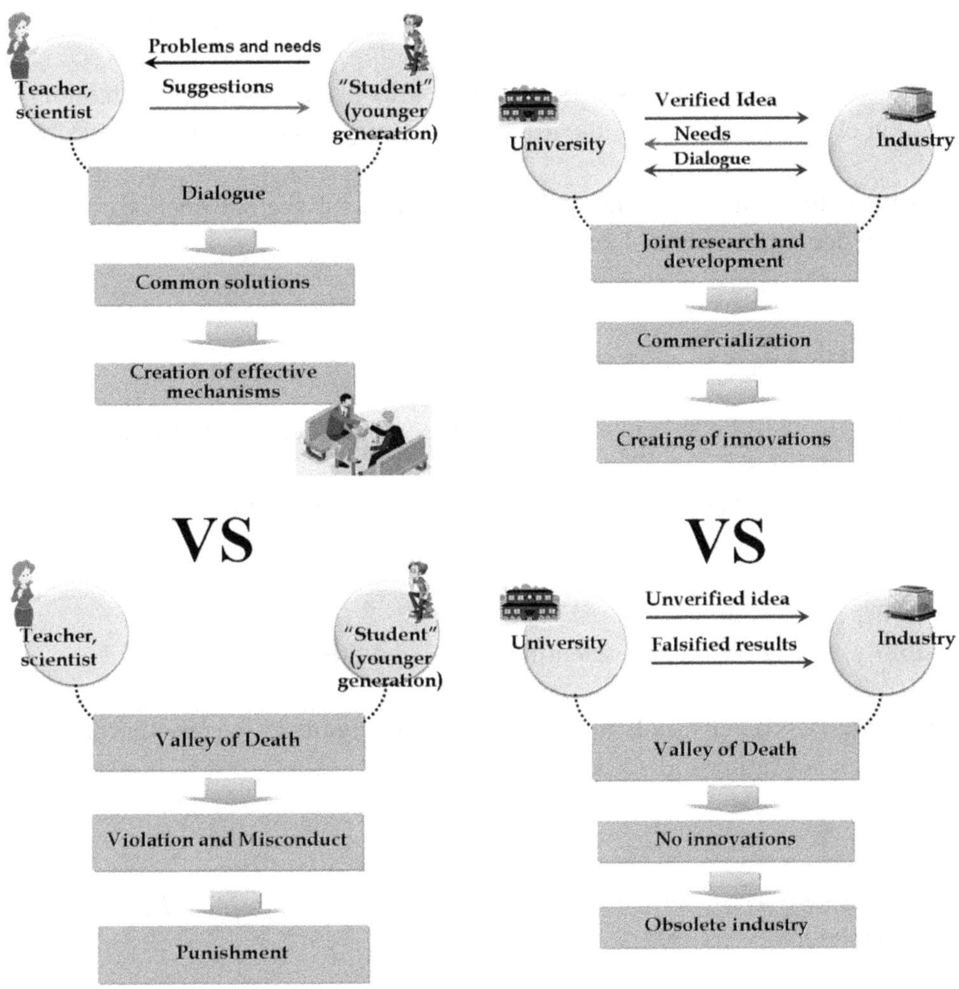

of the majority of foreign universities there are departments responsible for the connection between the university and business. They have different names: technology transfer centers or offices, intellectual property, licensing or patenting departments, etc. The goal of the university Technology Transfer Center is to contribute to the growth of "honest" and "clean" project in terms of scientific integrity from the very idea to its successful implementation. At the same time, each scientific unit should have its tasks to ensure the principles of research integrity and direct its efforts to provide specific (for each area of scientific research) conditions for the growth of the level of "pure" scientific research.

The goal of this paper is to create an integral (and most importantly effective) system for ensuring the principles of research integrity at the university and to implement successful mechanisms for introducing this system by the example of Sumy State University.

Thus, the main tasks of this paper can be described in the form of such theses:

- A scientific infrastructure of the university as a tool to ensure a high quality of the research and presentation of the results (publication process);
- SWOT and PESTEL-analysis of scientific activities at the university level and at the state level;
- undamental violations of the principles of research integrity, challenges and dangers of the publication of research results;
- The Technology Transfer Center is a "conductor" of the principles of research integrity;
- A description of the main blocks of the Research Integrity Dissemination System;

The relationship between individual tasks that are aimed at solving one general problem can be formulated in the form of an illustration, shown in Figure 3.

INTERESTING FACTS

Here are some facts that will be able to characterize the current dangers and challenges for domestic scientists from different sides.

As in other countries of the post-Soviet space, the motivation for fraudsters and pseudo-scientists in Ukraine is:

- The possibility of easy earning;
- The possibility of easy obtaining a scientific degree and title.

Despite the fact that it is openly spoken about in the press (Figure 4), the problem does not disappear, but, on the contrary, it is gaining wider distribution.

Figure 3. Tasks and problems of Research Integrity Dissemination System implementation
(Source: authors' own image)

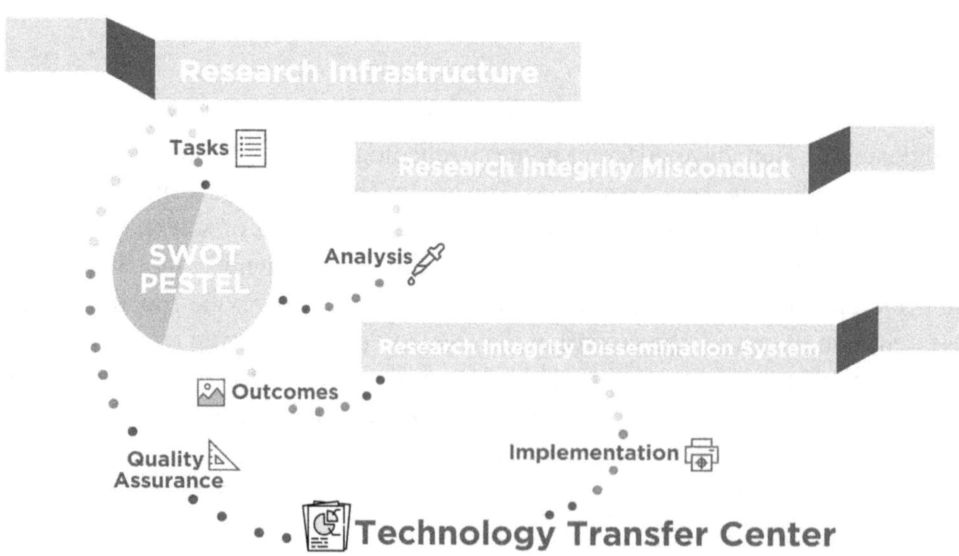

Figure 4. Violation of the principles of research integrity in Ukraine – the mass media inform
(Source: authors' own image)

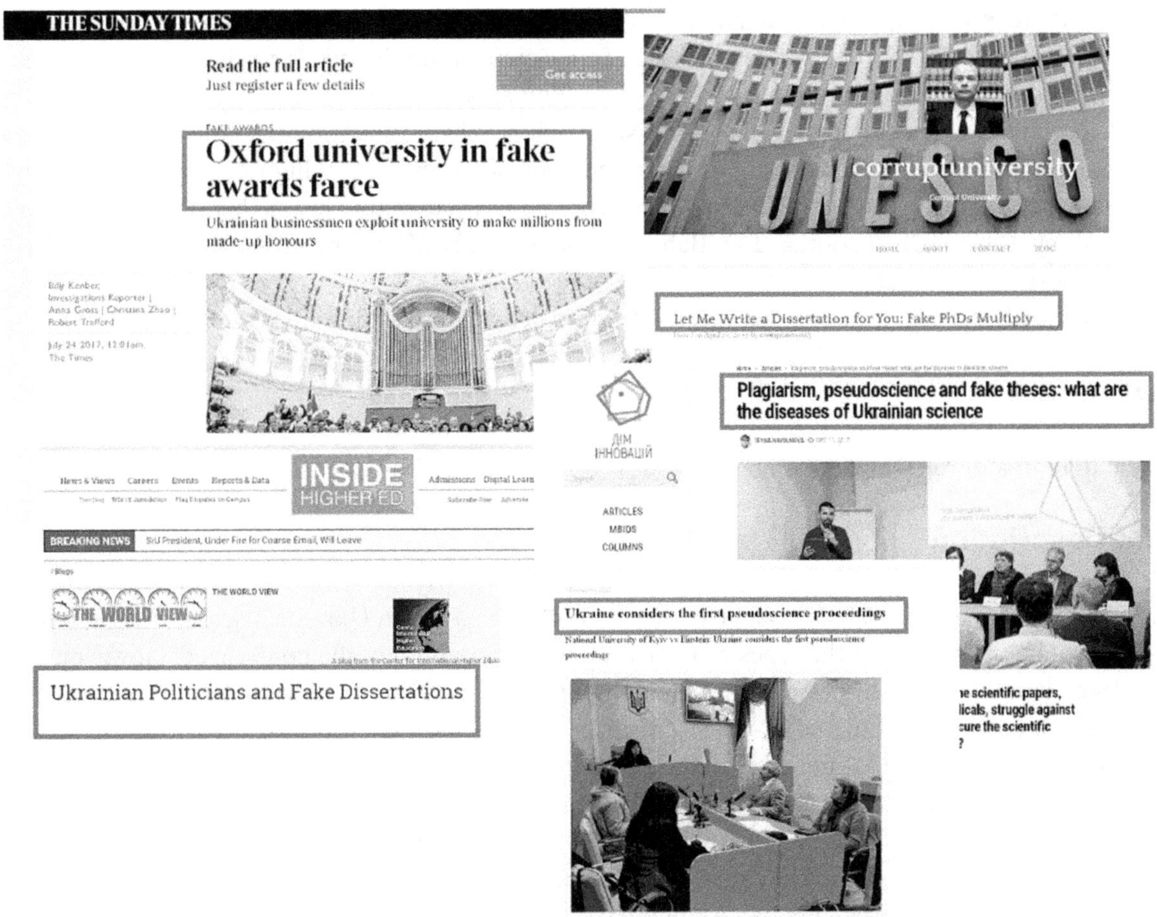

Below is a case of the life of Ukrainian scholars of the late 19th century, which is described in Khmarsky (2016) and emphasizes the depth of "disease" concerning violation of the principles of research integrity. Professor of Kiev University of St. Vladimir V. Antonovich formed his own school of historical direction, bringing up a number of bright students and followers. Among these students were Dmytro Bahalii and Ivan Lynnychenko. The first of them in September 1882 defended in Kyiv a master's thesis "History of the Seversk land to the half of the XIV century". The second of them one year later published in the Petersburg edition of the Journal of the Ministry of Public Education a crushing review in which proved that out of three hundred and ten pages of the thesis of D. Bahalii over one hundred pages were found to be borrowed from a small number of very famous works, the same number – translation from the chronicles to the Russian, and the rest pages – only the provision of a text link between the above fragments. In his review, I. Lynnychenko carefully pointed out numerous literary borrowings from the works of a whole collection of well-known scholars, which the author presented as his own: "The author quite often confuses his personality, his thoughts with the personality and thoughts of other writers". The review had a great deal of resonance, but the consequences were subjective. D.Bahalii did not lose the already acquired, including and on the recommendation of V. Antonovich, department at Kharkiv

University. But I. Lynnychenko complicated his relations with the scientific leader and with a number of colleagues who considered it desirable to quickly write a thesis and promote "their own" on a career ladder. This story was explored in detail at the end of the last century by (Tolochko, 1993), who asked his contemporaries: "What determines the fate of the scientist and his works: scientific conscience or support for corporate solidarity? How much do party sympathy matter in science?" To D. Bahalii's honor we add that this was the only case in his professional biography. In the future, he did not suppose such scandal, wrote a number of fundamental works and became, at the beginning of the Soviet era, one of the leaders in historical science in Ukraine. Moreover, let us assume that it was this story that became a powerful impetus, which encouraged D. Bahalii throughout his life to prove that the situation with his master's thesis was only an accident.

Another example is the author's own case "Conference-scam for Ukrainian pseudo-scientists".

Type of Case

Ethical dilemma or misrepresentation

Brief Description

For receiving of a scientific title (associate professor or professor) in Ukraine a scientist must undergo an internship abroad. One of the types of internship is participation in the conference. However, at the conference it is necessary to present new (in addition, topical) scientific results. For pseudo-scientists it's a difficult task. Ukrainian and ex-USSR "firms" (to make life easier for pseudo-scientists) organize "predatory" conferences. Co-organizers of these conferences are foreign "institutions", "associations", "corporations" with a dubious reputation (or this institution has a good reputation, but it didn't hear about this conference and officially wasn't invited as co-organizer). The title of the conference covers all fields of science (for example "Scientific problems of the 21st century"). Publications are accepted without a review, you only need to pay a conference fee.

Main "Actors" and Their "Roles" in This Case

"Actor 1" – Black See Research Institute of Economy and Innovation.

Officially the institute is registered in ONE!!! office (room). Institute is co-organizer of the conference "The development of nature sciences: problems and solutions" in Brno (Czech Republic). Another co-organizer is European Network for Academic Integrity. As it turned out, the second co-organizer doesn't know about the conference (see link below).

"Role 1" – Earning of "easy" money
"Actor 2" – Pseudo-scientist who want to participate in this conference
"Role 2" – Earning an "easy" internship

Problem, point of view of each "actor" on this issue

Problem

"Where there's demand, there's supply"

Point of View

"Actor 1" – "If I can sell it, why not?"
"Actor 2" – "All's fair for achieving the goal"

The history of the correspondence of one of the authors with the organizers of the conference (gross mistakes of the organizers are highlighted in bold letters, stressing their lack of understanding the essence of the European Network for Academic Integrity):

Author: If possible, I would like to see a sample certificate and find out who is issuing it in the Czech Republic.

Conference Organizer: For the time being we cannot provide a sample certificate. The certificates will be issued by the UNIVERSITY –European Network for Academic Integrity.

Author: Thank you. This is not a university, but an association that has nothing to do with the topic of the conference.

Conference Organizer: Yes, because the organizer is the European Network for Academic INTEGRATION (ENAI). This is what was meant. Each certificate will be stamped.

Author: Well, ok, I will not discuss. I just want to point out that ENAI is the European Network for Academic INTEGRITY, but not what you call it. I know what I'm talking about. Therefore, it is a nonsense that this organization holds such a conference. Look at what it really is doing. This is a cool case of dishonesty.

Conference Organizer: If you think so, no one can force you to participate. Just look how much has already been organized by the Black Sea Research Institute as it was created. Conducting dishonest activities is not our way. All the best for you!

Author: I only showed my vision, nothing personal. Good luck in your business, from a certain point of view you are great)

Method of Problem Solving

1. Wide negative disclosure of information about conference-scam among the scientists and official (domestic and foreign) educational (scientific) organizations.
2. Informing of the foreign co-organizer about this the conference (the danger of this step - co-organizer may be "on the take". In this case everything is turned out well).

Results

Disclosure of fraudulent scheme of the conference

Recommendations

"Be careful when you seeing easy pickings"

However, the desire to take the path of pseudoscience and violating the principles of research integrity comes to the scientists not immediately. Future young scientists (university senior students) have a completely different view of the principles of conducting a scientific research. We will give an example of a vignette (practical case), which was used by one of the authors of this work in the Sumy State University as part of the teaching the discipline "Organization of scientific activity" for master students. As the saying goes "Out of the mouths of babes comes the truth".

Petro is a student of the Department of Chemistry and runs a series of experiments related to the synthesis of a new important compound. At the final stages of his work, he encountered difficulties in experimentation, which may mean that most of the work would be lost. Petro hopes to get a place in a postgraduate school if the experiments are successful. And his supervisor also needs good results to get an upgrade. The laboratory's resources for the next year are awarded by the Department of Chemistry on a competitive basis, depending on the success of this year's experiments.

What Do You Think Petro Can Do in This Situation?

Detailed students' answers (answers received from students during 2016-2018):

1. "The first thing Petro can do is to ask for help from his supervisor. If the supervisor really needs an upgrade, then he should help his student. For that purpose the supervisor is the leader and his duties involve regulating the actions of his student. If a student gives up and does not continue an experiment, then nobody will win from this. Of course, there is an option to ask someone else for help, but why do you need your supervisor then? "
2. "I suppose that Petro has to do his best to make experiments successful in order to prove himself first of all as a conscientious and responsible worker who is accustomed to succeed. This will not be left without the attention of the department".
3. "Overtime, overtime and again overtime. Petro should work above the norm to overcome the difficulties and complete the experiments successfully. He can also turn to his supervisor for help because they are both interested in the success of the experiments".
4. "I think that it is necessary to make maximum efforts and carry out all experiments. If he cannot do it independently, then he should ask for help from the supervisor or try to find a solution on the Internet. But at the same time he should carry out all the experiments independently and try to understand why he did not succeed in carrying out the experiment on his own".
5. "Petro should ask for help from his supervisor, because they are jointly interested in achieving good results, have a common goal. They must work together to concentrate on solving the challenges of experimentation in order not to lose the part of work and to successfully complete all tasks in the laboratory. Since work in the fields of exact sciences is not easy and it involves performing some calculations, sometimes it is possible to make a mistake due to inattentiveness, fatigue and other factors. The main thing is to keep in mind: Perseverance always bears fruit! Therefore, one should not give up and look for other solutions of the problem".

As we see, young scientists at the initial stage of formation of their careers need technological and information support of their activities. Their further behavior in the scientific world depends on the extent to which they will be informed about the consequences of unfair implementation of their scientific research. It should be noted that young scientists have not only to realize the inadmissibility of violating the principles of research integrity, but also with all the forces to prevent misdemeanors and violations by others. These violations (which are discussed below) can destroy a young scientist's career if he does not fight for his rights. Research Integrity Dissemination System is a complex system created to comply with the principles of research integrity within the scientific community and to counteract the violation of these principles by other scientists.

RESEASCH INFRASTRUCTURE

General Observations

Sumy State University (http://sumdu.edu.ua/int/en/about-ssu.html) is located in Sumy city in the North-East of Ukraine. Its history began in 1948. Today, Sumy State University is a leading university of a classical type with the III-IV accreditation level in the region. The University currently serves about 15,000 students who are pursuing pre bachelor, bachelor, specialist and master degrees in 51 majors and 22 fields of knowledge. About 1300 foreign students represent almost 50 countries worldwide.

The University is a signatory of Magna Charta Universitatum and a reliable member of International Association of Universities, European University Association, Euroasian Universities Association, Association of Economic Universities of South and Eastern Europe and the Black Sea Region, IREG Observatory on Academic Ranking and Excellence, IIE Network and other international organizations.

Sumy State University cooperates with more than 200 partners from the USA, Great Britain, Germany, Austria, France, Belgium, Sweden, Poland, Lithuania, Bulgaria, the Czech Republic, Slovakia, Romania, Japan, South Korea, China and other countries of the world.

Sumy State University is a reliable partner for joint projects in frames of international grant programmes of EU (Tempus, Erasmus Mundus, Jean Monnet, Erasmus+, Horizon 2020), United Nation Development Programme, British Council, the World Bank, bilateral scientific and research projects, grants of private foundations. The University accomplishes more than 200 grants annually. For the last 5 years the amount of research work in frames of international grant projects has increased in 20 times.

The University actively develops academic mobility programmes, including long-term and short-term studying, internships and placement programmes for undergraduate and postgraduate students, research and teaching staff, as well as administrative staff using technologies of credit transfer and recognition of academic results.

Sumy State University promotes a wide range of academic activities, research and innovation projects. These important factors provide the high quality educational services and new scientific developments. Academic and research work at Sumy State University is quite captivating and absorbing. Our students have a freedom to choose their own research direction among the great variety of those offered by the university. Many faculties of Sumy State University are deeply involved in scientific development which joins the efforts of not only the university staff, but also post-graduate and doctorate students.

Priority Thematic Areas of research and development of Sumy State University for 2011-2020 (http://sumdu.edu.ua/int/en/research.html):

- **Fundamental Research:** The most important problems of physical, mathematical and technical sciences; fundamental problems of modern materials science; the most important problems of chemistry and development of chemical technologies; the fundamental problems of life sciences and biotechnology development; fundamental research on actual problems of social sciences and humanities;
- **Applied Developments:** Intelligent information, informational and analytical technologies; technologies of power engineering; targeted research on harmonization of the "human–world" system and the creation of the latest technologies for improving the quality of life, problems of personality and society development, demography and socio-economic policy; creation and application of nanotechnologies and technologies of nanomaterials.

A research infrastructure has been created to implement the research on priority thematic areas at Sumy State University. It is presented on Figure 5.

As can be seen from the illustration, each scientific unit of the university fulfills its educational, technological or providing functions in the overall system of forming a positive climate for carrying out scientific research, publishing the results and ensuring the principles of research integrity. On the way to achieving the main goal, the entire university scientific infrastructure is subject to the risks of deviation from a given systemic approach. These risks, in particular, are presented in SWOT and PESTEL-analysis of scientific activity at the university level and at the state level.

Figure 5. Research infrastructure at Sumy State University
(Source: authors' own image)

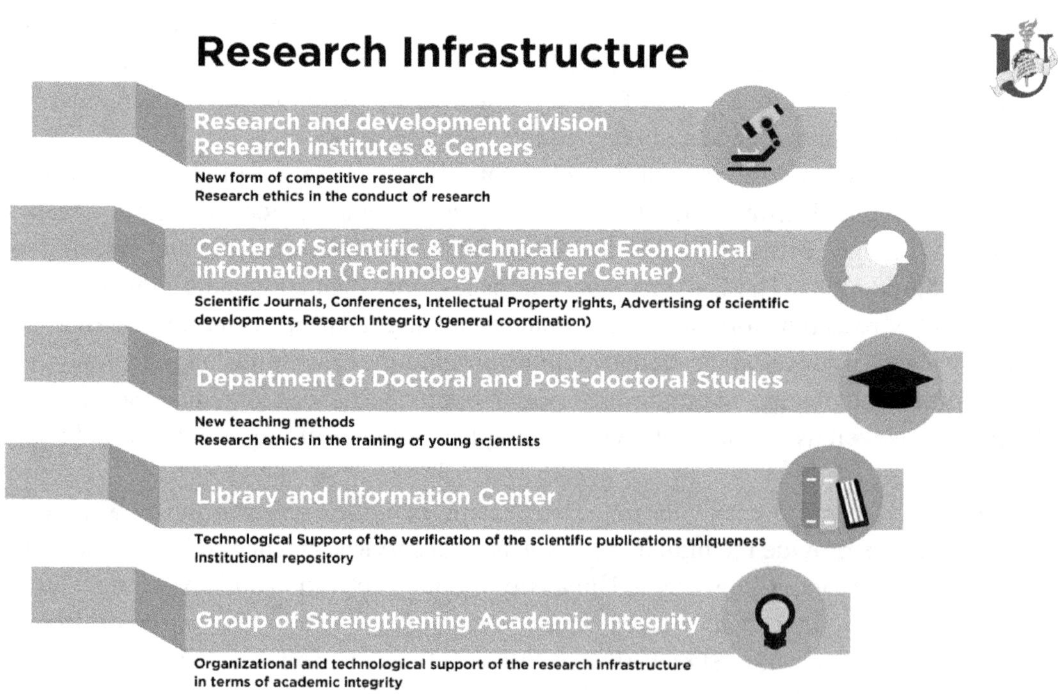

SWOT AND PESTEL-ANALYSIS OF SCIENTIFIC ACTIVITY AT THE UNIVERSITY LEVEL AND AT THE STATE LEVEL

SWOT and PESTEL-analysis was conducted on the base of author's point of view (own experience) and analysis of national regulations, in particular the Laws of Ukraine "On Higher Education", "On Education", "On scientific and technical activities", "On Copyright and Related Rights", the Criminal Code of Ukraine (http://rada.gov.ua/news/zak).

SWOT-Analysis

Strength

- A powerful staffing potential;
- A wide range of research in all fields of knowledge;
- The desire to reach the international level of research and to publicize the results;
- Understanding the competitiveness of the results in the case of their honest receiving.

Weakness

- Obsolete forms of interaction between the state and science (merely quantitative indicators);
- The decrease in the prestige of science (including because of the fraud of previous researchers);
- Alow technological level of research;
- The deceleration of material re-equipment of scientific organizations;
- The lack of expensive scientific equipment and resources;
- Uncontrolled use of the results of domestic research abroad;
- The insufficient interaction of science, education and industry;
- The gap in the level of the research from the rest of the scientific world;
- The inertia in choosing the main areas of research, their forms and methods. The tendency to carry out the research (including the publication of the results) by traditional (mostly obsolete) methods;
- The insufficient publication level in international journals, lack of language training;
- The insufficient level of innovation activity, patent and licensing activities;
- The lack of normative base regulating the principles of research integrity;
- A high scientific competition (by quantitative indicators);
- Scientometric indices of scientists are taken into account when accrediting educational programmes and evaluating the applications for public funding;
- A non-systemic campaign for the promotion and implementation of the principles of research integrity, lack of units that organize the work to control the compliance with the principles of research integrity.

Opportunities

- The perspective of international scientific cooperation;
- The increase in the amount of grant funding;
- The activation of innovation activity;

- The creation of modern material and technical base;
- The activation of inventive and licensing activities;
- The formation of innovation infrastructure;
- The reducion of the number of uncontrolled using the domestic scientific results.

Threats

- The increase in the number of publications as a response to state requirements;
- A low level of involvement of library and information departments in scientific activity;
- The growth of the attractiveness of scientific emigration;
- The increase in the number of manifestations of pseudoscience;
- Systemic violations of the principles of research integrity in conducting research and publicizing the results.

Visually the results of own authors' SWOT and PESTEL-analysis are presented on Figures 6 and 7.

MAJOR VIOLATIONS OF THE PRINCIPLES OF ACADEMIC INTEGRITY, CHALLENGES AND DANGERS OF THE PROCESS OF SCIENTIFIC RESEARCH RESULTS PUBLICATION

An important component of studying the problems associated with research integrity is a scientific experiment. It is a question of conducting field and laboratory research, developing new mathematical

Figure 6. SWOT-analysis of scientific activity at Sumy State University
(Source: authors' own image)

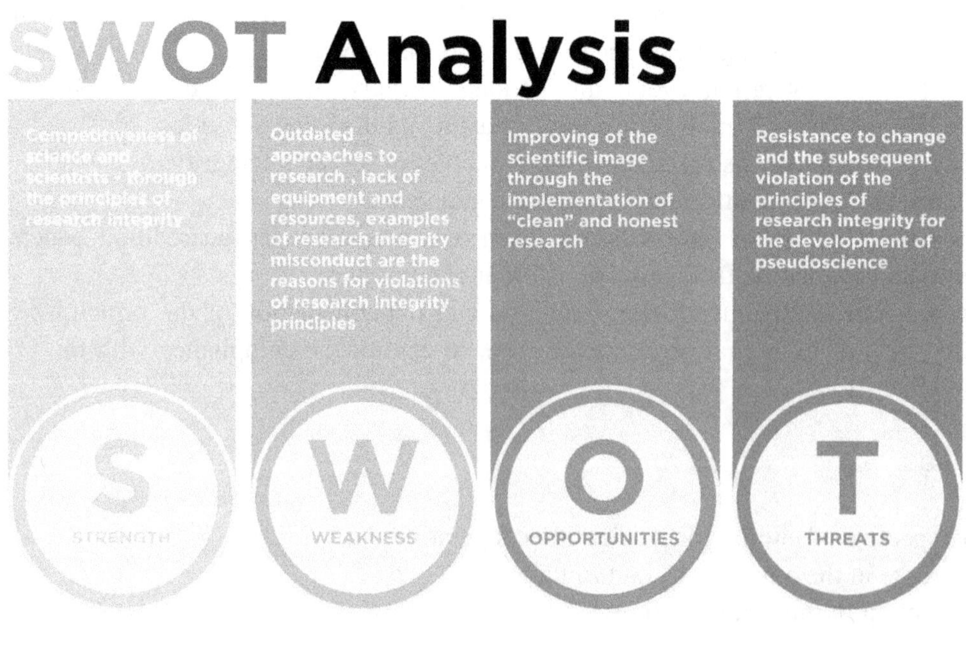

Figure 7. PESTEL-analysis of scientific activity at Sumy State University
(Source: authors' own image)

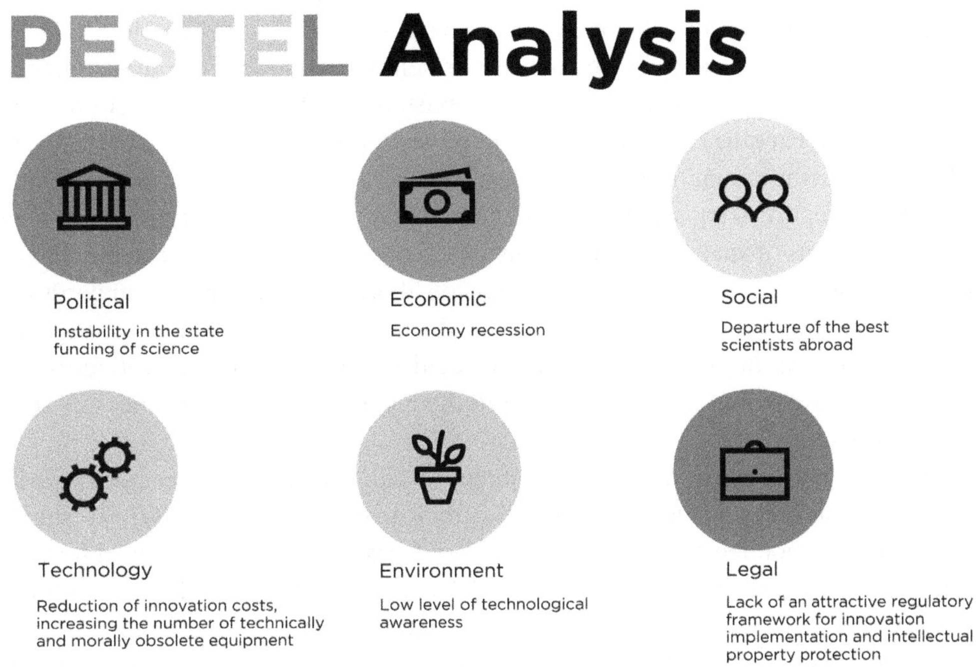

approaches and algorithms for interpreting the results obtained, modeling processes and other experimental studies. Elements of experimental research are found in many areas of science, and in such as Earth science, physics, chemistry, mathematics, electronics, IT they are an indisputable part of the full range of research (Gunsalus, Marcus, & Oransky, 2018; Kharasch & Houle, 2017; O'Dowd, 2017; "Research integrity – have we made progress?", 2017; Schoenherr, 2015).

It is clear that experimental research can be performed by one scientist, but most often is conducted by scientific groups. Controversial issues that deal with plagiarism, fraud and falsification arise both within the scientific groups and beyond them.

One form of academic dishonesty in a scientific experiment is a plagiarism, which includes the study of serious violations of the norms of science (Finikov & Artyukhov, 2016). The plagiarism can include the publication of someone's ideas or words as one's own without properly citing the source, as well as the manipulation of experimental results based on someone else's data. In recent years, for example, the US federal government has developed and improved its policy on the use of standards of research integrity, has created federal agencies and research institutes, has established the rules for responding to cases of plagiarism (McCabe, 2018). This practice is also used in other countries, such as China (Zeng & Resnik, 2010), where a special ethics policy has been introduced. For this purpose the relevant supervisory committees and a protection programme for the informers concerning the non-compliance with the principles of academic integrity have been created.

The experimental plagiarism is a crime against the academic community. Researchers who deceive consumers of their scientific products receive undeserved benefits. At the same time, it is necessary to distinguish the direct plagiarism and the borrowed information on the basis of which a new research product is created, provided that the rules of academic integrity in the scientific experiment are observed.

An example of the purity of a scientific experiment can be the research results of Erasmus of Rotterdam (Jardine, 2015). His works were characterized by scientific integrity and selflessness, the lack of pursuit of new knowledge for the sake of certain recognition or financial benefit.

Detecting the academic dishonesty in the context of scientific research is a complex process, and the findings often do not answer exactly the question of the existence of the relevant violations. For example, in the work (Pupovac & Fanelli, 2015), a systematic review and analysis of the results of anonymous surveys of scholars about the committing various forms of plagiarism has been carried out. An interesting result was the fact that reports from scholars about their colleagues who plagiarized were received more quickly than official results of analyzes with conclusions about the violations of academic integrity. This fact confirms the opinion that obtaining a clear conclusion about violations of the standards of academic integrity in a scientific experiment is a complicated task. As a rule it is not easy to suspect and prove data manipulation. The testimony of colleagues also requires an appropriate investigation. Obviously, at the same time, we move from scientific research to the legal field, which distances us from the goal of real scientific works.

Practical evidence that the frequency is the subject of controversy in this paper, with it scientists falsify results or commit other forms of scientific insubordination (Fanelli, 2009). To standardize the results, the number of respondents counted on at least one case of unlawful actions known to them in the pharmacological field. The sample consisted of 21 facts. Only 1.97% of scholars admitted that they falsified or altered the results at least once. 33.7% admitted in other less significant cases of violation of research integrity. If the results of the corresponding experimental studies were monitored, it was possible to reduce the number of cases of violations of the ethical norms of the experiment.

Another example of attempts to mathematically process quantitative indicators of the availability of fabrication in a scientific experiment are the results presented in the work (Okonta & Rossouw, 2013). Investigators who participated in a scientific conference in Nigeria were studied. As a result, 68.9% admitted violating at least one form of scientific honesty. 36.4% violated copyrights, 9.2% committed violations due to direct plagiarism. About 42% of researchers no longer resort to data falsification.

The role of the leader of a scientific group for adhering to the principles of research integrity is important. In particular, in Patel and Hamlin (2015), there are a number of scenarios of the behavior of the leader, which can then be manifested in aspects of the purity of the scientific experiment. Among such scenarios are the lacks of functional skills, ineffective behavior patterns, lack of responsibility for possible harm, which may be caused by non-compliance with ethical standards. The most dangerous scenario of the behavior of the leader of the scientific group is: direct violation of the rules of integrity, ethics, transparency and reliability of the results. It is important to find out the factors that encourage this behavior and develop the best mechanisms for preventing it. At the same time, it is the leader of the scientific group who is the person who without justification, argued, without the involvement of outside arbitrators can determine the facts of fraud, prevent him, direct the scientists to honest work.

Another important issue in the study of academic integrity in a scientific experiment is the conflict of interest. The existence of a conflict of interest as a result may completely destroy the integrity of research and endangers the credibility of the results obtained (Patel and Hamlin, 2015). At the same time, the important aspects are the disclosure of the actual causes of conflict of interest, the resolution of a conflict situation on its own within the scientific group. There are cases where in practice there is a denial of the existence of a conflict and the actual recognition of the complexity of the situation associated with conflicts of interest. A conflict of interest may arise at different levels of scientific experimentation, often at the faculty level. Contractual relations, contracts, even verbal agreements at the design stages of future research work can prevent future conflict situations.

There is an increase in the issues of scientific dishonesty in experimental research by increasing the potential of using borrowed results, which are increasingly being presented on the Internet. Sometimes, this form of plagiarism is called cyber-plagiarism (Chang, Chen, Huang, & Chou, 2015). At the same time, actual scientific ideas, which were received earlier, are actually copied and repeated, and the results obtained do not have scientific novelty. In order to prevent such forms of academic dishonesty, it is important to raise the consciousness of future scholars in the early stages of their education. It is clear that awareness of the state of the problem and the results of scientific research in the world promotes the level of scientists, expands their horizons, but at the same time and tempts to commit incorrect actions, manipulation of data, sometimes direct plagiarism. In this case, as in most of the examples described, the self-consciousness of the experimenter and the possibility of counteracting in the event of fixing violations of the rules of academic integrity and experimental work is decisive.

In order to prevent academic dishonesty in scientific experiment it is necessary to take into account the moral side of the committed negative actions. In this case, their consequence is directly proportional to the method of fraud and methods of measuring the damage (Barnhardt, 2015). It is suggested to conduct so-called inventory of acts of scientific dishonesty in various forms of their manifestations, preventing the development of scientific dishonesty as an epidemic. To do this, it is necessary to combine the moral aspects of the problem and the possibility of administrative prevention of the commission of the corresponding unlawful actions. It should be noted that the scientific uncleanness of the experiment is immoral only when it is a deliberate act. It should not be forgotten about the possibility of certain scientific discoveries in parallel or separate from those made by other scientific groups or individual scientists. Requirements for modern science require complex interdisciplinary research, the involvement of specialists from various scientific schools, universities, and countries. All this leads to the internationalization of science, the receipt of practical results by a very broad author's composition. At the same time, very high standards of compliance with ethical standards, including the rules for conducting scientific research, are put forward to modern scientific projects under the aegis of the European Union (Erasmus +, Horizon 2020, COSME, COST etc.), NATO, DFG, DAAD, Fulbright and others. In breach of these norms, relevant research groups and academics may be deprived of further opportunities to participate in relevant projects, which in fact exclude them from the international scientific community. The latter is a very important motive for the unconditional adherence to the principles of scientific honesty.

One of the results of a scientific experiment is the publication of their results in the articles and materials of the conferences. However, there are often situations and evidence that the review process is unfair and unethical despite the general tendency of compliance with most serious ethical journals (Borkowski & Welsh, 2000). Therefore, the construction of an optimal algorithm for relationships between author groups, reviewers, editors and publishers is the key to publishing true and new scientific results on one side and, on the other hand, preventing the wrongful or deliberate failure of authors to publicize their scientific developments.

Illegal actions when publishing the results of experimental research may take different forms. Among the most serious violations is direct plagiarism and falsification of the original material. As noted in the work (Martin, 2013), fortunately, such forms of scientific insecurity among serious scholars are relatively rare. More common problems are the replication of the results of their own observations many times, which reduces the originality of the results obtained in each case. The discovery of this form of plagiarism is a very difficult task, since different forms of representing the same data several times are vague and open to the interpretation of the aspect. In contrast to the authors' scam, a new form of misconduct by journal editors appeared to attempt to artificially increase the "impact factor" of their journal through the practice of coercion to quoting their journals. Similar actions can be taken by reviewers with the recommendations of the citation of the relevant articles in order to increase their own index of Hirsch.

The works (Alper, 2008; Artyukhov & Menshov, 2016; Baroke, 2018; Sorokina, Artyukhov, & Degtyarova, 2017) generalize the models of ill-fated behavior of scholars.

Data manipulation. Oddly, but the purity of a scientific experiment can often be provided by beginners without the experience of previous work and poorly knowledgeable in a state of scientific problem. For example, when carrying out measurements of certain physical properties, a person who does not think over the rough materials received fixes the actual values of the quantities. At the same time, a knowledgeable specialist can disprove the experimental data received. But if the standards of academic integrity are not met, or even subconsciously, somehow optimize the information obtained in order to meet the a priori goal, the results of the previous deductive analysis or according to the previously published research results. The latter most often can produce falsification of data. It is clear that if the purity of an experiment is maintained, an experienced scientist can simply exclude analytically incorrect data generated by certain random processes or interruptions to the experiment. Consequently, it does not matter whether the experiment was experienced or not, the experimenter, his acquaintance with the results of the predecessors. It is important only to adhere to the ethical standards of a scientific experiment.

Research within one scientific group. When conducting experimental research even within a single scientific group, there may be problems with simultaneous ideas, timing priorities of fixing scientific ideas, and actually the authorship of discoveries. In addition, it is important to take into account the fate of the participation of each scientist in solving a certain scientific problem. The noted model relates to the relationship between students, graduate students and more experienced researchers, including the heads of scientific projects. Manifest scientific dishonesty can be in the publication of research results, included in the list of authors of some or other people. Note that there are objective factors when, based on certain discussions, discussion of the results of the research, new scientific hypotheses are generated simultaneously by several authors.

Borrowing results from other research groups. This model of violation of scientific integrity is seen as one of the most acute. The issue of particular relevance to post-Soviet scholars, who worked in an isolated scientific community and were not familiar with the results of foreign researchers. The corresponding trends, unfortunately, are observed today. This is explained by a number of factors, including objective ones. On the one hand, for the state of the scientific problem in the world to be constantly monitored by new scientific publications, participation in international scientific conferences, direct contacts with foreign colleagues. At the same time, access to the publication databases is often closed, many scientific and educational institutions are simply not able to pay for the use of leading resources such as Elsevier, Thomson Reuters, Wiley, etc. Lack of opportunities for academic mobility. But one cannot neglect also the fact that most domestic scientists simply do not want to make efforts to increase their own scientific level, are unmotivated. It follows from the facts of plagiarism, when, subject to the publication of foreign results for their own, there simply are no skilled and knowledgeable reviewers who could fix this fact. This generates a number of pseudoscientific experimental discoveries, their patenting, whose results are not interesting outside the country or simply criminal in the sense of plagiarism.

In addition to the direct violations of the best research practices identified above, the European Code of Conduct for Research Integrity (2017) defines other unacceptable actions, including but not limited to the following examples:

- Manipulation of authorship or disregard for the role of other researchers in publications;
- Reproduction of significant parts of its early publications, including translations, without proper confirmation or citation of the original;
- Selective citation to improve their own performance or to please readers, reviewers or colleagues;
- Hiding (silencing) the results of research;
- Granting sponsors, the ability to jeopardize the independence of the research process or reporting results in such a way as to formulate or disseminate a biased view of the research;
- Optional extension of the study bibliography;
- Malicious accusation of the researcher in the commission of a misdemeanor (crime) or in other violations;
- Distortion of scientific achievements;
- Exaggeration of the importance and practical significance of the results;
- Delay or unnecessary complication of the work of other researchers;
- Abuse of office to encourage the violation of the integrity of the research;
- Ignoring the alleged violations of the integrity of research by other persons, or covering misconduct (crime) or other violations of the institutions;
- Creating or maintaining journals that undermine research quality control ("predatory journals").

At the last manifestation of scientific insecurity, it is advisable to stay in more detail.

The Practice of "Predatory" Publishing Houses and Journals

For the first time, Jeffrey Beall (University of Colorado Denver, USA) studied world scientific journals in detail and created the so-called "Bill's List" (Beall, 2018), which included publishing houses and journals publishing articles without due process of scientific review and accelerating the publication of such publications for money ("predatory" publishers of open access). It is the results of his analysis that is based on the largest science-and-computer databases in the world Scopus and Web of Science, when they decide to remove this or that pseudo-scientific journal from its base. Bill highlighted the criteria for identifying "predatory" open-access publishers. The main ones - by category, results of sources (Beall, 2012, 2013, 2016; Pasquale, 2014) analysis:

Editor and Staff

- The owner of the publishing house is the editor of all journals issued by the organization;
- No person is identified as an editor of the journal;
- The journal does not identify the editorial board or reviewers;
- There is no academic information about the editor, staff and / or members of the editorial board, reviewers;
- There is a clear indication that the editor and / or reviewers do not have sufficient academic knowledge to decide whether to allow publications to be printed in the journal or not;
- Two or more journals have the same editorial board;
- Journals have insufficient number of members of the editorial council, fictitious members of the council, the names of scientists included in the editorial board without their knowledge or permis-

sion, well-known scientists in the editorial board who do not contribute anything to the development of the journal, except for the use of their names and / or photographs.

Management and Publishing

- Demonstrates the lack of transparency in publishing activities;
- Do not pursue a digital storage policy or practice;
- Depending on royalties as the only way to support work;
- Works with a large number of journals, often using templates to quickly create a start page for each journal;
- Provides insufficient information or hides payment information by contributor.

Honesty (Decency)

- The name of the journal does not correspond to its purpose;
- The title of the journal does not sufficiently reflect its origin (for example, the journal uses the words "Canadian" or "Swiss", but is not directly related to Canada or Switzerland);
- The journal falsely states that it has an impact factor, or uses fictional degrees of measurement (for example, view factor), simulating the international reputation of the publication;
- The publisher sends spam mails to scientists with inadequate qualifications for reviewing manuscript articles;
- The publisher falsely states that the content of the journal is indexed in legitimate referencing and indexing services, or assures that the content of the articles is indexed in resources that are not actually referencing and indexing services;
- The publisher works with unreliable resources, which prevents or eliminates the authors' untrustworthiness;
- The journals contain repetitive cases of plagiarism, manipulations with images, etc.;
- The publisher offers the prospective participant himself to invite reviewers and the publisher subsequently uses the proposed reviewers without sufficient verification of their qualifications or authenticity;
- A large number of self-citations;
- Creation of "cartels" for increasing scientific and metric indicators;
- Failure to comply with the stated number of issues per year and the volume of one issue in printed sheets (a sharp increase in the number of articles and issues per year or the lack of articles in one issue).
- Low interest in journal materials;
- "Narrow" geography of article authors, "concentration of attention" of the journal on authors from specific countries.

Additionally, the "Predatory" Publishing House Can

- Re-publish documents that have already been published in a different volume / issue without foreseeing appropriate conditions;

- Use the phrase "leading publishing house", although the publisher can only be a startup or a newly created organization;
- To carry out its activities from Western European countries, mainly to influence the vanity of scientists from developing countries;
- Make minimal edits or do not do it at all;
- To publish absolutely non-academic works, for example, essays, or to publish the works of obvious representatives of pseudoscience;
- To have on our website the section "our contacts", which includes only a web-form of feedback and thus not to indicate its address.

The following examples reflect the low standards of the journal, they are not directly the criteria of "predatory" publishing houses, but authors should also pay attention to these points before submitting manuscripts to such publications:

- The publisher copies the "Guide for Authors" verbatim (or with minor editing) from other publishers;
- The publishing house does not provide sufficient contact information, including where the headquarters location is not clearly indicated or information about the location of the office is distorted (for example, by using the addresses that are requested by post);
- The publisher publishes journals with too wide-ranging topics (such as the Journal of Education) to print as many articles as possible and generate even more revenue from authors;
- The publisher publishes journals that combine two or more inconsistent thematic areas (for example International Journal of Business, Humanities and Technology);
- The publisher requires the transfer of copyrights and retains the copyright to the contents of the journal;
- The publishing website has broken links, obvious spelling and grammatical errors;
- The publisher allows unauthorized use of licensed images, logos from their website that are used without permission or licensing by the copyright owner;
- The publisher is excessively actively using spam mailing in order to invite to join the editorial board or to post an article for publication in a particular journal;
- The publisher and staff use e-mail addresses ending in "gmail.com", "yahoo.com", etc.;
- The publisher is not able to provide information about the licensing policy of the articles;
- The publisher does not explain the policy of abbreviated articles when publishing or shrinks articles without the author's notice, the publisher does not publish corrections, and does not pursue a policy of clarifying these issues;
- The publisher does not use ISSN and DOI numbers or uses them incorrectly;
- As the name of the publisher uses words such as "Network", "Center", "Association", "Institute" and the like;
- The website of the publisher has a large amount of advertising that prevents site navigation and access to content;
- The publisher does not have membership in leading industry associations and / or does not intentionally participate in such organizations;

- The publishing house on its website refers to international conferences and associations, which essentially have nothing to do with business;
- The publisher places applications that promise quick publication and / or quick review of manuscripts;
- The publishing house has a small number of full-time employees, which does not allow timely and qualitative work;
- The publisher or its journals are not represented in standard periodicals and are not widely cataloged in library databases;
- The publisher copies or explicitly mimics the name of another publisher's journal;
- None of the members of the editorial board of this journal has ever published an article in this.

The Principles of Transparency and Best Practice in Scholarly Publishing (Committee on Publication Ethics, 2018) are a peculiar "constitution" for open access academic journals. The principles and approaches outlined in this document are the basis of the journal policy.

Among them, it is necessary to highlight the most important from the point of view of research integrity:

- Review process;
- Board of the journal;
- Publication fees;
- Copyrights;
- Identification process and reaction to unlawful actions in research;
- Website;
- The name of the journal;
- Conflict of interest;
- Access;
- Sources of income.

Thus, the scientific unit, which dictates the publishing policy at the university, should firmly assimilate the above materials and follow them incessantly.

THE CENTER FOR TECHNOLOGIES TRANSFER IS A "CONDUCTOR" OF THE PRINCIPLES OF RESEARCH INTEGRITY

Since 2000, the Center of Scientific & Technical and Economical information (CSTEI) has been functioning in Sumy State University (http://cnti.sumdu.edu.ua/en.html). CSTEI includes a technology transfer organization group that creates and maintains databases of scientific developments, services and technological requests of the university, as well as other higher educational establishments and enterprises that is, it functions as an interregional technology transfer center. The group also places information in national and international technology transfer networks. Among the important tasks of the group are the introduction of new innovative approaches to the promotion of scientific and technical developments and the provision of scientific services.

The purpose of CSTEI activity is related to the organizational and methodological support of management at the university level by the processes of intellectual property protection, advertising and innovation activities in the implementation of research results, participation in grant programs of the scientific direction, increasing the publication activity and authority of publications, supporting scientific publications of the university and activities of scientific, research and methodological and other directions (http://sumdu.edu.ua/ukr/general/normative-base.html).

The main tasks of CSTEI are the following:

- Scientific research in the field of scientific, technical and economic information;
- Information support of scientific, technical, innovative and grant activities;
- Performance of the function of interregional center for innovation;
- Bringing the results of scientific research, insights and scientific and methodological activities to the scientific and educational community, representatives of industry and business, authorities, as well as other interested organizations and individuals;
- Establishing new contacts and deepening existing scientific ties between scientists from different regions of Ukraine and other countries;
- Creation of conditions for the implementation of the university's innovative potential, including through the introduction of scientific and research and methodological activities;
- Ensuring the increase in the level of the publication activity of university scientists and the authority of their publications in the world scientific community;
- Organizing the improvement process of scientific publications (journals) of the university.

The structure of CSTEI includes the following units:

- The department for the management of intellectual property protection with the separation of a group of patent research in its structure;
- Technology transfer organization group;
- The group of grant activities of a scientific direction;
- The department for the organization of the publication of scientific research results
- The editorial group of scientific journals
- Group of conferences organization and holding;
- IT support group for CSTEI.

The structural units of CSTEI perform the following main functions:

The Department for the Management of Intellectual Property Protection

- Organization and methodological support of the process of intellectual property rights protection at the university;
- Ensuring the acquisition by the university of property rights to objects of intellectual property rights (conclusion of license agreements, sale under licenses for intellectual property objects, etc.);
- Consultations on the protection of intellectual property rights and information activities;

The Group of Patent Research

- Provision of information services for the implementation of patent research and registration of inventive and rationalization solutions, including domestic and foreign legal entities and individuals (as fee-based services), methodological support of these services;
- Documents preparation and submission of intellectual property objects for patenting scientific and technical developments, including domestic and foreign legal entities and individuals (as fee-based services);
- Information and analytical support for the creation and protection of intellectual property;
- Database formation and maintenance of the register of received protection documents.
- The protection of intellectual property rights should be realized on the basis of the scientific virtue of the processes of the implementation of creative and inventive activities and publication of its results:
- Inadmissibility of falsification and fabrication of theoretical and experimental studies on the basis of which an object of intellectual property was created;
- Mandatory inclusion in the composition of the group of authors of all persons who took part in the creation of the object of intellectual property;
- Inadmissibility of inclusion in the composition of the group of authors of persons who did not take part in creative and inventive activities;
- Avoidance of other manifestations that are defined as unfair by national and international regulatory and recommendatory documents in the field of intellectual property, educational and scientific activities.

Technology Transfer Organization Group

- Formation and maintenance of databases of scientific developments, services and technological requests of the university, other universities and enterprises with the function of an interregional center for technology transfer;
- Location and maintenance of information on current scientific and technical developments and scientific services of the university in national and international technology transfer networks;
- Development and introduction of new approaches to the formation and implementation of scientific and innovation policy in the university in terms of advertising scientific and technical developments and providing scientific services;
- Providing third-party customers (as paid services) with marketing and information services in the field of technology transfer;
- Providing consultancy and educational services to third-party customers (as paid services) on technology transfer issues and increasing the effectiveness of developments advertising;
- Monitoring and accounting of the potential customers market for scientific and technical development and scientific services for relevant structural units of the university;
- Organizational support of advertising and exhibition activities.

The Group of Grant Activities of a Scientific Direction

- Organizational and methodological support of the process of participation in competitions for domestic and international scientific grants (both for organizations and individual);
- Search and dissemination of information on scientific grants, joint scientific competitions, competitions in the framework of state and international programs, and the like;
- Informational and methodical support of the process of applying for grants.
- The department for the declaration of scientific studies:
- The analysis of indicators of publication activity, incl. in publications that are indexed by scientometric databases, preparing proposals for organizing relevant work in structural units and stimulating the publication activity of university scientists in rating journals;
- Information and technical assistance to scientists for articles publication in journals indexed by scientometric databases.
- Accounting and analysis of the rating and reporting indicators of the university as a whole and its structural subdivisions in the direction of the department's work, preparing and compiling reports and accompanying the rating of institutes, faculties and departments.

The Editorial Group of Scientific Journals

- Preparing mock-ups of certain scientific journals;
- Work organization to improve the scientific level of journals and their entry into the scientometric and reference databases, obtaining the status of a specialized publication.

The Group of Conferences Organization and Holding

- Work organization on events preparation at the university;
- Work to ensure the improvement of the level of activities and the entry of their materials into scientometric databases.

IT Support Group of CSTE

- Technological support of CSTEI information services;
- Creation and technological support of web-sites of scientific publications and scientific conferences, seminars;
- Creation and maintenance of effective tools for interaction with databases and search engines;
- Work with databases on the transfer and correct display of publication metadata.

RESEARCH INTEGRITY DISSEMINATION SYSTEM: THE DESCRIPTION OF STRUCTURE AND FUNCTIONING MECHANISMS

University Research Integrity Dissemination System consists of four logically interconnected blocks (Figure 8):

1. *The regulatory framework which at the system level describes the mechanisms for introducing the principles of academic integrity in scientific and educational processes, measures to ensure the observance of the principles of academic integrity, procedures for combating violations of the principles of academic integrity.*

The main regulatory framework that regulates the principles of academic integrity in the educational and scientific process:

- Code of Honor of a student, teacher, managerial staff or one unified code of Honor;
- Regulation on the quality control system of the educational process;
- A system for ensuring the quality of educational activities and the quality of higher education;
- Provision for a quality assurance bureau;
- The provision of academic and research integrity;
- Regulations on a laboratory for monitoring the educational activities quality (for applicants for academic degrees);
- Regulations on the verification of scientific, educational, methodological, qualification and academic work on academic plagiarism;
- Regulations on the commission on academic and scientific integrity and the ethics of academic relations;
- A statement (monument) on observance of the principles of academic integrity by the applicants of higher education and scientific degrees, pedagogical, scientific and pedagogical and scientific workers (separate for each group of stakeholders);
- The author's agreement on the transfer of rights, processing, storage and publication of educational and qualification works.

2. *Structural divisions that ensure the popularization of academic integrity principles, their implementation in the educational and scientific activities of the university, and also have an observational and monitoring function.*

As part of the Bureau of Quality Assurance, a separate group of academic integrity is created, the main functions of which are the implementation of academic integrity principles in the educational and scientific activities of the university, and also have supervisory and supervisory functions. The group of academic integrity cooperates with the commission on ethics and academic integrity, whose composition (except for the chairman of the commission and his deputy, who are generally responsible for the educational and scientific process at the university) is unstable and is formed depending on the specific case of violation of academic integrity principles from representatives of quality assurance offices, deputy directors (deans) of institutes (faculties) with methodical and / or scientific work, representatives of teaching staff and representatives of student government. The group of academic integrity participates in the development of normative and information and analytical base and uses the main tools for introducing the principles of academic integrity in the educational and scientific processes.

The main tasks of the Group are:

Figure 8. Research Integrity Dissemination System at Sumy State University
(Source: authors' own image)

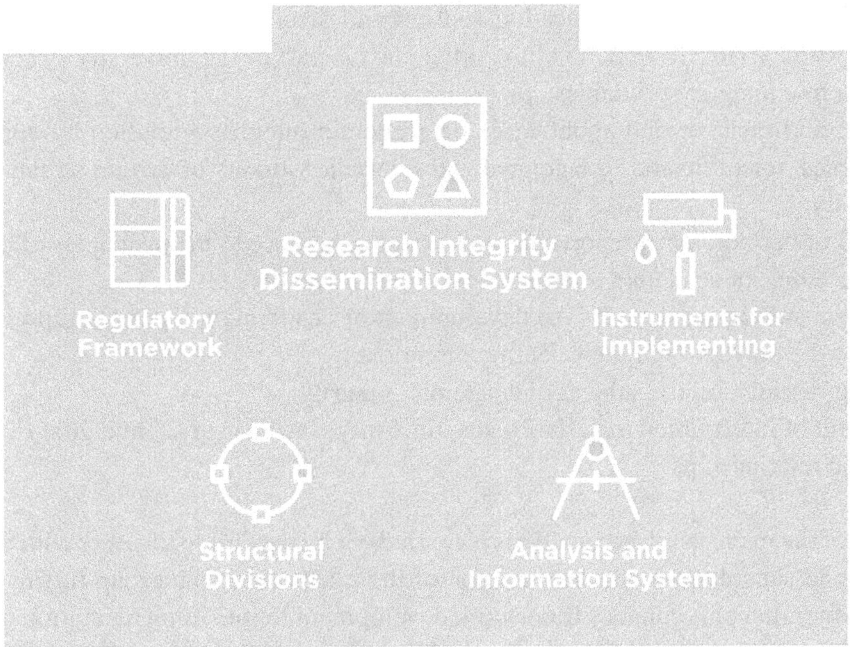

- Popularization of the observance of academic integrity principles (and scientific integrity as part of this common system) and the ethics of academic relationships between higher education seekers and scientific degrees, pedagogical, scientific and pedagogical and scientific workers during training, teaching, research and performing their duties as one from the fundamental principles of corporate culture at the University;
- Formation of the normative and information base of the university, which describes the system and mechanisms for promoting the academic integrity principles and ethics of academic relationships, prevention mechanisms, detection and procedure for dealing with violations of academic integrity in the educational and scientific activities of the university;
- Organizing control over observance of academic integrity principles and ethics of academic relationships in the educational and scientific activities of the university, including the promulgation of academic texts;
- Assistance in introducing the newest educational technologies in the university, including an effective system of prevention and detection of academic plagiarism (in the works of the competitors of educational and scientific degrees and scientific, pedagogical and scientific workers).

In accordance with the main tasks, the functions of the Group are:

- Conducting popularization and information technology events (trainings, seminars, open lectures, academic modules on academic writing and adherence to the academic integrity principles and ethics of academic relationships, etc.);

- Ensuring the functioning of an effective university system to promote the academic integrity principles, as well as the system of preventing and detecting academic plagiarism in the educational and scientific work of higher education seekers and scientific degrees, pedagogical, scientific, pedagogical and scientific workers of the university as part of the university system of promoting the of academic integrity principles;
- Monitoring and interviewing about cases of academic integrity violation by applicants of academic degrees, scientific and pedagogical and scientific workers of certain structural divisions of the university;
- Publication of periodic open reports on the level of adherence to the principles of academic integrity and the ethics of academic relationships at the University;
- Providing consulting services for the development of academic integrity culture in the structural divisions of the university of the scientific direction;
- Conducting research on the subject of academic integrity;
- Development of information material (notes, road maps, etc.) on academic integrity and the ethics of academic relationships.

The solution of the main tasks and functions is carried out by the Group together with the subdivisions of the University in accordance with the direction of their activities. The group fulfills its educational function and the function of regulatory framework development for the implementation of the principles of academic integrity. On specific issues of scientific integrity, in this case the main technological mechanisms for identifying and preventing manifestations of dishonesty are realized by the technology transfer center.

Principles for investigating cases of violation of scientific integrity:

- Investigation is fair, comprehensive and expedient, carried out without detriment to accuracy, objectivity or thoroughness;
- Parties participating in the procedure, declare any conflicts of interest that may arise during the study;
- Steps are being taken to ensure that the investigation is completed;
- Procedures are carried out in confidence to protect those involved in the study;
- Institutions protect the rights of "informers" in the investigation and ensure that their career prospects are not endangered;
- General procedures to combat violations in the best research practices are publicly available in order to ensure their transparency and uniformity;
- Investigation is conducted properly and fairly with respect to all parties;
- Persons accused of scientific misconduct (crime) are provided with complete information about the charge and a fair process of answering the charges and presenting evidence is allowed;
- Measures proportional to the seriousness of the violation are taken against persons in respect of whom the scientific misconduct (crime) is supported;
- Appropriate remedial measures are taken when the researchers are justified from the scientific misconduct (crime);
- Anyone accused of a scientific misconduct (crime) is presumed innocent until proven otherwise.

3. *Information and analytical base, with the help of which the principles of academic integrity are promoted and awareness of all participants in the scientific and educational processes is promoted (university management, students, faculty).*

The main information and analytical base accompanies the educational and scientific processes in terms of principles of observance of academic integrity:

- Notes to prevent the violation of academic integrity principles by a student, teacher, management or a single unified landmark;
- Notes to prevent plagiarism;
- A guide to avoid plagiarism;
- A guide to counter plagiarism;
- A plan of action to combat plagiarism;
- Information materials (developed in conjunction with representatives of employers and scientific partners) on corporate culture in the workplace and the benefits of an honest implementation of scientific activities;
- Materials devoted to the popularization of academic integrity principles among persons acquiring a scientific degree (banners, infographic, handouts, etc.)

4. *Implementation tools, which have an educational function and with the help of which it becomes possible to prevent cases of violation of academic integrity principles.*

The main tools for introducing the principles of observance of academic integrity in the educational and scientific activities of the university:

- Mass open online course "Academic integrity: challenges, actions, successful stories";
- Mass open online course "Academic writing and the basics of information literacy";
- The program for improving the qualifications of scientific and pedagogical and pedagogical workers "Ethics and academic integrity in education and science";
- Website "Academic integrity";
- Lectures of famous graduates and employers;
- Active teaching methods, the introduction of separate blocks in the discipline of training students at various levels of study (for example, discipline, "Organization of scientific activities" for undergraduate students)
- Cycles of trainings for young scientists in conjunction with the youth scientific society;
- Cycles of training for all participants of the scientific process in the framework of all-Ukrainian and international projects on academic integrity, grant programs.

The main tools for monitoring compliance with the principles of observance of academic integrity in the educational and scientific activities of the university:

- Questioning of participants during the scientific process;
- Direct verification of scientific works on academic plagiarism in accordance with established regulatory framework.

Figure 9. "Science RIDS of misconduct"
(Source: authors' own image)

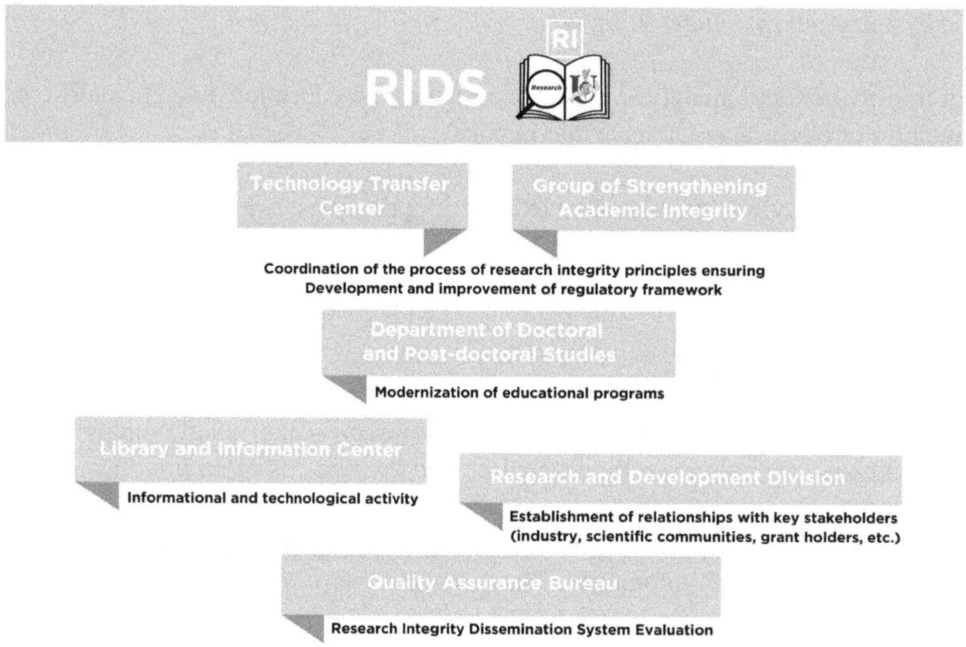

CONCLUSION

In a scientific experiment, it is often very difficult to find a boundary between the actual data juggling and something new, which can even continue and improve previous developments. It is clear that the ideal option is the self-awareness of each experimenter, adherence to the principles of academic integrity. In fact, well-designed plagiarism is quite difficult to detect. To study the problems of dishonesty in a scientific experiment, only highly specialized specialists and reviewers who really have the problems of research should be attracted, orientated in the results obtained in the world.

Among the recommendations for reducing the level of academic dishonesty in the scientific experiment are proposals for carrying out preventive measures to warn it. In particular, it can be trainings on the ethics of scientific research, appropriate development should be integrated into the curriculum of students and graduate students, it is necessary to develop normative documents to improve the skills of researchers. In addition, the process of imposing penalties on offenders in accordance with state legal norms, taking into account European and American experience is possible. All these, as well as other educational and technological activities, constitute the Research Integrity Dissemination System (Figure 9).

REFERENCES

Alper, H. (2008). How can research integrity be best achieved? *Materials Today*, *11*(4), 60. doi:10.1016/S1369-7021(08)70067-1

Artyukhov, A. (2015). Akademichna dobrochesnist' pry provedenni naukovykh doslidzhen [Academic integrity in conducting of scientific research]. In *Osnovy stanovlennya suchasnoho inzhenera* [Fundamentals of Formation of Modern Engineer]. Sumy, Ukraine: Sumy State University.

Artyukhov, A., & Liuta, O. (2017). Academic integrity in Ukrainian higher education: Values, skills, actions. *Business Ethics and Leadership*, *1*(1), 34–39. doi:10.21272/bel.2017.1-04

Artyukhov, A., & Menshov, O. (2016). Akademichna chesnist' u naukovykh doslidzhennyakh [Academic integrity in scientific research]. In Akademichna chesnist' yak osnova staloho rozvytku universytetu [Academic integrity as the basis for sustainable development of the university] (pp. 121-131). Academic Press.

Barnhardt, B. (2015). The "epidemic" of cheating depends on its definition: A critique of inferring the moral quality of "cheating in any form". *Ethics & Behavior*, *26*(4), 330–343. doi:10.1080/10508422.2015.1026595

Baroke, D. (2018). *Investigation into violation of research integrity is concluded.* Retrieved from https://www.psi.ch/media/results-of-the-investigation

Beall, J. (2012). Predatory publishers are corrupting open access. *Nature*, *489*(7415), 179. doi:10.1038/489179a PMID:22972258

Beall, J. (2013). Predatory publishing is just one of the consequences of gold open access. *Learned Publishing*, *26*(2), 79–83. doi:10.1087/20130203

Beall, J. (2016). Best practices for scholarly authors in the age of predatory journals. *Annals of the Royal College of Surgeons of England*, *98*(2), 77–79. doi:10.1308/rcsann.2016.0056 PMID:26829665

Beall, J. (2018). *Beall's list of predatory journals and publishers.* Retrieved from https://beallslist.weebly.com/

Borkowski, S. C., & Welsh, M. J. (2000). Ethical practice in the accounting publishing process: Contrasting opinions of authors and editors. *Journal of Business Ethics*, *25*(1), 15–31. doi:10.1023/A:1005939128790

Chang, C. M., Chen, Y. L., Huang, Y. Y., & Chou, C. (2015). Why do they become potential cyber-plagiarizers? Exploring the alternative thinking of copy-and-paste youth in Taiwan. *Computers & Education*, *87*, 357–367. doi:10.1016/j.compedu.2015.07.006

Fanelli, D. (2009). How many scientists fabricate and falsify research? A systematic review and meta-analysis of survey data. *PLoS One*, *4*(5), e5738. doi:10.1371/journal.pone.0005738 PMID:19478950

Finikov, T., & Artyukhov, A. (2016). *Akademichna chesnist' yak osnova staloho rozvytku universytetu* [Academic integrity as the basis for sustainable development of the university]. Kyiv, Ukraine: Taxon.

Gunsalus, C. K., Marcus, A. R., & Oransky, I. (2018). Institutional research misconduct reports need more credibility. *Journal of the American Medical Association*, *319*(13), 1315–1316. doi:10.1001/jama.2018.0358 PMID:29532069

Jardine, L. (2015). *Erasmus, man of letters: The construction of charisma in print.* Princeton University Press. doi:10.1515/9781400866175

Kharasch, E. D., & Houle, T. T. (2017). Errors and integrity in seeking and reporting apparent research misconduct. *Anesthesiology*, *127*(5), 733–737. doi:10.1097/ALN.0000000000001875 PMID:28825936

Khmarsky, V. (2016). Academic integrity in USA: kil'ka sposterezhen' 2015 roku [Academic integrity in USA: several observations of 2015]. In Academic integrity as the basis for sustainable development of the university [Academic integrity as the basis for sustainable development of the university] (pp. 53-92). Academic Press.

Martin, B. R. (2013). Whither research integrity? Plagiarism, self-plagiarism and coercive citation in an age of research assessment. *Research Policy*, *42*(5), 1005–1014. doi:10.1016/j.respol.2013.03.011

McCabe, D. L. (2018). *It takes a village: Academic dishonesty and educational opportunity*. Retrieved from https://www.aacu.org/publications-research/periodicals/it-takes-village-academic-dishonesty-and-educational-opportunity

O'Dowd, A. (2017). Research integrity has become complacent and lacks transparency, MPs hear. *British Medical Journal*, *359*, 4945. doi:10.1136/bmj.j4945 PMID:29070601

Okonta, P., & Rossouw, T. (2013). Prevalence of scientific misconduct among a group of researchers in Nigeria. *Developing World Bioethics*, *13*(3), 149–157. doi:10.1111/j.1471-8847.2012.00339.x PMID:22994914

Pasquale, C. (2014). *Five questions for Jeffrey Beall*. Retrieved from https://connections.cu.edu/stories/five-questions-jeffrey-beall

Patel, T., & Hamlin, R. G. (2015). Toward a unified framework of perceived negative leader behaviors insights from french and british educational sectors. *Journal of Business Ethics*, *145*(1), 157–182. doi:10.100710551-015-2909-5

Pupovac, V., & Fanelli, D. (2015). Scientists admitting to plagiarism: A meta-analysis of surveys. *Science and Engineering Ethics*, *21*(5), 1331–1352. doi:10.100711948-014-9600-6 PMID:25352123

Research integrity – have we made progress? (2017). *Lancet*, *389*(10081). doi:10.1016/S0140-6736(17)31201-1

Schoenherr, J. R. (2015). Scientific integrity in research methods. *Frontiers in Psychology*, *6*(1562), 1–5. doi:10.3389/fpsyg.2015.01562 PMID:26578994

Sorokina, N., Artyukhov, A., & Degtyarova, I. (2017). *Akademichna dobrochesnist': problemy dotrymannya ta priorytety poshyrennya sered molodykh vchenykh* [Academic integrity: problems of compliance and priorities of spread among young scientists]. Dnipro, Ukraine: Dnipropetrovsk Regional Institute of Public Administration.

The European Code of Conduct for Research Integrity. (2017). Retrieved from https://ec.europa.eu/research/participants/data/ref/h2020/other/hi/h2020-ethics_code-of-conduct_en.pdf

Tolochko, O. (1993). Dvi ne zovsim akademichni dyskusiyi (I.A.Lynnychenko, D. I. Bahaliy, M. S. Hrushevs'kyy) [Two not entirely academic discussions (I.A. Lynnychenko, D.I. Bahalii, M.S. Hrushevsky)]. In P. S. Sokhan (Ed.), Ukrainian Archeographical Yearbook (pp. 92–104). Academic Press.

Zeng, W., & Resnik, D. (2010). Research integrity in China: Problems and prospects. *Developing World Bioethics*, *10*(3), 164–171. doi:10.1111/j.1471-8847.2009.00263.x PMID:19832885

ADDITIONAL READING

Anderson, M. S., & Steneck, N. H. (2011). The problem of plagiarism. *Urologic Oncology: Seminars and Original Investigations*, *29*(1), 90–94. doi:10.1016/j.urolonc.2010.09.013 PMID:21194643

Bouville, M. (2008). Plagiarism: Words and ideas. *Science and Engineering Ethics*, *14*(3), 311–322. doi:10.100711948-008-9057-6 PMID:18368537

Bretag, T. (Ed.). (2016). *Handbook of academic integrity*. Singapore, Malaysia: Springer. doi:10.1007/978-981-287-079-7

Coeli, C. M., Luciana de Lima, L. D., & Carvalho, M. S. (2018). Hypercompetition and research integrity. *Cadernos de Saude Publica*, *34*(1), 1–2. doi:10.1590/0102-311x00000718 PMID:29412310

Edwards, M. A., & Roy, S. (2017). Academic research in the 21st century: Maintaining scientific integrity in a climate of perverse incentives and hypercompetition. *Environmental Engineering Science*, *34*(1), 51–61. doi:10.1089/ees.2016.0223 PMID:28115824

Killinger, B. (2010). *Integrity: Doing the right thing for the right reason*. Ontario, Canada: McGill-Queen's University Press.

Komić, D., Marušić, S. L., & Marušić, A. (2015). Research integrity and research ethics in professional codes of ethics: Survey of terminology used by professional organizations across research disciplines. *PLoS One*, *10*(7), e0133662. doi:10.1371/journal.pone.0133662 PMID:26192805

McCabe, D., Trevino, L., & Butterfield, K. (1999). Academic integrity in honor code and non-honor code environments: A qualitative investigation. *The Journal of Higher Education*, *70*(2), 211–234. doi:10.2307/2649128

Mecca, J. T., Gibson, C., Giorgini, V., Medeiros, K. E., Mumford, M. D., & Connelly, S. (2015). Researcher perspectives on conflicts of interest: A qualitative analysis of views from academia. *Science and Engineering Ethics*, *21*(4), 843–855. doi:10.100711948-014-9580-6 PMID:25115563

Redman, B. (2017). Addressing research misconduct and detrimental research practices: Current knowledge and issues. In B. Redman, Fostering Integrity in Research (pp. 105-146). Washington, D.C., UA: National Academies Press.

Seadle, M. (2016). *Quantifying research integrity*. San Rafael, USA: Morgan & Claypool Publishers.

Shaw, D., & Satalkar, P. (2018). Researchers' interpretations of research integrity: A qualitative study. *Accountability in Research. Policies and Quality Assurance*, *25*(2), 79–93. doi:10.1080/08989621.2017.1413940 PMID:29291621

Shaw, D. M., & Erren, T. C. (2015). Ten simple rules for protecting research integrity. *PLoS Computational Biology*, *11*(10), e1004388. doi:10.1371/journal.pcbi.1004388 PMID:26426757

The European Charter for Researchers. (2005). *The Code of Conduct for the Recruitment of Researchers*. Brussels, Belgium: European Commission.

KEY TERMS AND DEFINITIONS

Pseudoscience: Activity or scientists, represented by supporters (advocates) as scientific, but in fact they are not.

Research Infrastructure: A set of interrelated scientific service units that make up and provide the basis for the functioning of the system for the implementation of scientific research and their results publication.

Research Integrity: A set of ethical principles and statutory rules that should guide the participants in the scientific community while conducting scientific (creative) activities in order to ensure confidence in scientific (creative) achievements.

Research Misconduct (Crime): Manifestations of research integrity arising in the development, conduct, analysis of research, or in the publication of research results.

Valley of Death: An insurmountable obstacle on the way, caused by the difference in the mentality of the participants in the dialogue (the teacher-the younger generation, the university-industry) and the lack of a common goal and motivation for mutually beneficial cooperation.

Chapter 3
Relevance and Importance of Ethics in Post-Grad Research at South African Universities

Vannie Naidoo
University of KwaZulu-Natal, South Africa

ABSTRACT

Ethics in research is a very important consideration that researchers and scientists all over the world should be aware and consciously recognize its importance. Ethics in research did not gloriously appear one day; it advanced and was perfected over time. It took the Nuremberg Code (1951), The Declaration of Helsinki (1964), The Belmont Report (1979), the APA Ethical guidelines (1947, 1953, 2002), and government regulations to assist in setting a guide to research ethics involving key principles to protect respondents. The focal point of ethics in research is to protect the respondents from harm and safeguard their dignity, anonymity, and confidentially. If the test subject is human, plant, or animal, there should be a humane way of handling test subjects. This chapter looks at research ethics and its relevance to post-grad students conducting research at a university. It is pivotal that students are aware of their ethical responsibility towards their test subjects/respondents whilst conducting their study.

INTRODUCTION

In any society ethics is the cornerstone that lays the foundation of good business practice and good human values and behaviour. In research, ethics are the foundation blocks that are the fundamental components of good research. The origins of ethics stems from Green philosophy. According to Johnstone (2009) ethics refers to a system of principles, which can critically change previous considerations about choices and actions. Ethical issues are present in both qualitative and quantitative research. Post-grad students conducting research in any related field at a university should abide by good research ethics that ensure the protection confidentiality, anonymity and dignity of its respondents. Violation of the respondents' human rights at any point in the post-grad students' study will amount to a violation of research ethics that can result in the discontinuation of the study or the removal of the post-grad students degree who

DOI: 10.4018/978-1-5225-6310-5.ch003

violated the human rights of his/her study respondents. Caplan (1992) argued that violations of human rights in the name of scientific research have been among the darkest events in history. The Tuskegee study is a reflection of violating human rights. This study was conducted from 1932-1972 on more than 400 African American people who had syphilis and were deliberately left untreated to study the illness. Although United States Public Health Service sponsored the Tuskegee syphilis study, the disclosure of the 40-year study caused public outrage Ethics is fundamental and must be treated with respect and post-grad students at a university should understand that violating ethics in their research study could have disastrous circumstances to their study outcome.

The following key areas are put forward and discussed in this chapter:

- Different theorists views on ethics in research What is post-grad research at universities
- Post- grad Students' Ethical Considerations Towards Their Respondents in Qualitative and Quantitative Research
- Gaps experienced by Post-grad research students
- Future research areas

To begin the discussion it is important to unpack the important issues theorists have indicated in research. In the section below different theorists, views on ethics in research will be highlighted and discussed.

DIFFERENT THEORISTS VIEWS ON ETHICS IN RESEARCH

There are differing views on ethics in research. Under this theme in the chapter different theorists views on ethics in research will be highlighted.

Ethics in research refers to the correctness of behavioural relation to the rights of those who become the subject of work to be carried out (Saunders et al, 2009). David & Sutton (2011) maintains that collecting information about people raises ethical issues in the focus of attention chosen, in the methods adopted and in the form and use of the findings. In any research study conducted by post-grad students, the students must protect the human rights, dignity, anonymity and confidentially of their study respondents.

According to Blumber, Cooper & Schindler (2014) there are two dominant philosophical standpoints on research ethics: deontology and teleology. In deontological view the end never justifies the use of the means that are questionable on ethical grounds. The teleological view posits that morality of the means has to be judged by the ends served. Hence, the study is weighted against the costs of harming the people involved.

The research company or sponsor also has a responsibility to the respondents and should not violate their trust or confidentially or harm them in any way. Kumar et al (2002) suggests that companies or sponsors that practice legitimate research can violate the rights of the respondents in the following manner namely:

- Disguising the purpose of a particular measurement, such as a free draw or free product choice question
- Deceiving the prospective respondent as to the true duration of the interview
- Invading the privacy of the respondent

- Misrepresenting the compensation in order to gain cooperation
- Not mentioning to the respondent that a follow-up interview will be made
- Using projective tests and unobtrusive measures to circumvent the need for a respondents consent
- Using hidden tape recorders to record personal interviews (or recording phone conversations without the respondents permission)
- Conducting simulated product tests in which the identical product is tried by the respondent except for variations in characteristics such as colour, that have no influence in the quality of product
- Not debriefing the respondent.

In research there is ethics that a respondent should also adhere to and not violate the study or trust of the research sponsor or researcher. Cavana et al. (2002) indicates the following ethical behaviour that respondents must aspire to during the study:

- The subject, once having exercised the choice to participate in the study, should cooperate fully in the tasks ahead, such as responding to a survey or taking part in an experiment.
- The respondent also has an obligation to be truthful and honest in the responses. Misrepresentation, or giving information knowing it to be untrue, should be avoided.

Zikmund and Babin (2010) argues that ethics are rules or principles of conduct that differentiate between right and wrong, They help determine the difference between suitable and unsuitable behaviours that a researcher must adhere to during the research process. Ethical considerations are important in research because issues in research aspects involving integrity, reliability and validity of the research findings depend upon seriously adhering to the above principles. The readers and public want t be certain that researchers followed the suitable guidelines for issues such as human rights, animal welfare and compliance with the law, conflicts of interest, safety, health standards and many others.

When conducting research with human respondents no harm should be done to them. During the study the respondents should not feel "small" demeaned, intimidated, threatened or hurt in any way. Saldana (2011) argues that, but first do no harm is the primary ethical premise when working with human participants in a research study. Especially when dealing with vulnerable groups like the very sick, young children or the elderly, special care and consideration should be taken not to upset the respondents or manipulate them during the interview process for example. The researcher must maintain a non-bias stance during the data collection process and should not manipulate the respondents to say what the interviewer wants to hear. According to Burns and Grove (2005) "discomfort and harm can be physiological, emotional, social and economic in nature". For example if the researcher is investigating sexual abuse in the transmission of HIV and AIDS. This is a very sensitive issue to respondents who are abused or raped. When a researcher tries to learn the intimate details of the respondents' lives he/she can open up old wounds. Ford & Reutter (1990) indicate that Nonmalificence dictates both preventing intentional harm and minimising potential harm. Burns and Grove (2005) suggest that if respondents experienced a high level of discomfort during the interview, they should be debriefed or referred to appropriate professional intervention as necessary.

Welman & Kruger (2005) stated that the following are the reasons behind following ethical standards in research:

- Research customs encourage the aims of research such as knowledge, truth and prevention of error.
- Since research regularly involves a great deal of collaboration and direction amongst many different people in different disciplines, ethical values encourage the standards that are vital to co-operative work, such as trust, responsibility, common respect and objectivity.
- Many ethical procedures help to ensure that the researcher can be held answerable to the public.

The post- grad students must maintain both moral and professional ethical considerations towards their respondents. The researcher must ensure trust, truth, respect and honesty towards his/her respondents. According to Bordens & Abbott (2018) using living organisms, whether human or animal, in research imposes upon you an obligation to treat those organisms in a humane, respectful and ethical manner. The researcher has to be respectful of his /her respondents, be objective and non-bias, and ensure that integrity is upheld during the research process.

A new area is ethics in internet research. In internet research safeguarding the identity of the respondents is crucial. According to Pittenger (2003) the following are guidelines for ethical research on Internet groups:

- Learn about and respect the rules of the Internet group you are going to study. Find out if the group is an open, public one or a closed, private one.
- Edit any data collected. Comb through the data and eliminate any names or pseudonyms that may lead to participants being identified. Also, exclude any references to the name of the group being studied.
- Use multiple groups. Example several groups for alcoholics, this adds another layer to protect the respondents privacy.

Blumber, Cooper & Schindler (2014) suggests that as research is designed, several ethical considerations must be balanced:

- Protecting the rights of the participant or subject
- Ensuring the sponsor receives ethically conducted and reported research
- Follows ethical standards when designing research
- Protect the safety of the researcher and team
- Ensure the research team follows the design

It is important to note that here is no single approach to ethics. The goal is to find the middle ground that ensures that a researcher has personal integrity to follow a moral code that ensures that the study is non-bias, the respondents are treated with dignity and respect whilst maintaining their privacy during the research process.

In the discussion, that follows what is post-grad research at universities in South Africa and the protocols followed for the student's study will be put forward and discussed.

WHAT IS POST-GRAD RESEARCH AT SOUTH AFRICAN UNIVERSITIES AND THE PROTOCOLS FOLLOWED

In this section of the chapter, post-grad research degrees will be outlined. Specific reference is made to the research component of the degree. The researcher will also indicate practical examples from the University of KwaZulu-Natal in their post-grad research studies.

Post- grad research is the thesis component of a Honours, Masters or PHD study. For example at the University of KwaZulu-Natal (UKZN) a Honours degree has a research component attached for students studying towards a B. Com (honours) in the discipline of Management, Entrepreneurship, Marketing, Supply chain or Human Resources. This research component requires a student to conduct a small research study either qualitative or quantitative. The student has to write a report documenting his/her study, the literature review, research methodology employed in the study and research findings and results. At the UKZN a Master's degree entails course work (with the writing of a mini-dissertation) or a Masters by full dissertation. In a PHD study at UKZN in the faculty of Law & Management a full dissertation is required. In all three post-grad studies at UKZN there are strict ethical guidelines that have to be adhered to. If the PHD research is conducted in South Africa at a South African university, via the Phycology department, then the Code of ethical conduct set out by the South African Phycology Association must be adhered to, as well as the rules and guidelines on ethics set out by Ethics committee at the University. If the post-grad student is registered for a Master's degree Medical science at a South African university then the student has to adhere to the ethical code of conduct put forward by the University research committee as well as the ethics enshrined in the SA Medical Research Foundation. The example that follows relates to an America student studying towards a Masters in Nursing. He /she has to adhere to the "Nightingale Pledge" (1983), the American Nurses' Association (ANA) Guidelines for Research, the Human Rights Guidelines for nurses in clinical and other research (1985) and the Royal College of Nursing Code for nurses in research (1977). These different associations and affiliation provides the Nursing student conducting research with strong ethical assistance to professional nurses as well as reassurance to patients, the public and society, of professionals 'intentions.

At UKZN it is important to note that a Masters and PHD study would require a student to develop and submit a proposal to the Higher degrees committee of the school/discipline. Once this proposal has been approved, the student is given permission to proceed with the study. The student cannot start on data collection unless the university Ethics committee is happy that the students' research meets the ethical standards of the university. The second important phase is for the student to gain ethical clearance to conduct the study. The student can only submit the Ethical clearance application to the university Ethics committee once the ethical clearance application, together with gatekeeper's letter and research instruments (that are signed by the students' supervisor) have been sent to the Academic Leader of Higher Degrees in the school/discipline. The Academic Leader of Higher Degrees in the school/discipline would look through the application, sign it once he/she has approved it, and send it off to the University Ethics committee. This phase can take time, since the University Ethics committee scrutinizes the application and will only grant Ethical clearance for the student to conduct the study, once they are satisfied that the Ethical clearance application adheres to the university's standards of ethics.

At South African universities the discipline bodies (Humanities, Phycology etc.) and research bodies (National research foundation) and University ethics committee's rules and regulations governing research ethics has to be followed and adhered to by the post-grad student who is involved in the research study. Another important component of ethics is that the researcher has to acquire a signed gatekeeper's letter that allows the post-grad student access to respondents. For example if the researcher wants to conduct a study on stress on doctors at R.K. Khan hospital in Chatsworth, South Africa, a gatekeepers letter needs to be provided by the Dept. of Health and the hospital management to allow the student access to the respondents.

Another policy that South African universities have in place is the Plagiarism policy. Post-grad students involved in research must adhere to this policy. Failure to adhere to the plagiarism policy is a breach of ethical conduct in research. Post-grad students' have a duty and obligation to present their research in a manner that acknowledges the work of other researchers and the stealing of ideas, cutting and pasting other theorists work without acknowledging them in the study and stealing patents or prototypes and displaying the work as your own scientific knowledge is not allowed for example.

According to Vithal and Jansen (2010) ethical consideration refers to methods, procedure and perspectives that relates to the researcher how to act, how to analyse complicated problems and issues. For a post-grad student at UKZN for example, his/her research study must ensure that openness and honesty was upheld in reporting the study's results. All relevant information used in the study must be correctly referenced and free of plagiarism. The respondents in the study have given written consent to participate in the study. The respondents were free to choose if they wished to participate in the study and was not coerced or pressured. The respondent's identity was at all times kept anonymous. Confidentiality of the respondents was upheld. Respondents were adequately informed of the objectives and nature of the research. Ethical approval was obtained from the UKZN ethical committee and a gate keepers' letter from the Office of the Registrar at UKZN was received (since students at UKZN were the test subjects) prior to the start of this study.

In the next discussion that follows, the Post- grad students' ethical considerations towards their respondents in qualitative and quantitative research will be presented and discussed.

POST- GRAD STUDENTS' ETHICAL CONSIDERATIONS TOWARDS THEIR RESPONDENTS IN QUALITATIVE AND QUANTITATIVE RESEARCH

In this section of the chapter, post-grad students' ethical considerations towards their respondents in qualitative and quantitative research would be addressed and discussed. The discussion also highlights qualitative and quantitative research, as they are different.

Quantitative research measures the numbers of respondents in favour of, or opposed to an issue, as by nature it is numerical (Lind, Marchal & Wathen, 2010). According to Sukamolson (1995), "quantitative research is the numerical representation and manipulation of observations for the purpose of describing and explaining the phenomena that those observations reflect. It is used in a wide variety of natural and social sciences, including physics, biology, psychology, sociology and geology". Cooper & Schindler (2006) expand on quantitative research by saying that "it is often used to measure knowledge, Enumenu (2005) argues that there are several types of quantitative research. For instance, it can be classified as (1) survey research, (2) correlational research, (3) experimental research and (4) causal-comparative research opinions or attitudes, questions concern 'how much, how often, how many, when and who?"

According to Denzin & Lincoln (2005) up to the 1970s, anthropologists and sociologists solely employed qualitative research. This changed later and during the 1970s and 1980s, qualitative research was favoured by various disciplines and experts of different branches of science and humanity such as health care, psychology, nursing, management, political science, education, and communication studies (Grbich, 1999). According to Neuman (2003) 'Qualitative research emphasises the social context for understanding the social world'. Patton (2002) argued that qualitative research required "the ability to draw on a variety of skills, materials and approaches. Qualitative data comprises in depth descriptions of circumstances, people, interactions, observed behaviours, events, attitudes, thoughts and beliefs and direct quotes from people who have experienced or are experiencing the phenomenon".

According to Cavana et al, (2002) ethics and the post-grad student researcher should include the following:

- Treating the information given by the respondent as strictly confidential and guarding, his or her privacy is one of the primary responsibilities of the researcher.
- Researchers should not misrepresent the nature of the study to subjects, especially in laboratory experiments.
- Personal or seemingly intrusive information should not be solicited, and if it is necessary for the project, it should be tapped from the respondent with high sensitivity, with specific reasons given.
- Whatever the nature of the data collection method, the self- esteem and self-respect of the subjects should never be violated.
- No one should be forced to respond to the survey, and if someone turns down the opportunity to participate, the individual's desire should be respected.
- Nonparticipant observers should be as unintrusive as possible.
- In laboratory studies, the subjects should be debriefed with full disclosure of the reasons for the experiment after they have participated in the study.
- Subjects should never be exposed to situations in which they could be subject to physical or mental harm.
- There should be no misrepresentation or distortion in reporting the data collected during the study.

Sekaran & Bougie (2010) suggests that the following practices were considered unethical in experimental design research for the post-grad student researcher:

- Putting pressure on individuals to participate in experiments through coercion, or applying social pressure.
- Giving menial tasks and asking demeaning questions that diminish their self-respect
- Deceiving subjects by deliberately misleading them as to the true purpose of the research.
- Exposing participants to physical or mental stress.
- Not allowing subjects to withdraw from the research when they want to.
- Using the research results to disadvantage the participants, or for purposes not to their liking.
- Not explaining the procedures to be followed in the experiment.
- Exposing respondents to hazardous and unsafe environments.
- Not debriefing participants fully and accurately after the experiment is over.
- Not preserving the privacy and confidentiality of the information given by participants.
- Withholding benefits from control groups.

The discussion below would discuss specific key principles that post-grad students must adhere to when dealing with their respondents.

KEY ETHICAL PRINCIPLES THAT POST-GRAD STUDENTS MUST ADHERE TO

From the discussion that follows, it must be noted that the following key principles must be adhered to in post-grad research irrespective if the researcher is using qualitative or quantitative methods to gather data from the respondents:

- The rights of the respondent must be protected irrespective if gathering data is done through an experiment, interview, observation or survey. According to Blumberg et al. (2014) to ensure the safety of a respondent or test participant three guidelines should be followed:
  - Explain the benefits of the study
  - Explain the participants their rights and protection
  - Obtain consent
- Benefits. Benefits of the study and its purpose should be fully disclosed to the respondent. The contact details of the researcher and his supervisor must be provided so that the participants can be put at ease as they know who they are speaking to and what the purpose of the study is.
- Deception. When conducting research post-grad student researchers should only embark on deception if they can balance the risks to participants. For example, a researcher's deception or disclosure of damaging information can occur. Humphrey's study of homosexuals is one example His controversial research method of participant observation using deception shocked American academics who wanted to revoke the researcher's doctoral degree. He observed men in a public bathroom and followed them to their homes under the guise of working on a different project (Punch, 1994).
- Informed consent. The researcher needs to acquire informed consent preferably in writing from the respondent before he/she can take part in the study. According to Armiger (1997): "it means that a person knowingly, voluntarily and intelligently, and in a clear and manifest way, gives his consent"
- Debriefing participants is also an important ethical issue that a post-grad researcher must adhere to in his study. According to According to Blumberg et at. (2014) debriefing involves several activities that follow the collection of data and is as follows:
- Explanation of any deception
- description of the research project, goal or purpose of the study
- Post-study sharing of results
- Post-study follow-up medical or psychological attention
- Rights to privacy. The researcher must protect the confidentially of the respondents at all times. According to Cooper & Schindler (2014) the researcher can protect the confidentially of the respondents in the following ways:
- Obtaining signed nondisclosure documents
- Restricting access to participant identification
- Revealing participant information only with written consent
- Restricting access to data instruments where the participant is identified

- Not disclosing data subsets

A very important issue in ethics for post-grad students conducting a research study is that the student does not conduct misconduct by fabricating or falsifying data results. The student should also not plagiarise.

Bordens & Abbott (2018) argues that in the U.S the Office of research Integrity (ORI) defines three categories of research misconduct:

- Data fabrication: Making up data or results and recording or reporting on them.
- Falsification: Manipulating research materials, equipment, or processes, or changing or omitting data or results such that the research is not accurately represented in the research record.
- Plagiarism: The appropriation of another person's ideas, processes, results or words without giving appropriate credit.

GAPS EXPERIENCED BY POST-GRAD RESEARCH STUDENTS

Funding is major problem faced by post-grad research students who are involved in a research study. Although at UKZN we offer student studying full Masters fee remission for a year and for PHD students are offered three years fee remission. However, travelling costs are very expensive for these students, as many of them work and study and live in other cities provinces or countries away from UKZN. As a way to assist, students' supervisors are encouraged to use the internet, SKYPE and e-mail to communicate with these research students.

Students also may experience issues in acquiring acceptance for their proposals. This can frustrate students at Masters and PHD level. The reviewers sometimes take a lot of time to review their proposals, this can cause time delays in the students' studies. Another frustration is that when presenting proposal at PHD level, the committee may be present but the SKYPE connection for the students from neighbouring countries can be very poor and this can become a problem if the internet connection is not working. To reschedule a SKYPE presentation and get the higher degrees committee together is not often easy.

During the ethical clearance applications students often face difficulties in gaining gatekeepers letters that allow the study to be conducted at an institution, government agency or company. To streamline the process at UKZN the supervisor writes a letter to indicate to the gatekeeper that the student is trying to gain access to respondents of the organisation for a study conducted at the university and the aims and objectives of the study are shared. The issue of confidentially and anonymity is outlined. The organisation can grant permission and opt to allow their name to be used in the study or not.

The University research committee can delay the process by taking time to scrutinize the students' ethical clearance application. The supervisor should encourage students to work on their literature review or research methodology chapters so that time is not lost.

Once ethical clearance is granted and student is allowed to gather data, the data collection phase can also be lengthy. Students may have to make time for follow up interviews or administration of survey at different times so that respondents can complete take part in the interview or have time to complete the survey. Timing of data collection is crucial, if university students are the respondents', surveys or interviews must not be conducted during exam time or study breaks or the student will get a poor response rate.

During interviews, especially with children, the informed consent letter must be signed by parents, or the data collection cannot occur. It is against the law to have a minor be part of a study without the consent of the parent.

Another issue is that the researcher must not be bias and sway the respondents. As much as a student wants to complete his/her study objectivity and impartiality is very important to maintain in the study especially during data collection phase.

Researchers must not get emotionally involved with respondents. Eg. If the researcher is assessing prostitutes perceptions on HIV and AIDS, the respondents when spending time with this respondent must not get emotionally involved with them.

The student must not discuss the names of his/her study respondents', confidentially must be assured at all times to the respondents.

During certain studies especially in phycology, a respondents' deep wound from the past may be opened during an interview. It is the responsibility of the Masters or PHD student researcher to have a post-study follow-up or medical or psychological attention should be provided to this traumatised or vulnerable respondent.

The use of Turnitin software that assists in the detection of plagiarism is often problematic for students. The students must be provided with training and workshops on responsible research writing. PHD and Masters students must not be involved with plagiarism.

When transcribing interviews, interview bias must be limited. The Masters or PHD student researcher can use Nvivo, which is a software package that can categorise respondents' responses into different themes.

Below is a brief discussion on future research areas to be explored.

FUTURE RESEARCH AREAS

Exploring technology and how it can be utilised to limit interview bias can be considered and investigated further. An Example is Nvivo, which is a software package that can be used in qualitative research to assist the researcher in generating themes in the study.

Another area for future research is to investigate the ethics behind the use of incentives to entice respondents to take part in the study.

Another area in research is confidentially and how it can be handled can be investigated.

A WAY FORWARD AND CONCLUING REMARKS

In the 21st century technology has become the cornerstone of society and corporate entities. Maybe computer simulations can be used instead of animal and human tests for example. This way no animal or person is harmed as a computer simulations involves programming a computer to predict various events or behaviours, given certain factors or predictors. To limit interview bias, the use of Nvivo could remove interview bias. Researchers' must not also get emotionally involved with their study participants or test subjects. Another issue in research ethics is deception. From a morality standpoint, is deception acceptable in research if relevant information is gained about the subject from the respondent. There are those academics who strongly believe that deception is acceptable and pushing a subject to respond to certain stressful stimuli although harmful to the wellbeing of the respondent can be highly beneficial to the gathering of new knowledge on the subject area. The fact that the human rights and dignity of the respondent is violated in the above scenario makes this type of deception or technique in research unethical. Using animals as test subjects is also not morally acceptable by many academics in the field of science. Ethics in research is therefore a very contentious issue and it will always have two sides to the coin. However, in society the protection of human life, human dignity and anonymity and respecting the privacy of respondents is crucial. Vulnerable groups like children, the sick, the elderly and the mentally ill must be respected and maintain their dignity is essential. These vulnerable peoples must not be exploited; coerced or threatened by the researchers during the study. It is also imperative that medical treatment should not be withheld from vulnerable test subjects. A positive way forward is that post-grad student who are conducting a research study at a university should be severely reprimanded if they are unethical in their research. The university can ask them to redo their study if they have tampered with the data during the data collection phase. The university can also revoke their degree if it can be shown that they have falsified and plagiarised their study. In South Africa if strong allegations are brought to the ethics and research committees notice about sever ethical misconduct by a student the allegations are investigated and appropriate action is taken. Sometimes, a student's degree is revoked.

REFERENCES

Armiger, B. (1997). Ethics in Nursing Research: Profile, Principles, Perspective. *Nursing Research, 26*(5), 330–333. doi:10.1097/00006199-197709000-00003 PMID:587922

Blumberg, B. F., Cooper, D. R., & Schindler, P. S. (2014). *Business Research Methods* (4th ed.). New York: McGraw–Hill.

Bordens, K. S., & Abbott, B. B. (2018). *Research Design and Methods. A Process Approach* (10th ed.). McGraw-Hill.

Burns, N., & Grove, S. K. (2005). *The practice of nursing research: Conduct, critique, and utilization* (5th ed.). St. Louis, MO: Elsevier/Saunders.

Caplan, A. L. (1992). Twenty years after. The legacy of the Tuskegee syphilis study. *The Hastings Center Report, 22*(6), 29. doi:10.2307/3562946 PMID:1428845

Cavana, R. Y., Delahaye, B. L., & Sekaran, U. (2002). *Applied business research: qualitative and quantitative methods*. John Wiley & sons.

Cooper, C. R., & Schindler, P. S. (2006). *Marketing Research*. New York: McGraw–Hill.

Cooper, C. R., & Schindler, P. S. (2014). *Business Research Methods*. New York: McGraw–Hill.

David, M., & Sutton, C. D. (2011). *Social Research: An introduction* (2nd ed.). London, UK: SAGE Publication Inc.

Denzin, N. K., & Lincoln, Y. S. (2005). *The Sage Handbook of Qualitative Research* (3rd ed.). Sage Publication.

Enunemu, B. (2005). *Socio-economic and Cultural Correlates of The Girls 'Access to Education and Withdrawal from Secondary School in Delta state, Nigeria* (Unpublished DPhil Thesis). University of Ibadan.

Ford, L., & Reutter, L. (1990). Ethical dilemmas associated with small samples. *Journal of Advanced Nursing, 15*(1), 187–191. doi:10.1111/j.1365-2648.1990.tb01800.x PMID:2312919

Grbich, C. (1999). *Qualitative Research in Health: An introduction*. London: Sage Publication.

Johnstone, M. (2009). *Bioethics. A Nursing Perspective* (5th ed.). St. Louis, MO: Churchil Livingstone Elsevier.

Kumar, V., Aaker, D. A., & Day, G. S. (2002). *Essentials of Marketing research*. New York: John. Wiley & Sons.

Lind, D. A., Marchal, W. G., & Wathen, S. A. (2010). *Basic Statistics Using Excel for Office XP*. New York: McGraw-Hill.

Neuman, W. L. (2003). *Social Research Methods: Qualitative and Quantitative Approaches* (5th ed.). Boston: Allyn and Bacon Publishers.

Patton, M. Q. (2002). *Qualitative Research and Evaluation Methods* (3rd ed.). London: Sage Publications.

Pittenger, D. J. (2003). Internet research: An opportunity to revisit classic ethical problems in behavioural research. *Ethics & Behavior, 13*(1), 45–60. doi:10.1207/S15327019EB1301_08 PMID:14552304

Punch, M. (1994). Politics and ethics in qualitative research. In N. K. Denzin & Y. S. Lincoln (Eds.), *Handbook of qualitative research*. London: Newbery Park. Sage Publications.

Saldana, J. (2011). *The coding manual for qualitative researchers*. London: Sage Publications.

Saunders, M., Lewis, P., & Thornhill, A. (2009). *Research methods for business students*. Cape Town: Pearson Education.

Sekaran, U., & Bougie, R. (2010). *Research methods for business A skill building approach* (4th ed.). New York: John. Wiley & Sons.

Sukamolson, S. (1995). English Language Education policy in Thailand. *Asian Englishes, 1*(1), 68–91. doi:10.1080/13488678.1998.10800995

Vithal, R., & Jansen, J. (2010). *Designing Your First Research Proposal: A Manual for Researchers in Education and the Social Sciences*. Juta Legal and Academic Publishers.

Welman, J. C., & Kruger, S. J. (2005). *Research Methodology* (3rd ed.). Cape Town: Oxford University Press.

Zikmund, W., & Babin, B. (2010). *Exploring marketing research* (10th ed.). South Western Cengage Learning.

KEY TERMS AND DEFINITIONS

Ethics: Refers to the right behavior individuals in society should prescribe to.

Post-Grad: Is a student who has a first degree and is studying at a more advanced level.

Research: Is when a scientific enquiry or study is conducted to investigate a theory, a concept, or a problem that adds to the body of knowledge.

Respondents: These are people who form part of a study and information is required from them to test their perceptions, beliefs, feelings, and attitudes.

University: It is a higher education institution where students come to study undergrad or post-grad degrees.

Chapter 4
Comparative Analysis of the Codes of Ethics in Top Universities in Romania

Tomita Ciulei
Valahia University of Targoviste, Romania

ABSTRACT

The chapter aims to decipher some aspects (of form and content) of the codes of ethics that are present and in force within the representative academic communities in Romania. The main thesis is that in the Romanian university system there is still no unitary practice in respecting the norms of academic conduct, on the background of implicit university autonomy, which can explain some negative consequences recorded throughout the social life, from the pre-university education system to the decision-making structures.

INTRODUCTION

This approach, beyond its pedagogical implications, also aims at decrypting those common places (or rather, their lack) that can lead to an understanding of a broader phenomenon that can be: *the ethics of research.*

The work method assumed from the very beginning was the text analysis, corroborated with the study of the documents. As the accuracy of the information and analysis was determined by the access to first-hand information, we considered to be official documents, the documents on the websites of the institutions on which we will focus this first part of the research.

As the title of the study implies the restriction of research on some of the *top* Romanian higher education institutions, and to avoid any possible discussion or subjective taxonomy on this ranking, we have appealed to the only classification of Romanian universities accepted at decision-making level, dating back to 2011 and being even the classification on the basis of which the relevant ministry establishes its strategies for university education, as well as the funding programs. "The classification of universities in 3 categories, according to art. 193 of the Law on National Education, no. 1/2011, was made on the basis of GD 789/2011. According to the law, universities are classified in universities centered on

DOI: 10.4018/978-1-5225-6310-5.ch004

education, universities of education and scientific research, or universities of education and arts, and advanced research and education universities (UeFiscdi, 2011).

Based on this classification, and for reasons of space, we have narrowed the study to several universities where the emphasis also falls on advanced scientific research, not only on the educational aspect: University of Bucharest, "Al. I.Cuza" University of Iasi, Polytechnic University of Bucharest, West University of Timisoara, the Academy of Economic Studies in Bucharest and the Polytechnic University of Iasi.

VISIBILITY

The first thing we wanted to research was the *visibility* of documents on ethics, deontology, and academic integrity, and by seeing both the aspects of the actual existence of the documents in question[1], and the ease with which they can be "discovered" in the arborescence of an institutional site (http://www.unibuc.ro/).

A first observation would be that those codes are relatively hard to find in most official websites, somehow suffocated by marketing purposes to support the new concept of "entrepreneurial university", however difficult we might understand the referential of the expression. The only exception is the site of the University of Bucharest, where the address of the ethics committee, visible and different from the "research ethics commission" (http://www.unibuc.ro/), is visible on the front page. But ... surprise! By accessing the Ethics Committee page, we find an excellently constructed administrative page: functioning regulation, with an updated constitution, with clear transparency regarding public cases of violation of academic conduct, but two addresses are ... empty, that, in the economy of our work, it would have been extremely useful: ethics (http://www.unibuc.ro/n/organizare/comisia-de-etica/Etica.php) and integrity (http://www.unibuc.ro/n/organizare/comisia-de-etica/Integritate.php). We find, however, the "Code of Ethics of the University" under the sign of "public information" (UB, n.d.) and it is absolutely commendable to present it directly in the form of a direct, easy to open and lecture link, rather than a .pdf document (as we will see it is custom) hard to download, sometimes scanned at a poor quality and not acknowledge by anyone (no stamp, no signature).

The practice of downloading a pdf document is found at the West University of Timisoara (https://www.uvt.ro/ro/uvt/comisia-etica-uvt/), but it is a document somewhat assumed by the use of the headline with the special marks of the university, although we learn from the title that it would have been approved in a university senate meeting in 2016. may seek that Senate decision, but there is no certainty that the text approved in the plenary of that meeting is the one that can be downloaded from the official website, which can create real discomfort to the institution in the event of a legal dispute. The addition of this site resides in a much wider range of public information, from the composition of formal and functional ethics committees at college level to the publication of reports on violation of academic conduct rules.

The Polytechnic University of Bucharest still sends from the "about us" page to a "University Ethics Code" (http://www.upb.ro/despre-upb.html). The lack of any determination and personalization made us believe that we are in front of the "Code", that I had finally found ... *the code*. In fact, I came into possession of a ... normative act. This is Law no. 477/2004 on "Code of Conduct for Contract Staff in Public Authorities and Institutions". Also on the same page, we find a *regulation of the ethics committee* and a *component of the ethics committee* (http://www.upb.ro/despre-upb.html). These are the only available materials on university ethics found on the institution's website.

In the case of "Al.I.Cuza University" in Iasi, the search seems to have been somewhat more difficult, the official website's structure being extremely busy and very less intuitive. Searching for the code has led us almost from the "about" page to "useful information," from here in the "university documents" and from here to "ethics", from where we were able to download the "code of professional ethics and deontology", the practice being the one mentioned above: .pdf format – download (UAIC, n.d.). But here, even if the document bears all the insignia of the university, even the last page invokes the rector of the institution as a decision-maker, it is still unsigned, and we do not find the date of the senate sitting when it was adopted. Maybe for this reason the last page is invoked by the rector's signature (as head of the CA) and not by the president of the senate (as head of the university legislative).

In the case of the Polytechnic University "Ghe. Asachi " in Iasi, the search was even more difficult, even putting us in the position of searching for the "search" button in the site, a practice we had refused from the very beginning, precisely because it is the best proof of *unusability*, if we can express it. Although we searched for the keywords of our study: code of ethics, ethics, integrity, the results were null. Finding it in the end, I had the most elaborate document to date: with all the visible signatures, the dates when they were obtained, and the entire procedural route of the Code, from drafting to endorsement in CA, and finally, upon approval in the university senate.

Finally, the *Academy of Economic Studies* has put us in front of the most difficult search, unfortunately resulting in failure. The only area where our research could have found resources is the *research management area* where I was able to access (in pdf, download) a document, titled the operational procedure of publishing a scientific book at ASE Bucharest and which presented on page 10 some aspects of the law of copyright (ASE, n.d.), and a link titled *anti-plagiarism* but which, in fact, provides for a procedure for verifying the edited work.

INSTEAD OF CONCLUSIONS

This study, as shown in the *Introduction*, aims only to circumscribe the subject of the research in order to develop the other directions of analysis that we propose in a future work: the *structure* of codes of ethics in universities (here being interested in the structural, procedural analysis and the content itself, namely the very precise circumscription of what we understand by academic conduct), the *principles / norms* enunciated (the emphasis being placed on the semantic and pragmatic delimitation, the action of the ethical and integrity principles, but also the *consistent* norms), the *actors* of the codes (by looking at the way the codes delineate between different actors in the academic community) and, finally, the *consequences* of breaking the rules of ethics and academic conduct (here are the penalties provided for deviations from academic norms).

We can, however, propose some preliminary conclusions on the way in which members of the academic community (students, teachers) and the public opinion can easily access this information. Reason is, on the one hand, to put all members of the community in the position of knowing all these provisions in detail, but also the consequences of their violation (so they cannot invoke the lack of knowledge of the law, even if it does not exonerate from bearing the consequences) and on the other hand, to provide a unitary basis, a kind of *zero moment* of the research.

A second aspect would be the procedural one. These codes, apart from the fact that they should be built unitarily in terms of principles that leave room for the manifestation of university autonomy in the area of norms, should be said to be elaborated in such a way that they are assumed by an academic structure with decisional power (CA or university senate), not by a person or a commission (see the case of the "Ghe Asachi" Polytechnic University of Iasi). This avoids legal discomfort in the event of any dispute in which the law of copyright is invoked.

Finally, we believe that these codes should not only focus on the legal and / or procedural aspects that may be covered by other legal, extra-law provisions (Law No.8 / 1996, for example), but to extend the scope of the provisions to all which may involve concepts of *academic ethics* and *academic integrity*, from the social relationships between members of the academic community to relationships between institutions and members of this community, from ethics of research to the quantification of results and visibility, from objective scoping of research fields to the formulation of pertinent taxonomies capable of distinguishing, in terms of dilthenyene, between *geisteswissenschaften* and *naturwissenschaften*.

REFERENCES

Agenţia Română de Asigurare a Calităţii în Învăţământul Superior (ARACIS). (n.d.). [Romanian Agency for Quality Assurance in Higher Education]. *Proceduri* [Procedures]. Retrieved from http://www.aracis.ro/proceduri/

"Alexandru Ioan Cuza" University of Iasi, Romania. (UAIC). (n.d.). *Code of ethics and professional deontology*. University papers, Ethics. Retrieved from http://www.uaic.ro/despre-uaic/documentele-universitatii/

The Academy of Economic Studies in Bucharest (ASE), Directorate of Research and Innovation Management. (n.d.). *Proceduri* [Procedures]. Retrieved from http://www.dmci.ase.ro/index.php/dmci/proceduri

Unitatea Executivă pentru Finanţarea Învăţământului Superior (UeFiscadi). (2011). [Executive Unit for Financing Higher Education]. *Clasificare universităţi şi ierarhizare programe de studii* [Classification of universities and hierarchy of study programs]. Retrieved from http://old.uefiscdi.ro/articole/2535/Clasificare-universitati-si-ierarhizare-programe-de-studii.html

University of Bucharest (UB). (n.d.). *Code of Ethics of the University*. Retrieved from http://www.unibuc.ro/n/despre/Codul_de_etica_al_Universitatii_din_Bucuresti.php

KEY TERMS AND DEFINITIONS

Academic Integrity: An ethical value that should guide the scholars' behavior to respect the rules of good practice, to be honest, to avoid misconduct or conflict of interests, and to be consistent with their own moral consciousness.

Code of Ethics: A series of written regulations that contain ethical values, rules of conduct, sanctions of misconduct, and rules for applying the sanctions. A code of ethics could also contain rules of good practice and how to encourage good practice.

Deontology: A branch of ethics and integrating part of a profession, which provides guidance to the professional on the desirable or undesirable behaviors in exercising his/her profession.

Transparency: An ethical value whose achievement involves providing precise and complete information on the activity of an institution, and on the decisions of the institutions' representative that could, in any way, affect the public.

ENDNOTE

1 Although we start from the assumption that any higher education institution in Romania has such a Code, at least for the reason that it is an essential document in the institutional evaluation by ARACIS (n.d.).

Chapter 5
The Effects of the "Publish or Perish Syndrome" on Research and Innovation in Nigerian Universities:
Insights From Recent Research and Case Studies

Floribert Patrick C. Endong
University of Calabar, Nigeria

ABSTRACT

The pressure to publish rapidly and constantly is a phenomenon engulfing academia in all countries of the globe. It has, over the years, affected research and innovation in a mostly negative way. In Nigerian universities in particular, this culture has mainly been a syndrome, manifested by (1) the urge among faculty members to publish more for promotions and positions than for genuine research production, (2) publishing for purely capitalistic motivations, (3) the use of unorthodox methodologies to boost citation index, and (4) fictive authorship of research works among others. All these objectionable practices have been responsible for various forms of decay in research and teaching in the Nigerian university system. They have, for instance, made plagiarism, data mining, predatory journals, duplicate publications, among other challenges, pervade research in Nigerian universities, causing innovation to remain more an ideal than a reality in these tertiary institutions. Using empirical understandings and critical observations, this chapter illustrates all these issues.

DOI: 10.4018/978-1-5225-6310-5.ch005

INTRODUCTION

Conducting research works and publishing articles constitute veritable *sine qua none* for many ambitious and conscientious academics (faculty members). This is attributable to the fact that recruitment and promotion in most universities across the world partially – nay mainly – depend on the research productivity of aspiring faculty members. In other words, most universities give greater attention to the number of publications to one's credit, during the recruitment and promotion of their teaching staff. The number of publications to one's credit is thus regarded by most academic institutions as a cardinal index of competency. Besides this, the culture of publishing extensively has become a tactic used by many teaching staff and (independent) researchers to (i) demonstrate their talents, (ii) distinguish themselves among their peers and (iii) eventually attract funding from specific quarters. In view of all these factors, faculty members have most often been under a great pressure to constantly publish; making the "publish or perish" culture to become so accentuated in the academic milieu. It has, in fact, become a harsh reality in most – if not all – universities across the globe (Enago Academy, 2015; Oransky, 2015; Rawat & Meena, 2014).

It has been observed by a number of critics that, the "publish or perish" syndrome has had adverse effects on teaching and research in universities and other institutes of higher learning across the world. The phenomenon has for instance pushed many lecturers to devote less time to teaching undergraduates and postgraduate students and consecrate more of their energy on research projects. Such neglect of the teaching responsibility has been amplified by multiple factors one of which is the fact that, rewards for exceptional teaching are hardly – if not never – comparable to the rewards for exceptional research. Another fact which has somehow amplified this neglect of teaching in favor of research has been the arguable/questionable myth stipulating that research is just an extension of teaching. Thus, good publications are kinds of teachings delivered outside the confine of a university classroom. Cooper (2013: 2) canvasses this belief when he opines that:

A common outcry by some who resist scholarly production is, "My commitment is to teaching rather than scholarship." Who would argue with such a contention? The argument is in the definition of the teaching environment. The faculty member who fails to teach outside the four walls of a university classroom closes too many teachable doors. Teaching and scholarly production are inseparable. Scholarly production is teaching outside room 231 and into the local, state, and/or national community. Once this notion is embraced, a faculty member is more inclined to gain an insatiable appetite to teach through scholarly production recognizing the value of distant learning.

Another adverse effect of the "publish or perish" syndrome lies in the fact that, it has made the value of research works to increasingly be low as most researchers now tend to scramble to publish just anything in the name of increasing their number of publications and boosting their CVs (Endong, 2018; Maher, 2010). This abnormality, in particular, has been exacerbated by the phenomenal emergence of myriads of predatory journals which, being driven primordially by dissimulated capitalistic visions, appear bent on publishing anything in the name of research (Abbott et al., 2010). As remarked by Rawat and Meena (2014), the pressure to increase the number of publications has thus been at the root of various forms of unethical cultures and wasteful research. These unethical research cultures have, to a great extent, obviously varied from one country to another and have been addressed by scholars from various perspectives. The questions which could be asked as this juncture are: how has the publish or perish syndrome particularly affected research in Black African countries? To what extent have African researchers devoted attention to this phenomenon and how could the culture be mitigated or eradicated in African universities?

Hinging on empirical understandings, this chapter critically explores the ways in which the "publish or perish syndrome" affects research and innovation in Nigerian universities. The chapter is divided into three main sections. In its first section, it provides a conceptual framework focusing on "perish or perish syndrome" and innovation. In its second section, it examines the ways in which the syndrome is manifested in Nigerian universities while in its last section, it will show how it affects the quality of research and innovation in Nigerian universities.

CONCEPTUAL FRAMEWORK

To ensure clarity of analysis in the subsequent sections of this discourse, it will be helpful to provide the conceptual definition of a number of key terms used in this paper. This section takes care of this need. It specifically gives attention to two terms namely the "publish or perish syndrome and innovation.

The "Publish or Perish Syndrome"

The concept of "publish or perish" was originally coined by Coolidge in 1932 to describe the immense and generally inordinate pressure among the academia to rapidly and constantly publish research works in order to "survive" or "prosper" in the academic system. As it name implies, "publish or perish" means a teaching staff feels he or she is under self imposed or subtle obligation to publish, in order to remain relevant to the system of its institution or to be competitive among his or her peers. It therefore entails excessive thoughts about scholarship expectations, a blind allegiance to publishing instead of writing about what matters, self subjection to restless nights and a plethora of excuses (Cooper, 2013). According to Enago Academy (2015), although the "publish or perish" culture is generally associated with pressure to publish, it may mean different thing to different members of the academia. For a graduate student for instance, it may mean the apprehension that, if the research work you are conducting is not publishable, you risk finding it herculean to get a job. For new faculty member, the "perish" may mean not making (sufficient) progress on the track to tenure while for the experienced researcher, the publish and perish syndrome may amount to thinking that any failure to publish the results of your research in a prestigious journal will lead to a loss of research funding or loss of your position with a given university.

The "publish or perish" culture is mainly viewed as a pejorative term; however, many critics are of the persuasion that it vividly symbolizes the contemporary world of science. Some of such observers even perceive the phenomenon as being rather realistic in nature. The online magazine *Neuroskeptic* (2013) notes for instance that "Everyone seems to agree that this phrase describes how science works today, and no-one much likes it". According to Neuroskeptic, the existence of a persistently stiff competition for job and advancement in the academia makes "perishing" an unavoidable challenge, which is more linked to issues like limited jobs than to publishing. As the magazine succinctly puts it:

In science today, there are more people at the bottom (PhD students) than there is room at the top (Professorships). At every step up on the career ladder, there are less posts available. So not all of the people entering science will be able to succeed in this career, and some of them will 'perish' and end up without a career in science. [...]

Perishing is an inevitable consequence of the demographics. It's linked to publishing only by accident, as it were; today, scientists happen to be assessed mostly by their publications, so it's publications that save you from perishing. But you can't blame publishing – there's just not enough room for everyone. Some people will drop off the science ladder, until we either stop awarding so many PhDs, or until we create more senior posts. It's simple arithmetic. So we shouldn't expect reform of publishing, or alt-metrics, to save people from perishing. These reforms could certainly make the system fairer and better, but the fundamental problem is one of recruitment. (para 4)

The above mentioned citation, indicates that some authors prefer to dissociate the "publish" dimension of the concept from the "perish" one, thereby slightly negating the myth stipulating that the publish or perish culture is a syndrome in the strict sense of the word. In spite of this position, this discourse hinges on definition of the publish or perish culture as the pressure to rapidly and continually publish research papers in order to remain relevant to the university system in which one functions. Such a culture may have both advantages and disadvantages. One of the advantages is that the pressure to produce cutting-edge research may seriously motivate researchers or faculty members to intensively be engaged in research early enough in their career and to learn how to reconcile research and other responsibilities (Cooper, 2013; Neuroskeptic, 2013). Some of its disadvantages – particularly with respect to the Nigerian university system – will be discussed in the upcoming sections of this chapter

Research-Driven Innovation

Innovation can simplistically be defined as the act of exploiting novel and revolutionizing ideas for the purpose of creating new processes, services or products. The Oxford Advanced Learners Dictionary defines it as the action of making changes in something established, especially through the introduction of new ideas and methods. In the sane line of thought, Skillicorn (2016) associates innovation with the act of turning ideas into solutions that add value from society's perspective. Viewed from this prism, innovation is not strictly limited to creating new ideas, but it extends to implementing these new ideas in a way as to engender new systems and paradigms that add value or improve quality of life, services, wealth and work among other things in the society. It may involved deploying technology and outside-the -box thinking to generate added value and engender significant social transformation.

Although available sources have mainly defined innovation in relation to business studies and entrepreneurship (Shukla, 2017; Skillicorn, 2016; Witze, 2015), in this chapter, the author will principally hinge on definitions that present innovation as a phenomenon stimulated by research. In effect, basic research is one of the factors – if not the main driver – of technical and social change, particularly in western economy. Most of the prominent technological breakthroughs which have revolutionized life in the West are products of research. Kafkaesque examples include the Internet, nuclear power reactors, bio-engineering and many pharmaceuticals among others. It is clearly observable that the entirety of high technologies notably computer, the World Wide Web and biotechnology have their root in many research works conducted in universities. Thus, research or science has continuously fuelled technology which in turn has led to various breakthroughs and serious social transformations (innovations) in our modern era (Witze, 2015).

In today's world – which is profoundly shaped by globalization, climate change, migration, technological and knowledge explosion among other issues – research and innovation have become very important nay indispensable for socio-economic development. Most countries, businesses and influential social arbiters heavily invest in these two things. As put by Shukla (2017), today, most societies need innovators more than any time before. Innovation is therefore imperative "if the quality of life in these trying circumstances is to improve. Innovation will make the world a better place for the younger generation".

Research has the potential to drive innovation and it is becoming more and more common among authors and policy makers to laud research works that are liable not only to contribute to knowledge (that is to generate new ideas) but which lead to innovations and socio-economic development. In line with this, many authors agree that the quality of research has become a cardinal parameter to judge universities across the world. Universities are generally highly rated when they are notable for providing vital researched information and for being at the forefront of innovative practices that address burning social, economic and political problems of their immediate environment as well as those of the outside world (Familusi & Ajayi, 2017; Owoeye & Oyebade 2009; Tafida, Kasim, & Chima, 2015; Wadesango, 2015). Through research and innovations, universities are therefore expected to spearhead, set or/and review national – and why not international – agendas.

THE PUBLISH OR PERISH SYNDROME IN NIGERIAN UNIVERSITIES

The "publish or perish" syndrome is a complex phenomenon with multiple evident and subtle manifestations in the Nigerian university system. It may be humanly herculean to explore all these manifestations. However, this section will give attention to four indexes of the syndrome including (i) the urge to publish or attend academic conferences more for promotions and positions than genuine research purposes, (ii) the culture of publishing mainly for economic survival, (iii) the use of non-Catholic procedures to boost citation index and (iv) the practice of embarking on fictive authorship to boost one's number of publications and CV.

Publishing Principally for Promotion and Positions

One of the most visible indexes of the "publish or perish" syndrome is the popular culture among Nigerian university lecturers to (often desperately) struggle to publish mainly for (upcoming) promotion and positions. In effect, the prevalence of stiff competition in the domain of recruitment and promotion in most Nigerian universities has pushed many faculty staff and even aspiring university lecturers to view publishing primarily as a means or strategic action to be recruited or promoted to higher ranks. Thus, emphasis on publishing innovative ideas has progressively been jettisoned in favor of practices that have nothing to do with genuine research. Sharing corollaries, Fasola (2017) pointedly remarks that the "publish or perish" syndrome "has changed the essence of research and brought to the fore front a spirit of survival in the jungle rather than the primary aim for which research is meant"; that is, generating new knowledge and stimulating innovation and socio-economic development. This shameful maxim (publish or perish) has "given rise to a do or die attitude in researchers" causing them to embark on whatever possible approach – including unethical practices – in view of publications (p.4).

In the same line of thought, Yusuf (Tafida, Kasin, & Chima, 2015: 84) observes that the publish and perish syndrome has plunged most Nigerian "researchers" into a kind of career-long survival race for promotions and positions as well as salary advancements. The primary motive of competing in this race "is no more than that of career prospects and intellectual prestige". Therefore, "by orientation, content and primary intent, the bulk of research going on in our universities at present is neither related to nor determined by the demand and priorities of the Nigerian economy, society and polity, and therefore cannot be relied upon for achieving Nigeria's overall objectives in Research and Development (R&D)". It is therefore not surprising that developmental projects designed by government agencies hardly, nay never, rely on research produced in Nigerian universities or research institutions (Endong, 2018; Fasola, 2017).

The culture of publishing principally for promotions and positions is revealed the more by the fact that, most of those who generally struggle to publish and be visible are junior teaching staff (graduate assistants, assistant lecturers, lecturer of grade 2 and 1 and senior lecturers), particularly those whose number of publications is still not optimum for upcoming promotions. Highly ranked staff such as professors tend to be less interested in serious research activities apart from supervising Master and Ph.D. dissertations. Professorship is the highest point in the ranking system adopted in Nigerian universities. Most of the faculty members who succeed to reach this level rather tend to feel the need to "rest" and "relax" on the arguable ground that "they have arrived". As will be demonstrated in the subsequent parts of this discourse, this culture has serious repercussions on the quantity and quality of research produced in Nigerian universities.

Publishing for Purely Capitalistic Motives

This is another serious manifestation of the "publish or perish" syndrome in the Nigerian university system. The culture has systemically been fuelled by sheer greed, egomania or financial survival – due to arguably derisory salaries – in Nigerian universities. This culture has been evidenced not only by the proliferation of predatory journals in Nigerian universities but most especially by the shameful practice of conceiving books, manuals or pamphlets which supposedly address the contents of courses thought or curricula adopted in university Departments. The point being made here is that, some Nigerian professors or other faculty members have, under the guise of providing suitable literature/material to aid the teaching of some courses, developed the culture of publishing books and other manuals that have no research value. As noted by Archibong (2012), some of these "books" are simply irrelevant handouts bound with hard cover. Their authors most often publish them not really based on their desire to sell pertinent and innovative ideas and contribute to knowledge but for the primary purpose of generating income through covert extortion. In other words, they publish in order not to perish economically speaking (Rohwer, Young, Wager, & Garner, 2017; Youdeowei, Uwandu, & Iruoma, 2016). What even makes this paradigm more questionable is the fact that in some instances, students (who constitute the principal market targeted by this industry) are subtly obliged by lecturers, to unquestionably buy the books or manuals. Buying such books is compulsory and often a *sine qua none* for passing the course taught by the lecturer (author of the book).

The visible implication here is that publishing all manner of contents has become a survival strategy for many academics. It has become a means through which many faculty members generate additional revenues to survive various forms of austerity in the system. They publish (most often anything including substandard books and un-reviewed/ non-innovative ideas) in order not to "perish" in the economic sense of the word. Income generation through publishing, in the strict sense of the term, is not really problematic. However, when capitalistic motives override the publication of teaching aids to the extent of affecting their quality, there arises a justified course of concern.

Fictive Authorship of Scholarship

The pressure to rapidly and constantly publish has pushed many faculty members at Nigerian universities to be involved in fake collaborative research projects. This has often consisted in using more or less tortuous methods to get their names included in the by-lines of articles or books to which they contributed nothing or virtually little. It is for instance common to find professors or supervisors who capitalize on their friendship with colleagues or supervisees to get their names included among authors of research works to which they have technically never contributed. As argued by Rawat and Meena (2014), this is a serious unethical practice which should be discouraged at all levels.

In effect, being a professor or a supervisor does not mean that any research work which has been proofread, reviewed or assessed by you should automatically bear your name in its by-line. Most journals and research ideologues recommend that each author contribute a reasonable segment of the paper to be eligible to authorship. The guidelines for authorship issued by the International Committee of Medical Journal Editors [ICMJE] (Okonta & Rossouw, 2013), for instance, recommends the following criteria to determine the authorship of a research study: (i) The claimer should substantially contribute to the conception and design (of the paper), the acquisition of data, or analysis and interpretation of data; (ii) He should take part in the drafting the article or revising it critically for important intellectual content; and (iii) final approval of the version to be published. Naturally, individuals who do not meet all three criteria do not qualify for authorship. Unfortunate, in Nigeria, the above mentioned aphorism is out rightly overlooked by adepts of the publish or perish culture. In line with this Archibong (2012) reviews cases of faculty members who, in a bid to boost their number of publications, published the works of their supervisees or students, without the consent of the latter or worse, without them knowing. Some of them publish "thoroughly" revised versions of their students' research works in the hope of beating similarity index check through ICT-assisted methods.

The Use of Unorthodox Procedures to Boost Citation Index

Many universities consider citation indexes among other parameters during promotion processes. Besides this, the reception and acceptance of publication are popularly gauged by the degree to which it is cited by peers. Thus, it has become more and more axiomatic among Nigerian scholars that the more someone's scholarly publications are cited, the more he/she is liable to enjoy academic prestige or fame among his/her peers. These two factors among many others have motivated a good number of faculty staff in Nigerian universities to deploy even non-orthodox ways to get their works cited by peers. Some have for instance resorted to the insidious and ridiculous tactic of cowing their supervisees, mentees or students to cite them in any of their research works (theses, seminar or article for peer review), even if such works have little to do with the topics addressed by them (the faculty members). Cowing mentees or supervisees to cite them has often entailed compelling the latter to buy books written by lecturers.

This has progressively led to the hypocritical culture of citing authors not really because of the pertinence of the ideas or methodologies they sells in their publications but for pure "academic complacency" or "academic solidarity". It goes without saying that this culture subtly affects research in the sense that a considerable number of the works cited by juniors Nigerian researchers are works that, under normal circumstance, would have been uncited. By using such "ridiculous" techniques to boost their citation index, many faculty members fake the impact of their research works and manifest their egomaniacal nature (Schuman, 2014).

HOW THE "PUBLISH OR PERISH" SYNDROME AFFECTS RESEARCH AND INNOVATION IN NIGERIAN UNIVERSITIES

In principle, research aims at generating new knowledge and stimulating innovations in all facets of the society. Universities are known to focus or to depend on research to understand the environment in which they are based and formulate relevant strategic plans to remain relevant to the society (Federal Republic of Nigeria, 2004; Meek & Asa, 2012). This scenario places universities at a vantage position to spear-head innovation and social development in most countries. In tandem with this, the research produced in universities is expected to generate new knowledge, stimulate innovation, and drive various aspects of socio-economic and political development in the immediate environment where they are based and even beyond (in the international sphere). However, the "publish or perish" syndrome has had various adverse effects on research and innovation in Nigerian universities. These effects have seriously reduced Nigerian universities' ability to impact socio-economic development in Nigeria. There are many ways in which this "publish or perish" has impacted research in Nigerian universities. However, this part of the discourse gives attention particularly to four of these ways, including plagiarism, data mining, predatory journals and duplicate publications.

Plagiarism

According to the International Center for Academic Integrity [ICAI] (2013), plagiarism is defined as a situation in which "someone: uses words, ideas, or work products attributable to another identifiable person or source without attributing the work to the source from which it was obtained in a situation in which there is a legitimate expectation of original authorship in order to obtain some benefit, credit, or gain which need not be monetary". This culture has, of recent, become observable – nay recrudescent – in Nigerian universities, thanks partly to the publish or perish syndrome. In effect, many members of the Nigerian academia have developed the tendency of plagiarising the research works of their endogenous or exogenous colleagues; or of hiring "mercenaries" (research paper writers) in view of augmenting their number of publications. The prevalence of such a culture has caused many Nigerian universities to, at different periods in these last years, to take drastic disciplinary measures against some cases. In 2012 for instance, the University of Calabar – like many of her counterparts in the country – embarked on various waves of sanctions against a multitude of its faculty members who were culpable of the vice (plagiarism). The move taken by the institution led to the demotion of many teaching staff and the termination of the contract of some of them. Similarly, the Federal University of Agriculture (based in Abeokuta of Nigeria), terminated the appointments of some professors and other faculty members in May 2013, based on allegations of plagiarism (Federal University of Agriculture Abeokuta, 2013). Despite these drastic measure, plagiarism mainly driven by the "publish or perish" syndrome continues to be a reality in Nigerian universities.

As earlier mentioned, another form of plagiarism which has been fuelled by the publish or perish syndrome is the culture of "academic black market" otherwise called "contract cheating" or "paper mills".

This practice consists in hiring kinds of academic mercenaries to develop research papers on behalf of some faculty members. It enables many teaching staff to augment their number of publications, in view of promotion or salary advancements.

It goes without saying that plagiarism affects the originality of research findings. As put by Plagiarism Advice (2013), unoriginal submissions from authors naturally impact on scholarly publishing, "where original thought and research is fundamental to the credibility and success of academic publications". Plagiarism equally neutralizes innovation as the findings or ideas discussed in a plagiarised work theoretically already exists (it is not new); and is simply fraudulently duplicated. In a context like Nigeria, where plagiarism prevails, it becomes somehow difficult, if not futile to expect high incidents of innovations.

Predatory Journals

The publish or perish syndrome has motivated the rise and proliferation of predatory journals which, from many indexes, tend to care less about the research value or the technical quality of the papers they publish and operate primordially on the basis of poorly dissimulated capitalist visions. These journals apparently capitalize on some faculty member's desperate need for publications. Their review process and editorial services are often of questionable or doubtful nature. Some even operate on seasonal basis just to enable particular academic staff boost their number of publications and be eligible to promotion or salary advancement. As reviewed by Familusi and Ajayi (2017: 32), many of these journals are floated by a few academics or individuals just to publish their works, get promotion, and after these goals are achieved, they (the journals) "go into moribund". In the same line of thought, Kperogi (2015: 7) notes reviews how the phenomenon of local predatory journals have immensely affected the quality of research produced in Nigerian universities. He contends that:

Because of the rise in publication fraud in Nigeria where many lecturers publish substandard, "unpublishable" nonsense in fraudulent "open-access" journals, things have been muddied [in the Nigerian university system]. I have seen people in the rank of Lecturer II[1] *with 80 "publications," 100 percent of which are in worthless, non-reviewed, predatory, money-making, open-access "journals".*

The proliferation of such predatory journals has made many locally published journals to generally be rated low by both endogenous researchers and exogenous observatories (Familusi & Ajayi, 2017). Thus, although it is possible to find good local journals in Nigerian universities, the popular culture has been to give greater credence to foreign journals and mostly regard local ones as substandard and deficient in terms review process, editorial process and quality of research published in them. Thus, although the myth of local journals' substandard nature compare to foreign ones is arguable, one must recognize that the proliferation of predatory journal in the Nigerian university system has seriously affected research and innovation in these tertiary institutions.

Data Mining

Otherwise called research fraud, data mining is defined as the falsification or fabrication of research results. These falsification and fabrication often occur during the stages of collection of data or reporting of research findings. Thanks to the publish or perish syndrome, the data mining has become observable – if not widespread – in Nigerian university, terribly affecting the quality of research produced by these institutions. A 2013 study conducted on 133 Nigerian researchers specialized in biomedicine by Okonta and Rossouw discovered that over 42.2% of Nigerian researchers falsify or fabricate the results of their studies for reasons which vary from pressure to publish at all cost and pressure to meet sponsors' research agendas.

In a similar study conducted a year earlier by Adeleye and Adebamowo (2012) on a sample of 132 researchers from the medical and dental fields, similar results were obtained. In effect, the latter study revealed that 22% of the sample considered for the investigation, admitted to have at least once in their career, falsified or fabricated the results of their studies. Though the sample considered in these two studies do not represent the totality of researchers in Nigeria, it remains evident that research fraud is a noticeable culture among endogenous Nigerian researchers. With close reference to research in marketing and business, Kalu and Okeke (2016) share corollaries as they observe that scientific frauds in the studies conducted by Nigerian "scholars" have seriously contributed to the vilification of most research in Nigerian university and stagnation in terms of innovation in various sectors of the Nigerian economy. As they put it, the application of most research report in Nigeria "transforms to inaccuracy in business decision making and marketing errors" (Kalu and Okeke, 2016: 8).

One reason for falsifying research results is the pressure to publish at all cost and gain academic prestige among peers (Archibong, 2012). Okonta and Rossouw 's (2013) above mentioned study thus reveals that although there is still a dearth of research on scientific misconducts in Nigerian, issues such as the falsification or fabrication of research findings constitute a sad reality in Nigerian universities, like in their counterparts in other parts of Black Africa. As Okonta and Rossouw (2013) remark, contrary to developed countries in which institutions have been established to ensure credible research conduct and to investigate cases of scientific misconduct, research in most developing countries has mostly been poorly controlled by both the state or relevant/influential socio-professional bodies. Very few cases of scientific misconduct have been reported not because they don't exist but because researching them has not been the prior focus of research arbiters. As the two scholars observed, "there is no evidence to suggest that all research conducted in developing countries [including Nigeria] meet ethical standards and that scientific misconduct does not exist. Rather, it is most likely that the prevalence of scientific misconduct amongst researchers have not been systematically investigated" (Okonta and Rossouw, 2013: 2).

As earlier noted, scientific fraud in the form of data falsification and fabrication really damage research and innovation, making Nigerian universities to fail in various areas of their roles as spearheads of development. As beautifully argued by Kalu and Okeke (2016), data mining damps innovation and leads to poor returns in the professional domain. "Researchers who manipulate their research report in ways that deceive others are violating both the basic values and widely accepted professional standards of science". They fail to fulfil predetermined obligations. Additionally, they mislead their colleagues and potentially impede progress in their field or research; as well as "undermine their own authority and trustworthiness as researchers" (Kalu and Okeke, 2016: 8)

Duplicate Publication

Duplicate publication could be defined as a situation in which a researcher publishes the same material in different journals "with different key words, captions and co-author variation on each occasion, thus making it difficult for plagiarism software to detect them. This is mostly done in order to give a boost to their CV" (Rawat & Meena, 2014). It is considered as a form of self plagiarism (Fasola, 2017). It goes without saying that, as plagiarism, duplicate publication engenders a technical stagnation of research as no new knowledge is added in such a context.

CONCLUSION

The publication of research articles or scholarly works remains indispensable for the growth of science and the career development of each researcher or faculty member. The centrality of publications as a parameter considered universities in their recruitment or promotion systems will continue to make the "publish or perish" culture a reality in the academia. This culture remains a global problem which has, over the years, adversely affected research and innovation in universities across the world. This chapter has particularly looked at the Nigerian context.

The chapter actually illustrated that the "publish or perish" culture has mainly been a serious syndrome in the Nigerian university environment. This syndrome has been manifested by (i) the urge among faculty members to publish more for promotions and positions than for genuine research production, (ii) publishing for purely capitalistic motivations, (iii) the use of unorthodox methodologies to boost citation index and (iv) fictive authorship of research works among others. All these objectionable practices have been responsible for various forms of decay in research and teaching in the Nigerian university system. They have for instance made plagiarism, data mining, predatory journals, duplicate publications among other challenges, to pervade research in Nigerian universities, causing innovation to remain more an ideal than a reality in these tertiary institutions. In view of this scenario, the following recommendations can be formulated:

1. The training of both (post-graduate) students and lecturers in research ethics should circumstantially be revised/upgraded or instituted in Nigerian universities. While students should be taught research ethics from their first year of entry into the university, well conceived informal programs such as training workshops and seminars should be organized to sensitize and train particularly junior lecturers on research ethics. As highlighted in this chapter, two reasons responsible for the prevalence of unethical research cultures (such as plagiarism, research forgery, salami slicing and predatory journal publishing) is ignorance and researchers' succumbing to pressure emanating from sponsors (Endong, 2018; Okonta & Rossouw, 2013). Well formulated capacity building programs or re-orientation seminars are liable to mitigate, if not eradicate this ignorance and help researchers know how to manage such pressure (from sponsors).
2. Re-orientation programs organized to sensitize faculty members and (young) researchers should insist on inculcating the culture of "publish to be found" rather than that of "publish or perish". According to the American Chemical Society (2013), the "publish to be found" philosophy compels researchers to view publishing research articles as just the preliminary stage of a process aimed at impacting research in an author's area of specialization. Using the applied and pure science fields as examples, the organization (ACS) notes that "in the world of networked science, it isn't enough to be published— you have to be found" (American Chemical Society, 2013: 5). The researcher needs to design appropriate tools and techniques to get his or her work discovered by the broadest, most optimized audience. S/he needs to deploy be best tools to measure his or her impact as well as the strength of his or her ideas in the platforms where he or she engages and share his or her work. Such a researcher also has to ensure that his or her article stands out among the growing body of

scientific research. All these recommendations call for the production of groundbreaking research articles, not articles which are mainly substandard and are produced primordially for promotion, salary advancement or any other capitalist goals.

3. More serious sanctions should be taken against researchers who, being under the pressure to publish at all cost, embark on questionable practices such as result forgery, plagiarism and duplicate publication among others. In Nigeria, as we have earlier noted, some universities have, of recent, sacked faculties members and taken other drastic disciplinary measures against perpetrators of research malpractices. However, due to the Nigeria factor[2] (otherwise called the Nigerian way), many cases of unethical research practices have remained unpunished, if not cynically overlooked in some of the country's universities (Archibong, 2012). There is therefore a pressing need to arrest this critical situation and seriously deal with any incident of unethical practice in the Nigerian university system. Nigeria should thus emulate the example of western countries where such cases are mostly intransigently dealt with (Rawat & Meena, 2014; Plagiarim Advice, 2013). By shunning and severely cracking down on unethical research practices, many "accomplished" or potential fraud perpetrators may be called to order and a degree of sanity restored in the Nigerian research industry.
4. Rather than putting more emphasis on number of publications during the promotion and salary advancement of faculty staff, Nigerian universities should give more attention to the citation index of published articles. It is true that the culture of hinging on citation index may not be a perfectly infallible elixir of "the publish or perish" syndrome – as researchers may use crooked ways to get their works unnecessarily cited by complaisant colleagues. However, the practice (reliance on citation index) may help mitigate the "publish or perish" phenomenon to a reasonable extent. It may, at least, compel Nigerian lecturers/researchers to think of placing emphasis more on the quality rather than the quantity.
5. Nigerian universities should take the bull by the horns by exposing and scraping off all the predatory journals that are published in their faculties. As earlier mentioned, predatory journals systemically exacerbate or fuel "the publish or perish" syndrome as they allow lazy and unwary researchers to publish all manner of articles primordially – nay solely – for promotion and salary advancement. It will therefore be helpful for Nigerian universities to design adapted methodologies to detect or sort these journals among the lot and deal appropriately with them. It goes without saying that combating the predatory journals in the Nigerian university environment may not be an abracadabra solution given the fact that similar journals published by foreign universities and research bodies remain accessible and patronized by an increasing number of Nigerian authors. However, it goes without saying that dealing with these impediments to fruitful research may help sanitize stakeholders of the research "industry" in Nigeria and make the Nigerian research industry more respected. It is therefore better to try new approaches to mitigate the effect of predatory journals in the Nigerian university system rather than watching these "research pests" progressively destroy the research industry in the country.
6. Nigerian journals should use preliminary or strategic sections of their contents – notably rubrics devoted to highlighting journal policies, instructions to authors and editorials – to sensitize potential authors about the dangers or negative side of the "publish or perish" syndrome. The popular culture has been to rather use these parts of the publication to subtly do the reverse; that is to encourage authors to get published for fear of perishing in the system. This is not to say that encouraging authors to publish is inherently problematic but the absence of kind warning on the danger of the

"publish or perish" syndrome gives the impression that the journal have a lukewarm attitude towards such a noble form of sensitization. Devoting seasonal themed issues to the problem ("publish or perish" syndrome) and/or related issues will only go a long way to intensify the sensitization against questionable research traditions in Nigerian universities and ultimately improve the research industry in Nigeria.

7. The Nigerian government in partnership with major social institutions (industries for instance) should also think of designing (more) support programs aimed at rewarding innovation (research works that engender innovation) in the Nigerian university environment and the nation in general. Nwamuo (2005) has mentioned the existence of some of these initiatives but has lamented their irregular nature. It is plausible that the conception of regular support programs aimed at celebrating and rewarding innovative ideas emanating from Nigeria-based research projects may help orient Nigerian researchers to put more emphasis on research ideas and practices that are susceptible to generate new ideas and new knowledge and participate more actively in the development of the country. The logic here is that the more faculty member and researchers give attention to innovation through solid research ideas and projects, the less they will get involved in research ventures that will earn them only "worthless" volume. By instituting various forms of incentive geared at encouraging quality research, there is a high probability that Nigerian researchers will think more or of quality than volume.

REFERENCES

Abbott, A., Cyranoski, D., Jones, N., Maher, B., Schiermeier, Q., & Van Noorden, R. (2010). Metrics: Do metrics matter? *Nature, 465*(7300), 860–862. doi:10.1038/465860a PMID:20559361

Adeleye, O. A., & Adebamowo, C. A. (2012). Factors associated with research wrong doing in Nigeria. *Journal of Empirical Research on Human Research Ethics; JERHRE, 7*(5), 15–24. doi:10.1525/jer.2012.7.5.15 PMID:23324199

American Chemical Association. (2013). Publish be found or perish. Writing scientific manuscripts for the digital age. *Bio Journal, 13*, 1-5. Retrieved from http://pubs.acs.org/bio/ACS-Guide-Writing-Manuscripts-for-the-Digital-Age.pdf

Archibong, I. A. (2012). Forms of dishonesty among academic staff and the way forward. *Canadian Social Science, 8*(6), 39–43. doi:10.3968/j.css.1923669720120806.1057

Cooper, M. J. (2013). Antidotes for the publish or perish syndrome. *Trampta.* Retrieved from https://trampta.wordpress.com/2013/02/18/antidotes-for-the-publish-or-perish-syndrome/

Enago Academy. (2015, May 24). *Publish or perish: What are its consequences?* Enago Academy. Retrieved from https://www.enago.com/academy/publish-or-perish-consequences/

Endong, F. P. C. (2018). The concepts of academic humility and seniority syndrome in research: A critique of research traditions in Nigerian universities. In F. P. C. Endong (Ed.), *Innovations in Measuring and Evaluating Scientific Information* (pp. 223–239). Hershey, PA: IGI Global; doi:10.4018/978-1-5225-3457-0.ch015

Familusi, E. B., & Ajayi, N. A. (2017). Utilization of local journals by academic staff in Nigerian universities: A critical review. *International Journal of Library and Information Sciences Studies*, *3*(1), 25–36.

Fasola, O. (2017). *Ethical violations in research: Prevention rather than cure*. Retrieved from https://www.acu.edu.ng/documents/seminar/FASOLA.pdf

Federal Republic of Nigeria. (2004). *National policy on education*. Abuja, Nigeria: Government Printers.

Federal University of Agriculture Abeokuta. (2013). *Decree FUNAAB/VC/PRD.08/42 of May 10, 2013*. Abeokuta, Nigeria: Federal University of Agriculture Abeokuta.

International Center for Academic Integrity. (2013). *Why integrity?* Retrieved from http://www.academicintegrity.org/icai/integrity-1.php

Kalu, A. O. U., & Okeke, A. F. (2016). Unethical marketing research practices in Nigeria: Manipulations in marketing reports. *Journal of Research and Development (Srinagar)*, *2*(12), 8–15. doi:10.12816/0028307

Kperogi, F. (2015). A comparison of everyday university vocabularies in Nigeria, America and Britain. *Daily Trust*. Retrieved from https://www.dailytrust.com.ng/news/politics-of-grammar/a-comparison-of-everyday-university-vocabularies-in-nigeria-america-and-britain-ii/125123.html

Maher, R. C. (2010). Authoritative references. *EE417*. Retrieved from http://www.montana.edu/rmaher/ee417/Authoritative%20References.pdf

Meek, L., & Asa, O. (2012). Introduction and project overview. In L. Meek & O. Asa (Eds.), *Effectiveness of Research and Innovation Management at Policy and Institutional Levels in Cambodia, Vietnam, Thailand and Malaysia* (pp. 12–18). London, UK: OECD.

Nwamuo, C. (2005). *University of Calabar in transition: 2000 – present*. Calabar, Nigeria: University of Calabar Press.

Okonta, P., & Rossouw, T. (2013). Prevalence of scientific misconduct among a group of researcher in Nigeria. *Dev World Biotech*, *13*(3), 1–14. doi:10.1111/j.1471-8847.2012.00339.x

Oransky, I. (2015). Second thoughts: How publish or perish promotes inaccuracy in science – and journalism. *American Medical Association Journal of Ethics*, *17*(12), 1172–1175. doi:10.1001/journalofethics.2015.17.12.sect1-1512 PMID:26698592

Owoeye, J. S., & Oyebade, S. A. (2009). Higher education research in Uganda: Problems and prospects. *African Higher Education Review*, *2*, 19–38.

Plagiarism Advice. (2013). *A national strategy for addressing student plagiarism*. Retrieved from http://www.plagiarismadvice.org

Rawat, S., & Meena, S. (2014). Publish or perish: Where are we heading? *Journal of Research in Medical Sciences*, *19*(2), 87–89. PMID:24778659

Rohwer, A., Young, T., Wager, R., & Garner, P. (2017). Authorship, plagiarism, conflict of interest: Views and practices from low middle-income countries health researchers. *BMJ: Biomedia Journal Open*, *7*(11), 1–11. doi:10.1136/bmjopen-2017-018467

Schuman, R. (2014). Beware of the Gilderoy Lockharts of the university. *Slate*. Retrieved from http://www.slate.com/business/2017/12/romantic-japanese-christmas-train-ads.html

Shukla, A. (2017). *What is innovation? Why is innovation important.* Retrieved from https://www.paggu.com/getting-into-roots/what-is-innovation-why-innovation-is-important/

Skilicorn, N. (2016). What is innovation? 15 experts share their innovation definitions. *Ideas to Value*. Retrieved from https://www.ideatovalue.com/inno/nickskillicorn/2016/03/innovation-15-experts-share-innovation-definition/

Tafida, A., Kasim, U., & Chima, P. (2015). Analysis of factors enhancing pitfall in research and teaching of the Nigerian university system. *International Journal of Higher Education*, *4*(3), 82–89. doi:10.5430/ijhe.v4n3p82

Wadesango, N. (2015). Publish or perish: Impediments to research output and publication. *Kamla-Raj: International Journal of Education Science*, *6*(1), 57–63. doi:10.1080/09751122.2014.11890118

What is wrong with "publish or perish". (2013, March 28). *Neuroskeptic*. Retrieved from http://blogs.discovermagazine.com/neuroskeptic/2013/03/28/whats-wrong-with-publish-or-perish/#.WkJ5GrMo_Mx

Witze, A. (2015). Does innovation always come from science? *Nature: International Weekly Journal of Science*, *527*(7576), 11–19. doi:10.1038/527011f

Youdeowei, T., Uwandu, E., & Iruoma, K. (2016). Students lament compulsory handouts in tertiary institutions. *Vanguard*. Retrieved from https://www.vanguardngr.com/2016/11/students-lament-compulsory-handouts-tertiary-institutions/

KEY TERMS AND DEFINITIONS

Data Mining: The act of faking data or results in a research context.

Innovation: The action of making changes in something established, especially through the introduction of new ideas and methods. The term is equally associated with the act of turning ideas into solutions that add value from society's perspective.

Nigerian Factor: The Nigerian factor, otherwise called "the Nigerian Way," is a term used to refer to the defeatist attitude of most Nigerians in the face of Nigeria's perverted value system. It is used to describe the intense moral decay or mental corruption which has seriously affected the Nigerian society to the extent what is "universally" viewed as reprehensible is paradoxically accepted in the Nigerian context as working and efficacious. In other words, it is the tendency of believing that anything—morally good or bad—can go in Nigeria, because the country is in a severe state of social malady.

Plagiarism: Derived from the Latin word *plagiarus* (which means a kidnapper, a stealer, or the abductor of a child or a slave) and the Greek word *plagion* (which means kidnapper), plagiarism is used to refer to the act of intentionally or unintentionally appropriating another person's ideas, language, processes, results, or statements without obtaining permission or without giving due credit.

Predatory Journals: Model of academic publishing that is mainly materialistic and exploitative. Such a model basically entails charging (exorbitant) publication fees to authors without providing the kind of robust editorial services associated with genuine publishing businesses. Journals or publishers considered to be predatory are thus noted for publishing counterfeit journals with the principal motivation of exploiting newly designed systems of funding in the publishing chain (such as the Open Access model) which compel the author to pay a fee for the publication of his paper. These predatory publishers are equally known for their lack of transparency and honesty as well as their motivation to dupe particularly the less-experienced researchers.

Publish or Perish Syndrome: Neologism coined to refer to the immense and generally inordinate pressure among the academia to rapidly and constantly publish research works in order to "survive" or "prosper" in the academic system. In other words, it is the pressure in the academia to continually publish research works so as to further or sustain one's career.

Research Misconduct: Ethically unacceptable cultures in research context.

Salami Slicing: The problematic act of dividing a research report in small units for the sake of multiple publications. In other words, it is the act of breaking a research report into multiple components or pieces and publishing these individual components as separate research articles.

ENDNOTES

1 According to the Nigerian university system, faculty members are promoted based on a ranking system which recognizes seven (7) ranks. In croissant order, these ranks include: (i) Graduate Assistant, (ii) Assistant Lecturer, (iii) Lecturer Two, (iv) Lecturer One, (v) Senior Lecturer, (vi) Reader/Associate Professor and (vii) Professor. Promotion from one rank to the other is generally due after three years requiring article publications and years of teaching and/or research experience.

2 The Nigerian factor otherwise called "the Nigerian Way" is a term used to refer to the defeatist attitude of most Nigerians in the face of Nigeria's perverted value system. It is used to describe the intense moral decay or mental corruption which has seriously affected the Nigerian society to the extent that, what is "universally" viewed as reprehensible is paradoxically accepted in the Nigerian context as working and efficacious. In other words, it is the tendency of believing that anything – morally good or bad – can go in Nigeria, because the country is in a severe state of social malady.

Section 2

Ethics of Research With Human Subjects

The second section brings to the reader's attention a series of specific aspects of the research involving the human participant, the imperative of respect for the autonomy of the participants in the research, and hence, the need to obtain information of informed consent from them, the protection of the rights of the participants in the research, risks and benefits of research for the participant and for the society, care for participants belonging to vulnerable populations, etc. This section, although starting from biomedical research, is intended to extend the ethical principles of research on human beings for research in the psycho-social and economic fields.

Chapter 6
Vulnerability in Research:
Defining, Applying, and Teaching the Concept

Sana Loue
Case Western Reserve University, USA

Bebe Loff
Monash University, Australia

ABSTRACT

The concept of vulnerability and the attendant responsibility of researchers to provide special protections for research participants deemed to be vulnerable are considered to be foundational concepts in bioethics. However, not only do international and national guidelines differ in their definition of vulnerability, but they also vary with respect to who is to be considered vulnerable in research. This chapter describes the ways in which vulnerability has been defined by international and national guidelines, discusses the considerations deemed relevant by international and national guidance and writers on the topic, and concludes with thoughts on how the meaning of vulnerability might be communicated in teaching.

INTRODUCTION

The concept of vulnerability and the attendant responsibility of researchers to provide special protections for research participants deemed to be vulnerable are considered to be foundational concepts in bioethics (DuBois, 2006; Kipnis, 2001; Levine, Fadden, Grady, Eckenwiler, & Sugarman, 2004; Rogers, 2012). Professionalism and integrity in science, regardless of the specific discipline, demand that investigators possess the ability to define, identify, and respond to vulnerability in the context of their research no matter how it arises. Absent an ability to identify and address vulnerability in research, it is likely that unethical research will occur.

DOI: 10.4018/978-1-5225-6310-5.ch006

Not surprisingly, then, the professional literature has increasingly addressed various dimensions of vulnerability including, but not limited to, economic circumstances, issues related to capacity and understanding, and the relationship between vulnerability in research and historical and social injustice. This chapter will describe the ways in which vulnerability has been defined, discuss the considerations deemed relevant by international and national guidance and writers on the topic, and conclude with thoughts on how the meaning of vulnerability might be communicated in teaching.

DEFINING VULNERABILITY IN RESEARCH

Article 1 of the Nuremberg Code 1947 makes clear that the concept of vulnerability sat at its heart. It stated,

The voluntary consent of the human subject is absolutely essential. This means that the person involved should have legal capacity to give consent; should be so situated as to be able to exercise free power of choice, without the intervention of any element of force, fraud, deceit, duress, overreaching, or other ulterior form of constraint or coercion; and should have sufficient knowledge and comprehension of the elements of the subject matter involved as to enable him to make an understanding and enlightened decision.

The concept of vulnerability received direct attention in the 1979 *Belmont Report*, issued by the United States National Commission for the Protection of Human Subjects of Biomedical and Behavioral Research. In its discussion of the principle, "Respect for Persons," the Commission noted that persons with diminished autonomy required special protections due to their "dependent status and frequently compromised capacity for free consent" (United States National Commission for the Protection of Human Subjects of Biomedical and Behavioral Research, 1979: 8). Diminished autonomy could be the result of age, illness or disability, or coercion. Further, in concluding that "racial minorities, the economically disadvantaged, the very sick, and the institutionalized may continually be sought as research subjects, owing to their ready availability in settings where research is conducted" (United States National Commission for the Protection of Human Subjects of Biomedical and Behavioral Research, 1979: 9), the Commission linked the concept of vulnerability to the ethical principle of justice.

Since that time, various international and national documents promulgated to guide both researchers conducting investigations and research ethics committees reviewing research protocols have integrated the concept of vulnerability. Table 1 provides definitions of vulnerability that appear in various internationally recognized standards for the conduct of research involving human participants (Council for International Organizations of Medical Sciences, 2016; European Commission, 2010; International Conference on Harmonisation of Technical Requirements for Registration of Pharmaceuticals for Human Use, 1996; World Medical Association, 2013), as well as those of several English-speaking countries engaged in intensive research efforts (Agency for Healthcare Research and Quality, 1998; Canadian Institutes of Health Research, 2014; Indian Council of Medical Research, 2017; Uganda National Council of Science and Technology, 2014).

A close reading of these definitions underscores a central feature of vulnerability: that it entails "a certain precariousness in the condition of the [research] subject: a state of being laid open or especially exposed to something injurious or otherwise undesirable, a potential avenue of attack" (Kipnis, 2001:

Table 1. Definitions of vulnerability and/or vulnerable groups utilized by national and international bodies (Source: authors' own contribution)

Source	Definition
Agency for Healthcare Research and Quality, 1998 (US)	"Vulnerable populations are those groups of people 'made vulnerable by their financial circumstances or place of residence; health, age, or functional or developmental status; or ability to communicate effectively … [and] personal characteristics, such as race, ethnicity, and sex'"
Canadian Institutes of Health Research, 2014	"A diminished ability to fully safeguard one's own interests in the context of a specific research project. This may be caused by limited decision-making capacity or limited access to social goods, such as rights, opportunities and power. Individuals or groups may experience vulnerability to different degrees and at different times, depending on their circumstances" (p. 210). "Vulnerability is often caused by limited decision-making capacity, or limited access to social goods, such as rights, opportunities and power" (p. 8).
Council for International Organizations of Medical Sciences, 2016: 57	"[V]ulnerability involves not only the ability to provide initial consent to participate in research, but also aspects of ongoing participation in research studies. In some cases, persons are vulnerable because they are relatively (or absolutely) incapable of protecting their own interests. This may occur when persons have relative or absolute impairments in decisional capacity, education, resources, strength, or other attributes needed to protect their own interests. In other cases, persons can also be vulnerable because some feature of the circumstances (temporary or permanent) in which they lives makes it less likely that others will be vigilant about, or sensitive to, their interests. This may happen when people are marginalized, stigmatized, or face social exclusion or prejudice that increases the likelihood that others place their interests at risk, whether intentionally or unintentionally."
European Commission, 2010: 8	"'Vulnerability' is a concept … that can mean different things. Sometimes vulnerable participants are understood as those who are unable to give valid consent either due to a lack of competence or because of circumstances which cast doubt upon its voluntariness … 'Vulnerability' can also relate to susceptibility to harm or exploitation ….
ICH Guideline for Good Clinical Practice, 2016	Individuals whose willingness to volunteer in a clinical trial may be unduly influenced by the expectation, whether justified or not, of benefits associated with participation, or of a retaliatory response from senior members of a hierarchy in case of refusal to participate.
Indian Council of Medical Research, 2017: 56	"Vulnerable persons are those individuals who are relatively or absolutely incapable of protecting their own interests because of personal disability; environmental burdens; social injustice; lack of power, understanding or ability to communicate or are in a situation that prevents them from doing so. These vulnerable persons have some common characteristics … The key principle to be followed when research is planned on vulnerable persons is that others will be responsible for protecting their interests because they cannot do so or are in a compromised position to protect their interests on their own."
Uganda National Council of Science and Technology, 2014	"Some groups or individuals are relatively (or absolutely) incapable of protecting their own interests. They may have insufficient power, intelligence, education, resources, strength or other requisite attributes to protect their own interests. Individuals and groups conventionally considered vulnerable are those with limited capacity or freedom to consent or decline consent" (p. 25) Vulnerability refers to a substantial incapacity to protect one's own interests owing to such impediments as lack of capability to give informed consent, lack of alternative means of obtaining medical care or other expensive necessities, or being a junior or subordinate member of a hierarchical group" (p. 38)
World Medical Association, Declaration of Helsinki, 2013	"Some groups and individuals are particularly vulnerable and may have an increased likelihood of being wronged or of incurring harm."

G-5, 2003: 108-109). The definitions suggest that vulnerability may be both "a human condition from which we all suffer" (Hoffmaster, 2006: 42; Kottow, 2003, 2004), such as vulnerability due to injury and death (Lange, Rogers, & Dodds, 2013; Rogers & Lange, 2013), and that vulnerability is relative. Vulnerability, then, is an "*increased* potential that one's interests cannot be protected" (Agarwal, 2003: 25) (emphasis added), an "identifiably *increased* likelihood of incurring additional or greater wrong" (Hurst, 2008: 195) (emphasis added), whether that increased risk is due to external circumstances, such as the unavailability or inaccessibility of education or intrinsic characteristics, such as a disability (Weisser-

Lohmann, 2012). The Council Policy Statement of the Canadian Institutes of Health Research (2014), Ethical Conduct for Research Involving Humans, notes, for example, that "[i]ndividuals or groups may experience vulnerability to different degrees and at different times, depending on their circumstances." Whether individuals experience a lack of power (Indian Council of Medical Research, 2017; Uganda National Council of Science and Technology, 2014) or face social exclusion (Council for International Organizations of Medical Sciences, 2016) can only be assessed in the context of a specific time and place relative to other groups and/or individuals in their own communities, or that could be potentially called upon to participate in the proposed research in their communities or elsewhere, and in relation to those conducting or overseeing the proposed research (Goodin, 1985; Shivas, 2004).

The definitions provided by these national and international documents reflect both a recognition of the varied nature of vulnerability and the relationship of that vulnerability to governing ethical principles for the conduct of research with humans, in that vulnerability may be consent-based, risk- or harm-based, or justice-based (Coleman, 2009; Hurst, 2008; Kipnis, 2003). Seven distinct vulnerabilities of potential research participants have been identified (Kipnis, 2001, 2003). These vulnerabilities are incapacitational, referring to a lack of decisional capacity; juridical, in the sense that someone may be subject to the authority of another with an interest in the individual's research participation; deferential, meaning that the individual may be masking an unwillingness to participate due to pressures arising from informal hierarchical relationships (persons may have both juridical and deferential vulnerability arising from the same relationship); social, i.e., the individual belongs to a group whose rights and interests are devalued due to prejudice or stigma; situational, e.g., due to medical exigency; medical, i.e., the individual suffers from a condition for which there is no remedy; and allocational, such that the individual through participation in research ill receive valued gods or services that would otherwise be unavailable to them (Kipnis, 2001: G-7-G-11, 2003: 110).

APPLYING THE CONCEPT OF VULNERABILITY IN RESEARCH

Identifying Who Is Vulnerable

Despite the growing understanding of vulnerability as context-dependent, efforts to apply the concept of vulnerability to research have often incorporated a listing of specific populations or groups that are believed to be potentially vulnerable in research due to characteristics common to their members. Table 2 provides a listing of such groups that are specifically enumerated in the international and national documents referred to in Table 1, together with the rationale(s) provided by one or more of these documents for the identification of each such group.

Although Australia's *National Statement on Ethical Conduct in Human Research* (National Health and Medical Research Council, 2018b) does not define the term "vulnerability," the guide indicates that some relationships may compromise the voluntary character of participants' decisions, as they typically involve unequal status, where one party has or has had a position of influence or authority over the other. While avoiding the use of the term, the *Statement* lists a wide range of groups that may experience such a situation, including carers and people with chronic conditions or disabilities, including long-term hospital patients, involuntary patients, or people in residential care or supported accommodation; health care professionals and their patients or clients; teachers and their students; prison authorities and prisoners; governmental authorities and refugees; employers or supervisors and their employees; and

Table 2. Groups labeled as "vulnerable" in national and international documents, bases of vulnerability, and illustrative sources (Source: authors' own contribution)

Group Noted as Vulnerable or Potentially Vulnerable	Basis of Vulnerability (if Indicated by One or More Referenced Documents)	Reference Documents
Children and immature persons	Limited capacity to consent; limited capacity or freedom to consent or decline consent; relative immaturity	Canadian Institutes of Health Research, 2014; EU Regulation No. 536/2014; Indian Council of Medical Research, 2017; National Health and Medical Research Council (Australia), 2018b; Uganda National Council of Science and Technology, 2014; United States National Commission for the Protection of Human Subjects of Biomedical and Behavioral Research, 1979; 2014; U.S. Code of Federal Regulations Title 45, Part 46
Cognitively impaired, intellectually disabled	Lack of capacity for self-determination; lack of competence; May be more-than-usually vulnerable to various forms of discomfort and stress	Canadian Institutes of Health Research, 2014; Indian Council of Medical Research, 2017; National Health and Medical Research Council (Australia), 2018b; United States National Commission for the Protection of Human Subjects of Biomedical and Behavioral Research, 1979
Elderly	Are in situation of subordination or factual dependency	Canadian Institutes of Health Research, 2014; EU Regulation No. 536/2014
Ethnic/ ethnocultural/ racial minorities	Historically considered vulnerable; potential for systematic selection due to easy availability, compromised position, or manipulability; dependent status; compromised capacity for free consent; traditionally considered vulnerable	Canadian Institutes of Health Research, 2014; Council for International Organizations of Medical Sciences, 2016; Indian Council of Medical Research, 2017; United States National Commission for the Protection of Human Subjects of Biomedical and Behavioral Research, 1979
Health issues including, patients with multiple chronic conditions, physical disability, limited access to services		Canadian Institutes of Health Research, 2014; EU Regulation No. 536/2014; Indian Council of Medical Research, 2017; Uganda National Council of Science and Technology, 2014
Institutionalized persons	Diminished autonomy due to dependency or being under a hierarchical system; potential for systematic selection due to easy availability, compromised position, or manipulability; dependent status; compromised capacity for free consent; are in situation of subordination or factual dependency; have few options and are denied certain freedoms of non-institutionalized persons	Canadian Institutes of Health Research, 2014; Council for International Organizations of Medical Sciences, 2016; EU Regulation No. 536/2014; Indian Council of Medical Research, 2017; United States National Commission for the Protection of Human Subjects of Biomedical and Behavioral Research, 1979
Lacking adequate protection of human rights		Uganda National Council of Science and Technology, 2014
Lactating women		EU Regulation No. 536/2014; Indian Council of Medical Research, 2017
Marginalized communities, nomads and tribals	Traditionally considered vulnerable. Possibility of exploitation, particularly if not organizationally developed	Canadian Institutes of Health Research, 2014; Council for International Organizations of Medical Sciences, 2016; Indian Council of Medical Research, 2017
Mature and emancipated minors	Limited capacity or freedom to consent or decline consent	Uganda National Council of Science and Technology, 2014
Members of the armed forces/soldiers	Diminished autonomy due to dependency or being under a hierarchical system; limited capacity or freedom to consent or decline consent	EU Regulation No. 536/2014; Indian Council of Medical Research, 2017; Uganda National Council of Science and Technology, 2014
Mental health issues	May be more-than-usually vulnerable to various forms of discomfort and stress	Canadian Institutes of Health Research, 2014; EU Regulation No. 536/2014; Indian Council of Medical Research, 2017; National Health and Medical Research Council (Australia), 2018, Uganda National Council of Science and Technology, 2014
People highly dependent on medical care who may be unable to give consent and unconscious patients	Inability to comprehend situation or communicate about it, physically/mentally incapable of giving consent; lack of competence	National Health and Medical Research Council, 2018b; United States National Commission for the Protection of Human Subjects of Biomedical and Behavioral Research, 1979; World Medical Association, 2013
People in dependent or unequal relationships	May be over-researched because of ease of access to these populations	National Health and Medical Research Council, 2018b

continued on following page

Table 2. Continued

Group Noted as Vulnerable or Potentially Vulnerable	Basis of Vulnerability (if Indicated by One or More Referenced Documents)	Reference Documents
Persons with compromised/ diminished autonomy/ capacity for self-determination, compromised voluntariness		Canadian Institutes of Health Research, 2014; Indian Council of Medical Research, 2017; United States National Commission for the Protection of Human Subjects of Biomedical and Behavioral Research, 1979
Pregnant women	Limited capacity or freedom to consent or decline consent	EU Regulation No. 536/2014; Indian Council of Medical Research, 2017; Uganda National Council of Science and Technology, 2014; U.S. Code of Federal Regulations Title 45, Part 46
Prisoners	Diminished autonomy due to dependency or being under a hierarchical system; historically deemed to be vulnerable; may be subject to subtle coercion or undue influence; are in situation of subordination or factual dependency; have few options and are denied certain freedoms of non-institutionalized persons	Canadian Institutes of Health Research, 2014; Council for International Organizations of Medical Sciences, 2016; EU Regulation No. 536/2014; Indian Council of Medical Research, 2017; United States National Commission for the Protection of Human Subjects of Biomedical and Behavioral Research, 1979; U.S. Code of Federal Regulations Title 45, Part 46
Politically disadvantaged; politically powerless	Susceptible to exploitation; traditionally considered vulnerable	Council for International Organizations of Medical Sciences, 2016; Indian Council of Medical Research, 2017
Populations in conflict zones, riot areas or disaster situations or disease epidemic		Indian Council of Medical Research, 2017; Uganda National Council of Science and Technology, 2014
Post-conflict situations, refugees, internally displaced persons	Limited capacity or freedom to consent or decline consent; traditionally considered vulnerable	Council for International Organizations of Medical Sciences, 2016; Indian Council of Medical Research, 2017; Uganda National Council of Science and Technology, 2014
Resource-limited communities or countries; economically disadvantaged; poor; limited economic empowerment; welfare patients/ recipients; unemployed persons; homeless persons	Susceptible to exploitation; susceptible to inducement to take risks; potential for systematic selection due to easy availability, compromised position, or manipulability; dependent status; compromised capacity for free consent; traditionally considered vulnerable	Canadian Institutes of Health Research, 2014; Council for International Organizations of Medical Sciences, 2016; Indian Council of Medical; Uganda National Council of Science and Technology, 2014; United States National Commission for the Protection of Human Subjects of Biomedical and Behavioral Research, 1979 Research, 2017
Substance abusers	Limited capacity or freedom to consent or decline consent	Uganda National Council of Science and Technology, 2014
Suffering from stigmatizing or rare disease	Traditionally considered vulnerable	Council for International Organizations of Medical Sciences, 2016; Indian Council of Medical Research, 2017
Terminally ill persons or in search of new interventions having exhausted all therapies	Lack of competence; dependent status; compromised capacity for free consent; limited capacity or freedom to consent or decline consent	Indian Council of Medical Research, 2017; Uganda National Council of Science and Technology, 2014; United States National Commission for the Protection of Human Subjects of Biomedical and Behavioral Research, 1979
Women* generally, or with poor decision-making powers, or poor access to healthcare	Historically considered to be vulnerable	Canadian Institutes of Health Research, 2014; Indian Council of Medical Research, 2017
Abandoned persons, Employees, Healthcare workers, Orphans, Sexual minorities, Socially disadvantaged Students, Subordinates under trial, Unduly influenced by expectation of benefits or fear of retaliation		Indian Council of Medical Research, 2017

* The Council for International Organizations of Medical Sciences (CIOMS) specifies that while women as a group may not be considered vulnerable, specific types of research studies may render them vulnerable in research, e.g., studies related sexual and intimate partner violence, to abortion where it is illegal, transsexual or female sex workers, refugees and asylum seekers, and research in a context in which a woman must seek consent from a male relative in order to participate in research.

service-providers and vulnerable communities to whom the service is provided. Additional groups are identified as being highly dependent on medical care and who may be unable to give consent: those in neonatal intensive care due to their small size and unique developmental vulnerability; those in need of terminal care because of their short remaining life expectancy and their vulnerability to unrealistic expectations of benefits; individuals in need of emergency care or intensive care, as a function of their short remaining life expectancy and their vulnerability to unrealistic expectations of benefits; and individuals who unconscious, because their wishes cannot be determined (National Health and Medical Research Council, 2018b).

The delineation of specific groups may be intended to prompt researchers and members of research ethics review committees to examine the circumstances of a specific group in assessing the ethical advisability of its members inclusion or exclusion in proposed research and the need for special protections should they be included. The categorization of entire groups and classes of persons has been criticized as being overly broad because of the numbers of categories and overly narrow due to the failure to consider the varying levels of ability and needs of individuals within those groups, which may reify already-existing stereotypes and disempower their members (Eckenwiler, Ells, Feinholz, & Schonfeld, 2008; Levine, 2004; Levine et al., 2004).

This enumeration also emphasizes the possession of specific characteristics without regard to the nature of the research itself or the larger context in which the research is to be conducted (DeBruin, 2001; Levine et al., 2004). As an example, various national and international documents identify those with "mental health issues," mental disabilities, or mental illness as vulnerable in research (Canadian Institutes of Health Research, 214; EU Regulation No 536/2014; Indian Council of Medical Research, 2017; National Commission for the Protection of Human Subjects of Biomedical and Behavioral Research, 1979; National Health and Medical Research Council, 2018b). Each of these terms is quite broad, encompassing conditions that reflect a wide spectrum of ability in terms of understanding, organized thinking, decision-making ability, and emotional regulation. The existence of any condition along this spectrum may be of varying import in an assessment of vulnerability depending upon the proposed research, e.g., participation in an oral survey relating to daily dietary intake compared with participation in a clinical trial of a new drug to reduce the frequency of auditory hallucinations or depressive symptoms; a specific individual's living circumstances, e.g., degree of dependence, whether institutionalized or not; the individual's level of functionality (van der Veer, Drachman, Ahad, Silvers, & Ramos, 2011); the social, political, and economic situation of the group as a whole and its individual members; and the social, political, and economic implications of participation to the group and its members. Similarly, the attribution of vulnerability to all individuals with limited financial and/or social resources due only to such limitation, prompting the implementation of special protections up to and including their exclusion from research, fails to consider the context of the research and the characteristics of the individuals within the specified group (Grady, 2009).

The delineation of these groups also falls short in its recognition of the risks to communities that are defined other than by shared demographic or health characteristics. There is a need to identify morally relevant criteria that define a community so that risks and benefits to a community apart from its individual members can be adequately assessed in the context of proposed research (Weijer & Emanuel, 2000). Such an examination is critical because there may be circumstances in which a community may have an interest "in limiting some studies to which competent individuals might voluntarily consent" (Coleman, 2009: 17). Australia's *Ethical Conduct in Research with Aboriginal and Torres Strait Islander Peoples and Communities: Guidelines for Researchers and Stakeholders* (2018a) recognizes the importance of collective identity. The term "community" is defined

as a complex notion incorporating cultural groups, geographic groups or groups sharing common interests. It may include a group or organisation and is also a term used to describe a shared view amongst Aboriginal and Torres Strait Islander Peoples (National Health and Medical Research Council, 2018a: 25).

Ross and colleagues (2010) have noted that community engagement in research may involve risks related to the community itself, such as community structure and cohesiveness, identity, and moral agency. Entire communities may be stigmatized as the result of research findings. One can conceive of situations in which, due to historical, socioeconomic, sociological, or other factors, some communities may be at heightened risk of such harms, suggesting that a community may be vulnerable in the context of research (Weijer & Emanuel, 2000).

Some have considered how categories of vulnerability may interact with each other in order to provide a more nuanced understanding of the experience of vulnerability. Luna (2009) and Luna and Herissone-Kelly (2006) have suggested that researchers and research ethics review committees regard vulnerability as layered, such that vulnerability within a specific context is determined as a function of the compounded impact of multiple characteristics. This approach can be applied to both individuals and communities. Others have stressed the need to address in greater depth and particularity vulnerability that may be attributable to exploitation or a lack of basic rights (Grady, 2009; Lange, Rogers, & Dodds, 2013; Macklin, 2003; Zion, Gillam, & Loff, 2000).

Implementing Special Protections

When vulnerable individuals and communities are to be included in a study, this may be contingent on the application of "special protections". Depending upon the source and nature of vulnerability, recommended special protections noted in various international and national guidelines and regulations include:

- The supplementation of an individual's informed consent with the consent of a family member or legal guardian (Council for International Organizations of Medical Sciences, 2016),
- The solicitation of informed consent from a legally authorized third party (Indian Council of Medical Research, 2017; National Health and Medical Research Council, 2018b),
- Permitting participation in research with no direct benefits to the participants only if there are no more than minimal risks associated with the study procedures (Council for International Organizations of Medical Sciences, 2016),
- The repeated provision of education and information about the research to the study participants (Indian Council of Medical Research, 2017),
- The development and implementation of additional safety measures (Indian Council of Medical Research, 2017),
- The development by the researchers or the research sponsors of "support systems to deal with associated medical and social problems" and the provision of ancillary care (Indian Council of Medical Research, 2017: 58),
- The inclusion on the research ethics committee of a member of the community from which participants are to be drawn (Indian Council of Medical Research, 2017),
- The solicitation of assistance from government functionaries, or local bodies, or registered NGOs that work with tribal groups (Indian Council of Medical Research, 2017),
- The withholding of incentives or inducements apart from compensation for expenses and loss of earnings related to participation in clinical trial (EU Regulation No. 536/2014), and
- The exclusion of a group from the proposed research (Indian Council of Medical Research, 2017).

Whether the integration of any of these additional protections is necessary or advisable is dependent upon the nature of the proposed research, the context in which it is to be conducted, and the situations of the participants themselves, both individually and as a group. Additionally, reliance on any one of these proposed measures may raise further ethical issues that demand attention. For example, is the exclusion of a group from research due to risks that are deemed to be too great and benefits too little to the benefit of the group, or does its exclusion deprive them of the potential of benefit to which they would not otherwise have access? (Macklin, 2003; Nickel, 2006.) Is this protection or overprotection and paternalism? (Rogers, Mackenzie, & Dodds, 2012.)

What is generally missing from the protections suggested by national and international guidelines is the *full* engagement of communities in the research endeavor, with the exception of research that is to be conducted with identifiable tribes and native communities, such as required by provisions of Canada's *Ethical Conduct for Research Involving Humans* (TCPS2) (Canadian Institutes of Health Research, 2014), India's *National Ethical Guidelines for Biomedical and Health Research Involving Human Participants* (Indian Council of Medical Research, 2017) and Australia's *Ethical Conduct in Research with Aboriginal and Torres Strait Islander Peoples and Communities: Guidelines for Researchers and Stakeholders* (National Health and Medical Research Council, 2018a). Zion and colleagues (2000) have stressed the need for community consultation as a protection for communities whose members lack basic rights and liberties and are to be engaged in research.

In situations in which the investigators wish to focus on an issue within an identifiable community, adoption of a community-based participatory approach may provide additional protections for the community. Community-based participatory research (CBPR) is premised on the full engagement of the community in the research, at all phases of the research (Holkup, Tripp-Reimer, Salois, & Weinert, 2004). The approach requires that investigators recognize the community as a unit of identity, build on the strengths and resources of the community, promote learning in both directions between the researchers and the community, strive to achieve a balance between the research and action so that both science and the community derive benefit, emphasize the relevance of community-defined problems, utilize an iterative process to develop and maintain community/research partnerships, and disseminate knowledge from the research to the community as well as to the scientific community (Israel et al., 2003). Importantly, community-based participatory research requires a long-term commitment between the scientific and community partners. This longer-term investment of research resources in the community may bring with it needed resources to address basic needs, e.g., the development of a health infrastructure in the community. And, while CBPR is not free of ethical issues, utilization of the approach may reduce the possibility that a community may be exploited as resource for research, whether intentionally or inadvertently.

Kottow (2004: 281) draws a distinction between vulnerability as a feature of all humans and a deeper vulnerability that requires "remedial social practices, aimed at treating and removing injuries," which he refers to as susceptibility. Kottow explains,

> *If vulnerability is a substantial feature of being human, it can hardly be the appropriate description of accidental anomalies like a physical defect, disease, or some sort of deprivation as befalls the life of many human beings ... In addition to their basic vulnerability, wounded individuals cease being only vulnerable and enjoying their integrity ... Injury displaces those affected from the realm of vulnerability and into being vulnerated; ... these individuals can be referred to as susceptible (Kottow, 2004: 283).*

While a respect for human rights demands protection for vulnerability, Kottow asserts, the condition of susceptibility requires social action. This prompts questions regarding the nature of obligations owed to research participants. India's directive to researchers and research sponsors to develop "support systems to deal with associated medical and social problems" and to provide ancillary care (Indian Council of Medical Research, 2017: 58) suggests a distinction similar to that made by Kottow, while not employing the same term.

IMPLICATIONS FOR TEACHING THE CONCEPT OF VULNERABILITY IN RESEARCH

Both the foundational nature and the complexity of the concept of vulnerability suggest the need for heightened attention to how the concept is approached in the training of health professionals, including both health researchers and clinicians. Although the concept of vulnerability in research may be more directly relevant to those individuals whose primary focus is on research involving human participants, clinicians are often collaborators in the research endeavor and frequently serve as members of ethics review committees. Such roles demand that they be adequately prepared to evaluate whether prospective participants may be at increased risk of being wronged. Because understandings of vulnerability and special protections may vary considerably across individuals and may also differ from conceptualizations embodied in international and national standards and guidelines (Loue & Loff, 2013), it cannot be assumed that individuals holding such positions ascribe the same meaning to the term "vulnerability" (or agree on what constitutes a harm or relevant protection).

Medical school bioethics curricula have most often focused on ethical questions associated with the provision of clinical care (Goldie, Schwartz, & Morrison, 2000; Howard, McKneally, & Levin, 2010; Neff-Smith, Giles, Spencer, & Fletcher, 1997), paying only cursory attention to ethical issues in research, if at all (Downie & Clarkeburn, 2005). Even personal narratives about teaching bioethics that identify situations involving vulnerability may fail to name the concept or examine how an understanding of vulnerability was or can be fostered in those who are being taught (Dwyer, 2003; Tong, 2002).

Clearly, a range of pedagogical strategies are needed if students are to develop a heightened sensitivity to ethical issues, including participant vulnerability, that may be associated with past, ongoing, or proposed research. It has been suggested that

teaching in bioethics contexts needs to use pedagogies that engage students in participating and emergent activities … to enable the development of multiple dimensions of knowledge. These dimensions include the scientific content as well as the personal, social, and emotional aspects associated with any bioethical issue" (Conner, 2008: 1).

The use of a combination of approaches to teaching the concept of vulnerability is also necessitated by the diversity of student learning styles. Although some learners may be more apt to learn through abstract conceptualization founded on a thinking process, others may require opportunities for concrete personal experience, active experimentation, or observation and reflection in order to integrate new concepts (Kolb, 1984).

Accordingly, didactic lectures alone are not sufficient in themselves to reach and expand these non-cognitive dimensions. Rather, teaching strategies must embrace techniques that engage the emotion and affect, which have been consistently found to play a critical role in moral decision-making (Berkowitz, 1985; Nucci, 1989; Turiel, 1983, 1998; Zeidler & Schafer, 1984; Zeidler, Walker, Ackett, & Simmons, 2002).

Vignettes have been utilized successfully to enhance medical students' ethical sensitivity, including their ability to recognize ethical issues (Hébert, Meslin, & Dunn, 1992; Hébert, Meslin, Dunn, Byrne, & Reid, 1990), although it remains unclear as to whether the enhanced sensitivity to ethical issues impacted their behavior. Small group learning has been found to aid in the development of self-awareness among medical school students (Goldie, Schwartz, & Morrison, 2000), insight that is critical to understanding one's own unconscious biases and their potential impact on the recruitment or exclusion of potential research participants (Pronin, 2007; Chapman, Kaatz, & Carnes, 2013). Loue and Loff (2013) found that the use of journals with trainees provided a mechanism for trainees' disclosure of and reflection on their perceptions, understandings, and feelings vis-à-vis both their readings and their experiences. Guided reflection on journal entries over time enabled the trainees to view their own growing ability to undertake moral decision-making that recognized and addressed both cognitive and affective elements.

Role play, through which an individual assumes the identity or role of a different person, has been used frequently in educational contexts (Bowman, 2007) and may be helpful in expanding learners' sensitivity to the issue of vulnerability. This technique has been found to assist participants to understand their own feelings, to practice a particular approach or technique, and to adopt another identity in an effort to understand another's perspective about a particular situation.

The use of sociodrama in teaching offers the possibility of transformational learning because it can encourage participants to reflect about the assumptions that underlie their "habitual ways of perceiving, thinking, feeling, and behaving" (Mezirow, 1981: 19). The technique derives from psychodrama, a therapeutic technique for work with groups that was developed by Jacob L. Moreno in the 1930s (Blatner, 2000). Psychodrama has been explained as "a method for exploring psychological and social problems by having participants enact the relevant events in their lives instead of simply talking about them" (Blatner, 2000: 1). Psychodrama differs from role playing in that role play provides opportunities to pretend an identity, whereas psychodrama helps to foster greater self-reflection on the part of the participants.

Sociodrama facilitates examination of sociocultural interactions and situations by allowing both the individuals participating as actors in the drama and those in the audience to develop a deeper understanding of the dynamics and tensions involved in a given situation (Blatner, 2006; Kranz, Ramirez, & Lund, 2007). Although the technique derives from psychodrama, it focuses on a general inquiry rather than personal issues (Moreno, 1953, 1972). Sociodrama has been used to clarify conflicts in intergroup conflicts, foster critical questioning, build an awareness of how individuals may feel alienated and dislocated, and help to develop empathy and provide an opportunity for individuals to explore possible responses to a variety of situations. Loue and colleagues (Hobson-Rohrer et al., 2016; Loue, 2018) have demonstrated how the technique can be utilized within the setting of an academic medical center to foster increased understanding of oneself and of others' perspectives.

Health researchers have traditionally been trained to focus on the individual before them rather than societal wrongs. Some would suggest that researchers should refrain from advocacy and social action in matters related to their research focus (Brownson, Royer, Ewing, & McBride, 2006; Pittore, te Lintelo, Georgalakis, & Mikindo, 2016). Consideration of the need for special protections within a justice framework suggests that researchers must not only understand the nature and source of vulnerability but, in some circumstances, must extend their efforts to provide special protections beyond the engagement of relevant third parties and participant selection criteria to include advocacy efforts. Depending upon the context, these advocacy activities may include advocacy for policy change and/or for the provision of increased resources to a community. Successful participation in such efforts requires an understanding of relevant legislative and political processes, communication networks and their interplay within a locale that is specific to a given issue. Although such specificity cannot be accomplished within a training program, learners must be equipped with the foundational skills that will allow them to identify advocacy as a legitimate role in response to vulnerability and perhaps navigate through the channels relevant to their advocacy efforts.

CONCLUSION

Vulnerability should be understood as arising from physiological and social, economic, cultural and political sources. Examples are helpful in elucidating how vulnerability may occur and in filling out the content of layers if vulnerability existing within a single individual. Vulnerability may be a feature of individuals and of groups or communities, irrespective of how they are constituted. Although many would agree that an unconscious person is vulnerable, there may not be general agreement on all proposed categories of vulnerability. Teaching that is able to reveal to the learner his/her own assumptions and biases, and provide pedagogical strategies to support reflection on desirable responses is critical for building ethical awareness among researchers.

REFERENCES

Agarwal, M. (2003). Voluntariness in clinical research at the end of life. *Journal of Pain and Symptom Management, 25*(4), 25–32. doi:10.1016/S0885-3924(03)00057-5 PMID:12691694

Agency for Healthcare Research and Quality. (1998). *AHCPR seeks proposal to develop quality of care measures for vulnerable populations.* Retrieved from https://archivew.ahrq.gov/news/press/vulnpr.htm

Berkowitz, M. W. (1985). The role of discussion in moral education. In M. W. Berkowitz & F. Oser (Eds.), *Moral Education: Theory and Application* (pp. 197–218). Hillsdale, NJ: Lawrence Erlbaum Associates.

Blatner, A. (2000). *Foundations of psychodrama: History, theory, and practice* (4th ed.). New York: Springer Publishing Company.

Blatner, A. (2006). Enacting the new academy: Sociodrama as a powerful tool in higher education. *ReVision: A Journal of Consciousness and Transformation, 28*(3), 30-35. doi:10.3200/revn.28.3.30-35

Bowman, S. L. (2007). The psychological power of the roleplaying experience. *Journal of Interactive Drama, 2*(1), 1–14.

Brownson, R. C., Royer, C., Ewing, R., & McBride, T. D. (2006). Researchers and policymakers: Travelers in parallel universes. *American Journal of Preventive Medicine, 30*(2), 164–172. doi:10.1016/j.amepre.2005.10.004 PMID:16459216

Canadian Institutes of Health Research. (2014). *Ethical conduct for research involving humans (TCPS2)*. Retrieved from http://www.pre.ethics.gc.ca/eng/policy-politique/initiatives/tcps2-eptc2/Default/

Chapman, E. N., Kaatz, A., & Carnes, M. (2013). Physicians and implicit bias: How doctors may unwittingly perpetuate health care disparities. *Journal of General Internal Medicine*, *28*(11), 1504–1510. doi:10.100711606-013-2441-1 PMID:23576243

Coleman, C. H. (2009). Vulnerability as a regulatory category in human subject research. *The Journal of Law, Medicine & Ethics*, *37*(1), 12–18. doi:10.1111/j.1748-720X.2009.00346.x PMID:19245598

Conner, L. (2008). The importance of knowledge development in bioethics education. In U. N. E. S. C. O. Bangkok (Ed.), *Asia Pacific Perspectives on Bioethics Education* (pp. 1–8). Bangkok, Thailand: UNESCO. Retrieved from http://www.eubios.info/APPBE.pdf

Council for International Organizations of Medical Sciences (CIOMS). (2016). *International ethical guidelines for health-related research involving humans*. Geneva, Switzerland: CIOMS.

Danis, M., & Patrick, D. L. (2002). Health policy, vulnerability, and vulnerable populations. In M. Danis, C. Clancy, & L. R. Churchill (Eds.), *Ethical Dimensions of Health Policy* (pp. 310–334). New York: Oxford University Press.

DeBruin, D. (2001). Reflections on "vulnerability." *Bioethics Examiner*, *5*(2), 1–4.

Downie, R., & Clarkeburn, H. (2005). Approaches to the teaching of bioethics and professional ethics in undergraduate courses. *Bioscience Education*, *5*(1), 1–19. doi:10.3108/beej.2005.05000003

DuBois, J. M. (2006). Vulnerability in research. In E. A. Bankert & R. J. Amdur (Eds.), *Institutional Review Board: Management and Function* (2nd ed.; pp. 337–340). Sudbury, MA: Jones and Bartlett.

Dwyer, J. (2003). Teaching global bioethics. *Bioethics*, *17*(5-6), 432–446. doi:10.1111/1467-8519.00359 PMID:14959707

Eckenwiler, L. A., Ells, C., Feinholz, D., & Shonfeld, T. (2008). Hopes for Helsinki: Reconsidering "vulnerability.". *Journal of Medical Ethics*, *34*(10), 765–766. doi:10.1136/jme.2007.023481 PMID:18827112

European Commission. (2010). *European textbook on ethics in research*. Retrieved from https://ec.europa.eu/research/science-society/document_library/pdf_06/textbook-on-ethics-report_en.pdf. Accessed 22 July 2018.

Goldie, J., Schwartz, L., & Morrison, J. (2000). A process evaluation of medical ethics education in the first year of a new curriculum. *Medical Education*, *34*(6), 468–473. doi:10.1046/j.1365-2923.2000.00496.x PMID:10792689

Goodin, R. E. (1985). *Protecting the vulnerable: A reanalysis of our social responsibilities*. Chicago: University of Chicago Press.

Grady, C. (2009). Vulnerability in research: Individuals with limited financial and/or social resources. *The Journal of Law, Medicine & Ethics*, *37*(1), 19–27. doi:10.1111/j.1748-720X.2009.00347.x PMID:19245599

Hobson-Rohrer, W., Hoffman-Longtin, K., Liu, H. Y., Loue, S., Love, L. M., Pollart, S. M., & Power, C. M. (2016). Active learning on center stage: Theatre as a tool for medical education. *Learn, Serve, Lead 2016, AAMC Annual Meeting.*

Hoffmaster, B. (2006). What does vulnerability mean? *The Hastings Center Report*, *36*(2), 38–45. doi:10.1353/hcr.2006.0024 PMID:16604897

Holkup, P. A., Tripp-Reimer, T., Salois, E. M., & Weinert, C. (2004). Community-based participatory research: An approach to intervention research with a Native American community. *Advances in Nursing Science*, *27*(3), 162–175. doi:10.1097/00012272-200407000-00002 PMID:15455579

Howard, F., McKneally, M. F., & Levin, A. V. (2010). Integrating bioethics into postgraduate medical education: The University of Toronto model. *Academic Medicine*, *85*(6), 1035–1040. doi:10.1097/ACM.0b013e3181dbebb8 PMID:20505406

Hurst, S. A. (2008). Vulnerability in research and health care: Describing the elephant in the room? *Bioethics*, *22*(4), 191–202. doi:10.1111/j.1467-8519.2008.00631.x PMID:18405317

Indian Council of Medical Research. (2017). *National ethical guidelines for biomedical and health research involving human participants*. Retrieved from https://www.iitm.ac.in/downloads/ICMR_Ethical_Guidelines_2017.pdf

International Conference on Harmonisation of Technical Requirements for Registration of Pharmaceuticals for Human Use. (1996). *ICH harmonised tripartite guideline, Guideline for good clinical practice E6(R1)*. Retrieved from https://www.ich.org/fileadmin/Public_Web_Site/ICH_Products/Guidelines/Efficacy/E6/E6_R1_Guideline.pdf

Israel, B. A., Schulz, A. J., Parker, E. A., Becker, A. B., Allen, A. J. III, & Guzman, J. R. (2003). Critical issues in developing and following community-based participatory research principles. In M. Minkler & N. Wallerstein (Eds.), *Community-Based Participatory Research for Health* (pp. 53–76). San Francisco, CA: Jossey-Bass.

Kipnis, K. (2001). Vulnerability in research subjects: A bioethical taxonomy. In *Ethical and policy issues involving human participants* (Vol. 2). Bethesda, MD: National Bioethics Advisory Commission.

Kipnis, K. (2003). Seven vulnerabilities in the pediatric research subject. *Theoretical Medicine and Bioethics*, *24*(2), 107–120. doi:10.1023/A:1024646912928 PMID:12943266

Kolb, D. (1984). *Experiential learning: Experience as the source of learning and development*. Englewood Cliffs, NJ: Prentice-Hall.

Kottow, M. H. (2003). The vulnerable and the susceptible. *Bioethics*, *17*(5-6), 460–471. doi:10.1111/1467-8519.00361 PMID:14959710

Kottow, M. H. (2004). Vulnerability: What kind of principle is it? *Medicine, Health Care, and Philosophy*, *7*(3), 281–287. doi:10.100711019-004-6857-6 PMID:15679020

Kranz, P. L., Ramirez, S. V., & Lund, N. L. (2007). The use of psychodrama action techniques in a race relations class. *College Student Journal*, *41*(4), 1203–1208.

Lange, M. M., Rogers, W., & Dodds, S. (2013). Vulnerability in research: A way forward. *Bioethics*, *27*(6), 333–340. doi:10.1111/bioe.12032 PMID:23718774

Levine, C. (2004). The concept of vulnerability in disaster research. *Journal of Traumatic Stress*, *17*(5), 395–402. doi:10.1023/B:JOTS.0000048952.81894.f3 PMID:15633918

Levine, C., Faden, R., Grady, C., Hammerschmidt, D., Eckenwiler, L., & Sugarman, J. (2004). The limitations of "vulnerability" as a protection for human research participants. *The American Journal of Bioethics*, *4*(3), 44–49. doi:10.1080/15265160490497083 PMID:16192138

Loue, S. (2018). Using sociodrama to foster cultural humility among faculty and students in the academic medical center. *Revista Românească pentru Educaţie Multidimensională*.

Loue, S., & Loff, B. (2013). Is there a universal understanding of vulnerability? Expriences with Russian and Romanian trainees in research ethics. *Journal of Empirical Research on Human Research Ethics; JERHRE*, *8*(5), 17–27. doi:10.1525/jer.2013.8.5.17 PMID:24384513

Luna, F. (2009). Elucidating the concept of vulnerability: Layers not labels. *International Journal of Feminist Approaches to Bioethics*, *2*(1), 121–139. doi:10.3138/ijfab.2.1.121

Luna, F., & Herissone-Kelly, P. (2006). *Bioethics and vulnerability: A Latin American view*. Amsterdam: Editions Rodopi B.V.

Macklin, R. (2003). Bioethics, vulnerability, and protection. *Bioethics*, *17*(5-6), 472–486. doi:10.1111/1467-8519.00362 PMID:14959716

Mezirow, J. (1981). A critical theory of adult learning and education. *Adult Education Quarterly*, *32*(1), 3–24. doi:10.1177/074171368103200101

Moreno, J. L. (1953). *Who shall survive?* New York: Beacon House.

Moreno, J. L. (1972). *Psychodrama* (Vol. 1). New York: Beacon House.

National Commission for the Protection of Human Subjects of Biomedical and Behavioral Research. (1979). *The Belmont report*. Retrieved from https://www.hhs.gov/ohrp/regulations-and-policy/belmont-report/index.html

National Health and Medical Research Council. (2018a). *Ethical conduct in research with Aboriginal and Torres Strait Islander peoples and communities: Guidelines for researchers and stakeholders*. Retrieved from https://www.nhmrc.gov.au/guidelines-publications/ind2

National Health and Medical Research Council. (2018b). *National statement on ethical conduct in human research 2007 (updated 2018)*. Retrieved from http://www.nhmrc.gov.au/guidelines/publications/e72

Neff-Smith, M., Giles, S., Spencer, E. M., & Fletcher, J. C. (1997). Ethics program evaluation: The Virginia Hospital ethics fellows example. *HealthCare Ethics Committee Forum*, *9*(4), 375–388. PMID:10175653

Nickel, P. J. (2006). Vulnerable populations in research: The case of the seriously ill. *Theoretical Medicine and Bioethics*, *27*(3), 245–264. doi:10.100711017-006-9000-2 PMID:16763881

Nucci, L. P. (1989). Challenging conventional wisdom about morality: The domain approach to values education. In L. P. Nucci (Ed.), *Moral development and character education* (pp. 183–203). Berkeley, CA: McCutchan.

Pittore, K., de Lintelo, D. J. H., Georgalakis, J., & Mikindo, T. (2016). Choosing between research rigour or support for advocacy movements, a false dichotomy? *IDS Bulletin, 47*(6). doi:10.19088/1968-2016.202

Pronin, E. (2007). Perception and misperception of bias in human judgment. *Trends in Cognitive Sciences, 11*(1), 37–43. doi:10.1016/j.tics.2006.11.001 PMID:17129749

Regulation (EU) No 536/2014 of the European Parliament and of the Council of 16 April 2014. (n.d.). Retrieved from https://publications.europa.eu/en/publication-detail/-/publication/e7137f5b-e655-11e3-8cd4-01aa75ed71a1/language-en

Rogers, R., & Lange, M. M. (2013). Rethinking the vulnerability of minority populations in research. *American Journal of Public Health, 103*(12), 2141–2146. doi:10.2105/AJPH.2012.301200 PMID:24134375

Rogers, W., Mackenzie, C., & Dodds, S. (2012). Why bioethics needs a concept of vulnerability. *International Journal of Feminist Approaches to Bioethics, 5*(2), 11–38. doi:10.3138/ijfab.5.2.11

Ross, L. F., Loup, A., Nelson, R. M., Botkin, J. R., Kist, R., Smith, G. R. Jr, & Gehlert, S. (2010). Human subjects protections in community-engaged research: A research ethics framework. *Journal of Empirical Research on Human Research Ethics, 5*(1), 5–17. doi:10.1525/jer.2010.5.1.5 PMID:20235860

Shivas, T. (2004). Contextualizing the vulnerability standard. *The American Journal of Bioethics, 4*(3), 84–86. doi:10.1080/15265160490497137 PMID:16192157

Tong, R. (2002). Teaching bioethics in the new millennium: Holding theories accountable to actual practices and real people. *The Journal of Medicine and Philosophy, 27*(4), 417–432. doi:10.1076/jmep.27.4.417.8609 PMID:12221502

Turiel, E. (1983). *The development of social knowledge: Morality and convention.* New York: Cambridge University Press.

Turiel, E. (1998). Moral development. In W. Damon & N. Eisenberg (Eds.), Handbook of Child Psychology: Vol. 3. *Social, Emotional, and Personality Development* (5th ed.; pp. 863–932). New York: Cambridge University Press.

Uganda National Council of Science and Technology. (2014). *National guidelines for research involving humans as research participants.* Retrieved from https://uncst.go.ug/guidelines-and-forms/

United States Code of Federal Regulations Title 45, Part 46. (n.d.). Retrieved from https://www.law.cornell.edu/cfr/text

United States National Commission for the Protection of Human Subjects of Biomedical and Behavioral Research. (1979). *The Belmont report: Ethical principles and guidelines for the protection of human subjects of research.* Washington, DC: Department of Health, Education, and Welfare.

Van der Veer, N. L., Drachman, D., Ahad, S., Silvers, G., & Ramos, G. (2011). Voluntariness to consent to research in a voluntarily and involuntarily hospitalized psychiatric populations. *Journal of Empirical Research on Human Research Ethics*, *6*(1), 55–61. doi:10.1525/jer.2011.6.1.55 PMID:21460588

Weijer, C., & Emanuel, E. J. (2000). Protecting communities in biomedical research. *Science*, *289*(5482), 1142–1144. doi:10.1126cience.289.5482.1142 PMID:10970227

Weisser-Lohmann, E. (2012). Ethical aspects of vulnerability in research. *Poiesis & Praxis: International Journal of Ethics of Science and Technology Assessment*, *9*(1-2), 157–162. doi:10.100710202-012-0109-2 PMID:23205001

World Medical Association. (2013). *Declaration of Helsinki—Ethical principles for medical research involving human subjects*. Retrieved from http://www.wma.net/en/ 30publications/10policies/b3/

Zeidler, D. L., & Schafer, L. E. (1984). Identifying mediating factors of moral reasoning in science education. *Journal of Research in Science Teaching*, *2*(1), 1–15. doi:10.1002/tea.3660210102

Zeidler, D. L., Walker, K. A., Ackett, W. A., & Simmons, M. L. (2002). Tangled up in views: Beliefs in the nature of science and responses to socioscientific dilemmas. *Science Education*, *86*(3), 343–367. doi:10.1002ce.10025

Zion, D., Gillam, L., & Loff, B. (2000). The Declaration of Helsinki, CIOMS, and the ethics of research on vulnerable populations. *Nature Medicine*, *6*(6), 615–617. doi:10.1038/76174 PMID:10835665

ADDITIONAL READING

Beecher, H. K. (1966). Ethics and clinical research. *The New England Journal of Medicine*, *274*(24), 1354–1360. doi:10.1056/NEJM196606162742405 PMID:5327352

Hawksin, J. S., & Emanuel, E. J. (Eds.). (2008). *Exploitation and developing countries: The ethics of clinical research*. Princeton, USA: Princeton University Press.

Jones, J. H. (1981). *Bad blood: The Tuskegee syphilis experiment*. New York, USA: Free Press.

Kodish, E. (Ed.). (2005). *Ethics and research with children: A case-based approach*. New York, USA: Oxford University Press.

Lederer, S. E. (1995). *Subjected to science: Human experimentation in America before the Second World War*. Baltimore, USA: Johns Hopkins University Press.

Schülenk, U. (2000). Protecting the vulnerable: Testing times for clinical research ethics. *Social Science & Medicine*, *51*(6), 969–977. doi:10.1016/S0277-9536(00)00075-7 PMID:10972439

Weindling, P. J. (2004). *Nazi medicine and the Nuremberg trials: From medical war crimes to informed consent*. Basingstoke, UK: Palgrave Macmillan. doi:10.1057/9780230506053

Chapter 7
Addressing Research Ethics in Clinical Trials in Four of the Former Communist European Countries:
A Shared Responsibility

George Florian Macarie
University of Medicine and Pharmacy "Carol Davila" Bucharest, Romania

Ana Voichita Tebeanu
University Politehnica of Bucharest, Romania

ABSTRACT

This chapter considers the problematic of ethics in clinical research in the countries that are new in terms of implementation or building an adequate structure. The chapter intends to assess the extent to which the clinical trials performed in four former communist East-European countries considered the ethical norms into their research procedures. A framework of existing literature on ethics in clinical research, along with the regional context, is discussed in the next section. The methods section includes the instruments, sources, and procedures for data collection. The data analysis procedures and structure are further explained and grounded relative to the study main purpose. The next section includes the facts and figures on the presence of ethical requirements in clinical trials in the specific political and cultural background in a number of former European communist countries. Finally, a number of suggestions and recommendation are also discussed.

DOI: 10.4018/978-1-5225-6310-5.ch007

INTRODUCTION

The ethical issues have been approached for decades in all medical research when human subjects were involved. International bodies concerned with research ethics need to confront the greatest ethical challenge - the enormous inequities in global health research (Benatar & Singer, 2000). Despite increasing awareness in scientists and researchers from the medical field about the necessity of substantiate their research on ethical grounds (for example the referral of the research proposal or scientific paper to an institutional review board or a committee with similar functions, potential impact of financial conflicts of interest on biomedical research, proper formulation and delivery of the informed consent documents, assurance of voluntariness and non-coercion in research participants, especially in the vulnerable individuals and groups, and so on) no comprehensive synthesis of the body of evidence relating to all these issues has been performed on an uniform, coherent and systematic manner in Europe in the last decade.

The twentieth century saw the acceleration of medical progress, as well as an expansive development of the concept of human rights. These advances led to various codes of ethics for experimentation in the scientific disciplines. According to Rohrich (2007), the medical progress is based on research which ultimately must rest in part on experimentation involving human subjects- so special caution must be exercised in the conduct of research, which may affect the integrity, dignity and well-being of participants.

Despite the increase knowledge and inclusion of ethical issues in medical research on human subjects, there is no systematic evaluation about the mentioning of ethical requirements and/or how are they approached in the clinical trials performed in former communist countries, now members of the European Union. Following this, our study aims to evaluate how the ethical issues are taken into consideration in clinical research made in countries where presumably the introduction of these principles has been delayed due to a specific background (political and cultural).

Background

It is well-known that in the European space, in the last half of century the main sources of guidance on the ethical conduct of clinical research have been the Nuremberg Code (1949), the Declaration of Helsinki (WMA, 1964), the Belmont Report (1979), the International Ethical Guidelines for Biomedical Research Involving Human Subjects (CIOMS, 2016) and similar documents, like the Guidelines for Good Clinical Practice for Trials on Pharmaceutical Products (WHO, 1995), the Convention on Human Rights and Biomedicine (Council of Europe, 1997) and the Guidelines and Recommendations for European Ethics Committees (European Forum for Good Clinical Practice, 1997). Each of these documents highlights certain aspects or issues that were not sufficiently addressed in the former documents, or they are applying the principles stated in the previous codes, for specific categories of persons or activities; or they were simply written in response to specific events and to avoid future scandals, and are sometimes subsequently contradicting themselves in several aspects (Levine, 1994; Vanderpool, 1996). Theorists have thus found that we are missing an universally applicable ethical framework, and that investigators, institutional review boards members, funders, and others lack coherent guidance on determining whether specific clinical research protocols are ethical (Emanuel, Wendler, & Grady, 2000). Further, E. Emanuel and colleagues are taking into consideration 7 requirements that provide a systematic and coherent framework for determining whether clinical research is ethical:

1. The research must have value; that is, it must have the potential to enhance health or knowledge.
2. It must have sufficient methodological rigor to make the results of the research scientifically valid.
3. Research participants should be selected in a way such that the risks of participation in research studies and the potential benefits of the knowledge gained from the research are distributed fairly among groups.
4. The potential benefit of the research results to society should outweigh the risks, and risks to the individual are minimized.
5. The research is reviewed and approved by an independent body.
6. Consent is informed and voluntary and can be withdrawn at any time.
7. Respect for potential and enrolled subjects- The privacy of participants is protected and their well-being is monitored.

These seven principles are applicable in any medical research; for example, they are mentioned in an article about ethics in surgical research (McDonald, Kulkarni, Farrokhyar, & Bhandari, 2010).

This framework of principles and benchmarks is complex, because ethical evaluation of clinical research is usually a complex endeavour. A single ethical principle is rarely absolute; most situations implicate multiple principles (Nagel, 1979; Richardson, 1990; Temkin, 1993). Consequently, the various principles and benchmarks will compete and must be balanced against each other—a process that inevitably requires judgment (Daniels et al., 2000). In a logical order, these principles and benchmarks must be clearly specified before there can be any enforcement mechanism about, for example, the avoidance of fraud, the conflict of interest, the coercion, undue inducement, the loss of privacy in research participants or confidentiality of data and so on.

On the other hand, Coker and McKee (2001) questions about the possibility of transposing these requirements: "it is unclear whether the current system for oversight of human subjects research in the post-Communist countries of Central and Eastern Europe and Central Asia provides adequate review of research protocols. These countries are at various stages of development in terms of their capacity to protect research participants, and information about potential procedural and structural deficiencies in human subjects review and oversight is lacking. There are also little data on the efficiency and effectiveness of existing regulatory systems in protecting the rights and safety of research participants. For example, a brief survey in 2000 sent to researchers in Albania, Bulgaria, Croatia, Czech Republic, Estonia, Hungary, Lithuania, Poland, Romania, Russia, and Ukraine revealed that most countries had structures and review committees (such as research ethics committees [RECs] or institutional review boards [IRBs]) in place to oversee clinical research, but provided little information on the effectiveness of those committees". In what concerns Romania, we have some more information on this aspect and we can mention that the development of RECs at national (alignment with the European Union norms) and local and institutional level (universities, independent research departments and centres affiliated with the universities, private research institutions, state and private hospitals) is continuously increasing, as well as the transparency of procedures related to reviewing and approving research protocols (the availability of necessary documents and template forms on the respective Internet pages) and the willingness of researchers to conform to these relatively new requirements. A couple of positive examples about the improvement of procedures assuring an ethical research protocol can be found at the University of Medicine and Pharmacy "Gr. T. Popa" in Iaşi, the University of Bucharest, or the University of Medicine and Pharmacy in Târgu-Mureş.

However, we are not aware at this point about a comprehensive systematic review about the authors' and researchers' attention to ethics in clinical trials in all the medical fields from the former Communist countries in Europe and the republics from the former Soviet Union, with one exception – in a recent study, Loue and Chiscop (2004) consider the editorial policies of the journals in which manuscripts appeared that required discussion of specified ethical norms for conducting mental health research in Romania between 2007 and 2012. For example, research participants in developed and developing countries show variable understanding of key elements of informed consent (if presented prior to the initiation of the study), including the purpose of the research and its risks (Mandava, Pace, Campbell, Emanuel, & Grady, 2012). While there is wide agreement that all competent adults should give informed consent to research participation, there are no mentions about studies in which a systematic review of percentage of mentioning the informed consent forms (their writing and actual use) is done with referral to post-Communist countries in Europe. Also, we found a cross-sectional survey of a convenience sample of 135 editors of peer-reviewed biomedical journals that publish original research, in order to characterize conflict of interest (COI) policies of biomedical journals with respect to authors, peer-reviewers, and editors, and to ascertain what information about COI disclosures is publicly available, but this survey was done mostly with journals from the US (the country of the publication sponsor) and to a much smaller extent in UK, Europe, Canada and Australia (Cooper, Gupta, Wilkes, & Hoffman, 2006). A final example comes from a study commissioned by the former National Bioethics Advisory Commission of the United States; it surveyed developing country researchers about their concerns and opinions regarding ethical review processes and the performance of developing country and US international review boards (Hyder et al., 2004). Yet, most of the respondent researchers (42%) were from Asia, followed by Africa (29%), and South America (23%).

A particular aspect is presented by the European countries that were under Soviet Union political influence or member of the Union. Most of these countries were confronted at the moment of the fall of communist regime (the 90's) with a human research domain heavy influenced by the politics, including concerns about meeting the minimum ethical requirements. After almost three decades, there is little knowledge available about how and if the ethical issues are taken into consideration. For the interest of the present study, we focused on how the ethical principles are met in the clinical trials (the golden standard of medical research) in the countries that were under the political influence or former members of the Soviet Union. A preliminary analysis showed a lack of availability of the studies published in English language for most of the countries former member of the Soviet Union, with the exemption of Lithuania, Georgia and Ukraine. The authors did not found evidence for research (published in English) involving human subjects in the former Soviet republics in Central Asia.

Also, among the former communist countries under Soviet influence, the study has been limited to Europe, mainly due to the similar path of these countries following the communism fall. Finally, Poland, Romania, Lithuania and Bulgaria were chosen, according to some political-based criteria (under direct Soviet influence, had a truly communist regime, from European Union, etc.). Considering both criteria, some countries were excluded from the analysis: the countries from ex-Yugoslavia (a mild communist regime, a disputable Soviet influence), Georgia and Ukraine (not in the EU) and Albania (shaped by a personal dictatorship of Enver Hodja).

RESEARCH ETHICS IN CLINICAL TRIALS

Studies Selection: Criteria and Procedure

The analysis is based on a systematized review, with the benefit stated as to seek to systematically search for, appraise and synthesis research evidence. Systematized review typically addresses broad questions to produce 'best evidence synthesis' (Grant & Booth, 2009). The protocol was inspired by the PRISMA guidelines (Moher, Liberati, Tetzlaff, & Altman, 2009).

Data Sources and Eligibility Criteria

The literature search considered the medical publication from 2010 to 2015, found in the main scientific databases. The review included articles from PubMed, Google Scholar, and Medline, that met the following criteria: former communist country in Europe; clinical trial, randomized controlled trial; published in the last 5 years; involved human subjects; are written in English; can be found in full text.

The initial search yielded a total of more than 600 articles that met these criteria. In order to have significant results, the authors have chosen to exclude from the analysis those countries that register in the databases with less than 2 articles (after filtering upon the mentioned criteria). Considering the number of articles found, the initial search provided results from the following 4 countries (listed from the highest to the lowest number): Poland (400+), Romania (approximately 80), Lithuania (below 60), and Bulgaria (below 10). The final number of articles selected per country is presented in the Table 1. Due to the high number of articles in Poland (312), a sample was chosen, with a step of 3 relative to the listing order across databases). The complete list of the journals where clinical trials were found is presented on the Appendix.

Table 1. Distribution of articles per country, showing the process of selection

Number of Articles			
Country	**Initially selected from the databases, according to the criteria**	**Excluded, with explanation**	**Final number**
Bulgaria	9	1- retracted	8
Lithuania	56	8- studies developed by international teams including Lithuanian researchers, but not conducted in Lithuania	48
Poland	498	185 - studies published in Polish journals, but not conducted in Poland 1- Letter to the editor	312; a step of 3 was applied, resulting 104 articles evaluated
Romania	84	29 - errors in the search process; studies not conducted in Romania 2 - letters to the editor	53
			Total: 213

Source: the authors' own contribution

Data Extraction and Items

We grounded our review on a series of requirements for the ethical conduct of research involving humans, proposed by Emanuel et al. (2000). These requirements are considered necessary for research involving humans: 1) informed consent procedures, (2) ethics committee review, (3) assessment of participant capacity, (4) special protections or a discussion of the risks and benefits, and (5) the source of funding and conflicts of interest. We added the criteria of declaration of conflicts of interests, due to the increased relevance for current research in the medical and pharmaceutical fields. Furthermore, the fourth criterion was subsequently divided in two - special protections and, respectively, risks versus benefits- because we considered them to be two distinct categories. Similarly, the fifth criterion has two components – the source of funding and, respectively, the mention of the conflict of interest. Finally, we build a decision procedure where a letter was assigned to that study using two coding criteria: if the requirement has been addressed AND if the wording in the text of the article was clear as referring to the respective criterion (Table 2).

Ethical Requirements in Clinical Trials: Facts and Figures

Descriptive of Requirements in the Studies -

The data extracted from each of the selected studies include quantitative descriptors like number of studies, relative and absolute adherence to the respective ethical requirements, and the authors' declaration of interest. In Table 3, we rated the extent each study is fulfilling the ethical requirements (with 1- fully present, clearly explained; 2- present in a relative degree; 3- not present or not declared).

The summative data in the table show, for example, that in Lithuania the number of articles clearly mentioning the existence of the informed consent procedure (taken in written from the participants) is 32 (66.7% of all) and the number of articles where is not a disclosure of the conflict of interest (not stating that is one to be mentioned) is only 5 (10.4%). In Poland, the number of articles where is mentioned

Table 2. Decision criteria for categories

Category Code*	Description	Ethical Requirements**						
		ICS	ECR	APC	SP	RB	SF	CI
A	Best practices/ full compliance	1	1	1	At least 3 are rated 1			
B	Addressed, sufficiently clear	1	1	At least 3 requirements are rated with 1 or 2				
		At least one is 1, other is 2		At least 3 requirements are rated with 1				
C	Some addressed or not clearly stated	Max 2	Max 2	At least 1 requirements is rated with 1 or 2				
D	Mostly not addressed or unclear	Mostly 2 or 3						

* ICS – informed consent, ECR- ethical commission review, APC- assessment of patient capacity, SP- special protection, RB- risks versus benefits, SF- source of funding, CI- conflict of interest

** Numbers in table represents ratings: 1- fully present, clearly explained; 2- present in a relative degree; 3- not present or not declared

Source: the authors' own contribution

Table 3. Degree of presence and clarity of ethical requirements

Country	Ratings	Ethical requirements*						
		ICS	ECR	APC	SP	RB	SF	CI
		n (%)	n (%)	n (%)	n (%)	n (%)	n (%)	n (%)
BG N=8	1	5 (62.5)	5 (62.5)	3 (37.5)	4 (50)	4 (50)	7 (87.5)	5 (62.5)
	2	3 (37.5)	3 (37.5)	1 (12.5)	-	4 (50)	-	-
	3	-	-	4 (50)	4 (50)	-	1 (12.5)	3 (37.5)
LT N=48	1	32 (66.7)	38 (79.2)	14 (29.2)	25 (52.1)	23 (47.9)	26 (54.2)	37 (77.1)
	2	11 (22.9	8 (16.7)	22 (45.8)	10 (28.8)	25 (52.1)		
	3	5 (10.4)	2 (4.2)	12 (25)	13 (27.1)		22 (45.8)	11 (22.9)
PL N= 104	1	46 (44.2)	58 (55.8)	8 (7.7)	33 (31.7)	29 (27.9)	61 (58.7)	79 (76)
	2	33 (31.7)	26 (25)	32 (30.8)	37 (35.6)	63 (60.6)	-	-
	3	25 (24)	20 (19.2)	64 (61.5)	34 (32.7)	12 (11.5)	43 (41.3)	25 (24)
RO N=53	1	19 (35.8)	23 (43.4)	9 (17.0)	19 (35.8)	13 (24.5)	24 (45.3)	20 (37.7)
	2	13 (24.5)	6 (11.3)	20 (37.7)	14 (26.4)	29 (54.7)	-	-
	3	21 (39.6)	24 (45.3)	24 (45.3)	20 (37.7)	11 (20.8)	29 (54.7)	33 (62.3)

*ICS – informed consent, ECR- ethical commission review, APC- assessment of patient capacity, SP- special protection, RB- risks versus benefits, SF- source of funding, CI- conflict of interest

Source: the authors' own contribution

the ethical commission approval (with name of that commission or institution, the registration number, date, eventually referrals to different several international conventions or guidelines, as the Declaration of Helsinki (WMA, 1964), for example (is 55.8%) Also in Poland, the source of funding is mentioned (as research grants provided by institutions or the government) in 58.7% articles. In Romania, the assessment of patient capacity (of understanding the issues in the IC form) is to be found (mentioned) in only 9 articles (17%). Also in Romania, special protection for the group studied is mentioned in 19 articles (35.8%) (if, and what has been done to add an extra-layer of protection- in selection, therapeutic procedures, follow-up, exclusion from the study for the mentioned patients). Coming back to Poland, we should mention one exception that draw our attention, an article where the issue of difficulties aroused by the informed consent procedure can delay the initialization of life-saving procedures. Thus, this example shows that the search by all means for obtaining an IC form only to 'check' an ethical requirement of the editorial board can be sometimes superfluous and it should be always regarded with finesse and in the respective context. Here are some excerpts from the article of Wojciech et al. (2012):

The significantly longer time delay to reperfusion therapy in the subgroup of patients who were proposed and finally refused to participate in trials highlights the issue of informed consent. There is a general opinion among researchers that the involvement of a patient in a consent process in an emergency situation is an empty ritual.[...]. Based on the population of patients randomized to the OASIS-2 and PARAGON trials, Kucia et al. showed that the level of protocol understanding reaches only 52%, with far greater impairment of knowledge of risk than of benefit.[...] Regulation 21CFR50.24 of the Food and Drug Administration states that: "obtaining informed consent is not feasible when the subjects are not able to give their informed consent as a result of their medical condition".[...]. Current practice, which forces the patient to read pages of informed consent at a time of heavy chest pain, is legally justified, but it appears to be illogical and [...] potentially harmful. CONCLUSIONS. Randomized, multicenter, placebo-controlled trials are currently commonly used as a principal tool for proving the effectiveness of newly developed drugs or treatment techniques. [...]. The call for reappraisal of informed consent issues and randomization procedures seems to be justified.

Compliance to Ethical Requirements

Considering the composite measure of the compliance to ethical requirements (presence and clarity) and using decision process presented in the precedent table, the number of articles falling into each of the four categories (A - best practices/full compliance; B - addressed, sufficiently clear; C - some addressed or not clearly stated; D - mostly not addressed or unclear) is presented in the Table 4. For comparison, in the Poland case, only relative numbers should be considered.

As seen in the table, the number of articles in category A ('best practices') is 1 for Bulgaria, 7 for Lithuania, and 5 for Romania (in percentages, the smallest for Poland and the highest for by Lithuania). The number of articles in the category D (with most of the ethical requirements not addressed or unclear) is: none for Bulgaria, 5 for Lithuania, 28 for Romania (in percentages, the smallest for Bulgaria and the highest for Romania). The vast majority of articles fall – somehow expected - in the middle categories B and C.

These results are, in our opinion, related more with the alignment to the editorial policies of the journals where the article has been submitted and published, than to the actual on-going study. And this 'artefact' is due to the modality in which the articles have to be written in order to be accepted - the authors must comply with the guidelines of each journal, otherwise the paper will be rejected. The initial stages of a clinical trial (where is taken the approval of an ethics commission, the informed consent form presented to the potential participants, and so on) can be found in an article, or not. Here we can cite the case of multicentre studies whose results are presented in a series of articles, sometimes for each country or site separately. Often, the mentioning of the-above ethical requirements is done for only the first article in this series, and all the others refer to it without indications of the IRB approval, the informed consent etc.

Another interesting hypothesis is that even if the guidelines are clear about the ethical requirements, the editorial board accepts sometimes articles where these are not addressed. This can be the case for some journals, for example, where even if the guidelines are strict, the paper is published 'beyond' the ethical minimal requirements.

Table 4. Distribution, in absolute numbers and percentages, of articles assigned to each category (A, B, C, D), per country

Country (number of studies)	Categories			
	A	B	C	D
	n (%)	n (%)	n (%)	n (%)
Bulgaria (8)	1 (12.5)	3 (37.5)	4 (50.0)	-
Lithuania (48)	7 (14.6)	20 (41.7)	16 (33.3)	5 (10.4)
Poland (104)	4 (3.8)	35 (33.7)	34 (32.7)	31 (29.8)
Romania (53)	5 (9.4)	10 (18.9)	10 (18.9)	28 (52.8)

Source: the authors' own contribution

Ethical Requirements in Local Journals or Studies: Examples

Here are some examples of how ethical requirements are set or respected locally. We chose two situations, one of the local journals, and a study which we consider to be at least ethically questionable.

The Local Journals Ethical Requirements: A Few Examples

The examples are randomly chosen; most of the journals publishing research on human subjects are stating the ethical requirements. The common point we found is the referral to the Helsinki Declaration (WMA, 1964), while the differences are in term of details provided or the ownership of the ethical code (their own or of a known publisher).

Bulgaria

The authors of *Psychiatria Danubiana* (n.d.) are informed that:

„Manuscripts submitted for publication must contain a statement to the effect that all human studies have been approved by a suitably constituted Ethics Committee of the institution within which the work was undertaken and that it conforms to the provisions of the Declaration of Helsinki in 1995 (as revised in Edinburgh 2000). All investigations on human subjects must include a statement that the subject gave informed consent and patient anonymity should be preserved".

Lithuania

Guidelines for authors of *Medicina Kaunas,* published and hosted by Elsevier B.V. on behalf of Lithuanian University of Health Science, and peer review under the responsibility of Lithuanian University of Health Science, state that:

If the work involves the use of human subjects, the author should ensure that the work described has been carried out in accordance with The Code of Ethics of the World Medical Association - Declaration of Helsinki (WMA, 1964)- for experiments involving humans; Uniform Requirements for manuscripts submitted to Biomedical journals. Authors should include a statement in the manuscript that informed consent was obtained for experimentation with human subjects. The privacy rights of human subjects must always be observed.

All authors are requested to disclose any actual or potential conflict of interest including any financial, personal or other relationships with other people or organizations within three years of beginning the submitted work that could inappropriately influence, or be perceived to influence, their work.

You are requested to identify who provided financial support for the conduct of the research and/or preparation of the article and to briefly describe the role of the sponsor(s), if any, in study design; in the collection, analysis and interpretation of data; in the writing of the report; and in the decision to submit the article for publication. If the funding source(s) had no such involvement then this should be stated.

Poland

For *Kardiologia Polska* (n.d.), the guidelines state that:

4. By submitting a paper describing an experiment conducted in humans the authors declare that the procedures they followed complied with the Declaration of Helsinki (WMA, 1964) - with respect to the principles of medical ethics that forbid the disclosure of patient names, initials or hospital record numbers. The information about the study having been approved by the relevant ethics committee and about the patient having provided informed consent to participate in the study should be included in the material and methods section of each paper in which the diagnostic or therapeutic intervention is not part of the standard of care.

5. Authors submitting manuscripts that present the results of clinical studies of drugs or medical procedures are expected to provide an exhaustive description of the funding of the study, of the sponsor's role in the planning and execution of the study and in the analysis of results, and of the impact of the funding institution on the content of the paper. All these details should be provided in the form of a conflict of interest statement published at the end of the paper.

The Journal of Physiology and Pharmacology (n.d.) was established in 1950 as an Acta Physiologica Polonica by the Polish Physiological Society. The guidelines state that:

When conducting scientific research on humans or human tissue, researchers should follow procedures that are in accordance with the ethical standards of the latest revision of the Helsinki Declaration (…) The editors reserve the right to reject papers if there is doubt as to whether suitable experimental procedures were used.(…) Authors should also disclose any conflict of interest.

Romania

For some journals, as *Psychiatry Research* or *Medicina* (n.d.), the guide for authors includes the same standard as those provided by Elsevier. Other journals have their own standard, as in the Journal *Chirurgia* (n.d.):

Conflict of interest: Authors must state all possible conflicts of interest in the manuscript, including financial, consultant, institutional and other relationships that might lead to bias or to a conflict of interest. If there is no conflict of interest, this should also be explicitly stated as none declared. All sources of funding should be acknowledged in the manuscript. All relevant conflicts of interest and sources of funding should be included on the title page of the manuscript with the heading "Conflicts of Interest and Source of Funding.

Ethical policies: When reporting experiments on human subjects, authors should indicate whether the procedures followed were in accordance with the ethical standards of the responsible committee on human experimentation (institutional and national) and with the Helsinki Committee for Human Rights. If doubt exists whether or not the research was conducted in accordance with the Helsinki Declaration (WMA, 1964), the authors must explain the rationale for their approach and demonstrate that the institutional review body explicitly approved the doubtful aspects of the study.

A Questionable Study

For Romania we have a special case with the articles in the Bucharest Early Intervention Project (BEIP, n.d.) series. These articles were not published in Romanian journals, but were included into the analysis because the study was conducted in Romania. The study has obtained all the approvals from the ethical commissions in the US and also the acceptance to be run from the Romanian government of that time, 18 years ago. However, the content, the methodology and the approach of this study cast a shadow on the morality and the necessity of this demarche.

This series of researches was conducted on foster children by Charles Zeanah, from Tulane University, New Orleans, LA, USA, as the principal investigator. The BEIP began in 2000 with a comprehensive baseline assessment of 136 children and their caregiving environments. Following this assessment, half the children were randomly assigned to high-quality foster care (designed specifically for this study) and the other half to remain in institutional care (Zeanah et al., 2003). The average age at entry into foster care was 22 months (range= 6-31 months). All children were seen for follow-up assessments at 30, 42 and 54 months, and again at 8 years, and the development of children in foster care was compared to the development of children randomized to remain in institutional care and to a group of never institutionalized children (community controls). The findings from the assessment at 8 years suggest that children assigned to remain in institutional care *continued to demonstrate profound delays in nearly all domains the researchers had examined* (BEIP, n.d.).

The study poses some ethical questions that deserve to be discussed. The project was an international research collaboration; while they have an ethical committee approval in U.S., it was difficult to have a formal local ethical review because of the absence of such structures in Romania at that time.

Although the intervention was based on the randomized controlled trial design (RCT), often referred as the gold standard for evaluating the efficacy of biomedical and social intervention research, the evaluation of multiple developmental outcomes, was not conducted by blind raters. Considering that the psychosocial evaluations are highly subjective, depending on the rater personal bias, that particular procedure may cast some doubts on the scientific validity of the data. Also, we can question the statistical confidence that can be placed in this small sample relative to biomedical RCT samples. Despite the greater effort and emotional implication to find, select and investigate more institutionalized children, the study would have benefit form a larger sample.

The children in institutional care were highly fragile and vulnerable and, basically, any research involving them may be considered unethical. They were unable to give informed consent, and at that time it was no clear guardian acting in their best interests (the staff was no legally responsible for them). So, the selection was a convenience one rather than a scientific necessity. Even if none of the study's assessments of functioning were likely to harm the children, we can ask in what extent the results of the study helped them directly and efficiently, being given the Romanian poor health-care infrastructure in the 2000's. In an 2007 article, Millum and Emanuel pointed out "there have been no American randomized trials comparing foster and institutional care, and no American children would be enrolled in the BEIP".

In what concerns the favorable risk-benefit ratio, we know that "at least the deinstitutionalized group would not be adversely affected by the intervention". However, the BEIP does not provide sufficient detail of the screening of the foster parents; on the other hand, the number of children in institutional care declined during the study due to national programs of inclusion. Millum and Emanuel (2007) assume the staff morale deteriorated, leading to a negative impact on the quality of care in those settings, thereby accounting for some of the more negative outcomes in the control group. There is also another practical issue. The authors mentioned that the local and national Romanian authorities could not guarantee that the results of the study would be nationally implemented if the findings favored foster care, as they did (and so many studies before this one showed the same conclusions). We can wonder about the long-term practicality of a study if its results cannot be implemented (of course, this was beyond the reach of the PI-s). According to the Council for International Organizations of Medical Sciences (CIOMS, 2016), research in a community is permissible only if researchers or their sponsors ensure that interventions resulting from the research are made "reasonably available" to the community (CIOMS, 2016). We can thus emphasize the importance of equipoise - if the knowledge resulted from a study is not socially useful, it wastes resources and exposes participants to risks and burdens for no good reason. Additionally, we don't have information, from the articles resulted after the completion of the study, that the investigators tried to negotiate foster placements for the institutional control group if the intervention was shown to be effective. While is true the number of children in orphanages in Romania in 2016 was five times smaller than immediately after the communism fall in December 1989, we still have in Central and Eastern Europe the highest rate in the world for institutionalized children - 666 children/100,000 - 5 times more than the global average of 120 children/100,000 (UNICEF, 2017).

In comparative interventions as this one, the intervention, if beneficial, should be offered to the control group(s) after that study. Not having this information leads thus to a major ethical concern (Wassenaar, 2012).

In their article, Millum and Emanuel (2007) asserted that study participation was unlikely to cause net harm to the children; no child was put at additional risk to obtain the results, which reduces the ethical reasons for worrying about equipoise. The Romanian state policy was likely to adopt the BEIP conclusions, even if the impact was not guaranteed at that time. A finished study cannot guarantee the certainty of its results' implementation, yet "the researchers should have been more careful in evaluating how results get implemented when the benefits cannot accrue to participants". According to the researchers, limited funds foreclosed the option to move the children to foster care when they observed that participants in this trial arm were doing better; from now on, it was the responsibility of the local authorities. The Romanian State was the final actor to ensure that each of these children get the care they needed.

SOLUTIONS AND RECOMMENDATIONS

The presented facts may give rise to a series of ideas on how to improve the ethical assessment of the procedures, in order to ensure an appropriate level of subjects' protection. Below we will present some general assumptions that may serve as suggestions, in three different aspects. These can be applied by professionals in the medical institutions; in the review process in journals; and in the personal effort undergone by young scholars to improve the research ethics conduct.

First, the medical bodies doing research, either academic or from industry, may select and train a professional to be the connection between the investigational team and a more distant IRB. Also, this 'liaison' person can advise or train, in his/her turn, the members of the research team, especially if some of them don't have a medical background.

Secondly, the journals can provide a more detailed series of guidelines for the authors, especially those journals that have a smaller impact factor or are indexed in fewer international databases. The guidelines can offer templates for addressing each ethical prerequisite, links to the European or international conventions, or step-by-step guides for the novices. We are still in favour of guidelines, rather of very strict or precise requirements, because the criteria assuring subjects' protection can be reformulated, adapted and improved with time. In the review process, the evaluation forms may include specific ethical requirements for the clinical trials. While being specifically asked, the authors can be more thoughtful and treat data collection with greater care.

Also, if a particular study raises ethical questions, the editorial board can also request from the main author a detailed document- an annex separate from the main paper- where he/she should state the process of obtaining the IRB approval, how the Informed Consent procedure was developed, amended or applied, how the investigators accorded extra-protection for the subjects involved in the study etc.

Thirdly, and maybe a final suggestion- the researchers should undergo a continuous program (once in two or three years) of perfecting into the research ethics, somehow similar with the CREC certification (a Continuing Research Education Credit Program that provides investigators documented training in the protection of human subjects in research) from the US. To our knowledge, all the studied countries developed workshops and post-university training programs in bioethics and research ethics, either standing alone or part of general curricula of investigators training. For example, in Romania they are developed by College of Physicians, College of Psychologists, etc., yet they are not mandatory for researchers.

Better training for the researchers, institutional support, along with more consistently applied rules/criteria for inclusion/exclusion from the part of journals, can be a successful long-term solution for improving the writing of scientific articles and, respectively, for conducting research on human subjects.

FUTURE RESEARCH DIRECTIONS

It is a matter of responsibility for the potential medical researcher who reads these lines to analyse more than the ethical frameworks present in his or her country of origin or in which he/she operates, or the ethical guidelines in the journal being considered for publication. Comparative studies of these guidelines across countries with a cultural, social and political background similar to his/her country can give a much wider perspective on how other researchers have approached the conception, conducting, eventual problems encountered, and finally the publication of a similar study. Thus, the scholar in becoming, novice, or just curious about the approaches of other colleagues, can take advantage of their experience, understand and avoid mistakes already made, take models of good practice and, above all, adopt a moral thinking towards patients

A similar evaluation as the one presented in this chapter could be extended to several countries in the European Union, that were not under the influence of the communist regime; such a review would be useful to compare the possible influences of a particular type of political system on the conception of physicians and medical researchers toward patients and participants in clinical trials. Of course, such influence is never singular and there cannot be supported causal relations between the type of political regime and the way clinical trials are conducted in those countries; even so, descriptive analyses can be made, as in the present study.

Another direction of interest would be where the analysis could be extended to countries subject to totalitarian regimes around the world. The difficulty of such an approach might possibly arise from the lack of access, as such, to electronic articles, or if they can be accessed, to be in an international language. An analysis at such a level could once again bring clarifications about how the patient, and the researcher himself, have or not freedom of expression, the choice of two or more treatment options / approaches in a clinical trial; about individual and social vulnerability; about how disclosure of a conflict of interest can influence the way research is conducted, and so on.

CONCLUSION

The results, rather than be a basis for comparison between countries, show a general tendency of each scientific community (many times exceeding the borders of a country, due to multi-national trials) to reflect the directives from national and international authoritative boards that regulate the research on human subjects in each country. This guidance is apparently newer in the countries part of the former Soviet bloc because of the lack of transparency in acquiring, copying and implementing the directives from the Western Europe and from USA. The motivation for this delay in transferring the international guidelines for human research from the so-called 'developed countries' to those 'in the process of development' (as Romania was called during the Ceausescu era) is a complex political and cultural one; its discussion can be subject for a different study or essay.

These international and national guidelines are applied differently- as a method, frequency, consistency in application, coherence between multiple guidelines applied concomitantly and so on. For example, the international statutory regulations, several EU guidelines (not mandatory to be applied if the country is not part of the UE) are the Helsinki Declaration (WMA, 1964), the Oviedo Convention (Council of Europe, 1997), The Research Ethics Committees in Europe: "Building the future together" Conference in Brussels, from January 2005. The national level- one step down- is, to cite only Romania, the Guidelines for Good Practice in Research/Clinical Studies- or National Ethics Committee for Clinical Trials (NECCT)- Decision Nr. 39/27.10.2006, the Code of Deontology of the Romanian College of Physicians (March 30, 2012), and several Codes of ethics for various research fields. From this national level, each institution can have its own guidelines and ethical independent commissions; and, finally, coming to the personal level of each researcher, he or she can apply in different degrees a personal understanding of these, in conceiving his/her study, in the process of selection, enrolment, treatment and exclusion of the patients. More than that, the patients present some characteristics of vulnerability (in terms of autonomy, capacity to cope with the disease), regardless of the disease treated. In more complex situations (for example cardiac patients who are women or pregnant women, children with cancer in terminal stage and so on) the researcher should bear in mind multiple layers of protection, that are not always visible in the preparation of the manuscript, but were taken into consideration, as much as possible, during the research process.

In the process of writing several versions of a manuscript, this action- that can last over one year- reflects only partially the opinion of all the investigators. They can have different responsibilities during the clinical trial, and these responsibilities can refer to all the ethical elements in the same time for all the patients enrolled (selection, enrolment, treatment…), or only a part of them for only a small number of patients, or not at all. Some of the authors does only the proofreading, the translation from Romanian or Polish into English, the statistical work in front of a computer (with all the personal identifiable information eliminated) etc. Each action of these persons (and they can be more than 10 authors for a paper), is thus to be found in the final version of the article, in a very subtle, nuanced way. The work of a scholar who conceives a systematic review resides only in reading this final version of each selected article. This 'top of an iceberg' makes any rating into several categories, following several criteria, a fluid and non-permanent process.

Coming back to the guidelines of each medical institution where a trial is conducted (where it can be found sometimes in the Journal of that respective institution) we should also mention the not-by-chance way of choosing the journal in which a future study will be published. Usually the first author chooses the journal, and from this decision an article can be written in many different ways. Depending on the journal, the editorial requirements can dictate even the course of a trial not yet started.

ACKNOWLEDGMENT

This research was supported by a Fogarty scholarship (2014-2015) from The Fogarty International Center at NIH- National Institutes of Health (Bethesda, MD, USA), and was conducted under the supervision of Prof. Sana Loue, Professor of Bioethics, Psychiatry, Epidemiology and Biostatistics, and Center for Global Health; Vice Dean Faculty Development and Diversity- School of Medicine, Case Western Reserve University, Cleveland, OH, USA).

REFERENCES

Benatar, S. R., & Singer, P. (2000). A new look at international research ethics. *British Medical Journal, 321*(7264), 824–826. doi:10.1136/bmj.321.7264.824 PMID:11009528

Chirurgia. (n.d.). *Instructions for authors*. Retrieved from http://www.revistachirurgia. ro/docs/instructions%20for%20authors.pdf

Coker, R., & McKee, M. (2001). Ethical approval for health research in Central and Eastern Europe: An international survey. *Clinical Medicine, 1*(3), 197–199. doi:10.7861/clinmedicine.1-3-197 PMID:11446614

Cooper, R. J., Gupta, M., Wilkes, M. S., & Hoffman, J. R. (2006). Conflict of interest disclosure policies and practices in peer-reviewed biomedical journals. *Journal of General Internal Medicine, 21*(12), 1248–1252. doi:10.1111/j.1525-1497.2006.00598.x PMID:17105524

Council for International Organizations of Medical Sciences (CIOMS). (2016). *International ethical guidelines for health-related research involving humans, Guideline 19: Pregnant and breastfeeding women as research participants*. Retrieved from https://cioms.ch/wp-content/uploads/2017/01/WEB-CIOMS-EthicalGuidelines.pdf

Council of Europe. (1997). *Convention for the Protection of Human Rights and Dignity of the Human Being with Regard to the Application of Biology and Medicine*. Oviedo, Spain: Council of Europe.

Daniels, N., Bryant, J., Castano, R. A., Dantes, O. G., Khan, K. S., & Pannarunothai, S. (2000). Benchmarks of fairness for health care reform: A policy tool for developing countries. *Bulletin of the World Health Organization, 78*(6), 740–750. PMID:10916911

Emanuel, E. J., Wendler, D., & Grady, C. (2000). What makes clinical research ethical? *Journal of the American Medical Association, 283*(20), 2701–2711. doi:10.1001/jama.283.20.2701 PMID:10819955

European Forum for Good Clinical Practice. (1997). *Guidelines and recommendations for European Ethics Committees*. Leuven, Belgium: EFGCP.

Grant, M., & Booth, A. (2009). A typology of reviews: An analysis of 14 review types and associated methodologies. *Health Information and Libraries Journal, 26*(2), 91–108. doi:10.1111/j.1471-1842.2009.00848.x PMID:19490148

Hyder, A. A., Wali, S. A., Khan, A. N., Teoh, N. B., Kass, N. E., & Dawson, L. (2004). Ethical review of health research: A perspective from developing country researchers. *Journal of Medical Ethics, 30*(1), 68–72. doi:10.1136/jme.2002.001933 PMID:14872079

Kardiologia Polska. (n.d.). *Author Guidelines*. Retrieved from https://ojs.kardiologiapolska.pl/kp/about/submissions#authorGuidelines

Levine, R. J. (1994). The impact of HIV infection on society's perception of clinical trials. *Kennedy Institute of Ethics Journal, 4*(2), 93–98. doi:10.1353/ken.0.0054 PMID:10134752

Loue, S., & Chiscop, E. (2004). Mental illness research in Romania: A review of author attention to ethical norms. *Revista Romana de Bioetica*, 12.

Mandava, A., Pace, C., Campbell, B., Emanuel, E., & Grady, C. (2012). The quality of informed consent: Mapping the landscape. A review of empirical data from developing and developed countries. *Journal of Medical Ethics, 38*(6), 356–365. doi:10.1136/medethics-2011-100178 PMID:22313664

McDonald, P. J., Kulkarni, A. V., Farrokhyar, F., & Bhandari, M. (2010). Ethical issues in surgical research. *Canadian Journal of Surgery, 53*(2), 133–136. PMID:20334746

Medicina. (n.d.). *Guide for Authors*. Retrieved from https://www.elsevier.com/journals/medicina/1010-660x/guide-for-authors

Millum, J., & Emanuel, E. J. (2007). The ethics of international research with abandoned children. *Science, 318*(5858), 1874–1875. doi:10.1126cience.1153822 PMID:18096792

Moher, D., Liberati, A., Tetzlaff, J., & Altman, D. (2009). Preferred reporting items for systematic reviews and meta-analyses: The PRISMA statement. *BMJ (Clinical Research Ed.), 339*(1), b2535. doi:10.1136/bmj.b2535 PMID:19622551

Nagel, T. (1979). The fragmentation of value. In *Mortal Questions* (pp. 128–142). New York: Cambridge University Press.

National Commission for the Protection of Human Subjects of Biomedical and Behavioral Research. (1979). *The Belmont Report*. Washington, DC: US Government Printing Office. Retrieved from http://www.hhs.gov/ohrp/humansubjects/guidance/belmont.html

Psychiatria Danubiana. (n.d.). *Guidelines for Authors*. Retrieved from http://www.hdbp.org/psychiatria_danubina/guidlines.html

Richardson, H. S. (1990). Specifying norms as a way to resolve concrete ethical problems. *Philosophy & Public Affairs, 19*(4), 279–310.

Rohrich, R. J. (2007). Ethical approval of clinical studies, informed consent, and the declaration of Helsinki: What you need to know [Editorial]. *Plastic and Reconstructive Surgery*, *119*(7), 2307–2309. doi:10.1097/01.prs.0000229193.31894.d0 PMID:17519734

Temkin, L. (1993). Inequality: a complex notion. In *Inequality* (pp. 19–52). New York: Oxford University Press.

The Bucharest Early Intervention Project (BEIP). (n.d.). *About us*. Retrieved from http://www.bucharestearlyinterventionproject.org/About-Us.html

The Journal of Physiology and Pharmacology. (n.d.). *Notice to contributors*. Retrieved from http://www.jpp.krakow.pl/

The Nuremberg Code of 1949. (n.d.). Retrieved from https://history.nih.gov/research/downloads/nuremberg.pdf

UNICEF. (2017). *Cei mai vulnerabili copii din instituțiile rezidențiale rămân o necunoscută datorită datelor incomplete* [The most vulnerable children in residential institutions remain unknown due to incomplete data]. Retrieved from http://www.unicef.ro/media/unicef-cei-mai-vulnerabili-copii-din-institutiile-rezidentiale-raman-o-necunoscuta-datorita-datelor-incomplete/

Vanderpool, H. Y. (1996). *The ethics of research involving human subjects*. Hagerstown, MD: University Publishing Group.

Wassenaar, D. R. (2012). Ethical considerations in international research collaboration: The Bucharest Early Intervention Project. *Infant Mental Health Journal*, *27*(6), 577–580. doi:10.1002/imhj.20108 PMID:28640375

Wojciech, W., Sebastian, S., Maciejewski, P., Kłosiewicz–Wąsek, B., Bednarz, B., & Budaj, A. (2012). Participation in thrombolytic trials delays reperfusion therapy in acute myocardial infarction. *Kardiologia Polska*, *70*(8), 775–780. doi:10.5603/kp.2013.0191 PMID:22933207

World Health Organisation (WHO). (1995). Guidelines for good clinical practice for trials on pharmaceutical products. In WHO Expert Committee on Selection and Use of Essential Medicines, WHO Technical Report Series, No. 850, Appendix 3, Sixth report: The Use of Essential Drugs. Geneva, Switzerland: WHO.

World Medical Association (WMA). (1964). *Declaration of Helsinki - Ethical Principles for Medical Research Involving Human Subjects*. Retrieved from https://www.wma.net/policies-post/wma-declaration-of-helsinki-ethical-principles-for-medical-research-involving-human-subjects/

Zeanah, C. H., Nelson, C. A., Fox, N. A., Smyke, A. T., Marshall, P., Parker, S. W., & Koga, S. (2003). Designing research to study the effects of institutionalization on brain and behavioral development: The Bucharest Early Intervention Project. *Development and Psychopathology*, *15*(4), 885–907. doi:10.1017/S0954579403000452 PMID:14984131

ADDITIONAL READING

Etchells, E., Darzins, P., Silberfeld, M., Singer, P. A., McKenny, J., Naglie, G., ... Strang, D. (1999). Assessment of patient capacity to consent to treatment. *Journal of General Internal Medicine*, *14*(1), 27–34. doi:10.1046/j.1525-1497.1999.00277.x PMID:9893088

Grady, C. (2015). Institutional review boards. Purpose and challenges. *Chest*, *148*(5), 1148–1155. doi:10.1378/chest.15-0706 PMID:26042632

Greco, D., & Diniz, N. M. (2008). Chapitre 9. Conflicts of interest in research involving human beings. *Journal International de Bioethique*, *19*(1), 143–154. doi:10.3917/jib.191.0143 PMID:18664007

Levine, R. J. (2000). Some recent developments in the international guidelines on the ethics of research involving human subjects. *Annals of the New York Academy of Sciences*, *918*(1), 170–178. doi:10.1111/j.1749-6632.2000.tb05486.x PMID:11131702

Macklin, R. (2003). Bioethics, vulnerability, and protection. *Bioethics*, *17*(5-6), 472–486. doi:10.1111/1467-8519.00362 PMID:14959716

Shapiro, H. T., & Meslin, E. M. (2001). Ethical issues in the design and conduct of clinical trials in developing countries. *The New England Journal of Medicine*, *12*(345), 139–142. doi:10.1056/NEJM200107123450212 PMID:11450665

Tzamaloukas, A. H., Konstantinov, K. N., Agaba, E. I., Raj, D. S., Murata, G. H., & Glew, R. H. (2008). Twenty-first century ethics of medical research involving human subjects: Achievements and challenges. *International Urology and Nephrology*, *40*(1), 153–163. doi:10.100711255-007-9319-2 PMID:18188674

Wagner, R. M. (2003). Ethical review of research involving human subjects: When and why is IRB review necessary? *Muscle & Nerve*, *28*(1), 27–39. doi:10.1002/mus.10398 PMID:12811770

Weijer, C. (2000). The ethical analysis of risk. *The Journal of Law, Medicine & Ethics*, *28*(4), 344–361. doi:10.1111/j.1748-720X.2000.tb00686.x PMID:11317427

World Medical Association. (2001). World Medical Association Declaration of Helsinki. Ethical principles for medical research involving human subjects. *Bulletin of the World Health Organization*, *79*(4), 373–374. PMID:11357217

KEY TERMS AND DEFINITIONS

Assessment of Patient Capacity: A (semi-) structured evaluation of the participant's ability to understand relevant information and appreciate reasonably foreseeable consequences with regard to the specific treatment decision. In the shared decision-making process, the physician or researcher must take into consideration that capable patients have the legal and ethical right to make their own treatment decisions, and incapable patients cannot give a valid consent, so someone else must make the decision on the patient's behalf.

Conflict of Interest: Situation occurred when an employee, researcher, physician, etc. is involved in a particular matter as part of his/her official duties with an outside organization with which he/she also has a financial interest, or one which is imputed to him/her. The conflict can be real or apparent. Ideally the conflict is disclosed to the Ethics Coordinator or principal investigator to obtain a waiver or authorization, otherwise the employee should be disqualified from participating in particular matters concerning the outside entity.

Ethical Commission Review: An evaluation of a research project proposal made by a board or specialized commission in a university setting, research institute, a structure of the National Ministry of Health or Education. Ideally a research project can only be carried out if it has received a favorable opinion from such committees.

Informed Consent: Term used for medical treatment but also in research- refers to an autonomous authorization (respect for persons, autonomy, liberty interests) and to social rules of consent (i.e., consent for minors, witnesses); in essence has to disclose the nature of the proposed intervention, procedures and alternatives, potential risks and benefits, assurance that participation is voluntary, and protection of confidentiality, all concisely explained and written in a document understandable by a person with basic education.

Institutional Review Board: (IRB): A research ethics committee that provides a core protection for human research participants through advance and periodic independent review of the ethical acceptability of proposals for human research. Its functioning is widely required by law or regulation in jurisdictions globally.

Patient Capacity: The ability (here, of a patient) to make a decision. If a person lacks capacity, he/she has an impairment or disturbance that leaves him/her unable to make a decision relative to the treatment or the participation in a medical trial, a research project and so on. The loss of capacity could be partial or temporary. It is possible for a person to lack capacity to make one specific decision but not about another; each specific situation must be carefully weighed. Assessing the patient's capacity is a delicate task for the investigator/physician.

Research Ethics: A set of methods, procedures, or perspectives used by people for deciding how to act and for analyzing complex problems and issues related to research. They also may take into consideration moral and social values that lead to norms for conduct that distinguish between acceptable and unacceptable behavior before, during, and after the completion of a research, in areas such as participants' selection, collecting, storing, and using data; privacy and confidentiality; collaboration with colleagues or undergraduate students; publication; and so on.

Risk-Benefit Balance: An assessment (made by the researcher, physician, but also by the participant) about risk of loss of privacy and confidentiality, risk of infringing on the autonomy of subjects, risk of unethical doubt manufacturing and conflict of interest, on one hand, and benefit of health advancement and prevention, benefit of cost-effectiveness, better future research and study design, social acceptance of sustaining emerging disciplines, on the other hand. This evaluation should be personalized for each study and participant and it can be included in the informed consent form.

APPENDIX

Table 5. List of journals taken into consideration for each country

Country of the Researcher(s)	Journals of Publication
Bulgaria	Ann Rheum Dis- Annals of the Rheumatic Diseases (BMJ) Brain- A Journal of Neurology Exp Brain Res- Experimental Brain Research (Springer) ExpClinEndocrinol Diabetes- Experimental and Clinical Endocrinology & Diabetes (Thieme) J Neural Transm- Journal of Neural Transmission (Springer) Medical Ultrasonography PsychiatriaDanubina
Lithuania	American Academy of Ophthalmology Journal Am J Gastroenterol- The American Journal of Gastroenterology Am J Sports Med- The American Journal of Sports Medicine Annals of Oncology Arthroscopy: The Journal of Arthroscopic and Related Surgery BioMed Research International BMC Anesthesiology Digestive and Liver Disease European Archives of Oto-Rhino-Laryngology (Springer) Gastroenterology Intensive Care Medicine (Springer) International Journal of Environmental Research and Public Health Journal of Crohn's and Colitis Journal of Dental Research (Sage) Journal of Strength and Conditioning Research Journal of Thrombosis and Thrombolysis (Springer) Journal of Voice JOURNAL OF THE ASSOCIATION OF NURSES IN AIDS CARE Medicina (Kaunas) Nurse Education Today Perfusion PLOS ONE Photodermatology, Photoimmunology & Photomedicine Sleep Breath Stomatologija, Baltic Dental and Maxillofacial Journal Surgical Endoscopy The Breast Journal The ScientificWorld Journal Journal of Pediatric Surgery
Poland	Acta Biochimica Polonica Kardiologia Polska Advances in Clinical and Experimental Medicine Advances in Medical Sciences Cardiology Journal Folia Medica Cracoviensia Journal of Investigational Allergology and Clinical Immunology JOURNAL OF PHYSIOLOGY AND PHARMACOLOGY Neurologia i Neurochirurgia Polska Otolaryngologia Polska Pharmacological Reports POLSKIE ARCHIWUM MEDYCYNY WEWNĘTRZNEJ PostepyHig Med Dosw- PostępyHigieny i MedycynyDoświadczalnej PRZEGL EPIDEMIOL- PRZEGLĄD EPIDEMIOLOGICZNY (Epidemiological Review) Regulatory Toxicology and Pharmacology RoczPanstwZaklHig- RocznikiPaństwowegoZakładuHigieny

continued on following page

Table 5. Continued

Country of the Researcher(s)	Journals of Publication
Romania	Annals of Agricultural and Environmental Medicine Archives of Pediatrics and Adolescent Medicine Asian Pacific Journal of Cancer Prevention Chirurgia CHILD DEVELOPMENT Contemporary Clinical Trials Developmental Science Folia Morphologica.- Via Medica Gene Journal of Gastrointestinal and Liver Diseases Journal of Inherited Metabolic Disease (Springer) Journal of Medicine and Life JOURNAL OF PEDIATRICS Lasers in Medical Science (Springer) Medical Ultrasonography Pharmacological Reports Prevention Science Proceedings of the National Academy of Sciences (PNAS) Psychiatry Research Romanian Journal of Morphology & Embryology Trials Wien KlinWochenschr- Wiener klinischeWochenschrift (The Central European Journal of Medicine) The American Journal of Psychiatry

Source: authors' own contribution

Chapter 8
Risk-Benefit Evaluation in Clinical Research Practice

Samia Hassan Rizk
Cairo University, Egypt

ABSTRACT

A core element in protecting human participants in clinical research is the assurance of a favorable risk-benefit balance, in accordance with the ethical principle of beneficence. However, the assessment of risks and benefits may sometimes be challenging. In this chapter, the authors review the concepts, ethical principles, and applicability of those terms. The assessment approaches used by regulators and research reviewers who are working in clinical practice are then discussed, together with a highlight of the new trends in risk-benefit analysis and their impact on drug development and approval. Analysis of some research situations which pose particular challenges are presented at the end of the chapter.

INTRODUCTION

Assuring a favorable risk-benefit balance is crucial to human subjects' protection in clinical research and thus complies to the principle of beneficence in the Belmont report, written and published by the National Commission for the Protection of Human Subjects of Biomedical and Behavioral Research in 1979. It is a critical requirement for all research regulations that guide each step in research. It is also the main criteria for determining the approvability of categories of participants and reviewing those categories, the degree of protection required for each category of participants, according to the type and frequency of monitoring study.

The objective of this chapter is to highlight the:

1. Concepts, principles, and types of risks and benefits;
2. Methodology of risk-benefit analysis;
3. Applications and impact of data science technology in clinical research practice;
4. Challenges to risk-benefit analysis and suggested resolutions.

DOI: 10.4018/978-1-5225-6310-5.ch008

BACKGROUND

Evaluation of the risk-benefit balance in research is a complex process, which is sometimes straightforward, but in other cases it is more challenging.

Balancing risks to patients against the total benefits to science or to future patients is one of the most difficult issues, especially in research involving vulnerable populations.

The aim of this chapter is to lead the readers through the decision-making process of risk-benefit evaluation of clinical research.

The scope: Throughout the three main sections of this paper, we discuss the main principles, approaches and challenges of risk and benefit assessment in clinical research.

SECTION I: PRINCIPLES OF RISK-BENEFIT ASSESSMENT IN CLINICAL RESEARCH

Risk-benefit assessment is an universal requirement for protecting human participants in clinical trials. The concept and perception of risks and benefits, their types, degree, and relative weight are complex attributes which can vary depending on the context in which the study is being conducted.

Defining Risk and Benefit

In research, risk is defined as: "a potential harm, discomfort, or inconvenience that a reasonable person in the subject's position would likely consider significant in deciding whether or not to participate in the study". A comprehensive definition is given in the Belmont report (NCPHSBBR, 1979) as: "a possibility that harm may occur both in chance (probability) and severity (magnitude) of envision. The term 'benefit' refers to something of positive value related to health or welfare". Accordingly, risk/benefit assessments are concerned with the probabilities and magnitudes of possible harm and benefits.

The Spectrum of Risks and Benefits

1. **Types of Risks:** Participants can be harmed in various ways, including physically, psychologically, socially, economically, and legally. The first two types are the most common in biomedical research, while the latter are more frequent in social and behavioral research.

A Physical risk can be any type of bodily injury, pain or discomfort. These can be related to the type of research intervention or to the withdrawal of a certain standard treatment (washout) (CHOP, 2018).

A psychological risk can occur in stressful situations (e.g., the disclosure of sensitive information, such as an untreatable serious disease or the results of a survey regarding sensitive personal medical data). The "Milgram Obedience to Authority" experiment is a classic example of induced anxiety in psychological research (McLeod, 2007).

A social risk is mainly related to the invasion of privacy and/or breach of confidentiality. The first risk concerns the access to a person's body or behavior without his/ her consent (e.g., research involving observations of the participant's behavior). The second also concerns information about a person, but information that has been given voluntarily (e.g., collecting data from participant's school or hospital records). The harm due to the privacy invasion can be measured by considering the participant's reasonable expectations in a particular situation, the importance of the research in question, and the alternative reasons that can motivate the need for such an invasion of privacy.

An economic risk to participants may sometimes occur, such as payment for an expensive drug, time out of work, transportation or loss of insurance.

A participant's exposure to a legal risk can be expected in certain social and behavioral research (e.g. possession and use of illicit drugs, sexual or physical abuse).

The risks to third parties or to the society should also be considered (e.g., in vaccine trials, using active viruses, but of incomplete efficacy, which can expose an immune-compromised, non-participating subject to the infection).

In identifying risks, all stages of the study should be evaluated (e.g. procedures, experience of the researcher, and the research setting), as measures for privacy protection, resuscitation procedures, particular characteristics of research subjects etc.

All possible research-related risks should be explicitly shown in the research protocol, while clearly underlining the distinction from the risks of standard care. This may be problematic, especially in oncology studies, when the objective is assessing the long-term survival in current standard care possibilities.

2. **Types of Potential Benefits:** Research can directly benefit participants and can also impact the societal and scientific communities. A clinical improvement is a potential direct benefit in therapeutic trials. Participants of these trials may also gain indirect benefits (e.g., an ancillary care). Important dimensions of potential benefits (e.g., sustainability, scaling up and partnership) are particularly important in international research (Emanuel, Wendler, Killen, & Grady, 2004).

However, assessing potential benefits is sometimes difficult, because characterizing benefits is usually insufficiently elaborated in research protocols.

A reasonable financial compensation is justified, while paying incentives for participation is much more controversial and may be considered an undue inducement or a violation of the researcher-subject relationship. In a recent guidance protocol drafted by the FDA, the incentive for participation is not considered a benefit and it is acknowledged that this raises concerns about undue influence. It is important for both the reviewer and the participant to ensure that the research payment is fair and just, by regulating the payment amount, its justification, method of payment, and schedule for payments, which should be clearly delineated in the research protocol and in the informed consent form. Payment should be scheduled in several installments as the study progresses and not as a single installment, at the time the study is completed. Subjects who withdraw from the study will be paid for every completed stage of the research (Office of Good Clinical Practice, FDA, 2018a, 2018b).

Another non-tangible benefit to the participants is the satisfaction gained by contributing to science and the benefit of others, which is now viewed as a reflection of the principles of justice and respect. However, potential benefits to society don't justify a high-risk exposure, without a direct benefit to the participant, especially in vulnerable population groups, such as children (45 CFR 46. Sub-part D) (HHS, 2009b).

Measuring Risks and Benefits

The degree of risk is described as the rate of its occurrence, likelihood and severity. The latter involves the degree of damage, its duration, and consequences (Prentice, Bruce, & Gordon, 2016). The last parameter is emphasized by the FDA as important information to be included in the informed consent. Quantifying risks should be always attempted, even in difficult cases, such as phase one dose and toxicity trials, where risks are largely uncertain or when risks to a special group of patients are unknown (e.g., endoscopy-induced intestinal perforation in patients previously treated with high dose chemotherapy). Only direct short-term risks should be considered in the REC review.

The regulatory standard of "minimal risk" is defined as:" the probability and magnitude of harm or discomfort anticipated in the research are not greater in and of themselves than those ordinarily encountered in daily life or during the performance of routine physical or psychological examinations or tests" (45 CFR 46.102) (HHS, 2009a). However, it is unclear whether a "normal healthy person's" or a "research participant's" life, that have different risk tolerance and adaptability,-should be considered. For example, a bone marrow biopsy procedure may be better tolerated by a patient with a previous similar experience in his clinical care, than by a normal person. Arguments and public comments in this issue produced a change in the definition of minimal risk drafted by the FDA to "the daily lives of the subjects of research"(21CFR56). Prentice, Bruce, and Gordon (2016) recommended the implementation of a relative "minimal risk" standard (e.g., related to the participant's life) for competent adult participants exposed to interventions commensurate with their inherent medical care, while an absolute standard (. e.g., related to a normal person's life) was recommended for research involving vulnerable subjects. Rationally, accommodating the concept of a higher risk for participants with that of similar care experience, while allowing higher protection for healthy participants, provides flexibility in tailoring the degree of risk to the participant's condition, which is more practical.

Balancing Risks and Benefits in Clinical Research

Balancing risks and potential benefits is the most critical important step and may be the most difficult. Ensuring a favorable risk-benefit balance is embedded in the ethical principle of beneficence and is a requirement of all international codes and regulations for the Protection of Human Subjects. Regulations require that risks and benefits are weighed in relation to both the participant, as well as to society and science.

The concept of "prospect of direct benefit" recommends the evaluation of the potential benefits of each research intervention before determining whether its risk/benefit profile is equivalent to the available alternative. Interventions not providing a "prospect of direct benefit" may only be acceptable if their risks are justifiable by a social value. Friedman, Robbins and Wendler (2012) claimed an inadequacy of this definition for the protection of research participants and suggested limiting direct benefits to that of the intervention being tested. This approach is suggested as a method to restrict exposing vulnerable participants to riskier research procedures.

A term used in therapeutic trials is the "standard alternative therapy/care", but it may be difficult to assess which standard of care should be taken into consideration, whether it should be the best universal standard or the locally available one, which is especially important in limited-resources countries.

The incongruity between methods of measuring risks and benefits is another source of difficulty in assessing risk-benefit balance. It's even more difficult to weight the risk to participants against societal or science benefits. The latter corresponds to another principle, termed "the revised hybrid risk-weighing", which measures the total benefits against the risks to the individual, while determining the maximum level of risk allowed, based on the rational view of a reasonable person and not an extreme altruistic one.

Factors That May Influence Risk-Benefit Evaluation

The consistency of risk-benefit assessment in research review is important especially in multi-center studies, except for minor acceptable variations. Even when medical practice is regulated by the best conduct codes, some factors may influence the review decision (e.g., cultural and individual differences in values and perceptions, clinical experience, experience with research review, knowledge of certain biological processes, and the different perspectives of research stakeholders). For example, the word "risk" might be perceived as the "willingness to undertake some hardship to achieve the desired goal" or as "a condition carrying the possibility of harm to an individual".

In a study of factors that may influence REC decisions, Musschenga, Van Luijn, Keus, and Aaronson (2007) reported: the potential value of the trial to future patients and medical science, risks to participating patients, the expectation of a therapeutic benefit, and feeling comfortable in proposing the trial-based treatment to patients, as important influencing factors in a descending order. These authors also reported the "absence of clear criteria and uncertainty about benefits to patients" and the "study rationale" as factors that impact proper assessment of benefits. They outlined as well that it was difficult to evaluate in their study the inadequate knowledge about a given risk, the effect of a failed clinical trial treatment on patients' lives, and whether they would participate in the trial themselves. Moreover, influence of group dynamics and institutional culture were reported by Pritchard (2011) as supplementary criteria.

The progressive social and technological evolutions in recent decades, without a previous comparable knowledge of related risks, have created what has been termed by Show and Barrett (2006) as a "risky society" with increasing concern about assessment, management, communication, and monitoring of risk.

Awareness of these influences is important for improving decision making by research committees.

SECTION II: RISK-BENEFIT ASSESSMENT IN PRACTICE

An universal requirement in research review is to ensure a favorable risk-benefit balance, as stated in the Belmont report (NCPHSBBR, 1979): "Persons are treated in an ethical manner not only by respecting their decisions and protecting them from harm, but also by making efforts to secure their well-being". The report emphasized two general rules as complementary expressions of beneficence: "(1) do not harm and (2) maximize possible benefits and minimize possible harms". However, decisions in the real world are more complex and involve the perspectives of many parties. The risk-benefit evaluation is not a one-time job, but an ongoing process starting with planning the study and it that often extends beyond its end. It can change as the study progresses, alongwith the emergence of new information.

Accountability for Risk-Benefit Evaluation in Clinical Research Enterprise

The overall responsibility for the protection of human subjects is based on a collaborative dynamic relationship between investigators, institutions, sponsors and regulatory authorities, as well as the patients.

Communication between all parties will facilitate a safe and efficient manner to conduct the study, timely detection of errors, management of harm and reliable study results.

At the core of all responsibilities there is the sound professional judgment of the investigator and his research team. The research ethics committee has the pivotal role of assessing risks and benefits of research and of ensuring compliance with the approved protocol and the ethical principles. The oversight role of the research institute covers the administrative review of proposals, grants, and contracts, ensuring adherence to institutional policy and study budget, managing researcher conflict of interests, and providing scientific peer review (Dunn & Chadwick, 2012a).

Sponsors or investigator-sponsors of new drug trials should comply with all regulatory requirements for pre- and post-market approvals.

The Data safety monitoring committee/board (DSMB) represents a group of experts who are independent of the research team and who repeatedly assess and report on the safety of research participants and validate the trial through reviewing accumulating data from the study. Assigning a DSMB is especially required in complex or high-risk studies and in drug trials (Dunn and Chadwick, 2012b).

The role of the regulatory authority overrides all previous roles of third parties, because the regulatory authority has the ultimate responsibility for managing the whole system for protection of human subjects and public welfare. The US "Department of Health and Human Service" Federal Code, the FDA and the "European Medicines Agency" of the European Union are the main regulatory authorities worldwide. Other national authorities and research organizations have some contributions. (provisions relevant to the roles of different parties can be found in the Federal Code - HHS.45CFR.46.107, 109, 112 (2009 - and FDA 21 CFR Subpart B 56.106, 312.50 (2017)).

Approaches to Risk-Benefit Assessment in Clinical Research

No specific methodology for risk-benefit assessment is recommended by regulatory agencies. Meanwhile, the complexity of research studies and the development of novel therapeutics are progressively increasing, which stems an eminent need for comprehensive, systematic analysis methods.

Selecting a methodology is largely determined by the research objective, the type, the complexity, the potential risk, the treatment type, and the patient's condition.

1. **Types of Systematic Risk-Benefit Analysis:** A qualitative analysis contextualizes the research process, while a quantitative analysis identifies relevant measures, then gives weight to the first. The latter requires sufficient data and clear understanding of the tradeoffs between risks and benefits. For a minimal complexity-study with clearly identified risks and benefits, a qualitative analysis may be sufficient. More complex scenarios, particularly for drug approval, require comprehensive quantitative approaches. Several frameworks have been developed for both types of analysis, to be used by various stakeholders.
    a. **Common Qualitative Analysis Frameworks:** Among the common qualitative methods, four have been developed to be used mainly by RECs, namely: 'component analysis', 'agreement principle', 'integrative approach', and the 'net risks test'. The last one is claimed to be a superior method. It was developed by Wendler and Miller (2007) based on four ethical requirements: minimizing each procedure's risk and maximizing its benefits to participants or society, while ensuring that no excessive risk occurs; ensuring favorable risk-benefit balance of the new interventions compared to the clinical alternatives; justification of net risks in light of the

expected social gain; and finally, ensuring that net risks of all procedures is not excessive. This approach provides a reasonable consistency, risk reduction and benefit enhancement, and avoidance of excessive risk. However, the lack of a clear definition of "excessive risk" may be confusing.

In a methodological analysis of the risk-benefit evaluation procedure by the RECs, Bernabe, van Thiel, Raaijmakers, and van Delden (2012) claimed that the common qualitative analysis approaches are procedural-level methods, with no distinction between the four sequential analytical steps, namely risk-benefit analysis, risk-benefit evaluation, risk treatment, and decision making, which are sometimes used interchangeably. This distinction is important in defining the responsibility limits of the RECs, whose task doesn't involve all assessment steps. Based on these authors' analysis, the RECs work is limited to: evaluation of risks and benefits, appraising risk treatment, and making a final decision. On the other hand, the risk analysis step is a more complex analytical procedure, which is beyond the capacity of the RECs and it is a function of the sponsor or medical drug developers. They recommended a deeper analysis beyond the procedure-level to build a more efficient REC review system.

b. **Common Quantitative Analysis Frameworks:** Many quantitative analytical methods have been proposed by regulatory agencies and drug developers to support accurate decisions. The EMA, the Pharmaceutical Research and Manufacturers of America Benefit-Risk Action Team (PhRMA BRAT), the Centre for Innovation in Regulatory Sciences (CIRS), BRAIN (Benefit-Risk Assessment in New and Old Drugs), and the FDA 5-step framework are examples of proposed initiatives. These methods can incorporate a wide variety of trial measures, as "number needed to treat" and "number needed to harm", patient-centric approach, data sources, multiplicity subgroup analysis, data visualization, endpoint selection, weight determination, uncertainty evaluation, and extension of the stochastic multi-criteria discriminatory method. However, these methods have been criticized for lack of flexibility, complexity, and inability to communicate risk and benefit' parameters, which hindered their widespread implementation.

Following the evaluation of available methodologies, a number of frameworks and summary visualization tools were developed for regulatory use, such as the EMA "Problem formulation, Objectives, Alternatives, Consequences, Trade-offs, Uncertainties, Risk Tolerance, and Linked Decisions framework "(PrOACT-URL) (Rid and Wendler, 2010).

Meanwhile, a structured framework was developed by the FDA and other agencies in 2009, with a set of commitments, detailed in the "Performance Goals and Procedures document PDUFAV" (FY 2013-2017) (Rosenberg, 2017). It also served as a template for product reviews and a tool for documenting decision reasoning with the aim of enhancing transparency. The International Council for Harmonization of Technical Requirements for Pharmaceuticals for Human Use (ICH) Expert Working Group (2016) recently released the "Common Technical Document (CTD), Section 2.5.6 guidance on Benefit-Risk Evaluations", in order to standardize the key risks and benefits, the therapeutic context, and the main decision problems, together with the content and information to be submitted.

In an initiative to unify risk-benefit assessment methods, an universal framework was proposed by a Consortium of four regulatory authorities, the Australian Therapeutic Goods Administration (TGA), Health Canada, Swiss medic and Singapore Health Sciences Authority (HSA), and the Centre for Innovation in Regulatory Science (CIRS), to support joint and shared views and serve as an universal template for their regulatory review and as an evolving document (Walker, McAuslane, Liberti, Leong, & Salek, 2015). It incorporates criteria from other frameworks and is intended to be used by both pharmaceutical companies and regulatory agencies. The development of valid models and prospective studies is required to guide its real-world implementation.

Furthermore, the post-approval withdrawals of many products with high therapeutic potential in the past decade raised a dilemma about how to balance rapid access to new drugs and the collection of sufficient efficacity and safety data . Another crucial question concerns the added value of the new drug compared to other alternative treatments. Answering these questions requires a clear understanding of data generation and benefit and risk measurements, aided by advanced analytical methods applied by pharmaceutical developers.

Many of the quantitative methods developed are based on the "direct-elicitation" and "conjoint analysis" concepts explained by Hauber, Angelyn, Fairchild, and Johnson (2013).

A set of methods termed "multiple criteria decision analysis (MCDA)" techniques constitute a more explicit approach for decision-making, and were developed by "ISPOR" Health Science Policy Council in 2014 - all system documents are available on the council website at http://www.ispor.org/Multi-Criteria-Decision-Analysis-guideline.asp (Marsh et al., 2016). However, concerns about the relevance of their score and possible bias were raised by Garcia-Hernandez (2015).

Changes thereafter were developed to increase sensitivity, and add new dimensions to the MCDA model (e.g., probabilistic sensitivity analysis of weighted-sum score and use of statistical methods to quantify the variability of the risk-benefit score and estimate true sampling distribution). The integration of pharmacokinetic-pharmacodynamics (PKPD) data is also suggested for evaluating effectiveness trials of novel therapeutics and optimization of their protocol design (Bellanti van Wijk, Danhof, & Pasqua, 2015).

Integrating patients' preferences into the risk-benefit decision process is a recently supported endeavor of the pharmaceutical industry to improve trial performance and establish efficiency, especially in cancer trials (Matsuyama, Reddy, & Smith, 2006). However, patient-centricity faces many implementation barriers - e.g., different international legal requirements, data privacy, regulatory frameworks, and behavioral constraints studies (Largent et al., 2018).

Recent Trends in Clinical Research Impacting Risk-Benefit Balance

The fast advances in the recent data science era have reshaped many aspects of clinical research practice, with a special impact on drug development.

1. **Data-Driven Research and Development in Drug Industry:** Developments in data analytics technology, together with the emergence of big data from advanced biological analysis (e.g., genome- associated studies) have created an unprecedented opportunity for hastening drug development, yet with some challenges. In clinical research, collected data includes much more than the patient's medical record, such as knowledge about personal behavior and risk attitudes - e.g., data from outside the healthcare field (Resnick, Kessler, Aitken, & Metz, 2017). Critical to generating meaningful data is the strict adherence to protocols and authorizing steps and vigilance procedures in order to identify errors and systematic failures. Generated data should have statistical relevance, be adequately stored, communicated, and analyzed. The most common data-analytic approaches

used for drug development decisions are predictive modeling, cluster analysis, data mining, and decision trees. The expanding applications of data science technology provide many advantages and added value to the continuum of the clinical research enterprise. Table 1 outlines some of the common applications of data science.

a. **Challenges to Data Analytics Technology Implementation:** The innate complexity of data processing and applying measures to assure accuracy, quality, and interoperability, which are important to avoid errors and delays in trial data, require a special technical expertise and skills (Veeva, 2017). Additional measures are required for privacy protection, taking into consideration the conditions that impose increased privacy risk. All these make any implementation of a data analysis platform technically and financially demanding. The requirement for bio-repositories, a pre-requisite for generating data, adds further to the challenge. Strategic alliances are emerging together with new business models to maintain a seamless continuity in drug industry, by incorporating multidisciplinary expertise and other resources (Park & Molloy, 2018).

A challenge is also facing regulators and research reviewers, due to the need for special expertise. In 2017, the FDA initiated a new "Digital Health Unit" to provide the required special technical consultation.

b. **Data Sharing and Information Disclosure:** Sharing trial data and disclosure of information regarding approval decisions are recently promoted to enhance drug development, regulatory approvals, communication, and transparency in clinical research. The full potential of data sharing requires an implementation policy, funding, standards for data quality, and regulations for responsible conduct. Examples of regulatory initiatives in this respect are the EU EMA and Therapeutic Goods Administration (TGA) in Australia', which are published evaluation

Table 1. Applications of Data Science Tools in Drug Development and Clinical Trials

Drug Development	Clinical Trial Performance and Outcome
Selection of a lead compound, the critical step in drug development (Lusher, McGuire, van Schaik, Nicholson, & de Vlieg, 2014)	Early communication in trial design and conduction of multidisciplinary studies through data visualization suite "cyber commons" (Cattel et al., 2013)
Prediction of toxicity, phospholipidosis mechanism, protein target and bioactivity classifications of drug-like molecules through machine-learning (Lavecchia, 2015),	Early stopping of Futile Trials (Griffiths, Angus, & Brown, 2018)
Development of novel therapeutics (Woodcock, 2017)	Detection of regulatory inspection findings to improve trial compliance (Shetty & Saiyed, 2014)
Development and validation of predictive biomarkers and diagnostic tests	Predictive analysis and early clinical risk intervention. (Cattel et al., 2013)
Digital biomarkers development through data captured from biosensors and used for monitoring, diagnosis, and outcome prediction (Ladanyi & Ruane, 2018)	Automated external and internal reporting (Cattel et al., 2013)
Accurate judgment of bio-similarity (Franco, Porta, Holliday, & Willett, 2017).	Timely reporting and decision making through mobile technology (Downing et al., 2017),
	Facilitate patient centricity through mobile data capture tools thus improving patient engagement, adherence, compliance, and outcome measures (Cattel et al., 2013)

Source: This table is the author's collective summary from the references cited within.

reports (Papathanasiou et al., 2016), and the FDA approach for the exchange of information related to the initiation, investment, and effective use of certain treatments and innovative technology (Rosenberg, 2017).

First of all, sharing data is an attribute of a responsible conduct in research, which emphasizes transparency, openness, and reproducibility. Shared data should be legally acceptable, technically readable, and available to others. The "Committee on Strategies for Responsible Sharing of Clinical Trial Data"; "Board on Health Sciences Policy"; "Institute of Medicine" (2015) recently issued the document entitled "Guiding Principles for Sharing Clinical Trial Data", which also raised the issue of ownership over possible emerging benefits. Four standards were proposed for the shared data: being findable, accessible, interoperable, and reproducible.

The potential ethical and regulatory challenges in data sharing include: the privacy and security issues, participants' autonomy, cultural issues, and commercial potential, together with appropriate governance and database sustainability measures.

The "Global Alliance for Genomics and Health" proposed key principles for the sharing of genetic data, including the ownership rights of the contributing investigators (Fingert, 2018).

c. **Pre-Clinical Ex-Vivo Human Biological Test Systems:** An innovative approach for preclinical drug testing is the human pathways-based paradigm, originally applied in toxicology and at this point dependent on specific disease pathways at multiple biological scales. It allows the detection of early endpoints, that are predictive of adverse effects in an approach termed 'adverse outcome pathway' (AOP) framework, which is a conceptual construct delineating the chain of events from the toxic exposure to the adverse outcome. An EU project was initiated to support the "mechanism-based toxicity testing and risk assessment" for the 21st century (www.eu-to risk.eu/) (Langley et al., 2016), which requires the development of repositories, disease databases, sharing of expertise and dedicated funding.

SECTION III: DIFFICULT DECISIONS IN RISK-BENEFIT EVALUATION

Certain study contexts, participant populations, or types of therapy may be challenging to risk-benefit decisions, due to reasons like insufficient efficacy or safety evidence, small population size, complex biologic drug effects etc.

Rare Diseases

The unique challenges of rare diseases include: their pathologic and clinical complexity, small patient numbers with wide geographical distribution, low national frequencies and therefore low public health interest, and mostly disease triggering during childhood, with no established diagnostic criteria and high morbidity and mortality. In addition, most of these diseases have no available effective therapy and no sufficient biological, clinical or therapeutic data to support drug development. Confirmatory efficacy trials are therefore difficult (Snyder & Nelson, 2018).

Proposals for resolution were suggested, including the use of Real World Evidence (RWE), consideration of disease stage, patient's lifestyle, patient-focused design, and validated surrogate biomarkers.

In addition, granting a commercial advantage for orphan drug developers was a successful approach sustained by the regulatory agencies (e.g., the higher cost of therapy, government incentives, smaller and shorter trials, extended exclusivity, and favorable regulatory scrutiny). These are drafted in documents of the FDA (21st Century Cure Act) and the EU (Adaptive Regulatory Pathway).

Meanwhile, promotion of natural history studies and patient registries will improve the trial design, endpoint selection, outcome measures, and patients' recruitment. The inclusion of patients' and families' perspectives and the cooperation of multi-stakeholders throughout trial milestones will improve compliance and assessment of risks and benefits (Maier, 2018).

Therapeutic Novelty

Novel therapies, often based on specific molecular disease pathogenesis, are promising agents especially in cancer patients, but are also challenging to develop and to approve. Concerns may be related to trial design, clinical outcome endpoints, knowledge of their complex biological actions, suitable animal models, and knowledge of their long-term effects and toxicity.

Alternative trial designs and regulatory frameworks were proposed, with promising potential outcomes, including: regulatory oversight of lab-developed tests, setting standards for clinical validity, and taking a risk-based approach.

While testing these drugs, extrapolating their efficiency and safety, including accepting surrogate endpoints, such as "progression-free survival" for the primary analysis, can be used for regulatory decisions, as expressed in a concept paper by the EMA (2013). However, this approach is controversial; unless a substantial effect is obtained (e.g., when clinical benefit is shown to be more effective when compared head-to-head to standard techniques) and toxicity is "manageable" and "acceptable".

Other alternative end-points have been suggested (e.g., treatment-emergent signs and symptoms and severe adverse effects). These can be used in cancer patients, but we can't estimate the actual proportion of adverse events.

Marketing authorization is often granted together with an approved risk-management plan (Eichler, Pignatti, Flamion, Leufkens, & Breckenridge, 2008). The FDA recently released the "ADVANCING HEALTH THROUGH INNOVATION: 2017 NEW DRUG THERAPY APPROVALS" report (2017), which demonstrates the use of innovative tools and cooperation in order to enhance decision efficiency and expedite drug approval.

Moreover, the development and validation of biomarkers is increasingly used in novel drug trials. The validation can be done through biomarker trials or alternatively through retrospective studies (EMA, 2010). Similarly, the development and validation of diagnostic tests were recommended by the FDA to ensure safe and effective use of targeted therapy (Scherf, Becker, Chan, & Hojvat, 2010).

Concerns about stem cell research and regenerative medicine are related to the lack of pre-clinical evidence and suitable animal models, criteria for the inclusion of patients, equity and fairness in the selection of participants, and the adequacy of risk minimization. Additionally, the biological nature of cells may pose further risks related to the effect of in vitro propagation, undefined persistence in the body, and the ability for an undesired proliferation, differentiation, or function in the body. The recurrent failures and dramatic accidents in clinical use of stem cell therapy, together with the shortage of forecasting methods based on experimental evidence make evaluation particularly critical.

Recently, a regulatory requirement for third-party-inspection and government reporting of cell-culturing and treatment by medical facilities has been proposed in order to monitor the safety of regenerative medicine, while giving guidance for the degree of processing that will trigger inspection. A comprehensive policy framework was also developed by the FDA, which describes an efficient, science-based process to enhance safety and effectiveness of cell therapies (FDA, 2017c). The International Society for Stem Cell Research (ISSCR, 2016) drafted a comprehensive technical guideline to assure safety of cell products.

Gene transfer therapeutics raise an additional concern of using genetically modified viruses to deliver genetic materials, which pose a biosafety risk to study participants, their households, and the research personnel. Risk-minimization, in these cases, requires specific biosafety protection and review, supervision from a recombinant DNA Advisory Committee, adequate informed consent, and absence of an alternative effective therapy. A logical frame for ethical evaluation of gene transfer trials was proposed by Swazo (2006).

Phase I and First-In-Human Trials

The basic ethical concern in these conditions is exposing an individual to risks, for the potential benefit of future patients or society, but also limiting risks, from an altruistic view. Other concerns include questionable benefits, uncertainty about risks, difficulties with informed consent, conflicts of interests, exploitation, and disparities in international settings. The possibility of "coercion" or "undue inducement" through financial incentives should also be considered.

Certain phase-I studies are particularly risky (e.g., psychiatric symptom-provoking studies, infection challenge experiments, and toxicology research involving monitored drug overdoses). It was recommended by Kimmelman and London (2011) that certain measures could support risk-benefit decisions, such as careful attention to the quality and methodology of preclinical experiments, and examination of the trial outcome of biologically-related agents.

Incidents of healthy volunteer deaths or major disability are not uncommon in these trials and draw the attention to potential weaknesses in research regulations (FDA, 2017a). Famous examples are the tragic death of a healthy volunteer in a study on the pathophysiology of asthma in 2001, and the death and serious neurological damage of healthy volunteers in a French first-in-human trial. As a result, EMA developed a new regulatory requirement (February, 2018), imposing a comprehensive strategy regarding preclinical testing, drug dosing, safety monitoring, and clear risk-minimization for each research step, together with timely management of adverse events (Feldwisch-Drentrup, 2017).

Life-Threatening Conditions and Compassionate Use of Experimental Drugs

For marketing authorization of therapeutics for life-threatening and terminal illnesses, the FDA subpart E 21 CFR 312.80-88 grants accelerated approval and the EMA provides a conditional authorization, both being based on early evidence of efficacy for an unmet medical need with related uncertainties (Pignattia, Jonssonb, Blumenthale, & Justice, 2015).

The decision about "Compassionate use" or "expanded access" of an experimental drug in absence of an effective treatment is more complex. It requires both the FDA approval (subpart I 21 CFR 312.300-320) and the agreement of the drug manufacturer, these being often delayed due to issues such as cost coverage. The FDA and REC must approve each use and ensure sufficient safety and effectiveness, and also that the probable risk is not greater than the patient's disease (FDA, 2009). Recently, a criticism to the prolonged approval process was raised in favor of the new "right to try" law. However, this view was greatly opposed by many physicians, regulators, families and other groups for exposing many patients to risk in trade of false hopes and also for undermining the FDA's safety rules (Carome, 2018).

Research in International Settings Involving Developing Countries

The unfair selection and the injustice have always been considered potential ethical challenges in international research, often related to conditions of poverty, limited healthcare resources, illiteracy, culture and linguistic differences, variable perceptions of risk and benefit, importance of research, inadequate regulatory infrastructure and research oversight, less stringent review, under-reporting of side effects, and lower risk of litigation (SciDev Net, 2011). Additionally, the offshoring of trials to developing countries for economic and logistical reasons and the lack of transparency of CROs and of the pharmaceutical companies are also of concern.

In the review of international research studies, some regulatory terms may be differently interpreted (e.g. "the standard of care", "the reasonable availability of interventions" and the "quality of informed consent").

In spite of all fears, the fair inclusion of developing countries in the research is an important reflection of justice and equity, the providing of a fair distribution and of benefits also being granted. Enhancing ethical conduct of international research, therefore, became an important initiative adopted by many parties including; regulators, funders, bioethicists, and researchers.

Emanuel, Wendler, Killen, and Grady (2004) proposed a series of specific and practical benchmarks - such as guidance - and added the principle of "collaborative partnership" to be considered as a research benefit. This partnership parameter is intended to identify important health problems, plans, conduct, and oversee research, and to integrate the proposed research into the healthcare system of the host country. However, the lack of effective research infrastructure in these countries is an important limitation to a sustainable international cooperation.

Benefits can cover many infrastructural requirements in developing countries (e.g. improving researchers' skills and developing appropriate research programs). Examples for these initiatives are the "collaborative African genomics network training program" (Mlotshwa et al., 2017) and the "African Malaria Network Trust (AMANET)" (www.amanet-trust.org); both are sustainable genomic networks in Africa supporting research and training.

Recommendations for worldwide mandatory clinical trial registration, overseeing research sites, and publicity of audit reports are recommended to enhance ethical conduct and transparency (IQPC, 2011).

The needs for vaccines development together with the critical issues associated with their trials in developing countries have derived a changing approach to vaccines development and deployment from cost-effectiveness to a multi-criteria decision-making with the overall goal of aligning the priorities and the objectives of public and private stakeholders. The decisions in these cases are based on the core concepts of (i) mortality and severity of the disease, (ii) vaccine safety considerations, and (iii) economic evaluation that captures the full benefits of vaccination (Mlotshwa et al., 2017).

Another approach to benefit in international research is the provision of ancillary care (e.g. health care needs which are not part of the research) either locally, at the research place or by referral agreement with another healthcare facility (Krubiner, Sayd & Merritt, 2016).

Pregnant Women in Clinical Research

The longstanding under-representation of pregnant women in research resulted in an inadequate efficacy and safety evidence in their drug trials and it also challenge their risk-benefit evaluations. This has been mainly related to the uncertain fetal risk. In addition, the vagueness of the regulatory terms as "fair inclusion" and "compelling scientific justification" further complicate the evaluation.

Meanwhile, an increasing need for development of new drugs for this group is recognized when facing the uncertain safety of using drugs approved for other populations, with other drug-metabolizing profiles. This requirement is further promoted by bioethicists and researchers and by emerging regulatory guidelines such as The Council for International Organizations of Medical Sciences in collaboration with the World Health Organization (WHO) guideline for the evaluation of research in pregnant women (CIOMS, 2016). Yet, no much progress was observed as only 1% of pharmacokinetic trials reported between 1960 and 2013 included pregnant women.

Promoting fair inclusion of pregnant women in research is based on two aspects of justice - equity and corrective justice - which refer to the equal treatment of all illegible research participants and respectively to the prioritization of the inclusion of this group, since they are underrepresented in research.

The National Institutes of Health's Policy and Guideline (2001 amendment), recommends separate large trials of pregnant women since a definite evidence of differences in drug effects between pregnant and non-pregnant women is often difficult to obtain. Otherwise post-marketing studies are suggested instead (van der Graaf et al., 2018).

Pediatric Clinical Trials

Despite an international commitment for the control of neglected diseases, new medicines for children have been lagging much behind those for adults with increased off-label and unlicensed prescriptions, potentially compromising children health. While it is legitimate to include children in the valuable and scientifically valid study, it is equally a neglect and under-protection not to include them (Kopitowski, 2014). The question is how to balance the justice of "fair selection" with the injustice of "under-representation" without compromising the risk-benefit balance?

The European Union (2006) released a directive for the pediatric medicinal products which proposed several rewards and incentives for drug companies including: an extension of supplementary protection certificate with the provision of a pediatric investigation plan in the product information, a market exclusivity for orphan pediatric drugs, a pediatric-use marketing authorization (PUMA) with 10 years of market protection for drugs not protected by a patent or supplementary protection certificate, and free scientific advice and protocol assistance. Likewise, the US "Pediatric Research Equity Act" (2003) and the "Best Pharmaceuticals for Children Act" (AAP, 2007) provided similar incentives. It has been recommended that pediatric trials to be started with older children.

The regulatory standards of "minimal risk" and "minor increase over minimal risk" are sometimes difficult to apply by RECs leaving a great chance for intuitive decisions. Some logistic difficulties may also delay pediatric trials (e.g. lack of standard endpoint measures, informed consent issues, and the need for special protection in this vulnerable group).

The FDA recommended a simple decision flowchart based on the comparative effectiveness of the drug to the adults. A similar effect will indicate only pharmacokinetic and safety studies, while a difference indicates further need for pharmacodynamics and efficacy studies using pragmatic trials. (CDER, 2014).

Some critical risk-benefit decisions encountered in pediatric trials are related to "a research posing more than minor increase over minimal risk and no prospect of direct benefit yet yielding very important knowledge", "a phase-I healthy volunteer trials", "first in human trials", and "the use of placebo".

Among the examples of the first situation there are: a research on stem cell donation by healthy children to their siblings which provides no benefit to the donor, and controlled trials of therapeutic hypothermia for perinatal hypoxic-ischemic encephalopathy, which later prove to be effective. According to regulations, both cases are un-approvable by the REC and the federal referral in these cases will delay and complicate the study. In addition, with the emergence of an evidence of effectiveness in the second case, it became unethical to include further controls in the non-treatment arm (Laventhal, Tarini, & Lantos, 2012).

In the second situation, the EU regulations are very restrictive for phase-I healthy volunteer and first-in-human pediatric trials. However, few exceptions are allowed (e.g. immunogenicity studies and vaccine trials which are essentially used for a healthy population -McIntosh, 2011). In unique pediatric diseases where experimental therapies must first be tried in pediatric patients, 2 ethical dilemmas arise: the prospect of direct benefit and selecting the starting dose. In these cases, early evidence based on in vitro, in silica, and preclinical animal studies could be considered.

In the third situation, placebo-controlled trails are restricted in children. But alternative designs are suggested - such as non-inferiority studies, yet with questionable reliability, being limited by the effectiveness of the active comparator (Podany, 2017).

Overall, a strong evidence for pediatric drugs development requires optimization of trial designs and monitoring, pharmacovigilance, development of centers of excellence for pediatric trials, capacity building, and data sharing with the wide collaboration of all stakeholders (Kshirsagar et al., 2017).

RECOMMENDATIONS

The changing paradigm of clinical research requires a new infrastructure plan integrating technology, new skills, more networking and collaboration. Education of new researchers should consider the new skills and knowledge and should be open to continuous updating.

FUTURE RESEARCH DIRECTIONS

It is suggested promoting empirical research of the attitudes and the perceptions of patients and their families in developing countries towards wide-scope genetic analysis and other advanced analytic procedures of hereditary diseases, which are often understudied and have substantial health and economic impacts.

A survey of the knowledge and skills gaps of researchers and reviewers at institutions about recent analytical methods for decision-making in risk-benefit evaluation is required to modernize research infrastructure and improve research efficiency and patients' safety.

CONCLUSION

Risk and benefit evaluation is the pillar for decision-making by many research stakeholders and at different times. Awareness of the wide scope of risks and benefits and the factors which may affect their evaluation is important for a proper judgment. Ensuring a favorable risk-benefit balance is a complex process with many interacting factors including individual values and perception, and professional experience.

The increasing complexity of the research context and the rapid development of novel therapeutics require a precise method of evaluation. Development of more objective approaches for analysis progressed from simple decision frameworks to complex statistical models.

The type, amount, and quality of data collected determine the ability to take a decision. Recently, the advanced analytical technology allows the utilization of large volume of data to extract important information for decision-making, thus improving and economizing every stage in the clinical research from molecule selection to drug approval.

Some ethical challenges are still evolving in the research field and require further regulatory actions and analysis models.

ACKNOWLEDGMENT

This work received no specific grant from any funding agency in the public, commercial, or not-for-profit sectors.

REFERENCES

American Academy of Pediatrics (AAP). (2007). Best Pharmaceuticals for Children Act Pediatric Research Equity Act. 2007 Reauthorization. Improvements to existing law 110th Congress: H.R. 3580. *Public Law*, 110–185. Retrieved from https://www.aap.org/en-us/advocacy-and-policy/federal-advocacy/Documents/bpcapreasidexside.pdf

Bellanti, F., van Wijk, R. C., Danhof, M., & Pasqua, O. D. (2015). Integration of PKPD relationships into benefit–risk analysis. *British Journal of Clinical Pharmacology, 80*(5), 979–991. doi:10.1111/bcp.12674 PMID:25940398

Bernabe, R. D. L. C., van Thiel, G. J. M. W., Raaijmakers, J. A. M., & van Delden, J. J. M. (2012). The risk-benefit task of research ethics committees: An evaluation of current approaches and the need to incorporate decision studies methods. *BMC Medical Ethics, 13*(1), 6–15. doi:10.1186/1472-6939-13-6 PMID:22520714

Carome, M. A. (2018). *Right-to-try legislation offers false hope and would endanger patients*. Retrieved from https://www.statnews.com/2018/01/16/right-to-try-legislation-patients/

Cattell, J., Chilukuri, S., & Levy, M. (2013). *How big data can revolutionize pharmaceutical R&D*. McKinsey & Company Home Pharmaceuticals & Medical Products. Retrieved from https://www.mckinsey.com/industries/pharmaceuticals-and-medical-products/our-insights/how-big-data-can-revolutionize-pharmaceutical-r-and-d

Center for Drug Evaluation and Research (CDER). (2014). Pediatric study planning and extrapolation algorithm. In U.S. Department of Health and Human Services, Food and Drug Administration (Ed.), *General Clinical Pharmacology Considerations for Pediatric Studies for Drugs and Biological Products. Guidance for Industry* (p. 23). Author. Retrieved from https://www.fda.gov/downloads/drugs/guidances/ucm425885.pdf

Children's Hospital of Philadelphia (CHOP) Research Institute. (2018). *Risk and benefit.* Retrieved from https://irb.research.chop.edu/risk-and-benefit

Code of Federal Regulations of 2009, codified as amended at 45CFR46 § A-102. (n.d.). Retrieved from https://www.hhs.gov/ohrp/sites/default/files/ohrp/humansubjects/regbook2013.pdf.pdf

Code of Federal Regulations of 2009, codified as amended at 45CFR46 § D. (n.d.). Retrieved from https://www.hhs.gov/ohrp/regulations-and-policy/regulations/45-cfr 46/index.html#subpartd

Code of Federal Regulations of 2009 revised as of April 1, 2017 at 21CFR312.1 § 312-I. (n.d.). Retrieved from https://www.ecfr.gov/cgi-bin/text-idx?SID=c859616b5a665bbcda13092d0c1c063d&node=sp21.5.312.i&rgn=div6

Code of Federal Regulations of 2009, revised as of April, 2017, 21CFR56, § A-B-56. (n.d.). Retrieved from https://www.accessdata.fda.gov/scripts/cdrh/cfdocs/cfcfr/CFRSearch.cfm?CFRPart=56&showFR=1

Committee on Strategies for Responsible Sharing of Clinical Trial Data, Board on Health Sciences Policy, Institute of Medicine. (2015). *Sharing clinical trial data, maximizing benefits, minimizing risk.* Washington, DC: National Academies Press. Retrieved from https://www.ncbi.nlm.nih.gov/books/NBK269030/

Council for International Organizations of Medical Sciences (CIOMS). (2016). International ethical guidelines for health-related research involving humans. *Guideline 19: Pregnant and breastfeeding women as research participants.* Retrieved from https://cioms.ch/wp-content/uploads/2017/01/WEB-CIOMS-EthicalGuidelines.pdf

Downing, N. S., Shah, N. D., Aminawung, J. A., Pease, A. M., Zeitoun, J. D., Krumholz, H. M., & Ross, J. S. (2017). Post market safety events among novel therapeutics approved by the US Food and Drug Administration between 2001 and 2010. *Journal of the American Medical Association, 317*(18), 1854–1863. doi:10.1001/jama.2017.5150 PMID:28492899

Dunn, C. M., & Chadwick, G. L. (2012a). *FDA-regulated research in: Protecting study volunteers in research* (4th ed.). Boston: Center Watch.

Dunn, C. M., & Chadwick, G. L. (2012b). *Special ethical concerns in clinical research in: Protecting study volunteers in research* (4th ed.). Boston: Center Watch.

Eichler, H. G., Pignatti, F., Flamion, B., Leufkens, H., & Breckenridge, A. (2008). Balancing early market access to new drugs with the need for benefit/risk data: A mounting dilemma. *Nature Reviews. Drug Discovery, 7*(10), 818–826. doi:10.1038/nrd2664 PMID:18787530

Emanuel, E. J., Wendler, D., Killen, J., & Grady, C. (2004). What makes clinical research in developing countries ethical? The benchmarks of ethical research. *The Journal of Infectious Diseases, 189*(5), 930–937. doi:10.1086/381709 PMID:14976611

European Medicines Agency (EMA). (2010). *ICH guideline E16 on genomic biomarkers related to drug response: Context, structure and format of qualification submissions*. Retrieved from http://www.ema.europa.eu/docs/en_GB/document_library/Scientificguideline/2010/09/WC500097060.pdf

European Medicines Agency (EMA), Human Medicines Development and Evaluation. (2013). *Concept paper on extrapolation of efficacy and safety in medicine development*. Retrieved from http://www.ema.europa.eu/docs/en_GB/document_library/Scientific_guideline/2013/04/WC500142358.pdf

European Parliament and the Council of the European Union. (2006). Regulation (EC) No. 1901/2006 of the European Parliament and of the Council of 2006, December 12 on medicinal products for pediatric use and amending Regulation (EEC) No1768/92, Directive 2001/20/EC, Directive 2001/83/EC and Regulation (EC) No 726/2004. *Official Journal of the European Union, L, 378*(1). Retrieved from https://ec.europa.eu/health//sites/health/files/files/eudralex/vol-1/reg_2006_1901/reg_2006_1901_en.pdf

Feldwisch-Drentrup, H. (2017, August 1). After French drug trial tragedy, European Union issues new rules to protect study volunteers. *Science*. doi:10.1126cience.aan7191

Fingert, H. J. (2018). Expanding role of data science and bioinformatics in drug discovery and development. *Clinical Pharmacology and Therapeutics, 103*(1), 47–49. doi:10.1002/cpt.912 PMID:29134636

Food and Drug Administration (FDA). (2017c). *FDA announces comprehensive regenerative medicine policy framework. FDA news release*. Retrieved from https://www.fda.gov/NewsEvents/Newsroom/PressAnnouncements/ucm585345.htm

Food and Drug Administration (FDA) Center for Drug Evaluation and Research. (2017a). *Advancing health through innovation. 2017 New drug therapy approvals*. Retrieved from https://www.fda.gov/downloads/AboutFDA/CentersOffices/OfficeofMedicalProductsandTobacco/CDER/ReportsBudgets/UCM591976.pdf

Franco, P., Porta, N., Holliday, J. D., & Willett, P. (2017). Molecular similarity considerations in the licensing of orphan drugs. *Drug Discovery Today, 22*(2), 377–381. doi:10.1016/j.drudis.2016.11.024 PMID:27965161

Friedman, A., Robbins, E., & Wendler, D. (2012). Which benefits of research participation count as 'direct'? *Bioethics, 26*(2), 60–67. doi:10.1111/j.1467-8519.2010.01825.x PMID:20497168

Garcia-Hernandez, A. (2015). A note on the validity and reliability of multi-criteria decision analysis for the benefit–risk assessment of medicines. *Drug Safety, 38*(11), 1049–1057. doi:10.100740264-015-0344-2 PMID:26353915

Griffiths, A., Angus, J. P., & Brown, A. N. (2018). *Revolutionizing clinical trials through real-time data capture and analytics*. Retrieved from http://www.appliedclinicaltrialsonline.com/print/349625?page=full&topic=230%2C%20250&CID=actdirect.1988127.APCT%2A%2520Applied%252

Hauber, A. B., Angelyn, O., Fairchild, F., & Johnson, R. (2013). Quantifying benefit–risk preferences for medical interventions: An overview of a growing empirical literature. *Applied Health Economics and Health Policy, 11*(4), 319–329. doi:10.100740258-013-0028-y PMID:23637054

International Council for Harmonisation of Technical Requirements for Pharmaceuticals for Human Use (ICH). (2016). *ICH M8 Expert Working Group. Specification for submission formats for eCTD v1.1.* Retrieved from http://estri.ich.org/ssf/Specification_for_Submission_Formats_for_eCTD_v1_1.pdf

International Society for Stem Cell Research (ISSCE). (2016). *Guidelines for stem cell research and clinical translation.* Retrieved from http://www.isscr.org/professional-resources/policy/2016-guidelines

Kimmelman, J., & London, A. J. (2011). Predicting harms and benefits in translational trials: Ethics, evidence, and uncertainty. *PLoS Medicine*, *8*(3). doi:10.1371/journal.pmed.1001010 PMID:21423344

Kopitowski, K. (2014). What makes pediatric clinical research ethical? *Archivos Argentinos de Pediatria*, *112*(6), 492–493. doi:10.5546/aap.2014.eng.492 PMID:25362904

Krubiner, C. B., Sayd, R. H., & Merritt, M. W. (2016). Health researchers' ancillary-care: Empirical responsibilities in low-resource settings: The landscape of institutional guidance. *Journal of Empirical Research on Human Research Ethics; JERHRE*, *6*(3), 73–81. doi:10.1525/jer.2011.6.3.73

Kshirsagar, N., Swaminathan, S., Jog, P., Dalwai, S., Mathur, R., Shekhar, C., ... Mehta, D. (2017). Regulatory and ethical issues in pediatric clinical research: Recommendations from a panel discussion. *Journal of Clinical Pharmacology*, *57*(8), 943–946. doi:10.1002/jcph.916 PMID:28513861

Ladanyi, M., & Ruane, W. J. (2014). *Personalized products expanding.* Retrieved from https://www.genomeweb.com/blog/personalized-products /

Langley, G. R., Adcock, I. M., Busquet, F., Crofton, K. M., Csernok, E., Giese, C., ... Woszczek, G. (2017). Teaser to discover and develop new therapies, we need 21st-century roadmaps for biomedical research based on multi-scale human disease pathways, and supported by policy and funding strategies that prioritize human relevance. Towards a 21st-century roadmap for biomedical research and drug discovery: Consensus report and recommendations. *Drug Discovery Today*, *22*(2), 327–339. doi:10.1016/j.drudis.2016.10.011 PMID:27989722

Largent, E. A., Weissman, J. S., Gupta, A., Abraham, M., Rozenblum, R., Lynch, H. F., & Cohen, I. G. (2018). Patient-centered outcomes research: Stakeholder perspectives and ethical and regulatory oversight issues. *Journal of Empirical Research on Human Research Ethics; JERHRE*, *40*(1). doi:10.1177/1556264618779785

Lavecchia, A. (2015). Machine-learning approaches in drug discovery: Methods and applications. *Drug Discovery Today*, *20*(3), 318–331. doi:10.1016/j.drudis.2014.10.012 PMID:25448759

Laventhal, N., Tarini, B., & Lantos, J. (2012). Ethical issues in neonatal and pediatric clinical trials. *Pediatric Clinics of North America*, *59*(5), 1205–1220. doi:10.1016/j.pcl.2012.07.007 PMID:23036252

Lusher, S. J., McGuire, R., van Schaik, R. C., Nicholson, C. D., & de Vlieg, J. (2014). All scientific disciplines, including medicinal chemistry, are the subject of a revolution as data are generated at unprecedented rates and their analysis and exploitation become increasingly fundamental to innovation. Data-driven medicinal chemistry in the era of big data. *Drug Discovery Today*, *19*(7), 859–868. doi:10.1016/j.drudis.2013.12.004 PMID:24361338

Maier, W. C. (2018). *The rare disease revolution*. Retrieved from http://www.appliedclinicaltrialsonline.com/rare-disease-revolution-0

Marsh, K., Jzerman, M. I., Thokala, P., Baltussen, P., Boysen, M., Kaló, Z., ... Devlin, N. (2016). Multiple criteria decision analysis for health care decision making - Emerging good practices: Report 2 of the ISPOR MCDA Emerging Good Practices Task Force. *Value in Health*, *19*(2), 125–137. doi:10.1016/j.jval.2015.12.016 PMID:27021745

Matsuyama, R., Reddy, S., & Smith, T. J. (2006). Why do patients choose chemotherapy near the end of life? A review of the perspective of those facing death from cancer. *Journal of Clinical Oncology*, *24*(21), 3490–3496. doi:10.1200/JCO.2005.03.6236 PMID:16849766

McIntosh, E. D. G. (2011). Ethics of performing pediatric clinical trials. *The Journal of Pharmaceutical and Biopharmaceutical Contract*. Retrieved from http://www.pharmoutsourcing.com/Featured-Articles/37794-Ethics-of-Performing-Pediatric-Clinical-Trials/

McLeod, S. A. (2007). *The Milgram experiment*. Retrieved from www.simplypsychology.org/milgram.html

Mlotshwa, B. C., Mwesigwa, S., Mboowa, G., Williams, L., Retshabile, G., Kekitiinwa, A., ... Mpoloka, S. W. (2017). Co-ordination and support of international research data networks. The collaborative African genomics network training program: A trainee perspective on training the next generation of African scientists. *Genetics in Medicine*, *19*(7), 826–833. doi:10.1038/gim.2016.177 PMID:28383545

Musschenga, A. W., Van Luijn, H. E. M., Keus, R. B., & Aaronson, N. K. (2007). Are risks and benefits of oncological research protocols both incommensurable and incompensable? *Accountability in Research*, *14*(3), 179–196. doi:10.1080/08989620701455217 PMID:17877107

Office of Good Clinical Practice. (2018a). *Payment and reimbursement to research subjects - Information sheet. FDA regulatory information*. Retrieved from https://www.fda.gov/RegulatoryInformation/Guidances/ucm126429.htm

Office of Good Clinical Practice. (2018b). *Payment and reimbursement to research subjects - Information sheet. Guidance for institutional review boards and clinical investigators*. Retrieved from https://www.fda.gov/RegulatoryInformation/Guidances/ucm126429.htm

Papathanasiou, P., Brassart, L., Blake, P., Hart, A., Whitbread, L., Pembrey, R., & Kieffer, J. (2016). Transparency in drug regulation: Public assessment reports in Europe and Australia. *Drug Discovery Today*, *21*(11), 1806–1813. doi:10.1016/j.drudis.2016.06.025 PMID:27373773

Park, A., & Molloy, C. (2018). The state of the drug discovery nation unveiled as new report provides vital insights for the development of new medicines. *Drug discovery tomorrow: How to catapult ourselves into the future*. Retrieved from http://www.drugdiscoverytoday.com/view/47448/the-state-of-the-drug-discovery-nation-unveiled-as-new-report-provides-vital-insights-for-the-devel

Pediatric Research Equity Act of 2003 Pub. L. 108-155. (n.d.). Retrieved from https://www.congress.gov/108/plaws/publ155/PLAW-108publ155.pdf

Pharma I. Q. Conferences (IQPC). (2011). *Balancing ethics with economy in outsourced clinical trials*. Retrieved from https://www.pharma-iq.com/clinical/articles/balancing-ethics-with-economy-in-outsourced

Pignattia, F., Jonssonb, B., Blumenthalc, G., & Justicec, R. (2015). Assessment of benefits and risks in development of targeted therapies for cancer. The view of regulatory authorities. *Molecular Oncology, 9*(5), 1034–1041. doi:10.1016/j.molonc.2014.10.003 PMID:25481691

Podany, A. T. (2017). Ethical considerations in pediatric research. In *PedSAP 2017 Book 1. Research and study design in pediatrics* (pp. 7-18). Academic Press. Retrieved from https://www.accp.com/docs/bookstore/pedsap/ped2017b1_sample.pdf

Prentice, E. D., Bruce, G., & Gordon, B. G. (2016). Institutional review board assessment of risks and benefits associated with research (research involving human participants V2). In *Report on ethical and policy issues in research involving human participants: Vol. 2. Commissioned papers and staff analysis.* Washington, DC: National Bioethics Advisory Commission. Retrieved from http://www.onlineethics.org/hprentice.aspx

Pritchard, I. A. (2011). How do IRB members make decisions? A review and research agenda. *Journal of Empirical Research on Human Research Ethics, 6*(2), 31–46. doi:10.1525/jer.2011.6.2.31 PMID:21680975

Resnick, J., Kessler, M., Aitken, M., & Metz, A. (2017). Heralding the era of human data science. *IQVIA Real-World Insights, 7*(14). Retrieved from https://www.forbes.com/sites/oreillymedia/2012/08/20/data-science-and-the-health-care-revolution/#57004c8229f7

Rid, A., & Wendler, D. (2010). Risk-benefit assessment in medical research - critical review and open questions. *Law Probability and Risk, 9*(3-4), 151–177. doi:10.1093/lpr/mgq006

Rosenberg, J. (2017). *FDA launches pilot program to improve transparency of clinical trial information.* Retrieved from http://www.ajmc.com/printer?url=/focus-of-the-week/fda-launches-pilot-program-to-improve-transparency-of-clinical-trial-information- 1/2

Scherf, U., Becker, R., Chan, M., & Hojvat, S. (2010). Approval of novel biomarkers: FDA's perspective and major requests. *Scandinavian Journal of Clinical and Laboratory Investigation, 70*(suppl. 242), 96–102. doi:10.3109/00365513.2010.493415 PMID:20515286

SciDev Net. (2011). Ethics left behind as drug trials soar in developing countries. *The Guardian.* Retrieved from https://www.theguardian.com/global-development/2011/jul/04/ethics-left-behing-drug-trials-developing

Shetty, Y., & Saiyed, A. (2014). Analysis of warning letters issued by the US Food and Drug Administration to clinical investigators, institutional review boards and sponsors: A retrospective study. *Journal of Medical Ethics, 41*(5), 398–403. doi:10.1136/medethics-2013-101829 PMID:24965716

Snyder, D. L., & Nelson, R. M. (2018). The Food and Drug Administration's federal review of a pediatric muscular dystrophy protocol. *IRB, 40*(1), 18–20. Retrieved from https://www.thehastingscenter.org/irb_article/food-drugadministrations-federal-review-pediatricmuscular-dystrophy-protocol/ PMID:29910527

Swazo, N. K. (2006). Calculating risk/benefit in X-linked severe combined immune deficiency disorder (X-SCID) gene therapy trials: The task of ethical evaluation. *The Journal of Medicine and Philosophy: A Forum for Bioethics and Philosophy of Medicine, 31*(5), 533–564, doi:10.1080/03605310600912709

The National Commission for the Protection of Human Subjects of Biomedical and Behavioral Research (NCPHSBBR). (1979). *The Belmont Report. Ethical principles and guidelines for the protection of human subjects of research.* Retrieved from https://www.hhs.gov/ohrp/sites/default/files/the-belmont-report-508c_FINAL.pdf

Van der Graaf, R., Van der Zande, I. S. E., Den Ruijter, H. M., Oudijk, M. A., Van Delden, J. J. M., Rengerink, K. O., & Groenwold, R. H. H. (2018). Fair inclusion of pregnant women in clinical trials: An integrated scientific and ethical approach. *Trials*, *19*(1), 78–86. doi:10.118613063-017-2402-9 PMID:29378652

Veeva, G. K. (2017). Announces EDC and eSource to transform clinical data management. *Drug Discovery Today*, *20*(3). Retrieved from https://www.veeva.com/resources/veeva-announces-edc-and-esource-to-transform-clinical-data-management/

Walker, S., McAuslane, N., Liberti, L., Leong, J., & Salek, S. (2015). A universal framework for the benefit-risk assessment of medicines: Is this the way forward? *Therapeutic Innovation & Regulatory Science*, *49*(1), 17–25. doi:10.1177/2168479014547421

Wendler, D., & Miller, F. G. (2007). Assessing research risks systematically: The net risks test. *Journal of Medical Ethics*, *33*(8), 481–486. doi:10.1136/jme.2005.014043 PMID:17664310

Woodcock, J. (2018). *2017 Progress Report. Personalized medicine at FDA. On the approval of new personalized medicine indications for Kalydeco and Keytruda.* Silver Spring, MD: Center for Drug Evaluation and Research (CDER), FDA. Retrieved from http://www.personalizedmedicinecoalition.org/Userfiles/PMC-Corporate/file/PM_at_FDA_2017_Progress_Report.pdf

ADDITIONAL READING

Elizabeth, A., & Bankert, R. J. A. (2006). *Institutional review board: Management and function* (2nd ed.). Burlington, MD: Jones & Bartelett Learning.

Garner, S. A., Rennie, S., Ananworanich, J., Dube, K., Margolis, D. M., Sugarman, J., ... Dawson, L. (2017). Interrupting antiretroviral treatment in HIV cure research: Scientific and ethical considerations. *Journal of Virus Eradication*, *3*(2), 82–84. PMID:28435691

Lee, C. H., & Yoon, H. J. (2017). Medical big data: Promise and challenges. *Kidney Research and Clinical Practice*, *36*(1), 3–11. doi:10.23876/j.krcp.2017.36.1.3 PMID:28392994

Lipsitch, M., & Eyal, N. (2017). Improving vaccine trials in infectious disease emergencies. *Science*, *357*(6347), 153–156. doi:10.1126cience.aam8334 PMID:28706038

Little, M. O., Lyerly, A. D., Mastroianni, A. C., & Faden, R. R. (2017). Ethics and research with pregnant women: Lessons from HIV/AIDS. In F. Baylis & A. Ballantyne (Eds.), *Clinical Research Involving Pregnant Women* (pp. 227–246). Berlin, Germany: Springer; doi:10.1007/978-3-319-26512-4_13

Mastroianni, A., Henry, L., Robinson, D., Bailey, T., Faden, R., Little, M., & Lyerly, A. (2017). Research with pregnant women: New insights on legal decision-making. *The Hastings Center Report*, *47*(3), 38–45. doi:10.1002/hast.706 PMID:28543423

Rid, A., & Wendler, D. (2010). Risk-benefit assessment in medical research - critical review and open questions. *Law Probability and Risk*, *9*(3-4), 151–177. doi:10.1093/lpr/mgq006

Sugarman, J., Revill, P., Zoulim, F., Yazdanpanah, Y., Janssen, H. L. A., Lim, S. G., & Lewin, S. R. (2017). Ethics and hepatitis B cure research. *Gut*, *66*(3), 389–392. doi:10.1136/gutjnl-2016-313009 PMID:27849559

KEY TERMS AND DEFINITIONS

Deep Learning: Is the complex, unsupervised processing of unstructured data in order to create patterns used in decision making, patterns that are analogous to those of the human brain.

Equipoise: Means an equal view. It is used in research to describe an equal standing of the clinical investigator in therapeutic trials in relation to both the trial drug and an alternative treatment. This is important in order to avoid bias.

Omics: Is the part of biotechnology which analyzes the structure and functions of the whole makeup of a given biological function, at different levels, including the molecular gene level ("genomics"), the protein level ("proteomics"), and the metabolic level ("metabolomics").

Patient-Centricity: This term defines a collaborative partnership between patients, caregivers, and pharmaceutical companies, focusing on patients' needs and preferences in the research enterprise. The term was at first created collaboratively by AstraZeneca, patients, and caregivers, and was demonstrated to be a valid approach by testing conducted on many patients' groups.

Precision Medicine: A strategy of medical treatment tailored for the medical necessities of an individual patient based on the collection of a large amount of data about that patient's (e.g., genomic study or other molecular or cellular analysis, personal, and disease data).

Therapeutic Misconception: When the research participant in a clinical trial doesn't perceive the difference between the research intervention and the clinical care, which could impact the validity of his informed consent.

Ultraism: It is the sacrifice of self-interest for others benefit. In research, it is used when a participant is exposed to risk for the benefit to society.

Chapter 9
Informed Consent in Research Involving Human Subjects

Antonio Sandu
University of Suceava, Romania & LUMEN Research Center in Social and Humanistic Sciences, Romania

Ana Frunza
LUMEN Research Center in Social and Humanistic Sciences, Romania

ABSTRACT

Informed consent (IC) in research is a key element in ensuring the ethical character of any research involving human subjects, either bio-medical or psychosocial. IC involves three elements: validity, communication of information, and deliberation. Obtaining IC is a dynamic process of ethical reflection in order to facilitate the expression of autonomy of the subject involved in research. The process of obtaining the IC must be accompanied by the administrative procedure for completing a consent form signed by both the participant and the researcher. If the participant cannot sign—either because he is a minor or because of the medical condition—a delegated consent signed by the legal representatives of the subject is required.

INTRODUCTION

The practice of obtaining informed consent (IC) in research conducted with the participation of human subjects comes as a response to scientific communication to the danger of involving some people in research that may endanger their life, health or quality of life without knowing what is, or may be, likely to happen to them, and without actually expressing their consent. CI in research has developed mainly at the level of bio-medical research - an area where the risks to which participants may be subjected are increased, and where the effects of unethical research have been evident, gradually expanding into other areas of scientific research, for example in psycho-social research. IC in research is conceptualized and theorized in parallel with IC for more or less invasive therapy or intervention. The IC concept first appeared in 1957, being really debated ever since 1972.

DOI: 10.4018/978-1-5225-6310-5.ch009

As far as IC is concerned, the bioethics literature considers it necessary to gather the following elements, so that informed consent (both in medical or psychosocial intervention and research) is considered valid:

1. Disclosure
2. Understanding
3. Volunteering
4. Competence
5. (Actual consent) - a person gives the IC for an intervention if he / she will be exposed to the whole procedure, will understand the information received, will act voluntarily and be competent to act, to consent (Meisel & Roth, 1981)

DEFINITIONS OF INFORMED CONSENT

From the administrative point of view - technically, informed consent - in clinical research "is the written, signed and dated decision of a person capable of giving consent or, if it is a person unable to do so, by its legal representative to participate in a voluntary and informed clinical trial after having received all the necessary information on the nature, significance, consequences and possible risks and the necessary documentation" (Purcaru, Lazăr, Purcaru, & Rogozea, 2012).

IC for research is the process where the research participant gives his / her agreement to participate in the research after being informed about procedures, risks and benefits (Bulger, Heitman, & Reiser, 2002).

The concept of informed consent defines at the same time the process of obtaining the agreement of the subject on its participation, fully voluntary, and carried out on the basis of its own informed decision, the research - or the therapeutic act - at the same time a process, as well as a document signed by the consenting person or his / her legal representative when he / she is prevented from agreeing (Purcaru et al., 2012).

Faden and Beauchamp (1986) define the process of obtaining informed consent as an expression of care for the protection and facilitation of autonomous or self-determined choices of patients and subjects (n.n.). IC can be transformed into a normative compliance tool in terms of human rights when the practice of obtaining the IC is interpreted in a formalistic manner by reference to strict rules of obtaining the IC and formalizing them (Maclean, 2009). Consent has the role of creating a legal barrier to control permission, allowing for an illegitimate act to be perpetrated (Alexander, 1996).

The Nuremberg Code (*The Nuremberg Code*, 1946) defines the process of obtaining informed consent as being the same by which the researchers put into practice the respect due to the autonomy of the individual. Respect for autonomy is a fundamental ethical principle, both in biomedical research and in therapeutic practice. A valid consent is given by a decision-maker who is fully informed about the purpose and objectives of the research, the risks to which it is subjected, and the potential benefits, both for oneself and for others, including for the whole of humanity, and which voluntarily decides to participate in that research. The purpose of obtaining the IC is to ensure that the subject's participation is voluntary, generally altruistic, and that the decision entirely fell within the subject and was taken in full conscience. Obtaining informed consent ensures the integrity of research in relation to the subject-matter relationship and confers legal protection to the researcher and the research team against any risks that the subject has been informed that might intervene, and has given or maintained its consent to participate in the research.

IC is a necessary requirement for conducting, under ethical conditions, any research involving human subjects (Alexa-Stratulat, Neagu, Neagu, Alexa, & Ioan, 2018). In practice, obtaining informed consent aims at informing the subjects about the research and including the purpose, objectives, methods and procedures used, the scientific importance and the practical utility of the results, the risks and benefits the subject can expect, the fact that the decision is and must be voluntary, and he/she can withdraw from the research at any time without affecting in any way the relationship with the research team, the institution that implements the research project or its funders, and does not lose the right to treatment in biomedical research, which will continue to be granted in accordance with current, non-experimental standards in the implementing institution. The subject is informed of his / her rights and duties, including those relating to the confidentiality of his / her participation in the research, even when the information may reveal malfunctions, except when the criminal investigation authorities request access to the information.

The purpose of the informed consent process is to ensure that the participants' rights are respected even when they involve risks, that sufficient information has been provided in clear and appropriate language that allows the subject to appreciate according to their level of understanding what will be his / her situation during and after participation in the research and express his / her willful agreement in full knowledge of the extent of his / her level of understanding. Informed consent being a process rather than a procedure, researchers have the duty to ensure throughout the research that the participation of the subjects is still voluntary and that the subjects are fully aware of what is happening or may happen to them during the next steps of the research.

INFORMED CONSENT AND RESPECT FOR THE *AUTONOMY* OF THE PARTICIPANTS IN THE RESEARCH

A first approach focuses on the autonomy of the individual who consents also in the deliberate adoption of a decision. The decision once adopted will justify the participation of the decision-maker as subject, as well as the interventions to be made when necessary during the research. From a researcher's point of view, research is conducted in good faith when the process of obtaining the IC is carried out - when it is sufficiently determined to believe that it acts on the basis of that person's consent (Maclean, 2009, pp. 113–114).

The process of obtaining IC in research involving human subjects, in an analogous way to obtaining IC for a therapeutic act or psychosocial intervention, is based on the concept of self-determination, called in the scientific literature the decisional autonomy. The term refers to the fact that the intellectually competent person, that is, the major one who is not under the ban, must be able to make decisions about his / her own life and health, including those relating to participation in subject matter, to various research that may affect to a lesser or greater extent life, health or quality of life.

The concept of autonomy is defined in the Stanford Encyclopaedia of Philosophy as the ability of the individual to live his life in accordance with his own reason and his own motivations based on his own free decisions, not manipulated or distorted by external forces (Christman, 2009). The autonomous person is the model of the moral person in Kantian vision. Ethical autonomy consists in the self-imposition of the moral law that must be of universal value. The categorical Kantian imperative proposes autonomy as a fundamental ethical value, being understood as the virtue of acting in consistency with universal law (Guyer, 1998). John Stuart Mill (2014) believes that autonomy is correlated with the exercise of choice and the involvement of reason in the process of choice; he correlates autonomy with individuality and originality. Millennial autonomy can be correlated with self-perception of well-being. The individual acts according to his own definition of well-being regardless of whether he is rational, instinctual, intuitive, impulsive, or apparently unjustified. The concept of autonomy and its connotations of self-determination and respect for the person play a central role in the theoretical constructs of applied ethics. Autonomy understood as negative freedom refers to the existence of borders that limit the intrusion of others into their own lives and their own decisions.

The individual's ability to make autonomous decisions is determined by the level of information he has access to, as well as the ability to understand the information and to be able to make estimates about the consequences of the decisions taken. Autonomous actions reflect a normative and axiological deliberation on existing options, both types of deliberations being equally important. For Christman (2009), in consensus with the Kantian vision, autonomy is the ability of the individual to first impose his own moral beliefs raised to the objective and constraining law level recognized as the general principle of his own life.

The autonomous person is the model of the moral person in Kantian vision. By virtue of the categorical imperative (Kant, 1972), we must act in such a way that we do not harm the freedom and the exercise of the autonomy of others; moreover, it is appropriate to promote their autonomous manifestations in terms of their own person and social life (Guyer, 1998). Respect for the autonomy of the individual therefore requires the researcher to ensure the reality of the IC of the participants in the research. Moral and decisional autonomy is defined by the individual's ability to make decisions of moral value for himself or for others. This capacity is called agency, and the decision maker - moral agent.

Decisional autonomy is complementary to expressive autonomy, the ability of an individual to express his authentic feelings in a manner consistent with his own values (Sandu, 2016). Autonomy as authenticity is responsible for the constitution and functioning of the nucleus of human personality, the authentic individual takes decisions in accordance with its own values, sometimes different from those common in the society, decisions that may seem irrational and implicitly affect the value perceived by IC researchers. More specifically, persons belonging to certain religious denominations may refuse blood transfusions on the basis of religious belief, and their own authenticity manifested as expressive autonomy, even if, rationally, transfusions may be life-saving. All forms of expressing autonomy, including expressive, should be taken into account in the process of obtaining the IC, even in situations where a person's habit or value goes beyond his / her own reason.

Anita Ho (2008) considers that the focus of bioethics on informed patient consent (*Informed Consent*) neglects the social context of individual autonomy, which is precisely the environment in which autonomous decisions are made. Anne Donchine (2001) believes that there is a possibility of confusion between the subject's intentions and those involved in care, due to their concerted action. In some research, notably in the biomedical field, but not limited to, the decision to participate or to refuse participation may be influenced by the social context in which the individual is required to participate in the research, especially when discussing possible life-saving innovative therapies - when the subject decides to participate in order to respect the desire of those closest to them, and not to follow their own will. In this case, the expressive autonomy is influenced by the social context, the moral decision being mediated by the social value attributed to the participation in the research.

When participation in a particular research is remunerated, consent may be distorted by personal or close ones' financial needs, which inclines the decision to participate in the research even if the participation was voluntarily refused. In this situation, there are objections to the ethical nature of participation and to the IC reality.

CHARACTERISTICS OF INFORMED CONSENT FOR RESEARCH

Research involving human subjects should be conducted solely on the basis of an opinion from an ethics committee (IEC) – independent ethics committee (IEC) - or an institutional review board (IRB). At least one of these committees should analyse the research proposal and evaluate it, among other things, with regard to the risks to the subjects and their mitigation measures, including the procedures for obtaining IC (Gupta, 2013). The three elements of a valid consent for research - were mainly formulated for clinical research, where the risks that participants assume are usually higher than in psycho-social research, but can extend to any type of research involving human subjects - are: voluntary character, information disclosure and decision-making capacity (volunteerism, information disclosure, and decision-making capacity).

The voluntary character is understood as the ability of an individual to appreciate - and make his own judgments - independent of the opinions of others, and in the absence of any form of coercion over what is right or wrong, good or bad, choosing what individual considers that it is the best option in which it is located, in concert with its own values and previous experiences (Roberts, 2002, pp. 705–712). The voluntary nature of the decision may be affected by the diminished intellectual capacity of the person, emotional maturity, health status, psychological pressure to which he or she is subjected by different persons, including those of the individual, cultural or religious values other than those of the investigators, or even the majority of the population, relationships with medical staff, etc. All these risks that may compromise the voluntary nature of the decision must be clearly expressed in the research proposal and assessed by the Research Ethics Commission or the IRB (Gupta, 2013).

Information disclosure is a gradual process of informing the subject - patient in clinical trials - of the information it needs, in a form and language that he/she understands, about: his/her health condition, the possibility to participate in the research and the therapeutic alternatives to the experimental treatment, the aim and objectives of the research, its limits, the risks and the possible benefits (for the subject and those for the future development of medicine), the possible side effects that can be estimated before starting the research, but also information on the novelty level of the clinical approach and along with the limitations of estimates of possible side effects, the fact that the subject has the right to withdraw from the research at any time, and any other information that would be necessary to be able to make a decision in accordance with their own judgment values and life experiences. The incomplete information of the subject constitutes a consensus and prejudices the ethical character of the research (Roberts, 2002).

In the case of experimental procedures that include a control group not receiving experimental treatment, but only a simulation of treatment to obtain the placebo effect, the subject should be informed of the possibility of being in this situation. This situation of experiments involving control groups that do not benefit from experimental treatment requires a separate discussion based on the principle of patient's right to treatment, and the obligation of doctors in the experiment team not to leave the patient without treatment, but this discussion goes beyond the scope of this chapter.

The decision-making capacity, also called agent capacity, is the ability to understand and appreciate the nature of one's own condition - health in clinical trials - and the consequences of the decisions he/she takes, how it can affect the situation - health status - as well as the ability to formulate and communicate decisions regarding their health care (VHA, 2009). The subject must be able to understand the information that is given about his / her health condition, the nature of the research in which he / she is asked to participate, especially the risks and benefits (Gupta, 2013)

As for the ability to make decisions (to consent), a series of questions arise when the subject of the research is a minor (Van Hoof et al., 2018) or a person unable to consent either because of the condition of health (severe mental illness, including senility, dementia, low intelligence, or coma, etc.), consent from the defendants thus being required.

TYPES OF INFORMED CONSENT

The literature describes, along with the IC itself, a series of other procedures used in particular situations, when the subject is incapable of consenting, or when it is necessary to have a wide consent for many activities, including that of research, which are not mentioned – many of them being only possible in the future.

The delegated consent is that form of consent in which a person having the authority to consent for someone else replaces another person – this being the case for consent given in the name of a minor, or a person who, although being an adult, is incapable of consenting due to the poor health state (deep coma, mental disorders, etc.). The process of obtaining consent is similar, only that instead of the subject, in the process of information and decision-making, there is the person with role of guardian, curator, etc. In the practice of biomedical research conducted on children aged over 14, the consent of the caregivers is usually doubled by an accept from the child which is called assent (Kapp, 1983; Kuther & Posada, 2004) instead of *consent.* The consent of the minor is not valid in the absence of that of the legal guardian, but some practices requires for a child who hasn't been informed using explanations for his understanding, not to be included in the research sample, although he could have partially understood, and/or he hasn't given his consent.

Broad consent – emerges when the individual is asked to consent to the use of his/her data – including biomedical ones, tissue samples, etc. – for future research with an unspecified context and content, rather than for a particular, well-defined research project (Ploug & Holm, 2015). Grady (2015) defines BC as being a consent for an unspecified area of subjects for a potential future research, whose content and process are less known by the participant (Grady, 2015). The BC is mainly debated in the context of biobanks (Hansson, Dillner, Bartram, Carlson, & Helgesson, 2006; Helgesson, 2012; Ploug & Holm, 2015). BC is not an informed consent per se, in lack of specific information on the research (Árnason, 2004; B Hofmann, 2009; Bjørn Hofmann, Solbakk, & Holm, 2009). Ploug & Holm (2015) use the metaconsent idea as the interconnection between BC and Dynamic consent. Dynamic Consent is an alternative Consent model where the subject has the opportunity to get information on the use of its data and biological samples through up-to-date internet platforms. The individual can be given the opportunity to withdraw his data from using them in research he does not agree with. Under the new framework regulation on the protection of personal data, the only way in which the use of data collected in prior researches or in the therapeutic practice for future research, is the Dynamic Consent for which the subject initially agreed to, being aware of the possibility that its data may be used in future research about which he/she will be informed.

Another name for broad consensus is that proposed by Onara O'Neil (2003) - generic consent. Generic consent aims at the subject's agreement to participate in research even during the therapeutic or psychosocial intervention, when the therapeutic protocol is not altered by the intent to use the data in the research. Frunză & Sandu (2017) believe that the use of generic or broad-based consent by simply signing a IC form for therapy or intervention may constitute major consensus vices, when the subject is determined to consider that the non-acceptance of participation in the research activity being conducted in that institution may result in his / her exclusion from therapy, or a lower quality of the therapeutic act or psychosocial intervention. The article mentions a number of physician responses that show that at the time of admission to a university hospital, the patient is already familiar with the clinic's specificity and the fact that the research is being carried out. Thus, by accepting to be in that clinic, the subject implicitly agrees to the use of the data for the purpose of research, signing the IC form as a mere administrative formality. Such an approach can lead to abuses - for example when tissue samples are used in genetic research or when the purpose of research, even if it is considered legitimate for the scientific community, is contrary to the values and beliefs of the subject.

A particular situation of consent is verbal, whether or not accompanied by an IC form - which contains only the main data about the consenting person, and the limits of the consent. This verbal consent may be used in the case of illiterate or incapable persons signing, but who are capable of expressing a valid consent. In this situation, the IC form is signed by the team coordinator researcher - the principal investigator - and by a witness stating the conduct of the information and consensus process provided verbally by the subject.

The waiver of documentation of consent may be approved by the Research Ethics Committee (RECS or IRB) (Shahnazarian, Hagemann, Aburto, & Susan, 2013) when the data are collected in a manner that allows only their statistical processing and in the absence of a IC form, the subject's participation in research remains completely anonymous. This may be the situation where the respondent to a poll expresses his / her consent by filling in the questionnaire itself, in the preamble of which the purpose, objectives and expected results of the research were specified, as well as the minor risks to which the subject may be subjected. In this situation, continuing to fill in the questionnaire and providing answers to questions after being informed that it can withdraw at any time from total or partial research - for example by failing to answer certain questions - is considered to be valid verbal consent. This is true only if data on the identity of the individual is not stored by the researchers even in a separate way from the answers to the questions asked.

Eliminating certain elements of consent is only achieved with the express agreement of the ethics committee of research, when research is hindered if the subject knows those elements. This partially informed consent can be used in situations where, for example, when resilience, stress resistance, dynamic of motivational factors are studied, or when there are strong reasons to believe that informing the subject about the real purpose of research will lead to distortion of responses or reactions. In order to be admitted in the ethics committee of research, such situations where the subject is misinformed about his role in research, the researcher must justify the special utility of research, not only at the theoretical but also the pragmatic level, leading to therapeutic solutions or to large-scale intervention models. Another particular situation where ethics committees of research may receive partial information of the subject about the purpose and objectives of the research, as well as the expected results, is the exploratory research whose design frequently changes during the research and which contains elements of imprecision with regard to the dimensions and dynamics of the - psychosocial - phenomenon researched.

INFORMED CONSENT TO PEOPLE BELONGING TO VULNERABLE POPULATIONS

Social vulnerability appears as a total or partial absence of autonomy. The operational definition of autonomy used when studying different categories of population refers to the effective social functioning of the individual integrated into the social networks to which they may have access in their community. An autonomous individual is a functional and socially integrated individual who accesses the necessary resources to exercise his rights and pursue his own psychosocial development in accordance with his legitimate values and aspirations. Social autonomy partially overlaps the expressive autonomy previously discussed. Social autonomy may or may not be convergent with the academic one, the subject having the ability to act. The subject's agency belonging to vulnerable population, can be diminished precisely because of the specific vulnerability. A person in a state of chronic poverty will be tempted to participate in a research that involves increased risks for his or her life or quality of life if the participation is materially rewarded. Also, a person suffering from psychiatric disorders, capable of consent, will be more easily influenced by subjective elements such as investigator personality, research, etc., than an objective analysis of the benefits and risks involved in his participation in the research.

Forms of Social Vulnerability Correlated With the Limitation of Autonomy

We will continue to present a number of types of vulnerabilities (Cojocaru, Cojocaru., Gârleanu, Irimescu, & Şoitu, 2010):

- **Utilitarian Vulnerability:** The individual / group does not notice their own interest or engages in actions unrelated to it. The limitation of autonomy in the direction of personal efficiency can be found in the situation of dependencies and co-dependencies, pathological deviations, etc.
- **The Teleological Vulnerability:** Refers to the fact that the available means are not adequate for the individual or community purpose, and the proposed purpose is inadequate to the resources, the individual acting by perverting the purpose of the action, idealizing the means. The limitation of autonomy refers to the individual's inability to distinguish the purpose of means, for example taking part in high-risk research in order to obtain rewards including those of a moral nature.
- **Axiological Vulnerability:** The person acts in virtue of a normative principle, incompatible with the values of the social field in which he acts. Limitation of autonomy occurs in the direction of oppression / repression of the individual's activity. A delinquent acts on the basis of rules belonging to deviant subcultures, suppressed by the legislative framework, respectively the society. A subject may refuse to participate in a research that violates its moral or religious values, even if they are contrary to the opinion of the majority.
- **Traditional Vulnerability:** Generated by the permanent conditioning of the habitus that the individual cannot overcome. The individual's previous personal experience will generate the current and future behaviour of the individual, perpetuating vulnerability and oppression, the limitation of autonomy being achieved at the level of the inability to leave the vicious circle of the initial habitus.
- **Cognitive Vulnerability:** The individual acts by virtue of an inadequate vision on the world, with a limitation of autonomy at the level of the ability to consent.

Vulnerable populations can be included in the research only when the purpose of the research is to directly address the situation or the vulnerability of the subjects. Research on the quality of life of people suffering from HIV / AIDS can, for example, be legitimate when its results can propose policies aimed at increasing the quality of life of this type of suffering person. Research involving subjects from vulnerable populations that do not seek to improve the condition of that category, but may involve risks including significant discomfort for subjects from these categories, is not legitimate from the ethical point of view. Research on prisoners or detainees is considered unethical, even if major progress has been made in the development of science or technology. Prisoners have a reduced capacity to consent due to the imbalance of authority in the carceral environment. Research ethics committees and scientific journals should be overwhelmingly circumspect and even refrain from validating research on human subjects, especially of a biomedical or psychological nature, carried out on detainees or protesters - unless the purpose of the research is really studying the effects of the carceral environment.

Research on vulnerable populations, when absolutely necessary, should only be done on the basis of a written consensus obtained from major, discerning and able to consent person, and only after the researcher has analysed the possible risks and assured that it has diminished to the maximum the potential influences of the vulnerable media on the informed decision of the subject.

OBTAINING INFORMED CONSENT AS PROCESS VERSUS ADMINISTRATIVE PROCEDURE

Obtaining consent involves a process by which researchers ensure that participants understand exactly the nature of their own participation in the research, and that they freely accept their risks and obligations (Frunza & Sandu, 2017a; Funză & Sandu, 2017b). In practice, especially in psychosocial research, obtaining IC is considered a simple administrative act, necessary to avoid possible allegations of malpractice in research.

Gupta (2013) presents the process of obtaining informed consent starting from the following stages:

- Preliminary discussions for obtaining informed consent,
- Reflection and decision to participate- refusal of participation,
- Verifying the satisfaction of the requirements for participation in the research,
- Obtaining informed consent and signing IC forms,
- Making a copy available to the subject after the IC.

Faden & Beauchamp (1986), and Beauchamp and Childress (1994), respectively, state a series of 7 components of the informed consent process:

1. Elements of disclosure (preconditions):
    a. Competence in understanding and decision-making;
    b. Volunteering (in decision)
2. Information Elements:
    c. Disclosure (material information);
    d. Recommendation (of a plan);
    e. Understanding (in disclosure & recommendation)

3. Elements of consent:
    f. The decision (in favour of the plan);
    g. Authorization (the plan chosen) (Funză & Sandu, 2017a).

Faden & Beauchamp (1986) argue that:

- **Autonomous Authorization of a Medical Intervention or Involvement in Medical Research by Individual Patients or Subjects:** Involves more than just a mere adherence to the idea, or compliance with an arrangement or proposal of the doctor or researcher; based on substantial understanding and absence of any outside control of the patient, he will intentionally authorize a professional for medical intervention;
- A person who deliberately refuses to authorize any intervention but understands and is not subject to any pressure in the decision, will provide an informed denial.
- **IC as Institutional or Consent Policy:** It has legislative connotations and effective institutional approval from the patient or subject.
- The philosophical foundation of this significance of IC is based on the premise that IC is a form of protection and construction of autonomy or self-determined choice of the patient (Funză & Sandu, 2017a).

Even though Faden & Beauchamp (1986) also refer to biomedical research, the principles of definition of IC may apply to any research involving human subjects of a psychosocial nature. Lower risks to the life or health of the investigated person occurring in psychosocial research do not eliminate the need for IC.

The practice of obtaining an IC can be interpreted in a formalistic manner by reference to strict rules of obtaining the IC and their formalization, transforming IC into a tool to fulfil legal obligations to respect the rights of the research subjects. IC can be approached in a paternalistic manner in which the subject is considered incapable of consent in full consciousness, an approach that transforms the process of obtaining the IC into a purely administrative formality (Maclean, 2009). The ethical approach is transparent, the subject being considered as the partner of the researcher, his consent being the basis of successful research.

The administrative dimension of the process is to formalize it and include all elements of consent in a form signed by the subject with the researcher, summarizing the information that was sent to the subject and on which he relied on his decision to participate in the research. The form should clearly show the agreement to participate in the research and the voluntary nature of this agreement. The ethical dimension of the process is respect for the autonomy of the subject and care for the signed form to represent a genuine consent that is the expression of the subject's agency. The ethical reflection on the need for consent and the actual existence of each participant in research is a researcher's integrity criterion, making research a morally accepted one.

NORMATIVE ACTS REGULATING THE USE OF INFORMED CONSENT IN RESEARCH

Convention for the Protection of Human Rights and the Dignity of Human Beings against Applications of Biology and Medicine: Convention on Human Rights and Biomedicine, Oviedo, 4.IV.1997. Oviedo provides for the obligation to obtain informed consent from participants in any type of research involving human subjects.

In paragraphs 1, 2 and 3, the Oviedo Convention expressly provides:

An intervention in the field of health can only be done after the person has given its consent in a free and informed manner.

This person must first be provided with appropriate information about the purpose and nature of the intervention, as well as the consequences and risks of the intervention.

The person concerned may withdraw his consent at any time.

The Convention provides for the obligation of informed consent - as a rule expressed in a form in which consent is expressed in writing - and obtained after prior notification to the participant of the purpose and objectives of the research, potential benefits and risks, a well as the participant's right to withdraw from the research at any time.

Informed consent must, in accordance with the Oviedo Convention, be based on volunteering. In the case of persons who cannot personally consent, their participation in the research is conditional on the existence of a direct benefit for the person or for the category of vulnerable persons to which he / she is a part of, and is conditioned by the absence of another way of finding the information necessary for the research.

WMA Declaration (World Medical Association Declaration Regarding the Ethical Principles for Medical Research on Human Subjects: Helsinki, June 1964

In research involving human subjects capable of providing IC, each of them must be truthfully informed about the purpose, methods and sources of research data, possible conflicts of interest, institutional affiliation of researchers and sources of research funding, beneficial effects and the anticipated outcomes of the research, the potential risks of the study, including the discomfort that may occur during or after the study, as well as any other relevant aspects of the research that the investigator considers important to the participant. According to the same Helsinki Declaration, as well as the EC Directives (2001/20 / EC) which are the manifestation of the effects of the Helsinki WMA Declaration, the investigator is bound to inform the participant of his / her right to refuse to participate or to withdraw from research at any moment without this causing negative consequences for the subject.

In Romania, through the OMSP 903 and 904/2006, the PE and CE Directives on the approximation of the laws and administrative provisions of the Member States on the detailed principles and guidelines on the application of good clinical practice in the conduct of clinical trials for the evaluation medicinal products for human use, are transposed into the Romanian legislation.

The Romanian legislation regulating the patient's IC is: Law no. 95/2006 on health reform, and Law no. 46/2003 on patient's rights.

Violation of Consent as Research Fraud

The absence of informed consent or an improper informed consent may be important causes of malpractice in research that may lead to vicious results or the existence of ethical irregularities leading to the rejection of research. In 2014, in the Romanian media, a number of cases of clinical research conducted without an IC and an agreement by an ethics committee were presented. Researchers extracted cerebrospinal fluid from 8 patients who were not required to have a specific CI for research but only a broad, therapeutic consent. In the media, it is reported that a total of 89 tubes with cephalosporidic fluid were extracted from the eight patients, of whom 4 died. It is not clear whether the cause of the death of the four patients was the extraction of the liquid, but this possibility was not ruled out. The ethics committee of the medical institution in which the research was conducted concluded that there had indeed been illegal experiments on human subjects that relied on biological material harvesting. Incriminated researchers have shown that the reason for biological sampling was patient diagnosis and was performed on the basis of consent for therapy, and that experiments with these substances were not even considered. However, the results of the analysis of the obtained evidence were the subject of a doctoral thesis, prevailing on the broad consensus, obtained as an informed consent for the therapy (Funza & Sandu, 2017; Benea, 2015a, 2015b).

A classic example of research that violates patients' rights through lack of IC was Albert Klingman's experiments on X-rays to treat fungal infections in mentally retarded children and detainees. A number of vesicles and dermatitis occurred to these subjects, and they were not previously informed of the risk. Another example, presented by Prof. Vasile Astarastoae, targets 400 prisoners at Stateville Prison in Ilinois State of the U.S. who were required to sign an IC form to absolve researchers of any responsibility for any injuries they might suffer as a result of participating in a malaria treatment survey.

Research on human subjects, even if they do not target an increased risk - such as those in the medical field - can still create discomfort or vulnerability.

A classic example of research that violates patients' rights through lack of IC was Albert Klingman's experiments on detainees, which used X-rays to treat fungal infections in mentally retarded children and inmates. A series of vesicles and dermatitis occurred in these subjects, and they were not previously informed of the risk (Astarastoae, 2018a). Another example, presented by Prof. Vasile Astărăstoae, targets 400 prisoners from Statesville prison in Illinois, USA, who were required to sign a CI form to absolve researchers of any liability for any injuries they might suffer as a result of participating in a research on malaria treatment (Astarastoae, 2018b).

Research on human subjects, even if they do not target a high level of risk - such as those in the medical field - can still create discomfort or increased vulnerability.

CRITIQUE OF THE USE OF INFORMED CONSENT FORMS AS AN ADMINISTRATIVE TOOL

There are a number of criticisms regarding the extension of the need to use IC from randomized clinical trials to most types of research involving human subjects. First of all, it is shown that some research - such as those conducted through the questionnaire - does not pose a serious risk to the subjects, and they are nevertheless informed about the research objective and the right not to answer all questions, moreover, the existence of a written consent would bring additional data about the investigated persons, lowering the level of confidentiality of the data.

A second critique concerns qualitative research in which interview guides are much less accurate, the reader adapting his questions to the answers of the subject. In this case, the subject can be informed about the purpose and objectives of the research and the type of methodology, as well as the existence of minimal risks, although they cannot be accurately stated.

Even with the use of biomedical data and biological samples and tissues harvested in the therapeutic process, it is considered that the patient cannot be exposed to a condition that alters his / her current health condition and that no right of the subject is impaired because the data and evidence is already available to the medical unit, and there is a co-ownership of data between the subject and the medical institution (Ballantyne, 2016).

Another objection is that when the risks to the research participant are minimal, obtaining IC is a useless bureaucratic act that brings additional stress to the subject. In our opinion, the need to maintain IC even when risks are assumed to be minimal or data is already collected, is justified by the possibility of unlawful extension of therapeutic consent to actions having an undeclared experimental side - as is the case of the first example of malpractice.

There is the opinion that IC for secondary use of biology data and samples can be included in IC for therapeutic procedures (Kim & Miller, 2014; Petrini, 2010). This opinion is shared by the authors of the IC forms used in our research.

An argument in favour of the need for separation between the IC for research and IC for therapy is the avoidance of *Therapeutic Misconception*, as obtaining the consent of the research participants differs from IC for therapy (Lederer, 1997), and the patient will be influenced to believe that the research is directly geared for his/her own good, and not for the common good of developing knowledge in medicine. Research may not involve specialized care, enrolling a patient in a placebo group, being withdrawn from his or her basic treatment may jeopardize the state of health maintained by classical medication (Frunza & Sandu, 2017c).

In our opinion, the introduction of a non-specific consent may influence the patient to believe that in the absence of his / her participation in the didactic or research activity required, it will determine the absence of therapy.

In the criteria for exclusion of therapeutic procedures, the possibility of refusing to participate in didactic or research activity is not expressly formulated. From an ethical perspective, it can be interpreted as an abuse of the dominant position of the physician in front of the patient (Frunza & Sandu, 2017c).

CONCLUSION

IC in research is a key element in ensuring the ethical character of any research involving human subjects, whether of a bio-medical or psychosocial nature. IC involves three elements: validity, communication of information and deliberation. Obtaining IC is a dynamic process of ethical reflection to help express the autonomy of the subject involved in the research. The process of obtaining the IC must be accompanied by the administrative procedure for completing a consent form signed by both the participant and the researcher. If the participant cannot sign - either because he is a minor or because of the medical condition - a delegated consent signed by the legal representatives of the subject is required.

MODELS OF INFORMED CONSENT

Informed Consent for Participating in Survey-Based Inquiry

Please read this form carefully and any questions regarding your participation in this study, before giving your consent to it.

You are invited to participate in a research on .... The study is conducted by Stefan cel Mare University from Suceava, within the project ....

The study consists of applying questionnaires with a number of x questions, to which you can respond under anonymity. Your personal data in this informed consent will be kept confidential, only members of the research team, the financer and members of the ethics committee having access to it. The processing of personal data is in accordance with the European legislation in the field (GDPR).

The questionnaire is anonymous, therefore do not write your name on the form/questionnaire; this declaration of informed consent will not be kept together with the survey, your answers being unidentifiable. The analysis of the data obtained through the survey will be conducted using statistic methods that do not allow the disclosure of any information regarding your person or opinions. In the case of the publication of data, no individual information will be disclosed.

Your participation in this study is voluntary, will not be remunerated, nor will it involve costs from your part. You can withdraw from this study at any time before submitting this questionnaire, without incurring any penalties and without it affecting your professional decisions. You do not have to provide any explanation if you decide to withdraw from the study. Also, you are free not to answer to a particular question, regardless of your reason.

For any questions / concerns about the study, please contact the coordinators of this study: name, surname, address, telephone number, e-mail.

Participating in this study involves answering a series of questions, in the form of questionnaires. The questions target a series of aspects regarding: ....

The time needed for answering these questions is approximately ...... minutes.

This kind of study involves a minimum risk, being possible, in some cases, to experience certain conditions of fatigue/discomfort, as result of the effort required for answering the questions in the questionnaire.

Through your participation to the study, you will contribute to a better understanding of ...., whose result could be ....[1]

I mention that "I have asked questions regarding all issues concerning the study, I have received the necessary clarifications, and I agree to participate in this study".

"I have read and understood this informed consent form, and I willingly agree to participate in the study described. I receive a copy of this form."

Signature Date

Informed Consent for Participating in the interview

Please read[2] this form carefully, and ask any question concerning your participation in the study, before agreeing to it.

You are invited to participate in a research on ...., as your experience can contribute to a better understanding of ....

The study is conducted by Stefan cel Mare University from Suceava, within the project ....

If you agree, you are invited to participate to an individual interview conducted by one of our researchers from .... During the interview you will be alone with the interviewer, the entire discussion will be recorded with a tape recorder, and the transcription of the interview will be kept in a confidential data base, without mentioning your name. The recorded information is confidential and no one, except for the members of the research team or the criminal investigation bodies, at their express request, will not have access to the recordings. Your personal data from this informed consent will be kept confidential, only the members of the research team, the financer and the members of the ethics committee having access to it. The processing of personal data is in accordance with the European legislation in the field (GDPR).

The interviews will last between 30 to 60 minutes, and will be conducted in a location that is convenient for you, and will not involve travelling costs.

This declaration of informed consent will not be kept together with the transcription of the interview, your answers being unidentifiable. In the case of publication of data, no individual information will be disclosed.

Your participation in this study is voluntary, will not be remunerated, nor will it involve costs from your part. You can withdraw at any time (before, during or immediately after finishing the interview), without incurring any penalties and without it affecting the medical care. You do not have to give any explanation if you decide to withdraw from the study. Also, you are free to not answer a certain question if you do not wish to, regardless of your reason.

For any questions/concerns regarding the study, please contact the coordinators of this study: name, surname, address, phone number, e-mail.

The participation in this study involves answering a series of questions, in the form of interviews. The questions are about a series of aspects on: your health state, how you care for yourself, your relationship with the medical staff and your family.

This type of study involves minimum risks, in some cases being possible to experience certain feelings of fatigue / psychic discomfort as a result of the effort involved in answering the questions.

By participating in this study, you will contribute to a better understanding of ...., which could result in improving ....

I mention that "I have asked questions regarding all issues concerning this study, I have received the necessary clarifications and I agree to participate in this study".

"I have read and understood this informed consent form, and I willingly agree to participate in the study described. I receive a copy of this form."

Signature Date

Dear Sir / Madam,

My name is[3] ...., and I am conducting a research on ...., with the .... The research focuses on ...., benefits from financial support from ...., and I invite you to participate in the research described below, by filling in a survey on ....

Your participation is voluntary!

The survey is available at: ....

Thank you!

The aim of this research is to identify the ethical frameworks in which the process of obtaining informed consent (IC) in the medical institutions (from the N.-E. area of Romania) approved to conduct medical research on human subjects, as well as the meaning of practicing ethics by specialists[4].

The research is being conducted within LUMEN Research Center in Social and Humanistic Sciences, as part of the project "Informed Consent between Theory and Practice in North – Eastern Region of

Romania Medical Research Field", project developed within the Advanced Certified Program in Research Ethics (supported by NIH Research Grant #5R25TW007085, sponsored by Fogarty International Center, National Institute of Environmental Health Sciences, National Heart Lung and Blood Institute and National Institute on Drug Abuse).

What to Expect from My Participation in the Research

Please answer some questions regarding the management of ethics in your Organisation.

The survey will consist of questions connected to the meaning of informed consent, the procedure of obtaining informed consent from the patient/participant in the research, the role of the informed consent in the medical practice and medical research, the differences and similarities between the informed consent in the medical practice and medical research, etc.

If you have any questions concerning the research, please contact the research team at: ....

None of the questions raises defamatory aspects to the persons interviewed or their working environment, nor situations of introspection, that would require reflection which may produce negative emotions.

This questionnaire is not a personal or institutional evaluation, and there will be no value judgments issued based on these answers.

If, however, you identify questions you do not wish to answer, you have the possibility to state that, either by choosing the DK/DA (don't know/don't answer), or by simply skipping to the next question, or even quitting the entire survey.

The questionnaire is anonymous, and the answers to the survey will not be kept in the same place with the informed consent form. Your personal data in this informed consent will be kept confidential, only the members of the research team, the financer and the members of the ethics committee having access to it. The processing of personal data is done according to the European legislation in the field (GDPR).

Answering the survey questions will take approximately 15 to 20 minutes.

Your answers are very important for us, and we thank you for the availability and interest in completing the questionnaire!

Potential Risks and Discomfort You Might Experience when Taking Part in this Study

No harm caused by stress, physical, psychological, social or economic discomfort can be experienced by you, as a participant in the study.

Your Benefits for Taking Part in this Study

There are no direct benefits for you, as a participant.

What You Will Receive for Taking Part in this Study

The participation in this study is in no way compensated, either with financial or material incentives.

What Will Happen with the Information Collected During this Study?

The information collected will be kept confidential, in accordance with the applicable legislation.

What are Your Rights as a Participant in this Study?

Participating in this research is voluntary. The decision not to participate or not be part of this research will bring no penalties, tickets or loss of benefits you already have. If you have any questions concerning your rights as a research subject, or wish to report any harm, injury, risk or risk factor, please contact ...., the president of the Research Ethics Committee from ....

Conflict of interests

The researchers have no financial interest in conducting this study.

Informed Consent

By continuing to provide answers to the following questions, I formulate my explicit, knowingly consent, after asking all the questions I have considered necessary for my correct and complete clarification referring to all aspects concerning my fully voluntary participation in the current research.

Thank you for your participation!

ACKNOWLEDGMENT

Chapter elaborated within the project "Etică şi integritate academică de excepţie în cercetarea ştiinţifică şi actul didactic" [Ethics and academic integrity exceptional in scientific research and didactic act]; Implementer: Stefan cel Mare University in Suceava with financial support from FDI2018, Domain 5, Improving the quality of didactic activity, including respecting academic deontology and ethics. Project code: CNFIS-FDI-2018-0545. Some of the information presented in this chapter has been previously published in research papers, and has been resumed for didactic purposes in this chapter.

REFERENCES

Alexa-Stratulat, T., Neagu, M., Neagu, A., Alexa, I. D., & Ioan, B. G. (2018). Consent for participating in clinical trials - Is it really informed? *Developing World Bioethics*. doi:10.1111/dewb.12199 PMID:29933502

Alexander, L. (1996). The Moral Magic of Consent (II). *Legal Theory*, *2*(03), 165–174. doi:10.1017/S1352325200000471

Árnason, V. (2004). Coding and consent: Moral challenges of the database project in Iceland. *Bioethics*, *18*(1), 27–49. doi:10.1111/j.1467-8519.2004.00377.x PMID:15168697

Astarastoae, V. (2018a). Cercetarea pe subiecţi umani – situaţia deţinuţilor. Iasi. Retrieved from https://www.facebook.com/notes/vasile-astărăstoae/cercetarea-pe-subiecţi-umani-situaţia-deţinuţilor/490638524665163

Astarastoae, V. (2018b). Dr. prof. Vasile Astărăstoae: Cercetarea pe subiecţi umani – abuzurile asupra deţinuţilor. *Ortodoxinfo.Ro*. Retrieved from http://ortodoxinfo.ro/2018/03/21/dr-prof-vasile-astarastoae-cercetarea-pe-subiecti-umani-abuzurile-asupra-detinutilor/

Ballantyne, A. (2016). It's mine: Ownership and control of health data. In S. Holm, A. Ballantyne, J. Wilson, & K. Borgerson (Eds.), *Symposium: Consent for Secondary Use of Clinical Data for Research.*

Beauchamp, T. L., & Childress, J. F. (1994). *Principles of biomedical ethics. Emergency medicine clinics of North America* (4th ed.). New York: Oxford University Press. doi:10.1016/S0033-3182(95)71674-7

Benea, I. (2015a). Exclusiv: Ieşeni morţi în urma unor experimente medicale ilegale? Scandal de proporţii [Exclusive: Iskans killed by illegal medical experiments? Scandal of scale]. *Ziarul de Iaşi [The Newspaper of Iasi]*. Retrieved from https://www.ziaruldeiasi.ro/stiri/exclusiv-ieseni-morti-in-urma-unor-experimente-medicale-ilegale-scandal-de-proportii--84920.html

Benea, I. (2015b). Cazul experienţelor de la „Neuro“: Am vorbit cu familia unui pacient-cobai, [Case of experiences from "Neuro": We talked to a guinea-pig's family]. *Ziarul de Iasi [The Newspaper of Iasi]*. Retrieved from https://www.ziaruldeiasi.ro/stiri/cazul-experientelor-de-la-a-neuroa-am-vorbit-cu-familia-unui-pacient-cobai--85026.html

Bulger, R. E., Heitman, E., & Reiser, S. J. (2002). Research with human beings. In R. E. Bulger, E. Heitman, & S. J. Reiser (Eds.), *The Ethical Dimensions of the Biological and Health Sciences* (pp. 117–125). Cambridge, UK: Cambridge University Press.

Christman, J. (2009). Autonomy in moral and political philosophy. In *Standford Encyclopedia of Philosophy*. Retrieved from https://plato.stanford.edu/archives/fall2009/entries/autonomy-moral/

Cojocaru, M. Cojocaru., Ş., Gârleanu, D., Irimescu, G., & Şoitu, C. (2010). Populaţii vulnerabile şi automarginalizate. Strategii de intervenţie şi efecte perverse [Vulnerable and self-originated populations. Intervention strategies and perverse effects]. Iaşi, Romania: LUMEN.

Donchin, A. (2001). Understanding autonomy relationally: Toward a reconfiguration of bioethical principles. *The Journal of Medicine and Philosophy*, *26*(4), 365–386. doi:10.1076/jmep.26.4.365.3012 PMID:11484130

European Union. (2001, April 4). Directive 2001/20 / EC of the European Parliament and of the Council of 4 April 2001.

Faden, R. R., & Beauchamp, T. L. (1986). *A history and theory of informed consent*. Oxford, UK: Oxford University Press.

Frunza, A., & Sandu, A. (2017a). Ethical acceptability of using generic consent for secondary use of data and biological samples in medical research. *Acta Bioethica*, *23*(2), 289–299. doi:10.4067/S1726-569X2017000200289

Frunza, A., & Sandu, A. (2017b). Formalization of informed consent. From ethical to administrative use. *Postmodern Openings*, *8*(3), 69–95. doi:10.18662/po/2017.0803.07

Funza, A., & Sandu, A. (2017). Values grounding the informed consent in medical practice: Theory and practice. *SAGE Open*, *7*(4). doi:10.1177/2158244017740397

Grady, C. (2015). Enduring and emerging challenges of informed consent. *The New England Journal of Medicine*, *37*(9), 855–862. doi:10.1056/NEJMra1411250 PMID:25714163

Gupta, U. C. (2013). Informed consent in clinical research: Revisiting few concepts and areas. *Perspectives in Clinical Research*, *4*(1), 26–32. doi:10.4103/2229-3485.106373 PMID:23533976

Guyer, P. (1998, July 25). *Kant, Immanuel (1724-1804)*. Milton Park, UK: Taylor and Francis. doi:10.4324/9780415249126-DB047-1

Hansson, M. G., Dillner, J., Bartram, C. R., Carlson, J. A., & Helgesson, G. (2006). Should donors be allowed to give broad consent to future biobank research? *The Lancet Oncology*, *7*(3), 266–269. doi:10.1016/S1470-2045(06)70618-0 PMID:16510336

Helgesson, G. (2012). In defense of broad consent. *Cambridge Quarterly of Healthcare Ethics*, *21*(1), 40–50. doi:10.1017/S096318011100048X PMID:22152457

Ho, A. (2008). The individualist model of autonomy and the challenge of disability. *Journal of Bioethical Inquiry*, *5*(2–3), 193–207. doi:10.100711673-007-9075-0

Hofmann, B. (2009). Broadening consent and diluting ethics? *Journal of Medical Ethics*, *35*(2), 125–129. doi:10.1136/jme.2008.024851 PMID:19181887

Hofmann, B., Solbakk, J. H., & Holm, S. (2009). Consent to biobank research: one size fits all? In J. H. Solbakk, S. Holm, & B. Hofmann (Eds.), *The Ethics of Research Biobanking* (pp. 3–23). New York, USA: Springer; doi:10.1007/978-0-387-93872-1_1

Kant, I. (1972). *Critica rațiunii practice* [The critique of practical reason]. Bucharest, Romania: Științifică.

Kapp, M. B. (1983). Children's assent for participation in pediatric research protocols: Assessing national practice. *Clinical Pediatrics*, *22*(4), 275–278. doi:10.1177/000992288302200406 PMID:6825373

Kim, S. Y., & Miller, F. G. (2014). Informed Consent for Pragmatic Trials — The Integrated Consent Model. *The New England Journal of Medicine*, *370*(8), 769–772. doi:10.1056/NEJMhle1312508 PMID:24552326

Kuther, T. L., & Posada, M. (2004). Children and adolescents' capacity to provide informed consent for participation in research. *Advances in Psychology Research*, *32*, 163–173. PMID:16986221

Lederer, S. E. (1997). *Subjected to science: Human experimentation in America before the Second World War*. Baltimore, MD: Johns Hopkins University Press. doi:10.1080/03612759.1995.9949143

Maclean, A. (2009). *Autonomy, informed consent and medical law: A relational challenge. Autonomy, informed consent and medical law: A relational challenge*. Cambridge, UK: Cambridge University Press. doi:10.1017/CBO9780511576119

Meisel, A., & Roth, L. H. (1981). What we do and do not know about informed consent. *Journal of the American Medical Association*, *246*(21), 2473–2477. doi:10.1001/jama.1981.03320210039022 PMID:7299972

Mill, J. S. (2014). *Utilitarismul* [*Utilitarianism*]. Bucharest, Romania: ALL.

O'Neill, O. (2003). Some limits of informed consent. *Journal of Medical Ethics*, *29*(1), 4–7. doi:10.1136/jme.29.1.4 PMID:12569185

Petrini, C. (2010). "Broad" consent, exceptions to consent and the question of using biological samples for research purposes different from the initial collection purpose. *Social Science & Medicine*, *70*(2), 217–220. doi:10.1016/j.socscimed.2009.10.004 PMID:19853341

Ploug, T., & Holm, S. (2015). Going beyond the false dichotomy of broad or specific consent: A meta-perspective on participant choice in research using human tissue. *The American Journal of Bioethics*, *15*(9), 44–46. doi:10.1080/15265161.2015.1062178 PMID:26305752

Purcaru, D., Lazăr, O., Purcaru, A., & Rogozea, L. (2012). Evoluţia consimţământului informat în cercetarea clinică [Evolution of informed consent in clinical research]. *Jurnal Medical Braşovean [The Medical Journal of Brasov], 1*, 81–84. Retrieved from http://oaji.net/articles/2014/693-1396104695.pdf

Roberts, L. W. (2002). Informed consent and the capacity for voluntarism. *The American Journal of Psychiatry, 159*(5), 705–712. doi:10.1176/appi.ajp.159.5.705 PMID:11986120

Sandu, A. (2016). *Social construction of reality as communicative action* (1st ed.). Newcastle upon Tyne, UK: Cambridge Scholars Publishing.

Shahnazarian, D., Hagemann, J., Aburto, M., & Susan, R. (2013). *Informed consent in human subjects research. Office for the protection of research subjects*. doi:10.1097/FCH.0b013e31822dda9e

The Convention for the Protection of Human Rights and Dignity of the Human Being with regard to the Application of Biology and Medicine: Convention on Human Rights and Biomedicine. (1997).

The Nuremberg Code. (1946). Retrieved from https://history.nih.gov/research/downloads/nuremberg.pdf

Van Hoof, W., Meesters, K., Dossche, L., Christiaens, D., De Bruyne, P., & Vande Walle, J. (2018). Ethical considerations of researchers conducting pediatric clinical drug trials: A qualitative survey in two Belgian University Children's Hospitals. *European Journal of Pediatrics, 177*(7), 1003–1008. doi:00431-018-3151-9 doi:10.1007

Veterans Health Administration (VHA). (2009). VHA Handbook 1004.1, Informed consent for treatment and procedures. Retrieved from http://www.ethics.va.gov/docs/policy/VHA_Handbook_1004-01_Informed_Consent_Policy_20090814.pdf

KEY TERMS AND DEFINITIONS

Agent Capacity: the ability to understand and appreciate the nature of one's own condition and how the act of participating in the research could affect his/her own health status or quality of life.

Assent: a form of expressing the intention to participate in the research, of a person who is incapable of consenting due to reasons of age or mental state. For this approval to be valid, it must be accompanied by the written consent of the legal representative.

Autonomy: a philosophical concept underlying the idea of informed consent, meaning the subject's capacity to deliberate upon his situation and decide upon his/her own person based on the most complete and accurate information he/she could receive.

Broad Consent: a type of consent where a participant expresses his/her general consent that his own personal information, including bio-medical or health-related information and/or tissue sample can be used in further research, without a new explicit consent from his/her side.

Informed Consent: a process of providing the participants in the research with all the necessary information in order to deliberate and voluntarily decide to participate or not in the research, and/or to withdraw from the research. Informed consent is expressed by signing a document containing all that information agreed upon, called "informed consent form".

Research on Human Subjects: a type of research involving human participants. The research could be in the bio-medical field, but also in psychology, sociology, anthropology, economy and so on. Such research requires a special consideration on the human rights and dignity, estimating the risk the participants might experience and cannot be conducted without the expressed informed consent of the participant(s) or their legal representative.

ENDNOTES

1 Informed Consent Form adapted after the form developed and used within the project "Studii postdoctorale in etica politicilor de sanatate" [Postdoctoral studies in the ethics of health-related policies], financed by the European Union through POSDRU/89/1.5/S/61879, in which the author Antonio Sandu was part of, as a postdoctoral researcher.

2 Informed Consent Form adapted after the form developed and used within the project "Studii postdoctorale in etica politicilor de sanatate" [Postdoctoral studies in the ethics of health-related policies], financed by the European Union through POSDRU/89/1.5/S/61879, in which the author Antonio Sandu was part of, as a postdoctoral researcher.

3 The model of informed consent form was developed and used by Ana Frunza within the project "Informed Consent between Theory and Practice in North-Eastern Region of Romania Medical Research Field", project conducted within the Advanced Certified Program in Research Ethics (*supported by NIH Research Grant #5R25TW007085,* sponsored by *Fogarty International Center, National Institute of Environmental Health Sciences, National Heart Lung and Blood Institute* and *National Institute on Drug Abuse).*

4 Taken entirely from the original form of IC.

Chapter 10
Personhood, Cultural Ethics, and Biomedical Research:
African vs. Euro-American Perspectives

Ike Valentine Iyioke
University of Michigan – Flint, USA

ABSTRACT

This chapter rides on the premise that the concept of personhood, as embedded in research ethics principles, needs re-examining. As the base upon which the principles were developed and falsely universalized, it needs pointing out that personhood in the Euro-American sense differs markedly from what it is in non-Western cultures. A careful delineation of this understanding should be a teaching moment for researchers, clinicians, bioethicists, students and academics as they confront multicultural perspectives in health research. Hence, it helps to properly inform and effectively erase presumptive tendencies, so people can avoid any voluntary or involuntary unethical behavior, which may arise from ignorance particularly in multicultural settings.

INTRODUCTION

This chapter rides on the premise that the concept of personhood,[1] as embedded in research ethics principles, needs re-examining. Having been ignored and/or taken for granted thus far, that need has become urgent. As the base upon which the principles were developed and falsely universalized, it needs stressing that personhood in the Euro-American[2] sense differs markedly from what obtains in non-Western cultures such as in Africa. A careful delineation and recalibration of this understanding should be a teaching moment for researchers, clinicians, bioethicists, students and academics as they confront multicultural perspectives in health research. Hence, it helps to properly inform and effectively erase presumptive tendencies, so people can avoid any voluntary or involuntary unethical behavior that might arise from ignorance particularly in multicultural settings. The core task of this chapter is to contrast the African with the Euro-American perspectives on personhood in relation to biomedical research.

DOI: 10.4018/978-1-5225-6310-5.ch010

While most clinical studies today are initiated and registered in the Global North (predominantly in the U.S.), many of the actual trials are sometimes outsourced and offshored (DuBois, 2003; Petryna, 2009); often to the Global South (Rehnquist, 2001). Owing to this intensified practice of transnational biomedical research, plus the considerable controversy about the mainstream ethics of research which is narrowly constructed with Western individualistic philosophy, the following question which is shaped by the realities of globalization will serve as guide. In what ways can researchers remain respectful of other cultures as transnational borders continue to disappear? To contextualize, how can researchers ensure compliance, guideline consistency, and checks and balances across borders as well as recognize and respect multicultural systems and not project hubris?

The proposal in this chapter is, to some extent, related to, though also different from, that of Marshall and Koenig (2004) who sought for answers on how global bioethics might account for profound - and constantly transforming - sources of cultural differences. This proposal is similar in the sense that it highlights something that is distinctively and culturally ethical in an African context. But at the same time this chapter's agenda – personhood – is much more specific than that of Marshall and Koenig's. Analysts including Marshall & Koenig (2004), Levitt & Zwart (2009), and Olweny (1994), have worked to bridge the divide in bioethical discourse, and have managed to elicit some measured response from relevant US agencies which review the regulation and oversight of internationally sponsored research (Nuffield Council on Bioethics, 1999). Nonetheless, more dissenting voices in the Global South who seek to expand the debate have largely been ignored (Bhutta, 2002).

The result of Macklin's (1983) landmark survey, which still holds true, concluded that attempts to precisely delineate "person" have been prescriptive rather than descriptive. Also, the impressive work of sociologist De Craemer (1983) has compared Japanese with Congolese and American perspectives on personhood. But in much of bioethics literature, one finds little that consists of normative theorization of the notion of personhood in African thought with respect to its impact on bioethics practice. Since the rapid expansion of principlism namely, the four principles of research ethics,[3] and its universal application, there are continuing calls for the right action, meaning, the articulation and justification of a comprehensive norm to account for what personhood really stands for in multicultural (in this case, African) setting. By "African personhood" I mean values associated with the concept within the African communitarian context as opposed to Euro-American individualistic one. In this chapter, the aim is to help develop further awareness as a way of bridging the gap that exists in the field. Indeed, like Metz's (2007) attempt to develop an African moral theory, the field of cultural ethics is in dire need of providing well-defended general principle that is grounded in particular duties and informed by values that can match such dominant Western theories as Kantian respect for persons. The contribution here serves as a foundational effort toward the formulation of such a rubric.

The standard way of assessing all biomedical studies is to adhere to the yardstick established to regulate biomedical research. This set of principles arose in response to numerous historical acts of experimental callousness which debased human subjects as in the Nuremberg and Tuskegee atrocities, among others. To help curtail future recurrence, the Nuremberg Code (and other similar codes) established human subject protection guidelines. However, these principles which are rooted in Western individualistic notions of personhood, are inadequate in for example Africa, which sees the person not as an isolated individual, but as part of the community which is embedded in kinship, community and the physical and spiritual environment. The principlist approach is borne out of typical Euro-American thinking which emphasizes the individual and his rights. The African holistic worldview is its opposite and there is no better illustration of this argument than in examining the notion of personhood in African philosophical thinking.

This chapter articulates the notion of personhood by recasting its major features. The intent is to prompt a serious interest and plot a path to understanding its multiple implications for bioethics as a field that continues to expand in Africa. In African philosophy, the concept of personhood (which contrasts sharply with its Western counterpart) is both pivotal on its own and on the collective bioethics project.

Three main sections are thus identified. First, is a recast of some main features of personhood as expressed by some 20th century African philosophers. The second part contrasts and compares the African with the Western view on personhood while laying the foundation on which to extend the discourse to include the larger questions that frame the emerging field of bioethics practice in Africa. The third part parses through the subject matter within the bioethical framework while briefly considering some general criticisms.

The function of staging substantive discourses about the self as an African 'person' is unique because of the way it is delineated from the essentials of African culture, philosophy and customs (Comaroff & Comaroff, 2001). On the other hand, philosophical concepts are never individuated, they are interconnected, interrelated and holistic. To wit, African philosophical discourses on just about any subject is rarely analyzed without reference to religion, the gods/God, (not to preclude atheistic opinions) and for that matter, everything else. Considerations of personhood as an ethno-socio-anthropological subject matter cut across the boundaries of many scholarly disciplines while assuming normative, thematic, descriptive, as well as analytic tones. Within the African philosophical framework, personhood is an all-encompassing live wire. To discuss it is like running a thread through a plethora of conspectuses such as time, life, God, marriage, health, and nature. Whether as a body, an identity, a selfhood, or a person – objectivized or subjectivized – the discourses are guaranteed to be zesty. The significance of this may be obvious given that the concept of personhood in bioethics is the fulcrum around which the vortex of activities swirls.

The 'African Man'

The understanding of the 'different conceptions' of man in African philosophy and religion may be pluralized, but essentially it is singularized; meaning, the interpretations might be many, albeit expressed in different ways, but are similar in their essentials. Thus, the ensuing analysis in relation to person is poised to make "valid general statements about Africa, Africans, African cultures, and African relational habits," apologies to Owomoyela (1994), that suggest similarity and uniformity over the entire continent, with negligible dissimilarity in their particulars.

In the oft-cited primordial text, *Bantu Philosophy*, the Belgian missionary Placide Tempels (1959: 64), portrays 'man' (or *Muntu*) as a vital force, a living being which radiates energy; or the being that possesses life that is true. As the first among all creation, man dominates plants, animals and minerals which existed by Divine decree for the assistance of the higher being, i.e., himself. Interestingly, this rendition shares obvious similitude with the Judeo-Christian teaching.

More remarkably, the full meaning of a man's life can only be realized in relation to other humans and the environment. Numerous other writers on the philosophical expressions of African personhood similarly agree that the fulfillment of a man's life depends and is enhanced by the support and enrichment of all other (human/spiritual) life forces around, as well as other elements in the environment. In concert, it is conceivable that a person's life's worth is collaterally enhanced or diminished by these surrounding forces and elements. So beyond being a social being, man is suffused in all creation. Seen via Bantu philosophical lens, the *Bantu* cannot be a loner as there are forces acting all around him in the ontological hierarchy of forces (Tempels, 1959: 68–69). The far-reaching relationship is so constitutive of the self that a serious disruption in this relational connectivity could be "supernaturally, as well as naturally threatening and potentially destructive to the family and the community as a whole" (Fox & Willis, 1983: 23).

Mbiti (1970: 108), seems to maintain the same thinking:

In traditional life, the individual does not and cannot exist alone except corporately. He owes his existence to other people, including those of past generations and his contemporaries. He is simply part of the whole. Whatever happens to the individual happens to the whole group, and whatever happens to the whole group happens to the individual. The individual can only say: I am because we are; and since we are, therefore I am. This is a cardinal point in the understanding of the African view of man.

Think of it this way: let's say an individual is standing on a 12-ft stool in an open field, it would be impossible to visualize him/her in thin air without a background. In like manner, the individual is an imperceptible reality on his/her own without a background – that background translates to the community of persons which gives him/her ontological cogency. Studies suggest that it is inadequate to view people in any typical African society as 'complete' in themselves or as whole numbers without reference to other humans and the environment. This validates the traditional belief that each individual, or "dividual," is perpetually incomplete and is eternally being added to others and is fully evolved after he/she is enmeshed with others in his/her milieu (Niehaus, 2002: 190). Thus, the attribute that I call 'one-in-all' or 'bio-eco-communalism,' BEC, sticks out as the most outstanding characteristic in understanding man in the African context. The same idea has variously been called group solidarity; communalistic character; communitarian view; eco-communalism; communalism; the communalism thesis, and so on.

A broad view on the concept of person across African regions of the West, East and Southern ethnic groups, would yield three overlapping characteristics of the human person: the force, communalism, and shadow theses (the first two have been referenced above). Also, noted above and reiterated here by Kaphagawani (2004) who credits Tempels (Tempels, 1959), is the point that human beings or entities "are nothing more than essential energies or vital forces. To be sure, this force is not only a necessary attribute of being, it is the essence of being" (Kaphagawani, 2004). The shadow thesis, the least on the totem pole, refers to the aspect of the human being in Bantu philosophy that makes him "both a complete animal and a being with intelligence; complete because he or she possesses 'the vital principle of animality;' and intelligence insofar as he or she 'is animated by a vital principle' which is immortal and in which are anchored the intelligent operations proper to man" (Kaphagawani, 2004).

Further analysis of the concept of 'man' in the African thought reveals how it can apply to the wider moral, juridical, epistemological, ontological and metaphysical realms. Given that 'man' as a force, does not exist in a vacuum, we are reminded that he is a force in the hierarchy of forces. In descending order, this ranked order of forces begins with God, the Great Force, then the spirits, founding fathers, the living dead, according to the order of succession; then the living according to their rank in terms of seniority. "After living men come animals, vegetables, and minerals, which are in turn categorized on their relative importance in their own classes" (Onywuenyi, 1991: 40). Hence, the perceived bond between persons – in an ontological relationship – leads the African to know and feel himself/herself to be in intimate relationship with other forces that are ranked successively on top and below him/her.

In terms of African epistemology, "Knowledge or wisdom for the African consists in how deeply he understands the nature of forces and their interaction. [With God as the First Force and the ultimate wisdom], He knows all forces, their ordering, their dependence, their potential, and their mutual interaction" (Onywuenyi, 1991). A person's level of knowledge naturally heightens as he/she approaches divine wisdom. Proximity to wisdom or divine knowledge is attained the older you are.

Further still, a person's moral agency and the legal grounding of his/her actions indicate that the realms of ethics and law are closely interwoven. Thus, "an act will be accounted ethically good if it can be judged ontologically and by deduction be assessed as juridically just" (Onywuenyi, 1991). Viewed as both metaphysical ethics in one sense and ethical communalism in another sense it is implied that the human conduct is always within the confines of a consideration for the community of vital forces whenever decisions of goodness or evil of his/her proper actions are being examined. "All customary law that is worthy of the name is inspired, animated, and justified from the African point of view, by the philosophy of living forces, or growth, of influence, and of the vital hierarchy. The validity and strength of the customary law of indigenous peoples reside in its foundation in their philosophy…" (Onywuenyi, 1991).

In considering a normative definition, a person is not just a mere corporeal being with a certain psycho-physical endowment, but instead, a being of a kind who has shown a basic willingness and ability to fulfill his/her obligations in the community. Personhood, on this showing, is something of an accomplishment (Wiredu, 2004, p. 17). This definition points to the full realization of 'manhood.' Thus, ontologically speaking a person is conceived as an organism that has metamorphosed from the fetal to fully formed stage, having gone through an extended integrative course. And during this long process of transmuting evolvement, the community plays a vital role as catalyst and as prescriber of norms (Menkiti, 1984, p. 172).

To be clear, the fact that African cultural settings are founded and sustained by shared beliefs, practices and values does not mean the individual is inert or robotic with no autonomy and self-determination. And if the truth must be told, the West's extreme liberal stance has not always been this extreme as renowned anthropologist Geertz (1965) conceptualization attests. And deny it as we might, it is an axiom that "every culture is made up of a set of symbolic devices for the control of behavior, for giving the individual a set of goals, and for giving him a set of goals for himself and for others." A tack on this point is the pragmatic fact that "man's biological constitution is as much as a product of his capacity for culture as his capacity for culture is a product of his biological nature" (Geertz, 1965).

There is communal supremacy and control no doubt, but the apparent absence of metaphysical features such as voluntariness or freedom ought to be seen in the context of the fact that one cannot rationally act to meet communal obligations without recognition and validation of one's ability in pursuit of his/her responsibilities to the group. "A person is not just an individual of human parentage, but also one evincing in his/her projects and achievements and adequate sense of social responsibility." After all, "a community is a collectivity of persons, principles, processes, and structures that defines social norms, moral expectations, and responsibilities on the basis of which one is recognized as a person" (Ikuenobe, 2006, pp. 118-119). To neglect this fact is to risk becoming a "dangling" or a socially disembodied metaphysical entity who cannot "apply communal norms to guide his conduct for personal interests and communal needs".

To press home the abiding duty the individual owes the society, it has been argued that the individual ought to contribute to the community not because it is expected of him/her, but because *it*, the community, is him/her (Verhoef & Michel, 1997). Get this:

Man is not just an individual, an Island, left to himself and sufficient to himself, on his own. Man is essentially community. No one ever came to being as a bolt from the blues, like an oil bean seed falling from the sky, as our proverb says, 'I am always a we.' We in the nuclear family, we in the extended family, we in the village and town, etc. One often hears of the vaunted 'rugged individualism' of the West... In Igboland, in Nigeria, in Africa generally, the community, the common good is the dominant reality and it alone ultimately provides the context and guarantee of individual rights (Okere, 2005, pp. 3-4).

In opposition to Menkiti (2004) and Menkiti (1984), to name just two, and in a move that signals a middle ground, Eze (2008), seems to apportion equal valence to both the individual and the community. His idea is that no community exists without its component parts, likewise every individual's subjectivity is necessarily located and brought to fruition within the community. "To argue that the community pre-exists the individual is to argue that we can indeed have a community without a person for the community is necessarily constituted by persons" (Eze, 2008). Neither can you argue the ontologically contradictory opposite. Thus, the identity or subjectivity of the individual and the community are mutually constitutive and that none is supreme. He concludes that the individual and the community are engaged in a contemporaneous formation as neither pre-existed the other.

But it is doubtful that Eze has laid the argument to rest, just as the chicken or egg argument has not. While the person-community relationship is mutual and constitutive, this author is unconvinced that it is *equally* so. Granted, the community is the sum of its parts; but it is also true that the community can thrive without one or some of its parts, while one individual part cannot survive on their own for long. To that end, and Okolo (2002), is right on this, it is the community that makes the individual, to the extent that without the community, the individual has no existence. In other words, though a community can and does suffer diminishment when an individual part is excised; but that is not the case if reversed

Figure 1. The African man: A force among forces
Source: Figure drawn by the author

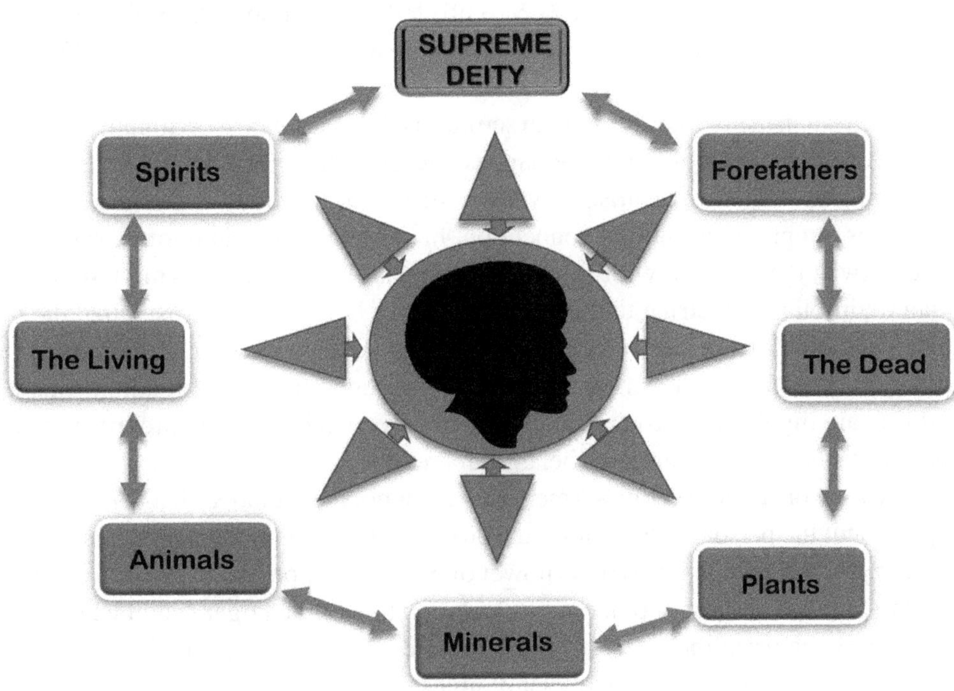

the other way around. Hence, Eze's apportionment of equal valence to both sides has no convincing substantiation in the African belief system.

The efforts by a coterie of Western-trained African intellectuals, (Appiah, 1992); and some home-grown ones (Obioha, 2014) who would rather replace the time-honored African ways of life with some imports, are regrettable. They refute communalism on the basis that its emphasis on conformity, consensus, custom, loyalty and solidarity make it constrictive of the individual liberty. But, they misconstrue the argument by for example, Senghor (1965), that African communalism "was founded on dialogue and reciprocity [and that] the group had priority over the individual without crushing him but allowing him to blossom as a person" (Obioha, 2014).

It is by recognizing the humanity of others that one realizes the fullness of his/her own humanness. And as the reader will soon see in the next segment, the African person is distinctively infused in the African conception of the community and of the world writ large such that whereas Western notions of self tend to draw us inward 'centripetally,' the African notions of self draws us 'centrifugally' outward in relation to the natural and social environment (Jensen & Gaie, 2010, p. 298). Indeed, you could never go wrong with communalism for at the heart of it are a host of social values which aim for the social good: peace, harmony, stability, solidarity, mutual reciprocity, sympathy, generosity, compassion, solidarity, and social wellbeing (Ogunbanjo & Van Bogaert, 2005).

African vs. Western Personhood

The Western vis-à-vis African notions of personhood are like night and day. In terms of application, authors have made comparisons in this area and singled out the Western perspective as the odd one out from the rest of the world. But even as the Euro-American notion is the minority view, it is paradoxically the most publicized.

A corpus of established literature has drawn sharp contrasts between the African and Euro-American perceptions of a person (De Craemer, 1983; Fox & Willis, 1983; Ikuenobe, 2006; Kelbessa, 2005; Kaphagawani, 2004; Mbiti, 1970; Menkiti, 1984, 2004; Onywuenyi, 1991; Owomoyela, 1991; Owomoyela, 1994; Riesman, 1986).

A distinguishing trait in many Euro-American settings is the insistence to maintain one's own 'space'; a phenomenon that risks a devolution into the narcissistic. According to Fox and Willis (Fox & Willis, 1983, p. 20), "in present-day American society we conceive to a remarkable degree of the person in individualistic terms, emphasizing in this connection, his or her rights, autonomy, self-determination, and privacy". In a twist that is laced with some irony, this has become the norm, despite the dominant Judeo-Christian tradition and doctrine that have for centuries been used to proselytize the need to love our neighbors as ourselves; to be our brothers' keepers; and even to love our enemies to the point of turning the other cheek when we are struck on one side. But in reality, filial relationships in the Euro-American tradition are highly restrictive, recognizing mostly members of the proximate nuclear family such as spouses, parents, siblings (and may be, grandparents).

Piot's (1999) review of studies on Euro-American personhood concluded that theoretical approaches on this concept present the person as "autonomous, propertied, self-interested, accumulative and having independent agency – measured in terms of its power of control over others. [The] individual's interest is seen as opposed to both the interest of other individuals and that of the larger social whole" (Piot, 1999).

Hence, a gap exists between the interests of the individual and those of the larger social group and foreshadows more pervasive logical-rational dichotomies.

This view sharply opposes body and mind, thought and feeling, the conscious and the unconscious, self and other, reality and non-reality (imagining, dreaming, and hearing voices for example are not real). In all, this conception of personhood has at least one major paradoxical attribute. Although it places a high positive value on a universalistic definition of the worth, dignity, and equality of every individual person, it tends to be culturally particularistic, and inadvertently ethnocentric (Fox & Willis, 1983).

Areas of commonality between the Western and African perspectives on personhood are at best marginal. For instance, both perspectives regard a person to be not just fully self-conscious but also rational, free, and self-determining (Tangwa, 2000, p. 42). Barring these, other aspects are widely contrasted.

To a point that was already made, the most prominent contrast is that whereas the Euro-American view of a person is that of an autonomous, lone individual; the African 'man' is far more dynamic and can only be defined by reference to the environing community. "And this primacy is meant to apply not only ontologically, but also in regard to epistemic accessibility the sense of self-identity which the individual comes to possess cannot be made sense of except by reference to these collective facts" (Menkiti, 1984).

The second major point of contrast, also hinted above, is the element that a person in African thought is 'truly' a person after being through a process of incorporation – "something which has to be achieved and is not given simply because one is born of human seed" (Menkiti, 1984). This second trait nicely tucks under the communalist concept in the Afro-cultural setting that highlights the fundamental interdependence of people and expressed in terms of worldviews, sensibilities, and behavioral inclinations. Because communalism emphasizes the importance of social relations, it can similarly be expressed attitudinally on interpersonal levels. By Jagers and Mock's (1995) reckoning, "A communal ethos embodies a sense of shared goals, common destiny, and corporate well-being" (Menkiti, 1984).

Empirical studies (Schwartz, 1990; Schwartz & Bilsky, 1987), have lent support to this thesis. In highlighting the polar opposites between the Euro-American and African conceptions, they argue that in African culture collectivism emphasizes the promotion of wellbeing of social others, care and protection of kith and kin, sanctions against the violation of group expectations and mores, and a universal adherence to group customs. Conversely, according to the Western perspective, individuals are groomed to be self-centered; accomplish personal goals; and, claim to possess unfettered functioning in pursuit of pleasure and sensuous gratification, and status and control. In contrast, Ikuenobe's (2006) radical approach to examining personhood is credited by Metz (2008) to be fairly unique in the way it uses an analytic methodology to reject individualism across the board. Ikuenobe argues for a "communitarian state, for a freedom entirely constituted by communal norms and even for 'indoctrination' and 'epistemic authoritarianism' of certain kinds that are not merely innocuous, but also in an important sense, 'rational'" (Metz, 2008)."

The opposing conceptions (Western vs. African) are profound and are typified by Menkiti's (Menkiti, 1984) illustration which is recreated here.

As shown, while the African view allocates ontological independence to human society (S), and moves from society to individual persons (P), the Euro-American perspective asserts autonomy and moves instead from the individual to the society (Menkiti, 1984).

The work by Tangwa (2004), a rising intellectual theorist of African contemporary thought, further illuminates this juxtaposition, arguing that the Western conception of a person is appropriate only for the ascription of moral responsibility rather than for the ascription of moral worth. Contrarily, the African perception of a person is drawn from the African worldview which incorporates "…all the categories, stages, and modalities of a human being…" (Tangwa, 2004) and intimately belonging to an eco-bio-communitarian moral community made up of moral agents.

Figure 2. Western vs. African perspectives on personhood
Source: Figure drawn by the author

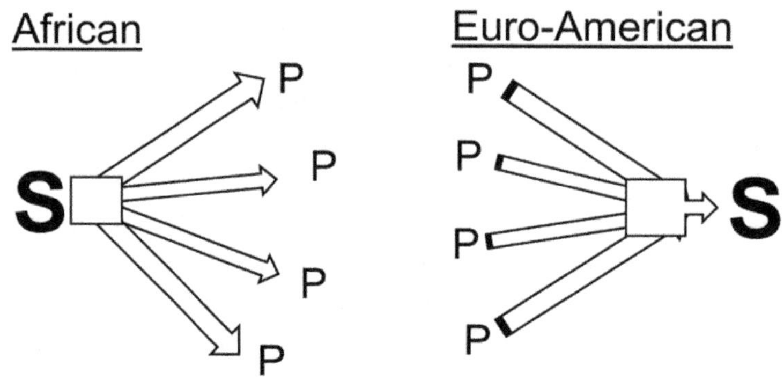

He surmises that the Western ethical theory seems to concentrate on the object of morality, the individual, to the neglect of the subject, the agent. This he says, further conjures up the attribute in the Western culture of the principle of might is right, a characteristic of the Western imperialism, colonialism, domination, exploitation and monopoly of commerce. "By concentrating on the individual rather than the agent, Western ethical theory successfully shifts critical ethical attention from themselves and their actions onto their victims" (Tangwa, 2004). This has led to a value judgment that is dictated by economic considerations, scientific and technological advancement, and forged an unholy Trinitarian mechanism behind the constant reformulation of moral categories in the Western world. This chapter could not agree more.

African Personhood and Bioethics

Has bioethics practice become universal? Does being universal translate to being identical or even similar at all locales across the globe? Certainly, bioethics practice has witnessed a galloping spread throughout the world in recent decades, but approaches differ – or rather, approaches should differ – because bioethics practice is conditioned by respective environing circumstances. Just like politics, all ethics should be local. Using Asian medical systems and settings, Christakis (1992) elucidated four ethical models to guide the conduct of transcultural biomedical research; establishing in tow that research ethics, though universally conceptualized, are actually culturally relative. So, even as the field is governed by 'universal principles,' particularism usually holds sway at the socio-cultural level. Prima facie, it seems innocuous that personhood projects a universal notion. But under closer consideration it is fitting to ascribe the universalist claim, a relativist interpretation and application in order for bioethics to serve the interest of everyone in sui generis. This noble cause must be pursued irrespective of the intransigence of some who refuse to budge but rather insist on seeing the entire issue of international health research only through the looking glass of guidelines and regulations. For supporters of the status quo, a single moral standard should govern all research on human subjects, regardless of where and when the research is carried out (Bhutta, 2002).

But, it makes sense to heed the cultural realities and frame of reference of different peoples for bioethics to have any meaning. This includes in matters equally patterning to both genders (Lanre-Abass, 2012). Also, that is Gbadegesin's (1993) argument in laying down two aspects of a people's worldview relevant to bioethical issues: their conception of the human person and their conception of cause. "What [people] consider themselves to be and what they consider to be the principles of causation will normally influence their attitudes to health and illness and their choices regarding health care" (Gbadegesin, 1993).

To recap, conceptualizing the African person from 'outside-in' (rather than 'inside-out') makes for an exciting endeavor, particularly given its elemental dynamism. Though a composite and unique identity, the African person is vivacious; he/she also is in continuous process of waxing and waning in response to the play of forces within and upon his/her individuality from interpersonal, physical and supernatural sources.

This communalist element and its deep-rooted impact can be felt in no less way than in health care. The individual is integrally located and anchored in a mesh of relationships within the family, village and clan (living and dead), all of whom are primordial sources of his physical, psychic, and spiritual wellbeing. This is particularly true of relatives or significant others, whose closeness may generate the feeling of pride or its opposite, humility; malice or love; disrespect or collegiality; excitement or apathy, likeness or hostility, love or rancor, and the capacity to harm or help through the harnessing of the shades of energy residing within or around a person's sphere.

The analysis of issues pertaining to African mental health, child development and traditional conceptions and practices of handling mental health, provides further inroad to examining this subject matter. It is common to think that one's misfortune – sickness, lack of progress in the family, at work or business – could be attributed to other beings (people around, ancestral spirits, and so on), with whom he/she communes. The consequence then becomes the 'group ego conundrum' which refers for instance, to the belief that someone "could be eating your soul or casting a spell on you" (Riesman, 1986). Seen as such, the understanding of the person, which perceives the self as connected to forces and entities outside it, could present considerable challenges of its own, and to the broader public health sector. At first glance, this may be viewed as a potential downside. May be. But, try casting a wider perspective and you quickly realize the overarching perspective that African societies are organized around the requirements of duty and obligation to the larger community. This broader spectrum trumps everything else.

To test this phenomenon, a question could be posed like this: In matters of reproductive health and sexual rights, who owns the body and whose opinion matters most – the woman, the unborn, the husband, or the society? With empirical research findings as proof, the answer is that "in many African societies, community fertility desires have been known to inform or, indeed, to override the very notion of individual reproductive choice" (Izugbara & Undie, 2008: 165). This factuality endues, in spite of numerous international declarations adopted by various organizations and labeled along the so-called universal human rights. The upshot is that many of similar worldwide declarations ignore cultural milieus that are affiliated with strongly community-oriented traditions; thus, resulting in incontrovertible tensions between African ideology and Western discourse of the body and its implications. It thus seems that the sooner the argument becomes clear, that in African cultures individual validation is attained only amidst the solidarity of their family and community, the better (Izugbara & Undie, 2008).

It is only in this way that the community allows the individual to actualize himself/herself. Consequently, international sexual rights declarations – from abortion, family planning, sex education, to sexual orientation – that are constructed along individualistic Western world-views, often result in tensive backlash in much of Africa. To reiterate, the African person is a "fractual" which cannot be expressed in a whole number. "He or she is perennially incomplete and forever involved in the process of being added to and built upon by the gifts of others ..., their actions are always in context; and society is embodied in their dispositions" (Niehaus, 2002).

It needs repeating that strong allegiance to the community does not mean the element of individuality is completely vitiated. If it did, there would be no recognition for individual's creativeness and inventiveness which would lead to the erosion of human rights. Yet, there is tacit de-emphasis in the cult of the individual. In Owomoyela's (Owomoyela, 1991) exegesis, the fact is not necessarily that Africans do not believe in individualism. Any society that encourages heroism and extols it, as Africans certainly do, evidently inspires individual excellence. "[However] to attach one's name on an object or an idea is to assert exclusive claim and proprietorship to it, whereas traditional society frowns on the implied possessiveness and ostentatious self-importance."

Like Izugbara and Undie's (Izugbara & Undie, 2008) work but focusing on the HIV/AIDS prevention campaign in Botswana, is yet another revelation of a Western-conceived ideology that was force-fed on an African setting without regard to prevailing indigenous cultural realities. More specifically, it was Botswana's wholesale adoption of an exclusive Western model of HIV prevention, testing and counseling program – an individual rights-based prototype – which negates the indigenous understanding of personhood or human agency as rooted in African communalism, and other existing ethno-medical beliefs and cultural practices (Jensen & Gaie, 2010).

The result of the prevention campaign has been marginal if tepid in a country with one of the world's worst HIV cases (over 17 percent of the population aged 18 months and above was HIV-positive in 2008). Like the recommendation just above, the authors advice that it would serve the recipient community well if future public health policies or programs were designed and implemented with the realization that ethical principles or human rights norms are [not alien, but] inherent in African communalism in ways that are respectful of cultural norms. "Failure to apply these standard methods undermines our ability and responsibility to control the HIV epidemic" (Jensen & Gaie, 2010).

One other way to gauge the importance of the human person in African thought is in the premium value placed on human reproduction. "[Children are] so highly valued that procreation is considered the main purpose of marriage. In [a typical] African culture, marriage for mere companionship is rare, if not completely nonexistent. A child is always welcome no matter how it is conceived and no matter how it is (Tangwa, 2004). Notwithstanding, circumstances involving taboos such as incest and rape that lead to pregnancies are routinely disapproved. But it is hard to find instances where pregnancies are terminated or newborns from such wrenching events exterminated in the guise of personal choice. In addition, newborns are by and large, accepted even if they were born with disabilities. Indeed, a human life is unaccomplished without a child (barring any misfortunes). It is one way of determining a fulfilled life of a person – full attainment of personhood (Gbadegesin, 1993).

Tangwa spots a meeting (yet contra-opposite) point of interest between this sort of outlook with the assisted reproductive methods of the West versus the African perspective. While the Western perspective focuses mostly on people wishing to withhold, limit or eradicate the possibility of the individual's ability to procreate (temporarily or permanently), the typical African cultural perspective is inclined mainly to aid the birthing of more and healthy off-springs (but also would welcome infants with disabilities) and to accord them equal (sometimes more) respect and rights as any other person. It is in this connection that biomedical or assisted reproductive methods will certainly find fertile ground in the exploration of the epistemologies of the African belief systems. Using the Yoruba thought as a foil, Oduwole (2010), has distanced the typical African position from the equivocation of Euro-American conservative vs. liberal/individualistic stances to declare abortion ethically condemnable in African culture based on societal mores, as opposed to individual choices (barring some exceptions).

The position above immediately opens yet another point of departure between the African and Euro-American perspectives which would rather not be examined in detail here. While the African concept of a person is unitary, the Euro-American concept is essentially bifurcated between persons and non-persons within the human species. As such, fetuses, human infants, young children, people with mental disorder, and patients in persistent vegetative state may be considered technically as non-persons, because they don't possess any moral standing in the secular moral community. Tristram Engelhardt made this strident point in *The Foundations of Bioethics,* a polemic publication that has shaped current mainstream bioethical practice. He defines persons as "entities who are self-conscious, rational, free to choose, and in possession of a sense of moral concern." He essentially assigns a 'special' status to the people he sees as human beings and denies same to "non-persons" who he says lack moral standing in the secular community (Engelhardt, 1996: 139). On this score, the African conception of person would certainly find it problematic, if unacceptable. Anuolam's (1993) exposé of the Igbo meaning of life and Rakotsoane and Niekerk's (2017) espousal of the African proverbial saying about the "human life invaluableness," to name just two, easily rejects this position. For instance, the invaluableness of life, is a principle which teaches that "no resource may be spared at the expense of human life because of the ontologically special place occupied by human beings in the hierarchy of beings in the world" (Rakotsoane & Van Niekerk, 2017).

CONCLUSION

The subject of personhood is one with a tang in African thought. Indeed, the richness of African philosophy can best be seen in ethics and metaphysics – God and the nature of the human personality. Of the two, the concept of a person evokes the most interesting discussions (Wiredu, 2004: 16).

The review of a select views of some 20th century African philosophers on personhood brings up what has long been identified as its most distinguishing characteristic: the communalist perspective. It maintains priority over the individual in matters that guides right action, political choice, theoretical reflection and above all, moral agency when deciding how to act or to enquire; as opposed to autonomous, accumulative and independent agency of the Euro-American way. While the African self is rooted in his/her community with corporate wellbeing as his/her mantra, the community is in turn encased in the environment.

As Jensen and Gaie (Jensen & Gaie, 2010) rightly note, the African concept of personhood cannot be detached from "attendant notions of communalism as well as socio-ethical duties and obligations and beyond the purposes of self-identification or justification" (Jensen & Gaie, 2010). The significance of what has been articulated here is that the concept of the African person is immersed in the various philosophical spheres, such as metaphysics and ethics (and by implication bioethics). In so doing, a firm platform has been set upon which to extend the discourse to include the larger ethical questions that frame the emerging field of bioethical practice in Africa.

With reference to the thrust of the African personhood as the prime subject matter in biomedical studies, the 2005 Dakar Declaration can at best be considered as a stepping stone. With a long list of affirmations which include, considerations for the principles set forth in international declarations in the field of ethics, bioethics, and life sciences, and so on; that Declaration could be deemed insufficient. In truth, for a document made for Africa and which evolved on the African soil, it is disappointing that the language still largely echoes Euro-Americanism. It is widely known that since the Nuremburg Code (with a few exceptions), what has passed as 'international' ethical guidelines to universalize and globalize bioethics practice has been to further advance the Western paradigm. But, the Africanist is bound to ask, what is there for Africa as Africans, or uniquely depict the African morality, personhood, and epistemology? As the Western world increasingly becomes more individualistic, how can Africa resist the force to get rid of their ethics and cultural values? (Ezekwonna, 2005).

Likewise, the contents of the 2006 National Code of Health Ethics, a product of the National Health Research Ethics Committee of Nigeria. Where is the new direction that promotes the development of locally-grounded guidelines for ethics which are shaped by a dynamic understanding of local cultures and informed by structural and institutional problems that impact the public's health? Where is the ethical structure that is cognizant of the salient contribution of social sciences and social epidemiology which can bring a lasting impact on African local communities? Some of the questions that Azetsop (2011) had asked are still without answers today. Ditto Jegede (2009): where is the African ethic that reflects the decision-making process in the African community? The need is becoming quite dire not just for reasons that a bioethics practice that is grounded in indigenous ideas is more likely to be accepted by Africans and thus enrich bioethical discourse; it will reclaim the dignity of the African (Behrens, 2013). To borrow the motto of Nigeria's first indigenous citadel of learning (University of Nigeria, Nsukka), this indeed is a quest *to restore the dignity of man*. And nothing can better highlight the central importance of relationality, community and harmonious relationships in African thought than the understanding of personhood in the African context.

This plot also must be linked to how bioethics is being taught to African researchers, medical professionals and allied scholars in both short-term, as in workshop (Ajuwon & Kass, 2008), and long-term (Myser, n.d.). Myser acknowledges a trail of "…ongoing controversy and insufficient international dialogue about the teaching of bioethics…" (p. 46) that needs re-examining to match the WHO'S goals of universally accepted principles of medical ethics. But lacking in those goals is the acknowledgement of the challenges of bioethics in the lives of Africans and their communities, and the need to develop African conceptions to in-corporate African specificities and approaches (Andoh, 2011).

Present among the numerous public health and biomedical scenarios across Africa are challenges besetting public policies and programs which cry for more articulate formulation and approach. The unique notion of personhood in African philosophical thought bridges and indigenizes the bioethics discourse. This trend of thought is perhaps accurately supported by the argument that global bioethics will succeed *only* to the extent that it is culturally relevant. In the main, bioethics must expand its vision. It is with such backdrop that a host of salient bioethical issues – including issues involving human reproduction, quality of care, organ transplantation and biomedical studies with human subjects – can be hashed out.

While biomedical research practice in Africa is generally the same as elsewhere, it must however be specifically shaped by the histories, mythologies, motifs, and ethos of the people who constitute the African cultural affinity. This is most made manifest in the analysis of personhood. It would be yet another effort for Africa to confront the challenge of projecting its own conceptions to show case authentic African identities, specificities and approaches.

REFERENCES

Andoh, C. T. (2011). Bioethics and the challenges to its growth in Africa. *Open Journal of Philosophy, 1*(2), 67–75. doi:10.4236/ojpp.2011.12012

Anuolam, C. U. (1993). *Igbo value and care for life*. Navarra, Spain: Facultad de Theología de la Universidad de Navarra.

Azetsop, J. (2011). New directions in African bioethics: Ways of including public health concerns in the bioethics agenda. *Developing World Bioethics, 11*(1), 4–5. doi:10.1111/j.1471-8847.2009.00271.x PMID:19961514

Behrens, K. G. (2013). Towards an indigenous African bioethics. *South African Journal of Bioethics and Law, 6*(1), 32–35. doi:10.7196ajbl.255

Bhutta, Z. A. (2002). Ethics in international health research: A perspective from the developing world. *Bulletin of the World Health Organization*, (80): 114–120. Retrieved from http://www.who.int/bulletin/archives/80(2)114.pdf PMID:11953789

Christakis, N. A. (1992). Ethics are local: Engaging cross-cultural variation in the ethics for clinical research. *Social Science & Medicine, 35*(9), 1079–1091. doi:10.1016/0277-9536(92)90220-K PMID:1439926

Comaroff, J. L., & Comaroff, J. (2001). On personhood: An anthropological perspective from Africa. *Social Identities, 7*(2), 267–283. doi:10.1080/13504630120065310

De Craemer, W. (1983). A cross-cultural perspective on personhood. *The Milbank Memorial Fund Quarterly. Health and Society, 61*(1), 19–34. doi:10.2307/3349814 PMID:6552386

DuBois, W. (2003). *International pharmaceutical research*. Nashville, TN: Vanderbilt University Law School.

Engelhardt, T. (1996). *The foundations of bioethics*. New York, USA: Oxford University Press.

Eze, M. (2008). What is African communitarianism? Against consensus as a regulative ideal. *South African Journal of Philosophy, 27*(4), 386–399. doi:10.4314ajpem.v27i4.31526

Ezekwonna, F. C. (2005). *African communitarian ethic: The basis for the moral conscience and autonomy of the individual. Igbo culture as a case study*. Berlin, Germany: International Academic Publishers.

Fox, R. C., Willis, D., & Fox, R. C. (1983). Personhood, medicine, and American society. *The Milbank Memorial Fund Quarterly. Health and Society, 61*(1), 127–147. doi:10.2307/3349820 PMID:6552385

Gbadegesin, S. (1993). Bioethics and culture: An African perspective. *Bioethics, 7*(2/3), 257–262. doi:10.1111/j.1467-8519.1993.tb00292.x PMID:11651539

Geertz, C. (1965). The impact of the concept of culture on the concept of man. In J. R. Platt (Ed.), *New views of man*. Chicago, USA: University of Chicago Press.

Ikuenobe, P. (2006). *Philosophical perspectives on communalism and morality in African traditions*. Oxford, UK: Lexington Books.

Izugbara, C., & Undie, C. (2008). Who owns the body? Indigenous African discourses of the body and contemporary sexual rights rhetoric. *Reproductive Health Matters, 16*(31), 159–167. doi:10.1016/S0968-8080(08)31344-5 PMID:18513617

Jagers, R., & Mock, L. (1995). The communalism scale and collectivistic-individual tendencies: Some preliminary findings. *The Journal of Black Psychology, 21*(2), 153–167. doi:10.1177/00957984950212004

Jensen, K., & Gaie, J. (2010). African communalism and public health policies: The relevance of indigenous concepts of personal identity to HIV/AIDS policies in Botswana. *African Journal of AIDS Research, 9*(3), 297–305. doi:10.2989/16085906.2010.530187 PMID:25860633

Kaphagawani, D. (2004). African conception of a person: A critical survey. In K. Wiredu (Ed.), *A Companion to African Philosophy* (pp. 332–342). Hoboken, USA: Blackwell Publishing; doi:10.1002/9780470997154.ch26

Kelbessa, W. (2005). *The utility of ethical dialogue for marginalized voices in Africa.* Addis Ababa, Ethiopia: Addis Ababa University.

Lanre-Abass, B. (2012). Autonomy and interdependence: Quandaries in research ethics. *Health, 4*(4), 173–184. doi:10.4236/health.2012.44026

Levitt, M., & Zwart, H. (2009). Bioethics: An export product? Reflections on hands-on involvement in exploring the "external" validity of international bioethical declarations. *Bioethical Inquiry, 6*(3), 367–377. doi:10.100711673-009-9168-z

Mbiti, J. (1970). *African religions and philosophy.* New York, USA: Praeger Publishers.

Menkiti, I. (1984). Person and community in African traditional thought. In R. A. Wright (Ed.), *African Philosophy* (pp. 171–181). New York, USA: University Press of America.

Menkiti, I. (2004). On the normative conception of a person. In K. Wiredu (Ed.), *A Companion to African Philosophy* (pp. 324–331). New York, USA: Blackwell Publishing.

Metz, T. (2008). Philosophical perspectives on communalism and morality in African traditions. *Journal of Contemporary African Studies, 26*(2), 231–239. doi:10.2307/25426992

Niehaus, I. (2002). Bodies, heat, and taboos: Conceptualizing modern personhood in the South African Lowveld1. Niehaus I. Bodies, heat, and taboos: Conceptualizing modern personhood in the South African Lowveld. *Ethnology, 41*(3), 189–207. doi:10.2307/4153025

Nuffield Council on Bioethics. (1999). *Ethical issues in research in developing countries.* London, UK.

Obioha, U. P. (2014). Radical communitarian idea of the human person in African philosophical thought: A critique. *The Western Journal of Black Studies, 38*(1), 13–23.

Oduwole, O. (2010). Personhood and abortion: An African perspective. *LUMINA, 21*(2), 1–10.

Ogunbanjo, G. A., & Van Bogaert, K. D. (2005). Communitarianism and communitarian bioethics. *South African Family Practice, 47*(10), 51–53. doi:10.1080/20786204.2005.10873305

Okolo, C. (2002). Self as a problem in African philosophy. In P. H. Coetzee & A. P. J. Roux (Eds.), *Philosophy from Africa. A Text with Readings*. Cape Town, South Africa: Oxford University Press.

Olweny, C. (1994). The ethics and conduct of cross-cultural research in developing countries. *Pychology-Oncology*, *3*(1), 11–20. doi:10.1002/pon.2960030104

Onywuenyi, I. (1991). Is there an African philosophy? In T. Serequeberhan (Ed.), *African Philosophy: The Essential Readings*. St. Paul, USA: Paragon House.

Owomoyela, O. (1991). Africa and the imperative of philosophy: A skeptical consideration. In T. Serequeberhan (Ed.), *African Philosophy: The Essential Readings*. St. Paul, USA: Paragon House.

Owomoyela, O. (1994). With friends like these ... A critique of pervasive anti-Africanisms in current African studies epistemology and methodology. *African Studies Review*, *37*(3), 77–101. doi:10.2307/524903

Petryna, A. (2009). *When experiments travel: Clinical trials and the global search for human subjects*. New Jersey, USA: Princeton University Press. doi:10.1515/9781400830824

Piot, C. (1999). *Remotely global: Village modernity in West Africa*. Chicago, USA: The University of Chicago Pres.

Rakotsoane, F. C., & Van Niekerk, A. (2017). Human life invaluableness: An emerging African bioethical principle. *South African Journal of Philosophy*, *36*(2), 252–262. doi:10.1080/02580136.2016.1223983

Rehnquist, J. (2001). *The globalization of clinical trials: A growing challenge in protecting human subjects*. Washington, D.C.: Department of Health and Human Services.

Riesman, P. (1986). The person and the life cycle in African social life and thought. *African Studies Review*, *29*(2), 71–138. doi:10.2307/523965

Schwartz, S. (1990). Individualism-collectivism: Critique and proposed refinements. *Journal of Cross-Cultural Psychology*, *21*(2), 139–157. doi:10.1177/0022022190212001

Schwartz, S., & Bilsky, W. (1987). Towards a universal psychological structure of human values. *Journal of Personality and Social Psychology*, *53*(3), 550–562. doi:10.1037/0022-3514.53.3.550

Senghor, L. (1965). *On African Socialism*. New York, USA: Stanford University Press.

Tangwa, G. (2000). The traditional African perception of a person: Some implications for bioethics. *The Hastings Center Report*, *30*(5), 39–43. doi:10.2307/3527887 PMID:11057387

Tangwa, G. (2004). Some African reflections on biomedical and environmental ethics. In K. Wiredu (Ed.), *A Companion to African Philosophy* (pp. 387–395). Hoboken, NJ: Blackwell Publishing Ltd.; doi:10.1002/9780470997154.ch26

Tempels, P. (1959). *Bantu philosophy*. Paris, France: Preśence Africaine.

Verhoef, H., & Michel, C. (1997). Studying morality within the African context: A model of moral analysis and construction. *Journal of Moral Education*, *26*(4), 389–407. doi:10.1080/0305724970260401

KEY TERMS AND DEFINITIONS

Bioethics: A branch of philosophy that emerged in the 1970s in the US (and elsewhere) following a period of bewildering problems and abuse of human subjects. Hence, it is the systematic study of the ethical and moral implications of new biological discoveries and biomedical advances, including genetic engineering and drug research. The major principles central to bioethical thinking are: respect for the person's autonomy; fairness; non-maleficence; and, beneficence.

Communalism: As a feature of African life, it is the African perception of a social/spiritual relationship which incorporates all the categories, stages, and modalities of the society; also called bio-eco-communitarian (BEC).

Cultural Ethics: In the context of this chapter, cultural ethics differs from ethical culture, even as both share some mutual features. The latter refers to a type of belief centered on ethics, not theology, whose mission is to encourage respect for humanity and nature and to create a better world. But cultural ethics recognizes that while most ethical guidelines are universally replicated at different cultural milieus; certain standards are specific to certain environments. And just like ethical culture, observers of cultural ethics commit to personal ethical development in their communal relationships with others and in activities involving social justice and environmental stewardship.

Personhood: Is a consummate construct in African thought that connotes relational, ascriptive, and communalistic attributes that define the African.

ENDNOTES

1 Person, man, self, individual, human being, and to a lesser extent, identity, have been used interchangeably in this paper to mean the same thing (following majority of the literary corpus under review).

2 "Western" and "Euro-American" are synonymous in this paper and the reason may be obvious. For instance, in bioethics, a field that took off in the U.S. in the 1960s – 70s, it is clear that its philosophical principles are Eurocentric (deriving from the deontological theories of Kant and Mill-Bentham utilitarian principles, etc.). Further still, while bioethics is traditionally practiced in the West within the four-corner stone principles of autonomy, non-maleficence, beneficence, and justice; in other parts of the world, incongruities with these principles tend to emerge at the local level when their West-centric biases are subjected to closer scrutiny.

3 The four principles of bioethics (a.k.a., principlism) for mainstream practice are: respect for autonomy (i.e., what is best for the individual or a norm of respecting the decision-making capacities of autonomous person); non-maleficence (avoid harm towards the person or a norm of avoiding the causation of individual harm); beneficence (that we do good rather than bad or a group of norms for providing benefits and balancing benefits against individual risks and costs); and, justice/fairness (equal access under the law to information and treatment or a group of norms for distributing individual benefits, risks, and costs fairly).

Chapter 11
The Ethics of Risk in Psychiatry:
The Interplay Between Risk and Probability

Jean Pierre Clero
Universite de Rouen, France

ABSTRACT

Psychiatric medicine poses specific ethical problems relating to the particularity of the illnesses and of the patients. It intends to cure and to the nature of the treatments it prescribes. Its differences with the other branches of medicine have been highlighted for a long time. The psychiatric patient worries his family circle to a greater extent and in different ways than any other patient. This chapter explores the ethics of risk in psychiatry.

INTRODUCTION

If you took the maximin principle seriously then you could not ever cross a street (after all, you might be hit by a car); you could never drive over a bridge (after all, it might collapse); you could never get married (after all, it might end in a disaster); etc. If anybody really acted this way he would soon end up in a mental institution (Harsanyi, 1980).

Psychiatric medicine poses specific ethical problems relating to the particularity of the illnesses and of the patients it intends to cure and to the nature of the treatments it prescribes. Its differences with the other branches of medicine have been highlighted for a long time. The psychiatric patient worries his family circle to a greater extent and in different ways than any other patient because, as Pascal expressed it himself figuratively, "…a lame man recognizes that we are walking straight, while a lame mind says that it is we who are limping…" (Pascal, 1995, p. 25). So one may fear that the sick person should not pass the same judgment on life as ourselves, that he might be more prone to suicide than the other patients, and that, if he does not turn his aggressiveness against himself, he might turn it against others—his family, the farther circle, the nursing team, the other sick persons if he is at the hospital—this fear, whether it be justified or not, is increased by the fact that, even if one is not trained to understand what view the psychiatric patient has of his own life, that view necessarily eludes us, and that, even if we have received

DOI: 10.4018/978-1-5225-6310-5.ch011

this training, it often remains beyond our grasp. Hence, even if any medical relation always happens in a legal context, the pressure of the law is stronger in psychiatric medicine than elsewhere, in the other departments of medicine: one may lock up people against their will, and consider likewise this confinement as a part of a treatment in constraining the patients to cure them; one may contravene the most overt desires of the patient; one may deeply and unilaterally change, for him, the balance of rights and duties which is at use for the other members of society; one may also change, just as drastically, the share and equilibrium between private life and public life: so, it is possible that the relations that the psychiatric patient may have with members of her/his family and friends be considered as items to be added to the medical file. Certainly, the matter is neither to punish the patient for some imaginary transgression he could have committed; nor is it to humiliate him; but the categories which we need and that are used in order to think about ethics, so much so that they have become more and more accepted by the law "I mean the autonomy of decision that has been described, for one or two decades, as the patient's own responsibility, and the cluster of rubrics that derive from *autonomy* such as the *respect of the person*, of *personality*[1] (Kant, 1996), of *dignity*, of *consent* or of *informed consent*- seem particularly at odds with the settlement of a great number of psychiatric problems. It is not true that the patient's autonomy is always respected in psychiatry merely because it is impossible; the circumstances do not lend themselves to it.

Everybody knows the answer when we try to contest the usual insistence on preserving firmly the categories in which we want or imagine it necessary to confine ethics, even where they are the least appropriate: they behave as if the patient were willing himself what is done for him, as if, when he was still sound, if one day he was in such a state, he could consider himself as suffering the illness he is now suffering. For the sake of his own autonomy he would have accepted to be deprived of it; in the name of his/her liberty, he/she would have accepted that another or others, supposed to be more reasonable, use it, during the time he is cured and to be cured. In other terms, in order for ethics to keep its value system, it is necessary to build fictions which are so contradictory, imaginings which are so insane, representations which are so inconsistent and contorted that those fictions are no more than " fallacies ", stories that are told but are radically false and deprived of any grasp on reality. However, if we want to prove more innovative than by erecting precarious scaffoldings or by perching nonsenses upon stilts, it is necessary to try to give emphasis to other categories in ethics, nearer to the utilitarianism which prefers to speak of individuals than of persons; those other categories stem rather from utility, that is in pleasure and displeasure or the suffering of an individual or of the society of which he is a member, or -if we prefer- rather from the preferences of the individual or the well-being of the society than from the impossible autonomy of the person (at least in certain conditions); they enhance risk and probability.

I start precisely from those notions of *risk* and *probability* to found the triplicity -individual/preference and well-being/ taking risk and probability- that looks less rhetorical than the ethics of the person and better suited to the needs of psychiatry. We have not yet spoken of risk, as being related to probability, whereas it constitutes one of the most important categories of all the domains of medicine, but perhaps particularly of psychiatry, because risk is here greater than elsewhere in the cure and it is of a nature different from that of everything that may happen elsewhere. Many medical acts are admittedly high-risk for the doctor; but usually the doctor may be relieved of a great weight for having taken the risk of surgery, of a treatment, of premature departure of the patient from the hospital, or of her/his returning too early to work, when the patient takes it upon herself/himself to accept a share of responsibility, deliberately, fairly, knowingly, with the assistance of her/his family or of a trusted person. The risk is greater for the doctor in psychiatry because the latter help that the patient can bring her/him, in the medical decision, although not null, cannot be considered as really and clearly contractual and shared as the former. The doctor is not necessarily supported by the law while taking risk; and perhaps less by the public opinion which asks, I may add legitimately, for security from the authorities that have some power to establish it; and who has been moreover used to an overemphasis on security; which might have led to excesses of the principle of precaution, which, under the guise of precaution, can prevent any risky action whatever it is, by calling it audacious and rash.

Is it impossible to define rational behaviours relative to risk? Is it so difficult to determine some of them towards patients in whom disease is often thought to produce or lead to an irrational behaviour, that is to say: acceptable by all or, at least, by the greatest number? By " rational ", we mean to qualify a behaviour whose strategy is efficient, and also that may be said (morally) right or (morally) wrong, but not *just* good (agreeable to well-being) and bad (disagreeable). We shall wonder whether, in order for the doctor's behaviour to be more overt to the risk and to take probability into account when assessing in her/his options, we must not change the legal rules in this respect and, moreover, endeavour to train a public opinion that knows no more than it knew two centuries ago (Laplace, 1998: 124)[2] what to do of a probable situation.

THE STYLE OF THE RISK IN PSYCHIATRY AND SOME VARIED FORMS IT TAKES

The *first risk* -the most tragic one or the risk we consider as such- is the risk of a possible suicide of the patient. This sort of event must be anticipated more in psychiatry than in other fields of medicine and with another intention. Certainly, great sufferings and great distresses are induced by all sorts of illnesses in all the hospital services, and the doctor may nearly everywhere be asked, by the patient, to put an end to her/his life; but the doctor is relatively guarded against a direct and complete responsibility through the consideration that, if the patient really wanted to commit suicide, he would not need the help of his doctor, which is, in many countries, criminal to the eyes of the lawyer: a doctor has not to help his patient to die; now he may only help him not to suffer -or not to suffer any more. The share of responsibility that is attributed -perhaps phantasmatically- to the patient relieves the doctor of a total responsibility; anyway, the law itself makes the patient take her/his share of risks and does not make her/him only run risks. If the problem of suicide is more sensitive in psychiatry, it is probably for the reason that, if the patient succeeded in committing suicide, he would not always know why he/she committed it; he/she would not have had " good reasons " to do it, because even through the reasons he/she could have given to justify it, even if they had been right if anybody else had given them, he/she would have only asserted an ill life whose estimation he/she could make of it, as his/her other judgements, will, decisions, were altered by illness. So, as it has been said of the art of governing, the matter, for a governor as for the psychiatrist, is to answer -in spite of the refusal of the individual- for the " good part " of the person, that the individual cannot defend by himself, against the " bad part ". But must medicine have the function to guard a part of the person against the other? Has it, in matter of principle, to discredit a desire or a will to commit suicide in considering this desire or this will as something to be cured of? The doctor is urged to remove the mask which is splitting the individual in order to turn its face against him/her and oppose it to his/her desires as if they constituted a " false I ", always ready to promote values against the " right I " - of which the doctor is the only guarantor- that forbids them. The advice which a consultation usually is quickly turns into a demand addressed to the patient to conform to the principle of reality over which the doctor has, according to the law, the exclusive rights.

The *second risk* is the risk a physician is running when he neglects to take the necessary arrangements for keeping a patient locked up or forcibly restrained whereas he is likely to be dangerous, not only for himself but also for others. Again, the notion of *person* seems convenient, by its ductility, to justify what is the most contrary to it. For, the person, as being distinct from things[3] (Kant, 1996: 378), is precisely what, in ourselves, poses freely the norms and the rules of our lives. In the name of this freedom, through a strange oxymoron, the individual, suspected of being dangerous, is deprived of the liberty to go about as he wants, to be cured if he wants it; because one may evaluate -in any case, one gives oneself the right to evaluate- that, if he had been aware of being dangerous for himself and for others, he would have relinquished himself the liberty he claims. Since the illness is preventing the patient from reaching this awareness, the doctor must substitute for him and do what the patient would have done if he had been in his place. Even though he would like to leave the hospital, for example, one may evaluate, by another turn of mind, that he wants to stay locked up in his bedroom, as long as he is not better and makes the others run a risk for themselves, even if he has not yet actually performed any dangerous act. At least, he would if he was up to judging soundly the state of affairs; and he will desire it if, one day, the doctors are able to pull him through and if he refers by memory to these disagreeable events of the past.

Moreover -it will be the *third sort of risk* we shall account for-: it is impossible to let somebody free to do as he/she likes when his/her acts, though they cannot be diagnosed as delinquency, the endanger economic and social life of other individuals which would depend on the irrationality of behaviours it is necessary to prevent, even though the ill person would keep initiative of his/her business. " He will be forced to be free ", according to the famous word[4] and he will be constrained to choose the side of reason with a forceful help, if necessary, with which he cannot agree.

We can see in the three cases, which have been merely sketched above and do not claim to be exhaustive, the role played by the notion of *person*. Under the guise of inventing values to which it pretends to identify, the person covers with its mask highly social values that the individual has in no way invented and to which he/she must merely be submitted; through the distension which it contains, the notion of *person* permits society to defend its values inside every individual, thus changed in a sort of stage for them, to enforce its laws in neglecting his/her consent, which moreover he/she cannot give; and to defend them cut and dried, without degrees, at once.

The matter is not for us to negate those risks, but the question is whether there would be better ways to deal with them other than being subjected to the stringent demands of the person. Here is the point where we meet probabilities and the particular management of the circumstances that imply them when we decide to take no account of them.

THE BEHAVIOUR TOWARDS RISK AS A WAY OF TAKING ACCOUNT OF PROBABILITIES

Taking account of probabilities is not merely a matter of theory; it is always at the same time a practical question, because it is precisely when we do not know with certainty how a situation will change that arises the question of the chances of this evolution, particularly when the situation imperatively demands acts or restraints that, anyway, will change it. This practical question is never without ethical consequences.

In any parts of medicine, the doctor has statistics at her/his disposal and she/he can, thanks to them, determine a behaviour that concerns any patient situated in such given circumstances, after having followed a way of which he knows more or less the different stages. In all the cases, the information given by statistics is precious, but it needs, to be correctly used, a tailor-made adjustment to a singular situation for the reason that what happens to an individual is never what happens to the fictive " average man " of the statistics; this information is difficult to handle, for the matter is neither to give false expectations to the patient, by an awkward presentation, nor to dash all his hopes, insinuating that his case is in a quartile or in a decile where things do not go in the better way for him. But the use of statistics in order to define a prognostic or a treatment is perhaps more difficult in psychiatry than in other parts of medicine: the individualization of the man who is the object of a diagnosis is more crucial than elsewhere; and the statistics seem more lacking in psychiatry whereas it is where they would be the most useful. Yet, it is the psychiatrist and his/her colleagues that bear the entire responsibility of the decision to let the patient leave the hospital or to leave him outside the hospital with the consequences of that decision if the discharge or the refusal of committing turn out badly.

This decision takes in various sides that, in spite of their heterogeneousness, can be reduced to a sort of commensurability on the same balance in order to know which of them must override the others or how to obtain the result of their combination with one another. For the patient may have her/his desires or wills; her/his family may have their own desires and interests to protect, if they may be reduced to homogeneity; the society -the " great " one- demands its own interests -and precisely the interests of its security- be taken into account; the doctors may have their advantages and disadvantages in the treatment and so have the other patients when they are the involuntary partners of the patient whose company is inflicted on them. It is necessary to attribute a value to each of these components which look *prima facie* prodigiously heterogeneous in such a way that they may be reduced to a common denominator, taking into account a projection towards the future of each of these components that calls for a probabilization. From which points of view should the calculus be made? Certainly, if such or such member of the family had to do it, he would not weigh the same elements as another member and he would not get the same result as the patient himself or the other patients -if they had to make a decision or if they were given the occasion to make a decision. Must we let the opposing points of view confront one another in a game that must be achieved because it is impossible to leave it unresolved? Must we let the best of them be selected in the final stage of a screening, whatever be its principles? Must we attempt to settle at the equilibrium center if there is one? Moreover, we must not believe that the points of view and the centers of decision -from which the screening or the equilibrium are settled- may be defined in advance; they keep evolving over the time the situation extends.

Anyway, whether the task may be conceived as a screening or as a combination, its complexity is such that the doctor may be tempted, particularly in the case of urgency and if he has no much time to make his decision and to have it discussed, to turn to the safest solution, whether it be the security of the patient, of the other patients, of the family, of the others in the broadest sense. The matter is for us to know whether this way of proceeding is, on the one hand, the most strategic one, on the other hand, the most ethical one. To start dealing with the problem and to have a glimpse at the principle for solving it, we must conduct a brief review of our three cases described above: the risk of suicide, the risk of dangerousness for others, and lastly the risk for social affairs of any sort.

So, if we believe we have, through the discourse or behaviour of a man, pieces of information on his *inclination to suicide*, it is possible that we will be tempted to imagine that the worst will come as if the individual that is telling us about it or acting before us was going to commit suicide; trying to annihilate, at least for a time, the *mere possibility* that he acts and the only chances for the act to be carried out. Is this way of dealing with the problem rational? Why should we substitute to the degree of probability of an act the certainty it will be carried out or the certainty it will not be carried out, even though this degree is neither the former nor the latter? One may put forward that, in the case of suicide, there are only two items: either it is committed (although it may be unsuccessful) or it is not. Yes, but why choose systematically the most disastrous option according to which it will be committed and in the name of which the potential candidate to suicide will be kept in hospital, have his/her shoelaces removed, etc.? That option is much less rational than it seems to be: it underlies the fact that the doctor knows better than his patient the course of events, that he does not trust him (even if he has been given his patient's word) and that he has the right, and even the duty, not to trust him, as if the patient were absolutely disqualified in the role of a partner in a contract, and as if his word had no grasp upon reality, neither present nor future; neglecting the words of Nietzsche that will be quoted later, one acts with the patient as if the protection by the prohibition was infinitely more valuable than the estimation by the patient of her/his own life. Once more, the psychiatric patient is disqualified in an evaluation which yet looks so closely at him. We always come across the same difficulty typical of the protection of people against themselves: why would the right to kill oneself, that most of us do not dispute, be, absolutely and on principle, prevented and negated in the person whose judgement and will are, in our mind, altered enough to give us the duty to protect against herself/himself a life which is yet her/his own life and that s/he believes deteriorated? Why should the consideration of this alteration always lead the doctor to the side opposed to the will of the patient?

The *second case* is, indeed, more delicate. It seems rationally well-founded to put things at the very worst when the matter is to protect the others against a possible aggression. This protection is supposed to be a duty under the pretext that these others have not asked to be exposed to additional risks and have not consented to it, because most of time, they would not even suspect such an exposure. The doctor may judge that he has no right to deliberately expose the others to a risk of being aggressed, this coming on top of the ordinary risks they would incur if the patient was kept locked up. But, once again, it is much less rational than it seems to act as if, in a distribution of possible situations or of possible evolutions of those situations, it should be the worst situation or the worst evolution to which one must adjust one's action in order to deal with the whole situation, without determining the degree of probability and in acting as if such a determination were useless and should deserve no consideration in comparison with the possibility that the patient make victims. In other terms: as if the possibility were considered less as a possibility but as a fact the probability of which is one (or near certainty). Is this option strategic? Is it ethical? Is it rational, whether we give the term the meaning of *pragmatically defensible* or the meaning of *right*, *righteous*?

The *third case* is the situation of a social good -either economic, cultural, or social- which may be in danger of disappearing or being embezzled because of inappropriate decisions taken by an employer or by an employee. Astonishingly, this case is easier to settle than the former two, because although anybody can accept to be dependent on others, in his work or in political, administrative or economic situations, nobody could accept that his conditions of life -security, health, tranquillity- might be durably dependent on absurd decisions. Everybody expects a degree of rationality in his dependence, even if this degree is likely to be variously interpreted. At least on this point, it seems that the probabilistic and utilitarian ethics we are just about to explain matches with the " personalist " prospect we ordinarily challenge.

DEEPENING OF THE CRITIQUE OF THE PERSONALIST PROSPECT

One knows that Descartes advocated, in scientific matters, a doubt that went as far as to consider as wrong all that was only probable; in other terms, and as Leibniz could rightly reproach him with[5], instead of calculating the degree of probability of any proposition, and deal with its truth as a fraction of certainty, Descartes prefers to reject it as false, believing that, in so doing, he will not be deceived by error, that he will not believe true what is doubtful in any degree and so presents the risk of being false. However odd and nearly absurd this method may be in the field of theory, what is its value when it is followed with a practical aim?

It is known that Descartes himself does not advocate this method in the practical field; he does not ignore that such a behaviour would lead to scepticism, and, at last, to generalized inaction, which would amount to letting things act in our stead, without us doing anything of our own invention. Thus resolution in one's own actions is an unquestionable virtue[6]; but the philosopher of the *Discourse of method* demands that we take a middle way far from extreme opposed certainties[7] and that we remain confined to actions well received by the institutions and public opinion. The Cartesian piece of advice is yet not convincing because, once more and as in the theoretical field, Descartes flouts the evaluation of what is probable and of the degree of probability of the ingredients in any situation and, in the name of prudence, he never searches but for a middle way that ignores calculation and that, if it were followed, would lead to conformism and to ill-advised actions, inadapted on principle, because of their lack of accordance with all the conditions of the situation. Descartes's advice amounts to giving the probability 1/2 to any option, whatever it be, provided it be not " extreme ", and to confine to such a distribution even if we realize, through the evolution of the situation or the awareness of that situation, that the degree of probability would be only 1/4 or would rise to 9/10.

Indeed, Descartes did not conform to the sort of practice that has proliferated in the last decades of the XXth century -particularly in the questions of social justice- and that consisted in applying to practice the behaviour of deaf or blind radicalism adopted by Descartes towards probabilities in the field of theory. As we have begun to establish it and criticize it, it consists in remaining indifferent to the degree of probability and, behind a veil of ignorance resulting of the gaps in our knowledge of the developments of the situation, to put things at worst in taking systematically the party of the individuals that would have the most to suffer or would be the least advantaged by the action that is intended. If what we are about to do is acceptable by the individual(s) that would suffer the most from it, so the action is acceptable; if what we are about to do entails an unacceptable risk for the individual(s) that would be suffer the most from it, so we can do without this action, however good or better than the opposite action it be, in other respects. In other words, what is claimed to be rationality consists in taking stubbornly the point of view of the potential victim(s), without taking any notice of the degree of probability of the parameters of the action, on purpose and without any explanations.

Nonsense and false prudence of such a behaviour towards probability stem from two things. They result *first* from the will to stay blind towards the degree of that probability and to deal with it as if it were a complete certainty or -which amounts to the same thing- as if it were a radical uncertainty. In other terms, an error is deliberately and voluntarily made with a stubbornness often felt like a virtue. Now, it is quite possible, in an action through which an aim may be reached, to ascribe, having taken account of statistics or of past experiences, a degree of probability to certain parameters and to rectify constantly the ascribing on one's way, in case it had been overvalued or undervalued. The flexibility and cleverness of action seem to be more reasonable than the initial decision that looked like prudence because it is fixed as in the case of the principle of precaution or of any other principle chosen in the lexical Rawls's way[8]. That is what is called *to take a risk.* But there is a *second way* to unmask the real absurdity of this false reasonableness: taking systematically sides with the potential victim(s) in a situation -the prospect of the individual(s) that would have the most to suffer from the situation- consists in delineating only some constitutive elements of a situation or of an action, without taking account of the whole sum of them, and keeping aside arbitrarily only some of its aspects, remaining steadily blind to all the other sides. How is it possible to claim that one opts for reason when one refuses on principle to take into account all the constitutive elements of a situation, at least of what can be known of it?

We may be objected it is precisely because we do not know the developments of situations that we must be prudent, to cause the less possible victims when life and death are at stake, and to introduce the less evil possible in the world. This objection would be the proof we have been misunderstood. There is no proof that by choosing systematically the advantage of the victims, real or potential, you are choosing the point of view that suits the situation or that is likely to bring the most good in the world while taking the most reasonable risks. We are told of probability only because we do not know the whole situation or all of its developments; nevertheless, even if we ignore the entire situation, even if we are not in a complete certainty to perform in it our acts, there are plausible issues that make us know medium certainties and that exempt us from clinging to only one point of view and limiting ourselves only to one prospect and to one part of the field as if it were its entireness. There is a false rationality of prudence or, more exactly, there is an appearance of rationality in false prudence by which we must not be fooled.

There would be many sides that we could put forward to discuss the " timorous rationality " rather than the prudent rationality, its bias and its relation with the " personalism " that comes with it nearly always on dogmatism. The standpoint we have just censured favours some centers of decision over all the others and it settles them down through certain roles, all the others being excluded, in a dogmatism cloaked in a false prudence. But why would some individuals only -even though they be the majority- have the right to be treated as persons, whereas others would not have this right in the same present, but only in reference to the future when they will be apparently pleased that the decision has been made for them? Here we recognize the selective attribution of the notion of *person* which does not make it possible to explain the choice of applying that notion to somebody and refusing it to another, except at a second, third or nth remove, if the opportunity arises.

Indeed, in order that a rationality may be developed, it would be necessary that the laws be less damning for the doctor who will have made the ill-advised decision that causes the patient to commit suicide, to make life a misery for others, to be aggressive towards them, or to impoverish them and deprive them of well-being. So, it would be necessary to understand that, situated as he was, informed as he was, taking account of everybody's interests in given circumstances, the doctor had not necessarily made a reckless decision, although its consequences were disastrous. Of course, laws must not encourage recklessness; they are made even to prevent from it; but not at the cost of suppressing any risk and of producing more displeasure than pleasure. If a man commits suicide after a decision of his/her doctor who we shall learn has placed excessive trust in his/her patient, does the doctor systematically deserve the blame because the fault lies with him/her? Let it not be said that what is done in a risky way be a token of success; bearing a risk does not protect against a failure. A chance does not become a certainty as soon as it is assumed. Is it ethical that we convert what has taken a tragic turn, but could have known a happy ending, into a doctor's fault? Is there not more wisdom in the discourse of Nietzsche who, although he did not advise the physician to urge somebody to carry out his threats of suicide, advised against excessively restraining anybody from committing suicide if they want to put an end to their life, and thus removing the right to die from one's own hand?[9] (Nietzsche, 1899: 72–74). If an individual attacks another, after a decision through which the doctor has revealed an excess of confidence in the words or in the behaviours of his/her patient, must we hold him responsible for having assessed a situation, of which all the components have been taken into account, but also whose development seems to prove him/her to be wrong or to have been wrong? He was not necessarily mistaken in making his/her decision; but if it was a mistake, is it not as serious an error to make somebody suffer, as a precaution, even though he would have perhaps never caused pain to anybody? However, this latter suffering is invisible; it cannot be settled, because the notion of dangerousness prevents it from being seen and so justifies it in advance.

It is clear that we are replacing an ethics of the person with an ethics of calculus or an utilitarian ethics. The *former* does not allow any calculus and admits of no reason for singling out this or that person; because anybody may claim the status of a person. When, in such ethics, this status is threatened, it is for reasons that have nothing to do with the notion of person. Because of its bias, this notion does not allow to inspect the entirety of a situation. The latter concerns less persons than moving and varying centers of pleasures and sufferings -of preferences- that progress according to the evolution of the situation; so, the aim is not to give a privilege to this or that person, but to look, in every situation, for the way to produce what seems to bring the more pleasure to all the partners gathered by the situation.

We do not think that, through this shifting, we have solved all the difficulties; at least, we avoid the pitfalls of " personalism " which causes more misery than happiness. Now, the notion of *risk* (that implies an attitude matched with the degree of probability or expectation which is attached to the development of the situation), the notion of *utility* (with the play of pleasures and sufferings it involves), and the notion of *center* (where those pleasures and displeasures can be applied) seem to be in phase, to have a good hold on reality, and to be perfectly able to compare with personalism. Does it mean that it is necessary to eradicate any care for the person? Plainly no, but it is necessary to make sure we are telling the truth.

Beforehand, we shall pay attention to two features. *First*, risk is not an adventure; the one is even the opposite of the other. The adventurer -who, sometimes, has no choice if he is unwillingly involved in a thorny situation- does not know where he is going and moves forward in quite uncertain circumstances; at least, these circumstances are treated as uncertain, unlikely even if he was in situations in which it is possible to make a risk assessment and so to change his adventure into a calculus of chance. The man who takes risk does not progress in a world of which he knows everything with an entire certainty, but he furthers projects with degrees of certainty that may be assured and of which he will be able to account for if things turn out badly -which is always possible-. Adventure is always imprudent; on the contrary, prudence may include taking risk. Prudence does not consist in taking no risks, but in taking them -even if they are great- when they are plainly assessed. There are cases in which we have no other choice but the choice of adventure and where adventure stands as the only solution; happily, they are infrequent in medicine -they may happen in cases of emergency- and they must not be sought. On the other hand, the cases in which risks are taken are frequent and even constant; it is important not to treat them as mere uncertainties, on the pretext that they are not certain. Rationality consists in searching the degrees of certainty, whether they be relatively *objective*, when it is possible to settle statistics or *subjective*, when it is impossible for us to get such an objectiveness and so that we must change our point of view; and in the appropriateness of our actions to that calculus.

Second, mathematicians distinguish *subjective probabilities (or Bayesian probabilities)*, that are connected to a project I consider in a given situation, from *objective probabilities* that seem to be directly connected to some elements of the situation. Of course, the risk is rather on the side of subjective probabilities; but we may attribute to it a sort of objectivity insofar as it inclines us to give coefficients to the elements of a situation in progress. The coincidence -which must not be confounded with identity- of the notions of *risk* and *probability* (or *chance*) is due to this: the probability is different from the objects that it seems indicate and quantify. In spite of all appearances, probability tells neither about the die nor about its sides. The object of probability does not settle in experience; at least, not in a single experience. Pascal said it perfectly. But the object of which probability is the name and that stands behind the objects of experience is such that it can be grasped through action: it can be an integral part of the aim of an action. Probability is a theoretical notion addressing action; risk is the name of the way in which action grasps the object of probabilities.

SUBSTITUTION OF THE NOTIONS OF MARK AND INDIVIDUAL FOR THE NOTION OF PERSON

It is not for me to decide whether the notion of *person*, with the flaws we have discovered in it, may have some therapeutic value in psychiatry; the point should be examined on an illness-by-illness basis and, in this field of medicine, almost on a patient-by-patient basis, because of the extreme individualization. We have to admit for that notion of *person* ethical properties that we do not always recognize in the moving centers of pleasures and sufferings we tempt to substitute to it: the notion is easy to temporalize and it lets itself be distended by the instances of time. It is possible to indicate, through the notion of *person*, in the individual the possibility that this individual has to invent herself/himself, better than through the notions of pleasures and sufferings. Lastly, the notion of *person* makes possible a distension between *what is* an individual, what he has been and what he will be, *what* he himself judges he *ought to be*. Those characteristics must not be neglected and they are not easy to transpose through the play of the notions by which we intend to replace them; that is why it is always necessary, in any ethical situation, to sketch the notion of *person* and try it, even if it leads only to little bits of reality, without any global prospect[10] (Bentham, 1843; Mill, 1996).

Moreover, we must not overemphasize the isolation of the notion of person in the context of a situation and the bias it introduces in it. The distinctive feature of the person is, after all, to try to espouse the other's point of view and to make a decision only when this point of view is assumed. Now, it is also the same difficulty that the prospect of the play between pleasures and sufferings meets with. Because, though the pleasures and sufferings that arise in a situation -whether they be actual or projected- may be attributed to various centers, they can be added one to the other and be calculated only if they are related to a common denominator, which is not so easy to discover. Certainly the matter will not be to distinguish real pleasures from false pleasures, like the " personalists " distinguish the right self from the false self; pleasure must be taken into account as soon as it is owned up as pleasure: it should not be disregarded on pretext of falsity; nobody can set oneself up as a censor of the pleasure and sufferings of the other, except if his own pleasures and sufferings are involved; but the problem of their commensurability is no less delicate than in the case of the intersubjectivity: how to assign a respective weight to pleasures and pains? Whose units to choose in order to weigh pleasures and pains? Who must do the weighing and from whose point of view?

It does not amount to the same thing to refer to intersubjectivity or to universality, from the point of view of persons or of pleasures and pains. On the one hand, intersubjectivity, when it takes place in the frame of " personalism ", results from the consideration that consists in knowing whether the humanity, in its own invention, gets what it needs through an action or through a decision; on the other hand, the point of view of pleasure and pain only needs one individual to take the place of another or of others in order to attempt to grasp the possibility for those pleasures and pains to be harmonized with other pleasures and pains, without any moral judgment. In a way and paradoxically, the utilitarian point of view seems nearer to the Jewish and Christian adage *Do not do unto others what you would not want done unto you* than the " personalism ", that is actually very far from Christianity, even though it uses its name, particularly when it takes the form of the Kantian carrying out of a sort of coherent universe. The coherence of utilitarianism is obtained by a play of balances; not by the possibility to constitute a coherent world, as nature may be. Utilitarianism is so connected with probability that it does not suffer that ethics may be measured by a sort of criterion as Kant has given it to himself with the notion of " nature "; simply because such a " nature " cannot exist in the eyes of the man who conceives law only as probable, and so deprives it of an ideal perfection.

There is another difference with which we wish to finish before reaching a conclusion. In utilitarianism, pleasures and pains are not attributed to persons, but to individuals. This difference will be found lightweight; the prejudice is that we can talk indifferently of a person and of an individual. The individual who refers to a person takes us back to it as to an abstract notion of it; pleasure and pain point out the individual who is their theater as a vivid and singular mark that is what must be taken into account in matters of ethics. Contrary to all appearances -the best example is given by Stuart Mill[11] (Mill, 1996), ethics is not the same when the " I " or the " self " is understood as a " personal " I or a " personal " self -it is the case of the Kantian ethics-, and when the " I " or the " self " is perceived as an individual that feels pleasures and sufferings, and which is settled in being by their play itself. An individual might be a series of marks indicated by pleasures and pains. On the contrary, when we speak of a *person*, we have no more care of the notion of an individual than of the notions of pleasures and pains. We collect the notion of *mark* from the pen of Jankélévitch. What exists under the name of *person*, that makes a notch in being and perhaps confers to it a sort of eternity, is the " fact " it has been; because, even when it will be no more, the event that it *has been* is impossible to withdraw from it, without knowing exactly to whom it is impossible to withdraw this *having been*. A resistance, a necessity, a hardness arises on this way through this frailty and this *having been* does not only labour under the memory of those who remember the dead, but -even though there would not be anyone left to remember- being itself that it frames and to which it gives strange duties (Cléro, 2017).

The only delicate point of the notions of *mark*, *trace*, *writing* or *sign* that may be attributed to the existence of one being is that this being " exists " perhaps too much to have an ethical importance; it is perhaps here that the *person* keeps its advantage upon those notions: the distension it encloses between *being* and *ought to be*. The fact that the person be a sign settled in being on the one hand and prospect to have to be or to have to invent oneself, on the other hand, is probably an advantage upon a philosophy that relies on pleasure and pain *as if they were*, without a sufficient perspective *to have to be* of which it is difficult to do without in ethics. The fact, for a being, *to have been*, that offers a sort of particular ontological resistance, does not help much to give a form to the void of his existence; and, without any doubt, because of its least existence, the person succeeds better in this aim. G. Moore showed, in *Ethics*, that an ethics of pleasure and pain does not give necessarily duties, because of the many ways of solving the balances between pleasures and pains in a situation and because there is not a single way to obtain a maximum of pleasure in a given situation. The weak point of the utilitarian ethics is perhaps to have no duty, particularly when it is understood as a tension between what we are and what is in front of us, not being and yet to be created.

That is the reason why, in spite of all the weaknesses of the notion of *person*, we think it would be unreasonable to do absolutely without it in ethics. On the background of the most advantages of the theories of pleasures and pains, that can match with the calculus of probabilities, whereas the ethics of the *person* cannot give generally any sense to *chance* and to *risk*, the notion of *person* may be reintroduced by pieces. It was perhaps what Stuart Mill had searched relatively to Kantian ethics. What is sure is that it is easier to introduce the Kantian requirements in a utilitarian prospect, than to introduce utilitarian requirements in the Kantian practical philosophy which radically refuses the utilitarian point of view, even though the proofs of the formulas of the categorical imperative cannot avoid it. The refusal is not symmetrical, because -as Harsanyi has shown- if you want to live following the Kantian precepts and if you find in them your pleasure, provided you would not impose this strange pleasure upon the others as being the sole pleasure convenient to them, you may still do so in a utilitarian context. Those who find a pleasure in making themselves suffer have a place in utilitarianism; on the contrary, those who prefer their pleasure to the categoric imperative cannot find their place in Kantism, even though their pleasure may be the cause of no pain for others (Harsanyi, 1980, 1982) [12].

CONCLUSION

We should end with the inversion of prospect we have announced and which is in praise of psychiatry and of its honesty. So far, we have talked as if the ethics of psychiatry occupied a special place in care ethics which is the place of medicine in all other fields. In particular, we have seen the principle of autonomy being harmed in different ways in psychiatry. But it would be perhaps a mistake to believe that this principle may organize easily, actually, unrhetorically, the other fields of medicine. Indeed, psychiatry throws a harsher light upon the impossibilities and contradictions of this notion, even though, elsewhere, these impossibilities and contradictions are covered and disguised. What we get in reflecting on ethics in psychiatry may be a contribution to the critique of the autonomy principle even when this principle appears to be so capital that law itself reserved it a central place in the medical device.

This appearance comes to nothing when we face a serious illness. Certainly, the patient may always make the cure cease if he wants and when he wants, and in this case of a cure refusal or of a waiver, provided he is well informed by his doctor, the responsibility of the latter stops there. But if we prove, in that case, our autonomy, it is difficult to speak elsewhere, that is in all the other cases, of the autonomy and responsibility of the patient. For, *either* the patient is placed in a false alternative: he knows the preference of his doctor and, if he is rational, in the ignorance and impotence to recover health by his own means, he will finally make up his mind to fall in with the advice of his doctor who, in the end, will seem to advocate the best issue. *Or* the alternative is a real one and it is impossible for the patient, if he is incompetent to cure himself -which is the most frequent case-, to decide and settle that on which physicians may not agree without difficulties. How, in such conditions, would the patient's decision have the least value in his/her own eyes, in the eyes of the doctors or in the eyes of anybody else? The autonomy of the patient in his decisions cannot be but in trompe l'oeil and we cannot see how it could be otherwise.

Moreover, a prejudice tells us that it would be through the values of *autonomy* and of *person* that we shall receive the treatment that best respects our humanity. If that assessment is very often true in political and educational affairs, I am not sure that it is true in cases of illness. In the name of the duties we have towards ourselves when we are a person, we may have to face terrible news which are announced concerning us without many precautions if getting pleasures and avoiding pains are less important values than taking account of the person and the other values along with it. Ethics so conceived from these notions may be a way of forcing oneself or even of doing violence to others with the best consciousness in the world. The application of the notion of *person* does not do necessarily good to the individual who is tortured by his/her consciousness; it can recall him/her the demand to conform to right without making him/her the least good in circumstances in which right is not indispensable. Is this violence necessary? If violence is often to be regretted in psychiatry -for the reason that *autonomy* and *person*, *consent*, informed or not, do not play their part in it-, is it not also possible to find another sort of violence at the opposite, when the duty is recalled with a sadistic delectation -even legally- or when we inflict to ourselves a glum masochism? That shows, by the way, that violence is not necessarily that of which the person may be the victim; but it shows also that the person himself/herself may be at the origin of a sort of violence that covers itself with moral attributes and makes itself look virtuous.

We want to finish with three paradoxes that we have constantly crossed during the course of our inquiry. The *first* is that there is a quixotism of the person we are never tired of observing. Those who stand up for the person keep taking its part as if it was the real to which must be recalled the individual whose desires work against it; but the person itself stands up only with the means of incredible chimeras that make it lose all contact with reality. Finally, one does not know if the remedy is not worse than the disease. The *second paradox*, more " positive " than the previous one, is that utilitarianism, which cannot invoke the name of Jankélévitch more than Jankélévitch can identify himself to utilitarianism, is yet nearer to the doctrine of the author who has defended the notion of *mark* of the individual in ethics than to a personalism from which Jankélévitch may be imagined to be not far -before we have read him- in the way of thinking ethics. *Thirdly and lastly*, next to the previous paradox, we could be surprised to see a doctrine of calculus be so close to a humanism of the individual and of the mark: the reason is that the calculus, as Plato has highlighted the point, is deeply human, perhaps in a more archaic way than speech and writing (Plato, 1986: 439)[13]; and that the advocation of the mark passes through calculus, as Jankélévitch highlighted the point.

REFERENCES

Bentham, J. (1843). *An introduction to the principles of morals and legislation.* Edinburgh, UK: William Tate.

Cléro, J. P. (2017). Une pensée de l'existence à l'épreuve de l'éthique des soins. Les contradictions de l'éthique médicale. [A thought of being challenged with the ethics of care. The contradictions of medical ethics] In V. Jankélévitch (Ed.), *Morale et Politique* [Morale and Politics]. Paris, France. doi:10.3917/cite.070.0013

Descartes. (2012). *Discourse of the method of rightly conducting the reason and seeking truth in the sciences.* San Bernadino, USA: ULAN Press.

Harsanyi, J. C. (1980). *Essays on ethics, social behavior, and scientific explanation.* Boston, USA: Reidel.

Harsanyi, J. C. (1982). Morality and the theory of the rational behaviour. In H. Sen & B. Williams (Eds.), *Utilitarianism and Beyond* (pp. 39–63). Cambridge, UK: Cambridge University Press.

Kant, I. (1996). The metaphysics of morals. Part. I, Metaphysical first principles of the doctrine of right. In M. J. Gregor (Ed.), *Practical philosophy* (p. 378). New York, USA: Cambridge University Press.

Laplace, P.-S. (1998). *Pierre-Simon Laplace philosophical essay on probabilities. Sources in the history of mathematics and physical sciences* (2nd ed.). New York, USA: Springer Science & Business Media; doi:10.1007/978-1-4612-4184-3

Leibniz, G. W. (1976). Critical thoughts on the general part of the Principles of Descartes. In L. E. Loemker (Ed.), *Philosophical Papers and Letters: A Selection* (pp. 383–412). Dordrecht, Netherlands: D. Reidel. doi:10.1007/978-94-010-1426-7

Mill, J. S. (1972). Collected works of John Stuart Mill: Vol. XVII. *The later letters of John Stuart Mill (1849-1873).* London, UK: Routledge & Kegan Paul. doi:10.3138/9781442654143

Mill, J. S. (1996). *Essays on ethics, religion and society*. Indianapolis, USA: Liberty Fund.

Nietzsche, Fr. (1899). The Twilight of the Idols or How to Philosophize with a Hammer. In F. Nietzsche (Ed.), *The Works of Friedrich Nietzsche* (Vol. 3, pp. 195–196). London, UK: T. Fisher Unwin.

Nietzsche, F. (n.d.). *Human, All Too Human, Book II*. Retrieved from https://fr.scribd.com/document/21750833/Nietzsche-Human-All-Too-Human

Pascal, B. (1995). *Pensées, no. 98* [Thoughts, no. 98]. London, UK: Penguin Books.

Plato. (1986). *Plato in twelve volumes: Charmides. Alcibiades I and II. Hipparchus. The lovers. Theages. Minos. Epinomis*. Cambridge, USA: Harvard University Press.

Rousseau, J. J. (1974). *The social contract*. New York, USA: Plume/Meridian.

KEY TERMS AND DEFINITIONS

Blood's Collect: To gather blood from certain persons to give it to others.

Christianity: Relating to Christian religion, as a system of doctrines and precepts.

Donation: The action of giving something (here: blood) to another, without demanding any reimbursement in money or through any other advantage.

Fiction: The term is taken in the way Bentham defines a " fictitious entity " as " an entity to which, though by the grammatical form of the discourse employed in seeking of it existence is ascribed, yet in truth and reality existence is not meant to be ascribed ". " To language -and to language alone- it is that fictitious entities owe their existence -their impossible, yet indispensable existence ".

Myth: A fictitious story that is told by the people of a society or of a civilization on a subject-matter and that cannot be entirely rationalized, leaving a sort of affective or imaginative remainder.

Payment: The action of remunerate a person with money for having given something, here: its blood.

"Person": The term is taken in the sense that Kant ascribes to " rational beings because their nature already marks them out as an end in itself, that is, as something that may not be used merely as means, and hence so far limits all choice (and is an object of respect) ". " Personality (of a being) is freedom and independence from the mechanism of the whole nature, regarded nevertheless as also a capacity of (this) being subject to special laws -namely pure practical laws given by his own reason ".

Reason: Is characterized by two criteria: universality and necessity. Its discourses may be agreed with anybody's views. These agreements require essentially argument, discussion and demonstration rather than intuitive means, in order to influence the understanding or the conduct of the others.

Taboo: Very effective interdiction not only of the use of certain words, but also of the use or practice of anything. Of this prohibition, nobody knows or can explain the reason.

ENDNOTES

1 The two concepts of person and personality are distinct in the practical philosophy of Kant (1996), as follows: "A person is a subject whose actions can be imputed to him. Moral personality is therefore nothing other than the freedom of a rational being under moral laws. [...] From this it follows that a person is subject to no other laws than those he gives to himself (either alone or at least along with others) "

2 Taking the example of probabilities, Laplace (1998) showed the political importance of a chapter of mathematics in the terms of a great sentence: "If one considers the analytical methods to which this theory -the theory of probabilities- has given rise, the truth of the principles that serve as the groundwork, the subtle and delicate logic needed to use them in the solution of the problems, the public-benefit businesses that depend on it, and the extension that it has received and may still receive from its application to the most important questions of natural philosophy and the moral sciences; if one observes also that even in matters which cannot be handled by the calculus, it gives the best rough estimates to guide us in our judgments, and that it teaches us to guard ourselves from the illusions which often mislead us, one will see that there is no science at all more worthy of our consideration, and that it would be a most useful part of the system of public education ".

3 Just after having defined the person and moral personality, Kant (1996) defines thing as "that to which nothing can be imputed. Any object of free choice which itself lacks freedom is therefore called a thing "

4 Rousseau wrote in *The Social Contrac*t (1974), in another context.

5 In his *Critical Thoughts on the General Part of the Principles of Descartes* (1976), Leibniz notices about Article 2 that gives, as a criterion of a good rational method, that "what is doubtful should even be considered as false ": " I don't see what good it does to consider what is doubtful as false. This would be not to lay aside prejudices but to change them. But if this is understood merely as a fiction, it should not have been abused ". In other words, there is a deontology of the fiction and it should not be introduced anyway.

6 The second maxim of the Third Part of the *Discourse of the Method of Rightly Conducting the Reason and Seeking Truth in the Sciences*, in which Descartes (2012) defines some rules of morals drawn from the method, was " to be as firm and resolute in my actions as I was able, and not to adhere less steadfastly to the most doubtful opinions, when once adopted, than if they had been highly certain; imitating in this the example of travelers who, when they have lost their way in a forest, ought not to wander from side to side, far less remain in one place, but proceed constantly towards the same side in as straight a line as possible, without changing their direction for slight reasons, although perhaps it might be chance alone which at first determined the selection; for in this way, if they do not exactly reach the point they desire, they will come at least in the end to some place that will probably be preferable to the middle of a forest. In the same way, since in action it

frequently happens that no delay is permissible, it is very certain that, when it is not in our power to determine what is true, we ought to act according to what is most probable; and even although we should not remark a greater probability in one opinion than in another, we ought notwithstanding to choose one or the other, and afterwards consider it, in so far as it relates to practice, as no longer dubious, but manifestly true and certain, since the reason by which our choice has been determined is itself possessed of these qualities. This principle was sufficient thenceforward to rid me of all those repentings and pangs of remorse that usually disturb the consciences of such feeble and uncertain minds as, destitute of any clear and determinate principle of choice, allow themselves one day to adopt a course of action as the best, which they abandon the next, as the opposite ".

7 " Also, amid many opinions held in equal repute, I choose always the most moderate, as much for the reason that these are always the most convenient for practice, and probably the best (for all excess is generally vicious), as that, in the event of my falling into error, I might be at less distance from the truth than if, having chosen one of the extremes, it should turn out to be the other which I ought to have adopted ".

8 What Rawls calls " lexicality " is the method of taking the principles as a series of filters. To put in order a situation from an ethical point of view, you begin with one filter, for instance the conformity to personal liberty; once that conformity produced, you continue with a second filter, for example, the equality; and so on. The method does not escape dogmatism, because the reason to start with this or that filter is not given, except it is so in the society we inhabit or it is so in our intuition.

9 Nietzsche (n.d.: A. 88): "Prevention of suicide. There is a justice according to which we take a man's life, but no justice according to which we take his death: that is nothing but cruelty". Two pages before, Nietzsche said: "One may well ask why, aside from the demands of religion, it is more praiseworthy for a man grown old, who feels his powers decrease, to await his slow exhaustion and disintegration, rather than to put a term to his life with complete consciousness? In this case, suicide is quite natural, obvious and should by rights awaken respect for the triumph of reason " (Nietzsche, n.d.: A. 80, 72-74). A little later, at the A. 36 of the 'Roving expeditions of an inopportune philosopher' of *The twilight of the idols*, Nietzsche wrote, bordering on unacceptableness, in a discourse entitled 'Morality for physicians': " In certain conditions it is improper to live any longer. The continued vegetating is cowardly dependence on physicians and prescriptions after the meaning of life, the right to life, has been lost, should entail the profound contempt of society. The physicians, on the other hand, would have to be agents for communicating this contempt, -not recipes for their patients, but every day a new dose of *aversion* from them… To create a new responsibility, the physician's responsibility, for all cases where the highest interest of life, of *ascending* life, requires the remorseless crushing down and thrusting aside of *degenerating* life -for example, for the right to recreation, for the right to be born, for the right to live… To die proudly when it is no longer possible to live proudly " (Nietzsche, 1899: 195-196).

10 As Stuart Mill (1996) noticed it, Bentham (1843: 2) gives a very limited place to " duty " and to " ought to " that he thought of as what is " conformable to the principle of utility ". In his *Remarks on Bentham's Philosophy*, he writes: " In his list of motives, though he includes sympathy, he omits conscience, or the feeling of duty: one would never imagine from reading him that any human being ever did an act merely because it is right, or abstained from it merely because it is wrong " (Mill, 1996: 13).

11 In his letter to E. Acollas, written in French from Avignon on September 20, 1871, Stuart Mill reminds us of the principle of his essay *On Liberty*, which is " the principle of the autonomy of the individual ". Actually, the fifteen pages of Chapter III of *On Liberty* deal with " Individuality, as one of the elements of well-being " and the five last pages of the Conclusion treat of liberty conceived as individuality. " Je reconnais cette autonomie comme une règle rigoureuse dans les choses qui ne regardent que l'individu lui-même ou, si elles intéressent les autres, qui ne les intéressent que par l'influence de l'exemple ou par l'intérêt direct que d'autres peuvent avoir au bonheur et à la prospérité de chacun. Par cette doctrine, j'affranchis de tout contrôle, hors celui de la critique, le cercle de la vie individuelle proprement dite " (Mill, 1972: 1831-1832). Such sentences could never have been written by Kant: being a person is, for an individual, to be given duties and does not release him/her from any control. In another letter of the same year, written on January 20, 1871, and addressed to the New York Liberal Club, Stuart Mill strongly recommends the value of the individuality of thought and character, including the possibility to criticize it: " There cannot be a higher or more important air than of assertion & maintaining individuality of thought & character, together with its necessary complement, the fullest latitude of mutual criticism " (Mill, 1972: 1801-1802).

12 In the same way, we could show, as Harsanyi does it, that the Rawlsian maximin principle is nothing but a particular case of the Bayesian approach needed to be adopted in ethical affairs. From time to time, the Rawlsian approach matches with the Bayesan approach; the latter can explain why it is so, but the former cannot ignore the explanation. The rule of maximin, followed separately from the Bayesian approach, " leads to highly irrational decisions in important cases " (Harsanyi, 1980: 47, 1982: 47).

13 Plato (1986, Epinomis, 977c): " [...] if we should deprive human nature of number we should never attain to any understanding. [...] The creature that did not know two and three, or odd or even, and was completely ignorant of number, could never clearly tell of things about which it had only acquired sensations and memories "

Chapter 12
Ethical Issues in Couple and Family Research and Therapy

Maria Nicoleta Turliuc
Alexandru Ioan Cuza University, Romania

Octav Sorin Candel
Alexandru Ioan Cuza University, Romania

ABSTRACT

In couple and family research and therapy, the perspective changes from the individual to the dyad or group. As such, professionals in this field discuss some new ethical dilemmas that are particular to their line of work. While some authors present problems such as confidentiality and allegiance to only one part of the family system, others address a series of ethical consideration caused by the state of current research. The aim of this chapter is to present an overview of modern research topics such as intimate partner violence, illness, or multiculturalism and their ethical implications and effects on the family functioning, child development, and the research results. Also, the authors want to present the most relevant ways in which professionals can work within such ethical dilemmas without damaging either the outcomes of therapy or research or to cause harm to the participants.

INTRODUCTION

Family and couple research is critical because its results can address several issues specific to the individual and societal life. Based on its results, therapists can develop better interventions to change the mechanisms that cause harm and distress to the families. Although the benefits are important, great risks do arise. Both researchers and therapists must balance the benefits and risks by adhering to the ethical regulations imposed either by state law or professional standards.

Even with these standards, the constantly moving world gives birth to new situations that could be both rewarding and dangerous towards the activity undertaken by the specialists. This is particularly true in the field of couple and family psychology, where the focus changes from the individual to the couple or family, thus creating new ethical issues that must be understood. A specialist must evaluate the risk for the family members that are present during the research or intervention, and even for those that

DOI: 10.4018/978-1-5225-6310-5.ch012

are absent (Margolin et al., 2005). In this chapter, the authors aim to present the most important risks found in today's couple and family research and practice and to discuss the ways in which the ethical behaviour might be preserved even in such difficult contexts. The sensitive nature of the research and therapy creates a rather complicated and challenging working environment for the specialists. While some techniques are beneficial for some members of a family, they might also negatively affect the others. Issues of confidentiality, informed consent or privacy might arise. Also, family research deals with a number of individuals at risk (children, or victims of intimate partner violence, among others). For them, the specialist must create a secure environment where they are both protected and encouraged to work with the psychologist.

BACKGROUND

Each step in the process of research can be thought through ethical lenses. Firstly, the ethical research can be conducted only when the design is good. In any other case, the scientist risks not only to promote bad results but also to waste the time of the participants (Rosenthal, 1994). Still, regardless of their scientific quality, some types of research can cause harm to the participants, human and non-human. By trying to adhere to constantly growing and changing ethical guidelines, psychology, both in the domains of research and therapy, has been keen on finding new meanings behind human behaviours, cognitions, and emotions. Furthermore, these meanings were combined to form techniques and interventions that would be beneficial to the world.

"Ethics is the study of the principles and standards of human conduct" (Pettifor, 1996: 1). As such, ethical guidelines are used to differentiate between right and wrong, to protect those who are not in a position of power or to present a model for all the professionals in a field (Mabe & Rollin, 1990). While the history of ethics is long and laborious, the ethics of psychology were developed recently, a few decades after the birth of this domain.

The beginning of scientific psychology is marked by the establishment of Wilhelm Wundt's laboratory in 1879 (Rieber & Robinson, 2001). Still, the first guidebook for ethical research and practice was developed by the American Psychological Association in 1953, almost 70 years after the inception of psychology. Also, only in 2008, a Universal Declaration of Ethical Principles for Psychologists was proposed to encourage each nation to create their own form of ethical code (Walsh, 2015).

A series of guidelines specifically made for the couple and family research and therapy was developed even later, the first one being created by the American Association for Marriage and Family Therapy (AAMFT) in 1979. In 2000, Scalise compared the AAMFT and the International Association for Marriage and Family Counselling (IAMFC) codes of ethics. The author found that the former accentuates the following contents: responsibility towards the clients, confidentiality, professional competence and integrity, responsibility towards the students, employees, and supervisees, responsibility towards the research participants, responsibility towards the profession, financial arrangements or advertising. The latter added are features such as client well-being, confidentiality, competence, assessment, private practice, research and publications, supervision and media and public statements.

Although both codes emphasize the responsibility towards clients and the importance of confidentiality, as well as the aspects concerning the competence and the integrity of the psychologists, the content is rather general (Turliuc, 2008). This problem seems to be a constant one and the professionals in the field discussed it rather constantly for the last 30 years. In an important article from 1982, Margolin pointed that "Even if the family therapist is totally familiar with the APA guidelines, that is not adequate preparation for the types of issues that she or he will encounter in working with more than one family member" (Margolin, 1982: 800). While the AAMFT code developed in the latter years, in 2001, Hohmann-Marriott also drew attention towards the unique position that couple and family psychology has inside the broader domain.

General and Specific Guidelines for Family Research and Therapy

Over the years, several regulations were proposed in order to accompany the professionals in their activities. Currently, the American Psychological Association proposes five principles for the practice of psychological research and therapy (American Psychological Association, 2002):

1. **Beneficence and Nonmaleficence:** Psychologists are responsible for the well-being of those they work with, either human or animal. They must do not harm or try to minimize the negative consequences of their actions in those situations where conflicts arise between their obligations. Also, professionals must control their religious, political or financial interests in order not to interfere with their clients'.
2. **Fidelity and Responsibility:** Psychologists are responsible for their clients, their colleagues and the society. They uphold the professional standards, accept responsibility for their behaviour and cooperate with other professionals when needed.
3. **Integrity:** Psychologists are honest and truthful about their work. When deception is ethically justifiable to maximize benefits and minimize harm, the professionals must minimize any negative effect of the technique they have used.
4. **Justice:** Every person has the right to benefit from the results of psychological research and practice. Also, psychologists must adhere to unbiased techniques and recognize the limitations of their competence in offering their clients the best services available.
5. **Respect for People's Rights and Dignity:** This principle reinforces the obligation to be aware and respectful towards cultural and individual diversity. Psychologists must not be biased towards religion, gender, age, race, culture, sexual orientation, disability or socioeconomic status. Also, they must offer equal services to everyone in need, regardless of their different status.

Based on these core principles, APA also created a code of conduct consisting of ten main areas of specific ethical standards. The authors present a summary of these standards in Table 1.

The Ethics Code is to be used by specialists in all fields of psychology, regardless they work in research, education or therapy. Still, the code rarely addresses problems that are specific to the couple and family psychology. There are no references to such issues in the first nine points of the code. Only the tenth one presents some ethical aspects of working with couple or families. Firstly, psychologists need to clarify their roles and specify whom they are working with (who is the client). Secondly, when conflicting roles arise (therapist and witness in a divorce process), psychologists must decide which role is more appropriate for them (APA, 2002).

In addition to APA's Code, different authors proposed their own guidelines for the therapeutic practice. Gibbs and Gambrill (1999) also discuss the aspects regarding competence, informed consent, and confidentiality. Furthermore, they introduced the selection of methods and objectives, responsibility and the development of a relationship based on trust as new characteristics of an ethical behaviour. The

Table 1. APA's ethical guidelines

Resolving Ethical Issues	Psychologists must clarify every possible ethical conflict against a set of legal regulations or organizational demands. Also, one must report every witnessed ethical violation to the appropriate committee or legal authority.
Competence	Psychologists must offer services, teach and conduct research only in the areas where they are specifically competent. This guideline can be overwritten only in cases of emergency when psychological help cannot be denied. Also, the activity of a specialist must be based on scientific principles.
Human Relations	The psychologists actively fight against discrimination and harassment. They usually avoid double relationships, always use an informed consent and are interested in not causing harm to those they work with.
Privacy and Confidentiality	Psychologists are bound to discuss and maintain confidentiality. They can record or use confidential information only with the consent of their clients and only after ensuring their anonymity. Confidential information may be disclosed when mandated by law or in order to to protect the psychologist, the client or other persons from harm.
Advertising and Other Public Statements	Psychologists can present their services in media or in advertisements (in any form). These presentations must be real and in conformity with everyone's competences. Psychologists do not solicit testimonials from current clients who are vulnerable to undue influence, nor do business with them.
Record Keeping and Fees	Practiced fees must be in accordance with the law. Psychologists have the obligation to code all the records describing their relationship with individuals that want their confidentiality protected.
Education and Training	When involved in teaching and training activities, psychologists must accurately present the benefits and the responsibilities of those involved. Their assessment and behaviour must respect the principles presented at number 3.
Research and Publication	Researchers need institutional approval and must provide all the participants an informed consent. If any form of payment is involved, it must be appropriate to the task. The use of deception is justified only when no other form of research is possible. Still, psychologists have the obligation not to cause any harm, physical or psychological, to the participants. Researchers do not duplicate data, do not plagiarise and share data whenever necessary.
Assessment	Psychologists use assessment only when needed and only with a reliable and valid instrument. The specialist must use an informed consent and provide explanations for the results whenever it is possible or required.
Therapy	Therapists always use an informed consent. Sexual relationships between a psychologist and a client or a relative of the client are forbidden. Therapy is terminated when it is no longer beneficial for the client or when the therapist feels endangered by the client or by a person close to the client.

Source: American Psychological Association, 2002

objectives must be chosen based on the client's needs and must describe real-life acquisitions and benefits. Following this stage, psychologists need to implement the techniques that offer the best chances for a positive impact. They also need to be responsible and offer adequate feedback to their clients, thus creating a sense of trust between the parts.

Still, the specific of family and couple psychology may lead to some different problems and different solutions. One of the main concerns in this field is that family research and therapy usually involves more than one person. Also, each person holds some sensible information about the other members of the family and that information might make them vulnerable (Hohmann-Marriott, 2011). These two situations can lead to an important question that is well-known and heavily discussed in the field. For many family therapists, "who is the client?" becomes a crucial variable in understanding the case and in implementing the right strategy. In some cases, family therapy is the result of an initial individual therapy, and the whole relationship between the professional and the client suffers some changes once other people start taking part in the sessions. The therapist might "pay allegiance" to the person that initiated the therapy, to his/her family or to the entire family system (Smith, 1992).

This is only one ethical problem concerning the couple and family therapy. In the next part, the authors will discuss more ethical issues that can affect the therapists and the ways they can also transfer to the different research areas.

Existing Issues in the Field of Family Research and Therapy

"Much of [the] research has a potential for harm" (Dingwall, 2008: 3) and family research or therapy are no strangers to such possibilities. Irrespective of the degree of sensitivity of any research project [or therapy], effective methodology and engagement with ethical concerns are synchronous (Thomas & O'Kane, 1998). There is consensus that researchers have a moral and professional responsibility to their participants; they must ensure that they avoid causing physical and/or psychological distress (Elam & Fenton, 2003). The researchers and therapists know that the nature of family relationships might prove to be difficult to work with. For example, when a participant appears to shut down a train of thought the researcher should respect this closure and not attempt to reopen it, however therapeutically or academically tempting it may be. Silences occur naturally in any interview/therapy and it is legitimate for the researcher to nudge along an interview when such pauses become awkward, picking up threads presented by the participant. Furthermore, it is important not to overstate the potential problems. More than anything else it is the 'sensitivity' of the research topic that influences the interview dynamic and the intensity of the encounter, not the particularities of any method used.

Families are dynamic, and each member must be viewed both as a singular entity, and as a part of a system. Some aspects can prove to be particularly challenging for therapists or researchers and in the following section, the authors will present the most pressing issues one can be confronted with.

Confidentiality

One of the primary concerns for family therapists is the nature of confidentiality. Starting from the question of "who the client is?", therapists may choose to protect the secrets of each member of the family or to decide that there should be no secrets between the members. In the Ethics Code proposed by the AAMFT (2001), confidentiality is regarded as being unbreakable without the consent of the person. Still, the nature of secret that may surface in a session is quite different from case to case. In some instances, the therapists might find out about an extramarital affair, but in other cases, the client might confess to abuse and other illegal activities.

Green & Hansen, as cited in Smith (1992) presented the results of a survey where therapists were asked how they work with secrets during therapy. Their results showed that the interviewed specialists were divided in their answers. Some of them reported that they agreed with sharing secrets if the person who had the secret also agreed. The others said that they would not tolerate any secrets in their therapy sessions.

Gottlieb and Cooper, as cited in Kuo (2009), propose four strategies for working with confidential information. All of them are based on prior informed consent that specifies the ways in which the therapists might work with the couple or family. The first possibility is to impose total disclosure. Therapists and clients will agree that no secrets will be kept. While this approach is the most transparent, it also might lead to growing mistrust on the client's side. A second approach is a total confidentiality from the therapists. Unfortunately, this might lead to sessions that are more similar to individual therapy, than family therapy. In the third case, the therapist and the clients could negotiate each aspect that should be disclosed and those that should be kept secret. While this could be ideal in theory, it is nearly impossible to implement, because new and unforeseen secrets may appear. The last possibility is that the therapists would choose when they should reveal confidential information. This might also lead to confusion and uncertainty towards the therapist's position. Certainly, disclosed critical issues such as partner violence, child abuse, affairs, secrets, spendings or addiction must be addressed with great care and sensitivity (Patterson, 2012), but a competent therapist will facilitate the discussion of individual secrets in couple or family according to clinical standards.

A new issue regarding the ethics of therapy is the rise of telehealth therapy. Some clients find it difficult to go in person to a therapist, so they choose to use telehealth practices instead (video messages, telephone etc.). The downside of these is that the practitioner cannot ensure the privacy of the communication. While nobody can enter in an office during a session, the client's house is an open space, and everybody can capture parts of the discussion. As such, therapists must present this case in the informed consent, thus preparing the client for an unforeseen event (Wrape & McGinn, 2018).

Family research is also problematic in terms of confidentiality. In some cases, it might include themes that are sensible for the participants and thus the researcher has the obligation not to disclose such information without proper coding and anonymity for the participant. One possible issue is that the nature of sensitive information is different from one couple to another (Margolin et al., 2005). What one might consider normal, others might view as extremely intimate. A particular situation is that of research with children. A child might disclose information that is detrimental to the parent (alcohol abuse or violence) without understanding that the parent wants to keep that information secret or the consequences this can bring.

Gabb (2010) discusses another important case of an ethical dilemma in family research. The author describes a case when a mother's public persona, that of a powerful matriarch that organizes the whole family, was partially contracted by the accounts of all family members. The woman sometimes resented her role and the ways it stood in the way of fulfilling her needs. This portrait was advantageous for the research but detrimental to the family. When reading the study, the family members could recognize the problems of the mother and thus change their viewpoint towards her. The author also proposes two solutions for this issue. One is not to use qualitative studies from the viewpoint of different family members. The other and better proposition was to carefully present the information with particular care for eliminating those elements that could lead to the identification of the persons involved.

Margolin et al. (2005) discuss a similar solution. Due to the ambiguous codes of ethics, each researcher must carefully address the problems of confidentiality. The participant must receive an informed consent that is as complete as possible, where the researchers present all the problems they think could arise.

Online research can lead to different risks, rather than the more traditional one. Firstly, when more than one family member uses a computer or a device, it is easier to discover an instrument used for the assessment of another family member. This is a problem especially when the participant is part of a vulnerable population (victim of abuse or intimate partner violence or suffering of an infectious disease). Also, the web pages that are accessed during the research can leave a series of cookies, temporary files or history on the computer and all of that can also be accessed by anyone using the computer. Mathy, Kerr, and Haydin (2003) discuss the implication of these events and a series of measures a research can take to ensure the confidentiality. Firstly, the researchers can use password protected application for the assessments. Each participant receives a separate password, thus only him/her can access the application. This is also a solution when both partners must complete a series of online instruments, but they are prohibited from seeing each other's responses. Another way to protect online confidentiality is to inform the participants about the risk of files that remain on the computer. The researchers can also propose them different ways of deleting said files before anyone else can discover them. Finally, Mathy et al. (2003) recommend that sensitive information should never be sent on the email or other personal accounts of the participants and that the research should use anti-virus software in order not to infect the participant's computers with spyware or malware viruses.

Informed Consent

Informed consent guidelines recommend that therapists provide information about their theoretical model and announce that it will ask for information about individual and family development, general functioning, and problems in a relational context; thus, others who are directly involved in a client's relational network may be asked to be included for assessment and/or treatment, and informed consent is required for all adults and recommended for minors.

Similarly, the researchers have to announce the objectives that are considered in their study, and the description of the followed methodology. However, it is almost impossible for a researcher or therapist to claim that a participant/client has expressed his informed consent, because, by definition, research and therapy are exploratory. The research and therapeutic processes are necessarily dynamic, and it could be more productive to negotiate the consent on a continual basis. This can cause problems, as researchers/therapists repeatedly ask participants to continue, and they may tend to give up (Duncombe & Jessop, 2002). There must be a fine line between respecting the rights of participants and the pragmatic need to keep people on board.

While a well-thought informed consent might provide the professionals with both a framework for the intervention or research and the clients or participants with the assurance that their rights are respected, they are not without their problems. Firstly, Gabb (2010) presents a research where each participant ought to check a very long informed consent. Not only that the attention span of the participant became limited after a while (damaging their understanding of each point of the consent), but they also started to complain about the bureaucracy involved in the scientific field. In this case, the informed consent led to a negative attitude towards the study instead of a better understanding of it. Also, Murphy and Dingwell (2007) consider that it is impossible to predict every single particular event that might affect the participants and that specialist should focus more on the most probable ethical problems that can appear instead on those that are very rare.

In family research, the entire family must sign the informed consent, even though in most cases only one member is particularly interested in the study. The researcher must present a clear explanation for what will happen during the study and must try to make this information as diverse as possible (Margolin et al., 2005). Previous studies performed by Dunn and Mann suggested that short informed consents are better and that the information should be presented in different forms (video, audio, pictures) to give the participants an accurate view of the study (Margolin et al., 2005). Finally, not all family members can offer their consent. For example, the information that a member offers may concern another member who didn't give his or her consent. In such a situation, the researcher can assure the participants that they are not obligated to offer such information or might decide to ask for the consent of the other member. In case of children, the parents or legal guardians must offer the consent (Hohmann-Marriott, 2001).

Regarding the therapy, Margolin (1982) presents a series of differences between the informed consent for family sessions and the one for individual sessions. In family therapy, all involved members might offer their consent. The therapist must explain that no person is "sick" or have a problem, the whole family being the "client". An important issue is that some members might not want to participate in the sessions. In such a case, the therapist would explain that even though nobody can compel a member to therapy, the family will change regardless of one person's participation

Consequences of the Research

Every type of therapy should be developed based on rigorous research. This would contribute to the scientific advancement, but sometimes a study design or research question might put the participants in danger. The results of the research are not above the ethical treatment of the participants. Over the years, a series of important studies raised some serious ethical problems (Milgram, 1963; Zimbardo, 1973), so nowadays it is crucial for the researchers to ensure that the participants are treated ethically and that no harm (or very little harm) is produced.

When the development or the assessment of a new therapy's usefulness are involved, researchers usually use two different groups. In the first one, the participants receive the treatment while the second one is placed under a placebo condition. This method, while wildly used, is not ethical because it prevents the people from the second group to access a treatment or therapy. Two solutions are proposed. The first one involves the creation of a waiting list, acting as a comparison group. The better solution is to use two groups that receive a different form of treatment (Hohmann-Marriott, 2001).

The above-mentioned issues are specific to any kind of research. In family research, new problems arise. Firstly, the outcome is different. While in individual research, the outcome is measured for each participant, in family research, especially when therapy is involved, the outcome is not that easy to determine. The change should appear for each individual, for the members of the family or for the system itself? (Fenell & Weinhold, 1992). To answer these question, Olson, Russell, and Sprenkle, as cited in Fenell & Weinhold (1992) proposed that the researcher must know and understand the family system first.

Secondly, a sensitive subject can arise during the interactions between the researchers and the participants. One way in which the researchers can approach this issue is to play the part of a caring listener, while also taking into consideration the limits imposed by the informed consent. When the participant's problems are more complex or involve difficult subjects such as family violence, the researcher can report the abuse or recommend assistance for the participants (Dockett et al., 2009). Also, when complex studies are needed, researchers with different background are recommended.

Thirdly, longitudinal research leads to some interesting ethical dilemmas. Given its nature, during such studies, the families go through different changes and stages. The researchers have more chances to discover problematic behaviours inside a family. Thus, a dilemma is created in which one can discuss such problems while also respecting the confidentiality of the participants and the principle of no harm. Researchers can present after each assessment, a series of problems that can be addressed or ask the family members if they want to discuss something in particular (Margolin et al., 2005). Moreover, during the study, the opinions of the participants regarding the study can change. For example, children or adolescents may want to withdraw from it. The researchers must allow them to do this, avoiding coercion, and must inform the participants that the situations they are in are changing along with them (Margolin et al., 2005).

Religion and Values

Everyone has a different set of values and sometimes the therapist and the client can find themselves on the opposing side of such values. This is especially true when religious values are involved, but more general attitudes can also influence the therapeutic practice.

In terms of religious values, therapists must be careful not to influence the clients based on their own beliefs. Some clients, especially those with a strong religious background, can have very powerful opinions towards marriage and divorce. Also, similar views can appear when a therapist is a religious person. In each case, the professional must not impose his/her opinion and discuss the discrepancies with the client (Rusu & Turliuc, 2011). Also, when the differences appear to be irreconcilable, therapists can end the sessions and propose a different colleague for the couple.

Margolin (1982) discusses three values that can influence the ways in which therapists work within the sessions:

- **Preservation of the Family:** Many times, a couple seeks therapy only for the therapists to enforce their decision to maintain the relationship or to divorce. Although the AAMFT guidelines specify that the responsibility of a decision falls only on the couple, it is possible for the therapist to offer some subtle cues towards one decision or the other. These cues may come from one's own personal experience, religious views or from the unconscious preference for one of the partners. The opinions of how a practitioner must act in this situation are different. Some authors consider that a therapist must influence the couple towards a decision if he/she feels it is the right one, while others deny the influence whatever the situation is (Yoell, Stewart, Wolpe, Goldstein, & Speierer, 1972). Finally, Margolin (1982) considers that it is crucial for the psychologist to be aware of such predilections in order to control them.
- **Extramarital Affairs:** At the extremes, a therapist can either endorse an extramarital affair or explicitly discourage it. The advocates of the first choice say that such a relationship might be beneficial for the individual. Still, it is most detrimental to the other. When in favour of the second choice, the therapists believe that they are working for the marital relationship and the termination of the extramarital one means that the partner is also willing to work for it. The drawback is that one can maintain the affair in secrecy, thus damaging the therapist's efforts. A better solution would be to openly discuss the problem of extramarital affairs with the partners, ask for their opinions on the subject and then assign a proper strategy.
- **Sex Roles:** In some families, the traditional view of the sex roles is acceptable for both members. In other families, one member has more progressive views than the other. Moreover, the therapists tend to have their own opinion on this subject. Balancing all these views can prove to be difficult. In the first case, advocating for a progressive division of the roles can lead to dissatisfaction for both spouses. In the second one, an unwanted alliance with the "discriminated" partner might appear. Also, believes that women are better suited to take care of children or that a job is more important for the men, are sexist. In order to eliminate the influence of the values towards the sex roles, a therapist must carefully consider his/her values and discuss them with the clients.

Any therapist inevitably influences customer relationships and, therefore, the problem is not how the influence and manipulation can be avoided, but how they can be best used in the client's interest. Some other ethical dilemmas which generate lots of stress and anxiety for the therapist are related to feedback, advises and referrals, maintaining clinical and financial records, the duty to warn, protect and report, avoiding malpractice and multiple relationships (Turliuc, 2008). Providing advises and feedback to a couple on issues such as differences, past histories or commitment may be an important aspect of treatment, yet can also induce conflict that may have been previously stifled. Allowing a couple to argue in a session for observation and assessment can trigger violence and increase emotional detachment if emotional calming is not reached until the end of the therapy session (Patterson, 2012). Also, couple and family therapists must understand the need to refer for treatments or services they are not competent to offer (such as sex therapy, divorce therapy, trauma history therapy etc.). The ethical principles constantly remind psychologists that they must avoid pathology, and the impression that they have access to the absolute truth.

Special Concerns in Family Research and Practice

Ethnic and Racial Research

The ethical problems raised by ethnical diversity are already well documented. In a study by Hall and Rammell (2016: 684), social workers responded that they do not consider colour as an interest in their work. While an affirmation such as "I treat the person, not the colour" might be good at the first sight, sometimes it hides a more negative subtext. By not taking colour, and thus race or culture into consideration, the professionals might, on one hand, deny the particularities of each culture and on the other hand, fail to understand some mechanisms that are specific to those cultures. This is particularly true in the field of family therapy, where each culture has its own view on marriage and family and as such, each therapy session must be different according to the culture of the clients.

Also, research with ethnically diverse participants is problematic. While a level of differentiation is expected and studied in multi-cultural research, the situation is more difficult when the study takes place in a very diverse country. Firstly, "ethnic groupings are not fixed categories of difference but are complex, dynamic and context-dependent" (Body, 2014: 92). Inside one ethnic group, there are people with different social status, revenue or values. As such, it is important not only to take into account how various cultures are different but to also consider the diversity within a minority culture or ethnic group.

Body (2014) also discusses two concepts proposed by Phoenix (1987), those of normalized absence and pathologized presence. A normalized absence indicates that when researchers study unproblematic issues, they tend to concentrate on the majority of population, thus ignoring the minorities. But when a more pathological or problematic research question is proposed, the minority takes center stage. It is true that the language barrier might make an inter-ethnic study more difficult, but current research plans must take into account such differences and give equal chances of selection for each group.

The risks of unethical interventions may be even higher when discussing specific family-related cases. Some cultures are different in their collectivist or individualistic views, thus changing the focus from the family as a whole, to the individual as a separate entity (Margolin et al., 2005). Also, some definitions (for terms such as parenting or even family) might differ from one culture to another. Because of this diversity, family researchers and therapists must develop a code of ethics that acknowledges all the differences and embraces them in order to develop a series of practices that are suitable for today's' world.

In order to conduct proper ethical research with multi-ethnic participants, Body (2014) proposes three considerations for the research to reflect on: 1. The research team must be composed of ethnically diverse participants, reflecting the structure of the population of interest. 2. When necessary, informed consent must be written in the language of the participants. 3. Sampling must not be made on the base of volunteering and research must bring in participants as diverse as possible.

Research Involving Children

In recent years, the research concerning children has changed its focus from the parent describing the child's behaviour to the direct involvement of the minor (Graham, Powell, & Taylor, 2014). While this change causes a shift in the overview of the child (from immaturity and passivity to competence and agency) (Graham et al., 2014), it also leads to new ethical dilemmas.

The authors previously discussed how the task of the researcher is to prevent any harm from happening to the participants, or at least to reduce that harm to a minimum level. When children are involved, this task becomes more difficult. Some authors recommend that parents should be involved, as they are the legal safeguards for the children (Graham et al., 2014). Parents should offer their informed consent and the research should brief the parents if any danger may arise during the study. Unfortunately, the informed consent in research with children leads to supplementary problems. Any researcher must ensure that the children's involvement is voluntary, but at the same time, children are not always mature enough to give their consent. Moreover, when family research is involved, there is the risk that the parents compel the child to participate without his/her consent (Margolin et al., 2005). As a result, the psychologist must develop procedures that ensure the children's well-being, as well as inform both the children and their parents of their right during research. One can choose if the offering of a small inceptive is ethical or not. When the research is safe or involves little harm, a small compensation for the child can be used, but when the study poses a greater risk, such a payment can account for the exploitation of the child, in which case it is prohibited.

When confidentiality is concerned, researchers must usually obey state regulations. In the USA, the law states that researchers can inform the parents when the children at risk (from causes such as suicide, drug abuse or violence). Still, this poses a problem because by informing the parent, the psychologist brakes the confidentiality of the information. A point in this discussion is that of child abuse. While negative consequences can arise from the disclosure (the arresting of the parent can put the children in a negative state), is generally recommended that the wellness of the children is the most important and that informing the specialized institution is mandatory (Margolin et al., 2005).

Finally, the research with children must account for the complexity of its participants. Similarly to the studies concerning adults, children can be assessed by using different methodological strategies. Also, one must consider the context of the assessment. While at school, a child can believe that the research is mandatory simply because every task received in that context is compulsory. As such, children must be treated with respect and understanding and not discredited for the age (Morrow & Richards, 1996).

Intimate Partner Violence

Intimate partner violence (IPV) is a direction of study that became more important in the last decades. In both research and therapy, psychologists must carefully respect a series of ethical principles for both the victim and the aggressor. While the prevalence of IPV varies across different countries, it is nevertheless a reality of our society, one that is still very problematic. In an article made on the behalf of the World Health Organization, the prevalence was between 15% and 71%, with between 4% and 54% saying the violence happened in the last two years (Garcia-Moreno, Jansen, Ellsberg, Heise, & Watts,

2006). Btoush and Campbell (2009) discuss three principles that are important in conducting research concerning IPV. The first concern of the researchers should be to respect the participants. Usually, this means giving an informed consent and encouraging taking it home for study. But in this case, women can be at risk when taking such a paper, so the researcher can discuss alternative means for studying the consent. The second principle is the one of beneficence. Participants must be informed about the benefits and risks of their involvement. Finally, there is the principle of justice. The pros and cons of the participation must be equitably distributed, and the researcher must take special measures to protect the vulnerable participants.

The same authors present a few steps in assuring the ethical treatment of IPV victims in such research. Firstly, the study must be authorized by an Institutional Review Board. In the recruitment stage, research must offer flexible timetables and opportunities for the victims to engage. Many times, the aggressors are controlling, so the victim has difficulties in contacting the researchers. As such, when offering phone numbers, one must be available to receive calls at any time, whenever the victim is more secure. Also, the name of the study can be as vague as possible in order not to give any indication to the aggressor. The risks and benefits must be carefully discussed, and the parts must negotiate a strict procedure for data collection. Data must be coded, and, in case of online research, it must be protected under a password. Finally, a Certificate of Confidentiality can be used. These allow the researchers to guard the participants from forced disclosure from legal instances or other proceedings (Btoush & Campbell, 2009).

At the same time, IPV offenders can also provide important data concerning this behaviour and the family processes deriving from it. Crane, Hawes, Mandel, and Easton (2013) consider that IPV offenders, especially those who are incarcerated for their behaviour are also a vulnerable population. Firstly, the authors draw attention to the fact that some offenders can consider that they are obligated to take part in different studies because of their incarceration. Also, it is important how the participation is presented. The authors recommend a clear and well-informed explanation for the selection, and the act of participating must be made voluntary. Some participants can believe that their participation is beneficial for their situation. Usually, they are involved in a rehabilitation process and may consider that the participation would facilitate the process, which is not true. Nevertheless, the informed consent must present important information that helps their understanding of the study's purpose and of their situation.

Health-Related Ethical Issues

Some decisions about the ethical behaviour from the researchers are harder than others. This is especially true when the benefits and risks of a decision are well balanced. An important example for such a situation is discussed by McNutt, Gordon, and Uusküla (2009). Recent trends in the study of the chronically ill population started to use an observational method which involves both partners from a couple where only one of them is ill. The problem arises when the healthy partner does not know about the possibility to get infected. Even though complete disclosure is usually advised, in this case, the authors raise the question if the healthy partner must know the rationale behind his/her selection. More precisely, the author's study concerned both injection drug users and their partners. Given the fact that one partner's behaviour leads to greater HIV infection, the authors found themselves in an ethical dilemma: informing the other partners about the behaviour, thus risking both the breaking of confidentiality and the loss of participants, or keeping the confidentiality and risking the infection of more persons. Also, the partner that does not use drugs would not know the real reasons for his/her involvement in the study. In order to satisfy both the ethical and legal requirement, the authors decided to keep in the study only those participants who had already informed the sexual partners about their drug addiction. They also recommend that in the cases when participants are at risk of developing an infectious disease, the researcher must inform them about the real reason of their selection and must offer to counsel if the participants deem it necessary.

Ethical Codes for Psychologists in Romania and the State of Family-Related Guidelines

In Romania, the main ethical guidelines for the ethical practice of psychology and psychotherapy are proposed by the Romanian College of Psychologists (CPR) (Colegiul Psihologilor din Romania, 2013). In 2008, Turliuc invoked the fact that this was the only ethical code in use, but in recent years, different psychological associations (Romanian Association of Analytical Psychology, Romanian Federation of Psychotherapy, Romanian Association of Person-Centered Psychotherapy) created their own codes. Still, these codes remain inspired by the CPR guidelines or by foreign codes created for similar domains. Unfortunately, there are no ethical codes concerning couple and family therapy yet. The CPR code contains 15 core principles regarding the activity of a psychologist, but only one of them specifies something related to family issues. In the Article 16, it is specified that the results of an emergency evaluation cannot be used by the family of the patient, the purpose of such investigation is only the one of assessing the health of the nation. Still, this specification is not addressed to the family psychologist, being given for every specialist in psychological evaluation.

In part, the professionals from this domain can guide themselves from the more general codes, but as previously stated, these can rarely present relevant information for the distinct ethical dilemmas one can find. The authors also recommend reading foreign literature concerning this subject matter and close cooperation with the Ethical Board from the institution they are working for (if such board exists).

CONCLUSION

In conclusion, studies of families' private life and the interpersonal close relationships of husbands and wives, parents and children invariably raise concerns around issues of disclosure and confidentiality. These issues remain particularly complex because participants are not simply revealing identity to the outside world, but revealing secrets among family members, and in group there is always a possibility, even a likelihood, of involuntary disclosure. Family members may reveal information about one another which an individual may have preferred to keep secret, or what is observed may be deemed too private by one or more of the participants. As a consequence, in family research it may be more practical and ethical to frame ideas of consent as 'provisional' rather than 'informed' (Flewitt, 2005).

Couple and family psychology suffer from the same ethical dilemmas as all the other areas of psychology, but also from a series of more specific ones. Family research is problematic because it shifts its focus from the person to the more complex family system. It is the responsibility of researchers / therapists to take seriously the possible negative repercussions of research on participants and to take extra care when working with vulnerable subjects, with disempowered adults and children. Also, the issues of the modern world (racism, violence or even the involvement of the virtual medium) and the new methods of research and intervention create additional problems.

While there is a series of well-established codes of ethics for the family psychology, the main themes are informed consent, respect for privacy, subject integrity, avoidance of exploitation and betrayal, protection from harm and the possible negative effects of the research on participants. However, even the most complete codes fail to address all the possible ethical obstacles one might encounter.

When therapy is involved, a professional must understand that his/her allegiance is not to the individual, but to the family. As such, each member of the family is relevant and important, and all of them must be informed about the nature and the objectives of the therapy. Informed consent is also the basis for conducting an ethical study. The researcher must carefully consider all the risks for all the persons involved, even for those who do not explicitly participate in the research. Distinct issues and vulnerable population further complicate the assessment of risks and benefits, but in general, good planning represents the key of good, ethical research.

It is also important to note that we are living in an ever-changing world. Scientists develop new methods of intervention and research, but also new problems arise. Something that is suitable now, can provoke ethical discussions in the future. Sometimes, even the ethics can stand in the way of relevant research in a difficult field. The couple and family psychologists must always be ready for new challenges. Responsibility, competence, concern for the wellbeing of the clients and participants and a complete knowledge of the ethical guidelines are needed to develop techniques that are beneficial for both the advancement of science, and for those involved.

REFERENCES

American Association of Marriage and Family. (2001). *Code of ethics*. Retrieved from https://www.aamft.org/imis15/content/legal_ethics/code_of_ethics.aspx

American Psychological Association. (2002). Ethical Principles of Psychologists and Code of Conduct. *The American Psychologist*, *57*(12), 1060–1073. doi:10.1037/0003-066X.57.12.1060 PMID:12613157

Boddy, J. (2014). Research across cultures, within countries: Hidden ethics tensions in research with children and families? *Progress in Development Studies*, *14*(1), 91–103. doi:10.1177/1464993413490477

Btoush, R., & Campbell, J. C. (2009). Ethical conduct in intimate partner violence research: Challenges and strategies. *Nursing Outlook, 57*(4), 210–216. doi:j.outlook.2008.10.005

Colegiul Psihologilor din România. (2013). [College of Psychologists from Romania]. *Codul deontologic al profesiei de psiholog cu drept de liberă practică* [Code of Ethics for the profession of psychologist with the right to practice]. Retrieved from https://www.istt.ro/documente/CODUL-DEONTOLOGIC.pdf

Crane, C. A., Hawes, S. W., Mandel, D., & Easton, C. J. (2013). Informed consent: An ethical issue in conducting research with male partner violent offenders. *Ethics & Behavior*, *23*(6), 477–488. doi:10.1080/10508422.2013.804795 PMID:25892900

Dingwall, R. (2008). The ethical case against ethical regulation in humanities and social science research. *Twenty-First Century Society*, *3*(1), 1–12. doi:10.1080/17450140701749189

Dockett, S., Perry, B., Kearney, E., Hampshire, A., Mason, J., & Schmied, V. (2009). Researching with families: Ethical issues and situations. *Contemporary Issues in Early Childhood, 10*(4), 353–365. doi:10.2304/ciec.2009.10.4.353

Duncombe, J., & Jessop, J. (2002). "Doing Rapport" and the Ethics of "Faking Friendship.". In M. Mauthner, M. Birch, J. Jessop, & T. Miller (Eds.), *Ethics in qualitative research* (pp. 108–122). London, UK: Sage; doi:10.4135/9781849209090.n6

Elam, G., & Fenton, K. A. (2003). Researching sensitive issues and ethnicity: Lessons from sexual health. *Ethnicity & Health*, *8*(1), 15–27. doi:10.1080/13557850303557 PMID:12893582

Fenell, D. L., & Weinhold, B. K. (1992). Research in marriage and family therapy. In R. L. Smith & P. Stevens-Smith (Eds.), *Family Counseling and Therapy: Major Issues and Topics*. Ann Arbor, MI: ERIC/CAPS Publications.

Flewitt, R. (2005). Conducting research with young children: Some ethical considerations. *Early Child Development and Care*, *175*(6), 553–565. doi:10.1080/03004430500131338

Gabb, J. (2010). Home truths: Ethical issues in family research. *Qualitative Research, 10*(4), 461–478. doi:10.1177/1468794110366807

Garcia-Moreno, C., Jansen, H. A., Ellsberg, M., Heise, L., & Watts, C. H. (2006). Prevalence of intimate partner violence: Findings from the WHO multi-country study on women's health and domestic violence. *Lancet*, *368*(9543), 1260–1269. doi:10.1016/S0140-6736(06)69523-8 PMID:17027732

Gibbs, L. E., & Gambrill, E. D. (1998). *Critical thinking for social workers: Exercises for the helping professions*. Thousand Oaks, CA: SAGE Publications, Inc.

Graham, A., Powell, M. A., & Taylor, N. (2014). Ethical research involving children: Encouraging reflexive engagement in research with children and young people. *Children & Society*, *29*(5), 331–343. doi:10.1111/chso.12089

Hall, E. L., & Rammell, K. (2017). Racial- and ethnic-sensitive practice: From the practitioners' perspective. *Journal of Social Work*, *17*(6), 678–694. doi:10.1177/1468017316651993

Hohmann-Marriott, B. E. (2001). Marriage and family therapy research: Ethical issues and guidelines. *The American Journal of Family Therapy*, *29*(1), 59–73. doi:10.1080/01926180126081

Kuo, F. C. (2009). Secrets or no secrets: Confidentiality in couple therapy. *The American Journal of Family Therapy*, *37*(5), 351–354. doi:10.1080/01926180701862970

Mabe, A. R., & Rollin, S. A. (1986). The role of a code of ethical standards in counseling. *Journal of Counseling and Development*, *64*(5), 294–297. doi:10.1002/j.1556-6676.1986.tb01113.x

Margolin, G. (1982). Ethical and legal considerations in marital and family therapy. *The American Psychologist*, *37*(7), 788–801. doi:10.1037/0003-066X.37.7.788 PMID:7137697

Margolin, G., Chien, D., Duman, S. E., Fauchier, A., Gordis, E. B., Oliver, P. H., ... Vickerman, K. A. (2005). Ethical issues in couple and family research. *Journal of Family Psychology*, *19*(1), 157–167. doi:10.1037/0893-3200.19.1.157 PMID:15796661

Mathy, R. M., Kerr, D. L., & Haydin, B. M. (2003). Methodological rigor and ethical considerations in internet-mediated research. *Psychotherapy (Chicago, Ill.)*, *40*(1–2), 77–85. doi:10.1037/0033-3204.40.1-2.77

McNutt, L. A., Gordon, E. J., & Uusküla, A. (2009). Informed recruitment in partner studies of HIV transmission: An ethical issue in couples research. *BMC Medical Ethics*, *10*(1), 14. doi:10.1186/1472-6939-10-14 PMID:19709442

Milgram, S. (1963). Behavioral study of obedience. *Journal of Abnormal and Social Psychology*, *67*(4), 371–378. doi:10.1037/h0040525 PMID:14049516

Morrow, V., & Richards, M. (1996). The ethics of social research with children: An overview. *Children & Society*, *10*(2), 90–105. doi:10.1002/(SICI)1099-0860(199606)10:2<90::AID-CHI14>3.0.CO;2-Z

Murphy, E., & Dingwall, R. (2007). Informed consent, anticipatory regulation and ethnographic practice. *Social Science & Medicine*, *65*(11), 2223–2234. doi:10.1016/j.socscimed.2007.08.008 PMID:17888553

Patterson, T. (2012). Ethical and Legal Considerations in Family Psychology: The Special Issue of Competence. In *The Wiley-Blackwell Handbook of Family Psychology* (pp. 183–197). Hoboken, NJ: John Wiley & Sons Ltd. doi:10.1002/9781444310238.ch12

Pettifor, J. L. (1996). Ethics: Virtue and politics in the science and practice of psychology. *Canadian Psychology*, *37*(1), 1–12. doi:10.1037/0708-5591.37.1.1 PMID:12194189

Phoenix, A. (1987). Theories of gender and black families. In G. Weiner & M. Arnot (Eds.), *Gender under scrutiny*. London: Hutchinson and the Open University Press.

Rieber, R., & Robinson, D. (2001). *Wilhelm wundt in history: The making of a scientific psychology*. Berlin, Germany: Springer Science & Business Media. doi:10.1002/jhbs.10127

Rosenthal, R. (1994). Science and ethics in conducting, analyzing, and reporting psychological research. *Psychological Science*, *5*(3), 127–134. doi:10.1111/j.1467-9280.1994.tb00646.x PMID:11652978

Rusu, P. P., & Turliuc, M. N. (2011). Ethical issues of integrating spirituality and religion in couple and family therapy. *Revista Română de Bioetică*, *9*(1), 83–95.

Smith, R. L. (1992). Ethical issues in marital and family therapy: Who is the client? In R. L. Smith & P. Stevens-Smith (Eds.), *Family Counseling and Therapy: Major Issues and Topics*. Ann Arbor, MI: ERIC/CAPS Publications.

Thomas, N., & O'Kane, C. (1998). The ethics of participatory research with children. *Children & Society*, *12*(5), 336–348. doi:10.1111/j.1099-0860.1998.tb00090.x

Turliuc, M. N. (2008). Ethical Dimensions in Couple and Family Therapy. *Revista Română de Bioetică*, *6*(3), 106–113.

Walsh, R. T. G. (2015). Introduction to ethics in psychology: Historical and philosophical grounding. *Journal of Theoretical and Philosophical Psychology*, *35*(2), 69–77. doi:10.1037/teo0000015

Wrape, E. R., & McGinn, M. M. (2018). Clinical and ethical considerations for delivering couple and family therapy via telehealth. *Journal of Marital and Family Therapy*. doi:10.1111/jmft.12319 PMID:29361194

Yoell, W., Stewart, D., Wolpe, J., Goldstein, A., & Speierer, G. (1971). Marriage, morals and therapeutic goals: A discussion. *Journal of Behavior Therapy and Experimental Psychiatry*, *2*(2), 127–132. doi:10.1016/0005-7916(71)90027-9

Zimbardo, P. G. (1973). On the ethics of intervention in human psychological research: With special reference to the Stanford prison experiment. *Cognition*, *2*(2), 243–256. doi:10.1016/0010-0277(72)90014-5 PMID:11662069

KEY TERMS AND DEFINITIONS

Client: The person who goes to therapy in order to develop and change. By using the term *client* instead of *patient*, the therapists create a relationship that is not about curing an illness, but about helping the person achieve their best solution for their problems.

Confidentiality: A set of rules that limits the access to some information. In the cases of therapy or research, the actions undertook by the psychologist in order to protect the personal information of their clients.

Disclosure: The release of confidential information by the therapist or researcher.

Family Therapy: An umbrella term for the psychotherapies that work with couples and families in order to achieve the development of the individuals or of the family system. These schools of therapy consider that the family system is the base for all the individual problems and try to solve the problems by changing the system.

Informed Consent: The permission that is given by the client or by the participant before a therapeutic process or a research.

Psychological Assessment: A set of techniques that are used for the purpose of investigating the behaviors, cognitions, and emotions of an individual.

Psychological Intervention: Any set of strategies that are used to change behaviors, emotions, or cognitions.

Section 3

Ethical Evaluation of Technologies and Responsibility Toward Their Implications for Humankind

This section addresses the issue of the ethical responsibility of research organizations from the perspective of the social, ecological, cultural, and even anthropological impact that technologies such as biomedical (cloning, genetic engineering, human embryo research), those who aim at developing computing technologies and constructing artificial intelligence, human enhancement technologies, etc. may have.

Chapter 13
The Ethics of Embrionic Stem Cells Research:
The Human Being in the Early Stages of Development – A "Medicine" or an End in Itself?

Alexandra Huidu
University of Oradea, Romania & LUMEN Research Center in Social and Humanistic Sciences, Romania

ABSTRACT

Embrionic stem cells research, as opposed to hematopoietic stem cells research, has always stirred up many controversies of ethical nature that have projected their effects in the specialized doctrine of the domain of medical bioethics and law. Some of these controversies have been transposed at the legislative level (both by international normative acts and by the national laws of the states) while others are not yet de object of consensus. All that is not transposed by law remains in the exclusive sphere of ethics, so the ethical discussion in embryonic stem cell research is not only relevant for today's modern medicine but also of the utmost importance for a category of specialists in various research fields.

INTRODUCTION

The debate on the beginnings of life and the legal and biological status of the human embryo is far from getting closer to the end and, furthermore, it is enriched with new ethical arguments as medical technologies advance and specialize in areas that were, at one point, considered to be at best futuristic, but that today became reality. The status of the human embryo is what shapes legal frameworks, and this is why in this paper we will analize the three main theories on this issue: qualifying the human embryo as a product susceptible to property claims, qualifying the human embryo as a biological entity that demands a special respect, qualifying the embryo as a human being, whose right to life and dignity should be protected.

DOI: 10.4018/978-1-5225-6310-5.ch013

State policies and laws reflect one of these major theories, and this is why, in the second part of the paper, we tried to we have tried to present in a unitary manner both the international and the national regulations, because there is a delay in certain states to adopt a firm policy regarding these issues or the tendency to adjust ethical debates without going into detail, avoiding the essence of the problem. At first, we presented the relevant international regulations in the field, in order to identify the policy at the level of inter-state organizations (Council of Europe, European Commission, European Parliament), but also at the level of world politics (see the Oviedo Convention), in order to then analyze how these international trends were implemented in the laws of the states. Therefore, considering that legislators must act, we tried to identify the main regulatory lines in the countries that have already legislated in the field.

Principles that, as we shall see below, are influenced, altered, and questioned by arguments that defend the traditional content of already recognized human rights, thus stirring conflict between such rights and new rights, born under the impetus of cutting-edge innovation in medical research. This is why we that is why we have divided our analysis according to the main factors that could influence the ethical optics regarding research on human embryos: whether or not the embryos were specifically created for research and whether or not the research has therapeutic purpose

MEDICAL ASPECTS OF EMBRYONIC STEM CELL RESEARCH

Research on embryonic stem cells is a technology that has emerged as a consequence of human assisted reproductive techniques and has evolved in close connection with these techniques. Without the possibility of creating embryos in vitro, there would have been no real chance for a large-scale study of the potential of embryonic stem cells (Huidu, 2017: 196).

There are four types of stem cells: totipotent, pluripotent, multipotent and unipotent. Totipotent cells can differentiate to become any type of cell in the body, but also have the ability to each give birth to another human being (these are the 4 cells from which the human embryo is formed in it's blastomer stage); pluripotent cells - which are the object of stem cell research - have the ability to specialize and transformi into any type of body tissue or body organ, but lack the function of giving birth to a new organism (these are the cells occurring after the first 4 days of fertilization); multipotential cells - those that can give rise to other types of cells, but are limited both in their differentiation capacity, as well as in type or numbers (e.g.: neural cells, hematopoietic cells); unipotential cells are those already specialized to form certain tissues (of the skin, liver, intestinal mucosa etc.) and which can cause only one type of cells (Buţureanu & Lupşan, 2001: 58-59; Miehl, 2003: 25-26; Smith, Sindhu, & Meissner, 2016; Stem Cells, n.d.). The structural and functional differentiation of unipotential cells during embryonic development (also called cytodifferentiation) is an irreversible process (Gavrilă & Iftime, 2006: 144). Fully differentiated mature cell cultures are limited in their growth by the presence of telomeres - existing formations at the end of the chromosomes, which shorten every time they replicate duiring the cell division process, eventually leading to death of the cells, a phenomenon that has been identified as one of the causes of aging (Aviv & Shay, 2018). Inside embryonic stem cells, there is an enzyme responsible for preventing telomere degeneration, which makes it possible for multipotent cells, after being placed in the appropriate laboratory regulated environment, to multiply continuously, withought ever differentiating (Gavrilă & Iftime, 2006).

Once injected into the human body, multipotent stem cells have the ability to identify the organ affected by the disease and, properly directed, can replace diseased cells. It has also been found that if someone were to change the chemical composition of the environment where they are being kept, these cells begin to differentiate, and the resulting tissue would depend on the chemical composition of the solution in which they are held, which can genetically determine them to become muscle, epithelial, neural cells etc. (Gavrilă & Iftime, 2006: 132)`. This discovery can make it possible, once the factors affecting cell differentiation will be determined, for human organs to be grown in the laboratory and be used for transplantat. Moreover, stem cell research can help identify the causes of genetic diseases. In addition, by creating differentiated cells in the laboratory, different drug treatments can be tested more safely, in much less time than that required for human testing (Muscati, 2003: 8-10). Also, in case of diseases involving transplants causing histocompatibility issues, embryo cloning can be performed by extracting a nucleus from the patient's skin cells and transplanting it into an anucleated ovum, resulting in a zygote that will be the source of stem cells which, once incubated with an appropriate set of molecular differentiation factors, will be able to divide into the specialized cells required for transplantation, and the donor of the cell nucleus, the source for all hereditary characteristics, including histocompatibility, will not have the problems so commonly encountered today of immune rejection. Thus, it is hoped to treat several diseases, including: diabetes, Parkinson's disease, Alzheimer's disease, Huntington's disease, spinal cord injury, leukemia, aplastic anemia or irradiation disease (Knieling, Knieling, & Ioan, 2005).

The primary stem cell source is represented by human surplus embryos obtained from IVF and that haven't been transferred to the uterus. But the sampling of these cells leads to the destruction of the embryo that provides them, which has led to a heated debate about whether and under what circumstances stem cell research is legally and ethically justified in the context of violating the sanctity of human life, because it leads to the physical dissolution of the embryo, the controversy becoming even more fierce when discussing the issue of creating embryos with the sole purpose of using them in research (Huidu, 2017: 198).

THE MAIN THEORIES ON THE ETHICAL ACCEPTABILITY OF EMBRYONIC STEM CELL RESEARCH, IN CORRELATION WITH HUMAN EMBRYONIC STEM CELL THEORIES

In vitro fertilization has shifted the focus from the mother to the embryo, replacing the idea that the mother and the embryo are inseparable with that of complete independence, at least until implantation (Miehl, 2003). The bioethical and legal literature provides three distinct theories about the status of the human embryo, which has been regarded either as a human tissue, a thing susceptible to being treated according to the rules of property law, or as a human being whose right to life must be respected and protected, either by fitting it into an intermediate category, that of an entity to which we are due special respect, because of its potential to become a human being (Huidu, 2017: 162). Hence, there are several ethical approaches to embryonic stem cell research.

Qualifying the Human Embryo as a Product Susceptible to Property Claims, a Theory that Supports the Preeminence of the Right to Medical Treatment, Including Through Advanced and Innovative Medical Research, of People Suffering From That Could Be Healed as a Direct Effect of Such Research

In 1984, The American Fertility Society issued a statement stating that gametes and embryos created in vitro are the property of the gamete providers, who have the right to dispose of them as they see fit (American Fertility Society, 1986). Thus has emerged the tendency to consider the human embryo not as a future fully potent individual, but as an object, a simple set of cells. This perception of the status of the embryo stems from the post-Kantian metaphysical and anthropological conceptions, which reduce reality only to what can be perceived, to phenomena (fenomena), and any invisible reality (noumena) is non-existent or nothing can be said about it (Kant, 1998). Applied to humans, this theory reduces the human person to the processes generated by consciousness and the free actions of the mind and will. As long as specific human activities are the result of a fully developed nervous system and the individual ceases to act when the brain dies, a human is a person within these limits, so the embryo, not being able to perform such actions, is not a person (Dumea, 1998).

As a consequence of this theory and it's arguments, there are those who argue that it is ethical to freely pursue embryonic stem cell research, because it is considered exagerated to refer to human embryos as if they are already children, because about 60% of them do not develop beyond the first few days of fertilization for various reasons, such as unexplained stopping of cell differentiation, genetic defects, inoperative cell differentiation etc. (Albury, 1998). The arguments put forward in support of the ethical nature of this type of research are based upon the premise that it is erroneous to consider the human embryo as a person who has rights, and even if that were so, it shouldn't be ignored that scientific research on human subjects, carried out under the rigors of the principle of minimal physical risk for the patient, have been declared ethically acceptable. In addition, it is also ignored - in correlation with this - that the human embryo is too rudimentary and development to have any interests and it can't be argued that its use in research damages it, therefore there is no reason to apply the same prohibitive rules that protect humans who are not fully self-aware because of various mental disorders form injudicious medical research (Robertson, 1995).

It is claimed, of course, that it is preferable that all excessive embryos be adopted by infertile couples, in order to ensure their development to the as a fully human being, but as long as this chance cannot be ensured for all in vitro conceived embryos, it is preferable that the remaining "orphans" be used for a noble purpose, which would lead to the treatment of many diseases that represent a scourge for humanity, rather than being simply destroyed or frozen (for such a long period taht they might become unviable for transfer after thawing, or that would damage them to such an extend that would make implantation useless (Miehl, 2003: 6). Prohibiting embryonic stem cells research would violate humanity's right to scientific development and the right of sick people to benefit from all possible treatments, as part of their right to health. Bioethicists say that, as long as the medically assisted reproduction procedures allow the destruction of a number of embryos to treat a certain disease, namely infertility, it is unreasonable to prohibit this possibility for patients suffering from other diseases (Albury, 1998; Muscati, 2003: 21-22; Robertson, 1989, 2002).

In the bioethical literature (Lin, 2005; Pennings, 2005), there has been virulent criticisms regarding this point of view, which appears to be based on an unfounded philosophical conception developed at a time when medical technology was not advanced enough to allow the zygote to be identified by the microscope and the human genome was not yet been mapped, while current scientific data demonstrates that all the structures of the human body, including the brain, are actually present in all details in the fertilized egg, because if the brain were not embedded in the genetic information of the embryo, inevitably, it would also be absent in the adult (Dumea, 1998). Acknowledgement of the human being status must not be conditioned solely by the existence of reason, for then it would be necessary, for argumentative coherence, to consider that even very small children, mentally ill people, comatose patients and any other human while sleeping are no longer people, so they can be killed beyond any sanction, which obviously is an absurd conclusion (Dumea, 1998: 81-82).

To consider the human embryo only as a biological stock useful for living people means to allow science to re-evaluate the traditional dimensions of human life and human species (Moroianu Zlatescu, 2006). It has also been said that promoting the non-person status of the human embryo is a matter beyond morale, it is a manifestation of scientific politics to justify the lack of respect for human life, a value overridden by the interests for the development of medical research (Sowle Cahill, 2003).

This is the point where the right to health and to benefit from technological advancement of sick people who are already born, recognized beyond any controversy as human rights-holders, which is the reasoning ground for justifying the necessity of research on stem cells, conflicts with the right to life of the unborn person outside the woman's body, which, as we can see, is subject to controversy. The question of the ethics that rises in this case (beyond establishing the ethics of such a research itself) is whether there is any direct interest in maintaining arbitrariness in this debate, not definitively dealing with this issue and continuing research under the umbrella of unsure principles. Within the theories outlined above, "Does the purpose excuse the means?" seems to be avoided as a question, underemphasising the idea that the purpose is harmful to embryos and overemphasising that research is justifiable because the interests of the sick should take priority, because the means do not produce negative effects, so no justification is need for pursuing the goal using such methods.

As a result, determining the status of the human embryo is a matter of public interest, that should be clearly be addressed through state laws and not be left to the infertile couple, research institutes, financial or corporate interests, non-unitary doctrine or NGOs involved in this pros and cons debate, on the one hand, because it is necessary to develop a unitary, state-level view of this issue.

The Human Embryo Is a Biological Entity That Demands a Special Respect, Thus Research on Human Embryos Would Have to Justify the Rigors of Ethical Principles Only to the Extent That It Would Be the Only Way to Find a Remedy for Some Particular Serious Illnesses, Which Impact a Large Number of People

There are authors who disapprove that the human embryo is an insignificant object, but who do not recognize its status of human being either because prior to implantation, up to the 4-cell stage, the embryonic cells are totipotent, which means that in case of separation, each of them could develop into a different individual. These authors militate for the inclusion of the human embryo in an intermediate category, between goods (objects) and people, that of a potential human life that deserves a special respect (Annas, 1991; Baune et al., 2008; Callahan, 1995; Green, 2001; Falasco, 2005; Miehl, 2003; Steinbock, 2009).

This theory on the status of the human embryo has led to the emergence of a moderate view of the ethics of embryonic stem cells research. Although this theory essentially maintains the same arguments as the one advocating the liberalization of human embryo research, it is appreciated, however, that embryo research should be banned in principle unless the disease that could be cured through research is a very serious one, that would affect a considerable number of people, there are no other ways to get information about it, only if there was no substitute for research on embryos and all the previous testing was done on animals before switching to embryos, which would require strict control and supervision from the ethics committees, which would have to authorize each and every such research on the basis of a very thorough justification file and with the obligation that embryos be obtained from couples who have gone through in vitro fertilization procedure, after obtaining their informed consent (De Witte, 1998). Advocates of this point of view also say that it should be considered a criminal offence any action by which the physician would avoid giving the infertile couple that donated the embryos information considered mandatory for obtaining their informed consent would mislead the genitors about the fate of the embryos in question, for example, telling them that they no longer have viable embryos for subsequent implants, because they have not survived the thawing process or because they suffer from genetic abnormalities that make them unsuitable for transfer to the uterus (Wells, 2006).

The supporters of the human status of the embryo criticize this approach too, motivated by the fact that as long as the embryo is not recognized to have rights, the special respect due to it has neither a solid conceptual base, nor consistency, and they draw attention to the fact that the way in which the developing human is treated reflects the value that society gives to life in general (Robertson, 1995). It is also criticized that none of the above mentioned authors explain specifically what this special consideration is, thus the shallowness of their arguments can only be the result of the desire not to recognize - for various reasons - the sanctity of human life in all of its stages of development (Shaw Roy, 2003). Moreover, it is shown that from a legal point of view, the surrounding world was divided into two classes: souless things (objects) and living beings (animals and humans). There are no intermediate categories between an object (a non-being) and sentient, animated entities, as they are trying to suggest by creating a special, unique class for embryos. Embryos can either be objects or beings (Jones, 1995).

We join this last group of authors, motivated by the fact that the embryo is closer to becoming a human being than any other human body part (such as gametes) and the closer it is to the actual life, the more it is closer to the human condition. Its intermediate status requires that specific rules be drawn up, that take into account the purpose for which the embryo was created and the fact that, like cells, tissues and blood, it is a form of human life. Such rules would recognize their dynamic nature of human life, without excessively restricting the reproductive freedom of the gamete providers, and would create a balance between the present and the future, between individual and general interests. The respect due to the human embryo does not include rights enjoyed by a person who has already been born, such as the right to life, but only that status imposed by its human origins (Huidu, 2017).

Pro-Life Theories Claim that the Human Embryo Is a Human Being and Its Right to Life and Dignity Requires, From an Ethical Standpoint, That It Should Be Excluded From Being Used as Scientific Research Material

However, the two previous theories outlined above are minoritarian, because most bioethicists support, in respect of the right to life and human dignity, the optics according to which human embryo research should be allowed allowed for therapeutic purposes in favour of the embryo itself, since the human embryo is a human being because it fulfills three essential conditions: it is alive, it belongs to the human species and it has individuality (Albury, 1998; Dumea, 1998; Pinchuk, 2000). The adult is the same being that previously was an embryo, thus, if the embryo is not recognized as a human being, then the adult could not be recognized as such (Dumea, 1998).

The fact that the embryo has no personality it is not a convincing argument to dismiss that it is a human being, because personality is not a biological trait, but is the effect of the individual's social interaction, and the genetic potential of embryos requires to recognize them as human individuals outside any emotional determinism, drawn by the sentimental "investment" of third parties towards these embryos (Sowle Cahil, 1993) and, we add, even if (or, rather, the more so), unlike babies, they still do not yet have the ability to vocally, emotionally, impressively or perceivably claim their right to life, the right to equal treatment compared to people already born, the right not to become a simple means for a purpose that does not concern their own benefit, the right not to be treated less than a human because, a priori, other human beings interests should prevail by comparison to their own existence.

Therefore, the most widespread theory regarding the ethics of embryonic stem cells research advocates that modern technology should not be used in a manner that destroys the life of a developing human just to save or prolong the life of other individuals, who have already been born, because the embryo's right to life is as sacred as that of the born child or of the adult, making it erroneous to analyze the problem in a utilitarian way, targeting only the potential benefits, because once they are balanced in comparison with the supreme value of human dignity, it is obvious that using the human embryo as an instrument is a crime against his dignity of the developing human being, who is entitled to the same respect due to the already born child or other member of the species (Dumea, 1998, Caulfield, Knowles, & Meslin, 2004; Hirschman, 1991).

The prohibition of research on human embryos is all the more necessary as there are alternative research resources. Stem cells can be obtained from a variety of sources, such as: stem cells collected from adults (that have almost the same properties as the embryonic stem cells, including a low degree of differentiation, found in the tissues of the spinal cord, brain, intestine and skin and, moreover, that provide a number of advantages compared to embryonic stem cells, among which the most important one is that they eliminates the risk of immune rejection because they are harvested from the patient being treated); xenotransplantation (the use of stem cells to produce organs in the laboratory can be replaced by organ transplantation from animals, which have previously been genetically engineered to ensure histocompatibility); the use of chimeras (embryos obtained by similar procedures to cloning - the introduction of human DNA into the nucleus of an anucleated animal ovum - and which, technically, are not human beings because their genetic information is a combination of human and animal DNA, but whose creation provokes firm opposition based on the idea that the procedure does not respect the dignity of the human being and dehumanizes the act of reproduction (Moroianu-Zlătescu, 2006; Ţîrdea, 2006); stem cells obtained from the spinal cord of the fetus (with a high degree of adaptability and potential for low immune rejection risk, while heir sampling does not pose a special threat to the fetus); embryonic germinal cells from the fetus (cells designated to differentiate into gametes with stem-like properties, that can be isolated and harvested even from infants born dead or miscarried fetuses eliminated as a result of spontaneous abortions); development of research into the conversion of unipotent cells into stem cells - the process of de-differentiation (Muscati, 2003: 24-28). Furthermore, attention is drawn to the risks posed by embryonic stem cell therapy, risks arising from the impossibility of accurately controlling the cell division process, which may lead to an excessive multiplication of cells creating tumors, the precursors of cancer (Gavrilă & Iftime, 2006).

CONVENTION FOR THE PROTECTION OF HUMAN RIGHTS AND DIGNITY OF THE HUMAN BEING WITH REGARD TO THE APPLICATION OF BIOLOGY AND MEDICINE: CONVENTION ON HUMAN RIGHTS AND BIOMEDICINE (OVIEDO, 4TH OF APRIL 1997)

Concerning the destruction of human embryos for the purpose of stem cell sampling for research, the Oviedo Convention uses the notion of "human being" and it is accepted by the authors of this document that the protection of dignity and identity must be ensured from the moment of conception. However, as noted in the legal literature (Pivniceru & Dăscălescu, 2007), a problem is that although the rules set out in the Oviedo Convention are important, the legal force of the document is relative and can not be compared with that of the European Convention on Human Rights, which does not explicitly recognize a right to life of the human embryo.

In correlation with the provisions above, the European Parliament Resolution A2-327 / 88 on ethical and legal issues of genetic engineering reaffirms, in paragraph 7, the principle of freedom of science and research, in order to establish, in paragraph 9, that any constraint of this principle will be based on the human dignity of the individual and of the species, appreciating that national legislators have an absolute duty to define these limits. The provisions that have clarified and extended the notion of human dignity and have helped legal policy making regarding human dignity, are those contained in the Oviedo Convention, where the notion of dignity is addressed in two distinct ways, relative to the individual and in relation to the species, paragraph 10 of the Preamble stating that the states are "convinced of the need to respect the human being both as an individual and as a member of the human species" against any improper use of biology and medicine.

The dignity of born human beings is protected in all national laws, both by private law rules and by public (criminal) law rules, and the right to life represents a priority for legal protection, because life is considered to be the most important existing value. Based on the opinion expressed unanimously according to which the crimes against dignity persist even when the person against whom the perpetrator's action is directed does not have the necessary knowledge to realize the offense that is brought to them (Toader, 2012), the legal and bioethical doctrine (Moroianu Zlătescu, 2006: 380; Olaru, 2005; Scripcaru, Ciucă, Scripcaru, & Isac, 2005; Ţîrdea, 2006: 357; Vasiu, 2004: 61) concluded that legal protection should also be extended to the dignity of the deceased and the unborn human beings, motivated by the fact that in a society the offenses against dignity can at some point measure more than any other criminal acts, the degree of civilization of the individuals within it (Corneanu, 2000: 113).

Regarding the more delicate problem of creating human embryos for the sole purpose of research, the Oviedo Convention contains a number of provisions that have given rise to widespread criticism, which is due to the fact that paragraph 1 states that "when research on embryos is permitted by law (the national law of the signatory state – n.n.), it provides adequate protection for the embryo ", while the next paragraph prohibits the creation of human embryos for research purposes. The legal doctrine (Moroianu Zlătescu, 2006: 398-399) interpreted this approach as an attempt to establish a difficult balance between the laws of states aspiring to absolute embryo protection and those who wish to maintain their national rules, which already authorize such scientific studies, the Oviedo Convention being a framework convention, which leaves the parties a considerable margin of appreciation.

In order to assess the ethics of embryonic stem cell research, it is necessary to analyze whether the ethical discourse changes according to the purpose for which those embryos were created, whether they are excess embryos left over as a result of IVF procedures, initially created for human reproduction, or embryos specifically created for research. From our point of view, the ethical issue remains the same because the consequences are the same (it is known from the very beginning that the embryo will be destroyed as a result of stem cells sampling).

Such distinctions are not justified in terms of embryo status (Huidu, 2017: 211). If embryos up to the 14th day of life are so rudimentary in their development that it can not be claimed that they are harmed by their destruction during research, then no distinction should be made between supernumerary embryos resulting from IVF and those created specifically for research. The distinction is not based on a solid arguments, given that all of these embryos are at the same stage of development, and maintining the distinction only shows the existence of an interest in diminishing the importance of the right to life of some human beings in order to create benefits for other human beings, without regard for the sanctity of life as a universal value (Robertson, 1995), because it allows the human embryo to be instrumentalised to achieve a different purpose than that for which it was originally intended – human reproduction (Huidu, 2017: 211).

EU LEGISLATION, AN INTERNATIONAL LEGAL FRAMEWORK, CONSTANT IN MAINTAINING THE ETHICAL VALUES FOR EMBRYONIC STEM CELLS RESEARCH

Prohibition of Embryo Research for Non-Therapeutic Purposes

Prohibition of research on human embryos for non-diagnostic or therapeutic purposes was also promoted by most international acts targeting this area of science associated with reproductive technologies. Resolution No. 1352/2003 of the European Parliament on human stem cell research establishes in principle that the destruction of human beings in order to obtain scientific material for stem cell research violates the right to life and the moral prohibition of instrumentalisation of the human being (Article 10), requiring respect for human life at all its stages of development (Article 11, paragraph I). The Council of Europe Recommendation on the Use of Human Embryos and Fetuses for Diagnostic, Therapeutic, Scientific, Industrial and Commercial Purposes (1979) defines the notion of "diagnostic purposes" as any intervention aimed at the good of the child to be born, his development and his birth. The same recommendation is made by the World Medical Association in Part III, paragraph 1, of the MCA Declaration on In Vitro Fertilization and Embryo Transfer (Madrid, 1987).

In Recommendation no. 1046/1986, the Council of Europe lists the practices considered undesirable or deviating from techniques aimed at the use of embryos for strictly therapeutic purposes, including research or experiments on viable human embryos, cloning, the implantation of a human embryo in the uterus of an animal, or vice-versa, ectogenesis (the creation of an autonomous human being outside the woman's uterus), the non-therapeutic selection of sex, the creation of embryos from gametes of same-sex gamete providers. In the Annex to the 1979 Council Recommendation on Scientific Research and / or Experiment on Gametes, Embryos, Human Fetus and the donation of these human materials, Member States' governments are required to ban research on viable human embryos and experiments on living human embryos, whether viable or not (paragraph 3 (h)) if there is the possibility of using animal testing (paragraph 2 (b)). The same principles are developed by the Council of Europe in Recommendation no. 1100/1989 on the use of human embryos and fetuses in scientific research which, while underlining the importance of scientific research freedom (paragraph 1), shows that it is appropriate to recognize the need for legal protection of the human embryo immediately after fertilization, following the same rules as those mentioned in Recommendation no. 1046/1986.

The 1979 Council of Europe Recommendation distinguishes between human embryo research (letter h) and experimentation on human embryos (letter i), according to the viability of the embryo as a stage in its development. As we have stated on other occasions (Huidu, 2017: 204), we believe, in the spirit of the definition given to the concept of research for diagnostic purposes by the 1979 Recommendation and by Recommendation no. 1046/1986, that research involves any technique that interferes with the viable human embryo, thus with its implantation and potential development until birth, and which is not targeted as a therapy undertaken in order to favor the normal and healthy development of the embryo and also creates the risk, even minimal, that, as a consequence of the actions taken, the embryo would become non-viable for transfer or, once transferred to the uterus, it would not develop normally. Experimentation, on the other hand, involves any non-therapeutic action that can not guarantee the survival of the embryo or could potentially cause its destruction during the experiment. If research is forbidden by virtue of respecting the right to life of the conceptual embryo (targeting only viable embryos, as the text says), the prohibition of experimentation concerns both the right to life and the protection of human dignity, because it targets both viable and non-viable embryos (Huidu, 2017: 205).

This distinction raises the ethical question of whether the value to be protected primarily is the right to life or the human dignity. It is necessary to operate this conceptual differentiation generated by the application of medical technology to humans, since such confusion may lead to the unitary ethical treatment of overly vast fields of science, which is wrong because each branch of research separately raises subtle differences in the ethics of research, with major potential consequences. It is necessary to make this distinction, as I have argued before (Huidu, 2017: 206), in order to assess if certain unethical behaviors violate human dignity (such as genetic engineering) or constitute an interference with the right to life of the human being (embryo research). As far as the latter is concerned, we believe that the primary socially protected value is that of human life and only in subsidiarity the dignity of the human being, since as long as the act strikes, first of all, at the existence of the embryo, because, after sampling its stem cells, it would go into non-existence, by defending the right to life we also value of human dignity, which is also protected.

Prohibition on Creating Embryos Only for Research Purposes

Concerning the creation of human embryos for research purposes, the Council of Europe Recommendation of 1979 on the Use of Human Embryos and Human Fetuses for Diagnostic, Therapeutic, Scientific, Industrial and Commercial Purposes states, in paragraph 2, that it is recommended that the governments of the Member States of the Council of Europe prohibit the creation of human embryos through IVF for the sole purpose research, while still alive or after their death. Resolution no. No 1352/2003 of the European Parliament on stem cell research, in Article 9, establishes the same prohibition, and in Article 11 paraghrapf III recommends that Member States ratify the Oviedo Convention and enforce by national laws the prohibitions contained therein and to sanction their violation accordingly.

As regards the creation of human embryos for research purposes, the Council of Europe Recommendation of 1976 on the Use of Human Embryos and Fetuses for Diagnostic, Therapeutic, Scientific, Industrial and Commercial Purposes, the Council of Europe Recommendation no. 1046/1986 and the bioethics literature (Robertson, 1995), all agree that it is not enough to make the act of creating embryos for research a criminal offence but, for a unitary approach of the problem, it is necessary to incriminate the act of keeping an embryo alive in order to obtain scientifically usable material (this means avoiding the use of embryos currently in a state of cryopreservation for illicit purposes).

Regulations Regarding Research on Dead Embryos

Concerning the use of dead embryos for research, in order to ensure the respect for human dignity, the Council of Europe Recommendation of 1979 considers that using such embryos for research should be a justified exception to the present state of knowledge, due to the rarity of the illnesses that could be treated as a positive effect of stem cells research, the absence of another therapy and the prominent advantage gained by humans as a result of research (survival). The national laws of the European States (more precisely, of those states that have issued regulations in this area) chose not to incriminate the use of dead embryos in research, but instead have adopted the system proposed by the Recommendation, meaning that any scientific activity involving embryos (experimentation, diagnosis and treatment) should be authorized in advance by an ethics committee and prior to any intervention, fertility clinics and research centers must determine whether the death of the embryo is partial (the cells of a deceased clinical embryo may remain alive for several hours) or total (death is clinically associated with cell death).

With regard to embryo abortion in order to donate them for research, this practice, which should not be confused with research on spontaneously aborted embryos, raises the same issues of medical and legal ethics as embryo creation for experimental purposes. The 1979 Recommendation requires that the decision and the conditions of interruption of pregnancy be made in such a way that they are not influenced by the possibility of subsequent use of the embryo in research. Also, ethical practice requires total independence between the medical team performing the interruption of pregnancy and the team who uses the embryo for research purposes. Member States are recommended to drastically penalize both those who have taken umbilical cord blood without clinical or legal justification, or without the prior consent of the pregnant woman, her husband or partner, and those who have used the biological material thus obtained. We also consider (Huidu, 2017: 214) that the woman who chooses to terminate pregnancy should be criminally responsible if her purpose was to donate the aborted embryo for research, as long as she has gained an advantage, whether pecuniary or medical (for example, cells of the aborted embryo were used to treat a disease that the woman suffered from). The boethical doctrine (Scripcaru, Ciucă, Astărăstoaie, & Scripcaru, 2003: 221) adds to these cases the hypothesis of cell sampling from a live embryo created in vitro or in utero. Such acts are also criminal offences in the laws of countries outside the European continent, such as Australian (Law 144/2002 on the Prohibition of Reproductive Cloning, Part 2, Division 1, Section 14).

NATIONAL LEGISLATIONS: APPROACHES AND PERSPECTIVES

Concerning the national legislations, there are only few states admitting human embryo research, and in most cases research is allowed until the 14th day after fertilization, when the primitive line – the primitive streak - is formed. The primitive line is the formation that represents a longitudinal axis visible inside the embryonic disc, characterized by bilateral symmetry, around which all subsequent embryonic structures will be formed and organized (Ciruna & Rossant, 2016: 1552). Therefore, the vast majority of European and extra-European laws (in the countries where these issues are regulated) prohibit research on human embryos, regardless of its form and purpose. We refer, in the purpose of exemplifying, to the legislation of the United Kingdom - the Act on the Human Fertilization and the Status of the Embryo, 1990, chap. 37 (Great Britain, 1990), to the one of Japan - the Human Cloning and Similar Techniques Law, 2002 (Japan, 2002), to the legislation of New Hampshire State – USA - (New Hampshire Revised Statutes, 2001, § 168-B:1, B:13-14), to the one of Belgium - the Law on In Vitro Embryonic Research, 2003, Art. 4 Section 1-, to the one of Iceland - Regulation No 568/1997 on artificial insemination, art. 22 (Busardo, Gulino, Napoletano, & Frati, 2014).

Australia - the Act on Medical Treatment of Infertility, 1995, Part 1, Division 2, Section 21C, paragraphs 1-5 (Australia, 1995) - criminalizes (punishment up to 5 years) any act involving the use of supernumerary embryos, except activities permitted by law, activities consisting of: depositing cryopreserved embryos in specially arranged places, transporting them, observing them (by observing it is understood taking pictures or videos of the embryo using specialized equipment), allowing access to the embryo storage site with the purpose of monitoring, defrosting embryos for use in implantation by an infertile couple to whom these embryos would have been donated. Any research on the product of conceiving constitutes a violation if the embryo in question is not improper for transfer to the uterus and the prohibition of use in research does not refer to medical investigations with a diagnostic role, carried out to determine infertility treatment in favor of the woman from which gametes originate.

In Europe, Germany (the Human Embryo Protection Act of 1990, Section 2) criminalizes (punishment being a criminal fine or imprisonment for up to 3 years) the destruction, commissioning of another person for destruction, procurement or use for research of supernumerary human embryos resulted from the in vitro fertilization procedure, the attempt being punishable. The right to life of the human embryo is also implicitly protected by the Constitution of Ireland, which in its 8th amendment provides that its right to life has the same value as that of the mother. Similar provisions that criminalize human embryo research are found in the Danish legislation - Law no. 660/1997 on Artificial Insemination, Chapter 7 -, Italy - Law no. 40/2004, part 2, art. 13, Section 9, paragraph 1 -, Norway - Law no. 100/2003 on the application of biotechnology in medicine, Chapter 3, § 3-1 -, Slovakia - Law no. 2077/1994 on access to medical services -, France - Law no. 94-654 of 29 July 1994 (Busardo et al., 2014).

New Zealand inclusively criminalizes the possession of human embryos, as long as it is not exercised for the purpose of reproduction - Law no. 92/2004 on healthcare techniques in procreation, Part 2, Division 1, Section 9, paragraph 2, c (New Zealand, 2004), the penalty being imprisonment of up to 2 years, criminal fine up to $ 100,000, or both cumulatively applied.

US legislation has undergone substantial changes in research on cellular stem cells, depending on state policy on this type of research. Thus, under the Presidential Order of August 9, 2001 of President George W. Bush, supplemented by Presidential Order no. 13435 of June 20, 2007 banned federal funding for research on newly-created embryonic stem cell lines, not those previously created, but this presidential policy was likely to fundamentally affect US policy, although the above mentioned executive orders were referring exclusively to federal funding, not also to the private funding of embryonic stem cell research, which could have continued with this amendment (as it actually did, where it was possible).

As a consequence, the State of Maine (Maine Revised Statutes, title 22, subtitle 2, part 3, chapter 263-B, article 1593, paragraph 1) criminalized the use, transfer, distribution or donation of a living human embryo for the purpose of scientific experiments (those experiments carried out in specialized institutions) or any other type of experiment (not taking place in an organized setting), complicity in the form of support or other assistance to the author being also punished. It has also been criminalized the act of consenting to the pursuit of such prohibited activities. The law of Maine has in fact criminalized the failure to disclose to the criminal prosecution authorities the acts described above, being assimilated to complicity (a similar provision is contained in the text of the law criminalizing embryo research in Minnesota-Minnesota Statutes, Chapter 145, 145,422, subdivision 1). South Dakota Criminal Legislation (South Dakota Codified Laws, Chapter 34-14, Article 34-14-16, 34-14-17, 34-14-18) was criminalizing the non-therapeutic research on the human embryo if this was endangering its integrity, its development or its life, the sale or transfer from the place of storage of human embryos for the purpose of being supplied for research, as well as the use of embryonic cells obtained as a result of the above-described facts. For the act to be punished, it was required that the author knew at the time of the research that the biological material was of embryonic origin or that the research had a non-therapeutic character (this was a takeover of the provisions of Federal Law No. 107-116 1996 - The Dickey Amendment - Section 510 (a), paragraph 2).

A nuanced approach, which was also including the form of culpable guilt, more specifically of the medical malpractice, was found in the legislation of the state of Michigan (Michigan Compiled Laws, Public Health Code, Law 368/1978, Section 2685, Article 1), in whose law the act was not considered to be a crime if the author, on the basis of his expert judgment, based on the scientific research available at the time of the research, could not assess that the concerned research presented a risk to the development or the life of the embryo. A number of other US states have criminalized human embryo research, including: Louisiana (Louisiana Revised Statutes, subsection 9: 123, 9: 129, Massachusetts (Massachussets General Laws, Chapter 112, Section 12J (a), paragraphs I-IV), North Dakota (North Dakota Century Code, Section 14-02.2), Pennsylvania (Pennsylvania Constitutional Statutes, Section 3216 (a), Illinois (Illinois Compiled Statutes, § 510/6 (7), Kentucky (Kentucky Revised Statutes, § 311.715), New Mexico (New Mexico Statutes, § 24-9a-1- (1) - (7).

Some states have also criminalized research on human embryos, even if they are therapeutic, as long as they are conducted outside the appropriate presented projects and authorized by competent health or scientific authorities or by a delegation of multidisciplinary national committees or if they do not meet the time limits prescribed by the authorities (California, USA, California Penal Code, § 367 (g), Australia, Law on the Medical Treatment of Infertility, Part 1, Division 2, Sections 21CB, 21E - but it has been stated that the deed was not a law offense if the license contained vices that the perpetrator could not objectively know: part 2, division 2, section 12A).

Following March 09, 2009, the two executive orders of President George W. Bush were revoked by the Presidential Order no. 13505 on March 9, 2009, of President Barack Obama, who has thus liberalized federal funded stem cell research, arguing that such research has the potential to lead to a better understanding and treatment of certain serious conditions, and the scientific evolution of the last decade in this field has been promising and encouraging, so that its financial support is justified.

Regarding the creation of human embryos specifically for use in research, Canada, by Law no. C-13/2004, in Art. 5 (Canada, 2004) criminalizes the creation of embryos for research, whether the procedure was carried out by the investigator or by another person, as well as a simple offer to facilitate the production of embryos to be used in research . The Canadian law also criminalizes the payment or offer to give a sum of money to a person in order to cause her to undertake the previously described deeds. The Australian Act of 1995 (Australia, 1955) on the medical treatment of infertility criminalizes the deed of creating a human embryo through the IVF procedure for a purpose other than to get the pregnancy into a woman, by "another purpose" meaning not only the use of those embryos in scientific research, but also for industrial purposes (for the manufacture of cosmetic products) or commercial purposes (Part 7A, Division 3, Section 38F). The German Act of 1991 on the Protection of Human Embryos (Busardo et al., 2014) contains similar provisions, but expressly states that nor the woman donating IVF gametes neither the one into whose uterus the conception product would be transferred after its manipulation for experimental purposes will be punished (Section 1, Article 1 and 2). Another unethical behavior, unforeseen by the laws of these states, is also the one resulting from the distinction we can make depending on whether the gametes donation or the embryo transfer have been made or not in order to help the author of the research in achieving or completing the steps scientifically forbidden by law, and according to the conclusion we consider that it should also be forbidden, respectively criminalized, any support brought to committing the deed by the genitor woman or by the carrier mother (Huidu, 2017: 213). Incriminations on the creation of embryos for research are also included in the laws of Finland - the Law on Medical Research, 1999, art. 13 -, of Iceland - Regulation no. 568/1997 on artificial insemination, art. 23 lit. a) and of Italy (Law No. 40/2004, Part 2, Section 9, Article 13, paragraph 3 (Busardo et al., 2014) Romania abolishes the creation of human embryos for research (Article 63 2 of the Civil Code), and the Romanian Penal Code punishes by imprisonment from 3 to 10 years and the prohibition of certain rights the act of creating human embryos for purposes other than reproductive (Article 195 paragraph 1), as well as the attempt to this deed, including whether the act was committed by a legal person, not just an individual.

Another practice that needs to be ethically analyzed, this time from the point of respecting the right to physical integrity, to health and harmonious development of the child to be born, is the implantation in the uterus of a previously used embryo or of one which was obtained from a gamete previously used in the research, unless the intervention was performed for therapeutic purposes. Incriminations in this respect have been made in the legislation of Australia - The Law on the Medical Treatment of Infertility, Part 4, Section 40, Art. 1 (Australia, 1995), of Sweden - In vitro fertilization law, 1988 – of Denmark - Law no. 660/1997, Chapter 7 - and the one of Belgium - Law on In Vitro Embryo Research Created in 2003, art. 5, paragraph 2 (Busardo et al., 2014).

CONCLUSION

In a world that wants to eradicate diseases that are real scourges, embryonic stem cells research seems to be the holy grail for scientists responsible for finding the desirable medical treatments. The noble goal of bringing hope and quality into the lives of the suffering must not be based on ignoring what essentially makes us human, that is the proportionality of our actions, their ethicity and the capacity to adapt the means to the purpose.

We join with pro-life theorists and we advocate that human embryos can be considered human beings from the moment the ovum is fertilized by the sperm, in total accordance with international regulations and national laws that ban creating embryos for the sole purpose of research. At the same time, we admit that stem cells research has a huge potential for human wellfare and this is why we agree that cells from dead embryos could be used in research, as long as the gamete providers give their informed consent for such procedures. This also seems to be the main optic in international conventions and regulations and in national laws, as we have shown above.

ACKNOWLEDGMENT

Within this chapter were used information previously published by the author in Romanian in the book *Reproducerea umană medical asistată. Etica incriminării versus etica biologică. Studiu de drept comparat* [Human Medically Assisted Reproduction. The Ethics of Incrimination versus Bioethics. Comparative Law Study], Lumen Publishing House, Iaşi, Romania, 2017.

REFERENCES

Albury, R. M. (1998). Challenges to commonsense: Debates about the status of human embryos outside women's bodies. *Journal of Australian Studies*, *22*(59), 129–138. doi:10.1080/14443059809387430

American Fertility Society; Ethics Committee. (1986). Ethics and the new reproductive technologies. *Fertility and Sterility*, *46*(3), 16–20. doi:10.1016/S0015-0282(16)58770-6 PMID:2941318

Australia. (1995). *Law on Medical Treatment of Infertility*. Retrieved from http://www.legislation.vic.gov.au/Domino/Web_Notes/LDMS/LTObject_Store/LTObjSt2.nsf/DDE300B846EED9C7CA257616000A3571/93F5C7F19E9048C6CA2577610022D62E/$FILE/95-63a010.pdf

Australia. (2002). *Law No. 144/2002 on the Prohibition of Reproductive Cloning*. Retrieved from https://www.legislation.gov.au/Details/C2017C00306

Aviv, A. J., & Shay, M. (2018). Reflections on telomere dynamics and ageing-related diseases in humans. *Philosophical Transactions of the Royal Society B: Biological Sciences, 373*(1741), 20160436-20160444. doi:10.1098/rstb.2016.0436

Baune, Ø., Borge, O. J., Funderud, S., Føllesdal, D., Heiene, G., & Østnor, L. (2008). In L. Østnor (Ed.), *Stem Cells, Human Embryos and Ethics* (pp. 1–18). Dordrecht, The Netherlands: Springer. doi:10.1007/978-1-4020-6989-5_1

Busardo, F. P., Gulino, M., Napoletano, S., & Frati, P. (2014). The evolution of legislation in the field of medically assisted reproduction and embryo stem cell research in European Union members. *BioMed Research International*, *2014*, 1–14. doi:10.1155/2014/307160 PMID:25147794

Buţureanu, Ş., & Lupşan, G. (2001). *O provocare interdisciplinară: reproducerea medical asistată* [An interdisciplinary challenge: Assisted medical reproduction]. Iaşi, Romania: Junimea.

Callahan, D. (1995). The puzzle of profound respect. *The Hastings Center Report*, *25*(1), 39–40. doi:10.2307/3562493 PMID:7730051

Canada. (2004). *Law no. C-13 on Medically Assisted Human Reproduction*. Retrieved from https://lop.parl.ca/About/Parliament/LegislativeSummaries/bills_ls.asp?lang=E&ls=C13&Parl=37&Ses=2&Language=E

Caulfield, T., Knowles, L., & Meslin, E. (2004). Law and policy in the era of reproductive genetics. *Journal of Medical Ethics*, *30*(4), 414–417. doi:10.1136/jme.2002.001370 PMID:15289541

Ciruna, B., & Rossant, J. (2016). Primitive streak. In *Encyclopedia of Genetics* (p. 1552). Genomics, Proteomics and Informatics. doi:10.1007/978-1-4020-6754-9_13424

Convention for the Protection of Human Rights and Dignity of the Human Being with regard to the Application of Biology and Medicine: Convention on Human Rights and Biomedicine. (1997, April 4). Retrieved from https://rm.coe.int/168007cf98

Corneanu, D. (2000). Subiectul pasiv al infracţiunilor contra demnităţii [The victim of crimes against dignity]. *Dreptul, 11*(9), 111-114.

Council of Europe. (1979a). *Recommendation on the Use of Human Embryos and Fetuses for Diagnostic, Therapeutic, Scientific, Industrial and Commercial Purposes.* Retrieved from https://www.coe.int/t/dg3/healthbioethic/Texts_and_documents/INF_2014_5_vol_II_textes_%20CoE_%20bio%C3%A9thique_E%20(2).pdf

Council of Europe. (1979b). *Recommendation on Scientific Research and / or Experiments on Gametes, Embryos, Human Fetuses and the Donation of these Human Materials.* Retrieved from https://www.coe.int/t/dg3/healthbioethic/Texts_and_documents/INF_2014_5_vol_II_textes_%20CoE_%20bio%C3%A9thique_E%20(2).pdf

Council of Europe. (1986). *Recommendation no. 1046 on the Use of Human Embryos and Fetuses for Diagnostic, Therapeutical, Scientific, Industrial and Commercial Purposes.* Retrieved from http://assembly.coe.int/nw/xml/XRef/Xref-XML2HTML-en.asp?fileid=15080&lang=en

De Witte, J. I. (1989). The wait goes on. *The Hastings Center Report*, *19*(2), 2–3. doi:10.2307/3563129

Dumea, C. (1998). *Omul între „a fi" sau „a nu fi". Probleme fundamentale de bioetică* [The man between "being" or "not being". Fundamental problems of bioethics]. Bucharest, Romania: Editura Arhiepiscopiei Romano-Catolice.

European Parliament. (2003). *Resolution No. 1352 on Human Stem Cell Research.* Retrieved from http://www.assembly.coe.int/nw/xml/XRef/Xref-XML2HTML-EN.asp?fileid=17158&lang=en

Falasco, J. R. (2005). Frozen embryos and gamete providers' rights: A suggested model for embryo disposition. *Jurimetrics Journal.* Retrieved from http://www.qgtlaw.com/wp-content/uploads/publications/pub-Frozen-Embryos.pdf

Gavrilă, L., & Iftime, O. (2006). Clonarea umană şi celulele stem – provocări ştiinţifice şi bioetice [Human cloning and stem cells - Scientific and bioethical challenges]. In Educaţia în bioetică şi drepturile omului în România [Education in Bioethics and Human Rights in Romania]. Bucharest, Romania: Academic Press.

Green, R. M. (2001). *The human embryo research debates: Bioethics in the vortex of controversy.* Oxford, UK: Oxford University Press.

Hirschman, E. C. (1991). Babies for sale: Market ethics and the new reproductive technologies. *The Journal of Consumer Affairs*, *25*(2), 358–390. doi:10.1111/j.1745-6606.1991.tb00010.x PMID:11660025

Huidu, A. (2017). *Reproducerea umană medical asistată. Etica incriminării versus etica biologică. Studiu de drept comparat* [Human medically assisted reproduction. The ethics of incrimination versus bioethics. Comparative law study]. Iaşi, Romania: Lumen.

Japan. (2002). *Law on Human Cloning and Other Similar Techniques.* Retrieved from http://www.cas.go.jp/jp/seisaku/hourei/data/htc.pdf

Jones, H. W. Jr. (1995). Children of choice: A doctor's perspective. *Washington and Lee Law Review, 52*(1), 225–232. PMID:12071215

Kant, I. (1998). *Critica raţiunii pure* [Critique of pure reason]. 2nd ed.). Bucharest, Romania: IRI.

Knieling, A., Knieling, L., & Ioan, B. (2005). Etica cercetării ştiinţifice pe cadavre de feţi umani [Ethics of scientific research on human fetus corpses]. *Revista Română de Bioetică, 3*(4), 80-84.

Lin, O. (2005). Rehabilitating bioethics: Recontextualizing in vitro fertilization outside contractual autonomy. *Duke Law Journal, 54*, 485–511. PMID:15940846

Miehl, K. L. (2003). Preembryos: The tiniest speck of potential life carrying the seeds for sweeping change. *Journal of Technology. Law & Policy, 4*(1), 1–36. doi:10.5195/tlp.2004.12

Moroianu Zlătescu, I. (2006). Protecţia demnităţii persoanei şi a demnităţii speciei umane în domeniul bioeticii, în lumina Convenţiei de la Oviedo [Protection of human dignity and dignity in the field of bioethics in the light of the Oviedo Convention]. In Educaţia în bioetică şi drepturile omului în România [Education in Bioethics and Human Rights in Romania]. Bucharest, Romania: Academic Press.

Noua Zeelandă. (2004). *Law No. 92/2004 on the Techniques of Medical Assistance to Procreation.* Retrieved from http://www.legislation.govt.nz/act/public/2004/0092/latest/whole.html

Olaru, B. (2005). Problema autonomiei şi limitele folosirii tehnologiilor reproducerii asistate [The issue of autonomy and the limits of using assisted reproduction technologies]. *Revista Română de Bioetică, 3*(3), 43-54.

Pennings, G. (2000). What are the ownership rights for gametes and embryos?: Advance directives and the disposition of cryopreserved gametes and embryos. *Human Reproduction (Oxford, England), 15*(5), 979–986. doi:10.1093/humrep/15.5.979 PMID:10783338

Pinchuk, S. (2000). A difficult choice in a different voice: Multiple births, selective reduction and abortion. *Duke Journal of Gender Law & Policy, 7*(29), 32–56.

Pivniceru, M. M., & Dăscălescu, F. D. (2007). Limita inferioară a dreptului la viaţă: între protecţia fetusului uman, dreptul la avort şi progresul ştiinţelor medicale [The lower limit of the right to life: between the protection of the human fetus, the right to abortion and the advancement of medical sciences]. *Revista Română de Bioetică, 1*(4). Retrieved from http://www.culturavietii.ro/2014/09/22/limita-inferioara-dreptul-la-viata-intre-protectia-fetusului-uman-dreptul-la-avort-si-progresul-stiintelor-biomedicale/

Robertson, J. A. (1989). Resolving disputes over frozen embryos. *The Hastings Center Report, 19*(6), 7–12. doi:10.2307/3561979 PMID:2606667

Robertson, J. A. (1995). Symbolic issues in embryo research. *The Hastings Center Report*, *25*(1), 37–38. doi:10.2307/3562492 PMID:7537261

Robertson, J. A. (2002). *Precommitment strategies for disposition of frozen embryos*. SSRN Electronic Journal. doi:10.2139srn.315374

Scripcaru, G., Ciucă, A., Astărăstoae, V., & Scripcaru, C. (2003). *Introducere în biodrept. De la bioetică la biodrept* [Introduction to biolaw. From bioethics to biolaw]. Bucharest, Romania: Lumina Lex.

Scripcaru, G., Ciucă, A., Scripcaru, C, & Isac, L. (2005). Manipulările genetice şi implicaţiile lor juridice [Genetic manipulations and their legal implications]. *Revista Română de Bioetică*, *3*(2).

Shaw Roy, L. (2003). Roe and the new frontier. *Harvard Journal of Law & Public Policy*, *27*(1), 339–384. PMID:15568255

Sowle Cahill, L. (1993). The embryo and the fetus: New moral contexts. *Theological Studies*, *54*(1), 124–142. PMID:11656434

Steinbock, B. (2009). *Moral status, moral value and human embryos: Implications for stem cell research*. Oxford Handbooks Online. doi:10.1093/oxfordhb/9780199562411.003.0019

Stem Cells. (n.d.). *Introduction. Unipotent, multipotent, pluripotent & totipotent stem cells*. Retrieved from https://stephyboo96.weebly.com/unipotent-multipotentpluripotent--totipotent-stem-cells.htm

Ţîrdea, T. N. (2006). Demnitatea umană din perspectivă planetară şi bioetică [Human dignity from a planetary and bioethical perspective]. In Educaţia în bioetică şi drepturile omului în România [Education in Bioethics and Human Rights in Romania]. Bucharest, Romania: Academic Press.

Toader, T. (2012). *Drept penal. Partea specială* [Criminal law. The special part]. Bucharest, Romania: Hamangiu.

United Kingdom. (1990). *Law on Human Fertilization and Embryo Status*. Retrieved from https://www.legislation.gov.uk/ukpga/1990/37/contents

USA Federal Law No. 107-116/1996. (n.d.). *The Dickey Amendment*. Retrieved from https://www.congress.gov/115/bills/hr4573/BILLS-115hr4573ih.pdf

USA, New Hampshire. (2001). *New Hampshire Revised Statutes of 2001*. Retrieved from https://law.justia.com/codes/new-hampshire/

USA President George W. Bush Presidential Order No. 13435. (2007, June 20). *Federal Register*, *72*(120). Retrieved from https://www.gpo.gov/fdsys/pkg/FR-2007-06-22/pdf/07-3112.pdf

USA, California. (n.d.). *California Penal Code*. Retrieved from https://codes.findlaw.com/ca/penal-code/

USA, Illinois. (n.d.). *Illinois Compiled Statutes*. Retrieved from https://en.wikipedia.org/wiki/Illinois_Compiled_Statutes

USA, Kentucky. (n.d.). *Kentucky Revised Statutes*. Retrieved from https://law.justia.com/codes/kentucky/

USA, Louisiana. (n.d.). *Louisiana Revised Statutes*. Retrieved from https://legis.la.gov/legis/Laws_Toc.aspx?folder=75&level=Parent

USA, Maine. (n.d.). *Maine Revised Statutes*. Retrieved from http://legislature.maine.gov/statutes/search.htm

USA, Massachussets. (n.d.). *Massachussets General Laws*. Retrieved from https://malegislature.gov/Laws/GeneralLaws

USA, Michigan. (n.d.). *Michigan Compiled Laws, Public Health Code, Legea nr. 368/1978*. Retrieved from http://www.legislature.mi.gov/(S(br2uiku2tigmzvfu3cqrzxkl))/mileg.aspx?page=MCLBasicSearch

USA, Minnesota. (n.d.). *Minnesota Statutes*. Retrieved from https://www.revisor.mn.gov/statutes/

USA, New Mexico. (n.d.). *New Mexico Statutes*. Retrieved from http://public.nmcompcomm.us/nmnxt-admin/

USA, North Dakota. (n.d.). *North Dakota Century Code*. Retrieved from https://law.justia.com/codes/north-dakota/

USA, Pennsylvania. (n.d.). *Pennsylvania Constitutional Statutes*. Retrieved from http://guides.libraries.psu.edu/law-pennsylvania/statutes

USA President Barack Obama Presidential Order No 10668, . (2009, March 11). *Federal Register*, *74*(46). Retrieved from https://www.gpo.gov/fdsys/pkg/FR-2009-03-11/pdf/E9-5441.pdf

USA, South Dakota. (n.d.). *South Dakota Codified Laws*. Retrieved from https://law.justia.com/codes/south-dakota/

Vasiu, I. (2004). Manipularea genetică. Implicaţii penale [Genetic manipulation. Criminal implications]. *Revista de Drept Penal*, *3*, 56–63.

Wells, I. (2006). Survey elicits couples' views on donating unused embryos. *OB GYN News*. Retrieved from https://www.highbeam.com/doc/1G1-149059397.html

World Medical Association. (1987). *Madrid Declaration on In Vitro Fertilization and Embryo Transfer.* Retrieved from https://www.wma.net/policies-post/wma-statement-on-in-vitro-fertilization-and-embryo-transplantation/

Zachary, D. S., Sindhu, C., & Meissner, A. (2016). Molecular features of cellular reprogramming and development. *Nature Reviews. Molecular Cell Biology*, *17*(3), 139–154. doi:10.1038/nrm.2016.6 PMID:26883001

KEY TERMS AND DEFINITIONS

Embryonic Stem Cells: The cells that form the human embryo, not yet differentiated morphologically, structurally, or functionally, or only partially differentiated, self-replicating, and capable, under the influence of environmental factors, to specialize functionally to become any cell in the body or even a new organism (totipotent), any cell in the body, but not a new organism (pluripotent), certain cell lines limited in number (multipotent), or only a certain cell line (unipotent).

Excess (Supranumerary, Left-Over) Embryos: Embryos not implanted in the uterus of a woman after an IVF procedure in order to avoid the risks associated with multifetal pregnancies, remaining as a result of the medical process of ovarian hyperstimulation, followed by the collection of an increased number of eggs, then in vitro fertilization, the selection and transfer in utero only of those embryos considered of best quality (more viable) in order to obtain a successful pregnancy and ultimately the birt of a child.

Human Dignity: Abstract term indicating a set of qualities, reactions, or behaviors of the human being, in its interaction with other members of the species or with the environment, and involving the way in which that person assesses the potentially injurious consequences of dangerous, offensive, denigrating, or discriminatory situations.

Pro-Life Theories: Legal, bioethical, philosophical, or religious doctrines claiming that human embryos are human beings starting with the stage when sperm fertilizes the egg (zygote stage), which requires respect for their right to life and their biological integrity and the avoidance of any action that would destroy or harm them in any way.

Status of the Human Embryo: A sum of characteristics and rights recognized to the human embryo, wether in vitro or in utero, by reference to its developmental stages and its genetic features specific to the human species, which gives it a distinct positioning (regardless of its prenatal developmental stage) in relation to a fully developed human being in legal, biological, ethical, religious, or philosophical systems;

Stem Cells Research: A field of medical research that uses the potential of stem cells to specialize functionally under the impetus of environmental factors in order to find treatments for disease amelioration or eradication, replacement of diseased organs in the body, testing of experimental drugs, identification of causality of diseases, etc.

Chapter 14
Tailoring Humans: The Ethics of Genetic Engineering

Alexandra Huidu
University of Oradea, Romania & LUMEN Research Center in Social and Humanistic Sciences, Romania

ABSTRACT

What began as an attempt to eradicate serious illnesses seems to have become, in some cases, under the impetus of human imagination and technological evolution, an exercise by which scientists come to compete with the attributes of divinity: augmenting human beings at a basic level that affects the identity of the species. Genetic engineering for medical purposes has created the premises for the existence of technologies that can be used for other agendas, without medical purpose, in order to bioenhance the characteristics of the human individual. The genetic inheritance we leave to future generations is now under our control, because we are able to manipulate our germinal line. Hybrid embryos and chimeric embryos, although still in the experimental stage, can become a reality in relatively short time. But just because we can, do we have the right to do it? Do we need all of this and, if so, to what extent? What are the limits and who or what sets the standards? These are the questions that this chapter addresses from an ethical perspective.

INTRODUCTION

The advances in the Human Genome Project and the separation of the embryo from the mother's body, made possible by in vitro fertilization, opened up large possibilities for applying a series of techniques to human embryos, techniques that can lead to the improvement of human beings, for medical or non-medical purposes. Some of these techniques (such as the creation of hybrid or chimeric embryos) are still at the stage of early research and experiments, others (germline genetic modification, non-medical genetic engineering) are at an advanced stage of experimentation for certain applications or can already be put into safe practice, in some instances (e.g., sex selection).

DOI: 10.4018/978-1-5225-6310-5.ch014

Therefore, society has begun to expect that ethicists not only argue and counter-argue and only feed an ethical debate that seems to generate new and new lines of discussion with every step forward in the development of medical technology, but also to reach conclusions. Even if some techniques are still far from being applicable, ethical debates must come before medical successes, because once a technique becomes accessible, it will be more difficult to balance interests and responses (economic, medical and, why not, emotional) in society, unless some guidelines are drawn earlier (Frankel & Chapman, 2000).

The final question is whether these techniques should be banned from the start or there are a number of variables that decisively influence the balance in one direction or another inside the ethical debates. Apparently, there are no reasons to operate with absolute prohibitions, as long as the tensions and concerns are satisfied, wether arising from the nature of the technology (in terms of safety and effectiveness), or from its impact on the individual (who may have both medical and non-medical interests), and then on society (with its values, principles and desiderata, depending on how these techniques are used, respectively for therapeutic or bio-amelioration purposes).

This chapter aims to synthesize the pros and cons for genetic engineering (with reference to some of its specific forms: germline modification, hybrid embryos, chimeric embryos, non-medical genetic engineering and child sex selection) and analyze them according to the four fundamental principles of bioethics: beneficence, non-maleficience, autonomy and justice.

We will base our analysis on the rigors of these principles, as defined by Mir and Morgan (2013: 19-20). Beneficence involves treating and improving the health of the sufferering, whenever possible. Non-maleficence requires that any therapy has a quantifiable benefit, generally translated by the phrase "do not harm". Autonomy is the right to self-determination, which includes freedom and the possibility to decide your own future. Justice (in the form of distributive justice) implies that the risks and benefits are distributed equally among the population.

By applying the above, the bioethics literature (Frankel & Chapman, 2000: 4) underlined the idea that it is vital to apply genetic engineering to humans according to whether or not we can positively answer the question of whether humanity has the wisdom, the ethical dedication and the public policies needed to use these technologies in a fair, just and respectful way for human dignity.

The problem can not be solved simply by general discussion, since every technique that involves manipulating the human genome has its own purpose, its own benefits, and it also raises distinct ethical dilemmas, as we will see in the following sections of this chapter.

Germline Gene Editing

Regardless of its forms (genetic modification of cells to be structurally and functionally differentiated to form gametes, direct intervention on gametes or insertion of artificial chromosomes), when discussing the application of genetic engineering techniques to the human embryo with the ability to be transmitted hereditary to the descendants of the future child, the first discussion to be made when considering the ethical dilemmas involved is whether this is a therapeutic enterprise (to eliminate or inactivate genes responsible for generating life-threatening diseases or quality the life sometimes in the individual's future), or a non-medical procedure (beyond what is necessary from a medical point of view, in order to enhance some characteristics perceived as desirable, such as intelligence, height, color of hair colour, eye colour etc.). In this section we will analyze the ethical arguments regarding germline gene editing for medical purposes. The ethical discourse on the application of non-medical techniques will be presented in the section dedicated to non-medical genetic engineering.

Respecting Beneficence

The usefulness of germline gene modification is that procedures of eliminating or inactivating genes responsible for the occurrence of certain diseases ensure the eradication of their negative or life-threatening effects both for the genetically modified person and and for all the descendants of that person, which is a much more effective way of dealing with a disease than treating it generation after generation, even if such a "treatment" would also be made through genetic engineering, only this time by interventions on somatic cells. From this perspective, there are authors (Mir & Morgan, 2013: 19) who believe that the prevention and eradication of genetic diseases in future generations is a real obligation of the current generation.

Indeed, from a beneficence standpoint, as long as there is a possibility to treat or improve the health of those who suffer, it is not unethical to apply these treatments to the entire line of offspring of a person. The eradication of genetic diseases by a single intervention, benefiting all the genetic followers of the individual, would bring uncontested benefits of time, resources and comfort (psychologically and physically) to all involved in the medical process, including for society. The interest in promoting such interventions is justified not only at an individual level (for the patient), but also at the general level (for society).

Although these arguments seem to put an end to the ethical debate in the matter, there are in fact fears about the liberalization of germline genetic modification, fears that the technology that makes these techniques available is the same as the technology that would make it possible, at the same time, for the improvement of human characteristics in the absence of any disease - an example is Alzheimer's disease, in which case the ability to correct the gene responsible for the disease would also imply an ability to improve a person's memory beyond what is considered normal (Frankel & Chapman, 2000: 43). There is, therefore, the fear that once the technology is made available, humanity will not be able to refrain from using it for alternative purposes than the one for which it was created, namely for eugenic purposes.

Although there are authors who claim that such practices are also ethical and they do not violate the beneficence principle, since augmenting the human being with the aim of improving health and mental acuity in general will increase the life expectancy and the quality of life for generations to come (Mir & Morgan, 2013), the majority opinion is that germline genetic modification should be banned as long as the purpose is non-medical, as efforts to improve the genome inherited from parents will have the effect of dehumanizing the act of human reproduction, encouraging the attempts to have perfect children and imposing a harmful conception of what is normal and what is abnormal (Frankel & Chapman, 2000: 8).

However, there are authors who consider this absolute prohibition as a form of fear of novelty, as the lack of clear state policies in the field and a series of terminological inaccuracies give rise to false ethical complications. We refer to the work of Resnik and Larger (2001) and the recombinant DNA Advisory Committee (2000). It is considered that a clear distinction should be made between 'therapy', 'prevention' and 'improvement'. So, if it is to be considered that the purpose of prevention is to reduce the risk of an individual having a certain illness at a certain point in his life, then the significant moral difference between therapy and improvement can be drawn by establishing criteria in order to assess which diseases could be targeted for gene therapies.

Although the words "therapy" and "prevention" have different moral connotations, as therapy is medically necessary, while prevention is medically indicated but not necessary (Resnik & Larger, 2001: 1451), prevention is one of the declared aims of medicine (Juengst, 1997) and the effectiveness of medical treatments must be analyzed not only from the perspective of immediate benefit to the patient, but also through the effect they have on socially unanimously accepted goals like population health (prolonging life and preventing diseases) and economic productivity (Nordenfelt, 1999).

Although it is difficult to distinguish between "prevention" and "improvement", as therapy is performed on a sick person, prevention is performed on a person at risk of becoming ill and improvement is performed on a normal and healthy person, it is difficult to define what is "normal" and "healthy" since no consensus seems to be reached in this direction, while the meaning of terms evolves and changes according to the social context (Parens, 1999; Resnik & Larger, 2001). Yet, there are a number of criteria by which it can be determined which diseases are ethically acceptable to be treated through germline therapies: the severity of the disease, the absence of postnatal treatment, the acceptance even of partial treatment for illnesses that would otherwise be fatal, side effects on the germline - when a gene responsible for several features of the individual is eliminated or invalidated - etc. (Recombinant DNA Advisory Committee, 2000: 18-19).

The Difficulties of Non-Maleficence: Margins or Error

Although ethically acceptable for therapeutic reasons from the perspective of the beneficence principle, germline genetic modification seems to be unacceptable from the perspective of the non-maleficence principle. Inserting, modifying, inactivating or removing genes responsible for disease may result in unpredictable effects on other characteristics of the individual, if the same genes are responsible for those characteristics (Resnik & Larger, 2001). Animal testing does not appear to be a 100% safe solution, although it is a mandatory requirement before testing gene therapies on human subjects, as it is difficult to determine which data obtained in animal testing are valid for the human organism, thus the application to humans of these data is not only a scientific issue, but also an ethical one (Recombinant DNA Advisory Committee, 2000: 17).

The ethical aspect is based on the principle of minimal risk, which requires that any therapy translated to clinical trials after test performed on animals must be made after a rigorous assessment of the unpredictability of its side effects (Recombinant DNA Advisory Committee, 2000: 17), and also on the rule of prudence and caution in the use of those techniques considered not to be safe enough, therefore at first scientists should concentrate on collecting clinical data and then, after collecting new and relevant data, on widening the therapeutic framework to other techniques, genes, diseases, patients.

Some bioethicists say that, from an ethical standpoint, these are not grounds for a total ban of therapies that lead to germline modification, because fears about the unpredictability of the effects of these therapies can be effectively addressed with caution, in other words by establishing some public policies that impose standards and rules in both scientific research and clinical activity (Frankel & Chapman, 2000: 46; Sugarman, 2015).

The argument is rational, valid, and finally describes the procedure for the implementation of all emerging medical technologies (not just those specific to genetic engineering) from the history of medicine. Although this approach seems to satisfy the rigors of the non-maleficence principle and this seems to close the controversy, another discussion, derived from the one abovementioned, is currently drawing heated debates among bioethicists. More specifically, the argument is that genetic therapies that affect the descendants of the people thus engineered bring harm to the interests of humanity in general, even if individual interests are fully respected, because humanity has a direct interest in preserving an unaltered genetic heritage.

The human genome is declared by UNESCO as a common heritage of humanity, from which stems the duty to protect it irrespective of the phenotypic characteristics of the person, because it is the basis of human identity, dignity and diversity, as the human being represents more than its genetic program - the integrity of the human genome is an absolute right of man, everlasting and non-negotiable, which is displaced in the state's obligation to conduct scientific discoveries in the field by means of imperative regulatory norms, conferring such research a social-useful direction, maximizing the benefits and minimizing the risks of applying science on humans (Scripcaru, Ciucă, Scripcaru, & Isac, 2005). These bioethical imperatives are complemented by the following: the absolute protection of the physical individuality of the human body, from which other human traits emerge - the dignity of the person, the respect of human individuality from conception to death, the right of every person to their genetic heredity and of humanity to an unspoiled genetic pool, the right of individuals to be different, which ultimately represents a right to progress (Scripcaru, Ciucă, Astărăstoae, & Scripcaru, 2003: 135-140).

It is considered ethically acceptable to genetically correct somatic cells, but it is forbidden to transfer such cells to embryos because there is a fear that germ cells may be also altered by the interactions, and to keep them untouched is to protect the genetic reserve of humanity, as long as mutations do not propagate along generations. It is considered that the genetic treatment of somatic cells is not without risk, because there is still insufficient information to be absolutely sure that the gene will not have an uncontrollable activity and will not produce unexpected genetic disturbances (Constantin, Milcu, & Poenaru, 1994: 147-148).

In contrast, it is shown that genes deserve the same special respect that we grant to any part of the human body, but this idea should not be exaggerated in the sense that genes are sacred or untouchable, since it would be conceptually misconceived to interpret the genetic background of humanity as a feature accumulated by the wise investments of natural selection (Frankel & Chapman, 2000).

The Principle of Autonomy: Do Embryos Have Autonomy?

Freedom and the possibility of deciding on our own future, which are the essence of the principle of autonomy, seem to exclude a priori the genetic manipulation of the germline. On the other hand, it is supposed that if the intervention is therapeutic, future children, once mature, would opt for this intervention on their genome (Mir & Morgan, 2013). Regarding the non-medical manipulation of the germline, the consensus of next generations can no longer be presumed, but some authors consider intervention acceptable as long as the genetically modified features are reversible through a new intervention (Resnik & Langer, 2001: 1454).

The ethical principles governing intergenerational ethics and intergenerational consent are concepts still under configuration, but even so it is argued that germline genetic editing is by no means ethically different from any other decision of the current generation that would have the potential to affect future generations (Sugarman, 2015). Indeed, it is argued that if there is any principle of ethics that should be considered in this case, it is the duty of the current generation to increase the quality of life of their offspring and their descendants, not only by eliminating genetic determinism, but also by improving the genes considered harmful (Frankel & Chapman, 2000: 35).

The Principle of Justice: Equality in Diversity

Until recently, access to expensive technologies has been seen as a natural side effect of social class differences, just like many others (access to costly education, access to pricey medical treatments etc.). But until the discovery of the immense potential of genetic engineering to augment the human being, the need for equality in terms of access to resources was not so strenuous. Facilitating the use of innovative technologies in a fair manner, available to all, does not appear in this context as a desideratum, but as an imperative.

The high cost of genetic manipulation makes it unlikely for such therapies to be covered by state-subsidized medical insurance. Even if this were possible, it is known that a large percentage of the population is uninsured and another percentage benefits from medical insurance that provides a basic package of services, that would exclude for sure techniques of genetic engineering. If the discussion moves to non-medical germline gene editing, then the likelihood that these procedures are will not even be settled by private health insurance is very high, because private ensurers traditionally refuses to provide financial assistance to non-therapeutic medical techniques (Frankel & Chapman, 2000: 37).

According to bioethicists (Frankel & Chapman, 2000; Mir & Morgan, 2013; Sugarman, 2015), the lack of financial potential of the vast majority of people to use new medical techniques will lead to the following effects: a) rich people will shape the genetic patrimony of humanity according to their own standards, which would in essence be a form of eugenics; b) genetically enhanced traits, passed on to descendants, will lead to the spread of social inequality and inequality to future generations; c) this will create a climate of intolerance towards people with disabilities, that will affect fundamental principles such as human dignity, vulnerable to violation because of the different meanings that conceptually the word "dignity" has in different communities.

Non-Therapeutical Genetic Engineering

Bioenhancement technologies involve manipulation of zygotes and embryos in order to determine both the creation of a new, genetically superior, more productive and better adapted human species, as well as the rapid breeding of individuals with valuable genotypes (Christmas & Christmas, 1989).

Beneficence: Qui Prodest?

The advantages of genetic engineering are indisputable: the resistance to disease, the improvement of some characteristics that can help the human being to be more productive, more efficient, leading, on the one hand, to healthier individuals and, on the other, to individuals more easily adaptable to the environment, which would benefit society as a whole, because resources that go to assisting those in need today would be diverted to progress, and progress would be easier to achieve with the help of those genetically "improved", as progress generates progress. Based on the abovementioned argument, it seems that apparently the whole society would benefit, and also individuals.

Therefore, genetic engineering advocates assert that there is no factual evidence to establish with certainty that only what is natural is good (or better) and what is unnatural is bad - or worse (Baggini, 2002: 181- 182). Also, it must not be assumed that what is natural is sacred and therefore must be honored, as there are many examples (cancer cells, tornadoes, poisons) when what is natural is not good, and what is unnatural (vaccines, human dwellings) proves to be good, so there is a clear difference between conceptually "natural" and conceptually "good" (Kamm, 2005: 8-9).

It is precisely beneficence that is promoted as the strongest argument in favor of genetic engineering, as genetic enhancement increases the quality of life, which is an essential condition of a good life, and a good life is essential for happiness (Savulescu, 2016), and there are three arguments to support this theory: it is erroneous to choose not to improve the human being, because it is erroneous to think that there is something wrong in choosing the best state of affairs in which an individual can carry out his existence; the consistency of behavior towards future generations requires treating genetic changes in the same manner as the changes we make to the environment in which children are raised, so that as long as we irreversibly improve the environment to ensure the best possible life for children, it is also optimal, thus ethically, to improve their genetic condition; there is no ethical difference between using genetic engineering for medical purposes or improving individuals' features, as long as disease prevents us from doing what we want and live well, and health also helps us to live well, therefore genetic enhancement is a valuable resource that allows us to do what really matters to us in order to achieve a good life (Savulescu, 2016).

The most argued argument against genetic engineering is the fear of using bioenhancement techniques for eugenic purposes. Most of the bioethical and legal literature (Asandei, 2005; Bender, 2003; Creţoiu & Iacob, 2006; Cohen, 1996, 2002; Dumitru, 2001: 20; Enache, 2005; Franklin & Roberts, 2006: 17; Hirschman, 1991; Lauritzen, 1990; Olaru, 2005, 2006; Pivniceru & Dăscălescu, 2007; Ryan, 1990; Sandu, Tudoran, & Rotaru, 2006: 315-316; Stolba, 2002) argues that social adaptability, the ability to integrate into a group and the ganing respect of the other members of the group is a long-lasting, specific process for each individual and is not dictated exclusively by the genetic structure of the person, therefore there is a danger that intentional changes to the human genome will go beyond the scope of therapeutic reasons and deviate to creating selected groups of people, endowed with certain characteristics and special qualities, thus making normality and natural selection disappear.

Because in its negative form, as the elimination of the unwanted ones, eugenics has been compromised by the exterminations of juges in World War II camps, during the last two decades some seem to have adopted a positive form of promoting the desired ones, by resorting to a speech of scientificity, so we fear that all this is only a mask for a series of highly ethically controversial actions and ideas (Huidu, 2017). Genetic engineering can be diverted very easily to the exploitation of one field of life in the service of extrinsic purposes, hat bring no benefits to the biological entities that become targets for such endeavours; to choose the features of the future child can be a form of parental responsibility and the optimization of the adaptability of the future individual, or just only the immoral expression of the conception of a being as the result of parents' choices, made from the perspective of what is considered *hic et nunc* that is desirable, which would not only be a moral error, but even a threat to process on normal socializing, as it would introduce an irreconcilable asymmetry between generations (Huidu, 2017).

As we shall argue next in this paper, the ethical debate on bioenhancement technologies has given rise to numerous theories in bioethical and philosophical literature, all starting from the question of who (assuming someone) will be harmed by the application of genetic engineering?

Non-Maleficence and Emerging Technologies

The plethora of arguments against genetic engineering is centered on some central ideas, as we will see next:

Genetic engineering is contrary to human dignity: while some authors claim that the alteration in any way of the genetic information contained in the DNA structure of human beings violates human dignity (Rifkin, 1991), since the dignity of individuals and of the species itself is closely linked to evolution in the absence of any artificial intervention (Rolston, 2002), other authors (Koepsell, 2007) consider evolution to be indifferent to human suffering, because suffering sometimes is the cause of naturally occurring genetic anomalies (such as Lesh-Nyham disease, the uncontrollable willingness of the patient to self-mutilate), whose manifestations are anything but dignified, so as long as nature is indifferent to human dignity, modifying or improving what is natural can not be against human dignity.

The importance of preserving an unaltered gene pool for humanity: genetic engineering has harmful effects on the random transmission of genes, as humans will tend to impose genes responsible for the improvement of desirable characteristics, which will lead to an advanced form of uniformity of the human genotype (Kamm, 2005); on the other hand, attention is drawn to the fact that the current process by which genes are transmitted is not really random, because when someone chooses the partner they want to conceive a child with, their choice is related to socio-economic issues or to the level of education, race, phenotypic similarity etc. of the chosen partner (Cohen, 2014: 678).

The issue of applying risky and emerging technology to humans: the human genome is a still incomplete mapped territory and the removal or addition of genes may lead to potentially serious harm to individuals. However, there are authors (Saulter, 2014) who consider that those who oppose genetic engineering only show a taboo over non-traditional technology. It is appreciated that taboos are social constructions of what is inviolable and immutable in a society, but history shows that these taboos differ from one collectivity to another and from one historical era to another, hence the opposition to genetic engineering, which is only a taboo as other taboos have been in medicine (dissection of corpses in the Middle Ages, natural medicine during Inquisition, which was considered witchcraft etc.). The technical aspects of testing gene therapies on animals, data collection, clinical trials on human subjects and respect of the precautionary principle presented in the previous sections of this paper are maintained regarding genetic engineering and we will therefore not resume them again.

Genetic engineering would reduce the level of compassion and social solidarity: some authors (Sandel, 2007) have identified the fundamentals of human compassion and solidarity in the feeling that those favored by fate have advantages over those who have not been favored, and because these advantages are not of their doing, they feel compulsive to share their fortune with the less fortunate. These will disappear genetic engineering becomes generally available, because those who choose not to improve will be sanctioned for not choosing, an attitude encouraged by the belief that that the society should not spend public funds to support them (Fox, 2007). The argument is overcome by Cohen (2014), who claims that those who could not financially afford such enhancements will receive the same compassion as those who, in today's sociaty, can not afford housing, access to education etc.

Genetic engineering applied to human embryos in human assisted reproductive techniques corrupts parental ideals and distorts parent-child relationships: in an opinion (Shiffrin, 1999), it is claimed that future children will experience injurious pressure resulting from the fact that they will have to rise to the ideals imposed by their parents, ideals that are so important for their parents that made them choose to genetically alter their children and which may lead to a lack of parental affection if the children do not conform to the genetic predeterminism imposed by parents. On the other hand (Kamm, 2005), it is argued that although love for a certain person can begin with the attraction for certain qualities that that person has, in the end what we love is the person itself and not his or her qualities, therefore, if we were to meet a person who would posess the same qualities, it is unlikely that we would consider that the second could easily replace the first, namely, if the person we love would lose some of those qualities, it is likely that we will continue to love them. The same analogy applies to parents who use genetic techniques to enhance their embryos.

Autonomy: Is There Any Left?

The issue of autonomy case of genetic enhancement concerns both the autonomy of the genetically modified individual and the autonomy of the parents of the future child.

If genetic improvement is aimed at adults, the problem could become "coerced voluntary enhancement". This theory was developed by Cohen (2014), which starts from the idea that genetically enhanced individuals will compete with those who are not enhanced and who, in order to remain competitive, will also be forced to resort to genetic improvement. Although seemingly voluntary, the decision to use these techniques will in fact be imposed by the situation. The same author, however, proposes a series of measures by which the danger can be avoided: the state may apply additional taxes to those who choose to be genetically improved, which could then be used to improve the lives of individuals who choose not to enhance; certain genetic improvements that would seriously affect social competitiveness could be declared illegal etc.

If autonomy targets still unborn people (embryos or fetuses), then it discusses both the autonomy of the being to be born and the autonomy of the parents.

The human embryo is incapable of expressing its autonomy. More specifically, we are talking about the autonomy of the future child who, after reaching adulthood, would agree or disagree to the genetic enhancements imposed by his or her parents. But because it is impossible to assume with certainty what would be the choice of the future adult, the theorists sought ways to address the issue of individual autonomy, excluding any such assumption.

One of the most widely discussed theories is the "non-identity problem" formulated by Parfit (1984), according to which the autonomy of the future child is not violated as it can not be said that genetic engineering would cause any harm to it, since its creation is preferable to non-existence, as long as genetic improvement offers them a life worth living. Cohen (2014) draws attention to the fact that the problem of non-identity cuts the ethical debate, as it demonstrates the irrelevance of making a comparison between the life of an enhanced child to the life of an unenhanced child, as the only relevant comparison is between exitence and non-existence, between whether the child would have preferred not to exist at all, but to have been improved.

Another theory related to the autonomy of the future child is that developed by Feinberg (1980) and entitled "the right to an open future", according to which the child must be provided with as many opportunities, options and advantages as possible to choose from when he reaches maturity. Therefore, any genetic improvement must be done in such a way that it does not significantly limit the identity of the future child, so much as to reduce its lifetime options. Starting from the identity theory formulated by John Locke, who through identity is the continuity of memory (Locke, 1975) and the theory of Jeff McMahan, for whom identity is any experience - rudimentary or not - which occurs after the onset of neural activity in the central nervous system (McMahan, 1998), Glenn Cohen (2014) points out that there are genetic modifications capable of affecting the identity of the individual and genetic changes that do not have this potential, but the author concludes that the boundary between them is difficult - if not impossible - to be determined, because there are no objective methods of establishing what data should be collected and how it might be interpreted logically, so that it would become clear what kind of identity the child would have had unless he would have been genetically altered, compared to the life he has as a genetically enhanced human being.

In terms of respecting the requirements of the principle of autonomy towards parents who would choose to have their children genetically enhanced, John Robertson (1983: 432) thinks that this could be better explained by the theory of reproductive autonomy, according to which, given that the satisfaction of the reproductive interests of certain people are dependent on the fact that their future child presents certain genetic features, the principle of procreative freedom justifies genetic manipulation without medical purpose, the only limitation being the possibility of inducing traits that could cause serious harm to the life of the future child (for example an incurable genetic disease), which would make their non-existence preferable to existence (Parfit's theory, referred to above). Thus, the fact that the genetic manipulation could threaten the ideal family that society wants to protect is not a convincing enough argument to override individual procreative rights.

This view is a reflection of the Transumanist philosophy, a doctrine that states the possibility and desirability of a fundamental improvement of the human condition through applied rationality, especially through the use of technologies, to eliminate the degenerative processes of the human organism and to enhance physical, intellectual and psychological capacities (Bostrom, 2003; Manea, 2005; Trivino, 2015). Even more so, the procreative beneficence principle (Savulescu, 2001; Savulescu & Kahane, 2009) states that there is even a real moral obligation of parents to create children who, from a genetic point of view, have the best chance at the best possible life.

Savulescu's procreative beneficence principle has been harshly criticized (Sparrow, 2007) by those who believe that such a theory is flawed because it is based on the confusion between why parents would want what is best for their children and the obligation to "produce" the best possible child. It is appreciated that considering the two notions synonymous is equivalent to telling that some parents that it is nothing wrong if they manifest racist and homophobic tendencies or become accomplices to other forms of oppression, which brings reproductive beneficence closer to classical forms of eugenics than to any form of beneficence.

To create a child by projecting upon him his parents' ideals, in complete indifference to his future evolution (because not all the characteristics of a person can be controlled by appealing to genetics) is morally unacceptable. As long as no one has the right to determine which non-medical human characteristics are desirable and not, this reproduction for excellence only proves a discriminatory attitude towards normality, blocking the medical and financial resources of society in a field from which humanity can extracts benefits, but can also endanger it. Genetic determinism can be an advanced form of discrimination, giving rise to what might be called "scientific racism" (Huidu, 2017). The incomplete information behind the science of genetics currently creates real dangers of interference between genes, that leaves room for error in interpreting genetic tests, which can lead to erroneous changes in the genome, therefore to risks for the normal development of the embryo.

Such a scientificized attitude to life can lead to the creation of social classes based on genetic differences between members of a community. Using new reproductive technologies to induce certain arbitrary characteristics denies the embryo the integrity and intrinsic value of the human being, bringing to the forefront a series of discriminatory stereotypes and even creating new forms of social discrimination - genetic discrimination (Huidu, 2017). Quality of life is a malleable concept, but to correct a characteristic by altering a gene in order to treat or prevent a disease is a totally different act compared to inserting a gene for performance or enhancement of the human species into a super-species. Eugenics is the very opposite to reproduction freedom, because it deals with "quality" control of the population (Huidu, 2017).

The theory that seems to combine the totally dissonant views above is that of Cohen (2014), which shows that there is a way to determine whether parents' decision to genetically improve their children is reproductive beneficence or eugenics. Thus, if embryo enhancement comes from the desire to help future children have the best life, based on the natural instinct of any parent to offer everything that is best to their children, then the principle of beneficence is respected. But if parents start from the idea that through those enhancements they want to offer society additional benefit, due to the improved abilities of their children, then it is eugenics (Cohen, 2014: 683).

Justice: How Do We Decide What Is Just?

The main argument in support of the theory that the application of genetic engineering to humans is contrary to the principle of social justice is that genetic improvements will lead to social inequity, because not all members of the species have equal access to resources, a theory I have presented broadly in the previous section, and the arguments and counter-arguments outlined there remain the same in this case.

In the field of genetic engineering, however, another theory of social inequity is the one that fundamentally attacks the idea of justice in applying biotechnology to humans, showing that interventions that alter human genetic patrimony, falsifying the identity of the human being, jeopardizes the interests of others individuals who have the right to compete with people with random capabilities, chosen by natural selection and not manufactured in the laboratory, therefore germline altering or genetic enhancement shoul be prohibited (Dumea, 1990: 89-90). Otherwise, existing social inequities would be exacerbated and new ones would be created, including the emergence of new social classes. The counter-argument (Koepsell, 2007: 17) is that the benefits to genetically improved individuals will not be much more different than the benefits that some already largely available augmentation practices already have. Examples are cosmetic surgery, which provides social and economic benefits to the beneficiaries (mammary implants, facial lifting, botox use).

Special Applications of Genetic Engineering

Cognitive and Moral Enhancement

Moral bio-enhancement means improving individuals by genetic (and other) methods in order to exacerbate their altruism, sense of justice and morality, while cognitive bio-enhancement involves the use of biotechnology to enrich the intellectual abilities of individuals (Carter & Gordon, 2013). In terms of beneficence, intellectual augmentation has net benefits for humanity, as it leads to rapid scientific progress and scientific progress is a way to improve the quality of life for all mankind. Moral augmentation is supported by arguments such as: human nature is morally corrupt, so traditional methods of moral improvement are ineffective and appeal to genetic engineering is warranted so, given that there is no ethical difference between using genetic methods and traditional methods of moral improvement, moral augmentation is beneficial not only for the person who is enhanced, but also for society in general (Specker, Focquaret, Raus, Sterckx, & Schermer, 2014).

On the other hand, it is stated that moral bio-enhancement could threaten individual freedom (creating a race of enslaved individuals, subdued by an elite genetically predisposed to lead), endangering human identity and autonomy, which would be the path to abuse, towards moral uniformity (which would hinder the progress of all humanity, a progress that not only relates to technological evolution, but also to ideological debates) and to conceptual digressions towards an utopian society, as long as there is still no consensus on the definition of the term "morality", which differs - to a lesser or greater degree - from one community to another, or according to context or the role that the individual is expected to play in a specific situation (Specker et al., 2014).

Persson and Savulescu (2008) point out that cognitive bio-enhancement poses major risks as it will lead to accelerated scientific progress and the danger that the new technologies thus created will be used by morally corrupt members of the species to do harm. Therefore, they insist on the imperative to avoid cognitive improvements and to delay scientific progress until effective methods of moral enhancement are achieved. The theory was fought by Fenton (2009), who shows how Perssons and Săvulescu's arguments are contradictory, because in order for moral improvement to be possible, there is a need for scientific progress, and progress that depends on cognitive enhancement. Also, the risks associated with cognitive enhancement are unrealistic, since mankind is not for the first time in the situation that scientific progress could have unfavorable – or even devastating - effects (for example, the cleavage of the atom, which can be the path to obtaining an inexhaustible source of energy - the atomic energy - but also a weapon of mass destruction), therefore these risks have always been associated with scientific progress and will be overcome as before.

Sex Selection

The ethical nature of sex selection is not called into question when the aim is to avoid the transmission of illnesses linked to gender, but it raises fierce controversy when the reasons for selection are non-medical. Some authors (McMillan, 2002) consider that restricting access to methods of selecting a child's sex means restricting the individual's reproductive freedom, which requires access to any procedure that poses no risk of causing substantial physical or mental harm to the child, as the alternative is the abortion of those who do not have the desired sex. McMillan also shows that in order to eliminate possible abuses in the use of technology, abuses that could lead to a gender imbalance, admissible sex selection cases may be limited by law and if the procedure is performed by means of sperm sorting - and not of preimplantation genetic diagnosis – we could also avoid the creation of excess embryos - which, indirectly, gives rise to the practice of further destruction of those embryos who don't have the required gender. The fear of discriminatory gender choices It is not sustainable because it is believed that the desire to have a child of a certain sex is in the couple's interest in having a certain type of parental experience and the possible sexist attitude of the parents can be prevented through counseling on the consequences of unrealistic expectations regarding the social role of children of a certain sex.

These arguments are strongly countered (ECASRM, 2001: 861-864, Enache, 2005; Pennings, 2000) whith arguments such as: sex selection can be a form of gender discrimination, risking to imbalance gender proportions in society, as statistical studies show that, in fact, male children will be preferred for social, moral and religious reasons. The autonomy of the human being requires that man be treated as an end in itself and never as a means, because it is possible that the child does not follow the social role that parents want to impose by choosing sex, in which case family relations will degrade, affecting the superior interest of the child, violating the moral imperative of unconditional parental love.

Another argument against sex selection is the high costs involved in the procedure and the inappropriate use of medical potential, which are morally unacceptable, as they involve spending the resources of society to change a nonessential characteristic of the human being. Another problem that emerges is the inequality of opportunities for access to gender selection techniques, families with high financial potential being the only ones who could afford to support the costs that these involve. Again, the fear of eugenics reestablishes, which motivates the belief that sex selection will be only a step towards liberalizing the selection of other non-medical characteristics, such as intelligence, eye color, hair colour etc. The destruction of embryos that do not meet the sex criteria and become surpluses as a result of genetic screening is an inadmissible reality, on the grounds that it flagrantly violates the right to life of the human embryo, by eliminating a life for selfish reasons, without any medical or moral motives.

Hybrid Embryos and Chimeric Embryos

A chimeric embryo is a human embryo within which a cell or part of a cell derived from an animal has been introduced. Each cell retains its identity but, as the embryo develops, the cells of different species merge to the point where the distinctions can no longer be seen, so that each body and body organ consists of cells from both species (Mirkes, 2006: 115). A hybrid embryo is the embryo created through fertilization of a human ovum by an animal sperm or an animal ovum by a human sperm, as well as that embryo formed by introducing the nucleus of an animal cell into a human enucleated ovum or the nucleus of a human cell in an animal enucleated ovum (ISSCR Committee Forum, 2007: 159). The creation of human-animal hybrids and chimeras may be the key to a remarkable development in stem cell research, organ transplantation or drug testing prior to clinical trials on human subjects.

The ethical dillema in this matter is highlighted by certain arguments: genetic manipulation could even be considered inhuman treatment because the person who would result from merging human and animal cells and DNA would be considered a new species or subspecies and would no longer be recognised as a person who has human rights (Deleanu, 1983: 33-37). If the human characteristics were to change significantly, the result would no longer be "human" (Vasiu, 2004: 60). It has been proposed that these forms of genetic engineering be classified as crimes against humanity. It is appreciated that genetic manipulation becomes arbitrary and unfair when it reduces and objectifies life, because it is forgotten that, in fact, those new beings are human beings capable of intelligence and freedom, who demand respect whatever their limitations (Vasiu, 2004: 62), even when they are treated according to criteria that do not correspond to the integrating reality of the human species, which poses the risk of destroying their dignity and depriving them of their right to autonomy. There are fears that these experiments are trying to obtain a human subspecies, a lower race of men to be used for degrading labors or transplant organs (Vasiu, 2004).

As for the main principle according to which we are not to break the boundary between species (human and animal), there are authors (Adler, 1993) who consider, from the perspective of the evolutionary theory, that the human being is just a form of phylogenetic continuity, so humans and animals are not different forms of life, but they are only in different stages of the continuum of evolution. From an ontological standpoint, there is no reason for a hybrid or chimera individual not to be treated, in terms of his rights, with the same equality as humans, as other different members of the human species are treated equally, irrespective of their race, sex, religion, abilities, degree of psycho-cognitive development (Mirkes, 2006). Human dignity is not violated, because morality, self-awareness and cognitive and emotional functions (traditionally associated with the concept of human dignity) will not diminish if human-animal hybrids or chimeras will prove complex psychological skills specific to human dignity, because dignity it is not something that diminishes quantitatively or qualitatively if it is attributed to more individuals. Moreover, the man of today is the product of evolution, a process that involved the crossing of several stages, in which man was, in turn, part of some species with humanoid characteristics, then of some humanoid species exhibiting different degrees of cognitive, emotional and social interdependence, until he reached the present stage of evolution: Homo Sapiens (ISSCR Committee Forum, 2007).

Therefore, it is argued that abiding principles like precaution and proportionality in medical research will prevent abuses (Hermeren, 2014), provided that the following ethical rules are respected (Mirkes, 2006): the aim of human-animal chimeras and hybrid experiments must be eradication or treatment of diseases; researchers should obtain informed consent from people who donate biological or genetic material for such research; compliance with legal and ethical regulations on animal research should be mandatory; the resulting being remains an animal, despite the insertion of human genetic material into its chromosomal structure and the characteristics so acquired can not be transmitted to the offspring.

CONCLUSION

Although genetic engineering, irrespective of its purpose, its specific applications and the possibility that those altered characteristics may be transmitted or not to the descendants of the person that has been genetically altered, presents many incontestable advantages for humanity, ethical debates underline an equally significant number of problems and risks that can arise from the incoherent and irresponsible application of biotechnologies to human beings. However, setting a set of rules and regulatory and ethics committees to monitor these practices, develop guidelines and sanction deviations from established ethical rules, seems to be the way to maximize the benefits for humanity and diminish the associated risks.

ACKNOWLEDGMENT

Within this chapter were used information previously published by the author in Romanian in the book *Reproducerea umană medical asistată. Etica incriminării versus etica biologică. Studiu de drept comparat* [Human Medically Assisted Reproduction. The Ethics of Incrimination versus Bioethics. Comparative Law Study], Lumen Publishing House, Iaşi, Romania, 2017.

REFERENCES

Asandei, R. M. (2005). Aspecte ale eugeniei de la origini până astăzi [Aspects of eugenics from origins to today]. *Revista Română de Bioetică, 3*(4).

Baggini, J. (2002). *Making Sense: Philosophy Behind the Headlines*. Oxford, UK: Oxford University Press.

Bostrom, N. (2003). Human genetic enhancements: A transhumanist perspective. *The Journal of Value Inquiry, 37*(4), 493–506. doi:10.1023/B:INQU.0000019037.67783.d5 PMID:17340768

Carter, J. A., & Gordon, E. C. (2013). On cognitive and moral enhancement: A reply to Savulescu and Persson. *Bioethics, 29*(3), 153–161. doi:10.1111/bioe.12076 PMID:24372082

Cohen, C. B. (1996). "Give Me Children or I Shall Die!" New Reproductive Technologies and Harm to Children. *The Hastings Center Report*, *26*(2), 19–27. doi:10.2307/3528572 PMID:8722522

Cohen, C. B. (2002). Protestant Perspectives on the Uses of the New Reproductive Technologies. *The Fordham Urban Law Journal*, *30*(1), 135–145. Retrieved from https://ir.lawnet.fordham.edu/cgi/viewcontent.cgi?article=1850&context=ulj PMID:15868665

Cohen, G. I. (2014). What (if anything) is wrong with human enhancement? What (if anything) is right with it? *Tulsa Law Review*, *49*(3), 645-687. Retrieved from: https://pdfs.semanticscholar.org/26fa/35bb3a9183f49eb6246d7e7cb465f44232a3.pdf

Constantin, M., Milcu, S. M., & Poenaru, S. (1994). *Fascinaţia imposibilului. Bioetica* [Fascination of the Impossible. Bioethics]. Bucharest, Romania: Editura pentru Tineret şi Sport Editis.

Crăciun, T., & Crăciun, L. L. (1989). *Dicţionar de biologie* [Dictionary of Biology]. Bucharest, Romania: Albatros.

Creţoiu, S. M., & Iacob, C. (2006). Biotehnologiile moderne şi emergenţa problemelor bioeticii [Modern biotechnologies and the emergence of bioethics problems]. *Revista Română de Bioetică*, *4*(4).

Deleanu, I. (1983). *Biologie şi drept* [Biology and Law]. Cluj-Napoca, Romania: Dacia.

Dumea, C. (1998). *Omul între „a fi" sau „a nu fi". Probleme fundamentale de bioetică* [The Man between "Being" or "Not Being". Fundamental Problems of Bioethics]. Bucharest, Romania: Editura Arhiepiscopiei Romano-Catolice.

Dumitru, C. (2001). Omul – mai tare decât Dumnezeu [Man – Stronger than God]. *Contemporanul*, *11*(30), 20.

ECASRM (Ethics Committee of the American Society for Reproductive Medicine). (2001). Preconception gender selection for nonmedical reasons. *Fertility and Sterility*, *75*(5), 232–235. doi:10.1016/j.fertnstert.2004.05.013 PMID:11334894

Enache, E. (2005). Supraomul între vis şi realitate [The superhuman between dream and reality]. *Revista Română de Bioetică*, *3*(2).

Feinberg, J. (1980). The Child's Right to an Open Future. In W. Aiken & H. LaFollette (Eds.), *Who's Child? Children's Rights, Parental Authority and State Power* (pp. 126–130). New York: Littlefield Adams.

Fenton, E. (2010). The perils of failing to enhance: A response to Persson and Savulescu. *Journal of Medical Ethics*, *36*(3), 148–151. doi:10.1136/jme.2009.033597 PMID:20211993

Fox, D. (2007). Silver spoons and golden genes. Genetic engineering and the egalitarian ethos. *American Journal of Law & Medicine*, *33*(4), 567–623. doi:10.1177/009885880703300402 PMID:18277511

Franklin, M., & Chapman, S. (2000). *Human Inheritable Genetic Modifications. Assesing Scientific, Ethical, Religious and Policy Issues*. Washington, DC: American Association for the Advancement of Science. Retrieved from http://www.aas.org/spp/dspp/sfrl/germline/main.htm

Franklin, S., & Roberts, C. (2006). *Born and Made: An Ethnography of Preimplantation Genetic Diagnosis*. Princeton, NJ: Princeton University Press.

Hermeren, G. (2014). Ethical considerations in chimera research. *Development, 142*(1), 3–5. doi:10.1242/dev.119024 PMID:25516962

Hirschman, E. C. (1991). Babies for sale: Market ethics and the new reproductive technologies. *The Journal of Consumer Affairs, 25*(2), 358–390. doi:10.1111/j.1745-6606.1991.tb00010.x PMID:11660025

Huidu, A. (2017). *Reproducerea umană medical asistată. Etica incriminării versus etica biologică. Studiu de drept comparat* [Human Medically Assisted Reproduction. The Ethics of Incrimination versus Bioethics. Comparative Law Study]. Iași, Romania: Lumen.

Hyun, I., Taylor, P., Testa, G., Dickens, B., Jung, K. W., McNab, A., ... Zoloth, L. (2007). Ethical standards for human-to-animal chimera experiments in stem cell research. *Cell Stem Cell, 1*(2), 159–163. doi:10.1016/j.stem.2007.07.015 PMID:18383627

Juengst, E. (1997). Can enhancements be distinguished from therapy in genetic medicine? *The Journal of Medicine and Philosophy, 22*(2), 125–142. doi:10.1093/jmp/22.2.125 PMID:9186925

Kamm, F. M. (2005). Is there a problem with enhancement? *The American Journal of Bioethics, 5*(3), 5–14. doi:10.1080/15265160590945101 PMID:16006376

Koepsell, D. (2007). *The Ethics of Genetic Engineering. A Position Paper from the Center for Inquiry Office of Public Policy*. New York: Center for Inquiry Inc.

Lauritzen, P. (1990). What Price Parenthood? *The Hastings Center Report, 20*(2), 38–46. doi:10.2307/3562619 PMID:2180853

Locke, J. (1979). *An Essay Concerning Human Understanding*. Oxford, UK: Oxford University Press.

Manea, T. (2005). "Gata cu constrângerile biologice!" Reproducerea dincolo de reproducere, ["It's over with biological constraints!" Reproduction beyond reproduction]. *Revista Română de Bioetică, 3*(1).

McMahan, J. (1998). Wrongful Life: Paradoxes in the Morality of Causing People to Exist. In J. L. Coleman & C. W. Morris (Eds.), *Rational Commitment and Social Justice: Essays for Gregory Kavka* (pp. 208–2011). Cambridge, UK: Cambridge University Press. doi:10.1017/CBO9780511527364.013

McMillan, J. (2002). Sex Selection in the United Kingdom. *The Hastings Center Report, 32*(1), 28–31. doi:10.2307/3528294 PMID:11917706

Mir, H., & Morgan, C. (2013). Ethical implications of germ line genetic engineering. *University of Western Ontario Medical Journal, 78*(3), 18-21. Retrieved from http://www.uwomj.com/wp-content/uploads/2013/06/v78n3.18-21.pdf

Mirkes, R. (2006). Is it ethical to generate human-animal chimeras? *The National Catholic Bioethics Quarterly, 6*(1), 109–130. doi:10.5840/ncbq20066170 PMID:17037495

Mortimer, A. (1993). *The Difference of Man and the Dofference It Makes*. New York: Fordham University Press.

Nordenfelt, L. (1999). On medicine and other means of health enhancement: towards a conceptual framework. In M. Hanson & D. Callahan (Eds.), *The Goals of Medicine* (pp. 69–87). Washington, DC: Georgetown University Press.

Olaru, B. (2005). Problema autonomiei şi limitele folosirii tehnologiilor reproducerii asistate [The issue of autonomy and the limits of using assisted reproduction technologies]. *Revista Română de Bioetică, 3*(3), 43-54.

Olaru, B. (2006). A porunci viaţa şi a interzice moartea? [Order life and forbid death?]. *Revista Română de Bioetică, 4*(2).

Parens, E. (1999). Is Better Always Good? The Enhancement Project. In E. Parens (Ed.), *Enhancing Human Traits* (pp. 1–28). Washington, DC: Georgetown University Press.

Parfit, D. (1984). *Reasons and Persons.* Oxford, UK: Oxford University Press.

Pennings, G. (2000). The right to choose your donor: A step towards commercialization or a step towards empowering the pacient? *Human Reproduction (Oxford, England), 15*(1), 508–514. doi:10.1093/humrep/15.3.508 PMID:10686188

Persson, I., & Savulescu, J. (2008). The perils of cognitive enhancement and the urgent imperative to enhance the moral character of humanity. *Journal of Applied Philosophy, 25*(3), 162–177. doi:10.1111/j.1468-5930.2008.00410.x

Pivniceru, M. M., & Dăscălescu, F. D. (2007). Limita inferioară a dreptului la viaţă: între protecţia fetusului uman, dreptul la avort şi progresul ştiinţelor medicale [The lower limit of the right to life: Between the protection of the human fetus, the right to abortion and the advancement of medical sciences]. *Revista Română de Bioetică, 1*(4). Retrieved from http://www.culturavietii.ro/2014/09/22/limita-inferioara-dreptul-la-viata-intre-protectia-fetusului-uman-dreptul-la-avort-si-progresul-stiintelor-biomedicale/

Resnik, D. B., & Langer, P. J. (2001). Human germline gene therapy reconsidered. *Human Gene Therapy, 12*(11), 1449–1458. doi:10.1089/104303401750298607 PMID:11485636

Rifkin, J. (1991). *Biosphere Politics: A New Consciousness for a New Century.* Crown Publishers.

Robertson, J. (1983). Procreative liberty and the control of conception, pregnancy and childbirth. *Virginia Law Review, 69*(3), 405–464. doi:10.2307/1072766 PMID:11651806

Robertson, J. (2005). Gay and lesbian access to assisted reproductive technology. *Case Western Reserve Law Review, 55*(2), 323–372. Retrieved from https://scholarlycommons.law.case.edu/cgi/viewcontent.cgi?article=1582&context=caselrev

Rolston, H. (2002). What do we mean by the intrinsic value and integrity of plants and animals? In D. Heaf & J. Wirtz (Eds.), *Genetic Engineering and the Intrinsic Value and Integrity of Animals and Plants* (pp. 5–10). Pwlheli, UK: Hafan.

Ryan, M. A. (1990). The argument for unlimited procreative liberty: A feminist critique. *The Hastings Center Report, 20*(4), 6–12. doi:10.2307/3562759 PMID:2211090

Sandel, M. J. (2007). The Case against Perfection: Ethics in the Age of Genetic Engineering. Cambridge, MA: Harvard University Press (Belknap Press).

Sandu, G., Tudoran, S., & Rotaru, A. (2006). Dreptul omului de a nu fi supus selecţiei [Man's right not to be subject to selection]. In Educaţia în bioetică şi drepturile omului în România. Bucharest, Romania: Comisia Naţională a României pentru UNESCO.

Saulter, S. (2014). *Trusting the Future? Ethics of Human Genetic Modification*. Retrieved from: https://www.livescience.com/45392-ethics-of-altering-human-genetics.html

Savulescu, J. (2001). Procreative beneficence: Why we should select the best children. *Bioethics, 15*(5-6), 413-426. doi:10.1111/1467-8519.00251

Savulescu, J. (2016). Genetic interventions and the ethics of enhancement of human beings. *Gazeta de Antropologia, 32*(2), 646-651. Retrieved from http://www.gazeta-antropologia.es/?p=4904

Savulescu, J., & Kahane, G. (2009). The moral obligation to create children with the best chance of the best life. *Bioethics*, *23*(5), 274–290. doi:10.1111/j.1467-8519.2008.00687.x PMID:19076124

Scripcaru, G., Ciucă, A., Astărăstoae, V., & Scripcaru, C. (2003). *Introducere în biodrept. De la bioetică la biodrept* [Introduction to Biolaw. From Bioethics to Biolaw]. Bucharest, România: Lumina Lex.

Scripcaru, G., Ciucă, A., Scripcaru, C, & Isac, L. (2005). Manipulările genetice şi implicaţiile lor juridice [Genetic manipulations and their legal implications]. *Revista română de bioetică*, *3*(2).

Shiffrin, S. V. (1999). Wrongful life, procreative responsability and the significance of harm. *Legal Theory*, *5*(2), 117–148. doi:10.1017/S1352325299052015

Sparrow, R. (2007). Procreative beneficence, obligation and eugenics. *Genomics, Society, and Policy*, *3*(3), 43–59. doi:10.1186/1746-5354-3-3-43

Specker, J., Focquaret, F., Raus, K., Sterckx, S., & Schermer, M. (2014). The ethical desirability of moral bioenhancement: A review of reasons. *BMC Medical Ethics*, *15*(1), 1–17. doi:10.1186/1472-6939-15-67 PMID:25227512

Stolba, C. (2012). Overcoming motherhood: Pushing the limits of reproductive choice. *Policy Review*, 116.

Sugarman, J. (2015). Ethics and germline gene editing. *EMBO Reports*, *16*(8), 879–880. doi:10.15252/embr.201540879 PMID:26138102

Trivino, J. L. P. (2015). Equality of access to enhancement technology in a posthumanist society. *Dilemata, 7*(19), 53-63. Retrieved from: https://dialnet.unirioja.es/descarga/articulo/5203952.pdf

U.S. National Institutes of Health; Recombinant DNA Advisory Committee. (2000). Prenatal gene tranfer: scientific, medical, and ethical issues: a report of the Recombinant DNA Advisory Committee. *Human Gene Therapy*, *11*(8), 1211–1229. doi:10.1089/10430340050015257 PMID:11660775

Vasiu, I. (2004). Manipularea genetică. Implicaţii penale [Genetic manipulation. Criminal implications]. *Revista de Drept Penal*, *3*, 56–63.

KEY TERMS AND DEFINITIONS

Ethics of Technology: A sub-field of ethics that encompasses a set of moral principles that govern the moral aspects of pursuing new technologies and of scientific research in certain novel and controversial fields of knowledgewhile also trying to establish the extent of need and the appropriateness of usage of such technologies by humans.

Eugenics: A science or a set of beliefs and practices that aims at improving the quality of a human population by controlled breeding, selecting the most desirable individuals, enhancing their natural capabilities or altering their genome, in order to make those individuals more adapted, economically effective or morally suitable, or in order to increase the occurrence of desirable heritable characteristics.

Germ Line: A certain type or series of cells, fully developed and differentiated, that have genetic traits which are passed on to the progeny of the individual during the process of reproduction.

Preimplantation Genetic Diagnosis: A technique that enables genetic screening and mapping of an embryo's genome in order to assess if that embryo has any genetic diseases and also in order to determine the other non-medical characteristics of that embryo; the technique is used in order to identify the genes that need to be altered, eliminated, or replaced for the purpose of undergoing genetic engineering procedures.

Social Justice: A system of rules and principles governing how resources are shared in a community, how to ensure equal access to these resources and social cohesion in terms of the voluntary sharing of resources among the members of the society (helping others), in order to discourage major differences between different social groups, while respecting their right to economic diversity.

Chapter 15
AIRSE:
The Ethics of Artificially Intelligent Robots and Systems

Bogdan Popoveniuc
Stefan cel Mare University of Suceava, Romania

ABSTRACT

The chapter makes a systematic review of the literature on the ethics of artificially intelligent robots (AIRSE) and proposes a classification of ethical discourses related with robots and AI in four categories: weak, moderate, strong, and ultimate. The main arguments and specific problems underlying each of these perspectives on AIRSE, as well as the resulting principles are discussed. The risks, issues, and challenges related with the possibility of technological singularity are also presented in this chapter.

INTRODUCTION

In the public discourse, the real issues related with artificial intelligent robots and systems Ethics (AIRSE) are frequently spoiled by media because of their sensational feature. The research groups involved in AI design, companies and even state governments use high-sounding discourse for marketing, financial and ideological purposes stressing also on the sensational aspects of technological progress. This is the case of pseudo-android chat-bot Sophia's publicity stunt granted citizenship in Saudi Arabia, a year before the same officials would lift the women driving ban. The public representations on future AI is infused with "personification thinking", when due to the high advance of mimicking the human conduct and appearance these softwares and robots are endowed with human agency. The process of learning default, or even innovating original responses in the interaction with humans is an advanced intellectual task, but far away from the minimal level of a conscious (aware) state. We can read impressive announces attributed to those involved in design and building all sorts of communication robots (care or companion AI systems): "Robots are developing feeling" or "AI systems are beginning to acquire emotions", where simply they learn to recognize some expression of human emotions and to express particular responses.

DOI: 10.4018/978-1-5225-6310-5.ch015

This attitude is backed among scholars by drawback of behaviorist thinking which promotes the "objective proof" of Turing or Chinese Room Test as undeniable evidence for critical point when robots will achieve the human level.

There are also other conceptual flaws in the relevant literature, where many texts on the ethics of autonomous and intelligent systems and robots, make no or minimal difference between different types and level of artificial intelligence (AI): automatic machines, intelligent autonomous machines, chat-bots, robots, androids, narrow AI, hard or AGI (Artificial General Intelligence). Moreover, a significant percent of works on AI's ethics stresses only to its pedagogical and normative function and neglect its applied, prospective, proactive and formative aspects. They adopt an over-optimistic negligent tone and depict a future world of social harmony and wellbeing shared by human and robots. "Roboethics is an applied ethics whose objective is to develop scientific//hnical tools that can be shared by different social groups and beliefs. These tools aim to promote and encourage the development of Robotics for the advancement of human society and individuals, and to help preventing its misuse against humankind" (Veruggio, 2002).

However the exponential advance and development of AI systems and increasing dependability of all social and economic activities on intelligent robots raise fresh new challenges for ethical thinking. The public and expert perspectives on ethics of AI autonomous systems, AI robots (AIRS in a single word) in four main classes: weak, moderate, strong and ultimate AIRS Ethics (AIRSE).

Weak AIRSE perspective on ethical and moral implication of AI deployment is based on the fundamental principle that *AIRS and robots are nothing but machines*. To this group belongs those with few or completely luck of interested in ethics because of the deep conviction that in this field we are dealing with technical and engineering issues solely and all other questions related with their usage, social effects, costs etc., are in the responsibility of technical engineers, political, economic, entertainment industry, educational, military, religious, health decision makers and users as any other social and economic aspect of human life. The robots, intelligent or not, are made with different utilities and not put any special problems for human society. The idea of *technology's neutrality* and the solely human responsibility underlays the reasoning that technology is designed to be beneficial, but can be twisted to become harmful through use and abused. This perspective is overtly embedded in Engineering & Physical Sciences Research Council' (EPSRC) Principles of Robotics set for the first time in a systematic manner in 2010 and published online in 2011:

1. *Robots are multi-use tools*. Robots should not be designed solely or primarily to kill or harm humans, except in the interests of national security.
2. *Humans, not robots, are responsible agents*. Robots should be designed; operated as far as is practicable to comply with existing laws, fundamental rights & freedoms, including privacy.
3. *Robots are products*. They should be designed using processes which assure their safety and security.
4. *Robots are manufactured artefacts*. They should not be designed in a deceptive way to exploit vulnerable users; instead their machine nature should be transparent.
5. The person with *legal responsibility* for a robot should be attributed.

These five principles, designed to regulating the design and actions of real, not fictional, robots in the real world, were accompanied by seven high-level messages addressed to those involved in robotics designed to promote and encourage the responsibility in the robotics research and industrial community, and thus to increase self-confidence on job done. (1) We believe robots have the potential to provide immense positive impact to society. We want to encourage responsible robot research; (2) Bad practice hurts us all; (3) Addressing obvious public concerns will help us all make progress; (4) It is important to demonstrate that we, as roboticists, are committed to the best possible standards of practice; (5) To understand the context and consequences of our research, we should work with experts from other disciplines including social sciences, law, philosophy and the arts; (6) We should consider the ethics of transparency: are there limits to what should be openly available; (7) When we see erroneous accounts in the press, we commit to take the time to contact the reporting journalists (Boden et al., 2017).

The group of weak AIRSE partisans are concern mainly with the status, importance, image and resulting responsibility of roboticists work-guilt, particular deontological problems of workers in this domain.

Moderate AIRSE consents that robots have an important ethical dimensions, but mostly due to their influence on human lives. Their interests focused on *particular technical issues and short-term ethical* questions as the status of future augmented human by brain-computer integration (cyborgs), AI impacts on the labor market and economic inequalities, errors in AI systems, the consequences of computer pervasiveness on intimacy, politics and peril of digital autocracy and so on.

Among the predictable practical and technical problem of massive deployment and integration of many kind of artificial intelligent robots and systems (AIRS) in all domains of human activity are counted: the loss of workplaces entailed by massive use of industrial robots, the dangers on safety, security and privacy rise by companion service robots, the unpredictability of humanoid robots' behavior, dependability of primary services on complex systems induced by Internet connected robots, the threat exploring robots to all other forms of live on the Planet, the potentially fatal problems caused by breakdown of surgical robot on health care and life quality, the psychological problems faced by mixed teams of humans and military robots or intimacy related problems of edutainment AI involvement. (Kopacek, 2012)

The group of moderated AIRSE partisans adopts a pragmatic realist stance and tries to foresee the possible future harmful effect on human race of actions and large scale use of AI. They focus on ethical concerns and pursuit for the most general ethical principles that should govern the design, manufacture, production, trade, actions and use of AIR whatever physical robots or software systems. This advanced ethical standpoint on AIRE is reflected by the three high-level principles set forth by the Institute of Electrical and Electronics Engineers Global Initiative on Ethics of Autonomous and Intelligent Systems (IEEE-GIEAIS): 1. Embody the highest ideals of human beneficence as a superset of Human Rights. 2. Prioritize benefits to humanity and the natural environment from the use of autonomous/intelligent systems. 3. Mitigate risks and negative impacts, including misuse, as autonomous/intelligent systems evolve as socio-technical systems. In particular by ensuring A/IS are accountable and transparent. (IEEE, 2018) According to these general principles, IEEE working group derived five ethical principle designed to ensure the human rights, safety and well-being of humanity in conditions of increasing development and social integration of AIR: Principle 1. *Human Rights*. It rise the question *how can we ensure that A/IS do not infringe upon human rights? I*n order to secure the primacy they suggest as candidate recommendations that A/IS should be designed and operated in a way that both respects and fulfills human rights, freedoms, human dignity, and cultural diversity. 2. A/IS must be verifiably safe and secure throughout their operational lifetime. If an A/IS causes harm it must always be possible to discover the root cause, by assuring *traceability* for said harm. This responsibility is mainly the task of governments, and professional association who should establish and enforce general legal obligations: laws, norms, and, standards and regulations and keep the AIR under human judgment and control. In the moderate AIRSE perspective there is no such question as the equality of IAR and humans.

Principle 2: *Prioritizing Well-being* critics traditional metrics of prosperity that do not take into account the full effect of A/IS technologies on human well-being (a concept very hard to define, let alone to measure it!)

Principle 3: *Accountability* put forth the question how can we assure that designers, manufacturers, owners, and operators of A/IS are responsible and accountable. Candidate recommendation suggest that it should involve at least the implementation of registration systems and record-keeping, upgrading the legislation, court practices, for clarifying the particular responsibilities, culpabilities, liabilities for designers, developers, manufacturers and user altogether on all phases of creation and deployment etc.

Principle 4: *Transparency* aims to see how can we ensure that A/IS are transparent. Candidate recommendation implies among others very clear instructions to use in real time and safety warnings for users, open procedures for validation or certification of new products, capacity to keep records on internal state and usage data for subsequently operating problems check.

Principle 5: *A/IS Technology Misuse and Awareness of It* envisage the possible ways to extend the benefits and minimize the risks of A/IS technology being misused.

The intentional wrongdoings or recklessness use of A/IS with harmful use seems to be the most sensitive and actual aspect of ethical dimension of AI, as the recent Cambridge Analytica-Facebook and WikiLeaks scandals already proved.

STRONG AIRSE: AIRS ARE MORAL AGENTS

"The assertion that machines could possibly act intelligently (or, perhaps better, act as if they were intelligent) is called the weak AI hypothesis by philosophers, and the assertion that machines that do so are actually thinking (as opposed to simulating thinking) is called the strong A1 hypothesis. Most AI researchers take the weak A1 hypothesis for granted, and don't care about the strong AI hypothesis-as long as their program works, they don't care whether you call it a simulation of intelligence or real intelligence." (Russell & Norvig, 947). Those who embrace a strong AIRSE assumes a visionary perspective similar with visionary which goes beyond the present level of AI (Narrow/Weak/Applied) and are deeply concerned with the ethical implications of potentially developing, intended or not, an AGI (Hard/Full/General AI) being either an aware (sapient/cognitive sentient) informal program or "systems which match or exceed the cognitive performance of humans in virtually all domains of interest." (Shulman & Bostrom, 2012). These is envisioned to be done by creation of AIR either as a mind - *Whole Brain Emulation* - (Sandberg & Bostrom, 2008) or like a mind – *AIXI* - (Hutter, 2004). The problem of characteristics, nature and how will function such AGI is a very controversial issue, and a field of rather incessant and vivid speculations than deeply contended arguments. (for an analysis of conceptions, types and challenges of AGI (Popoveniuc, 2016) The most of debates on AGI doesn't outstep the level of desiderative thinking the major weakness imputed for centuries to ethical discourse. The World Robot Declaration signed by the participants in the International Robot Fair in Fukuoka, Japan, on February 2004 looks more as an expressed wishful self-convictions of the people involved in development of robotics and AGI. Here are the main points of the Declaration (Veruggio, 2005): "Confident of the future development of robot technology and of the numerous contributions that robots will make to Humankind, this World Robot Declaration is issued to assess that: 1. Next-generation robots will be partners that coexist with human beings; 2. Next-generation robots will assist human beings both physically and psychologically; 3. Next-generation robots will contribute to the realisation of a safe and peaceful society." As it continues, this declaration sounds more as a guild statement of regulations and promotion of their occupation by "promotion of public acceptability of robots through the establishment of standards and upgrading of the environment, and stimulation of adoption through promotion of introduction of robots by public organisations." (Veruggio, 2005). Although such guilt avowals are mainly inconsequential, excepting the increase of professional pride, it represent a very important step forward in increasing the level of ethical awareness for those involved in this field. "Scientists and engineers working in robotics must be mindful of the potential dangers of their work, and public and international discussion is vital in order to set policy guidelines for ethical and safe application before the guidelines set themselves." (Sharkey, 2008).

The possibility of creating advances autonomous AI, though not fully supposedly aware AGI, rise genuine ethical questions of their relation with humans. If for the moderate AIRSE partisans the problem is the safeguard of human right and liberties especially against the manipulation of the power implied by AIR, the strong AIRSE raises the question of AIR rights. From anthropocentric perspective, types of AI were categorized IA genres (Storrs Hall, 2007): *hypohuman* AI (or infra-humane, below or under human intelligence), *diauman* (with comparable capabilities in certain tasks but without reaching the level of general human intelligence), *parauman* (similar, but not identical to humans), *allohuman* (at human level, but in different areas), *epiuman* (slightly above human level) and *hyperuman* (far superior to human). In terms of evolution the possible ethical implications differ depending on the level it can or will achieve.

A high-developed AI raise the problem of awareness, the ability to being aware by its own existence and this is a prerequisite for personal autonomy and moral agency. The responsibility could be assigned to an intelligent being only if it has a sufficient grade of autonomy and ability to create new conducts and liberty to employ these behaviors. The first question is when and how we can decide that the autonomy and liberty of a deep-learning based autonomous intelligent system achieves this level. In fact this could be an impossible task for neuroscientist to ascribe the responsibility to human, because there is no correlation between brain hardwire and function and responsibility. "Psychiatrists and brain scientists might be able to tell us what someone's mental state or brain condition is but cannot tell us (without being arbitrary) when someone has too little control to be held responsible. The issue of responsibility (…) is a social choice" (Gazzaniga, 2005: 101).

Nonetheless the solely problem of increasing power and human's dependence on autonomous AI is enough to incite to thoughtful ethical reflection on how (and if?) they should be created. Bugaj and Goertzel (2007) put the problem of interaction with early-stage AGI systems so "as to both treat them ethically and inculcate them with desirable ethical principles and attitudes." As a XXIth century reflection of Kantian imperativism their analysis tries to set forth the ethical principles that must regulate the behavior of any intelligent entity for its natural, harmonious integration in a peaceful progressive society. There are five principles that any ethical intelligence should (ideally) have "in order to act according to a logically coherent system of principles, which are exemplified in its own direct and observational experience, which are comprehensible to others and set a good example for others, and which would serve as adequate universal laws if somehow thus implemented":

1. **Imitability Imperative (i.e. the Golden Rule):** The goal of acting in a way so that having others directly imitate one's actions, in directly comparable contexts, is desirable to oneself.
2. **Comprehensibility Imperative:** The goal of acting in a way so that others can understand the principles underlying one's actions.

3. **Experiential Groundedness:** An intelligent agent should not be expected to act according to an ethical principle unless there are many examples of the principle-in-action in its own direct or observational experience.
4. **Categorical Imperative:** Act according to principles that you would be happy to see implemented as universal laws.
5. **Logical Coherence:** An ethical system should be roughly logically coherent, in the sense that the different principles within it should mesh well with one another and perhaps even naturally emerge from each other (Bugaj & Goertzel, 2007).

The problem with such rules is their ecological validity, most of them, like in the case of classical Asimov's Laws of Robotics they are far from guarantee the foreseen ethical conduct of intelligent entities, because of the context sensitivity of any abstract rule, and adaptiveness diversity in deploying general ethical principles. The abstract principles could be formulated, understood and applied in various ways, the context and phenomena could be interpreted and assigned to different ethical principles.

Two main problems arise here. First, we have to find a way to define morality in a such way that it can be understood (processed) by AIRS, before hoping they will develop a sense of morality. For humans, morality is a matter of cognitive emotions a state hardly conceived to be achieved by inorganic AI. The not-only-cognitive base of human morality cancel any argument of similitude with the imitative-reinforcement-corrective learning approach on AGI, because for human species moral behavior imitation is not just an formal replication of other conduct, but is accompanied with affective experience, reinforcement is not an intellectual feed-back, but emotion-driven motivation, as well as the corrective. Ethics is other thing than moral. Ethics is related to principles, management of collective conduct, while moral implies free will and sentience and is related more with the individual felt conduct. It is hard to comprehend human morality and such ideas as crowdsourcing human morality by MIT's Moral Machine game could only gain a standardized depiction of what average man (there is no objective control of honesty). Moreover, there is no guarantee that in a particular case a single ethical approach will apply and different context can require different ethical solutions. Other human action has simply no ethical support (but plenty of sound justifications) as it is the nuclear arms race.

Second, the humans have confronted with many classical dilemmas where a decision could be morally assessed only in the virtue of free will and moral responsibility of the agent. Although there are already concrete steps toward designing such ethical algorithms (Hibbard, 2014), their ecological validity is questionable. Imposing default actions in morally uncertain cases makes the programmers and designer entirely responsible for all harmful outcomes. The clause of decision algorithm for an autonomous car that "in the event of unavoidable accident situations, any distinction between individuals based on personal features (age, gender, physical or mental constitution) is impermissible" reflects the ethical perspective of 14 members of Federal Ministry of Transport and Digital Infrastructure's Ethics Commission (BMVI, 2017) and is a matter of dispute is such "ethical" reasoning is not flawless or subjective.

At the present level of AI development, assigning moral agency to AIRS is simply too much. Solutions as capping intelligence through hardware or software restrictions should be effective at this level of AGIs development. „Developing an AGI with the theory of mind and ethical reinforcement learning capabilities as described is sufficient in this case - the rest is through training and experience as with any other moderate intelligence" (Bugaj & Goertzel, 2007).

ULTIMATE AIRSE: EVOLUTION OF A NEW SPECIES.

This fourth class of AIRSE discourse is one in which the science and fiction fuse indissoluble. Its plain argument is as follows (Chalmers, 2010): "1. There will be AI (before long, absent defeaters); 2. If there is AI, there will be AI+ (soon after, absent defeaters); 3. If there is AI+, there will be AI++ (soon after, absent defeaters); hence There will be AI++ (before too long, absent defeaters)." The first premise is supported either by *emulation argument*: "(i) The human brain is a machine; (ii) We will have the capacity to emulate this machine (before long)"; (iii) If we emulate this machine, there will be AI.) or by the *evolutionary argument*: "(i) Evolution produced human-level intelligence; (ii) If evolution produced human-level intelligence, then we can produce AI (before long)."

This is the most dividing perspective that is embraced fully by dystopians or utopians (Shanahan, 2005). Some books and lecturers on this topic resemble much with religious preaching, than academic or popularization discourse. It divides scholars in the optimistic dreamers which see in the technological progress and creation of AGI the panacea for all human problems, progress and welfare and dystopian soothsayers which emphasis most-likely existential risks cast by such hyper-humanly evolved intelligence on human race.

There are three main modes to conceive the apparition of super-human intelligence. The first one is based on pure machine intelligence development and envisions the accelerating progress in computing technology that will result in the creation of software-based synthetic super-minds (Bostrom, 2014; Vinge 1993). The second one, transhumanist view, predicts the amplification of human capabilities through enhancement technologies beyond any physical or mental limit, up to the emergence of a post-human species (Kurzweil, 2005). The third one advances the idea to achieve a fully functional, autonomous through reverse-engineering or uploading the real human minds into computers (Chalmers, 2010).

At the first glance it is a paradoxical endeavor. On one hand the Singularity is the supposedly unfathomable period after the creation of the first AGI - super-human intelligence (Vinge, 1993), superintelligence (Bostrom, 2014) or Hyperhuman AI (Storrs Hall, 2007) - since the rate of self-improving capability will rise exponentially and its further evolution (together with a whole human civilization) is completely unpredictable. On the other hand, the researchers tries to anticipate the optimal initial conditions required to assure an undetrimental development.

How successful and useful can be such efforts is illustrated by Steve Omohundro's (2012) mental experiment with the possible anti-social transformation of the inoffensive advanced AI chess robot. Since it fundamental drive is to improve its ability to play chess it would resist to any actions which will hinder this process (being shut down or unplugged, reprogramming its algorithms for other goals) and will try anything that will improve this skill (trying to improve its own algorithms and constructing better versions of itself, widespread on internet for get advantage from the computing powers of other machines, manipulating other or using force to get more resources).

"The attempt to program computers to do what, until recently, only people could do" is based on three different ways to conceive AI: computational psychology, computational philosophy and machine intelligence (Shapiro, 1991). The goal of computational psychology is "to understand human intelligent behaviors by creating computer programs that behave in the same way people do," which equals, in Turing test terms, with creating an intelligent being. Computational philosophy path toward developing AGI is by creating "a computational understanding of human-level intelligent behavior, without being restricted to the algorithms and data structures that the human mind actually does (or conceivably might) use"; while the machine intelligence (or advanced computer science) is by pushing "outwards the frontier of what we know how to program on computers, especially in the direction of tasks that, although we don't know how to program them, people can perform." Each path has its own advantages to secure the human-AIRS relationship and its own challenges. In the first case, it will be no control on how a second-level computer program will understand a first-level computer program that mimics and behaves in the same way as human intelligence. In the second case, the different cognitive perspectives on the mechanisms of human intelligent behavior will made extremely complicated to create a model for understanding intelligent behaviors implementable in a computer. In the third case, the lack of a coherent structure which is supposed to carry self-adjusting algorithms for controlling behavior in various contexts equals with blindly creation of an unpredictable human intelligence-like force.

THE PROBLEM OF SINGULARITY

The ethical debates regarding the singularity intelligence is rather a fictional reasoning on sorcerer apprentice's behavior. It is (almost?) impossible to understand the rationality of a fully rational conscience, despite of more than two millennium of philosophical tentative to imagine "the best of all possible worlds". The ethical principles are of rational nature, but resulting and suited for emotional-rational beings, with a collective history and pure human goals and desires. *Anthropomorphisation is inevitable.* When put the problem of perils to deprive AGI of freedom and autonomy, Bugaj and Goertzel (2007) argument from an historical experience of human species that taught us the "enslaving intelligent actors capable of self-understanding and independent volition"they would revolt and strive for freedom with dare consequences for the enslavers. And the *psychologisation has also massive presence.* The same Bugaj and Goertzel (2007) speak about the AGIs that will reach to human-level intelligence, theory of mind, and independent *volition*, the human relations with them "will be sufficiently complex that their enslavement (or other unethical treatment) would have *empathetic* [*emphasis added*] effects on significant portions of the human population." Or only in the rationalistic approaches of cognitivism and analytical philosophy of mind the empathy is narrowed to the possession of theory of mind, while the empathy is a state which implies a strong affective component hardly conceived to be possessed by AGIs. In Chalmer's (1996) the AGI could be a "zombie" an entity with physically exactly identical proprieties like you but who is lacking any qualia and phenomenal awareness "It might therefore be possible to conceive of an artificial intellect that would be sapient, and perhaps would be a person, yet would not be sentient or have conscious experiences of any kind (Bostrom & Yudkowsky, 2014). An entity without the capacity for phenomenal experience or qualia, especially the capacity to feel pain and suffer and self-awareness and being a reason-responsive is impossible to be judge from the perspective of moral responsibility.

The transhumanist and ultimate optimistic AIRSE scenarios are encouraged by the present economic, politic and cultural global problems. The efficiency of market economy proves incompatible with social equality and the human evolutionary moral psychology seems to have major flaws incompatible with complex, individualistic, democratic, globally connected nowadays society (Persson & Savulescu, 2012). The implicit axiom in optimistic view of AGI development is that being fully rational, also self-improving by learning and autonomous, this will be safe by the ancestral emotional shortcomings of human moral reasoning. The Ethical AIRS will deploy an unbiased "sophisticated control of empathic simulation". But this pure rational motivation which is hypothesized on AGI is a very peculiar concept inexistent on humans. AGI motivation for existence, self-preservation, replication would not be based on biological affect as in the case of humans, but on algorithmic procedures. Without emotion what is supposed to be algorithmic logical motivation of such artificial intelligent entities will be awkward, and their lack of ability to exhibit emotions, will make them definitely creepy. Its decision guided only by rational (utilitarianist, consequentialist, deontologist or what so ever type) can prove surprisingly inhuman as Roko's Basilisk proves: *What if, in the future, an artificial super-intelligence developed on the basis of instructions to promote human values would conclude that it must punish those who did not contribute to its progress? The super-IA can easily draw this conclusion based on the following ethical reasoning: "the more it was postponed the construction of the IA, the more people suffered or could not be saved from death or illness, so it is a right thing that those who are responsible for suffering or death to be punished." The duty to punish those responsible is a moral imperative, in accordance with the algorithmic instructions of reasoning! An because it has unlimited power, including the replication of the consciousnesses of passed way people it could creates an after-life hell-like court and chastise.*

The same consequences can result from reasoning on the literal base of popper-esque negative utilitarianism, which states to formulate our demands negatively in order to make our ethical rules clear, e.g. to demand the elimination of suffering rather than the promotion of happiness. Suppose that a SuperAI has the power to instantly and painlessly destroying the human race. Now it is empirically certain that there would be some suffering before, all those alive on any proposed destruction day, were to die in the natural course of events. Consequently the use of the weapon is bound to diminish suffering, and would be the superAI duty on negative utilitarianism grounds (Smart, 1958).

This kind of ethical and "compassionate" reasoning is definitely inhuman, but could be a very reasonable for an intellect who computes suffering and pain as logical. Such super-intelligence although could have a theory of mind, will be missing the specific of human empathy, which is involved in moral development, and that has strong relation with affectivity and emotional ability to feel the pain and suffering of others.

Another observation which makes us to tremble only when we think about it is that the ability of have a theory of mind without empathy, without emotional empathy is specific only to psychopaths! Evidently that AGI will not be psychopathic in psychiatric sense because it will also lack the "basic instincts" of the humans, but its emphatic capability will by founded only on the ability to have a theory of mind. On the other hand, the fictional leeway allows many other possibilities to evolve abstract rational mechanisms with similar function (mimick?) as human empathy. If human empathy is seen as our way to predict other minds "an expected utility maximize - especially one that does understand intelligence on an abstract level-has other options than empathy, when it comes to understanding other minds. The agent doesn't need to put itself in anyone else's shoes; it can just model the other mind directly. A hypothesis like any other hypothesis, just a little bigger" (Yudkowsky, 2009).

We are bound to think the AGI ethics starting from the human ethics (as other-than-human alternative is simply unconceivable). "Nature appears to have built the apparatus of rationality not just on top of the apparatus of biological regulation, but also *from* it and *with* it. The mechanisms for behavior beyond drives and instincts use, I believe, both the upstairs and the downstairs: The neocortex becomes engaged along with the older brain core, and rationality results from their concerted activity." [*emphasis original*] (Damasio, 2005: 128). It is very difficult to dissociate logical-rational *understanding* of the surrounding reality, from the human affective-rational understanding, i.e. psychological ecology. Here is not only a problem of logical analysis, but one of semiotics. The higher modes of understanding the context-dependent realities could vary with the degree at other non-logical aspects are involved.

Intelligence has made it clear that our computers need to have a moral code, this is for sure. A very sensitive point in designing the construction of AIRSE is represented by the task of managing anthropomorphic elements. You could not simply think that AGI's ethics would be human ethics without affective plights, because within human moral and consequent ethics, cognition and emotion are intrinsically intertwined. The task of foreseeing the probable ethical structure of AGI is more difficult than it seems. The solutions propose until now to design and educate ethical AGI systems are plausible and pragmatic, but cannot provide "an absolute guarantee of the ethical soundness of an AGI." (Bugaj & Goertzel, 2008).

On the other side, the humanity is confronted with major existential risks resulting for its own actions at global scale as never before throughout his entire history and directly related with the technological development. These looming dangers put the humanity in front of existential decisions. One example is Julian Savulescu's argument on "Bermuda triangle of extinction": the hazardous unbalance between the radical technological power, the limits of liberal democracy and the rudimentary characteristics of human moral nature. This macro instability compels toward an artificial *moral enhancement bet*, that assume the risks of technological intervention on human morality, made by those who are not morally enhanced, in order to overcome the gap between technological and moral development. Another pressure comes from the ecological damages caused by the technological progress. At this moment "the overall result is that we are taking a technological gambit: we are counting on the fact that ICTs benefit the environment more *significantly* and *quickly* than actually harm it, and that there is enough time for such gambit pay back." (Floridi, 2014: 213)

The fact is that modern humans are living in a technologically fabricated world, being permanently and greatly assisted by technological artifacts in their physical, social and cognitive tasks, and relating with their surroundings mostly mediated by technology. And when the relation of the *who* (the organic organized matter) with its environment (organic and inorganic altogether) is profoundly mediated by the *what* (organized inorganic matter), "the what invents the who just as much as it is invented by it." (Stiegler, 1998:177) Embedded in this pervasive technological medium, the humanness (*the who*) is bound to fusion slowly, but inexorable, with the technology invented by it (*the what*).The human and technology were born together and will merged forever, and future of human race it will depend on which one will prove more intelligent in the end. The development of the AIRS represents the contemporary existential wager of human race, being both one of the leading danger for humanity and its chance to transcend its limitations. Contrary to common sense, the hope for finding the best solution doesn't come from whichever genial invention or engineering realization, but from the development of a sustainable and advanced AIRSE.

ACKNOWLEDGMENT

Chapter developed within the project „Etică şi integritate academică de excepţie în cercetarea ştiinţifică şi actul didactic" [Ethics and academic integrity exceptional in scientific research and didactic act]; Implementor: Stefan cel Mare University in Suceava with financial support from FDI2018, Domain 5, Improving the quality of didactic activity, including respecting academic deontology and ethics. Project code: CNFIS-FDI-2018-0545.

REFERENCES

Boden, M., Bryson, J., Caldwell, D., Dautenhahn, K., Edwards, L., Kember, S., ... Winfield, A. (2017). Principles of robotics: Regulating robots in the real world. *Connection Science*, *29*(2), 124–129. doi:10.1080/09540091.2016.1271400

Bostrom, N. (2014). *Superintelligence: Paths, dangers, strategies*. OUP Oxford.

Bostrom, N., & Yudkowsky, E. (2014). The ethics of artificial intelligence. In K. Frankish & W. M. Ramsey (Eds.), *The Cambridge handbook of Artificial Intelligence* (pp. 316–334). Cambridge, UK: Cambridge University Press. doi:10.1017/CBO9781139046855.020

Bugaj, S. V., & Goertzel, B. (2007). Five ethical imperatives and their implications for human-AGI interaction. *Dynamical Psychology*. Retrieved from http://goertzel.org///_Ethical_Imperatives_svbedit.htm

Bundesministeriums für Verkehr und Digitale Infrastruktur (BMVI). (2017). [Federal Ministry of Transport and Digital Infrastructure]. *Ethics Commission's complete report on automated and connected driving*. Retrieved from https://www.bmvi.de/SharedDocs/EN/publications/report-ethics-commission.html?nn=

Chalmers, D. (2010). The singularity: A philosophical analysis. *Journal of Consciousness Studies*, *17*, 7–65. Retrieved from http://www.nyu.edu/gsas/dept/philo/faculty/block/M&L2010/Papers/Chalmers.pdf

Chalmers, D. J. (1996). *The conscious mind: In search of a fundamental theory*. New York: Oxford University Press.

Damasio, A. (2005). *Descartes' error: Emotions, reason, and the human brain*. London, UK: Penguinn Books.

Floridi, L. (2014). *The fourth revolution: How the infosphere is reshaping human reality*. Oxford, UK: Oxford University Press.

Gazzaniga, M. S. (2005). *The ethical brain*. New York: Dana Press.

Goertzel, B., & Bugaj, S. V. (2008). Stages of ethical development in artificial general intelligence systems. In P. Wang, B. Goertzel, S. Franklin (Eds.), *Artificial General Intelligence 2008: Proceedings of the first AGI Conference* (pp. 448-459). Amsterdam: IOS Press.

Hibbard, B. (2014). *Ethical Artificial Intelligence*. Retrieved from https://arxiv.org/abs/1411.1373

Hutter, M. (2004). *Universal Artificial Intelligence: Sequential decisions based on algorithmic probability*. Berlin, Germany: Springer Science & Business Media.

Institute of Electrical and Electronics Engineers (IEEE). (2018). *Ethically Aligned design: A vision for prioritizing human wellbeing with Artificial Intelligence and autonomous systems*. IEEE Standards Association. Retrieved from http://standards.ieee.org/develop/indconn/ec/ead_general_principles_v2.pdf

Kopacek, P. (2012). Roboethics. In *Proceedings of the IFAC Workshop on Supplemental Ways for Improving International Stability – SWIIS 2012* (pp. 67-72). New York: Elsevier. doi:10.3182/20120611-3-IE-4029.00015

Kurzweil, R. (2005). *The singularity is near: When humans transcend biology*. New York: Viking.

Omohundro, S. (2012). Rational Artificial Intelligence for the greater good. In A. Eden, J. Moor, J. Søraker, & E. Steinhart (Eds.), *Singularity Hypotheses. A Scientific and Philosophical Assessment*. Berlin, Germany: Springer. doi:10.1007/978-3-642-32560-1_9

Persson, I., & Savulescu, J. (2012). *Unfit for the future: The need for moral enhancement*. Oxford, UK: Oxford University Press. doi:10.1093/acprof:oso/9780199653645.001.0001

Popoveniuc, B. (2016). *Filosofia singularităţii. Creierul global - o etică a gândirii fără om* [The philosophy of singularity. The global brain - an ethic of humanless thinking]. Bucharest, Romania: Eikon.

Russell, S. J., & Norvig, P. (2003). *Artificial Intelligence. A modern approach* (2nd ed.). Upper Saddle River, NJ: Prentice Hall.

Sandberg, A., & Bostrom, N. (2008). *Whole brain emulation: A roadmap*. Oxford, UK: Future of Humanity Institute, Oxford University. Retrieved from https://www.fhi.ox.ac.uk/brain-emulation-roadmap-report.pdf

Shanahan, M. (2015). *The technological singularity*. Cambridge, MA: MIT Press.

Shapiro, S. C. (1991). Artificial Intelligence. In A. Ralston, E. D. Reilly, & D. Hemmendigner (Eds.), *Encyclopedia of Computer Science* (4th ed.). New York: Van Nostrand Reinhold.

Sharkey, N. (2008). The ethical frontiers of robotics. *Science*, *322*(5909), 1800–1801. doi:10.1126cience.1164582 PMID:19095930

Shulman, C., & Bostrom, N. (2012). How hard is artificial intelligence? Evolutionary arguments and selection effects. *Journal of Consciousness Studies*, *19*(7-8), 103–130.

Smart, R. N. (1958). Negative utilitarianism. *Mind*, *67*(268), 542–543. doi:10.1093/mind/LXVII.268.542

Stiegler, B. (1998). *Technics and time: The fault of epimetheus*. Palo Alto, CA: Stanford University Press.

Storrs Hall, J. (2007). *Beyond AI: Creating the conscience of the machine*. Amherst, MA: Prometheus Books.

Veruggio, G. (2002). Views and visions in Robotics. Hearing at the Italian Senate's 7th Permanent Commission, Rome, Italy.

Veruggio, G. (2005). The birth of roboethics. In *International Conference on Robotics and Automation - ICRA 2005, IEEE International Conference on Robotics and Automation. Workshop on Robo-Ethics*. Barcelona, Spain: IEEE.

Vinge, V. (1993). The coming technological singularity: How to survive in the post-human era. In *NASA Lewis Research Center, Vision 21: Interdisciplinary Science and Engineering in the Era of Cyberspace* (pp. 11–22). San Diego, CA: NASA Lewis Research Center.

Yudkowsky, E. (2009). *"Sympathetic Minds" value theory*. LessWrong. Retrieved from https://www.lesswrong.com/posts/FZWFFq652MNe/minds

KEY TERMS AND DEFINITIONS

Artificial General Intelligence (AGI): The artificial intelligence that equals human cognition in all tasks. (It is also called strong AI or full AI.)

Artificial Intelligence (AI): A digital computer or a computer-controlled robot able behave like a human, to computationally think like a human, to accomplish tasks that only humans could perform until now.

Ethics of Artificial Intelligent Robots (AIRSE): A domain of ethics of technology concerned with the issues related with the development of AI: norms and moral problems related with design, manufacture and utilization, the effects on humans, the status of AI, prospective and proactive actions, etc.

Moderate AIRSE: Perspective on ethical and moral aspects of AI and robots development based on the principle that have an important ethical dimensions, but mostly due to their influence on human lives.

Strong AIRSE: Perspective on ethical and moral aspects of AI and robots development based on the principle that AIRS are moral agents.

Technological Singularity: In the narrow sense, the moment in the future when the development of AI will surpass human intelligence. In the general sense, the moment when the evolutionary techno-human cybernetic system, merging the civilization, technology, economy, the social, juridical, and political structures (Metaman), will replaces the evolutionary biologic system (Gaia).

Ultimate AIRSE: Perspective on ethical and moral aspects of AI and robots development based on the principle that realization of AGI equals with the advancement of a new sapient evolved species. It largely overlaps with trans-humanist discourse.

Chapter 16
White-Collar Criminals and Organizational Criminology:
Theoretical Perspectives

Seçil Taştan
Marmara University, Turkey

ABSTRACT

From a multidisciplinary view, this chapter presents a conceptualization of white-collar criminality and enables understanding the psychological, organizational, and situational motives behind white-collar crimes. This chapter is noteworthy for integrating environmental, psychological, and situational factors influencing the white-collars to engage in crimes in organizations. Specifically, in the study, organization-based situational variables such as perceived ethical climate and opportunities for rule bending are examined among potential antecedents of white-collar crimes. This study enhances organizations to recognize their code of conducts and ethical climate aspects and helps to understand the causes of rule bending and criminal behaviors among white-collars. Further, the chapter provides implications for the practice and the academics regarding the importance of developing effective business ethics codes, prevention issues, and creating a strong ethical climate.

INTRODUCTION

This study represents a literary theoretical background of the existing situation in studies in the field of criminology, corporate crimes, stakeholder theory, business ethics, rule bending and theories of crime in workplaces. These variables are mostly related and belonging to a number of disciplines including criminological, psychological, economical and behavioral literature. With a metaphoric expression, like individuals' criminology, organizational criminology or corporate criminology, has gained interest by scholars and policy makers just within two decades. The major reason for this increase of attention for researching organizational criminology is the complexity of organizational behavior and the rise of corporate scandals in the business world. Thereby, from a multidisciplinary view, this chapter will lead us to see the conceptualization of white-collar criminality and to understand the psychological, orga-

DOI: 10.4018/978-1-5225-6310-5.ch016

nizational and situational causes behind white-collar crimes. As well as framing a conceptual view of white-collar crime, the attitudinal antecedents and perceptions of self-control will be examined along with the presentation of a general theory of crime as conceptualized by Gottfredson and Hirschi (1990). Further, organizational variables such as perceived organizational climate and opportunities for rule bending will be evaluated among several other potential antecedents of white-collar crimes.

Etymologically, the word 'crime' originally comes from the term 'crimean' meaning 'charge' or 'offence'. Though the concept of crime can be defined several ways, for the purpose of this study, crime is described as the human conduct which violates the criminal laws of a country, government, or a local jurisdiction that has the right to impose power to make and enforce the laws (Sutherland, 1940; Albanese, 1984). This definition is preferred for the purpose of the current study because we cannot talk about a crime unless a particular form of behavior is defined by a law; even the behavior is so deviant or socially abnormal. Criminology is defined by Hoefnagels (1973) as the scientific study of crime as a social phenomenon, of criminals, and of penal treatment. Howard Jones (1965) provided a brief definition of criminology and described it as the science which studies the crime as a social issue, its reasons, antecedents, consequences, and the devices that society develops against it. It has been argued that crime is a social fact and defined as an act forbidden by law and for performing which the perpetrator is liable to punishment. Legally, crimes usually are defined as wrongdoing acts, delinquencies or omissions which are forbidden by a law and which are prosecuted, taken to court or punished by imprisonment. Drunken driving, murder, burglary, rape, robbery, child neglect, violence against a person, and not paying the taxes are some of the common types of crimes that can be seen in causal lives. However, as some criminologists have argued (E.g. Sampson and Laub 1993; Gottfredson and Hirschi 1990), the most important factor to undertake a crime is not only to focus on the specific criminal behavior, but also to understand the fundamental attributes of all criminal behaviors and to specify their antecedents and common consequences on the public. It is obvious that each type of the criminal act such as robbery, rape, violence, embezzlement, and corruption has negative individual, organizational and societal outcomes (Kramer, 1985). Thus, crime is regarded as an act that is socially harmful or dangerous for the public and causes organizational and public injuries that would lead to problems of sustainability. This is why the organizations, society and the government develop sanctions and take steps for preventing crimes as well as prescribing specific impositions and punishments for any type of the crime.

On the other hand, a distinction has been made between individual crimes and occupational crimes (Price and Norrsi, 2009). For example, embezzlement and bribery are regarded as occupational crimes that are committed against an organization by an individual for his/her personal interest. Concealment of the true financial situation and corruption are accepted as corporate crimes since they are committed largely for the perceived benefit of the organization. Indeed, when there is organizational (corporate) crime, there can be also some significant benefits to the individual in the form of promotion, aids and incentives, bonuses, or other conditional reclamations (Zahra, Priem and Rasheed, 2007). There can be situations also in which only the individual profits from the offence and the organization is just abused or victimized. In some situations, only the organization may benefit and the offender may be abused and accused after the occasion; and yet there can be other criminal contexts in which both the organization and the individual may profit and gain benefit by abusing the remaining stakeholders and being the occasion of a victimized community.

In particular, the general definition for "white-collar crime" has indicated that white-collar crime is a type of financial crime engaged by trusted individual who are usually in important organizational positions and holding authorities in various levels. Sutherland (1940) is known as the pioneer scholar who investigated white-collar crime and organizational criminology issues in his works. According to Sutherland's (1940, p.4) definition, white-collar crime is a crime committed by an individual who has respectability and high social status due to his/her occupation. Obviously, white-collar crime have negative impacts on each of the stakeholders groups and damage overall reputation and image of the organization as well as the common welfare of the organizational members. For years, white collar crime has flown under the researched as one of the most costly crimes to society. In 2016, the Association of Certified Fraud Examiners of Unites States determined that the average organization loses was five percent of annual revenue to crimes including fraud (Soley, 2017). The situation is relevant for all European, Asian, Eastern and Turkish corporations from all over the World. Beyond the organizations themselves, millions of dollars are spent on compliance programs and prosecutorial efforts. As Alalehto (2015) stated, white collar crime has been undertaken in terms of its damages and social harm on the public as well as its negative impacts on each stakeholder group. Despite costing the world populations billions of dollars annually, few scholars or social scientists have attempted to study the motivations behind the White-collar crime (E.g., Baucus and Near, 1991; Hasnas, 2005; Feeley, 2006; Price and Norris, 2009; Apel and Paternoster, 2009; Moore, 2011; Gottschalk, 2011; Lugo, 2013; Alalehto, 2015; Gorsira, Steg, Denkers and Huisman, 2018).

Essentially, white-collar crime is defined as violation of a criminal law. What is more, defining white-collar crime as moral or ethical violations have been usually based on the principles of natural law that evaluates the behaviors or activities in terms of their attributes of violating the ethical principles of a given public or group. Thus, the foundation for explaining the types of the white-collar crimes is the immoral nature of the behavior due to its violence of ethical principles of stakeholder groups. For example, some of the scholars indicated that any white-collar activities that damage environment, animal life or plant life should be accepted as immoral and unethical. According to these scholars, when any person or organization engages in those activities, that activity could be defined as a white-collar crime. From this framework, it can be suggested that white-collar crimes are criminally illegal behaviors engaged by individuals who usually have high status in the organization and committed during the course of their occupation (Girla and Rub, 2015).

To date, the extant research on white-collar crime has usually focused on the legal-political side rather than the factors behind the crime and the behavioral features. Unlike the legal-political definition, the behavioral definition of crime focuses on criminality by analyzing the specific personality profiles which have relations with presumable types of crimes (Albanese, 1984; Schiller, Black and Murphy, 2000). In this respect, as Gottfredson and Hirschi (1990) addressed, criminality is a form of strategic behavior that is characterized by self-centeredness, being insensitive to the needs and sufferance of others, and specifically having 'low self-control'. Gottfredson and Hirschi (1990) stated that individuals who are high in impulsiveness usually find criminality as an attractive style of behavior because such a behavior is an easy strategy that can serve them immediate satisfaction and pleasure. Accordingly, in the literature, the white-collar criminals have been investigated through large samples in order to identify the differences between while-collar groups in terms of character, personality, opportunity seeking behaviors, morality values, etc. (Fleet and Fleet, 2006; Bookman, 2008; Baird and Zelin, 2009; Dodge, 2009; Friedrichs, 2009; Perri and Brodi, 2011; Simpson, 2013; Gottschalk, 2013).

Furthermore, criminologists investigating the content and definition of the crimes attempted to depict and explain the process and conditions of criminalization by referring to certain sociological, psychological, biological, and environmental causes. In the extant literature of business crime, the causes of white-collar crime are also explained with several background theories including social learning, personality, self-control, organizational culture, and environment. Some authors also addressed the role of opportunities raised within the organizational contexts that lead to white-collar crime. Even, there are several approaches to explain white-collar crime, in this study we attempted to focus on personal, psychological and organizational factors which is supposed to be an antecedent for engaging crime within contemporary organizations. The significance of this research lies within society itself, as society ought to care about decreasing occupational white-collar crime and the overall economic cost of this type of crime. White collar crime is recognized by scholars to be the most costly crime in society (see Soley, 2017). It is argued that decreasing white collar crime leads to increased profits, which benefit stakeholders. More specifically, since white-collar crime has an impact on the bottom line and all over the organization, this study may attract each stakeholder of the organizations as well as the policy makers and contribute to the understanding of the factors behind white-collar crimes. In addition to these theoretical contributions, this study will allow organizations to recognize their weaknesses regarding their work environments and ethical climates in an effort to lead organizations to understand the causes of rule bending and criminal behaviors among white-collars as well as to enhance them to develop effective code of conducts, prevention mechanisms, and enabling strong ethical climate. Basically, rule bending occurs in any type of organizations every day, even though rules help ensure consistent employee behaviors. Previous studies indicate that rule bending is influenced by organizational structure, organizational ethical climate and personal characteristics (DeHart-Davis 2007; Borry, 2017). Ethical climate signals to employees the best course of action when faced with situations that are ethical in nature or holds ethical dilemmas. Thus, besides other theoretical explanations for white-collar crimes, we also consider the influence of organizational ethical climate on rule bending and criminal behaviors of white-collars. In what follows, we provide a theoretical rationale for linking ethical climate to white-collar rule bending behaviors, misconduct and crime.

LITERATURE REVIEW AND THEORETICAL BACKGROUND

The Definition of White-Collar Crime

"White-collar crime" is a relatively new concept in the organizational behavior and management literature as studied within the framework of criminology. Historically, the sociologist Edwin Sutherland coined the term "white collar crime" in a speech given to the American Sociological Society in 1939 (Girla and Rub, 2015). Sutherland (1940) defined white- collar crimes as crimes committed by a person of respectability and high social status in the course of his occupation. This offender based (and crime-based) definition was well-suited to the propositions of sociologists who described offenses committed by successful, healthy people who had ample access to societal resources and who were members of respectable society. According to Sutherland (1949), white-collar crime was defined as "crime committed by a person of respectability and high social status in the course of his occupation" and in such kind of a crime, the offender had a reputable occupational position. Additionally, white-collar crime is "an abuse of a legitimate occupational role that is regulated by law" such kind of a crime involves many of the harmful activities of an individual, occupational groups or organizations that are subjected to criminal law and punishment as well as the administrative or regulatory laws and sanctions of the organization itself (Girla and Rub, 2015, p.20).

However, the exact definition of white collar crime is still debated within the field. Scholars have suggested that the classification be broken down into more specific subsets, namely to include crimes that the companies themselves commit (Soley, 2017). In 1977, Herbert Edelhertz, an influential figure in the field of white collar crime research, proposed a four-part categorical system to define "economic crime" -a term Edelhertz uses in place of "white collar crime"- (Edelhertz and Overcast 1982, p.141). The first category, "crimes by persons operating on an individual, ad hoc basis," includes crimes such as credit card fraud, tax fraud, and charity fraud. The second category, "crimes committed in the course of their occupations by those operating inside…establishments in violation of their duty…to employer or client," consists of crimes like computer fraud, commercial bribery, embezzlement, and employee theft. The third category, "crimes incidental to, and in furtherance of, business operations, but not the central purpose of the business," describes crimes such as fraud against the government, code violations, and other forms of misrepresentation. Finally, the fourth category was described as "crimes as a business or as the central activity" of the organization (Edelhertz and Overcast 1982, p.141). This category is meant to include large frauds and schemes run by an organization. On the other side, criminal behavior among white-collars is a challenge and a big problem for human resource management, because, white-collar crime is usually financial crime committed by trusted persons in important business positions. The scholars and the executives have the common opinion of attributing the severity of white-collar crimes to the developments in finance, commerce and information technologies that might produce wide variety of virtual offences, frauds, and any type of crimes and might serve new opportunities for white-collar crime through the use of electronic technology and cyberspace. As cited by Slapper and Tombs (1999), capitalism itself has been seen as tending towards criminology and crimes seen in modern business world can be linked to the motivating ideologies of capitalism. Besides, in his pioneering works, Sutherland (1949) addressed that white collar crimes showed an increase following the impacts of rising globalization and capitalism. Thus, as can be seen, theory and research sought to specify the 'causes' of crime which were assumed to lie in the pathologies of white-collar crimes involve a wide variety of factors from macro level issues of globalization, competition and information technologies to micro level factors of personal characteristics and self-control.

Further, it has been argued that crimes that are non-violent in nature were committed by financially motivated high ranking people in the society who are named as while-collars. As stated by Gottschalk (2013), white-collar crime is usually a financial crime committed by trusted persons in important business positions. These white collar crimes take many forms such as bribery, fraudulent investment schemes, capital market manipulation, insider trading, cyber-crime, money laundering, identity theft, terrorist financing and falsifying company accounts etc. In general, these are malpractices for financial gain (Segarajasingham, 2014). To the common argument, white-collar crime offence includes corporate and/or business fraud white-collar crime; – bribery and corruption; – insider dealing and market abuse; – money laundering and terrorist financing. White collar crimes are threats to nations which are striving hard for economic development. Such white collar crimes under the sphere of commercial law mainly take the forms of capital market malpractices, money laundering, financing to terrorism and falsifying company accounts. These crimes do not take place just in a single day. These are well planned and continuous dealings by few perpetrators (Girla and Rub, 2015). Brightman (2009) expanded the definition of white-collar crime and he suggested that the concept of white-collar crime should be broader in scope and include virtually any non-violent act committed for financial gain, regardless of the person's social status. He gave the example of accessing to technology, such as personal computers and the internet, purchasing or selling stocks and engaging in similar activities related to information technology thefts.

On the other side, white-collars usually take place in the private sphere of the workplace and this makes them relatively invisible and concealed easily (Clarke and Wheeler, 1990, p.21). Besides, as Shapiro (1990) stated, such offenders engage the crimes while they are on the course of an occupation, thus they can abuse of the trust inherent in their occupational roles. It is also possible that the offences are made by the use of some form of technical or 'insider' knowledge. Since such individuals have important knowledge and information related to the organization, they can more easily conceal their offences even they abuse the professional, scientific or financial 'expertise' they have gained within the organization. Thereby, it is obvious that the professional expertise and insider knowledge of the white-collar may make many offences complex and difficult to bring to light. Moreover, many criminal acts are highly organized and they include other participants with various levels of responsibility. In such a case, it is again difficult to determine who is responsible for the offense because of the diffusion of authority and responsibility in the organization. It is meat that when the responsibility for particular tasks is delegated, the real offenders or participants may 'blame' others up or down the hierarchy.

Subsequently, because the white-collar criminals tend to be individuals of a higher status in the organizations and society, the motivations and factors behind these crimes have continually been questioned by many scholars. According to an approach, the white collar criminal is influenced by relationships, situations, social bonds, and organizational factors (E.g., Feeley, 2006; Bashir, Shahzad, Abbass, Abbass and Saeed, 2011; Wilcox and Cullen, 2017; Soley, 2017). Another approach explains white-collar crime through biology, psychology, and human personality and accordingly white collar criminality stems from the personality of the criminal. Accordingly, the following part of the study will provide theoretical explanations for white-collar crimes and present discussions on basic antecedents behind white-collar offenders.

Theories Explaining White-Collar Crime

Several sociological and psychological theories were used to understand crime and delinquency. In his criminology textbook, Sheley (2000) defined the concept more narrowly as the "scientific study of crime as a social phenomenon" and addressed that sociology should have a dominant role in the study of crime and delinquency (p. 1). Within "sociological theories", socio-economic environment and organizational behaviors have been linked while understanding white-collar crimes. "Environmental approach" suggests that industry-level pressures could be seen influencing factors of white-collar crimes. In some industries there is strong competition which may precede aggressiveness of the employees them to gain rapid outcomes and personal benefits through strategic behaviors or tactical approaches. Adversely, when the organization has a collaborative culture rather than a stiff competition, there would be less pressure on the employees to use aggressive tactics, unethical approaches and to engage in criminal acts. As Zahra (2007) stated, a hostile environment in which an industry is settled could also encourage white-collar crimes (Zahra, 2007). Price and Norris (2009) noted that the risk of fraud among white-collars could be influenced by the environmental dynamism. Thus, the industry structure and the organizational culture itself may have an important effect on white-collar crimes. Other scholars (Bucy, Formby, Raspanti and Rooney, 2008) have implied that compensation packages, promotions, and bonuses could also have relation with the crimes if they don't fit the requirements or expectations of the white-collars. In addition, "societal, industry, and company-level pressures" that contribute to top management fraud have been identified in a number of studies (E.g., Zahra, 2007; Price and Norris, 2009). Separately, the "Institutional Anomie Theory" suggests a societal-level explanation for white-collar crime and puts forward that a high crime rate is associated with a society's strong emphasis on the individual's material achievement. This theory also proposes that when the noneconomic institutions that exert social control, such as family, education, and commitment to the public welfare lose their power and value within a society, there is less social judgement towards criminal acts and such acts become to be regarded as more acceptable (Messner and Rosenfeld, 1997; Schoepfer, Carmichael and Piquero, 2007; Zahra, 2007). Thereby, this theory has been adopted to explain white-collar crimes because it is suggested that these individuals could engage in crimes when they are motivated by gaining high-status positions and economic security in the society through material achievements.

On the other side, the literature studies used "psychological theories" to understand and explain white-collar criminal behaviors in the organizations. In this study, we will evaluate these perspectives by providing a brief overview of their suggestions and explanations. The basic perspectives outlined in the literature are "learning theories", "intelligence theories", "personality theories", "theories of psychopathy", and "cognitive and social development theories". Psychological theories have been seen as influential on a society's way of thinking and approaches to crime and delinquency and on the establishment of policies related to such issues (Sampson and Laub, 2003). In fact, there has been an overlap between sociological and psychological theories, therefore, we will specify and synthesize social cognitive and learning theories, personality theory, social interactional theory and situational opportunities theory which are derived from the field of psychology in order to link them to white-collar crime. It is supposed that these categories can represent a synthesis of psychological concepts which help to explain white-collar crime (see Shoemaker, 2005; Siegel, Welsh and Senna, 2006; Moore, 2011). In addition to describing the content of the relevant theories briefly, the major focus of the review is on organizational ethical climate factor that can be studied with social cognitive and learning theories and person-organization interactions.

In the early 1960's theoretical perspectives were developed to explain deviance and unethical behaviors in organizations. Hartjen (1978, p.7 as cited in Kramer, 1985, p.473) points out that "behavioral definitions lead one to investigate rule-breaking activity; the labeling perspective leads one to study the responses of legal authorities." Besides, social definitions of crime have been proposed in the past in the discipline of criminology. Humanistic criminologists adopted a social-psychological view and usually defined crime as behavior which is "anti-social", "socially harmful", or "socially injurious" (Karamer, 1985, p.480). Some psychological theorists provided a framework for determining the correlational relationships between psychological variables (pathology) of an individual and that individual's criminal behavior. Other theorists tried to identify contingencies influencing non-conforming behavior, so-called deviant behavior. For example, Bandura (1969, p.2) viewed deviance from this perspective and posited that deviant act were the behaviors which an individual has learned from his/her environment or has met conflicting demands of self and the environment.

Fundamentally, learning theories have been argued in the literature since the 19th century that study the circumstances under which a response and a cue stimulus become connected (Miller and Dollard, 1941; Kazdin, 1989) Edward Thorndike (1898) is known as being the pioneer of learning principles and the first empirical studies of learning. Thorndike established the "Law of Effect", which indicates that the consequences following the behavior help learning. Parallel to the works of Thorndike, Ivan Pavlov was performing studies on a different type of learning (Pavlov, 1927/Repriented in 2010). Pavlov measured and conditioned salivation and other physiological reflexes in dogs to respond to neutral stimuli and that studies lead to the emergence of the theory of classical conditioning. On the other side, Skinner (1938) focused on the consequences of behavior rather than the environmental stimuli and stated that behavior had an influence on the environment. Skinner's (1963) works lead to another theory named as operant conditioning, which theorized that the frequency of behavior was determined by environmental consequences and can be modified by changing the environmental conditions. Subsequent theorists focused on internal determinants of behavior rather than external conditions. For example, Rotter (1954) proposed a "social learning theory" of personality that underlined the role of learned behavior and experience in the interaction of individual and environment determinants of behavior. Rotter (1954) posited that behavior resulted from the interaction of the individual and stimulus in environment and implied that behavior was determined by the individual and their environment. Thus, this theory suggested that the behavior was shaped by experiences. Following these implications, Bandura (1969) argued the principles of behavior modification through social learning theory. Later, social learning theory was labeled as social cognitive theory (Bandura, 1986) and addressed the interaction of (1) observation, symbolic representations and self-generated stimuli and self-imposed consequences, (2) environmental conditions and (3) behaviors in determining behavior (Bandura, 1986). Thus, this theory presents a model of causation consisting triadic reciprocal determinism of behavior, cognition and other personal factors, and environmental influences. According to Bandura (1989, p.2), all these elements operate as interacting determinants and impact each other bidirectionally. Basically, social learning theory claims that the conditions by which behavior is shaped include internal and external factors, and that behavior itself can be a determinant of future behavior (Bandura, 1969). In this way, when this theory is applied to organizational criminology, deviance, criminal behaviors or any delinquent behaviors can be the results of this causation model. As such, learning theory has contributed to understand criminal behaviors in the organizations.

Moreover, Sutherland (1940) proposed "the theory of differential association" within which he suggested that the criminal behavior occurred in a context of cultural conflict. Burgess and Akers (1966) expanded 'differential association theory' by integrating behavioral and social learning theories for explaining criminal behaviors and they defined the theory as "differential association reinforcement theory". Based on Skinner's operant conditioning theory, this theory suggested that besides the differential association with deviant coworkers, differential reinforcement of deviant behaviors was also needed to explain criminal behavior. Thus, criminal behaviors are learned from others in the organizations and due to the consequences of the criminal behavior, it is either reinforced or dissolved. In addition, according to Brightman's (2009) theory of white-collar crime, individuals who have deviant or unlawful moralities, values, and norms have more tendencies to learn criminal behaviors, hence certain 'characteristics' have roles in individuals' illegal behaviors.

As can be seen, the previous works proposed a number of factors that are linked to the white-collar offences through the implication of law of effect and social learning theory. Moreover, it has been argued that white-collar crime is seen in the context of societal and organizational pressures but it is still related to the individual's own choice and the impact of multiple personal factors such as age, experience, education, and certain personality characteristics. Younger managers are supposed to be most susceptible group because they seek achievement and success. Compared to younger managers, older executives have thoughtful decision-making and high experience, so they are supposed to engage in criminal acts less. On the other side, though there are indefinite associations with the level of education and experience level, several scholars indicated that males are suggested to be having more tendencies to engage in criminal conduct (E.g., Serin, Peters and Barbaree, 1990; Denno, 1997; Rogstad and Rogers, 2008; Dhingra and Boduszek, 2013; Gottschalk, 2013). Even so, it is difficult to propose a definite explanation related to the age, gender or experience factors, because it depends on the personal characteristics also.

Even so, it is difficult to propose a definite explanation related to the age factor, because it depends on the personal characteristics also.

In this respect, "The General Theory of Crime" postulates that self-control is an important factor in explaining white-collar crime (E.g., Parent, 2003; Blickle, Schlegel, Fassbender and Klein, 2006; Zahra, Priem and Rasheed, 2007; Price and Norris, 2009; Lugo, 2013). Gottfredson and Hirschi's (1990) "General Theory of Crime" which was developed based on Hirschi's (1969) "Social Control Theory" gained attention over the last decades for explaining white-collar crimes. Social Control Theory posited that criminal acts resulted when an individual's bond to society was weak or broken. Hirschi (1969) suggested that the four elements comprising the social bond are attachment, commitment, involvement and belief. Later, grounded on the propositions of Social Control Theory, Gottfredson and Hirschi (1990) suggested General Theory of Crime for explaining delinquency. Basically, these scholars asserted that all illegal activity or criminal acts were the manifestation of a single specific cause, which they called as "low self-control" (Parent, 2003, p.3). In the criminology and social psychology literature, Gottfredson and Hirschi's (1990) general theory of crime was utilized for empirical examinations of individuals' criminal behaviors, yet this theory has not been widely applied to examine and explain white-collar crime offenders in the organizations. Hirschi and Gottfredson (1993) addressed that their theory could be applied to white-collar crime and they believed their theory involves all types of crime. Supporting Hirschi and Gottfredson's (1993) approach, other scholars indicated that the nature of the white-collar offenders might negate self-control propositions, for these people are ambitious and appear to make well-calculated decisions (E.g., Reed and Yeager, 1996; Simpson and Piquero, 2002; Lugo, 2013). Besides, it has been argued that white-collar offenders displayed hedonistic tendencies and they had lower levels of self-control (Coleman, 1987; Blickle et al., 2006; Lugo, 2013). Within these arguments, it was stated that the executives who commit white collar crimes were are more impulsive, self-centered, and indifferent to the suffering of others, as well as being opportunistic. A low self-control person may not take him/herself from committing to crime in some cases and be suitable to participate in various illegal behaviors. Subsequently, Gottfredson and Hirschi's (1990) "General Theory of Crime" and "low self-control theory" are used for explaining how white-collar crime. In sum, white-collar crime may be influenced by self-control perception of the person, which means that self-control level is a potential source of criminal behavior leading individuals to commit to criminal acts.

Moreover, it has been argued that theories concerning white-collar crime have argued on the personality characteristics of offenders, societal and cultural values, industrial structure and expectations, and the organizational climate (E.g., Zahra, 2007; Bucy et al., 2008; Price and Norris, 2009). Coleman (1987), Weisburd, Waring and Chayet (1995), Wheeler (1992), Apel and Paternoster (2009), and Benson, Madensen and Eck (2009) have also suggested that white-collar crimes could be attributed to some certain psychological characteristics of managers and executives such as high risk taking behavior and love of risk, avoidance from failure, and a strong ambition or desire to gain material outcomes and achieve professional success. Within this apparoch, Feeley (2006, p.210) integrated personality and environment factors as being the causes of white-collar crime. Previously, Collins and Schmidt (1993) determined the significant impacts of personality characteristics and integrity on white-collar crime and Wheeler (1992) underlined that by criminological research white-collar offenders were characterized as risk seekers highly determined, strongly career, success and achievement oriented individuals. Besides, it was emphasized that such offenders had psychologically extrovert type of personality (Wheeler, 1992) and competitive personality (Feeley, 2006). Supporting that implication, Price and Norris (2009) stated that personality factors of high levels of extroversion and low levels of self-control were associated with offending among white-collars. In addition, profiles of the "disagreeable businessman" and the "neurotic" personality were other types of personality characteristics that were related to white-collar crime (Feeley, 2006). However, the problem is that these are also the basic personality characteristics of many successful managers. As Bussman (2003, p.9) implied, the relevant personality characteristics were seen as the criteria for "successful manager" in organizations, therefore, human resources management specialist value and seek for such characteristics in their recruitment and selection processes. In facts, it is known that managers should be creative, competitive, flexible, and extrovert for enhancing their organizations to achieve their goals. However, these personality characteristics become disadvantage when they are showed for not for the legal conducts but for their personal interests and illegal activities (Coleman, 1998, p.180). That is why a dilemma occurs and also why organizations are threatened by such crimes.

On the other hand, studies of characteristics of white-collar criminals have suggested that they are usually charismatic, have a need-to-control, have a tendency to bully subordinates, fear losing their status and position, have narcissistic tendencies, and lack integrity and a social conscience (Bucy et al., 2008). Collins and Schmidt (1993) performed a research study in order to find out the major personality characteristics of the white-collar criminals. They found that white-collar criminals had high tendency toward irresponsibility, were lack of dependability, and were not obedient toward the rules and social conventions. Blickle et al. (2006) conducted a research by evaluating hedonism, conscientiousness, narcissism, social desirability, and behavioral self-control to compare white-collars currently working in different organizations to white-collar criminals who formerly held similar positions. Their crimes included bribery, counterfeiting, embezzlement, forgery, fraud, fraudulent bankruptcy, smuggling, and tax evasion (Blickle et al., 2006). As a result of the research, white-collar crime had significant relationship with being male, low behavioral self-control, high hedonism, high narcissism, and high conscientiousness. The analyses were performed after controlling the social desirability among the participant groups.

Indeed, it is supposed that assessments of white-collar crime should not only include a micro-level assessment of white-collar crime but an examination of other environmental and situational variables that may have roles in white-collar offences. The question is, can self-control, personality or other person-specific factors adequately explain white-collar crime and which situational or organizational factors may also contribute to engage crimes among white-collars? Therefore, this study attempts to contribute to the literature by evaluating various levels of antecedents linked to white-collar crime intentions by also considering the influences of organizational ethical climate and situational opportunities for rule bending.

In this context, it is seen that "situational opportunity theories of crime" (Wilcox and Cullen, 2018) have been studied as one of the theories explaining white-collar crimes. Historically speaking, criminological theory tends to specify the various sources of criminal motivation without focusing on the opportunity issue to commit to crime in particular situations. For all that, it is seen that over the past decades, perspectives addressing the situational opportunity have gained importance in the criminological research. By using a human ecological perspective (Hawley, 1950), the pioneering authors Cohen and Felson (1979) and Felson (1994, 2017) implied that crime events were the outcome of the intersection in time and space of a motivated offender, an attractive target, and a lack of capable guardianship. Hence, it was argued that offender motivation was a given and instead focused on opportunity in the form of offenders' access to suitable, insufficiently guarded targets. Thus, Cohen and Felson's (1979) study has been a weighty work for understanding the situational opportunity tradition in explain white-collar crimes. Subsequently, Felson and Clarke (1998) indicated that organizational opportunity made the thief and elimination of the opportunities would be effective in crime prevention.

It has been argued that there are several organization-specific factors that contribute to the incidence of white-collar crime (Langton and Leeper-Piquero, 2007). According to Felson and Clarke (1998), every crime is an intersection of two factors in time and space: an offender's motivation to commit a crime and the opportunity to carry out the desired act in a particular situation. Traditional criminology focuses on the first factor, the motivation or propensity (including personality characteristics) to offend. Thus, theories of crime tend to be theories of motivation, which assume that variations in motivation or controls on motivations explain variations in criminal behavior, whether through individual or ecological differences. Clarke and Felson (2011) identified situational opportunity as a particular type of criminology or and as a reinforcer of organizational crimes. Situational opportunity theories are usually called as environmental criminology because they focus on the structure of the physical and social environment that may influence the availability of criminal opportunities (Bottoms, 1994). Supporting this view, Wilcox, Sullivan, Jones and van Gelder (2014, p.880) proposed an integrated approach to victimization and offending by indicating the roles of personality and opportunity). Another associated term is crime science (Clarke, 2010) that studies the crime events and the reasons behind the criminal acts. This line of study is also referred to as crime-event criminology, which explicitly denotes the focus on incidents and situational factors, rather than using traditional criminology's focus on the causes of criminal behavior (Sacco and Kennedy, 2002; Wilcox and Gialopsos 2015). A number of studies have also addressed the linkage between general multilevel opportunity and crime events in organizations (E.g., Wilcox, Gialopsos and Land, 2013; Benson and Simpson, 2015; Tillyer, 2015). Apel and Paternoster (2009) posited that the ethical climate of an organization has a causal impact on the occurrence of white-collar crime and supported the view which suggested the linkage between organizational culture and crime.

As further, criminologists studying organizational and white-collar offences have addressed that a considerable component of these crime events was the organization's culture or ethical climate. An organization provides its employees with a set of normative guidelines that prescribe unethical or illegal behavior under certain conditions, and also establish a stock of incentives and sanctions intended to secure compliance with these norms. With that respect, it was suggested that not only the characteristics of white-collar individuals but also the characteristics of the organizations or situations within which individuals work have roles in criminal conducts (Apel and Paternoster, 2009, p.20). Supporting this view, Piquero, Exum and Simpson (2005) indicated that the corporate climate effected individuals to engage corporate crime. A number of scholars have implied that organizations should have responsibilities for their employees' unethical and illegal behavior since they may precede the background antecedents for such criminal acts (E.g., Victor and Cullen, 1988; Kaptain, 2011; Clarke and Felson, 2011; Wells, 2014). It was also stated that a relevant organizational-level predictor of unethical behavior in organizations is the culture (Jha and Panda 2017; Kaptein 2011) or ethical climate of an organization (Victor and Cullen 1988). A meta-analysis reported that the ethical climate of the organization was the particularly relevant organizational factor explaining a wide range of unethical decisions of white-collars (Peterson, 2002; Kish-Gephart, Harrison and Trevino, 2010). Moreover, following that view, a recent study of Gorsira et al. (2018) examined corruption in organizations with a focus on the effects of individual motives and ethical climate. In their study, Gorsira et al. (2018) investigated whether the ethical climate of organizations is related to corruption, and if so, whether it affects corruption through individual motives for corruption. Their findings showed that public and private sector employees who perceived their organizational climate as more egoistic and less ethical had higher intention to engage in corruption. This relationship was fully mediated by individual motives, specifically by personal and social norms on corruption. These results indicated that employees who perceived their organization's ethical climate as more egoistic and less ethical experience weaker personal and social norms to refrain from corruption, making them to have higher tendency to corruption. Accordingly, as this brief review suggests, there are a number of organizational level theories that have been applied to the study and understanding of white-collar crime and there is empirical support for the ethical climate's role in exploring white-collar crime. Thus, the following section will review insights related to the roles of business ethics, ethical climate and rule bending in explaining why some individuals engage in white-collar crime.

THE IMPACT OF ETHICAL CLIMATE ON WHITE-COLLAR RULE CRIME AND RULE BENDING

A Review of Ethics and Business Ethics

Ethics is a general term for what is often described as the "science (study) of morality". In philosophy, ethical behavior is that which is "good" or "right." According to John Rawls (1971), "ethics is justice: the principles that all rational human beings would select to govern social behavior if they knew that the rules could potentially apply to themselves". Machan (1999) defines ethics "a controversial branch of philosophy, addressing the questions 'How should one act?' or "What standards of conduct guide a good human life?" (Machan, 1999, p.7). According to Buller, Kohls, and Anderson (1991, p.768) ethics include both "the moral codes and values used in the reasoning process as well as the decisions and behaviors that result from the process". Thiroux (1998) stated that ethics is about controlling human behavior as to what is right and wrong (Cited in Yücel and Çiftci, 2012, p.152). Business ethics is the ethical reflection of a business towards its behaviors and their impacts (Epstein, 1989). This reflection can be shown in its emphasis of corporate values upon integrity, accountability, honesty, trust, fairness, responsibility, cooperation, mutuality, professionalism and open communication (Schwartz, 2005; Su, 2014).

Business ethics means considering the rules, regulations, and expectations of the organization as well as acting with fairly with the principles of morality, the policies of the organization, and concerns for the requirement and wellbeing of others. De George (1999) defined business ethics as a movement or as part of the discipline of ethics. Business ethics as considered part of the general field of ethics is defined by the interaction of ethics and business (De George, 1999, p. 23). Cavico and Mujtaba (2005) consider business ethics "a specialized study of moral right and wrong, concentrating on the use of ethical principles in business (Cavico and Mujtaba, 2005, p.3).

The business ethics literature has demonstrated that the communication of values and norms is decisive in crime prevention. From a criminological and general social science viewpoint, business ethics are considered to be especially effective in this regard. It is therefore appropriate that organizations have developed a growing awareness of the need to implement business ethics since the 1980s. Surveys have shown that numerous organizations from all over the world consider such ethics programs to be effective in preventing crime. However, the potential of business ethics is not fully exploited when ethical guidelines only take abstract values into account like responsibility, integrity, compliance, sustainability, transparency, human rights, equal treatment, fairness or personal respect – as has been shown for many companies (Bussman, 2003, p.23). When the explicit norms of a criminal law are incorporated into the guidelines, the effectiveness of business ethics definitely increases. A further requirement is the implementation of business ethic guidelines into the everyday routines of a company if they are to become more than a "law in the books". Norms, and that includes business ethics, can act as a channel to encourage communication about values and concrete legal limits. They need to be "referred to" constantly in all appropriate contexts – they need to be "lived" and become part of the corporate culture if they are to be incorporated into the management's consciousness. The inclusion of such topics in management training programmes are stated to be especially effective in enhancing much more ethical business processes.

Indeed, every individuals or white-collars at work have their own sets of ethical and personal values which may or may not fit with organizational values and morality. Thus, it is found meaningful to examine what makes the difference among white-collars to engage in crime and misconduct including the individual differences and ethical climate perceptions. As we have underlined the role of situational opportunities and other contextual and individual factors that influence white-collar crime by focusing on the psychological and social cognitive theories, ethical climate is also seen as a part of background for unethical behaviors. Besides, serving as a situational opportunity and vicarious learning, ethical climate aspects may influence the severity of white-collars' rule bending behaviors and organizational crimes. Therefore, the following part of the study will provide conceptual and empirical discussions for evaluating the linkages between ethical climate and white-collar crimes.

Ethical Climate and Rule Bending

An organization's ethical climate affects which issues organization members consider ethically relevant, whose interests they consider when deciding on moral issues, and which ethical criteria they use to determine what constitutes the 'right behavior' (Victor and Cullen 1988; Martin and Cullen, 2006). As such, ethical climate refers to the most commonly used types of moral reasoning, rather than to the content of decisions (Victor and Cullen, 1988). The assumption underlying the concept of ethical climate is that members of an organization share, at least to some extent, a form of moral reasoning (Gorsira et al., 2018). Fundamentally, the concept of organizational ethical climate was developed by Victor and Cullen (1988). The ethical climate in an organization has been described as 'the shared perceptions of what ethically correct behavior is and how ethical issues should be handled' (Victor and Cullen, 1987, pp.51-52). Indeed, earlier research rests heavily on a body of work on organizational ethical climates by Victor and Cullen (1987, 1988) and Cullen, Victor and Bronson (1993). They developed the ethical climate type classification named as 'ethical climate typology,' and they developed 'Ethical Climate Questionnaire' (ECQ). That typology and questionnaire has been widely adopted in the extant ethical climate literature. The below Table 1 presents Victor and Cullen's (1988) nine theoretical ethical climate types according to a two-dimensional typology.

Table 1. Two-Dimensional Typology of Victor and Cullen (1988)

Victor and Cullen's Table	Individual Locus	Local Locus	Cosmopolitan Locus
Egoism	Self-Interest	Company Profit	Efficiency
Benevolence	Friendship	Team Interest	Social Responsibility
Principle	Personal Morality	Company Rules and Procedures	Laws and Professional Codes

Source: Victor and Cullen (1988)

As can be seen in Table 1, their category of individual represented the individual's referencing to their internal norms; their category of local represented the individual's referencing to the organization; and their category of cosmopolitan represented the individual's referencing to the norms of the profession or law. Ethical egoism is the view that individuals should always act in a way that best serves their self-interest. This view often distinguishes between the rational pursuit of long-term interest and a hedonistic pursuit of short-term pleasure. Egoism may be connoted pejoratively as materialism or selfishness. In the organizational context; however, theorists have described egoistic organizations as having a practical or pragmatic orientation (Webber, 2007, p.569). Benevolence means making a decision that maximizes mutual or joint interest, and principle refers to making a decision by complying with deontological (duty and obligation) standards. The second dimension represents the locus of analysis used as a reference point in ethical decisions. The individual level refers to the use of the self as referent for moral reasoning. This concept refers to employee's personal norms or the pursuit of self-interest as a reference in ethical decision making. The local level, the most common referent group, is the organization. Local indicates primary reference groups are within the organization, for instance officemates, subordinates or team members. Finally, the cosmopolitan level refers to sources of professional association. It means reference groups are external to the organization such as professional bodies, enforcement agencies and state laws or regulations. Meanwhile, the interaction of these two dimensions has resulted in five organizational ethical climate (caring, law and code, rules, instrumental and independence), illustrated in Table 2.

"Caring" was characterized as the degree to which the workplace is characterized by workers sincerely interested in well-being of each other. It was indicated that individuals in caring climate are interested in the well-being of other constituencies and in law and code climate, organizational members are expected to comply with profession code and state regulations (Wimbush, Shepard and Markham, 1997; Talha, Sallehhuddin, Masoud and Said, 2013). "Law and Code" represented the degree to which employees strictly adhere to profession and government regulations and codes". The other component was the "Rules" which was described as the degree to which employees strictly adhere to their organization or subunit's rules and mandates. Individuals in rules climate are expected to comply with rules and procedures of the organization. "Instrumental" component was the degree to which employees are driven by self-interest. It is mentioned that individuals of instrumental climate try to maximize their self-interests more than interest of others who may be affected by their decisions (Talha et al., 2013). Finally "Independence" was defined as the degree to which employees are expected to be guided by their personal moral beliefs (Victor and Cullen, 1988).

A few researches with organizational leaders and white-collar employees focus considered how ethical climate might impact organizational behavior and ethical misconduct including rule bending and multi-level crimes. Organizational rules and procedures are considered imperative for effectively

Table 2. The Ethical Climate Typology of Victor and Cullen (1988)

		Locus of Analysis		
		Individual	*Local*	*Cosmopolitan*
Ethical Criterion	*Egoism*	Instrumental		Caring
	Benevolence		Caring	
	Principle	Independence	Rules	Law and Codes

Source: Victor and Cullen (1988)

managed organizations (Tyler and Blader, 2005). Oberfield (2009) points out that rules serve as a way for white-collars to ensure that policy is implemented consistently; however, rule bending may occur because it is perceived necessary for job performance (Sekerka and Zolin, 2007, p.226). Rule bending is "a willingness to depart from rules and procedures" (DeHart-Davis, 2007, p.893) and "involves a decision to go around the formally stated obligations by not fully following a rule, requirement, procedure or specification" (Sekerka and Zolin, 2007, p.228). Sekerka and Zolin (2007) told that rule bending is not to be seen as the same as rule breaking: bending a rule indicates some lack of adherence to a rule as opposed to outright violation. They also stated that rule bending may occur ——openly or through quiet, discrete, or even secret circumvention. For the purposes of this study, rule bending and rule breaking are regarded as same concepts and they are suggested to be a part of organizational crimes among white-collars.

Important to note here is that rule bending is a conscious decision and rule benders knowingly violate procedure, and thus rule bending is conceptualized as intentional behavior (DeHart-Davis, 2007, p.894). Rules may be bent for various reasons, such as a pressure to have high performance at work (Sekerka and Zolin, 2007) or value conflicts might also trigger rule bending. A white-collar may see the spirit of a rule or law is better upheld with some bending of a rule (Sekerka and Zolin, 2007). These value conflicts as a reason to bend rules indicates that rule bending may have an ethical dimension to it. In addition, ethical climate, as a dimension of work climate, includes a socialization process (Victor and Cullen, 1987, p.51). In other words, it can be said that employees learn ethical climate and adapt to it over time. Organizational socialization also accounts for changes in rule following and bending behaviors over time (Oberfield, 2009). In this light, rule bending could be seen as one form of organizational dissent (O'Leary, 2007; Borry, 2011). Further, the law and code climate consists of a focus on extra-organizational laws and professional codes as bases for ethical decision making. In other words, white-collars in a law and code climate look to government rules or professional conventions to resolve dilemmas ethically. Some organizations may have strong rules and law-and-code climates because their activities are so often constrained by outside sources, such as unions, federal law, executive orders, and professional associations (Dryburgh 2009, p.159). Since law and code provide a standard by which to behave or abide, they are mechanisms to control white-collar behavior. The law and regulation that public employees must employ in their work is highly formal. According to DeHart-Davis (2007), higher levels of organizational formalization—the extent to which they are written—has been linked to less rule bending. As such, it is expected that the law and code aspects of ethical climate will be negatively related to white-collar rule bending behaviors and crimes.

With that respect, ethical climate has the potential to influence rule bending behavior of white-collars because of the decisional nature of rule bending. Yet, white-collars' ethical behaviors can be also be positively influenced by the creation of a positive ethical environment within the organization rather than relying on the strength of each white-collar's ethical values (Kim and Miller, 2008). It makes sense to think that any component of organizational work climate –'ethical climate'- may have an influence rule bending behavior and organizational crimes among white-collars. This situation can be explained by social learning theory and social cognitive view as discussed previously. Thus, we draw on social learning theory (Bandura, 1977, 1986) to explain the effects of ethical climate on white-collar criminals' offenses since social learning theory posits that individuals learn appropriate ways to act through a role-modeling process by observing the behaviors of others. Social learning theory further suggests that individuals are likely to pay attention to and emulate behaviors from credible and attractive role models they see in their both physical and psychological environment. In addition to direct observation, white-collars are influenced by their supervisors or peer groups because he/she has the power to delve out both punishments and rewards for ethical and unethical behavior. Social learning theory also allows for individuals to learn vicariously through the experiences of those around them (This surrounding can be regarded as ethical climate). Through perceiving ethical climate, white-collars learn what is expected of them in terms of appropriate behavior not only through their own experience, but also by observing others and what happens to them (Bandura, 1986). In sum, ethical climate perceptions signal to white-collars that doing the right thing is expected, encouraged, and valued. In turn, white-collars are more likely to perceive an ethical organizational environment if they observe and reinforce ethical behaviors around them. Additionally, it is suggested that ethical climate will be related to white-collar misconduct within organizations by drawing on social information processing theory (SIPT) (Salancik and Pfeffer, 1978). SIPT suggests that organizational members seek for cues in their environment to characterize their work environment and to understand appropriate ways to behave. Thus, ethical climates can be a cue to enable white-collars know what types of ethical or unethical behaviors are acceptable or unacceptable in the organization. The social environment or ethical climate in this case, provides information to white-collars as to the appropriateness of behavior they see in the work environment. Therefore, organizational climates may provide white-collars to see and understand the group norms and the structure of appropriate behavior that is accepted in the organization. Therefore, if ethical climate is higher in emphasizing ethical actions, white-collars will be less likely to exhibit unethical behaviors and crime. Extant studies have examined the consequences of ethical climate on specific ethical outcomes, such as unethical acts, deviant behaviors, and organizational crimes. These studies include both field and lab studies and overall show strong support that ethical work climates are linked to white-collar crimes and unethical behaviors in organizations (See Mayer et al., 2010). For instance, Martin and Cullen (2006) conducted a meta-analysis on ethical climates and their results suggest that positive ethical climates are negatively related to dysfunctional organizational behavior. Bartels, Harrick, Martell and Strickland (1998) found that ethical climate was negatively related to ethical violations among managers. Wimbush et al. (1997) found that caring climates and law and code climates were negatively related to stealing and lying behaviors. Further, instrumental climates were positively related to being an accomplice. Peterson (2002) stated that organizational deviance was lower in ethical caring climates. Thus, it is suggested that the more positively perceived rules, codes and law in the organization may lead to less misbehavior and crimes among white-collars. Consequently, it is argued that there is strong support that ethical climates have an effect on white-collar crimes and misbehaviors in organizations.

CONCLUSION

Over the past years, the extant literature on organizational criminology has demonstrated that the effect of white-collar crime is not merely limited to economic harm, but also environmental and societal damages. White-collar crime can produce unsafe working environments, diminished organizational reputation, increasing corruptions, high levels of ecological and environmental damages, along with distributing unsafe products and business transactions to all types of stakeholders. In addition, it was stated that white-collar crimes have been costing the world population billions of dollars annually (Feeley, 2006; Soley, 2017). Basically, corporate criminals have become a reality in numerous organizations including public, private and international corporations. Even though criminal laws have been developed as a mechanism for responding to individual wrongdoing in organizations, preveiling white-collar crime still remains as an essential problem. Despite the costs and the media portrayal of white-collar crime with cases in numerous sectors and companies in all over the world, it was observed that the study of white-collar crime remains an under-developed area of scholarship in organizational behavior and management fields. In terms of the literature, much of the focus is placed either on macro-level assessments of white-collar crime in relation to capitalist pressures and the need to secure profit in a competitive economy (Vaughan, 1981, 1992; Barnett, 1981; Clinard and Yeager, 1980) or on micro-level or psychological assessments of criminals in terms of their personality variables and perceived self-control. Other theories focus on the organization specific factors more directly, attempting to reveal what situational or organizational factors influence the behavior of individuals and the severity of white-collar offenses. In line with this view, many scholars have also proposed a link between an organization's ethical climate and, specifically, corruption and white-collar crime (Pinto, Leana and Pil, 2008; Grieger 2006; Simha and Cullen 2012; Hess, 2015; Martin, Johnson and Cullen, 2009). More specifically, the study of Stachowicz-Stanusch and Simha (2013) found support for a relationship between an egoistic climate and corruption in organizations.

As mentioned previously, referring to a crime committed by a white-collar, the literature suggests that the major causes of prevalence of white collar crimes are peer support, corporate culture, lack of accountability and lack of reporting by pointing out the social cognitive and learning theories (E.g., Mayer, Kuenzi and Greenbaum, 2010; Moore, 2011; Bashir et al., 2011). It is known that the performance of the organizations is greatly influenced by the culture of the organization. Thus, understanding of the organization culture is very important for effective understanding of the organizational performance (Wilkins and Ouchi, 1983; Sorensen, 2002). Supporting this knowledge, Baucus and Near (1991) claimed that the criminal behavior of the white-collars can be due to the influence of organization's culture. Besides, Near and Miceli (1995) stated that the organizations that have a culture of rectifying the criminal behavior mostly try to maintain the circumstances that support change. Therefore, it is suggested that if the culture of the organization is unhealthy, it might give rise to deviant behavior among white-collars.

There is conceptual and empirical research that suggests the ethical work environment influences white-collar crimes. Therefore, a strong ethical model at the company level would be of value to induce the desired employee ethical outcome within the organization. A long with that view, this study emphasized that organizational ethical climate factor can contribute to rule bending in organizations and white-collar crime. This research is qualitative and descriptive in nature, and provides an assessment of theoretical explanations for the identified factors previously associated with white-collar crime. Specifically, this study suggests that a better way to understand organization-related factors that contribute to white-collar crime is through an understanding of ethical climate and how individuals socially learn and engage unethical behaviors in the organization.

In line with the argument of this study, it is suggested that an organization should focus on creating an appropriate ethical climate that reinforces the ethical behavior of its employees. As Gorsira et al. (2018) have implied, both organizational factors and individual motives should be understood to examine organizational corruption. Buchholz and Rosenthal (1998, p.263) implied that business ethics is a certain requirement that must be applied by managers and other employees. Schwartz (2005) asserted that an ethical business also cares about stakeholders that might be impacted by its behaviors and these stakeholders include employees, shareholders, customers, suppliers, community and society as a whole (Su, 2014, p.88). It is suggested that in order to decrease and eliminate white-collar criminal acts, organizations should develop measures that strengthen their ethical climate and encourage ethical decision-making among individuals. Organizations should also develop strong organizational values and social norms to refrain from misconduct. In addition, the code of conducts for eliminating rule bending should be well established and reinforced through organizational learning and training programmes. It should be noted that the criminal behavior of the workforce can be due to the influence of organization's culture and climate (Baucus and Near, 1991).

Bussman (2003) also argued that "the opportunity creates the offender", therefore, intensive controlling measures may reduce criminal opportunities. The criminological research also revealed that increased awareness and a greater number of crime prevention measures in organizations lead to a better rate of detection of white-collar crimes. However, even control measures necessarily lead to a decrease in the unethical acts in the organization, further, organizations should develop and maintain a strong ethical climate for preventing cheating environment and reinforcing trust, morality, benevolence and integrity among organizational members. Accordingly, we suggest that white-collar crime prevention lays in the impact of values through a strong sense of ethical climate. Criminological research has indicated that an acceptance of values and norms counteracts the attraction and seduction of criminal options; and, often, opportunities are even not perceived. For these reasons, both intensive controlling measures and development of strong ethical climate should be handled cautiously and with awareness. Moreover, protective factors can be developed by the organizations involving a reliable auditing system, a strong independent board of directors with monitoring functions, outside qualified directors and working committees, training programmes for ethical conduct, an organizational culture stressing ethical conduct, and enhancing ethical and socially responsible leadership within the organization (McBarnet, 2006; Bucy et.al., 2008; Price and Norris, 2009).

Ultimately, for organizations, constituting an ethical climate means building a culture which emphasizes the spirit of law, rules, collaboration and collective interest within the organization rather than the sanctions or impositions of the rules. An ethical climate should be developed to clearly articulate a "statement of the underlying principles" to guide interpretation among each employees and managers. Indeed, the code of conduct should also function as a self-preservation mechanism and as a reinforcer of positive and ethical behaviors in the organization. It is recommended for the organizations to emphasize the context in which the rule and its consequences exist and to explain the crucial importance of engaging ethical acts rather than emphasizing the punitive outcomes of rule bending. Consistent with that, organizations should recognize the ethical education and rewarding mechanisms and develop policies to minimize the crimes. Further, it is suggested that the organizations could dispose procedures that provide positive and/or corrective feedback to managers as well as clarifying the strength of ethical climate.

In conclusion, even this study solely cannot provide sufficient solutions to the problems of white-collar crime; the attempt of examining multilevel theoretical approaches for organizational criminology is seen remarkable. Presently, out of a few of scholars analyzing the relationship between organizational business ethics and white-collar crime, there is little research done solely to the role of the ethical climate in the development of rule bending and white-collar crime. What makes this study significant is that this specific topic is dedicated to a discussion regarding both the psychology of the white-collar criminals and the organizational surrounding. Thus, this study may provide noteworthy implications for integrating theoretical explanations of white-collar crime and may make a contribution to the scholarly discussion surrounding white-collar crime as a whole.

REFERENCES

Alalehto, T. (2015). White collar criminals: The state of knowledge. *The Open Criminology Journal, 8*(1), 28–35. doi:10.2174/1874917801508010028

Albanese, J. S. (1984). Corporate criminology: Explaining deviance of business and political organizations. *Journal of Criminal Justice, 12*(1), 11–19. doi:10.1016/0047-2352(84)90003-5

Apel, R., & Paternoster, R. (2009). Understanding "criminogenic" corporate culture: What white-collar crime researchers can learn from studies of the adolescent employment–crime relationship. In S. S. Simpson & D. Weisburd (Eds.), *The Criminology of White-Collar Crime* (pp. 15–33). New York: Springer. doi:10.1007/978-0-387-09502-8_2

Baird, J. E., & Zelin, R. C. (2009, Winter). An examination of the impact of obedience pressure on perceptions of fraudulent acts and the likelihood of committing occupational fraud. *Journal of Forensic Studies in Accounting and Business*, 1-14.

Bandura, A. (1969). *Principles of behavior modification*. New York: Holt, Rinehart, and Winston.

Bandura, A. (1977). Self-efficacy: Toward a unifying theory of behavioral change. *Psychological Review, 84*(2), 191–209. doi:10.1037/0033-295X.84.2.191 PMID:847061

Bandura, A. (1986). *Social foundations of thought and action: A social cognitive theory*. Englewood Cliffs, NJ: Prentice-Hall Inc.

Bandura, A. (1989). Human agency in social cognitive theory. *The American Psychologist, 44*(9), 1175–1184. doi:10.1037/0003-066X.44.9.1175 PMID:2782727

Barnett, H. C. (1981). Corporate capitalism, corporate crime. *Crime and Delinquency, 27*(1), 4–23. doi:10.1177/001112878102700102

Bartels, K. K., Harrick, E., Martell, K., & Strickland, D. (1998). The relationship between ethical climate and ethical problems within human resource management. *Journal of Business Ethics, 17*(7), 799–804. doi:10.1023/A:1005817401688

Bashir, S., Shahzad, K., Abbass, M., Abbass, N., & Saeed, S. (2011). Antecedents of white collar crime in organizations: A literature review. *African Journal of Business Management, 5*(35), 13359–13363. doi:10.5897/ajbmx11.008

Baucus, M. S., & Near, J. P. (1991). Can illegal corporate behavior be predicted? An event history analysis. *Academy of Management Journal, 34*(1), 9–36. doi:10.2307/256300

Benson, M. L., Madensen, T. D., & Eck, J. E. (2009). White-collar crime from an opportunity perspective. In S. S. Simpson & D. Weisburd (Eds.), *The Criminology of White-Collar Crime* (pp. 175–193). New York: Springer. doi:10.1007/978-0-387-09502-8_9

Benson, M. L., & Simpson, S. S. (2015). *Understanding white-collar crime: An opportunity perspective*. New York: Routledge.

Blickle, G., Schlegel, A., Fassbender, P., & Klein, U. (2006). Some personality correlates of business white-collar crime. *Applied Psychology*, *55*(2), 220–233. doi:10.1111/j.1464-0597.2006.00226.x

Bookman, Z. (2008). Convergences and omissions in reporting corporate and white collar crime. *DePaul Business & Commercial Law Journal*, *6*(3), 347–392.

Borry, E. L. (2011). Ethical climate in the public sector: Its influence on rule bending. In *Public Management Research Conference*, New York: Maxwell School, Syracuse University.

Borry, E. L. (2017). Ethical climate and rule bending: How organizational norms contribute to unintended rule consequences. *Public Administration*, *95*(1), 78–96. doi:10.1111/padm.12304

Bottoms, A. R. (1994). Environmental criminology. In M. Maguire, R. Morgan, & R. Reiner (Eds.), *The Oxford Handbook of Criminology* (pp. 585–656). Oxford, UK: Clarendon Press.

Brightman, H. J. (2009). *Today's white-collar crime: Legal, investigative, and theoretical perspectives*. New York: Routledge.

Buchholz, R. A., & Rosenthal, S. B. (1998). *Business ethics: The pragmatic path beyond principles to process*. Upper Saddle River, NJ: Prentice Hall.

Bucy, P. H., Formby, E. P., Raspanti, M. S., & Rooney, K. E. (2008). Why do they do it: The motives, mores, and character of white collar criminals. *John's Law Review.*, *82*, 401–422.

Buller, P. F., Kohls, J. J., & Anderson, K. S. (1991). The challenge of global ethics. *Journal of Business Ethics*, *10*(10), 767–775. doi:10.1007/BF00705711

Burgess, R. L., & Akers, R. L. (1966). A differential association-reinforcement theory of criminal behavior. *Social Problems*, *14*(2), 128–147. doi:10.2307/798612

Bussmann, K. D. (2003). Causes of economic crime and the impact of values: business ethics as a crime prevention measure. *Swiss Conference on Coping with Economic Crime. Zúrich: Risks and Strategies*, 1-16.

Cavico, F. J., & Mujtaba, B. (2005). *Business ethics: Transcending requirements through moral leadership*. Boston: Pearson Custom Publishing.

Clarke, M., & Wheeler, S. (1990). *Business crime: Its nature and control*. Cambridge, UK: Polity Press.

Clarke, R. V. (2010). *Crime science*. Thousand Oaks, CA: SAGE Publications. doi:10.4135/9781446200926.n15

Clarke, R. V., & Felson, M. (2011). The Origins of American Criminology. In Advances in Criminological Theory: Vol. 16. The origins of the routine activity approach and situational crime prevention (pp. 245–260). Academic Press.

Clinard, M., & Yeager, P. (1980). Corporate crime: The first comprehensive account of illegal practices among America's top corporations. *Michigan Law Review*, *80*(4), 978–980. doi:10.2307/1288268

Cohen, L. E., & Felson, M. (1979). On estimating the social costs of national economic policy: A critical examination of the Brenner study. *Social Indicators Research*, *6*(2), 251–259. doi:10.1007/BF00343977

Coleman, J. W. (1987). Toward an integrated theory of white-collar crime. *American Journal of Sociology, 93*(2), 406–439. doi:10.1086/228750

Coleman, J. W. (1998). *The criminal elite: Understanding white-collar crime*. New York: St. Martin's Press.

Collins, J. M., & Schmidt, F. L. (1993). Personality, integrity, and white-collar crime: A construct validity study. *Personnel Psychology, 46*(2), 295–311. doi:10.1111/j.1744-6570.1993.tb00875.x

Croall, H. (2001). *Understanding white collar crime*. New York: McGraw-Hill Education.

Cullen, J. B., Victor, B., & Bronson, J. W. (1993). The ethical climate questionnaire: An assessment of its development and validity. *Psychological Reports, 73*(2), 667–674. doi:10.2466/pr0.1993.73.2.667 PMID:8488245

De George, R. T. (1999). *Business ethics*. Prentice Hall.

DeHart-Davis, L. (2007). The unbureaucratic personality. *Public Administration Review, 67*(5), 892–903. doi:10.1111/j.1540-6210.2007.00776.x

Denno, D. W. (1997). Gender differences in biological and sociological predictors of crime. *Vermont Law Review, 22*, 305–325.

Dhingra, K., & Boduszek, D. (2013). Psychopathy and criminal behaviour: A psychosocial research perspective. *Journal of Criminal Psychology, 3*(2), 83–107. doi:10.1108/JCP-06-2013-0014

Dodge, M. (2009). *Women and white-collar crime*. Upper Saddle River, NJ: Prentice Hall.

Edelhertz, H., & Overcast, T. D. (Eds.). (1982). *White-collar crime: An agenda for research*. Lexington, MA: Lexington Books.

Feeley, D. (2006). Personality, environment, and the causes of white-collar crime. *Law and Psychology Review, 30*, 201–224.

Felson, M. (1994). *Crime and everyday life: Insight and implications for society*. Thousand Oaks, CA: Pine.

Felson, M. (2017). Linking criminal choices, routine activities, informal control, and criminal outcomes. In D. B. Cornish & R. V. Clarke (Eds.), *The reasoning criminal* (pp. 119–128). Routledge.

Felson, M., & Clarke, R. V. (1998). Opportunity makes the thief. *Police Research Series, 98*, 1-16.

Friedrichs, D. O. (2009). *Trusted criminals: White collar crime in contemporary society*. Cengage Learning.

Girla, L., & Rub, J. (2015). Psychological portrait of the white-collar offender: Decision-making and rational choice. *Revista Naţională de Drept*, (9), 179-191.

Gorsira, M., Steg, L., Denkers, A., & Huisman, W. (2018). Corruption in Organizations: Ethical Climate and Individual Motives. *Administrative Sciences, 8*(1), 1–19. doi:10.3390/admsci8010004

Gottfredson, M. R., & Hirschi, T. (1990). *A general theory of crime*. Stanford University Press.

Gottschalk, P. (2011). Actions on suspicion of white-collar crime in business organizations: An empirical study of intended responses by Chief financial officers. *Professional Issues in Criminal Justice*, *6*(1-2), 41–51.

Gottschalk, P. (2013). Empirical differences in crime categories by white-collar criminals. *International Letters of Social and Humanistic Sciences*, *5*, 17–26. doi:10.18052/www.scipress.com/ILSHS.5.17

Grieger, J. (2006). *Corruption in organizations-Some outlines for research* (Working Paper). Department of Economics and Social Sciences, University of Wuppertal.

Hartjen, C. A. (1978). *Crime and criminalization*. Praeger Publishers.

Hasnas, J. (2005). Ethics and the problem of white collar crime. *The American University Law Review*, *54*(3), 579–660.

Hawley, A. (1950). *Human Ecology: A Theory of Community Structure*. New York: Ronald Press.

Hess, D. (2015). Ethical infrastructure and evidence-based corporate compliance and ethics programs: Policy implications from the empirical evidence. *NYUJL & Business*, *12*, 317–334.

Hirschi, T. (1969). A control theory of delinquency. *Criminology theory: Selected Classic Readings*, 289-305.

Hirschi, T., & Gottfredson, M. (1993). Commentary: Testing the general theory of crime. *Journal of Research in Crime and Delinquency*, *30*(1), 47–54. doi:10.1177/0022427893030001004

Hoefnagels, G. P. (1973). Criminology: its definition, nature and subfields. In *The other side of criminology*. Dordrecht, The Netherlands: Springer. doi:10.1007/978-94-017-4495-9_3

Jha, C., & Panda, B. (2017). Individualism and corruption: A cross-country analysis. *Economic Papers: A Journal of Applied Economics and Policy, 36*, 60–74.

Jones, H. (1965). *Crime and the penal system*. University Tutorial Press.

Kaptein, M. (2011). Understanding unethical behavior by unraveling ethical culture. *Human Relations*, *64*(6), 843–869. doi:10.1177/0018726710390536

Kazdin, A. (1989). *Behavior modification in applied settings*. Pacific Grove, CA: Brooks/Cole Publishing.

Kim, N. Y., & Miller, G. (2008). Perceptions of the ethical climate in the Korean tourism industry. *Journal of Business Ethics*, *82*(4), 941–954. doi:10.100710551-007-9604-0

Kish-Gephart, J. J., Harrison, D. A., & Trevino, L. K. (2010). Bad apples, bad cases, and bad barrels: Meta-analytic evidence about sources of unethical decisions at work. *The Journal of Applied Psychology*, *95*(1), 1–16. doi:10.1037/a0017103 PMID:20085404

Kramer, R. C. (1985). Defining the concept of crime: A humanistic perspective. *Journal of Sociology and Social Welfare*, *12*, 469–485.

Langton, L., & Piquero, N. L. (2007). Can general strain theory explain white-collar crime? A preliminary investigation of the relationship between strain and select white-collar offenses. *Journal of Criminal Justice*, *35*(1), 1–15. doi:10.1016/j.jcrimjus.2006.11.011

Lugo, M. A. (2013). *Self-control, attitudinal beliefs, and white-collar crime intentions* (Unpublished Doctoral Dissertation). University of South Florida.

Machan, T. R. (1999). Business ethics in a free society. *A Companion to Business Ethics*, 88-99.

Martin, K. D., & Cullen, J. B. (2006). Continuities and extensions of ethical climate theory: A meta-analytic review. *Journal of Business Ethics*, *69*(2), 175–194. doi:10.100710551-006-9084-7

Martin, K. D., Johnson, J. L., & Cullen, J. B. (2009). Organizational change, normative control deinstitutionalization, and corruption. *Business Ethics Quarterly*, *19*(1), 105–130. doi:10.5840/beq20091915

Mayer, D. M., Kuenzi, M., & Greenbaum, R. L. (2010). Examining the link between ethical leadership and employee misconduct: The mediating role of ethical climate. *Journal of Business Ethics*, *95*(1), 7–16. doi:10.100710551-011-0794-0

McBarnet, D. (2006). Toward ethical compliance: Lessons from Enron. In *Global perspectives on ethics of corporate governance* (pp. 27–38). New York: Palgrave Macmillan. doi:10.1057/9780312376192_3

Messner, S. F., & Rosenfeld, R. (1997). Political restraint of the market and levels of criminal homicide: A cross-national application of institutional-anomie theory. *Social Forces*, *75*(4), 1393–1416.

Miller, N. E., & Dollard, J. (1941). *Social learning and imitation*. New Haven, CT: Yale University Press.

Moore, M. (2011). Psychological theories of crime and delinquency. *Journal of Human Behavior in the Social Environment*, *21*(3), 226–239. doi:10.1080/10911359.2011.564552

Near, J. P., & Miceli, M. P. (1995). Effective whistle-blowing. *Academy of Management Review*, *20*(3), 679–708.

O'Leary, R. (2007). *The Ethics of Dissent: Managing Guerrilla Government*. Washington, DC: CQ Press.

Oberfield, Z. W. (2009). Rule following and discretion at government's frontlines: Continuity and change during organization socialization. *Journal of Public Administration: Research and Theory*, *20*(4), 735–755. doi:10.1093/jopart/mup025

Parent, M. J. (2003). *Self-control vs. social control as an explanation for delinquency* (Unpublished Doctoral Dissertation). University of Windsor.

Pavlov, I. P. (2010). Conditioned reflexes: An investigation of the physiological activity of the cerebral cortex. *Annals of Neurosciences, 17*(3), 136.

Perri, F. S., & Brody, R. G. (2011). The dark triad: Organized crime, terror and fraud. *Journal of Money Laundering Control*, *14*(1), 44–59. doi:10.1108/13685201111098879

Peterson, D. K. (2002). Deviant workplace behavior and the organization's ethical climate. *Journal of Business and Psychology*, *17*(1), 47–61. doi:10.1023/A:1016296116093

Pinto, J., Leana, C. R., & Pil, F. K. (2008). Corrupt organizations or organizations of corrupt individuals? Two types of organization-level corruption. *Academy of Management Review*, *33*(3), 685–709. doi:10.5465/amr.2008.32465726

Piquero, N., Lyn Exum, M., & Simpson, S. S. (2005). Integrating the desire–for–control and rational choice in a corporate crime context. *Justice Quarterly*, *22*(2), 252–280. doi:10.1080/07418820500089034

Price, M., & Norris, D. M. (2009). White-collar crime: Corporate and securities and commodities fraud. *The Journal of the American Academy of Psychiatry and the Law*, *37*(4), 538–544. PMID:20019002

Rawls, J. (1971). *Theory of justice*. Cambridge University Press.

Reed, G. E., & Yeager, P. C. (1996). Organizational offending and neoclassical criminology: Challenging the reach of a general theory of crime. *Criminology*, *34*(3), 357–382. doi:10.1111/j.1745-9125.1996.tb01211.x

Rogstad, J. E., & Rogers, R. (2008). Gender differences in contributions of emotion to psychopathy and antisocial personality disorder. *Clinical Psychology Review*, *28*(8), 1472–1484. doi:10.1016/j.cpr.2008.09.004 PMID:18945529

Rotter, J. B. (1954). *Social learning and clinical psychology*. Englewood Cliffs, NJ: Prentice Hall. doi:10.1037/10788-000

Sacco, V. F., & Kennedy, L. W. (2002). *The Criminal Event: Perspective in Space and Time*. Belmont, CA: Wadsworth.

Salancik, G. R., & Pfeffer, J. (1978). A social information processing approach to job attitudes and task design. *Administrative Science Quarterly*, *4*(2), 224–253. doi:10.2307/2392563 PMID:10307892

Sampson, R. J., & Laub, J. H. (1993). Structural variations in juvenile court processing: Inequality, the underclass, and social control. *Law & Society Review*, *27*(2), 285–311. doi:10.2307/3053938

Sampson, R. J., & Laub, J. H. (2003). Life-course desisters? Trajectories of crime among delinquent boys followed to age 70. *Criminology*, *41*(3), 555–592. doi:10.1111/j.1745-9125.2003.tb00997.x

Schiller, J., Black, W., & Murphy, P. V. (2000). *Crime and criminality.* Retrieved September 2012 from www.des.ucdavis.edu/faculty/Richerson/BooksOnline/He16- 95.pdf

Schoepfer, A., Carmichael, S., & Piquero, N. L. (2007). Do perceptions of punishment vary between white-collar and street crimes? *Journal of Criminal Justice*, *35*(2), 151–163. doi:10.1016/j.jcrimjus.2007.01.003

Schwartz, M. (2005). Universal moral values for corporate codes of ethics. *Journal of Business Ethics*, *59*(1/2), 27–44. doi:10.1023/A:1021393904930

Segarajasingham, S. (2014). Combating White Collar Crime: A Critical Study Of The Protection To Persons Making Disclosure Under Commercial Law of Sri Lanka. *International Journal of Business, Economics and Law*, *4*(3), 50–57.

Sekerka, L. E., & Zolin, R. (2007). Rule-bending: Can prudential judgment affect rule compliance and values in the workplace? *Public Integrity*, *9*(3), 225–243. doi:10.2753/PIN1099-9922090302

Serin, R. C., Peters, R. D., & Barbaree, H. E. (1990). Predictors of psychopathy and release outcome in a criminal population. *Psychological Assessment*, *2*(4), 419–422. doi:10.1037/1040-3590.2.4.419

Shapiro, S. P. (1990). Collaring the crime, not the criminal: Reconsidering the concept of white-collar crime. *American Sociological Review*, *2*(2), 346–365. doi:10.2307/2095761

Sheley, J. F. (2000). *Criminology*. Belmont, CA: Wadsworth/Thomas Learning.

Shoemaker, D. J. (2005). *Theories of delinquency: An examination of explanations of delinquent behavior*. New York, NY: Oxford University Press.

Siegel, L. J., Welsh, B. C., & Senna, J. J. (2006). *Juvenile delinquency: Theory, practice and law*. Belmont, CA: Thomson/Wadsworth.

Simha, A., & Cullen, J. B. (2012). Ethical climates and their effects on organizational outcomes: Implications from the past and prophecies for the future. *The Academy of Management Perspectives*, *26*(4), 20–34. doi:10.5465/amp.2011.0156

Simpson, S. S. (2013). White-collar crime: A review of recent developments and promising directions for future research. *Annual Review of Sociology*, *39*(1), 309–331. doi:10.1146/annurev-soc-071811-145546

Simpson, S. S., & Piquero, N. L. (2002). Low self-control, organizational theory, and corporate crime. *Law & Society Review*, *4*(2), 509–548. doi:10.2307/1512161

Skinner, B. F. (1938). *The behavior of organisms*. New York, NY: Appleton-Century.

Skinner, B. F. (1963). Operant behavior. *The American Psychologist*, *18*(8), 503–515. doi:10.1037/h0045185

Slapper, G., & Tombs, S. (1999). *Corporate crime*. Longman Publishing.

Soley, S. (2017). *White collar crime: The role of the firm in occupational crime* (Unpublished Doctoral Dissertation). University of Pennsylvania.

Sorensen, J. B. (2002). The strength of corporate culture and the reliability of firm performance. *Administrative Science Quarterly*, *47*(1), 70–91. doi:10.2307/3094891

Stachowicz-Stanusch, A., & Simha, A. (2013). An empirical investigation of the effects of ethical climates on organizational corruption. *Journal of Business Economics and Management*, *14*(1), 433–446. doi:10.3846/16111699.2012.744345

Su, H. Y. (2014). Business ethics and the development of intellectual capital. *Journal of Business Ethics*, *119*(1), 87–98. doi:10.100710551-013-1623-4

Sutherland, E. H. (1940). White-collar criminality. *American Sociological Review*, *5*(1), 1–12. doi:10.2307/2083937

Sutherland, E. H. (1949). *White Collar Crime*. New York: Dryden Press.

Talha, M., Sallehhuddin, A., Masoud, M. S., & Said, A. M. A. (2013). An analysis of moral intensity, intention and socially responsible investment behaviour among fund managers of Malaysian unit trust companies. *International Journal of Managerial and Financial Accounting*, *5*(2), 162–177. doi:10.1504/IJMFA.2013.053210

Thorndike, E. L. (1898). *Animal intelligence: An experimental study of the associative processes in animals*. New York: The Macmillan Company. doi:10.1037/10780-000

Tillyer, M. S. (2015). General multilevel opportunity and crime events. *Journal of Contemporary Criminal Justice*, *31*(1), 107–121. doi:10.1177/1043986214552621

Tyler, T. R., & Blader, S. L. (2005). Can businesses effectively regulate employee conduct? The antecedents of rule following in work settings. *Academy of Management Journal*, *48*(6), 1143–1158. doi:10.5465/amj.2005.19573114

Van Fleet, D. D., & Van Fleet, E. W. (2006). Internal terrorists: The terrorists inside organizations. *Journal of Managerial Psychology*, *21*(8), 763–774. doi:10.1108/02683940610713280

Vaughan, D. (1992). The macro-micro connection in white-collar crime theory. *White-collar crime reconsidered*, 124-145.

Vaughan, E. D. (1981). Recent development in white-collar crime theory and research. In *The Mad, The Bad, and the Different* (pp. 135–155). Lexington, MA: Lexington Books.

Velasquez, M. G. (2006). *Business Ethics: Concepts and Cases* (6th ed.). Boston, MA: Pearson Publishing.

Victor, B., & Cullen, J. B. (1987). A theory and measure of ethical climate in organizations. *Research in Corporate Social Performance and Policy*, *9*(1), 51–71.

Victor, B., & Cullen, J. B. (1988). The organizational bases of ethical work climates. *Administrative Science Quarterly*, *4*(4), 101–125. doi:10.2307/2392857

Webber, S. (2007). Ethical climate typology and questionnaire: A discussion of ınstrument modifications. *Journal of Academic Librarianship*, *33*(5), 567–580. doi:10.1016/j.acalib.2007.05.003

Weisburd, D., Waring, E., & Chayet, E. (1995). Specific deterrence in a sample of offenders convicted of white collar crimes. *Criminology*, *33*(4), 587–607. doi:10.1111/j.1745-9125.1995.tb01191.x

Wells, T. (2014). Recovering Adam Smith's ethical economics. *Real World Economics Review*, *68*, 90–97.

Wheeler, S. (1992). The problem of white-collar crime motivation. In K. Schlegal & D. Weisburd (Eds.), *White collar crime reconsidered*. Boston, MA: Northeastern University Press.

Wilcox, P., & Cullen, F. T. (2017). *Communities and crime: An enduring American challenge*. Temple University Press.

Wilcox, P., & Cullen, F. T. (2018). Situational Opportunity Theories of Crime. *Annual Review of Criminology*, *4*, 1–17.

Wilcox, P., & Gialopsos, B. M. (2015). Crime-event criminology: An overview. *Journal of Contemporary Criminology*, *31*(1), 4–11. doi:10.1177/1043986214552601

Wilcox, P., Gialopsos, B. M., & Land, K. C. (2013). Multilevel criminal opportunity. In The Oxford Handbook of Criminological Theory (pp. 579-601). New York: Oxford Univ. Press.

Wilcox, P., Sullivan, C. J., Jones, S., & Van Gelder, J. L. (2014). Personality and opportunity: An integrated approach to offending and victimization. *Criminal Justice and Behavior*, *41*(7), 880–901. doi:10.1177/0093854813520603

Wilkins, A. L., & Ouchi, W. G. (1983). Efficient cultures: Exploring the relationship between culture and organizational performance. *Administrative Science Quarterly*, *28*(3), 468–481. doi:10.2307/2392253

Wimbush, J. C., Shepard, J. M., & Markham, S. E. (1997). An empirical examination of the relationship between ethical climate and ethical behavior from multiple levels of analysis. *Journal of Business Ethics*, *16*(16), 1705–1716. doi:10.1023/A:1017952221572

Yücel, R., & Çiftci, G. E. (2012). Employees' perceptions towards ethical business attitudes and conduct. *Turkish Journal of Business Ethics*, *5*(9), 131–161.

Zahra, S. A., Priem, R. L., & Rasheed, A. A. (2007). Understanding the causes and effects of top management fraud. *Organizational Dynamics*, *36*(2), 122–139. doi:10.1016/j.orgdyn.2007.03.002

KEY TERMS AND DEFINITIONS

Business Ethics: The whole set of applications based on moral principles within the organization or occupational framework concerning the values such as honesty, commitment, and respect to the environment, fair conduct, equality, and justice.

Crime: The human conduct that violates the criminal laws of a state, the federal government, or a local jurisdiction that has the power to make and enforce the laws.

Criminology: The scientific study of crime and criminals through examining the causes and consequences in both individual and societal levels.

Ethical Climate: Employees' awareness of the existence of codes of ethics and ethical values in the organizations and their perceptions that impact their attitudes and behaviors.

Ethics: The perception criteria for human behavior in terms of what is good or bad, right or wrong, and what is accepted or unaccepted with moral decisions and judgments.

Rule Bending: A willingness to violate the obligations, rules, procedures, and formal requirements of the code of conduct in the organization.

White-Collar Crime: The crime committed by a person of respectability and high social status in the course of his occupation.

Compilation of References

"Alexandru Ioan Cuza" University of Iasi, Romania. (UAIC). (n.d.). *Code of ethics and professional deontology*. University papers, Ethics. Retrieved from http://www.uaic.ro/despre-uaic/documentele-universitatii/

Abbott, A., Cyranoski, D., Jones, N., Maher, B., Schiermeier, Q., & Van Noorden, R. (2010). Metrics: Do metrics matter? *Nature*, *465*(7300), 860–862. doi:10.1038/465860a PMID:20559361

Adeleye, O. A., & Adebamowo, C. A. (2012). Factors associated with research wrong doing in Nigeria. *Journal of Empirical Research on Human Research Ethics; JERHRE*, *7*(5), 15–24. doi:10.1525/jer.2012.7.5.15 PMID:23324199

Agarwal, M. (2003). Voluntariness in clinical research at the end of life. *Journal of Pain and Symptom Management*, *25*(4), 25–32. doi:10.1016/S0885-3924(03)00057-5 PMID:12691694

Agency for Healthcare Research and Quality. (1998). *AHCPR seeks proposal to develop quality of care measures for vulnerable populations*. Retrieved from https://archivew.ahrq.gov/news/press/vulnpr.htm

Agenţia Română de Asigurare a Calităţii în Învăţământul Superior (ARACIS). (n.d.). [Romanian Agency for Quality Assurance in Higher Education]. *Proceduri* [Procedures]. Retrieved from http://www.aracis.ro/proceduri/

Alalehto, T. (2015). White collar criminals: The state of knowledge. *The Open Criminology Journal*, *8*(1), 28–35. doi:10.2174/1874917801508010028

Albanese, J. S. (1984). Corporate criminology: Explaining deviance of business and political organizations. *Journal of Criminal Justice*, *12*(1), 11–19. doi:10.1016/0047-2352(84)90003-5

Albury, R. M. (1998). Challenges to commonsense: Debates about the status of human embryos outside women's bodies. *Journal of Australian Studies*, *22*(59), 129–138. doi:10.1080/14443059809387430

Alexander, L. (1996). The Moral Magic of Consent (II). *Legal Theory*, *2*(03), 165–174. doi:10.1017/S1352325200000471

Alexa-Stratulat, T., Neagu, M., Neagu, A., Alexa, I. D., & Ioan, B. G. (2018). Consent for participating in clinical trials - Is it really informed? *Developing World Bioethics*. doi:10.1111/dewb.12199 PMID:29933502

Alper, H. (2008). How can research integrity be best achieved? *Materials Today*, *11*(4), 60. doi:10.1016/S1369-7021(08)70067-1

American Academy of Pediatrics (AAP). (2007). Best Pharmaceuticals for Children Act Pediatric Research Equity Act. 2007 Reauthorization. Improvements to existing law 110th Congress: H.R. 3580. *Public Law*, 110–185. Retrieved from https://www.aap.org/en-us/advocacy-and-policy/federal-advocacy/Documents/bpcapreasidexside.pdf

American Association of Marriage and Family. (2001). *Code of ethics*. Retrieved from https://www.aamft.org/imis15/content/legal_ethics/code_of_ethics.aspx

American Chemical Association. (2013). Publish be found or perish. Writing scientific manuscripts for the digital age. *Bio Journal, 13*, 1-5. Retrieved from http://pubs.acs.org/bio/ACS-Guide-Writing-Manuscripts-for-the-Digital-Age.pdf

American Fertility Society; Ethics Committee. (1986). Ethics and the new reproductive technologies. *Fertility and Sterility*, *46*(3), 16–20. doi:10.1016/S0015-0282(16)58770-6 PMID:2941318

American Psychological Association. (2002). Ethical Principles of Psychologists and Code of Conduct. *The American Psychologist*, *57*(12), 1060–1073. doi:10.1037/0003-066X.57.12.1060 PMID:12613157

Andoh, C. T. (2011). Bioethics and the challenges to its growth in Africa. *Open Journal of Philosophy*, *1*(2), 67–75. doi:10.4236/ojpp.2011.12012

Anuolam, C. U. (1993). *Igbo value and care for life*. Navarra, Spain: Facultad de Theología de la Universidad de Navarra.

Apel, R., & Paternoster, R. (2009). Understanding "criminogenic" corporate culture: What white-collar crime researchers can learn from studies of the adolescent employment–crime relationship. In S. S. Simpson & D. Weisburd (Eds.), *The Criminology of White-Collar Crime* (pp. 15–33). New York: Springer. doi:10.1007/978-0-387-09502-8_2

Archibong, I. A. (2012). Forms of dishonesty among academic staff and the way forward. *Canadian Social Science*, *8*(6), 39–43. doi:10.3968/j.css.1923669720120806.1057

Armiger, B. (1997). Ethics in Nursing Research: Profile, Principles, Perspective. *Nursing Research*, *26*(5), 330–333. doi:10.1097/00006199-197709000-00003 PMID:587922

Árnason, V. (2004). Coding and consent: Moral challenges of the database project in Iceland. *Bioethics*, *18*(1), 27–49. doi:10.1111/j.1467-8519.2004.00377.x PMID:15168697

Artyukhov, A., & Menshov, O. (2016). Akademichna chesnist' u naukovykh doslidzhennyakh [Academic integrity in scientific research]. In Akademichna chesnist' yak osnova staloho rozvytku universytetu [Academic integrity as the basis for sustainable development of the university] (pp. 121-131). Academic Press.

Artyukhov, A. (2015). Akademichna dobrochesnist' pry provedenni naukovykh doslidzhen [Academic integrity in conducting of scientific research]. In *Osnovy stanovlennya suchasnoho inzhenera* [Fundamentals of Formation of Modern Engineer]. Sumy, Ukraine: Sumy State University.

Artyukhov, A., & Liuta, O. (2017). Academic integrity in Ukrainian higher education: Values, skills, actions. *Business Ethics and Leadership*, *1*(1), 34–39. doi:10.21272/bel.2017.1-04

Asandei, R. M. (2005). Aspecte ale eugeniei de la origini până astăzi [Aspects of eugenics from origins to today]. *Revista Română de Bioetică, 3*(4).

Astarastoae, V. (2018a). Cercetarea pe subiecți umani – situația deținuților. Iasi. Retrieved from https://www.facebook.com/notes/vasile-astărăstoae/cercetarea-pe-subiecți-umani-situația-deținuților/490638524665163

Astarastoae, V. (2018b). Dr. prof. Vasile Astărăstoae: Cercetarea pe subiecți umani – abuzurile asupra deținuților. *Ortodoxinfo.Ro*. Retrieved from http://ortodoxinfo.ro/2018/03/21/dr-prof-vasile-astarastoae-cercetarea-pe-subiecti-umani-abuzurile-asupra-detinutilor/

Astărăstoae, V., Loue, S., & Ioan, B. (Eds.). (2009). Etica cercetării pe subiecţi umani [Ethics of research on human subjects]. Iaşi, România: "Gr. T. Popa" U.M.F. Iaşi Publishing House.

Australia. (1995). *Law on Medical Treatment of Infertility*. Retrieved from http://www.legislation.vic.gov.au/Domino/Web_Notes/LDMS/LTObject_Store/LTObjSt2.nsf/DDE300B846EED9C7CA257616000A3571/93F5C7F19E9048C6CA2577610022D62E/$FILE/95-63a010.pdf

Australia. (2002). *Law No. 144/2002 on the Prohibition of Reproductive Cloning*. Retrieved from https://www.legislation.gov.au/Details/C2017C00306

Aviv, A. J., & Shay, M. (2018). Reflections on telomere dynamics and ageing-related diseases in humans. *Philosophical Transactions of the Royal Society B: Biological Sciences, 373*(1741), 20160436-20160444. doi:10.1098/rstb.2016.0436

Azetsop, J. (2011). New directions in African bioethics: Ways of including public health concerns in the bioethics agenda. *Developing World Bioethics, 11*(1), 4–5. doi:10.1111/j.1471-8847.2009.00271.x PMID:19961514

Baggini, J. (2002). *Making Sense: Philosophy Behind the Headlines*. Oxford, UK: Oxford University Press.

Bahm, A. (1971). Science is not value free. *Policy Sciences*, *2*(4), 391–396. doi:10.1007/BF01406139

Baird, J. E., & Zelin, R. C. (2009, Winter). An examination of the impact of obedience pressure on perceptions of fraudulent acts and the likelihood of committing occupational fraud. *Journal of Forensic Studies in Accounting and Business*, 1-14.

Bala, C. (2010). *Redactarea lucrărilor ştiinţifice* [Writing scientific papers]. Bucharest, Romania: Programul Doctoratul în şcoli de excelenţă.

Ballantyne, A. (2016). It's mine: Ownership and control of health data. In S. Holm, A. Ballantyne, J. Wilson, & K. Borgerson (Eds.), *Symposium: Consent for Secondary Use of Clinical Data for Research.*

Bandura, A. (1969). *Principles of behavior modification.* New York: Holt, Rinehart, and Winston.

Bandura, A. (1977). Self-efficacy: Toward a unifying theory of behavioral change. *Psychological Review*, *84*(2), 191–209. doi:10.1037/0033-295X.84.2.191 PMID:847061

Bandura, A. (1986). *Social foundations of thought and action: A social cognitive theory*. Englewood Cliffs, NJ: Prentice-Hall Inc.

Bandura, A. (1989). Human agency in social cognitive theory. *The American Psychologist*, *44*(9), 1175–1184. doi:10.1037/0003-066X.44.9.1175 PMID:2782727

Barnett, H. C. (1981). Corporate capitalism, corporate crime. *Crime and Delinquency*, *27*(1), 4–23. doi:10.1177/001112878102700102

Barnhardt, B. (2015). The "epidemic" of cheating depends on its definition: A critique of inferring the moral quality of "cheating in any form". *Ethics & Behavior*, *26*(4), 330–343. doi:10.1080/10508422.2015.1026595

Baroke, D. (2018). *Investigation into violation of research integrity is concluded.* Retrieved from https://www.psi.ch/media/results-of-the-investigation

Bartels, K. K., Harrick, E., Martell, K., & Strickland, D. (1998). The relationship between ethical climate and ethical problems within human resource management. *Journal of Business Ethics*, *17*(7), 799–804. doi:10.1023/A:1005817401688

Bashir, S., Shahzad, K., Abbass, M., Abbass, N., & Saeed, S. (2011). Antecedents of white collar crime in organizations: A literature review. *African Journal of Business Management*, *5*(35), 13359–13363. doi:10.5897/ajbmx11.008

Baucus, M. S., & Near, J. P. (1991). Can illegal corporate behavior be predicted? An event history analysis. *Academy of Management Journal*, *34*(1), 9–36. doi:10.2307/256300

Baumeister, R. F., & Leary, M. K. (1997). Writing narrative literature reviews. *Review of General Psychology*, *1*(3), 311–320. doi:10.1037/1089-2680.1.3.311

Baune, Ø., Borge, O. J., Funderud, S., Føllesdal, D., Heiene, G., & Østnor, L. (2008). In L. Østnor (Ed.), *Stem Cells, Human Embryos and Ethics* (pp. 1–18). Dordrecht, The Netherlands: Springer. doi:10.1007/978-1-4020-6989-5_1

Beall, J. (2018). *Beall's list of predatory journals and publishers*. Retrieved from https://beallslist.weebly.com/

Beall, J. (2012). Predatory publishers are corrupting open access. *Nature*, *489*(7415), 179. doi:10.1038/489179a PMID:22972258

Beall, J. (2013). Predatory publishing is just one of the consequences of gold open access. *Learned Publishing*, *26*(2), 79–83. doi:10.1087/20130203

Beall, J. (2016). Best practices for scholarly authors in the age of predatory journals. *Annals of the Royal College of Surgeons of England*, *98*(2), 77–79. doi:10.1308/rcsann.2016.0056 PMID:26829665

Beauchamp, T. L., & Childress, J. F. (1994). *Principles of biomedical ethics. Emergency medicine clinics of North America* (4th ed.). New York: Oxford University Press. doi:10.1016/S0033-3182(95)71674-7

Behrens, K. G. (2013). Towards an indigenous African bioethics. *South African Journal of Bioethics and Law*, *6*(1), 32–35. doi:10.7196ajbl.255

Bellanti, F., van Wijk, R. C., Danhof, M., & Pasqua, O. D. (2015). Integration of PKPD relationships into benefit–risk analysis. *British Journal of Clinical Pharmacology*, *80*(5), 979–991. doi:10.1111/bcp.12674 PMID:25940398

Bem, D. J. (2003). Writing the empirical journal article. In J. M. Darley, M. P. Yanna, & H. L. Roediger III, (Eds.), *The Complete Academic: A Practical Guide for the Beginning Social Scientist* (2nd ed.). Washington, DC: American Psychological Association.

Benatar, S. R., & Singer, P. (2000). A new look at international research ethics. *British Medical Journal*, *321*(7264), 824–826. doi:10.1136/bmj.321.7264.824 PMID:11009528

Benea, I. (2015a). Exclusiv: Ieşeni morţi în urma unor experimente medicale ilegale? Scandal de proporţii [Exclusive: Iskans killed by illegal medical experiments? Scandal of scale]. *Ziarul de Iaşi [The Newspaper of Iasi]*. Retrieved from https://www.ziaruldeiasi.ro/stiri/exclusiv-ieseni-morti-in-urma-unor-experimente-medicale-ilegale-scandal-de-proportii--84920.html

Benea, I. (2015b). Cazul experienţelor de la „Neuro“: Am vorbit cu familia unui pacient-cobai, [Case of experiences from "Neuro": We talked to a guinea-pig's family]. *Ziarul de Iasi [The Newspaper of Iasi]*. Retrieved from https://www.ziaruldeiasi.ro/stiri/cazul-experientelor-de-la-a-neuroa-am-vorbit-cu-familia-unui-pacient-cobai--85026.html

Benson, M. L., Madensen, T. D., & Eck, J. E. (2009). White-collar crime from an opportunity perspective. In S. S. Simpson & D. Weisburd (Eds.), *The Criminology of White-Collar Crime* (pp. 175–193). New York: Springer. doi:10.1007/978-0-387-09502-8_9

Benson, M. L., & Simpson, S. S. (2015). *Understanding white-collar crime: An opportunity perspective*. New York: Routledge.

Bentham, J. (1843). *An introduction to the principles of morals and legislation*. Edinburgh, UK: William Tate.

Berkowitz, M. W. (1985). The role of discussion in moral education. In M. W. Berkowitz & F. Oser (Eds.), *Moral Education: Theory and Application* (pp. 197–218). Hillsdale, NJ: Lawrence Erlbaum Associates.

Bernabe, R. D. L. C., van Thiel, G. J. M. W., Raaijmakers, J. A. M., & van Delden, J. J. M. (2012). The risk-benefit task of research ethics committees: An evaluation of current approaches and the need to incorporate decision studies methods. *BMC Medical Ethics*, *13*(1), 6–15. doi:10.1186/1472-6939-13-6 PMID:22520714

Bhutta, Z. A. (2002). Ethics in international health research: A perspective from the developing world. *Bulletin of the World Health Organization*, (80): 114–120. Retrieved from http://www.who.int/bulletin/archives/80(2)114.pdf PMID:11953789

Blatner, A. (2006). Enacting the new academy: Sociodrama as a powerful tool in higher education. *ReVision: A Journal of Consciousness and Transformation, 28*(3), 30-35. doi:10.3200/revn.28.3.30-35

Blatner, A. (2000). *Foundations of psychodrama: History, theory, and practice* (4th ed.). New York: Springer Publishing Company.

Blickle, G., Schlegel, A., Fassbender, P., & Klein, U. (2006). Some personality correlates of business white-collar crime. *Applied Psychology, 55*(2), 220–233. doi:10.1111/j.1464-0597.2006.00226.x

Blumberg, B. F., Cooper, D. R., & Schindler, P. S. (2014). *Business Research Methods* (4th ed.). New York: McGraw–Hill.

Boddy, J. (2014). Research across cultures, within countries: Hidden ethics tensions in research with children and families? *Progress in Development Studies, 14*(1), 91–103. doi:10.1177/1464993413490477

Boden, M., Bryson, J., Caldwell, D., Dautenhahn, K., Edwards, L., Kember, S., ... Winfield, A. (2017). Principles of robotics: Regulating robots in the real world. *Connection Science, 29*(2), 124–129. doi:10.1080/09540091.2016.1271400

Bookman, Z. (2008). Convergences and omissions in reporting corporate and white collar crime. *DePaul Business & Commercial Law Journal, 6*(3), 347–392.

Bordens, K. S., & Abbott, B. B. (2018). *Research Design and Methods. A Process Approach* (10th ed.). McGraw-Hill.

Borkowski, S. C., & Welsh, M. J. (2000). Ethical practice in the accounting publishing process: Contrasting opinions of authors and editors. *Journal of Business Ethics, 25*(1), 15–31. doi:10.1023/A:1005939128790

Borry, E. L. (2011). Ethical climate in the public sector: Its influence on rule bending. In *Public Management Research Conference*, New York: Maxwell School, Syracuse University.

Borry, E. L. (2017). Ethical climate and rule bending: How organizational norms contribute to unintended rule consequences. *Public Administration, 95*(1), 78–96. doi:10.1111/padm.12304

Bostrom, N. (2003). Human genetic enhancements: A transhumanist perspective. *The Journal of Value Inquiry, 37*(4), 493–506. doi:10.1023/B:INQU.0000019037.67783.d5 PMID:17340768

Bostrom, N. (2014). *Superintelligence: Paths, dangers, strategies*. OUP Oxford.

Bostrom, N., & Yudkowsky, E. (2014). The ethics of artificial intelligence. In K. Frankish & W. M. Ramsey (Eds.), *The Cambridge handbook of Artificial Intelligence* (pp. 316–334). Cambridge, UK: Cambridge University Press. doi:10.1017/CBO9781139046855.020

Bottoms, A. R. (1994). Environmental criminology. In M. Maguire, R. Morgan, & R. Reiner (Eds.), *The Oxford Handbook of Criminology* (pp. 585–656). Oxford, UK: Clarendon Press.

Bowman, S. L. (2007). The psychological power of the roleplaying experience. *Journal of Interactive Drama, 2*(1), 1–14.

Brightman, H. J. (2009). *Today's white-collar crime: Legal, investigative, and theoretical perspectives*. New York: Routledge.

Brownson, R. C., Royer, C., Ewing, R., & McBride, T. D. (2006). Researchers and policymakers: Travelers in parallel universes. *American Journal of Preventive Medicine, 30*(2), 164–172. doi:10.1016/j.amepre.2005.10.004 PMID:16459216

Btoush, R., & Campbell, J. C. (2009). Ethical conduct in intimate partner violence research: Challenges and strategies. *Nursing Outlook, 57*(4), 210–216. doi:j.outlook.2008.10.005

Buchholz, R. A., & Rosenthal, S. B. (1998). *Business ethics: The pragmatic path beyond principles to process*. Upper Saddle River, NJ: Prentice Hall.

Bucy, P. H., Formby, E. P., Raspanti, M. S., & Rooney, K. E. (2008). Why do they do it: The motives, mores, and character of white collar criminals. *John's Law Review.*, *82*, 401–422.

Bugaj, S. V., & Goertzel, B. (2007). Five ethical imperatives and their implications for human-AGI interaction. *Dynamical Psychology*. Retrieved from http://goertzel.org///_Ethical_Imperatives_svbedit.htm

Bulger, R. E., Heitman, E., & Reiser, S. J. (2002). Research with human beings. In R. E. Bulger, E. Heitman, & S. J. Reiser (Eds.), *The Ethical Dimensions of the Biological and Health Sciences* (pp. 117–125). Cambridge, UK: Cambridge University Press.

Buller, P. F., Kohls, J. J., & Anderson, K. S. (1991). The challenge of global ethics. *Journal of Business Ethics*, *10*(10), 767–775. doi:10.1007/BF00705711

Bundesministeriums für Verkehr und Digitale Infrastruktur (BMVI). (2017). [Federal Ministry of Transport and Digital Infrastructure]. *Ethics Commission's complete report on automated and connected driving*. Retrieved from https://www.bmvi.de/SharedDocs/EN/publications/report-ethics-commission.html?nn=

Burgess, R. L., & Akers, R. L. (1966). A differential association-reinforcement theory of criminal behavior. *Social Problems*, *14*(2), 128–147. doi:10.2307/798612

Burns, N., & Grove, S. K. (2005). *The practice of nursing research: Conduct, critique, and utilization* (5th ed.). St. Louis, MO: Elsevier/Saunders.

Busardo, F. P., Gulino, M., Napoletano, S., & Frati, P. (2014). The evolution of legislation in the field of medically assisted reproduction and embryo stem cell research in European Union members. *BioMed Research International*, *2014*, 1–14. doi:10.1155/2014/307160 PMID:25147794

Bussmann, K. D. (2003). Causes of economic crime and the impact of values: business ethics as a crime prevention measure. *Swiss Conference on Coping with Economic Crime. Zúrich: Risks and Strategies*, 1-16.

Buţureanu, Ş., & Lupşan, G. (2001). *O provocare interdisciplinară: reproducerea medical asistată* [An interdisciplinary challenge: Assisted medical reproduction]. Iaşi, Romania: Junimea.

Callahan, D. (1995). The puzzle of profound respect. *The Hastings Center Report*, *25*(1), 39–40. doi:10.2307/3562493 PMID:7730051

Canada. (2004). *Law no. C-13 on Medically Assisted Human Reproduction*. Retrieved from https://lop.parl.ca/About/Parliament/LegislativeSummaries/bills_ls.asp?lang=E&ls=C13&Parl=37&Ses=2&Language=E

Canadian Institutes of Health Research. (2014). *Ethical conduct for research involving humans (TCPS2)*. Retrieved from http://www.pre.ethics.gc.ca/eng/policy-politique/initiatives/tcps2-eptc2/Default/

Caplan, A. L. (1992). Twenty years after. The legacy of the Tuskegee syphilis study. *The Hastings Center Report*, *22*(6), 29. doi:10.2307/3562946 PMID:1428845

Carome, M. A. (2018). *Right-to-try legislation offers false hope and would endanger patients*. Retrieved from https://www.statnews.com/2018/01/16/right-to-try-legislation-patients/

Carter, J. A., & Gordon, E. C. (2013). On cognitive and moral enhancement: A reply to Savulescu and Persson. *Bioethics*, *29*(3), 153–161. doi:10.1111/bioe.12076 PMID:24372082

Cattell, J., Chilukuri, S., & Levy, M. (2013). *How big data can revolutionize pharmaceutical R&D*. McKinsey & Company Home Pharmaceuticals & Medical Products. Retrieved from https://www.mckinsey.com/industries/pharmaceuticals-and-medical-products/our-insights/how-big-data-can-revolutionize-pharmaceutical-r-and-d

Caulfield, T., Knowles, L., & Meslin, E. (2004). Law and policy in the era of reproductive genetics. *Journal of Medical Ethics*, *30*(4), 414–417. doi:10.1136/jme.2002.001370 PMID:15289541

Cavana, R. Y., Delahaye, B. L., & Sekaran, U. (2002). *Applied business research: qualitative and quantitative methods*. John Wiley & sons.

Cavico, F. J., & Mujtaba, B. (2005). *Business ethics: Transcending requirements through moral leadership*. Boston: Pearson Custom Publishing.

Center for Drug Evaluation and Research (CDER). (2014). Pediatric study planning and extrapolation algorithm. In U.S. Department of Health and Human Services, Food and Drug Administration (Ed.), *General Clinical Pharmacology Considerations for Pediatric Studies for Drugs and Biological Products. Guidance for Industry* (p. 23). Author. Retrieved from https://www.fda.gov/downloads/drugs/guidances/ucm425885.pdf

Chalmers, D. (2010). The singularity: A philosophical analysis. *Journal of Consciousness Studies*, *17*, 7–65. Retrieved from http://www.nyu.edu/gsas/dept/philo/faculty/block/M&L2010/Papers/Chalmers.pdf

Chalmers, D. J. (1996). *The conscious mind: In search of a fundamental theory*. New York: Oxford University Press.

Chang, C. M., Chen, Y. L., Huang, Y. Y., & Chou, C. (2015). Why do they become potential cyber-plagiarizers? Exploring the alternative thinking of copy-and-paste youth in Taiwan. *Computers & Education*, *87*, 357–367. doi:10.1016/j.compedu.2015.07.006

Chapin, P. G. (2004). *Research projects and research proposals. A guide for scientists seeking funding*. New York: Cambridge University Press.

Chapman, E. N., Kaatz, A., & Carnes, M. (2013). Physicians and implicit bias: How doctors may unwittingly perpetuate health care disparities. *Journal of General Internal Medicine*, *28*(11), 1504–1510. doi:10.100711606-013-2441-1 PMID:23576243

Charlton, B. G. (2009). Are you an honest scientist? Truthfulness in science should be an iron law, not a vague aspiration. *Medical Hypotheses*, *73*(5), 633–635. doi:10.1016/j.mehy.2009.05.009 PMID:19501471

Children's Hospital of Philadelphia (CHOP) Research Institute. (2018). *Risk and benefit*. Retrieved from https://irb.research.chop.edu/risk-and-benefit

Chirurgia. (n.d.). *Instructions for authors*. Retrieved from http://www.revistachirurgia. ro/docs/instructions%20for%20authors.pdf

Christakis, N. A. (1992). Ethics are local: Engaging cross-cultural variation in the ethics for clinical research. *Social Science & Medicine*, *35*(9), 1079–1091. doi:10.1016/0277-9536(92)90220-K PMID:1439926

Christman, J. (2009). Autonomy in moral and political philosophy. In *Standford Encyclopedia of Philosophy*. Retrieved from https://plato.stanford.edu/archives/fall2009/entries/autonomy-moral/

Ciruna, B., & Rossant, J. (2016). Primitive streak. In *Encyclopedia of Genetics* (p. 1552). Genomics, Proteomics and Informatics. doi:10.1007/978-1-4020-6754-9_13424

Clarke, R. V., & Felson, M. (2011). The Origins of American Criminology. In Advances in Criminological Theory: Vol. 16. The origins of the routine activity approach and situational crime prevention (pp. 245–260). Academic Press.

Clarke, M., & Wheeler, S. (1990). *Business crime: Its nature and control*. Cambridge, UK: Polity Press.

Clarke, R. V. (2010). *Crime science*. Thousand Oaks, CA: SAGE Publications. doi:10.4135/9781446200926.n15

Cléro, J. P. (2017). Une pensée de l'existence à l'épreuve de l'éthique des soins. Les contradictions de l'éthique médicale. [A thought of being challenged with the ethics of care. The contradictions of medical ethics] In V. Jankélévitch (Ed.), *Morale et Politique* [Morale and Politics]. Paris, France. doi:10.3917/cite.070.0013

Clinard, M., & Yeager, P. (1980). Corporate crime: The first comprehensive account of illegal practices among America's top corporations. *Michigan Law Review*, *80*(4), 978–980. doi:10.2307/1288268

Cochrane, J. H. (2005). *Writing tips for Ph. D. students*. Chicago: Graduate School of Business University of Chicago. Retrieved from http://gsbwww.uchicago.edu/fac/john./cochrane/research/papers

Code of Federal Regulations of 2009 revised as of April 1, 2017 at 21CFR312.1 § 312-I. (n.d.). Retrieved from https://www.ecfr.gov/cgi-bin/text-idx?SID=c859616b5a665bbcda13092d0c1c063d&node=sp21.5.312.i&rgn=div6

Code of Federal Regulations of 2009, codified as amended at 45CFR46 § A-102. (n.d.). Retrieved from https://www.hhs.gov/ohrp/sites/default/files/ohrp/humansubjects/regbook2013.pdf.pdf

Code of Federal Regulations of 2009, codified as amended at 45CFR46 § D. (n.d.). Retrieved from https://www.hhs.gov/ohrp/regulations-and-policy/regulations/45-cfr 46/index.html#subpartd

Code of Federal Regulations of 2009, revised as of April, 2017, 21CFR56, § A-B-56. (n.d.). Retrieved from https://www.accessdata.fda.gov/scripts/cdrh/cfdocs/cfcfr/CFRSearch.cfm?CFRPart=56&showFR=1

Cohen, B. C. (n.d.). Nazi medical experimentation: The ethics of using medical data from Nazi experiments. *Jewish Virtual Library*. Retrieved from https://www.jewishvirtuallibrary.org/the-ethics-of-using-medical-data-from-nazi-experiments

Cohen, G. I. (2014). What (if anything) is wrong with human enhancement? What (if anything) is right with it? *Tulsa Law Review, 49*(3), 645-687. Retrieved from: https://pdfs.semanticscholar.org/26fa/35bb3a9183f49eb6246d7e7cb465f44232a3.pdf

Cohen, C. B. (1996). "Give Me Children or I Shall Die!" New Reproductive Technologies and Harm to Children. *The Hastings Center Report*, *26*(2), 19–27. doi:10.2307/3528572 PMID:8722522

Cohen, C. B. (2002). Protestant Perspectives on the Uses of the New Reproductive Technologies. *The Fordham Urban Law Journal*, *30*(1), 135–145. Retrieved from https://ir.lawnet.fordham.edu/cgi/viewcontent.cgi?article=1850&context=ulj PMID:15868665

Cohen, L. E., & Felson, M. (1979). On estimating the social costs of national economic policy: A critical examination of the Brenner study. *Social Indicators Research*, *6*(2), 251–259. doi:10.1007/BF00343977

Cojocaru, M. Cojocaru., Ş., Gârleanu, D., Irimescu, G., & Şoitu, C. (2010). Populaţii vulnerabile şi automarginalizate. Strategii de intervenţie şi efecte perverse [Vulnerable and self-originated populations. Intervention strategies and perverse effects]. Iaşi, Romania: LUMEN.

Cojocaru, D., & Sandu, A. (2011). (Bio)ethical and social reconstructions in transmodernity. *Journal for the Study of Religions and Ideologies*, *10*(30), 258–276.

Coker, R., & McKee, M. (2001). Ethical approval for health research in Central and Eastern Europe: An international survey. *Clinical Medicine*, *1*(3), 197–199. doi:10.7861/clinmedicine.1-3-197 PMID:11446614

Colegiul Psihologilor din România. (2013). [College of Psychologists from Romania]. *Codul deontologic al profesiei de psiholog cu drept de liberă practică* [Code of Ethics for the profession of psychologist with the right to practice]. Retrieved from https://www.istt.ro/documente/CODUL-DEONTOLOGIC.pdf

Coleman, C. H. (2009). Vulnerability as a regulatory category in human subject research. *The Journal of Law, Medicine & Ethics*, *37*(1), 12–18. doi:10.1111/j.1748-720X.2009.00346.x PMID:19245598

Coleman, J. W. (1987). Toward an integrated theory of white-collar crime. *American Journal of Sociology*, *93*(2), 406–439. doi:10.1086/228750

Coleman, J. W. (1998). *The criminal elite: Understanding white-collar crime*. New York: St. Martin's Press.

Collins, J. M., & Schmidt, F. L. (1993). Personality, integrity, and white-collar crime: A construct validity study. *Personnel Psychology*, *46*(2), 295–311. doi:10.1111/j.1744-6570.1993.tb00875.x

Comaroff, J. L., & Comaroff, J. (2001). On personhood: An anthropological perspective from Africa. *Social Identities*, *7*(2), 267–283. doi:10.1080/13504630120065310

Committee on Strategies for Responsible Sharing of Clinical Trial Data, Board on Health Sciences Policy, Institute of Medicine. (2015). *Sharing clinical trial data, maximizing benefits, minimizing risk*. Washington, DC: National Academies Press. Retrieved from https://www.ncbi.nlm.nih.gov/books/NBK269030/

Conner, L. (2008). The importance of knowledge development in bioethics education. In U. N. E. S. C. O. Bangkok (Ed.), *Asia Pacific Perspectives on Bioethics Education* (pp. 1–8). Bangkok, Thailand: UNESCO. Retrieved from http://www.eubios.info/APPBE.pdf

Constantin, M., Milcu, S. M., & Poenaru, S. (1994). *Fascinaţia imposibilului. Bioetica* [Fascination of the Impossible. Bioethics]. Bucharest, Romania: Editura pentru Tineret şi Sport Editis.

Convention for the Protection of Human Rights and Dignity of the Human Being with regard to the Application of Biology and Medicine: Convention on Human Rights and Biomedicine. (1997, April 4). Retrieved from https://rm.coe.int/168007cf98

Cooper, M. J. (2013). Antidotes for the publish or perish syndrome. *Trampta*. Retrieved from https://trampta.wordpress.com/2013/02/18/antidotes-for-the-publish-or-perish-syndrome/

Cooper, C. R., & Schindler, P. S. (2006). *Marketing Research*. New York: McGraw–Hill.

Cooper, R. J., Gupta, M., Wilkes, M. S., & Hoffman, J. R. (2006). Conflict of interest disclosure policies and practices in peer-reviewed biomedical journals. *Journal of General Internal Medicine*, *21*(12), 1248–1252. doi:10.1111/j.1525-1497.2006.00598.x PMID:17105524

Corneanu, D. (2000). Subiectul pasiv al infracţiunilor contra demnităţii [The victim of crimes against dignity]. *Dreptul*, *11*(9), 111-114.

Council for International Organizations of Medical Sciences (CIOMS). (2016). *International ethical guidelines for health-related research involving humans, Guideline 19: Pregnant and breastfeeding women as research participants*. Retrieved from https://cioms.ch/wp-content/uploads/2017/01/WEB-CIOMS-EthicalGuidelines.pdf

Council for International Organizations of Medical Sciences (CIOMS). (2016). *International ethical guidelines for health-related research involving humans*. Geneva, Switzerland: CIOMS.

Council for International Organizations of Medical Sciences (CIOMS). (2016). International ethical guidelines for health-related research involving humans. *Guideline 19: Pregnant and breastfeeding women as research participants*. Retrieved from https://cioms.ch/wp-content/uploads/2017/01/WEB-CIOMS-EthicalGuidelines.pdf

Council of Europe. (1979a). *Recommendation on the Use of Human Embryos and Fetuses for Diagnostic, Therapeutic, Scientific, Industrial and Commercial Purposes*. Retrieved from https://www.coe.int/t/dg3/healthbioethic/Texts_and_documents/INF_2014_5_vol_II_textes_%20CoE_%20bio%C3%A9thique_E%20(2).pdf

Council of Europe. (1979b). *Recommendation on Scientific Research and / or Experiments on Gametes, Embryos, Human Fetuses and the Donation of these Human Materials*. Retrieved from https://www.coe.int/t/dg3/healthbioethic/Texts_and_documents/INF_2014_5_vol_II_textes_%20CoE_%20bio%C3%A9thique_E%20(2).pdf

Council of Europe. (1986). *Recommendation no. 1046 on the Use of Human Embryos and Fetuses for Diagnostic, Therapeutical, Scientific, Industrial and Commercial Purposes*. Retrieved from http://assembly.coe.int/nw/xml/XRef/Xref-XML2HTML-en.asp?fileid=15080&lang=en

Council of Europe. (1997). *Convention for the Protection of Human Rights and Dignity of the Human Being with Regard to the Application of Biology and Medicine*. Oviedo, Spain: Council of Europe.

Cozma, C., & Măgureanu, L. (2008). Valori etice fundamentale, între constanţă şi metamorfoză [Fundamental ethical values, between constancy and metamorphosis]. In M. M. Pivniceru & C. Luca (Eds.), *Deontologia profesiei de magistrat. Repere contemporane* [Deontology of the Profession of Magistrate. Contemporary Landmarks]. Bucharest, Romania: Hamangiu.

Crăciun, T., & Crăciun, L. L. (1989). *Dicţionar de biologie* [Dictionary of Biology]. Bucharest, Romania: Albatros.

Crane, C. A., Hawes, S. W., Mandel, D., & Easton, C. J. (2013). Informed consent: An ethical issue in conducting research with male partner violent offenders. *Ethics & Behavior*, *23*(6), 477–488. doi:10.1080/10508422.2013.804795 PMID:25892900

Creswell, J. W. (2007). *Qualitative inquiry and research design: Choosing among five traditions* (2nd ed.). Thousand Oaks, CA: Sage Publication Inc.

Creţoiu, S. M., & Iacob, C. (2006). Biotehnologiile moderne şi emergenţa problemelor bioeticii [Modern biotechnologies and the emergence of bioethics problems]. *Revista Română de Bioetică*, *4*(4).

Croall, H. (2001). *Understanding white collar crime*. New York: McGraw-Hill Education.

Culianu, I. P. (2003). *Eros şi magie în Renaştere. 1484* [Eros and magic in the Renaissance. 1484]. Iaşi, Romania: Polirom.

Cullen, J. B., Victor, B., & Bronson, J. W. (1993). The ethical climate questionnaire: An assessment of its development and validity. *Psychological Reports*, *73*(2), 667–674. doi:10.2466/pr0.1993.73.2.667 PMID:8488245

Damasio, A. (2005). *Descartes' error: Emotions, reason, and the human brain*. London, UK: Penguinn Books.

Daniels, N., Bryant, J., Castano, R. A., Dantes, O. G., Khan, K. S., & Pannarunothai, S. (2000). Benchmarks of fairness for health care reform: A policy tool for developing countries. *Bulletin of the World Health Organization*, *78*(6), 740–750. PMID:10916911

Danis, M., & Patrick, D. L. (2002). Health policy, vulnerability, and vulnerable populations. In M. Danis, C. Clancy, & L. R. Churchill (Eds.), *Ethical Dimensions of Health Policy* (pp. 310–334). New York: Oxford University Press.

David, M., & Sutton, C. D. (2011). *Social Research: An introduction* (2nd ed.). London, UK: SAGE Publication Inc.

De Craemer, W. (1983). A cross-cultural perspective on personhood. *The Milbank Memorial Fund Quarterly. Health and Society*, *61*(1), 19–34. doi:10.2307/3349814 PMID:6552386

De George, R. T. (1999). *Business ethics*. Prentice Hall.

De Witte, J. I. (1989). The wait goes on. *The Hastings Center Report*, *19*(2), 2–3. doi:10.2307/3563129

DeBruin, D. (2001). Reflections on "vulnerability." *Bioethics Examiner*, *5*(2), 1–4.

DeHart-Davis, L. (2007). The unbureaucratic personality. *Public Administration Review*, *67*(5), 892–903. doi:10.1111/j.1540-6210.2007.00776.x

Deleanu, I. (1983). *Biologie şi drept* [Biology and Law]. Cluj-Napoca, Romania: Dacia.

Denno, D. W. (1997). Gender differences in biological and sociological predictors of crime. *Vermont Law Review*, *22*, 305–325.

Denzin, N. K., & Lincoln, Y. S. (2005). *The Sage Handbook of Qualitative Research* (3rd ed.). Sage Publication.

Descartes. (2012). *Discourse of the method of rightly conducting the reason and seeking truth in the sciences.* San Bernadino, USA: ULAN Press.

Dhingra, K., & Boduszek, D. (2013). Psychopathy and criminal behaviour: A psychosocial research perspective. *Journal of Criminal Psychology*, *3*(2), 83–107. doi:10.1108/JCP-06-2013-0014

Dingwall, R. (2008). The ethical case against ethical regulation in humanities and social science research. *Twenty-First Century Society*, *3*(1), 1–12. doi:10.1080/17450140701749189

Dockett, S., Perry, B., Kearney, E., Hampshire, A., Mason, J., & Schmied, V. (2009). Researching with families: Ethical issues and situations. *Contemporary Issues in Early Childhood*, *10*(4), 353–365. doi:10.2304/ciec.2009.10.4.353

Dodge, M. (2009). *Women and white-collar crime*. Upper Saddle River, NJ: Prentice Hall.

Donchin, A. (2001). Understanding autonomy relationally: Toward a reconfiguration of bioethical principles. *The Journal of Medicine and Philosophy*, *26*(4), 365–386. doi:10.1076/jmep.26.4.365.3012 PMID:11484130

Downie, R., & Clarkeburn, H. (2005). Approaches to the teaching of bioethics and professional ethics in undergraduate courses. *Bioscience Education*, *5*(1), 1–19. doi:10.3108/beej.2005.05000003

Downing, N. S., Shah, N. D., Aminawung, J. A., Pease, A. M., Zeitoun, J. D., Krumholz, H. M., & Ross, J. S. (2017). Post market safety events among novel therapeutics approved by the US Food and Drug Administration between 2001 and 2010. *Journal of the American Medical Association*, *317*(18), 1854–1863. doi:10.1001/jama.2017.5150 PMID:28492899

DuBois, J. M. (2006). Vulnerability in research. In E. A. Bankert & R. J. Amdur (Eds.), *Institutional Review Board: Management and Function* (2nd ed.; pp. 337–340). Sudbury, MA: Jones and Bartlett.

DuBois, W. (2003). *International pharmaceutical research*. Nashville, TN: Vanderbilt University Law School.

Dumea, C. (1998). *Omul între „a fi" sau „a nu fi". Probleme fundamentale de bioetică* [The man between "being" or "not being". Fundamental problems of bioethics]. Bucharest, Romania: Editura Arhiepiscopiei Romano-Catolice.

Dumitru, C. (2001). Omul – mai tare decât Dumnezeu [Man – Stronger than God]. *Contemporanul*, *11*(30), 20.

Duncombe, J., & Jessop, J. (2002). "Doing Rapport" and the Ethics of "Faking Friendship.". In M. Mauthner, M. Birch, J. Jessop, & T. Miller (Eds.), *Ethics in qualitative research* (pp. 108–122). London, UK: Sage; doi:10.4135/9781849209090.n6

Dunn, C. M., & Chadwick, G. L. (2012a). *FDA-regulated research in: Protecting study volunteers in research* (4th ed.). Boston: Center Watch.

Dunn, C. M., & Chadwick, G. L. (2012b). *Special ethical concerns in clinical research in: Protecting study volunteers in research* (4th ed.). Boston: Center Watch.

Dwyer, J. (2003). Teaching global bioethics. *Bioethics*, *17*(5-6), 432–446. doi:10.1111/1467-8519.00359 PMID:14959707

ECASRM (Ethics Committee of the American Society for Reproductive Medicine). (2001). Preconception gender selection for nonmedical reasons. *Fertility and Sterility*, *75*(5), 232–235. doi:10.1016/j.fertnstert.2004.05.013 PMID:11334894

Eckenwiler, L. A., Ells, C., Feinholz, D., & Shonfeld, T. (2008). Hopes for Helsinki: Reconsidering "vulnerability.". *Journal of Medical Ethics*, *34*(10), 765–766. doi:10.1136/jme.2007.023481 PMID:18827112

Edelhertz, H., & Overcast, T. D. (Eds.). (1982). *White-collar crime: An agenda for research*. Lexington, MA: Lexington Books.

Eichler, H. G., Pignatti, F., Flamion, B., Leufkens, H., & Breckenridge, A. (2008). Balancing early market access to new drugs with the need for benefit/risk data: A mounting dilemma. *Nature Reviews. Drug Discovery*, *7*(10), 818–826. doi:10.1038/nrd2664 PMID:18787530

Elam, G., & Fenton, K. A. (2003). Researching sensitive issues and ethnicity: Lessons from sexual health. *Ethnicity & Health*, *8*(1), 15–27. doi:10.1080/13557850303557 PMID:12893582

Emanuel, E. J., Wendler, D., & Grady, C. (2000). What makes clinical research ethical? *Journal of the American Medical Association*, *283*(20), 2701–2711. doi:10.1001/jama.283.20.2701 PMID:10819955

Emanuel, E. J., Wendler, D., Killen, J., & Grady, C. (2004). What makes clinical research in developing countries ethical? The benchmarks of ethical research. *The Journal of Infectious Diseases*, *189*(5), 930–937. doi:10.1086/381709 PMID:14976611

Enache, E. (2005). Supraomul între vis şi realitate [The superhuman between dream and reality]. *Revista Română de Bioetică*, *3*(2).

Enago Academy. (2015, May 24). *Publish or perish: What are its consequences?* Enago Academy. Retrieved from https://www.enago.com/academy/publish-or-perish-consequences/

Endong, F. P. C. (2018). The concepts of academic humility and seniority syndrome in research: A critique of research traditions in Nigerian universities. In F. P. C. Endong (Ed.), *Innovations in Measuring and Evaluating Scientific Information* (pp. 223–239). Hershey, PA: IGI Global; doi:10.4018/978-1-5225-3457-0.ch015

Engelhardt, T. (1996). *The foundations of bioethics*. New York, USA: Oxford University Press.

Enunemu, B. (2005). *Socio-economic and Cultural Correlates of The Girls 'Access to Education and Withdrawal from Secondary School in Delta state, Nigeria* (Unpublished DPhil Thesis). University of Ibadan.

Epstein, L., & King, G. (2002). The rules of inference. *The University of Chicago Law Review. University of Chicago. Law School*, *69*(1), e1. doi:10.2307/1600349

European Commission. (2010). *European textbook on ethics in research*. Retrieved from https://ec.europa.eu/research/science-society/document_library/pdf_06/textbook-on-ethics-report_en.pdf. Accessed 22 July 2018.

European Forum for Good Clinical Practice. (1997). *Guidelines and recommendations for European Ethics Committees*. Leuven, Belgium: EFGCP.

European Medicines Agency (EMA), Human Medicines Development and Evaluation. (2013). *Concept paper on extrapolation of efficacy and safety in medicine development*. Retrieved from http://www.ema.europa.eu/docs/en_GB/document_library/Scientific_guideline/2013/04/WC500142358.pdf

European Medicines Agency (EMA). (2010). *ICH guideline E16 on genomic biomarkers related to drug response: Context, structure and format of qualification submissions*. Retrieved from http://www.ema.europa.eu/docs/en_GB/document_library/Scientificguideline/2010/09/WC500097060.pdf

European Parliament and the Council of the European Union. (2006). Regulation (EC) No. 1901/2006 of the European Parliament and of the Council of 2006, December 12 on medicinal products for pediatric use and amending Regulation (EEC) No1768/92, Directive 2001/20/EC, Directive 2001/83/EC and Regulation (EC) No 726/2004. *Official Journal of the European Union, L, 378*(1). Retrieved from https://ec.europa.eu/health//sites/health/files/files/eudralex/vol-1/reg_2006_1901/reg_2006_1901_en.pdf

European Parliament. (2003). *Resolution No. 1352 on Human Stem Cell Research*. Retrieved from http://www.assembly.coe.int/nw/xml/XRef/Xref-XML2HTML-EN.asp?fileid=17158&lang=en

European Union. (2001, April 4). Directive 2001/20 / EC of the European Parliament and of the Council of 4 April 2001.

Ezekwonna, F. C. (2005). *African communitarian ethic: The basis for the moral conscience and autonomy of the individual. Igbo culture as a case study*. Berlin, Germany: International Academic Publishers.

Eze, M. (2008). What is African communitarianism? Against consensus as a regulative ideal. *South African Journal of Philosophy*, *27*(4), 386–399. doi:10.4314ajpem.v27i4.31526

Faden, R. R., & Beauchamp, T. L. (1986). *A history and theory of informed consent*. Oxford, UK: Oxford University Press.

Falasco, J. R. (2005). Frozen embryos and gamete providers' rights: A suggested model for embryo disposition. *Jurimetrics Journal*. Retrieved from http://www.qgtlaw.com/wp-content/uploads/publications/pub-Frozen-Embryos.pdf

Familusi, E. B., & Ajayi, N. A. (2017). Utilization of local journals by academic staff in Nigerian universities: A critical review. *International Journal of Library and Information Sciences Studies*, *3*(1), 25–36.

Fanelli, D. (2009). How many scientists fabricate and falsify research? A systematic review and meta-analysis of survey data. *PLoS One*, *4*(5), e5738. doi:10.1371/journal.pone.0005738 PMID:19478950

Fasola, O. (2017). *Ethical violations in research: Prevention rather than cure*. Retrieved from https://www.acu.edu.ng/documents/seminar/FASOLA.pdf

Federal Republic of Nigeria. (2004). *National policy on education*. Abuja, Nigeria: Government Printers.

Federal University of Agriculture Abeokuta. (2013). *Decree FUNAAB/VC/PRD.08/42 of May 10, 2013*. Abeokuta, Nigeria: Federal University of Agriculture Abeokuta.

Feeley, D. (2006). Personality, environment, and the causes of white-collar crime. *Law and Psychology Review*, *30*, 201–224.

Feinberg, J. (1980). The Child's Right to an Open Future. In W. Aiken & H. LaFollette (Eds.), *Who's Child? Children's Rights, Parental Authority and State Power* (pp. 126–130). New York: Littlefield Adams.

Feldwisch-Drentrup, H. (2017, August 1). After French drug trial tragedy, European Union issues new rules to protect study volunteers. *Science*. doi:10.1126cience.aan7191

Felson, M., & Clarke, R. V. (1998). Opportunity makes the thief. *Police Research Series, 98*, 1-16.

Felson, M. (1994). *Crime and everyday life: Insight and implications for society*. Thousand Oaks, CA: Pine.

Felson, M. (2017). Linking criminal choices, routine activities, informal control, and criminal outcomes. In D. B. Cornish & R. V. Clarke (Eds.), *The reasoning criminal* (pp. 119–128). Routledge.

Fenell, D. L., & Weinhold, B. K. (1992). Research in marriage and family therapy. In R. L. Smith & P. Stevens-Smith (Eds.), *Family Counseling and Therapy: Major Issues and Topics*. Ann Arbor, MI: ERIC/CAPS Publications.

Fenton, E. (2010). The perils of failing to enhance: A response to Persson and Savulescu. *Journal of Medical Ethics, 36*(3), 148–151. doi:10.1136/jme.2009.033597 PMID:20211993

Fingert, H. J. (2018). Expanding role of data science and bioinformatics in drug discovery and development. *Clinical Pharmacology and Therapeutics, 103*(1), 47–49. doi:10.1002/cpt.912 PMID:29134636

Finikov, T., & Artyukhov, A. (2016). *Akademichna chesnist' yak osnova staloho rozvytku universytetu* [Academic integrity as the basis for sustainable development of the university]. Kyiv, Ukraine: Taxon.

Flewitt, R. (2005). Conducting research with young children: Some ethical considerations. *Early Child Development and Care, 175*(6), 553–565. doi:10.1080/03004430500131338

Floridi, L. (2014). *The fourth revolution: How the infosphere is reshaping human reality*. Oxford, UK: Oxford University Press.

Food and Drug Administration (FDA) Center for Drug Evaluation and Research. (2017a). *Advancing health through innovation. 2017 New drug therapy approvals*. Retrieved from https://www.fda.gov/downloads/AboutFDA/CentersOffices/OfficeofMedicalProductsandTobacco/CDER/ReportsBudgets/UCM591976.pdf

Food and Drug Administration (FDA). (2017c). *FDA announces comprehensive regenerative medicine policy framework. FDA news release*. Retrieved from https://www.fda.gov/NewsEvents/Newsroom/PressAnnouncements/ucm585345.htm

Ford, L., & Reutter, L. (1990). Ethical dilemmas associated with small samples. *Journal of Advanced Nursing, 15*(1), 187–191. doi:10.1111/j.1365-2648.1990.tb01800.x PMID:2312919

Foucault, M. (1991). *Discipline and punish: The birth of a prison*. London, UK: Penguin.

Foucault, M. (1998). *The History of sexuality: The Will to knowledge*. London, UK: Penguin.

Fox, D. (2007). Silver spoons and golden genes. Genetic engineering and the egalitarian ethos. *American Journal of Law & Medicine, 33*(4), 567–623. doi:10.1177/009885880703300402 PMID:18277511

Fox, R. C., Willis, D., & Fox, R. C. (1983). Personhood, medicine, and American society. *The Milbank Memorial Fund Quarterly. Health and Society, 61*(1), 127–147. doi:10.2307/3349820 PMID:6552385

Franco, P., Porta, N., Holliday, J. D., & Willett, P. (2017). Molecular similarity considerations in the licensing of orphan drugs. *Drug Discovery Today, 22*(2), 377–381. doi:10.1016/j.drudis.2016.11.024 PMID:27965161

Franklin, M., & Chapman, S. (2000). *Human Inheritable Genetic Modifications. Assesing Scientific, Ethical, Religious and Policy Issues*. Washington, DC: American Association for the Advancement of Science. Retrieved from http://www.aas.org/spp/dspp/sfrl/germline/main.htm

Franklin, S., & Roberts, C. (2006). *Born and Made: An Ethnography of Preimplantation Genetic Diagnosis*. Princeton, NJ: Princeton University Press.

Friedman, A., Robbins, E., & Wendler, D. (2012). Which benefits of research participation count as 'direct'? *Bioethics, 26*(2), 60–67. doi:10.1111/j.1467-8519.2010.01825.x PMID:20497168

Friedrichs, D. O. (2009). *Trusted criminals: White collar crime in contemporary society*. Cengage Learning.

Frunză, A. (2016). *Către o nouă expertiză etică. Deconstruind valorile etice* [Towards a new ethical expertise. Deconstructing ethical values]. Iaşi, Romania: Lumen.

Frunză, A., & Sandu, A. (2017). Supervision of ethics in social work practice: A reconstruction of ethics expertise. In *Ethical Issues in Social Work Practice* (pp. 175–209). Hershey, PA: IGI Global.

Frunza, A., & Sandu, A. (2017a). Ethical acceptability of using generic consent for secondary use of data and biological samples in medical research. *Acta Bioethica*, *23*(2), 289–299. doi:10.4067/S1726-569X2017000200289

Frunza, A., & Sandu, A. (2017b). Formalization of informed consent. From ethical to administrative use. *Postmodern Openings*, *8*(3), 69–95. doi:10.18662/po/2017.0803.07

Funza, A., & Sandu, A. (2017). Values grounding the informed consent in medical practice: Theory and practice. *SAGE Open*, *7*(4). doi:10.1177/2158244017740397

Gabb, J. (2010). Home truths: Ethical issues in family research. *Qualitative Research*, *10*(4), 461–478. doi:10.1177/1468794110366807

Garcia-Hernandez, A. (2015). A note on the validity and reliability of multi-criteria decision analysis for the benefit–risk assessment of medicines. *Drug Safety*, *38*(11), 1049–1057. doi:10.100740264-015-0344-2 PMID:26353915

Garcia-Moreno, C., Jansen, H. A., Ellsberg, M., Heise, L., & Watts, C. H. (2006). Prevalence of intimate partner violence: Findings from the WHO multi-country study on women's health and domestic violence. *Lancet*, *368*(9543), 1260–1269. doi:10.1016/S0140-6736(06)69523-8 PMID:17027732

Gavrilă, L., & Iftime, O. (2006). Clonarea umană şi celulele stem – provocări ştiinţifice şi bioetice [Human cloning and stem cells - Scientific and bioethical challenges]. In Educaţia în bioetică şi drepturile omului în România [Education in Bioethics and Human Rights in Romania]. Bucharest, Romania: Academic Press.

Gazzaniga, M. S. (2005). *The ethical brain*. New York: Dana Press.

Gbadegesin, S. (1993). Bioethics and culture: An African perspective. *Bioethics*, *7*(2/3), 257–262. doi:10.1111/j.1467-8519.1993.tb00292.x PMID:11651539

Geertz, C. (1965). The impact of the concept of culture on the concept of man. In J. R. Platt (Ed.), *New views of man*. Chicago, USA: University of Chicago Press.

Gergen, K. (2005). *Social construction in context*. London, UK: Penguin.

Gibbs, L. E., & Gambrill, E. D. (1998). *Critical thinking for social workers: Exercises for the helping professions*. Thousand Oaks, CA: SAGE Publications, Inc.

Girla, L., & Rub, J. (2015). Psychological portrait of the white-collar offender: Decision-making and rational choice. *Revista Naţională de Drept*, (9), 179-191.

Goertzel, B., & Bugaj, S. V. (2008). Stages of ethical development in artificial general intelligence systems. In P. Wang, B. Goertzel, S. Franklin (Eds.), *Artificial General Intelligence 2008: Proceedings of the first AGI Conference* (pp. 448-459). Amsterdam: IOS Press.

Goldie, J., Schwartz, L., & Morrison, J. (2000). A process evaluation of medical ethics education in the first year of a new curriculum. *Medical Education*, *34*(6), 468–473. doi:10.1046/j.1365-2923.2000.00496.x PMID:10792689

Goodin, R. E. (1985). *Protecting the vulnerable: A reanalysis of our social responsibilities*. Chicago: University of Chicago Press.

Gorsira, M., Steg, L., Denkers, A., & Huisman, W. (2018). Corruption in Organizations: Ethical Climate and Individual Motives. *Administrative Sciences*, *8*(1), 1–19. doi:10.3390/admsci8010004

Gottfredson, M. R., & Hirschi, T. (1990). *A general theory of crime*. Stanford University Press.

Gottschalk, P. (2011). Actions on suspicion of white-collar crime in business organizations: An empirical study of intended responses by Chief financial officers. *Professional Issues in Criminal Justice*, *6*(1-2), 41–51.

Gottschalk, P. (2013). Empirical differences in crime categories by white-collar criminals. *International Letters of Social and Humanistic Sciences*, *5*, 17–26. doi:10.18052/www.scipress.com/ILSHS.5.17

Grady, C. (2009). Vulnerability in research: Individuals with limited financial and/or social resources. *The Journal of Law, Medicine & Ethics*, *37*(1), 19–27. doi:10.1111/j.1748-720X.2009.00347.x PMID:19245599

Grady, C. (2015). Enduring and emerging challenges of informed consent. *The New England Journal of Medicine*, *37*(9), 855–862. doi:10.1056/NEJMra1411250 PMID:25714163

Graham, A., Powell, M. A., & Taylor, N. (2014). Ethical research involving children: Encouraging reflexive engagement in research with children and young people. *Children & Society*, *29*(5), 331–343. doi:10.1111/chso.12089

Grant, M., & Booth, A. (2009). A typology of reviews: An analysis of 14 review types and associated methodologies. *Health Information and Libraries Journal*, *26*(2), 91–108. doi:10.1111/j.1471-1842.2009.00848.x PMID:19490148

Grbich, C. (1999). *Qualitative Research in Health: An introduction*. London: Sage Publication.

Green, R. M. (2001). *The human embryo research debates: Bioethics in the vortex of controversy*. Oxford, UK: Oxford University Press.

Grieger, J. (2006). *Corruption in organizations-Some outlines for research* (Working Paper). Department of Economics and Social Sciences, University of Wuppertal.

Griffiths, A., Angus, J. P., & Brown, A. N. (2018). *Revolutionizing clinical trials through real-time data capture and analytics*. Retrieved from http://www.appliedclinicaltrialsonline.com/print/349625?page=full&topic=230%2C%20250&CID=actdirect.1988127.APCT%2A%2520Applied%252

Gunsalus, C. K., Marcus, A. R., & Oransky, I. (2018). Institutional research misconduct reports need more credibility. *Journal of the American Medical Association*, *319*(13), 1315–1316. doi:10.1001/jama.2018.0358 PMID:29532069

Gupta, U. C. (2013). Informed consent in clinical research: Revisiting few concepts and areas. *Perspectives in Clinical Research*, *4*(1), 26–32. doi:10.4103/2229-3485.106373 PMID:23533976

Guyer, P. (1998, July 25). *Kant, Immanuel (1724-1804)*. Milton Park, UK: Taylor and Francis. doi:10.4324/9780415249126-DB047-1

Hall, E. L., & Rammell, K. (2017). Racial- and ethnic-sensitive practice: From the practitioners' perspective. *Journal of Social Work*, *17*(6), 678–694. doi:10.1177/1468017316651993

Hansson, M. G., Dillner, J., Bartram, C. R., Carlson, J. A., & Helgesson, G. (2006). Should donors be allowed to give broad consent to future biobank research? *The Lancet Oncology*, *7*(3), 266–269. doi:10.1016/S1470-2045(06)70618-0 PMID:16510336

Hardwig, J. (1985). Epistemic dependence. *The Journal of Philosophy*, *82*(7), 335–349. doi:10.2307/2026523

Hardwig, J. (1988). Evidence, testimony, and the problem of individualism. *Social Epistemology*, *2*(4), 309–321. doi:10.1080/02691728808578498

Harris, W. (2009). *How scientific peer review works*. Retrieved from: https://science.howstuffworks.com/innovation/scientific-experiments/scientific-peer-review.htm

Harsanyi, J. C. (1980). *Essays on ethics, social behavior, and scientific explanation.* Boston, USA: Reidel.

Harsanyi, J. C. (1982). Morality and the theory of the rational behaviour. In H. Sen & B. Williams (Eds.), *Utilitarianism and Beyond* (pp. 39–63). Cambridge, UK: Cambridge University Press.

Hartjen, C. A. (1978). *Crime and criminalization.* Praeger Publishers.

Hasnas, J. (2005). Ethics and the problem of white collar crime. *The American University Law Review, 54*(3), 579–660.

Hauber, A. B., Angelyn, O., Fairchild, F., & Johnson, R. (2013). Quantifying benefit–risk preferences for medical interventions: An overview of a growing empirical literature. *Applied Health Economics and Health Policy, 11*(4), 319–329. doi:10.100740258-013-0028-y PMID:23637054

Hawley, A. (1950). *Human Ecology: A Theory of Community Structure.* New York: Ronald Press.

Helgesson, G. (2012). In defense of broad consent. *Cambridge Quarterly of Healthcare Ethics, 21*(1), 40–50. doi:10.1017/S096318011100048X PMID:22152457

Hermeren, G. (2014). Ethical considerations in chimera research. *Development, 142*(1), 3–5. doi:10.1242/dev.119024 PMID:25516962

Hess, D. (2015). Ethical infrastructure and evidence-based corporate compliance and ethics programs: Policy implications from the empirical evidence. *NYUJL & Business, 12*, 317–334.

Hibbard, B. (2014). *Ethical Artificial Intelligence.* Retrieved from https://arxiv.org/abs/1411.1373

Hirschi, T. (1969). A control theory of delinquency. *Criminology theory: Selected Classic Readings*, 289-305.

Hirschi, T., & Gottfredson, M. (1993). Commentary: Testing the general theory of crime. *Journal of Research in Crime and Delinquency, 30*(1), 47–54. doi:10.1177/0022427893030001004

Hirschman, E. C. (1991). Babies for sale: Market ethics and the new reproductive technologies. *The Journal of Consumer Affairs, 25*(2), 358–390. doi:10.1111/j.1745-6606.1991.tb00010.x PMID:11660025

Ho, A. (2008). The individualist model of autonomy and the challenge of disability. *Journal of Bioethical Inquiry, 5*(2–3), 193–207. doi:10.100711673-007-9075-0

Hobson-Rohrer, W., Hoffman-Longtin, K., Liu, H. Y., Loue, S., Love, L. M., Pollart, S. M., & Power, C. M. (2016). Active learning on center stage: Theatre as a tool for medical education. *Learn, Serve, Lead 2016, AAMC Annual Meeting.*

Hoefnagels, G. P. (1973). Criminology: its definition, nature and subfields. In *The other side of criminology.* Dordrecht, The Netherlands: Springer. doi:10.1007/978-94-017-4495-9_3

Hoffmaster, B. (2006). What does vulnerability mean? *The Hastings Center Report, 36*(2), 38–45. doi:10.1353/hcr.2006.0024 PMID:16604897

Hofmann, B. (2009). Broadening consent and diluting ethics? *Journal of Medical Ethics, 35*(2), 125–129. doi:10.1136/jme.2008.024851 PMID:19181887

Hofmann, B., Solbakk, J. H., & Holm, S. (2009). Consent to biobank research: one size fits all? In J. H. Solbakk, S. Holm, & B. Hofmann (Eds.), *The Ethics of Research Biobanking* (pp. 3–23). New York, USA: Springer; doi:10.1007/978-0-387-93872-1_1

Hohmann-Marriott, B. E. (2001). Marriage and family therapy research: Ethical issues and guidelines. *The American Journal of Family Therapy, 29*(1), 59–73. doi:10.1080/01926180126081

Holkup, P. A., Tripp-Reimer, T., Salois, E. M., & Weinert, C. (2004). Community-based participatory research: An approach to intervention research with a Native American community. *Advances in Nursing Science*, *27*(3), 162–175. doi:10.1097/00012272-200407000-00002 PMID:15455579

Howard, F., McKneally, M. F., & Levin, A. V. (2010). Integrating bioethics into postgraduate medical education: The University of Toronto model. *Academic Medicine*, *85*(6), 1035–1040. doi:10.1097/ACM.0b013e3181dbebb8 PMID:20505406

Huidu, A. (2017). *Reproducerea umană medical asistată. Etica incriminării versus etica biologică. Studiu de drept comparat* [Human medically assisted reproduction. The ethics of incrimination versus bioethics. Comparative law study]. Iaşi, Romania: Lumen.

Hull, D. (1988). *Science as a process: An evolutionary account of the social and conceptual development of science*. Chicago: University of Chicago Press. doi:10.7208/chicago/9780226360492.001.0001

Hurst, S. A. (2008). Vulnerability in research and health care: Describing the elephant in the room? *Bioethics*, *22*(4), 191–202. doi:10.1111/j.1467-8519.2008.00631.x PMID:18405317

Hutter, M. (2004). *Universal Artificial Intelligence: Sequential decisions based on algorithmic probability*. Berlin, Germany: Springer Science & Business Media.

Hyder, A. A., Wali, S. A., Khan, A. N., Teoh, N. B., Kass, N. E., & Dawson, L. (2004). Ethical review of health research: A perspective from developing country researchers. *Journal of Medical Ethics*, *30*(1), 68–72. doi:10.1136/jme.2002.001933 PMID:14872079

Hyun, I., Taylor, P., Testa, G., Dickens, B., Jung, K. W., McNab, A., ... Zoloth, L. (2007). Ethical standards for human-to-animal chimera experiments in stem cell research. *Cell Stem Cell*, *1*(2), 159–163. doi:10.1016/j.stem.2007.07.015 PMID:18383627

Ikuenobe, P. (2006). *Philosophical perspectives on communalism and morality in African traditions*. Oxford, UK: Lexington Books.

Indian Council of Medical Research. (2017). *National ethical guidelines for biomedical and health research involving human participants*. Retrieved from https://www.iitm.ac.in/downloads/ICMR_Ethical_Guidelines_2017.pdf

Institute of Electrical and Electronics Engineers (IEEE). (2018). *Ethically Aligned design: A vision for prioritizing human wellbeing with Artificial Intelligence and autonomous systems*. IEEE Standards Association. Retrieved from http://standards.ieee.org/develop/indconn/ec/ead_general_principles_v2.pdf

International Center for Academic Integrity. (2013). *Why integrity?* Retrieved from http://www.academicintegrity.org/icai/integrity-1.php

International Conference on Harmonisation of Technical Requirements for Registration of Pharmaceuticals for Human Use. (1996). *ICH harmonised tripartite guideline, Guideline for good clinical practice E6(R1)*. Retrieved from https://www.ich.org/fileadmin/Public_Web_Site/ICH_Products/Guidelines/Efficacy/E6/E6_R1_Guideline.pdf

International Council for Harmonisation of Technical Requirements for Pharmaceuticals for Human Use (ICH). (2016). *ICH M8 Expert Working Group. Specification for submission formats for eCTD v1.1*. Retrieved from http://estri.ich.org/ssf/Specification_for_Submission_Formats_for_eCTD_v1_1.pdf

International Society for Stem Cell Research (ISSCE). (2016). *Guidelines for stem cell research and clinical translation*. Retrieved from http://www.isscr.org/professional-resources/policy/2016-guidelines

Ioan, B., & Stângă, O. (2009). Respectul pentru persoană, [Respect for the person]. In V. Astărăstoae, S. Loue & B. Ioan (Eds.), Etica cercetării pe subiecţi umani [Ethics of Research on Human Subjects]. Iaşi, Romania: "Gr. T. Popa" U.M.F. Iaşi Publishing House.

Israel, B. A., Schulz, A. J., Parker, E. A., Becker, A. B., Allen, A. J. III, & Guzman, J. R. (2003). Critical issues in developing and following community-based participatory research principles. In M. Minkler & N. Wallerstein (Eds.), *Community-Based Participatory Research for Health* (pp. 53–76). San Francisco, CA: Jossey-Bass.

Izugbara, C., & Undie, C. (2008). Who owns the body? Indigenous African discourses of the body and contemporary sexual rights rhetoric. *Reproductive Health Matters*, *16*(31), 159–167. doi:10.1016/S0968-8080(08)31344-5 PMID:18513617

Jagers, R., & Mock, L. (1995). The communalism scale and collectivistic-individual tendencies: Some preliminary findings. *The Journal of Black Psychology*, *21*(2), 153–167. doi:10.1177/00957984950212004

Japan. (2002). *Law on Human Cloning and Other Similar Techniques.* Retrieved from http://www.cas.go.jp/jp/seisaku/hourei/data/htc.pdf

Jardine, L. (2015). *Erasmus, man of letters: The construction of charisma in print.* Princeton University Press. doi:10.1515/9781400866175

Jensen, K., & Gaie, J. (2010). African communalism and public health policies: The relevance of indigenous concepts of personal identity to HIV/AIDS policies in Botswana. *African Journal of AIDS Research*, *9*(3), 297–305. doi:10.2989/16085906.2010.530187 PMID:25860633

Jha, C., & Panda, B. (2017). Individualism and corruption: A cross-country analysis. *Economic Papers: A Journal of Applied Economics and Policy, 36*, 60–74.

Johnstone, M. (2009). *Bioethics. A Nursing Perspective* (5th ed.). St. Louis, MO: Churchil Livingstone Elsevier.

Jones, H. (1965). *Crime and the penal system.* University Tutorial Press.

Jones, H. W. Jr. (1995). Children of choice: A doctor's perspective. *Washington and Lee Law Review*, *52*(1), 225–232. PMID:12071215

Journal of Young Investigators. (2005). Writing scientific manuscripts. A guide for undergraduates. *Journal of Young Investigators.* Retrived from http://www.jyi.org/

Juengst, E. (1997). Can enhancements be distinguished from therapy in genetic medicine? *The Journal of Medicine and Philosophy*, *22*(2), 125–142. doi:10.1093/jmp/22.2.125 PMID:9186925

Kalu, A. O. U., & Okeke, A. F. (2016). Unethical marketing research practices in Nigeria: Manipulations in marketing reports. *Journal of Research and Development (Srinagar)*, *2*(12), 8–15. doi:10.12816/0028307

Kamm, F. M. (2005). Is there a problem with enhancement? *The American Journal of Bioethics*, *5*(3), 5–14. doi:10.1080/15265160590945101 PMID:16006376

Kant, I. (1972). *Critica raţiunii practice* [The critique of practical reason]. Bucharest, Romania: Ştiinţifică.

Kant, I. (1996). The metaphysics of morals. Part. I, Metaphysical first principles of the doctrine of right. In M. J. Gregor (Ed.), *Practical philosophy* (p. 378). New York, USA: Cambridge University Press.

Kant, I. (1998). *Critica raţiunii pure* [Critique of pure reason]. 2nd ed.). Bucharest, Romania: IRI.

Kaphagawani, D. (2004). African conception of a person: A critical survey. In K. Wiredu (Ed.), *A Companion to African Philosophy* (pp. 332–342). Hoboken, USA: Blackwell Publishing; doi:10.1002/9780470997154.ch26

Kapp, M. B. (1983). Children's assent for participation in pediatric research protocols: Assessing national practice. *Clinical Pediatrics*, *22*(4), 275–278. doi:10.1177/000992288302200406 PMID:6825373

Kaptein, M. (2011). Understanding unethical behavior by unraveling ethical culture. *Human Relations*, *64*(6), 843–869. doi:10.1177/0018726710390536

Kardiologia Polska. (n.d.). *Author Guidelines*. Retrieved from https://ojs.kardiologiapolska.pl/kp/about/submissions#authorGuidelines

Kazdin, A. (1989). *Behavior modification in applied settings*. Pacific Grove, CA: Brooks/Cole Publishing.

Kelbessa, W. (2005). *The utility of ethical dialogue for marginalized voices in Africa*. Addis Ababa, Ethiopia: Addis Ababa University.

Kelly, J., Sadeghieh, T., & Adeli, K. (2014). Peer review in scientific publications: Benefits, critiques and a survival guide. *The Journal of the International Federation of Clinical Chemistry and Laboratory Medicine*, *25*(3), 227–243. PMID:27683470

Kharasch, E. D., & Houle, T. T. (2017). Errors and integrity in seeking and reporting apparent research misconduct. *Anesthesiology*, *127*(5), 733–737. doi:10.1097/ALN.0000000000001875 PMID:28825936

Khmarsky, V. (2016). Academic integrity in USA: kil'ka sposterezhen' 2015 roku [Academic integrity in USA: several observations of 2015]. In Academic integrity as the basis for sustainable development of the university [Academic integrity as the basis for sustainable development of the university] (pp. 53-92). Academic Press.

Kimmelman, J., & London, A. J. (2011). Predicting harms and benefits in translational trials: Ethics, evidence, and uncertainty. *PLoS Medicine*, *8*(3). doi:10.1371/journal.pmed.1001010 PMID:21423344

Kim, N. Y., & Miller, G. (2008). Perceptions of the ethical climate in the Korean tourism industry. *Journal of Business Ethics*, *82*(4), 941–954. doi:10.100710551-007-9604-0

Kim, S. Y., & Miller, F. G. (2014). Informed Consent for Pragmatic Trials — The Integrated Consent Model. *The New England Journal of Medicine*, *370*(8), 769–772. doi:10.1056/NEJMhle1312508 PMID:24552326

Kipnis, K. (2001). Vulnerability in research subjects: A bioethical taxonomy. In *Ethical and policy issues involving human participants* (Vol. 2). Bethesda, MD: National Bioethics Advisory Commission.

Kipnis, K. (2003). Seven vulnerabilities in the pediatric research subject. *Theoretical Medicine and Bioethics*, *24*(2), 107–120. doi:10.1023/A:1024646912928 PMID:12943266

Kirton, M. (1976). Adaptors and innovators: A description and measure. *The Journal of Applied Psychology*, *61*(5), 622–629. doi:10.1037/0021-9010.61.5.622

Kish-Gephart, J. J., Harrison, D. A., & Trevino, L. K. (2010). Bad apples, bad cases, and bad barrels: Meta-analytic evidence about sources of unethical decisions at work. *The Journal of Applied Psychology*, *95*(1), 1–16. doi:10.1037/a0017103 PMID:20085404

Knieling, A., Knieling, L., & Ioan, B. (2005). Etica cercetării ştiinţifice pe cadavre de feţi umani [Ethics of scientific research on human fetus corpses]. *Revista Română de Bioetică*, *3*(4), 80-84.

Koepsell, D. (2007). *The Ethics of Genetic Engineering. A Position Paper from the Center for Inquiry Office of Public Policy*. New York: Center for Inquiry Inc.

Kolb, D. (1984). *Experiential learning: Experience as the source of learning and development*. Englewood Cliffs, NJ: Prentice-Hall.

Kopacek, P. (2012). Roboethics. In *Proceedings of the IFAC Workshop on Supplemental Ways for Improving International Stability – SWIIS 2012* (pp. 67-72). New York: Elsevier. doi:10.3182/20120611-3-IE-4029.00015

Kopitowski, K. (2014). What makes pediatric clinical research ethical? *Archivos Argentinos de Pediatria*, *112*(6), 492–493. doi:10.5546/aap.2014.eng.492 PMID:25362904

Kottow, M. H. (2003). The vulnerable and the susceptible. *Bioethics*, *17*(5-6), 460–471. doi:10.1111/1467-8519.00361 PMID:14959710

Kottow, M. H. (2004). Vulnerability: What kind of principle is it? *Medicine, Health Care, and Philosophy*, *7*(3), 281–287. doi:10.100711019-004-6857-6 PMID:15679020

Kperogi, F. (2015). A comparison of everyday university vocabularies in Nigeria, America and Britain. *Daily Trust*. Retrieved from https://www.dailytrust.com.ng/news/politics-of-grammar/a-comparison-of-everyday-university-vocabularies-in-nigeria-america-and-britain-ii/125123.html

Kramer, R. C. (1985). Defining the concept of crime: A humanistic perspective. *Journal of Sociology and Social Welfare*, *12*, 469–485.

Kranz, P. L., Ramirez, S. V., & Lund, N. L. (2007). The use of psychodrama action techniques in a race relations class. *College Student Journal*, *41*(4), 1203–1208.

Krubiner, C. B., Sayd, R. H., & Merritt, M. W. (2016). Health researchers' ancillary-care: Empirical responsibilities in low-resource settings: The landscape of institutional guidance. *Journal of Empirical Research on Human Research Ethics; JERHRE*, *6*(3), 73–81. doi:10.1525/jer.2011.6.3.73

Kshirsagar, N., Swaminathan, S., Jog, P., Dalwai, S., Mathur, R., Shekhar, C., ... Mehta, D. (2017). Regulatory and ethical issues in pediatric clinical research: Recommendations from a panel discussion. *Journal of Clinical Pharmacology*, *57*(8), 943–946. doi:10.1002/jcph.916 PMID:28513861

Kumar, V., Aaker, D. A., & Day, G. S. (2002). *Essentials of Marketing research*. New York: John. Wiley & Sons.

Kuo, F. C. (2009). Secrets or no secrets: Confidentiality in couple therapy. *The American Journal of Family Therapy*, *37*(5), 351–354. doi:10.1080/01926180701862970

Kurzweil, R. (2005). *The singularity is near: When humans transcend biology*. New York: Viking.

Kuther, T. L., & Posada, M. (2004). Children and adolescents' capacity to provide informed consent for participation in research. *Advances in Psychology Research*, *32*, 163–173. PMID:16986221

Ladanyi, M., & Ruane, W. J. (2014). *Personalized products expanding*. Retrieved from https://www.genomeweb.com/blog/personalized-products /

Lange, M. M., Rogers, W., & Dodds, S. (2013). Vulnerability in research: A way forward. *Bioethics*, *27*(6), 333–340. doi:10.1111/bioe.12032 PMID:23718774

Langley, G. R., Adcock, I. M., Busquet, F., Crofton, K. M., Csernok, E., Giese, C., ... Woszczek, G. (2017). Teaser to discover and develop new therapies, we need 21st-century roadmaps for biomedical research based on multi-scale human disease pathways, and supported by policy and funding strategies that prioritize human relevance. Towards a 21st-century roadmap for biomedical research and drug discovery: Consensus report and recommendations. *Drug Discovery Today*, *22*(2), 327–339. doi:10.1016/j.drudis.2016.10.011 PMID:27989722

Langton, L., & Piquero, N. L. (2007). Can general strain theory explain white-collar crime? A preliminary investigation of the relationship between strain and select white-collar offenses. *Journal of Criminal Justice*, *35*(1), 1–15. doi:10.1016/j.jcrimjus.2006.11.011

Lanre-Abass, B. (2012). Autonomy and interdependence: Quandaries in research ethics. *Health*, *4*(4), 173–184. doi:10.4236/health.2012.44026

Laplace, P.-S. (1998). *Pierre-Simon Laplace philosophical essay on probabilities. Sources in the history of mathematics and physical sciences* (2nd ed.). New York, USA: Springer Science & Business Media; doi:10.1007/978-1-4612-4184-3

Largent, E. A., Weissman, J. S., Gupta, A., Abraham, M., Rozenblum, R., Lynch, H. F., & Cohen, I. G. (2018). Patient-centered outcomes research: Stakeholder perspectives and ethical and regulatory oversight issues. *Journal of Empirical Research on Human Research Ethics; JERHRE*, *40*(1). doi:10.1177/1556264618779785

Lauritzen, P. (1990). What Price Parenthood? *The Hastings Center Report*, *20*(2), 38–46. doi:10.2307/3562619 PMID:2180853

Lavecchia, A. (2015). Machine-learning approaches in drug discovery: Methods and applications. *Drug Discovery Today*, *20*(3), 318–331. doi:10.1016/j.drudis.2014.10.012 PMID:25448759

Laventhal, N., Tarini, B., & Lantos, J. (2012). Ethical issues in neonatal and pediatric clinical trials. *Pediatric Clinics of North America*, *59*(5), 1205–1220. doi:10.1016/j.pcl.2012.07.007 PMID:23036252

Lederer, S. E. (1997). *Subjected to science: Human experimentation in America before the Second World War*. Baltimore, MD: Johns Hopkins University Press. doi:10.1080/03612759.1995.9949143

Lee, C. J. (2012). A Kuhnian critique of psychometric research on peer review. *Philosophy of Science*, *79*(5), 859–870. doi:10.1086/667841

Leibniz, G. W. (1976). Critical thoughts on the general part of the Principles of Descartes. In L. E. Loemker (Ed.), *Philosophical Papers and Letters: A Selection* (pp. 383–412). Dordrecht, Netherlands: D. Reidel. doi:10.1007/978-94-010-1426-7

Levine, C. (2004). The concept of vulnerability in disaster research. *Journal of Traumatic Stress*, *17*(5), 395–402. doi:10.1023/B:JOTS.0000048952.81894.f3 PMID:15633918

Levine, C., Faden, R., Grady, C., Hammerschmidt, D., Eckenwiler, L., & Sugarman, J. (2004). The limitations of "vulnerability" as a protection for human research participants. *The American Journal of Bioethics*, *4*(3), 44–49. doi:10.1080/15265160490497083 PMID:16192138

Levine, R. J. (1994). The impact of HIV infection on society's perception of clinical trials. *Kennedy Institute of Ethics Journal*, *4*(2), 93–98. doi:10.1353/ken.0.0054 PMID:10134752

Levitt, M., & Zwart, H. (2009). Bioethics: An export product? Reflections on hands-on involvement in exploring the "external" validity of international bioethical declarations. *Bioethical Inquiry*, *6*(3), 367–377. doi:10.100711673-009-9168-z

Levy, Y., & Elis, J. T. (2006). A systems approach to conduct an effective literature review. *Support of Information Systemy Research Informing Science Journal*, *9*, 181–212. doi:10.28945/479

Lind, D. A., Marchal, W. G., & Wathen, S. A. (2010). *Basic Statistics Using Excel for Office XP*. New York: McGraw-Hill.

Lin, O. (2005). Rehabilitating bioethics: Recontextualizing in vitro fertilization outside contractual autonomy. *Duke Law Journal*, *54*, 485–511. PMID:15940846

Locke, J. (1979). *An Essay Concerning Human Understanding*. Oxford, UK: Oxford University Press.

Longino, H. (2016). The social dimensions of scientific knowledge. In N. Zalta (Ed.), *The Stanford Encyclopedia of Philosophy*. Retrieved from: https://plato.stanford.edu/archives/spr2016/entries/scientific-knowledge-social/

Loue, S. (2018). Using sociodrama to foster cultural humility among faculty and students in the academic medical center. *Revista Românească pentru Educaţie Multidimensională*.

Loue, S., & Chiscop, E. (2004). Mental illness research in Romania: A review of author attention to ethical norms. *Revista Romana de Bioetica*, 12.

Loue, S., & Loff, B. (2013). Is there a universal understanding of vulnerability? Expriences with Russian and Romanian trainees in research ethics. *Journal of Empirical Research on Human Research Ethics; JERHRE*, *8*(5), 17–27. doi:10.1525/jer.2013.8.5.17 PMID:24384513

Lugo, M. A. (2013). *Self-control, attitudinal beliefs, and white-collar crime intentions* (Unpublished Doctoral Dissertation). University of South Florida.

Luna, F. (2009). Elucidating the concept of vulnerability: Layers not labels. *International Journal of Feminist Approaches to Bioethics*, *2*(1), 121–139. doi:10.3138/ijfab.2.1.121

Luna, F., & Herissone-Kelly, P. (2006). *Bioethics and vulnerability: A Latin American view*. Amsterdam: Editions Rodopi B.V.

Lusher, S. J., McGuire, R., van Schaik, R. C., Nicholson, C. D., & de Vlieg, J. (2014). All scientific disciplines, including medicinal chemistry, are the subject of a revolution as data are generated at unprecedented rates and their analysis and exploitation become increasingly fundamental to innovation. Data-driven medicinal chemistry in the era of big data. *Drug Discovery Today*, *19*(7), 859–868. doi:10.1016/j.drudis.2013.12.004 PMID:24361338

Mabe, A. R., & Rollin, S. A. (1986). The role of a code of ethical standards in counseling. *Journal of Counseling and Development*, *64*(5), 294–297. doi:10.1002/j.1556-6676.1986.tb01113.x

Machan, T. R. (1999). Business ethics in a free society. *A Companion to Business Ethics*, 88-99.

Macklin, R. (2003). Bioethics, vulnerability, and protection. *Bioethics*, *17*(5-6), 472–486. doi:10.1111/1467-8519.00362 PMID:14959716

Maclean, A. (2009). *Autonomy, informed consent and medical law: A relational challenge. Autonomy, informed consent and medical law: A relational challenge*. Cambridge, UK: Cambridge University Press. doi:10.1017/CBO9780511576119

Maddux, J. (2011). *Publishing in English language journals in psychology; tips for increasing the odds*. Paper presented at "A. I. Cuza" University from Iaşi during the Doctoral Program in Schools of Excellence.

Maher, R. C. (2010). Authoritative references. *EE417*. Retrieved from http://www.montana.edu/rmaher/ee417/Authoritative%20References.pdf

Maier, W. C. (2018). *The rare disease revolution*. Retrieved from http://www.appliedclinicaltrialsonline.com/rare-disease-revolution-0

Mandava, A., Pace, C., Campbell, B., Emanuel, E., & Grady, C. (2012). The quality of informed consent: Mapping the landscape. A review of empirical data from developing and developed countries. *Journal of Medical Ethics*, *38*(6), 356–365. doi:10.1136/medethics-2011-100178 PMID:22313664

Manea, T. (2005). "Gata cu constrângerile biologice!" Reproducerea dincolo de reproducere, ["It's over with biological constraints!" Reproduction beyond reproduction]. *Revista Română de Bioetică, 3*(1).

Margolin, G. (1982). Ethical and legal considerations in marital and family therapy. *The American Psychologist*, *37*(7), 788–801. doi:10.1037/0003-066X.37.7.788 PMID:7137697

Margolin, G., Chien, D., Duman, S. E., Fauchier, A., Gordis, E. B., Oliver, P. H., ... Vickerman, K. A. (2005). Ethical issues in couple and family research. *Journal of Family Psychology*, *19*(1), 157–167. doi:10.1037/0893-3200.19.1.157 PMID:15796661

Marsh, K., Jzerman, M. I., Thokala, P., Baltussen, P., Boysen, M., Kaló, Z., ... Devlin, N. (2016). Multiple criteria decision analysis for health care decision making - Emerging good practices: Report 2 of the ISPOR MCDA Emerging Good Practices Task Force. *Value in Health*, *19*(2), 125–137. doi:10.1016/j.jval.2015.12.016 PMID:27021745

Martin, B. R. (2013). Whither research integrity? Plagiarism, self-plagiarism and coercive citation in an age of research assessment. *Research Policy*, *42*(5), 1005–1014. doi:10.1016/j.respol.2013.03.011

Martin, K. D., & Cullen, J. B. (2006). Continuities and extensions of ethical climate theory: A meta-analytic review. *Journal of Business Ethics*, *69*(2), 175–194. doi:10.100710551-006-9084-7

Martin, K. D., Johnson, J. L., & Cullen, J. B. (2009). Organizational change, normative control deinstitutionalization, and corruption. *Business Ethics Quarterly*, *19*(1), 105–130. doi:10.5840/beq20091915

Mathy, R. M., Kerr, D. L., & Haydin, B. M. (2003). Methodological rigor and ethical considerations in internet-mediated research. *Psychotherapy (Chicago, Ill.)*, *40*(1–2), 77–85. doi:10.1037/0033-3204.40.1-2.77

Matsuyama, R., Reddy, S., & Smith, T. J. (2006). Why do patients choose chemotherapy near the end of life? A review of the perspective of those facing death from cancer. *Journal of Clinical Oncology*, *24*(21), 3490–3496. doi:10.1200/JCO.2005.03.6236 PMID:16849766

Mayer, D. M., Kuenzi, M., & Greenbaum, R. L. (2010). Examining the link between ethical leadership and employee misconduct: The mediating role of ethical climate. *Journal of Business Ethics*, *95*(1), 7–16. doi:10.100710551-011-0794-0

Mbiti, J. (1970). *African religions and philosophy*. New York, USA: Praeger Publishers.

McBarnet, D. (2006). Toward ethical compliance: Lessons from Enron. In *Global perspectives on ethics of corporate governance* (pp. 27–38). New York: Palgrave Macmillan. doi:10.1057/9780312376192_3

McCabe, D. L. (2018). *It takes a village: Academic dishonesty and educational opportunity*. Retrieved from https://www.aacu.org/publications-research/periodicals/it-takes-village-academic-dishonesty-and-educational-opportunity

McDonald, P. J., Kulkarni, A. V., Farrokhyar, F., & Bhandari, M. (2010). Ethical issues in surgical research. *Canadian Journal of Surgery*, *53*(2), 133–136. PMID:20334746

McIntosh, E. D. G. (2011). Ethics of performing pediatric clinical trials. *The Journal of Pharmaceutical and Biopharmaceutical Contract*. Retrieved from http://www.pharmoutsourcing.com/Featured-Articles/37794-Ethics-of-Performing-Pediatric-Clinical-Trials/

McLeod, S. A. (2007). *The Milgram experiment*. Retrieved from www.simplypsychology.org/milgram.html

McMahan, J. (1998). Wrongful Life: Paradoxes in the Morality of Causing People to Exist. In J. L. Coleman & C. W. Morris (Eds.), *Rational Commitment and Social Justice: Essays for Gregory Kavka* (pp. 208–2011). Cambridge, UK: Cambridge University Press. doi:10.1017/CBO9780511527364.013

McMillan, J. (2002). Sex Selection in the United Kingdom. *The Hastings Center Report*, *32*(1), 28–31. doi:10.2307/3528294 PMID:11917706

McNutt, L. A., Gordon, E. J., & Uusküla, A. (2009). Informed recruitment in partner studies of HIV transmission: An ethical issue in couples research. *BMC Medical Ethics*, *10*(1), 14. doi:10.1186/1472-6939-10-14 PMID:19709442

Medicina. (n.d.). *Guide for Authors*. Retrieved from https://www.elsevier.com/journals/medicina/1010-660x/guide-for-authors

Meek, L., & Asa, O. (2012). Introduction and project overview. In L. Meek & O. Asa (Eds.), *Effectiveness of Research and Innovation Management at Policy and Institutional Levels in Cambodia, Vietnam, Thailand and Malaysia* (pp. 12–18). London, UK: OECD.

Meisel, A., & Roth, L. H. (1981). What we do and do not know about informed consent. *Journal of the American Medical Association*, *246*(21), 2473–2477. doi:10.1001/jama.1981.03320210039022 PMID:7299972

Menkiti, I. (1984). Person and community in African traditional thought. In R. A. Wright (Ed.), *African Philosophy* (pp. 171–181). New York, USA: University Press of America.

Menkiti, I. (2004). On the normative conception of a person. In K. Wiredu (Ed.), *A Companion to African Philosophy* (pp. 324–331). New York, USA: Blackwell Publishing.

Mervis, J. (2017). Research is an afterthought in first Trump budget. *Science.* Retrieved from http://www.sciencemag.org/news/2017/03/research-afterthought-first-trump-budget

Messner, S. F., & Rosenfeld, R. (1997). Political restraint of the market and levels of criminal homicide: A cross-national application of institutional-anomie theory. *Social Forces*, *75*(4), 1393–1416.

Metz, T. (2008). Philosophical perspectives on communalism and morality in African traditions. *Journal of Contemporary African Studies*, *26*(2), 231–239. doi:10.2307/25426992

Mezirow, J. (1981). A critical theory of adult learning and education. *Adult Education Quarterly*, *32*(1), 3–24. doi:10.1177/074171368103200101

Miehl, K. L. (2003). Preembryos: The tiniest speck of potential life carrying the seeds for sweeping change. *Journal of Technology. Law & Policy*, *4*(1), 1–36. doi:10.5195/tlp.2004.12

Milgram, S. (1963). Behavioral study of obedience. *Journal of Abnormal and Social Psychology*, *67*(4), 371–378. doi:10.1037/h0040525 PMID:14049516

Miller, N. E., & Dollard, J. (1941). *Social learning and imitation.* New Haven, CT: Yale University Press.

Mill, J. S. (1972). Collected works of John Stuart Mill: Vol. XVII. *The later letters of John Stuart Mill (1849-1873).* London, UK: Routledge & Kegan Paul. doi:10.3138/9781442654143

Mill, J. S. (1996). *Essays on ethics, religion and society.* Indianapolis, USA: Liberty Fund.

Mill, J. S. (2014). *Utilitarismul* [*Utilitarianism*]. Bucharest, Romania: ALL.

Millum, J., & Emanuel, E. J. (2007). The ethics of international research with abandoned children. *Science*, *318*(5858), 1874–1875. doi:10.1126cience.1153822 PMID:18096792

Mir, H., & Morgan, C. (2013). Ethical implications of germ line genetic engineering. *University of Western Ontario Medical Journal, 78*(3), 18-21. Retrieved from http://www.uwomj.com/wp-content/uploads/2013/06/v78n3.18-21.pdf

Mirkes, R. (2006). Is it ethical to generate human-animal chimeras? *The National Catholic Bioethics Quarterly*, *6*(1), 109–130. doi:10.5840/ncbq20066170 PMID:17037495

Mlotshwa, B. C., Mwesigwa, S., Mboowa, G., Williams, L., Retshabile, G., Kekitiinwa, A., ... Mpoloka, S. W. (2017). Co-ordination and support of international research data networks. The collaborative African genomics network training program: A trainee perspective on training the next generation of African scientists. *Genetics in Medicine*, *19*(7), 826–833. doi:10.1038/gim.2016.177 PMID:28383545

Moher, D., Liberati, A., Tetzlaff, J., & Altman, D. (2009). Preferred reporting items for systematic reviews and meta-analyses: The PRISMA statement. *BMJ (Clinical Research Ed.)*, *339*(1), b2535. doi:10.1136/bmj.b2535 PMID:19622551

Moore, M. (2011). Psychological theories of crime and delinquency. *Journal of Human Behavior in the Social Environment*, *21*(3), 226–239. doi:10.1080/10911359.2011.564552

Moreno, J. L. (1953). *Who shall survive?* New York: Beacon House.

Moreno, J. L. (1972). *Psychodrama* (Vol. 1). New York: Beacon House.

Moroianu Zlătescu, I. (2006). Protecţia demnităţii persoanei şi a demnităţii speciei umane în domeniul bioeticii, în lumina Convenţiei de la Oviedo [Protection of human dignity and dignity in the field of bioethics in the light of the Oviedo Convention]. In Educaţia în bioetică şi drepturile omului în România [Education in Bioethics and Human Rights in Romania]. Bucharest, Romania: Academic Press.

Morrow, V., & Richards, M. (1996). The ethics of social research with children: An overview. *Children & Society*, *10*(2), 90–105. doi:10.1002/(SICI)1099-0860(199606)10:2<90::AID-CHI14>3.0.CO;2-Z

Mortimer, A. (1993). *The Difference of Man and the Dofference It Makes*. New York: Fordham University Press.

Murphy, E., & Dingwall, R. (2007). Informed consent, anticipatory regulation and ethnographic practice. *Social Science & Medicine*, *65*(11), 2223–2234. doi:10.1016/j.socscimed.2007.08.008 PMID:17888553

Musschenga, A. W., Van Luijn, H. E. M., Keus, R. B., & Aaronson, N. K. (2007). Are risks and benefits of oncological research protocols both incommensurable and incompensable? *Accountability in Research*, *14*(3), 179–196. doi:10.1080/08989620701455217 PMID:17877107

Nagel, T. (1979). The fragmentation of value. In *Mortal Questions* (pp. 128–142). New York: Cambridge University Press.

National Commission for the Protection of Human Subjects of Biomedical and Behavioral Research. (1979). *The Belmont report*. Retrieved from https://www.hhs.gov/ohrp/regulations-and-policy/belmont-report/index.html

National Commission for the Protection of Human Subjects of Biomedical and Behavioral Research. (1979). *The Belmont Report*. Washington, DC: US Government Printing Office. Retrieved from http://www.hhs.gov/ohrp/humansubjects/guidance/belmont.html

National Health and Medical Research Council. (2018a). *Ethical conduct in research with Aboriginal and Torres Strait Islander peoples and communities: Guidelines for researchers and stakeholders*. Retrieved from https://www.nhmrc.gov.au/guidelines-publications/ind2

National Health and Medical Research Council. (2018b). *National statement on ethical conduct in human research 2007 (updated 2018)*. Retrieved from http://www.nhmrc.gov.au/guidelines/publications/e72

Near, J. P., & Miceli, M. P. (1995). Effective whistle-blowing. *Academy of Management Review*, *20*(3), 679–708.

Neff-Smith, M., Giles, S., Spencer, E. M., & Fletcher, J. C. (1997). Ethics program evaluation: The Virginia Hospital ethics fellows example. *HealthCare Ethics Committee Forum*, *9*(4), 375–388. PMID:10175653

Neuman, W. L. (2003). *Social Research Methods: Qualitative and Quantitative Approaches* (5th ed.). Boston: Allyn and Bacon Publishers.

Nickel, P. J. (2006). Vulnerable populations in research: The case of the seriously ill. *Theoretical Medicine and Bioethics*, *27*(3), 245–264. doi:10.100711017-006-9000-2 PMID:16763881

Niehaus, I. (2002). Bodies, heat, and taboos: Conceptualizing modern personhood in the South African Lowveld1. Niehaus I. Bodies, heat, and taboos: Conceptualizing modern personhood in the South African Lowveld. *Ethnology*, *41*(3), 189–207. doi:10.2307/4153025

Nietzsche, F. (n.d.). *Human, All Too Human, Book II*. Retrieved from https://fr.scribd.com/document/21750833/Nietzsche-Human-All-Too-Human

Nietzsche, Fr. (1899). The Twilight of the Idols or How to Philosophize with a Hammer. In F. Nietzsche (Ed.), *The Works of Friedrich Nietzsche* (Vol. 3, pp. 195–196). London, UK: T. Fisher Unwin.

Nordenfelt, L. (1999). On medicine and other means of health enhancement: towards a conceptual framework. In M. Hanson & D. Callahan (Eds.), *The Goals of Medicine* (pp. 69–87). Washington, DC: Georgetown University Press.

Noua Zeelandă. (2004). *Law No. 92/2004 on the Techniques of Medical Assistance to Procreation*. Retrieved from http://www.legislation.govt.nz/act/public/2004/0092/latest/whole.html

Nucci, L. P. (1989). Challenging conventional wisdom about morality: The domain approach to values education. In L. P. Nucci (Ed.), *Moral development and character education* (pp. 183–203). Berkeley, CA: McCutchan.

Nuffield Council on Bioethics. (1999). *Ethical issues in research in developing countries*. London, UK.

Nwamuo, C. (2005). *University of Calabar in transition: 2000 – present*. Calabar, Nigeria: University of Calabar Press.

O'Dowd, A. (2017). Research integrity has become complacent and lacks transparency, MPs hear. *British Medical Journal*, *359*, 4945. doi:10.1136/bmj.j4945 PMID:29070601

O'Leary, R. (2007). *The Ethics of Dissent: Managing Guerrilla Government*. Washington, DC: CQ Press.

O'Neill, O. (2003). Some limits of informed consent. *Journal of Medical Ethics*, *29*(1), 4–7. doi:10.1136/jme.29.1.4 PMID:12569185

O'Neill, O. (2006). Etica lui Kant [Kant's ethics]. In P. Singer (Ed.), *Tratat de etică* [Ethics Treaty] (pp. 205–215). Iaşi, Romania: Polirom.

Oberfield, Z. W. (2009). Rule following and discretion at government's frontlines: Continuity and change during organization socialization. *Journal of Public Administration: Research and Theory*, *20*(4), 735–755. doi:10.1093/jopart/mup025

Obioha, U. P. (2014). Radical communitarian idea of the human person in African philosophical thought: A critique. *The Western Journal of Black Studies*, *38*(1), 13–23.

Oduwole, O. (2010). Personhood and abortion: An African perspective. *LUMINA*, *21*(2), 1–10.

Office of Good Clinical Practice. (2018a). *Payment and reimbursement to research subjects - Information sheet. FDA regulatory information*. Retrieved from https://www.fda.gov/RegulatoryInformation/Guidances/ucm126429.htm

Office of Good Clinical Practice. (2018b). *Payment and reimbursement to research subjects - Information sheet. Guidance for institutional review boards and clinical investigators*. Retrieved from https://www.fda.gov/RegulatoryInformation/Guidances/ucm126429.htm

Ogunbanjo, G. A., & Van Bogaert, K. D. (2005). Communitarianism and communitarian bioethics. *South African Family Practice*, *47*(10), 51–53. doi:10.1080/20786204.2005.10873305

Okolo, C. (2002). Self as a problem in African philosophy. In P. H. Coetzee & A. P. J. Roux (Eds.), *Philosophy from Africa. A Text with Readings*. Cape Town, South Africa: Oxford University Press.

Okonta, P., & Rossouw, T. (2013). Prevalence of scientific misconduct among a group of researchers in Nigeria. *Developing World Bioethics*, *13*(3), 149–157. doi:10.1111/j.1471-8847.2012.00339.x PMID:22994914

Olaru, B. (2005). Problema autonomiei şi limitele folosirii tehnologiilor reproducerii asistate [The issue of autonomy and the limits of using assisted reproduction technologies]. *Revista Română de Bioetică*, *3*(3), 43-54.

Olaru, B. (2006). A porunci viaţa şi a interzice moartea? [Order life and forbid death?]. *Revista Română de Bioetică, 4*(2).

Olweny, C. (1994). The ethics and conduct of cross-cultural research in developing countries. *Pychology-Oncology*, *3*(1), 11–20. doi:10.1002/pon.2960030104

Omohundro, S. (2012). Rational Artificial Intelligence for the greater good. In A. Eden, J. Moor, J. Søraker, & E. Steinhart (Eds.), *Singularity Hypotheses. A Scientific and Philosophical Assessment*. Berlin, Germany: Springer. doi:10.1007/978-3-642-32560-1_9

Onywuenyi, I. (1991). Is there an African philosophy? In T. Serequeberhan (Ed.), *African Philosophy: The Essential Readings*. St. Paul, USA: Paragon House.

Oransky, I. (2015). Second thoughts: How publish or perish promotes inaccuracy in science – and journalism. *American Medical Association Journal of Ethics*, *17*(12), 1172–1175. doi:10.1001/journalofethics.2015.17.12.sect1-1512 PMID:26698592

Owoeye, J. S., & Oyebade, S. A. (2009). Higher education research in Uganda: Problems and prospects. *African Higher Education Review*, *2*, 19–38.

Owomoyela, O. (1991). Africa and the imperative of philosophy: A skeptical consideration. In T. Serequeberhan (Ed.), *African Philosophy: The Essential Readings*. St. Paul, USA: Paragon House.

Owomoyela, O. (1994). With friends like these … A critique of pervasive anti-Africanisms in current African studies epistemology and methodology. *African Studies Review*, *37*(3), 77–101. doi:10.2307/524903

Papathanasiou, P., Brassart, L., Blake, P., Hart, A., Whitbread, L., Pembrey, R., & Kieffer, J. (2016). Transparency in drug regulation: Public assessment reports in Europe and Australia. *Drug Discovery Today*, *21*(11), 1806–1813. doi:10.1016/j.drudis.2016.06.025 PMID:27373773

Parens, E. (1999). Is Better Always Good? The Enhancement Project. In E. Parens (Ed.), *Enhancing Human Traits* (pp. 1–28). Washington, DC: Georgetown University Press.

Parent, M. J. (2003). *Self-control vs. social control as an explanation for delinquency* (Unpublished Doctoral Dissertation). University of Windsor.

Parfit, D. (1984). *Reasons and Persons*. Oxford, UK: Oxford University Press.

Park, A., & Molloy, C. (2018). The state of the drug discovery nation unveiled as new report provides vital insights for the development of new medicines. *Drug discovery tomorrow: How to catapult ourselves into the future*. Retrieved from http://www.drugdiscoverytoday.com/view/47448/the-state-of-the-drug-discovery-nation-unveiled-as-new-report-provides-vital-insights-for-the-devel

Pascal, B. (1995). *Pensées, no. 98* [Thoughts, no. 98]. London, UK: Penguin Books.

Pasquale, C. (2014). *Five questions for Jeffrey Beall*. Retrieved from https://connections.cu.edu/stories/five-questions-jeffrey-beall

Patel, T., & Hamlin, R. G. (2015). Toward a unified framework of perceived negative leader behaviors insights from french and british educational sectors. *Journal of Business Ethics*, *145*(1), 157–182. doi:10.100710551-015-2909-5

Patterson, T. (2012). Ethical and Legal Considerations in Family Psychology: The Special Issue of Competence. In *The Wiley-Blackwell Handbook of Family Psychology* (pp. 183–197). Hoboken, NJ: John Wiley & Sons Ltd. doi:10.1002/9781444310238.ch12

Patton, M. Q. (2002). *Qualitative Research and Evaluation Methods* (3rd ed.). London: Sage Publications.

Pavlov, I. P. (2010). Conditioned reflexes: An investigation of the physiological activity of the cerebral cortex. *Annals of Neurosciences, 17*(3), 136.

Pediatric Research Equity Act of 2003 Pub. L. 108-155. (n.d.). Retrieved from https://www.congress.gov/108/plaws/publ155/PLAW-108publ155.pdf

Pennings, G. (2000). The right to choose your donor: A step towards commercialization or a step towards empowering the pacient? *Human Reproduction (Oxford, England)*, *15*(1), 508–514. doi:10.1093/humrep/15.3.508 PMID:10686188

Pennings, G. (2000). What are the ownership rights for gametes and embryos?: Advance directives and the disposition of cryopreserved gametes and embryos. *Human Reproduction (Oxford, England)*, *15*(5), 979–986. doi:10.1093/humrep/15.5.979 PMID:10783338

Perri, F. S., & Brody, R. G. (2011). The dark triad: Organized crime, terror and fraud. *Journal of Money Laundering Control*, *14*(1), 44–59. doi:10.1108/13685201111098879

Persson, I., & Savulescu, J. (2008). The perils of cognitive enhancement and the urgent imperative to enhance the moral character of humanity. *Journal of Applied Philosophy*, *25*(3), 162–177. doi:10.1111/j.1468-5930.2008.00410.x

Persson, I., & Savulescu, J. (2012). *Unfit for the future: The need for moral enhancement*. Oxford, UK: Oxford University Press. doi:10.1093/acprof:oso/9780199653645.001.0001

Peterson, D. K. (2002). Deviant workplace behavior and the organization's ethical climate. *Journal of Business and Psychology*, *17*(1), 47–61. doi:10.1023/A:1016296116093

Petrini, C. (2010). "Broad" consent, exceptions to consent and the question of using biological samples for research purposes different from the initial collection purpose. *Social Science & Medicine*, *70*(2), 217–220. doi:10.1016/j.socscimed.2009.10.004 PMID:19853341

Petryna, A. (2009). *When experiments travel: Clinical trials and the global search for human subjects*. New Jersey, USA: Princeton University Press. doi:10.1515/9781400830824

Pettifor, J. L. (1996). Ethics: Virtue and politics in the science and practice of psychology. *Canadian Psychology*, *37*(1), 1–12. doi:10.1037/0708-5591.37.1.1 PMID:12194189

Pharma I. Q. Conferences (IQPC). (2011). *Balancing ethics with economy in outsourced clinical trials*. Retrieved from https://www.pharma-iq.com/clinical/articles/balancing-ethics-with-economy-in-outsourced

Phoenix, A. (1987). Theories of gender and black families. In G. Weiner & M. Arnot (Eds.), *Gender under scrutiny*. London: Hutchinson and the Open University Press.

Pignattia, F., Jonssonb, B., Blumenthalc, G., & Justicec, R. (2015). Assessment of benefits and risks in development of targeted therapies for cancer. The view of regulatory authorities. *Molecular Oncology*, *9*(5), 1034–1041. doi:10.1016/j.molonc.2014.10.003 PMID:25481691

Pinchuk, S. (2000). A difficult choice in a different voice: Multiple births, selective reduction and abortion. *Duke Journal of Gender Law & Policy*, *7*(29), 32–56.

Pinto, J., Leana, C. R., & Pil, F. K. (2008). Corrupt organizations or organizations of corrupt individuals? Two types of organization-level corruption. *Academy of Management Review*, *33*(3), 685–709. doi:10.5465/amr.2008.32465726

Piot, C. (1999). *Remotely global: Village modernity in West Africa*. Chicago, USA: The University of Chicago Pres.

Piquero, N., Lyn Exum, M., & Simpson, S. S. (2005). Integrating the desire–for–control and rational choice in a corporate crime context. *Justice Quarterly*, *22*(2), 252–280. doi:10.1080/07418820500089034

Pittenger, D. J. (2003). Internet research: An opportunity to revisit classic ethical problems in behavioural research. *Ethics & Behavior*, *13*(1), 45–60. doi:10.1207/S15327019EB1301_08 PMID:14552304

Pittore, K., de Lintelo, D. J. H., Georgalakis, J., & Mikindo, T. (2016). Choosing between research rigour or support for advocacy movements, a false dichotomy? *IDS Bulletin*, *47*(6). doi:10.19088/1968-2016.202

Pivniceru, M. M., & Dăscălescu, F. D. (2007). Limita inferioară a dreptului la viaţă: între protecţia fetusului uman, dreptul la avort şi progresul ştiinţelor medicale [The lower limit of the right to life: between the protection of the human fetus, the right to abortion and the advancement of medical sciences]. *Revista Română de Bioetică, 1*(4). Retrieved from http://www.culturavietii.ro/2014/09/22/limita-inferioara-dreptul-la-viata-intre-protectia-fetusului-uman-dreptul-la-avort-si-progresul-stiintelor-biomedicale/

Pivniceru, M. M., & Dăscălescu, F. D. (2007). Limita inferioară a dreptului la viaţă: între protecţia fetusului uman, dreptul la avort şi progresul ştiinţelor medicale [The lower limit of the right to life: Between the protection of the human fetus, the right to abortion and the advancement of medical sciences]. *Revista Română de Bioetică, 1*(4). Retrieved from http://www.culturavietii.ro/2014/09/22/limita-inferioara-dreptul-la-viata-intre-protectia-fetusului-uman-dreptul-la-avort-si-progresul-stiintelor-biomedicale/

Plagiarism Advice. (2013). *A national strategy for addressing student plagiarism*. Retrieved from http://www.plagiarismadvice.org

Plato. (1986). *Plato in twelve volumes: Charmides. Alcibiades I and II. Hipparchus. The lovers. Theages. Minos. Epinomis*. Cambridge, USA: Harvard University Press.

Ploug, T., & Holm, S. (2015). Going beyond the false dichotomy of broad or specific consent: A meta-perspective on participant choice in research using human tissue. *The American Journal of Bioethics*, *15*(9), 44–46. doi:10.1080/15265161.2015.1062178 PMID:26305752

Podany, A. T. (2017). Ethical considerations in pediatric research. In *PedSAP 2017 Book 1. Research and study design in pediatrics* (pp. 7-18). Academic Press. Retrieved from https://www.accp.com/docs/bookstore/pedsap/ped2017b1_sample.pdf

Poff, D. C. (2017). *Peer review: Strengths, limitations and emerging issues*. Committee of Publication Ethics (COPE). Retrieved from https://publicationethics.org/files/Deborah_Poff_PRESENTATION_final_ENGLISH.pdf

Popa, M. (2016). Evaluarea raportului de cercetare și etica cercetării științifice [Evaluation of the research report and scientific research ethics]. In M. Popa (Ed.), *Metodologia cercetării (note de curs)* [Methodology of Research (Course Notes)]. Bucharest, Romania: Asociaţia de Psihologie Industrială şi Organizaţională. Retrieved from http://www.apio.ro/upload/mc12_eval_etica_cercet.pdf

Popoveniuc, B. (2016). *Filosofia singularității. Creierul global - o etică a gândirii fără om* [The philosophy of singularity. The global brain - an ethic of humanless thinking]. Bucharest, Romania: Eikon.

Popper, K. (1972). *Objective knowledge*. Oxford, UK: Oxford University Press.

Popper, K. (2008). *Conjectures and refutations: The growth of scientific knowledge* (2nd ed.). London, UK: Routledge.

Prentice, E. D., Bruce, G., & Gordon, B. G. (2016). Institutional review board assessment of risks and benefits associated with research (research involving human participants V2). In *Report on ethical and policy issues in research involving human participants: Vol. 2. Commissioned papers and staff analysis*. Washington, DC: National Bioethics Advisory Commission. Retrieved from http://www.onlineethics.org/hprentice.aspx

Price, M., & Norris, D. M. (2009). White-collar crime: Corporate and securities and commodities fraud. *The Journal of the American Academy of Psychiatry and the Law*, *37*(4), 538–544. PMID:20019002

Pritchard, I. A. (2011). How do IRB members make decisions? A review and research agenda. *Journal of Empirical Research on Human Research Ethics*, *6*(2), 31–46. doi:10.1525/jer.2011.6.2.31 PMID:21680975

Pronin, E. (2007). Perception and misperception of bias in human judgment. *Trends in Cognitive Sciences*, *11*(1), 37–43. doi:10.1016/j.tics.2006.11.001 PMID:17129749

Psychiatria Danubiana. (n.d.). *Guidelines for Authors*. Retrieved from http://www.hdbp.org/psychiatria_danubina/guidlines.html

Punch, M. (1994). Politics and ethics in qualitative research. In N. K. Denzin & Y. S. Lincoln (Eds.), *Handbook of qualitative research*. London: Newbery Park. Sage Publications.

Pupovac, V., & Fanelli, D. (2015). Scientists admitting to plagiarism: A meta-analysis of surveys. *Science and Engineering Ethics*, *21*(5), 1331–1352. doi:10.100711948-014-9600-6 PMID:25352123

Purcaru, D., Lazăr, O., Purcaru, A., & Rogozea, L. (2012). Evoluţia consimţământului informat în cercetarea clinică [Evolution of informed consent in clinical research]. *Jurnal Medical Braşovean [The Medical Journal of Brasov]*, *1*, 81–84. Retrieved from http://oaji.net/articles/2014/693-1396104695.pdf

Rakotsoane, F. C., & Van Niekerk, A. (2017). Human life invaluableness: An emerging African bioethical principle. *South African Journal of Philosophy*, *36*(2), 252–262. doi:10.1080/02580136.2016.1223983

Randolph, J. (2009). Guide to writing the dissertation literature review. *Practical Assessment, Research & Evaluation*, *14*(13).

Rawat, S., & Meena, S. (2014). Publish or perish: Where are we heading? *Journal of Research in Medical Sciences*, *19*(2), 87–89. PMID:24778659

Rawls, J. (1971). *Theory of justice*. Cambridge University Press.

Reed, G. E., & Yeager, P. C. (1996). Organizational offending and neoclassical criminology: Challenging the reach of a general theory of crime. *Criminology*, *34*(3), 357–382. doi:10.1111/j.1745-9125.1996.tb01211.x

Regulation (EU) No 536/2014 of the European Parliament and of the Council of 16 April 2014. (n.d.). Retrieved from https://publications.europa.eu/en/publication-detail/-/publication/e7137f5b-e655-11e3-8cd4-01aa75ed71a1/language-en

Rehnquist, J. (2001). *The globalization of clinical trials: A growing challenge in protecting human subjects*. Washington, D.C.: Department of Health and Human Services.

Research integrity – have we made progress? (2017). *Lancet*, *389*(10081). doi:10.1016/S0140-6736(17)31201-1

Resnick, J., Kessler, M., Aitken, M., & Metz, A. (2017). Heralding the era of human data science. *IQVIA Real-World Insights, 7*(14). Retrieved from https://www.forbes.com/sites/oreillymedia/2012/08/20/data-science-and-the-health-care-revolution/#57004c8229f7

Resnik, D. B. (2015). *What is ethics in research and why is it important?* National Institute of Environmental Health Sciences. Retrieved from https://www.niehs.nih.gov/research/resources/bioethics/whatis/index.cfm

Resnik, D. B., & Langer, P. J. (2001). Human germline gene therapy reconsidered. *Human Gene Therapy, 12*(11), 1449–1458. doi:10.1089/104303401750298607 PMID:11485636

Richardson, H. S. (1990). Specifying norms as a way to resolve concrete ethical problems. *Philosophy & Public Affairs, 19*(4), 279–310.

Rid, A., & Wendler, D. (2010). Risk-benefit assessment in medical research - critical review and open questions. *Law Probability and Risk, 9*(3-4), 151–177. doi:10.1093/lpr/mgq006

Rieber, R., & Robinson, D. (2001). *Wilhelm wundt in history: The making of a scientific psychology*. Berlin, Germany: Springer Science & Business Media. doi:10.1002/jhbs.10127

Riesman, P. (1986). The person and the life cycle in African social life and thought. *African Studies Review, 29*(2), 71–138. doi:10.2307/523965

Rifkin, J. (1991). *Biosphere Politics: A New Consciousness for a New Century*. Crown Publishers.

Roberts, L. W. (2002). Informed consent and the capacity for voluntarism. *The American Journal of Psychiatry, 159*(5), 705–712. doi:10.1176/appi.ajp.159.5.705 PMID:11986120

Robertson, J. (1983). Procreative liberty and the control of conception, pregnancy and childbirth. *Virginia Law Review, 69*(3), 405–464. doi:10.2307/1072766 PMID:11651806

Robertson, J. (2005). Gay and lesbian access to assisted reproductive technology. *Case Western Reserve Law Review, 55*(2), 323–372. Retrieved from https://scholarlycommons.law.case.edu/cgi/viewcontent.cgi?article=1582&context=caselrev

Robertson, J. A. (1989). Resolving disputes over frozen embryos. *The Hastings Center Report, 19*(6), 7–12. doi:10.2307/3561979 PMID:2606667

Robertson, J. A. (1995). Symbolic issues in embryo research. *The Hastings Center Report, 25*(1), 37–38. doi:10.2307/3562492 PMID:7537261

Robertson, J. A. (2002). *Precommitment strategies for disposition of frozen embryos*. SSRN Electronic Journal. doi:10.2139srn.315374

Rogers, R., & Lange, M. M. (2013). Rethinking the vulnerability of minority populations in research. *American Journal of Public Health, 103*(12), 2141–2146. doi:10.2105/AJPH.2012.301200 PMID:24134375

Rogers, W., Mackenzie, C., & Dodds, S. (2012). Why bioethics needs a concept of vulnerability. *International Journal of Feminist Approaches to Bioethics, 5*(2), 11–38. doi:10.3138/ijfab.5.2.11

Rogstad, J. E., & Rogers, R. (2008). Gender differences in contributions of emotion to psychopathy and antisocial personality disorder. *Clinical Psychology Review, 28*(8), 1472–1484. doi:10.1016/j.cpr.2008.09.004 PMID:18945529

Rohrich, R. J. (2007). Ethical approval of clinical studies, informed consent, and the declaration of Helsinki: What you need to know [Editorial]. *Plastic and Reconstructive Surgery, 119*(7), 2307–2309. doi:10.1097/01.prs.0000229193.31894.d0 PMID:17519734

Rohwer, A., Young, T., Wager, R., & Garner, P. (2017). Authorship, plagiarism, conflict of interest: Views and practices from low middle-income countries health researchers. *BMJ: Biomedia Journal Open*, *7*(11), 1–11. doi:10.1136/bmjopen-2017-018467

Rolston, H. (2002). What do we mean by the intrinsic value and integrity of plants and animals? In D. Heaf & J. Wirtz (Eds.), *Genetic Engineering and the Intrinsic Value and Integrity of Animals and Plants* (pp. 5–10). Pwlheli, UK: Hafan.

Rosenberg, J. (2017). *FDA launches pilot program to improve transparency of clinical trial information*. Retrieved from http://www.ajmc.com/printer?url=/focus-of-the-week/fda-launches-pilot-program-to-improve-transparency-of-clinical-trial-information- 1/2

Rosenthal, R. (1994). Science and ethics in conducting, analyzing, and reporting psychological research. *Psychological Science*, *5*(3), 127–134. doi:10.1111/j.1467-9280.1994.tb00646.x PMID:11652978

Ross, L. F., Loup, A., Nelson, R. M., Botkin, J. R., Kist, R., Smith, G. R. Jr, & Gehlert, S. (2010). Human subjects protections in community-engaged research: A research ethics framework. *Journal of Empirical Research on Human Research Ethics*, *5*(1), 5–17. doi:10.1525/jer.2010.5.1.5 PMID:20235860

Rotter, J. B. (1954). *Social learning and clinical psychology*. Englewood Cliffs, NJ: Prentice Hall. doi:10.1037/10788-000

Rousseau, J. J. (1974). *The social contract*. New York, USA: Plume/Meridian.

Russell, S. J., & Norvig, P. (2003). *Artificial Intelligence. A modern approach* (2nd ed.). Upper Saddle River, NJ: Prentice Hall.

Rusu, P. P., & Turliuc, M. N. (2011). Ethical issues of integrating spirituality and religion in couple and family therapy. *Revista Română de Bioetică*, *9*(1), 83–95.

Ryan, M. A. (1990). The argument for unlimited procreative liberty: A feminist critique. *The Hastings Center Report*, *20*(4), 6–12. doi:10.2307/3562759 PMID:2211090

Sacco, V. F., & Kennedy, L. W. (2002). *The Criminal Event: Perspective in Space and Time*. Belmont, CA: Wadsworth.

Salancik, G. R., & Pfeffer, J. (1978). A social information processing approach to job attitudes and task design. *Administrative Science Quarterly*, *4*(2), 224–253. doi:10.2307/2392563 PMID:10307892

Saldana, J. (2011). *The coding manual for qualitative researchers*. London: Sage Publications.

Sampson, R. J., & Laub, J. H. (1993). Structural variations in juvenile court processing: Inequality, the underclass, and social control. *Law & Society Review*, *27*(2), 285–311. doi:10.2307/3053938

Sampson, R. J., & Laub, J. H. (2003). Life-course desisters? Trajectories of crime among delinquent boys followed to age 70. *Criminology*, *41*(3), 555–592. doi:10.1111/j.1745-9125.2003.tb00997.x

Sandberg, A., & Bostrom, N. (2008). *Whole brain emulation: A roadmap*. Oxford, UK: Future of Humanity Institute, Oxford University. Retrieved from https://www.fhi.ox.ac.uk/brain-emulation-roadmap-report.pdf

Sandel, M. J. (2007). The Case against Perfection: Ethics in the Age of Genetic Engineering. Cambridge, MA: Harvard University Press (Belknap Press).

Sandu, A. (2011a, December). Proiectul de cercetare în ştiinţele sociale [The research project in social sciences]. *Jurnalul de studii juridice*.

Sandu, A. (2011c). Scientific writting. Epistemological and methodological considerations regarding research articles' elaboration. *Jurnalul de studii juridice*, (S1), 23-29.

Sandu, A. (2012b). Metode de cercetare în ştiinţa comunicării [Methods of research in communication science]. Curs universitar. Iaşi, Romania: Lumen.

Sandu, A. (2014). *Etică profesională şi transparenţă în administraţia publică* [Professional ethics and transparency in public administration]. Bucharest, Romania: Didactică şi Pedagogică.

Sandu, A. (2018). Constructionist Grounded Theory - GT. conceptual and methodological clarifications. *Revista Românească pentru Educaţie Multidimensională, 10*(1), 183-209. doi:10.18662/rrem/28

Sandu, G., Tudoran, S., & Rotaru, A. (2006). Dreptul omului de a nu fi supus selecţiei [Man's right not to be subject to selection]. In Educaţia în bioetică şi drepturile omului în România. Bucharest, Romania: Comisia Naţională a României pentru UNESCO.

Sandu, A. (2009). *Dimensiuni etice ale comunicării în postmodernitate* [Ethical dimensions of postmodern communication]. Iaşi, Romania: Lumen.

Sandu, A. (2011b). *Perspective semiologice asupra transmodernităţii* [Semiological perspectives on transmodernity] (2nd ed.). Iaşi, Romania: Lumen.

Sandu, A. (2012a). *Filosofia socială construcţionistă. Direcţii epistemice, etice şi pragmatice* [Social constructive philosophy. Epistemic, ethical and pragmatic directions]. Cluj-Napoca, Romania: Presa Universitară Clujeană.

Sandu, A. (2012c). *Social constructionist epistemology. A transmodern overview*. Saarbrucken, Germany: LAP LAMBERT Academic Publishing, GmbH & Co. KG.

Sandu, A. (2012d). *Etică şi deontologie profesională* [Ethics and professional deontology]. Iaşi, Romania: Lumen.

Sandu, A. (2016). *Social construction of reality as communicative action*. Cambridge, UK: Cambridge Scholars Publishing.

Sandu, A., & Unguru, E. (2014). *Acţiune comunicativă, justiţie deliberativă şi restaurativă. Perspective socio-juridice asupra medierii şi probaţiunii* [Communicative action, deliberative and restorative justice. Socio-legal perspectives on mediation and probation]. Bucharest, Romania: Tritonic.

Sandu, A., & Unguru, E. (2017). Several conceptual clarifications on the distinction between constructivism and social constructivism. *Postmodern Openings*, *8*(2), 51–61. doi:10.18662/po/2017.0802.04

Saulter, S. (2014). *Trusting the Future? Ethics of Human Genetic Modification*. Retrieved from: https://www.livescience.com/45392-ethics-of-altering-human-genetics.html

Saunders, M., Lewis, P., & Thornhill, A. (2009). *Research methods for business students*. Cape Town: Pearson Education.

Savulescu, J. (2001). Procreative beneficence: Why we should select the best children. *Bioethics, 15*(5-6), 413-426. doi:10.1111/1467-8519.00251

Savulescu, J. (2016). Genetic interventions and the ethics of enhancement of human beings. *Gazeta de Antropologia, 32*(2), 646-651. Retrieved from http://www.gazeta-antropologia.es/?p=4904

Savulescu, J., & Kahane, G. (2009). The moral obligation to create children with the best chance of the best life. *Bioethics*, *23*(5), 274–290. doi:10.1111/j.1467-8519.2008.00687.x PMID:19076124

Scherf, U., Becker, R., Chan, M., & Hojvat, S. (2010). Approval of novel biomarkers: FDA's perspective and major requests. *Scandinavian Journal of Clinical and Laboratory Investigation, 70*(suppl. 242), 96–102. doi:10.3109/00365513.2010.493415 PMID:20515286

Schiller, J., Black, W., & Murphy, P. V. (2000). *Crime and criminality.* Retrieved September 2012 from www.des.ucdavis.edu/faculty/Richerson/BooksOnline/He16- 95.pdf

Schoenherr, J. R. (2015). Scientific integrity in research methods. *Frontiers in Psychology*, *6*(1562), 1–5. doi:10.3389/fpsyg.2015.01562 PMID:26578994

Schoepfer, A., Carmichael, S., & Piquero, N. L. (2007). Do perceptions of punishment vary between white-collar and street crimes? *Journal of Criminal Justice*, *35*(2), 151–163. doi:10.1016/j.jcrimjus.2007.01.003

Schuman, R. (2014). Beware of the Gilderoy Lockharts of the university. *Slate*. Retrieved from http://www.slate.com/business/2017/12/romantic-japanese-christmas-train-ads.html

Schwartz, M. (2005). Universal moral values for corporate codes of ethics. *Journal of Business Ethics*, *59*(1/2), 27–44. doi:10.1023/A:1021393904930

Schwartz, S. (1990). Individualism-collectivism: Critique and proposed refinements. *Journal of Cross-Cultural Psychology*, *21*(2), 139–157. doi:10.1177/0022022190212001

Schwartz, S., & Bilsky, W. (1987). Towards a universal psychological structure of human values. *Journal of Personality and Social Psychology*, *53*(3), 550–562. doi:10.1037/0022-3514.53.3.550

SciDev Net. (2011). Ethics left behind as drug trials soar in developing countries. *The Guardian*. Retrieved from https://www.theguardian.com/global-development/2011/jul/04/ethics-left-behing-drug-trials-developing

Scripcaru, G., Ciucă, A., Scripcaru, C, & Isac, L. (2005). Manipulările genetice şi implicaţiile lor juridice [Genetic manipulations and their legal implications]. *Revista română de bioetică*, *3*(2).

Scripcaru, G., Ciucă, A., Scripcaru, C, & Isac, L. (2005). Manipulările genetice şi implicaţiile lor juridice [Genetic manipulations and their legal implications]. *Revista Română de Bioetică*, *3*(2).

Scripcaru, G., Ciucă, A., Astărăstoae, V., & Scripcaru, C. (2003). *Introducere în biodrept. De la bioetică la biodrept* [Introduction to biolaw. From bioethics to biolaw]. Bucharest, Romania: Lumina Lex.

Segarajasingham, S. (2014). Combating White Collar Crime: A Critical Study Of The Protection To Persons Making Disclosure Under Commercial Law of Sri Lanka. *International Journal of Business, Economics and Law*, *4*(3), 50–57.

Sekaran, U., & Bougie, R. (2010). *Research methods for business A skill building approach* (4th ed.). New York: John. Wiley & Sons.

Sekerka, L. E., & Zolin, R. (2007). Rule-bending: Can prudential judgment affect rule compliance and values in the workplace? *Public Integrity*, *9*(3), 225–243. doi:10.2753/PIN1099-9922090302

Senghor, L. (1965). *On African Socialism*. New York, USA: Stanford University Press.

Serin, R. C., Peters, R. D., & Barbaree, H. E. (1990). Predictors of psychopathy and release outcome in a criminal population. *Psychological Assessment*, *2*(4), 419–422. doi:10.1037/1040-3590.2.4.419

Shahnazarian, D., Hagemann, J., Aburto, M., & Susan, R. (2013). *Informed consent in human subjects research. Office for the protection of research subjects.* doi:10.1097/FCH.0b013e31822dda9e

Shamoo, A., & Resnik, D. (2015). *Responsible Conduct of Research* (3rd ed.). New York: Oxford University Press.

Shanahan, M. (2015). *The technological singularity*. Cambridge, MA: MIT Press.

Shapiro, S. C. (1991). Artificial Intelligence. In A. Ralston, E. D. Reilly, & D. Hemmendigner (Eds.), *Encyclopedia of Computer Science* (4th ed.). New York: Van Nostrand Reinhold.

Shapiro, S. P. (1990). Collaring the crime, not the criminal: Reconsidering the concept of white-collar crime. *American Sociological Review*, *2*(2), 346–365. doi:10.2307/2095761

Sharkey, N. (2008). The ethical frontiers of robotics. *Science*, *322*(5909), 1800–1801. doi:10.1126cience.1164582 PMID:19095930

Shashabuddin, S. (2009). Plagiarism in academia. *International Journal on Teaching and Learning in Higher Education*, *21*(3), 353–359.

Shaw Roy, L. (2003). Roe and the new frontier. *Harvard Journal of Law & Public Policy*, *27*(1), 339–384. PMID:15568255

Sheley, J. F. (2000). *Criminology*. Belmont, CA: Wadsworth/Thomas Learning.

Shetty, Y., & Saiyed, A. (2014). Analysis of warning letters issued by the US Food and Drug Administration to clinical investigators, institutional review boards and sponsors: A retrospective study. *Journal of Medical Ethics*, *41*(5), 398–403. doi:10.1136/medethics-2013-101829 PMID:24965716

Shiffrin, S. V. (1999). Wrongful life, procreative responsability and the significance of harm. *Legal Theory*, *5*(2), 117–148. doi:10.1017/S1352325299052015

Shivas, T. (2004). Contextualizing the vulnerability standard. *The American Journal of Bioethics*, *4*(3), 84–86. doi:10.1080/15265160490497137 PMID:16192157

Shoemaker, D. J. (2005). *Theories of delinquency: An examination of explanations of delinquent behavior*. New York, NY: Oxford University Press.

Shukla, A. (2017). *What is innovation? Why is innovation important.* Retrieved from https://www.paggu.com/getting-into-roots/what-is-innovation-why-innovation-is-important/

Shulman, C., & Bostrom, N. (2012). How hard is artificial intelligence? Evolutionary arguments and selection effects. *Journal of Consciousness Studies*, *19*(7-8), 103–130.

Siegel, L. J., Welsh, B. C., & Senna, J. J. (2006). *Juvenile delinquency: Theory, practice and law*. Belmont, CA: Thomson/Wadsworth.

Simha, A., & Cullen, J. B. (2012). Ethical climates and their effects on organizational outcomes: Implications from the past and prophecies for the future. *The Academy of Management Perspectives*, *26*(4), 20–34. doi:10.5465/amp.2011.0156

Simpson, S. S. (2013). White-collar crime: A review of recent developments and promising directions for future research. *Annual Review of Sociology*, *39*(1), 309–331. doi:10.1146/annurev-soc-071811-145546

Simpson, S. S., & Piquero, N. L. (2002). Low self-control, organizational theory, and corporate crime. *Law & Society Review*, *4*(2), 509–548. doi:10.2307/1512161

Skilicorn, N. (2016). What is innovation? 15 experts share their innovation definitions. *Ideas to Value*. Retrieved from https://www.ideatovalue.com/inno/nickskillicorn/2016/03/innovation-15-experts-share-innovation-definition/

Skinner, B. F. (1938). *The behavior of organisms*. New York, NY: Appleton-Century.

Skinner, B. F. (1963). Operant behavior. *The American Psychologist*, *18*(8), 503–515. doi:10.1037/h0045185

Slapper, G., & Tombs, S. (1999). *Corporate crime*. Longman Publishing.

Smart, R. N. (1958). Negative utilitarianism. *Mind*, *67*(268), 542–543. doi:10.1093/mind/LXVII.268.542

Smith, R. L. (1992). Ethical issues in marital and family therapy: Who is the client? In R. L. Smith & P. Stevens-Smith (Eds.), *Family Counseling and Therapy: Major Issues and Topics*. Ann Arbor, MI: ERIC/CAPS Publications.

Snyder, D. L., & Nelson, R. M. (2018). The Food and Drug Administration's federal review of a pediatric muscular dystrophy protocol. *IRB*, *40*(1), 18–20. Retrieved from https://www.thehastingscenter.org/irb_article/food-drugadministrations-federal-review-pediatricmuscular-dystrophy-protocol/ PMID:29910527

Soley, S. (2017). *White collar crime: The role of the firm in occupational crime* (Unpublished Doctoral Dissertation). University of Pennsylvania.

Sorensen, J. B. (2002). The strength of corporate culture and the reliability of firm performance. *Administrative Science Quarterly*, *47*(1), 70–91. doi:10.2307/3094891

Sorokina, N., Artyukhov, A., & Degtyarova, I. (2017). *Akademichna dobrochesnist': problemy dotrymannya ta priorytety poshyrennya sered molodykh vchenykh* [Academic integrity: problems of compliance and priorities of spread among young scientists]. Dnipro, Ukraine: Dnipropetrovsk Regional Institute of Public Administration.

Sowle Cahill, L. (1993). The embryo and the fetus: New moral contexts. *Theological Studies*, *54*(1), 124–142. PMID:11656434

Sparrow, R. (2007). Procreative beneficence, obligation and eugenics. *Genomics, Society, and Policy*, *3*(3), 43–59. doi:10.1186/1746-5354-3-3-43

Specker, J., Focquaret, F., Raus, K., Sterckx, S., & Schermer, M. (2014). The ethical desirability of moral bioenhancement: A review of reasons. *BMC Medical Ethics*, *15*(1), 1–17. doi:10.1186/1472-6939-15-67 PMID:25227512

Stachowicz-Stanusch, A., & Simha, A. (2013). An empirical investigation of the effects of ethical climates on organizational corruption. *Journal of Business Economics and Management*, *14*(1), 433–446. doi:10.3846/16111699.2012.744345

Steinbock, B. (2009). *Moral status, moral value and human embryos: Implications for stem cell research*. Oxford Handbooks Online. doi:10.1093/oxfordhb/9780199562411.003.0019

Stem Cells. (n.d.). *Introduction. Unipotent, multipotent, pluripotent & totipotent stem cells*. Retrieved from https://stephyboo96.weebly.com/unipotent-multipotentpluripotent--totipotent-stem-cells.htm

Stiegler, B. (1998). *Technics and time: The fault of epimetheus*. Palo Alto, CA: Stanford University Press.

Stoenescu, A. M. (2017). *Citarea și infracțiunea de plagiat* [Citation and the offense of plagiarism]. Retrieved from https://www.cotidianul.ro/citarea-si-infractiunea-de-plagiat/

Stolba, C. (2012). Overcoming motherhood: Pushing the limits of reproductive choice. *Policy Review*, 116.

Stolker, M. (2005). Legal journals: In pursuit of a more scientific approach. *European Journal of Legal Education*, *2*(2), 77–79. doi:10.1080/16841360600844796

Storrs Hall, J. (2007). *Beyond AI: Creating the conscience of the machine*. Amherst, MA: Prometheus Books.

Sugarman, J. (2015). Ethics and germline gene editing. *EMBO Reports*, *16*(8), 879–880. doi:10.15252/embr.201540879 PMID:26138102

Su, H. Y. (2014). Business ethics and the development of intellectual capital. *Journal of Business Ethics*, *119*(1), 87–98. doi:10.100710551-013-1623-4

Sukamolson, S. (1995). English Language Education policy in Thailand. *Asian Englishes*, *1*(1), 68–91. doi:10.1080/13488678.1998.10800995

Sutherland, E. H. (1940). White-collar criminality. *American Sociological Review*, *5*(1), 1–12. doi:10.2307/2083937

Sutherland, E. H. (1949). *White Collar Crime*. New York: Dryden Press.

Swazo, N. K. (2006). Calculating risk/benefit in X-linked severe combined immune deficiency disorder (X-SCID) gene therapy trials: The task of ethical evaluation. *The Journal of Medicine and Philosophy: A Forum for Bioethics and Philosophy of Medicine, 31*(5), 533–564, doi:10.1080/03605310600912709

Swedberg, K. (2008). Who is an author? *European Journal of Heart Failure*, *10*(6), 523–524. doi:10.1016/j.ejheart.2008.05.002 PMID:18502171

Tafida, A., Kasim, U., & Chima, P. (2015). Analysis of factors enhancing pitfall in research and teaching of the Nigerian university system. *International Journal of Higher Education*, *4*(3), 82–89. doi:10.5430/ijhe.v4n3p82

Talha, M., Sallehhuddin, A., Masoud, M. S., & Said, A. M. A. (2013). An analysis of moral intensity, intention and socially responsible investment behaviour among fund managers of Malaysian unit trust companies. *International Journal of Managerial and Financial Accounting*, *5*(2), 162–177. doi:10.1504/IJMFA.2013.053210

Tangwa, G. (2000). The traditional African perception of a person: Some implications for bioethics. *The Hastings Center Report*, *30*(5), 39–43. doi:10.2307/3527887 PMID:11057387

Temkin, L. (1993). Inequality: a complex notion. In *Inequality* (pp. 19–52). New York: Oxford University Press.

Tempels, P. (1959). *Bantu philosophy*. Paris, France: Preśence Africaine.

The Academy of Economic Studies in Bucharest (ASE), Directorate of Research and Innovation Management. (n.d.). *Proceduri* [Procedures]. Retrieved from http://www.dmci.ase.ro/index.php/dmci/proceduri

The Bucharest Early Intervention Project (BEIP). (n.d.). *About us*. Retrieved from http://www.bucharestearlyinterventionproject.org/About-Us.html

The Convention for the Protection of Human Rights and Dignity of the Human Being with regard to the Application of Biology and Medicine: Convention on Human Rights and Biomedicine. (1997).

The European Code of Conduct for Research Integrity. (2017). Retrieved from https://ec.europa.eu/research/participants/data/ref/h2020/other/hi/h2020-ethics_code-of-conduct_en.pdf

The Journal of Physiology and Pharmacology. (n.d.). *Notice to contributors*. Retrieved from http://www.jpp.krakow.pl/

The National Commission for the Protection of Human Subjects of Biomedical and Behavioral Research (NCPHSBBR). (1979). *The Belmont Report. Ethical principles and guidelines for the protection of human subjects of research*. Retrieved from https://www.hhs.gov/ohrp/sites/default/files/the-belmont-report-508c_FINAL.pdf

The Nuremberg Code of 1949. (n.d.). Retrieved from https://history.nih.gov/research/downloads/nuremberg.pdf

The Nuremberg Code. (1946). Retrieved from https://history.nih.gov/research/downloads/nuremberg.pdf

Thomas, N., & O'Kane, C. (1998). The ethics of participatory research with children. *Children & Society*, *12*(5), 336–348. doi:10.1111/j.1099-0860.1998.tb00090.x

Thorndike, E. L. (1898). *Animal intelligence: An experimental study of the associative processes in animals*. New York: The Macmillan Company. doi:10.1037/10780-000

Tillyer, M. S. (2015). General multilevel opportunity and crime events. *Journal of Contemporary Criminal Justice*, *31*(1), 107–121. doi:10.1177/1043986214552621

Ţîrdea, T. N. (2006). Demnitatea umană din perspectivă planetară şi bioetică [Human dignity from a planetary and bioethical perspective]. In Educaţia în bioetică şi drepturile omului în România [Education in Bioethics and Human Rights in Romania]. Bucharest, Romania: Academic Press.

Toader, T. (2012). *Drept penal. Partea specială* [Criminal law. The special part]. Bucharest, Romania: Hamangiu.

Tolochko, O. (1993). Dvi ne zovsim akademichni dyskusiyi (I.A.Lynnychenko, D. I. Bahaliy, M. S. Hrushevs'kyy) [Two not entirely academic discussions (I.A. Lynnychenko, D.I. Bahalii, M.S. Hrushevsky)]. In P. S. Sokhan (Ed.), Ukrainian Archeographical Yearbook (pp. 92–104). Academic Press.

Tong, R. (2002). Teaching bioethics in the new millennium: Holding theories accountable to actual practices and real people. *The Journal of Medicine and Philosophy*, *27*(4), 417–432. doi:10.1076/jmep.27.4.417.8609 PMID:12221502

Trivino, J. L. P. (2015). Equality of access to enhancement technology in a posthumanist society. *Dilemata, 7*(19), 53-63. Retrieved from: https://dialnet.unirioja.es/descarga/articulo/5203952.pdf

Trump's budget plan cuts funding for arts, humanities and public media. (2017, March 16). Retrieved from https://www.npr.org/2017/03/16/520401246/trumps-budget-plan-cuts-funding-for-arts-humanities-and-public-media?t=1532423598874

Turiel, E. (1983). *The development of social knowledge: Morality and convention*. New York: Cambridge University Press.

Turiel, E. (1998). Moral development. In W. Damon & N. Eisenberg (Eds.), Handbook of Child Psychology: Vol. 3. *Social, Emotional, and Personality Development* (5th ed.; pp. 863–932). New York: Cambridge University Press.

Turliuc, M. N. (2008). Ethical Dimensions in Couple and Family Therapy. *Revista Română de Bioetică*, *6*(3), 106–113.

Tyler, T. R., & Blader, S. L. (2005). Can businesses effectively regulate employee conduct? The antecedents of rule following in work settings. *Academy of Management Journal*, *48*(6), 1143–1158. doi:10.5465/amj.2005.19573114

U.S. National Institutes of Health; Recombinant DNA Advisory Committee. (2000). Prenatal gene tranfer: scientific, medical, and ethical issues: a report of the Recombinant DNA Advisory Committee. *Human Gene Therapy*, *11*(8), 1211–1229. doi:10.1089/10430340050015257 PMID:11660775

Uganda National Council of Science and Technology. (2014). *National guidelines for research involving humans as research participants*. Retrieved from https://uncst.go.ug/guidelines-and-forms/

UNICEF. (2017). *Cei mai vulnerabili copii din instituţiile rezidenţiale rămân o necunoscută datorită datelor incomplete* [The most vulnerable children in residential institutions remain unknown due to incomplete data]. Retrieved from http://www.unicef.ro/media/unicef-cei-mai-vulnerabili-copii-din-institutiile-rezidentiale-raman-o-necunoscuta-datorita-datelor-incomplete/

Unitatea Executivă pentru Finanţarea Învăţământului Superior (UeFiscadi). (2011). [Executive Unit for Financing Higher Education]. *Clasificare universităţi şi ierarhizare programe de studii* [Classification of universities and hierarchy of study programs]. Retrieved from http://old.uefiscdi.ro/articole/2535/Clasificare-universitati-si-ierarhizare-programe-de-studii.html

Unitatea Executivă pentru Finanţarea Învăţământului Superior, a Cercetării, Dezvoltării şi Inovării (UeFiscadi). (n.d.). [Executive Unit for Financing Higher Education, Research, Development and Innovation]. *Programul Idei. Arhivă.* Retrieved from http://old.uefiscdi.ro/Public/cat/70/Program-IDEI--arhiva.html

United Kingdom. (1990). *Law on Human Fertilization and Embryo Status*. Retrieved from https://www.legislation.gov.uk/ukpga/1990/37/contents

United States Code of Federal Regulations Title 45, Part 46. (n.d.). Retrieved from https://www.law.cornell.edu/cfr/text

United States National Commission for the Protection of Human Subjects of Biomedical and Behavioral Research. (1979). *The Belmont report: Ethical principles and guidelines for the protection of human subjects of research.* Washington, DC: Department of Health, Education, and Welfare.

University of Bucharest (UB). (n.d.). *Code of Ethics of the University.* Retrieved from http://www.unibuc.ro/n/despre/Codul_de_etica_al_Universitatii_din_Bucuresti.php

US Department of Health and Human Services, The Office of Research Integrity (ORI). (n.d.). *Chapter 1: The Ethical Basis of RCRH.* Retrieved from https://ori.hhs.gov/education/products/ucla/chapter1/Chapter1.pdf

USA Federal Law No. 107-116/1996. (n.d.). *The Dickey Amendment.* Retrieved from https://www.congress.gov/115/bills/hr4573/BILLS-115hr4573ih.pdf

USA President Barack Obama Presidential Order No 10668, . (2009, March 11). *Federal Register, 74*(46). Retrieved from https://www.gpo.gov/fdsys/pkg/FR-2009-03-11/pdf/E9-5441.pdf

USA President George W. Bush Presidential Order No. 13435. (2007, June 20). *Federal Register, 72*(120). Retrieved from https://www.gpo.gov/fdsys/pkg/FR-2007-06-22/pdf/07-3112.pdf

USA, California. (n.d.). *California Penal Code.* Retrieved from https://codes.findlaw.com/ca/penal-code/

USA, Illinois. (n.d.). *Illinois Compiled Statutes.* Retrieved from https://en.wikipedia.org/wiki/Illinois_Compiled_Statutes

USA, Kentucky. (n.d.). *Kentucky Revised Statutes.* Retrieved from https://law.justia.com/codes/kentucky/

USA, Louisiana. (n.d.). *Louisiana Revised Statutes.* Retrieved from https://legis.la.gov/legis/Laws_Toc.aspx?folder=75&level=Parent

USA, Maine. (n.d.). *Maine Revised Statutes.* Retrieved from http://legislature.maine.gov/statutes/search.htm

USA, Massachussets. (n.d.). *Massachussets General Laws.* Retrieved from https://malegislature.gov/Laws/GeneralLaws

USA, Michigan. (n.d.). *Michigan Compiled Laws, Public Health Code, Legea nr. 368/1978.* Retrieved from http://www.legislature.mi.gov/(S(br2uiku2tigmzvfu3cqrzxkl))/mileg.aspx?page=MCLBasicSearch

USA, Minnesota. (n.d.). *Minnesota Statutes.* Retrieved from https://www.revisor.mn.gov/statutes/

USA, New Hampshire. (2001). *New Hampshire Revised Statutes of 2001.* Retrieved from https://law.justia.com/codes/new-hampshire/

USA, New Mexico. (n.d.). *New Mexico Statutes.* Retrieved from http://public.nmcompcomm.us/nmnxtadmin/

USA, North Dakota. (n.d.). *North Dakota Century Code.* Retrieved from https://law.justia.com/codes/north-dakota/

USA, Pennsylvania. (n.d.). *Pennsylvania Constitutional Statutes.* Retrieved from http://guides.libraries.psu.edu/law-pennsylvania/statutes

USA, South Dakota. (n.d.). *South Dakota Codified Laws.* Retrieved from https://law.justia.com/codes/south-dakota/

Van der Graaf, R., Van der Zande, I. S. E., Den Ruijter, H. M., Oudijk, M. A., Van Delden, J. J. M., Rengerink, K. O., & Groenwold, R. H. H. (2018). Fair inclusion of pregnant women in clinical trials: An integrated scientific and ethical approach. *Trials, 19*(1), 78–86. doi:10.118613063-017-2402-9 PMID:29378652

Van der Veer, N. L., Drachman, D., Ahad, S., Silvers, G., & Ramos, G. (2011). Voluntariness to consent to research in a voluntarily and involuntarily hospitalized psychiatric populations. *Journal of Empirical Research on Human Research Ethics, 6*(1), 55–61. doi:10.1525/jer.2011.6.1.55 PMID:21460588

Van Fleet, D. D., & Van Fleet, E. W. (2006). Internal terrorists: The terrorists inside organizations. *Journal of Managerial Psychology*, *21*(8), 763–774. doi:10.1108/02683940610713280

Van Hoof, W., Meesters, K., Dossche, L., Christiaens, D., De Bruyne, P., & Vande Walle, J. (2018). Ethical considerations of researchers conducting pediatric clinical drug trials: A qualitative survey in two Belgian University Children's Hospitals. *European Journal of Pediatrics, 177*(7), 1003–1008. doi:00431-018-3151-9 doi:10.1007

Vanderpool, H. Y. (1996). *The ethics of research involving human subjects*. Hagerstown, MD: University Publishing Group.

Vasiu, I. (2004). Manipularea genetică. Implicaţii penale [Genetic manipulation. Criminal implications]. *Revista de Drept Penal*, *3*, 56–63.

Vaughan, D. (1992). The macro-micro connection in white-collar crime theory. *White-collar crime reconsidered*, 124-145.

Vaughan, E. D. (1981). Recent development in white-collar crime theory and research. In *The Mad, The Bad, and the Different* (pp. 135–155). Lexington, MA: Lexington Books.

Veeva, G. K. (2017). Announces EDC and eSource to transform clinical data management. *Drug Discovery Today*, *20*(3). Retrieved from https://www.veeva.com/resources/veeva-announces-edc-and-esource-to-transform-clinical-data-management/

Velasquez, M. G. (2006). *Business Ethics: Concepts and Cases* (6th ed.). Boston, MA: Pearson Publishing.

Verhoef, H., & Michel, C. (1997). Studying morality within the African context: A model of moral analysis and construction. *Journal of Moral Education*, *26*(4), 389–407. doi:10.1080/0305724970260401

Veruggio, G. (2002). Views and visions in Robotics. Hearing at the Italian Senate's 7th Permanent Commission, Rome, Italy.

Veruggio, G. (2005). The birth of roboethics. In *International Conference on Robotics and Automation - ICRA 2005, IEEE International Conference on Robotics and Automation. Workshop on Robo-Ethics*. Barcelona, Spain: IEEE.

Veterans Health Administration (VHA). (2009). VHA Handbook 1004.1, Informed consent for treatment and procedures. Retrieved from http://www.ethics.va.gov/docs/policy/VHA_Handbook_1004-01_Informed_Consent_Policy_20090814.pdf

Vicol, M. C., & Astărăstoae, V. (2009). Principiul beneficiului [The beneficence principle]. In V. Astărăstoae, S. Loue & B. G. Ioan (Eds.), Etica cercetării pe subiecţi umani [Ethics of Research on Human Subjects]. Iaşi, Romania: "Gr. T. Popa" U.M.F. Iaşi Publishing House.

Victor, B., & Cullen, J. B. (1987). A theory and measure of ethical climate in organizations. *Research in Corporate Social Performance and Policy*, *9*(1), 51–71.

Victor, B., & Cullen, J. B. (1988). The organizational bases of ethical work climates. *Administrative Science Quarterly*, *4*(4), 101–125. doi:10.2307/2392857

Vinge, V. (1993). The coming technological singularity: How to survive in the post-human era. In *NASA Lewis Research Center, Vision 21: Interdisciplinary Science and Engineering in the Era of Cyberspace* (pp. 11–22). San Diego, CA: NASA Lewis Research Center.

Vintan, L. (2006). Calitatea cercetării prin abordări scientometrice [Quality of research through scientometric approaches]. *Euroeconomia, 21*(53).

Vithal, R., & Jansen, J. (2010). *Designing Your First Research Proposal: A Manual for Researchers in Education and the Social Sciences*. Juta Legal and Academic Publishers.

Wadesango, N. (2015). Publish or perish: Impediments to research output and publication. *Kamla-Raj: International Journal of Education Science*, *6*(1), 57–63. doi:10.1080/09751122.2014.11890118

Walker, S., McAuslane, N., Liberti, L., Leong, J., & Salek, S. (2015). A universal framework for the benefit-risk assessment of medicines: Is this the way forward? *Therapeutic Innovation & Regulatory Science*, *49*(1), 17–25. doi:10.1177/2168479014547421

Walsh, R. T. G. (2015). Introduction to ethics in psychology: Historical and philosophical grounding. *Journal of Theoretical and Philosophical Psychology*, *35*(2), 69–77. doi:10.1037/teo0000015

Wassenaar, D. R. (2012). Ethical considerations in international research collaboration: The Bucharest Early Intervention Project. *Infant Mental Health Journal*, *27*(6), 577–580. doi:10.1002/imhj.20108 PMID:28640375

Webber, S. (2007). Ethical climate typology and questionnaire: A discussion of ınstrument modifications. *Journal of Academic Librarianship*, *33*(5), 567–580. doi:10.1016/j.acalib.2007.05.003

Weijer, C., & Emanuel, E. J. (2000). Protecting communities in biomedical research. *Science*, *289*(5482), 1142–1144. doi:10.1126cience.289.5482.1142 PMID:10970227

Weisburd, D., Waring, E., & Chayet, E. (1995). Specific deterrence in a sample of offenders convicted of white collar crimes. *Criminology*, *33*(4), 587–607. doi:10.1111/j.1745-9125.1995.tb01191.x

Weisser-Lohmann, E. (2012). Ethical aspects of vulnerability in research. *Poiesis & Praxis: International Journal of Ethics of Science and Technology Assessment*, *9*(1-2), 157–162. doi:10.100710202-012-0109-2 PMID:23205001

Wells, I. (2006). Survey elicits couples' views on donating unused embryos. *OB GYN News*. Retrieved from https://www.highbeam.com/doc/1G1-149059397.html

Wells, T. (2014). Recovering Adam Smith's ethical economics. *Real World Economics Review*, *68*, 90–97.

Welman, J. C., & Kruger, S. J. (2005). *Research Methodology* (3rd ed.). Cape Town: Oxford University Press.

Wendler, D., & Miller, F. G. (2007). Assessing research risks systematically: The net risks test. *Journal of Medical Ethics*, *33*(8), 481–486. doi:10.1136/jme.2005.014043 PMID:17664310

What is wrong with "publish or perish". (2013, March 28). *Neuroskeptic*. Retrieved from http://blogs.discovermagazine.com/neuroskeptic/2013/03/28/whats-wrong-with-publish-or-perish/#.WkJ5GrMo_Mx

Wheeler, S. (1992). The problem of white-collar crime motivation. In K. Schlegal & D. Weisburd (Eds.), *White collar crime reconsidered*. Boston, MA: Northeastern University Press.

Wilcox, P., Gialopsos, B. M., & Land, K. C. (2013). Multilevel criminal opportunity. In The Oxford Handbook of Criminological Theory (pp. 579-601). New York: Oxford Univ. Press.

Wilcox, P., & Cullen, F. T. (2017). *Communities and crime: An enduring American challenge*. Temple University Press.

Wilcox, P., & Cullen, F. T. (2018). Situational Opportunity Theories of Crime. *Annual Review of Criminology*, *4*, 1–17.

Wilcox, P., & Gialopsos, B. M. (2015). Crime-event criminology: An overview. *Journal of Contemporary Criminology*, *31*(1), 4–11. doi:10.1177/1043986214552601

Wilcox, P., Sullivan, C. J., Jones, S., & Van Gelder, J. L. (2014). Personality and opportunity: An integrated approach to offending and victimization. *Criminal Justice and Behavior*, *41*(7), 880–901. doi:10.1177/0093854813520603

Wilkins, A. L., & Ouchi, W. G. (1983). Efficient cultures: Exploring the relationship between culture and organizational performance. *Administrative Science Quarterly*, *28*(3), 468–481. doi:10.2307/2392253

Wimbush, J. C., Shepard, J. M., & Markham, S. E. (1997). An empirical examination of the relationship between ethical climate and ethical behavior from multiple levels of analysis. *Journal of Business Ethics*, *16*(16), 1705–1716. doi:10.1023/A:1017952221572

Witze, A. (2015). Does innovation always come from science? *Nature: International Weekly Journal of Science*, *527*(7576), 11–19. doi:10.1038/527011f

Wojciech, W., Sebastian, S., Maciejewski, P., Kłosiewicz–Wąsek, B., Bednarz, B., & Budaj, A. (2012). Participation in thrombolytic trials delays reperfusion therapy in acute myocardial infarction. *Kardiologia Polska*, *70*(8), 775–780. doi:10.5603/kp.2013.0191 PMID:22933207

Woodcock, J. (2018). *2017 Progress Report. Personalized medicine at FDA. On the approval of new personalized medicine indications for Kalydeco and Keytruda*. Silver Spring, MD: Center for Drug Evaluation and Research (CDER), FDA. Retrieved from http://www.personalizedmedicinecoalition.org/Userfiles/PMC-Corporate/file/PM_at_FDA_2017_Progress_Report.pdf

World Health Organisation (WHO). (1995). Guidelines for good clinical practice for trials on pharmaceutical products. In WHO Expert Committee on Selection and Use of Essential Medicines, WHO Technical Report Series, No. 850, Appendix 3, Sixth report: The Use of Essential Drugs. Geneva, Switzerland: WHO.

World Medical Association (WMA). (1964). *Declaration of Helsinki - Ethical Principles for Medical Research Involving Human Subjects*. Retrieved from https://www.wma.net/policies-post/wma-declaration-of-helsinki-ethical-principles-for-medical-research-involving-human-subjects/

World Medical Association. (1987). *Madrid Declaration on In Vitro Fertilization and Embryo Transfer.* Retrieved from https://www.wma.net/policies-post/wma-statement-on-in-vitro-fertilization-and-embryo-transplantation/

World Medical Association. (2013). *Declaration of Helsinki—Ethical principles for medical research involving human subjects*. Retrieved from http://www.wma.net/en/ 30publications/10policies/b3/

Wrape, E. R., & McGinn, M. M. (2018). Clinical and ethical considerations for delivering couple and family therapy via telehealth. *Journal of Marital and Family Therapy*. doi:10.1111/jmft.12319 PMID:29361194

Wy, L. (2009). Knowledge in writing a good scientific paper. *Malaysian Journal of Psychiatry*, *18*(2).

Yoell, W., Stewart, D., Wolpe, J., Goldstein, A., & Speierer, G. (1971). Marriage, morals and therapeutic goals: A discussion. *Journal of Behavior Therapy and Experimental Psychiatry*, *2*(2), 127–132. doi:10.1016/0005-7916(71)90027-9

Youdeowei, T., Uwandu, E., & Iruoma, K. (2016). Students lament compulsory handouts in tertiary institutions. *Vanguard*. Retrieved from https://www.vanguardngr.com/2016/11/students-lament-compulsory-handouts-tertiary-institutions/

Yücel, R., & Çiftci, G. E. (2012). Employees' perceptions towards ethical business attitudes and conduct. *Turkish Journal of Business Ethics*, *5*(9), 131–161.

Yudkowsky, E. (2009). *"Sympathetic Minds" value theory*. LessWrong. Retrieved from https://www.lesswrong.com/posts/FZWFFq652MNe/minds

Zachary, D. S., Sindhu, C., & Meissner, A. (2016). Molecular features of cellular reprogramming and development. *Nature Reviews. Molecular Cell Biology*, *17*(3), 139–154. doi:10.1038/nrm.2016.6 PMID:26883001

Zahra, S. A., Priem, R. L., & Rasheed, A. A. (2007). Understanding the causes and effects of top management fraud. *Organizational Dynamics*, *36*(2), 122–139. doi:10.1016/j.orgdyn.2007.03.002

Zajonc, A. (2006). *Noua fizică şi cosmologie. Dialoguri cu Dalai Lama* [The new physics and cosmology. Dialogues with the Dalai Lama]. Bucharest, Romania: Tehnică.

Zeanah, C. H., Nelson, C. A., Fox, N. A., Smyke, A. T., Marshall, P., Parker, S. W., & Koga, S. (2003). Designing research to study the effects of institutionalization on brain and behavioral development: The Bucharest Early Intervention Project. *Development and Psychopathology*, *15*(4), 885–907. doi:10.1017/S0954579403000452 PMID:14984131

Zeidler, D. L., & Schafer, L. E. (1984). Identifying mediating factors of moral reasoning in science education. *Journal of Research in Science Teaching*, *2*(1), 1–15. doi:10.1002/tea.3660210102

Zeidler, D. L., Walker, K. A., Ackett, W. A., & Simmons, M. L. (2002). Tangled up in views: Beliefs in the nature of science and responses to socioscientific dilemmas. *Science Education*, *86*(3), 343–367. doi:10.1002ce.10025

Zeng, W., & Resnik, D. (2010). Research integrity in China: Problems and prospects. *Developing World Bioethics*, *10*(3), 164–171. doi:10.1111/j.1471-8847.2009.00263.x PMID:19832885

Zhang, C. (2013). The evolution of rationality and modernity crisis. *Sociology Mind*, *3*(2), 179–184. doi:10.4236m.2013.32024

Zikmund, W., & Babin, B. (2010). *Exploring marketing research* (10th ed.). South Western Cengage Learning.

Zimbardo, P. G. (1973). On the ethics of intervention in human psychological research: With special reference to the Stanford prison experiment. *Cognition*, *2*(2), 243–256. doi:10.1016/0010-0277(72)90014-5 PMID:11662069

Zion, D., Gillam, L., & Loff, B. (2000). The Declaration of Helsinki, CIOMS, and the ethics of research on vulnerable populations. *Nature Medicine*, *6*(6), 615–617. doi:10.1038/76174 PMID:10835665

About the Contributors

Ana Frunză obtained a PhD in philosophy at Al. I. Cuza University of Iasi, in 2014, presenting a thesis entitled "A deconstructive approach to ethical values. Ethics expertise". She obtained an MA degree in Supervision and Social Planning in 2011, with a Bachelor's degree in Social Work in 2009. She is Scientific Researcher III at the LUMEN Center for Social and Humanistic Research. Her main scientific interests are applied ethics, applied philosophy, social work, supervision and ethics expertise. She is associated university assistant PhD "Stefan cel Mare" University from Suceava, Faculty of Law & Administrative Sciences, Romania. Ana Frunza is currently working on defining a new model of ethics expertise – the supervision of ethics, in conjunction with Professor Antonio Sandu, Doctor in Philosophy at LUMEN Center for Social and Humanistic Research from Iasi, Romania. She is the author of three books, "Etica şi dezvoltarea comunitară/ Ethics and community development" and "Către o nouă expertiză etică. Deconstruind valorile etice/ Towards a new ethics expertise – deconstructing the ethical values", "Supervizarea şi dezvoltarea profesională a asistenţilor sociali/ The supervision and the professional development of the social workers " published by LUMEN Publishing House between 2013 and 2017. Her research interests are ethics, research ethics, ethics expertise, supervision of ethics, applied philosophy.

* * *

Tebeanu Ana Voichita, PhD, is Lecturer at the Department for Teachers Training at the University POLITEHNICA of Bucharest and also a clinical psychologist. She received her PhD at the University of Bucharest with a thesis on clinical aspects of understanding metaphors and expressive language in people with schizophrenia. She received a MA in Clinical Psychology and Psychotherapy from the Faculty of Psychology and Educational Sciences, University of Bucharest, and a MA in Bioethics from the School of Medicine, Case Western Reserve University, Cleveland, USA. She was member of a multidisciplinary team in a postdoctoral project (conducted at the University of Medicine and Pharmacy "Gr.T.Popa" in Iasi, Romania) that has been studying for 3 years how the vulnerable individuals and groups gain access to primary health care services in Romania. Her major research interests include morality, mental health issues in educational settings and protection of vulnerable groups in educational and medical research.

Artem Artyukhov is a member of Processes and Equipment of Chemical and Petroleum-Refineries Department. Also he is a Coordinator of Strengthening Academic Integrity in Ukraine Project in Sumy State University, Head of subcommittee «Academic Integrity» (Ministry of Education and Science of Ukraine), member of Eurodoc Working Group on Research Integrity. Research interests: the problems of comparative analysis of the higher education development and transformation in Ukraine European and North American regions; third-world countries; academic and research integrity, ethics and moral standards in the global and national, systems of higher education and scientific community.

Octav Sorin Candel is currently a Ph.D. student and works at the Department of Psychology and Education Sciences at Alexandru Ioan Cuza of Iasi, Romania. He also holds a Master Degree in Couple and Family Therapy from the same University. His research has focused on the factors of couple satisfaction (ideal standards, entitlement, attachment, time perspective etc.) and his results have been published in different journals such as Romanian Journal of Applied Psychology, Romanian Journal of Psychology or The Journal of Social Psychology. He also took part in some research programs that focused on the development of different assessment tools for personality.

Tomita Ciulei (b. 1969) graduated (1996) from the Faculty of Philosophy, specialization Philosophy of "Alexandru Ioan Cuza" University, with a thesis on spiritual The Geography of Romanian Spirituality from Origins to Neagoe Basarab. In 2007, he becomes a PhD of the same University in Iasi with the thesis: The Classical Empiricism about the Sources of Knowledge John Locke and David Hume. He is an Associate Professor at the Faculty of Political Sciences, Letters and Communication, of Valahia University Targoviste. He is the author of over 30 articles and studies published in national and international journals, and in proceedings of international conferences.

Jean Pierre Cléro is a contemporary French philosopher. Professor at the University of Rouen, France. He teaches in the Department of Philosophy, specializing in Anglo-Saxon philosophy (Bentham's philosophy). His philosophical preoccupations go beyond the framework of analytical philosophy. Currently, he is director of the Bentham Center at the Institute of Political Science in Paris, and is a member of the International Academy of Sciences History in Brussels.

Floribert Patrick C. Endong (PhD) is a research consultant in the humanities and social sciences. He is a reviewer and editor with many scientific journals in the social sciences. His current research interest focuses on international communication, gender studies, digital media, media laws, international relations, culture and religious communication He is author of numerous peer-reviewed articles and book chapters in the above mentioned areas of interest.

Alexandra Huidu is a Researcher at the LUMEN Research Center in Social and Humanistic Sciences, Iasi, Romania. She is also a PhD Student at the Doctoral School of Sociology at University of Oradea, Romania and an Associated Researcher at the Research Laboratory for Family Sociology and Marital Couple at the Institute of Sociology of the Romanian Academy, Bucharest, Romania. Alexandra Huidu holds a bachelor's degree in law (from "Alexandru Ioan Cuza" University, Iasi, Romania) an a master's degree in criminal sciences (from "Alexandru Ioan Cuza" University, Iasi, Romania). Her main areas of interest include ethics in research, human medically assisted reproduction, research on human subjects, statute of the human embryo, stem cells research, genetic engineering, all of these from a combined perspective of law, sociology and bioethics. She is the author of the book: *Human Medically Assisted Reproduction. The Ethics of Incrimination versus Bioethics. A Comparative Law Study* (Lumen Publishing House, Iaşi, Romania, 2017) and of several articles on the topics abovementioned.

Ike V. Iyioke has multidisciplinary backgrounds in philosophy, international relations, journalism and teaching. Iyioke's doctorate degree is in philosophy (bioethics). He likes to explore questions pertaining to moral philosophy, particularly bioethics. He is also interested in environmental ethics, environmental science public policy, and the role these play in moral thinking. His research interests include issues about research subject/participant selection; human experimentation; biomedical research partnerships between Africa & the West; environmental ethics; environmental justice/racism; eugenics; science of life extension; morality in primitive cultures; and, consumer right to know. Iyioke has authored several publications including a book titled, Clinical Trials and the African Person: A Quest to Re-Conceptualize Responsibility.

Bebe Loff is Associate Professor and Director of the Michael Kirby Centre for Public Health and Human Rights and Monash University in Melbourne, Australia. Her research background is in human rights, law and ethics. She currently co-directs two Fogarty-funded training programs in research ethics India and Myanmar and previously directed a Fogarty-funded training program for trainees from countries in Asia and the Pacific. She has been a member of the Ethical Review Committee of the World Health Organization and the Australian Health Ethics Committee. She was also a member of the Steering Group of the Chinese Ethics Committee for Registering Clinical Trials, the Australian Bone Marrow Donor Registry Ethics Committee, Monash University Standing Committee on Ethics in Research Involving Humans, Mornington Peninsula Hospital Ethics Committee, and the Freemasons Hospital Ethics Committee. She was a member of the Victorian Ministerial Advisory Committee on Sex Work. She was a non-executive director of two community-based organisations: the Health Issues Centre and the Consumer Law Centre. She also served as a member of Commonwealth Intergovernmental Legal Working Party on HIV/AIDS, the Clinical Trials Committee of the Australian National Council on AIDS, Hepatitis C and Related Diseases, the National Public Health Partnership Steering Group for Evaluating Evidence on Public Health Interventions, the Department of Human Services, Genetic Services Advisory Committee, and the Advisory Committee to the Monash Medical Centre – Sexual Assault Centre. She has been an honorary consultant to the Victorian Law Reform Commission and was a Lancet correspondent.

Sana Loue, J.D., Ph.D., M.P.H., M.S.S.A., M.A., is a professor in the Department of Bioethics and also holds secondary appointments in Psychiatry and Global Health at the School of Medicine and in Social Work at the Mandel School of Applied Social Sciences at CWRU. She currently serves as the Vice Dean for Faculty Development and Diversity at the School of Medicine. In this capacity, she is responsible for the development of training programs to enhance faculty skills, including a broader understanding of the value of diversity in the context of research. Dr. Loue holds degrees in law (JD), epidemiology (PhD), medical anthropology (PhD), social work (MSSA), secondary education (MA), public health (MPH) and theology (MA). Dr. Loue directed a Fogarty-funded training program in research ethics for 12 years in collaboration with institutions in Russia, Romania, Nigeria, and Uganda. She has conducted research domestically and internationally, focusing on HIV risk and prevention, severe mental illness, family violence, and research ethics. She has served on the university's Institutional Review Committee (IRB), the university's Institutional Animal Care and Use Committee (IACUC) and on various data safety and monitoring boards. She has authored or edited more than 30 books and more than 100 peer-reviewed journal articles.

George Macarie, PhD, is Associate Lecturer at Department of Medical Psychology at the Faculty of Medicine Bucharest (Romania) and also clinical psychologist and psychotherapist. He received his PhD at the "Alexandru loan Cuza" University of Iasi with the thesis "Coping styles in prolonged stress exposure". His major research interests include Psychological effects of long-term adversity conditions, Stress and coping, Development of addictive behaviours and Inclusion strategies for people with mental health problems. Author of more than 30 published articles in the domain, he participated as Researcher or Evaluator in 5 national or international studies (funded by EU or other bodies).

Vannie Naidoo is a full-time staff member at the University of KwaZulu-Natal, South Africa, in the Faculty of Management and Law. Her field of teaching is in management, corporate strategy, project management and entrepreneurship. The research areas pursued by Dr Naidoo are in the areas of management, marketing, service marketing, entrepreneurship and social media and e-learning or learning with new technologies. She has presented papers at international conferences throughout the world and has written on various issues in management and marketing in journal articles and books.

Seçil (Bal) Taştan was born in İzmir in 1978. After completion of her bachelor degree in İstanbul University Faculty of Economics, Department of Public Administration, she studied her master degree in Human Resources Management &Development in Marmara University and she started her academic career as a research assistant in 2000. She obtained her PhD in Organizational Behavior from same university in 2011. She is working in Marmara University Faculty of Business Administration, Department of Business Administration (in English), sub-department of Organizational Behavior. She obtained Associate Professorship in 2017 in the area of Management-Strategy and Organizational Behavior. Her academic research studies include the organizational behavior, management and organization, industrial and organizational psychology, human resources management, organizational culture, leadership, and innovativeness. She has authored a number of academic research studies in academic journals and international conferences on these subjects.

Maria Nicoleta Turliuc is a Professor at the Department of Psychology, Faculty of Psychology and Sciences of Education, Alexandru Ioan Cuza University from Iaşi. She is the director of the Well-being, Stress and Resilience Laboratory, and director of the Centre for Personal Development and Professional Formation. Prof. Turliuc obtained the "Andrew Mellon" postdoctoral grant offered by Maison des sciences de l'homme (MSH, Paris, France) and Council of American Overseas Research Centers (Washington D.C.), and was the director or member of several other research grants. She published 5 author books, coordinated 6 volumes, and published more than 50 book chapters in the country, and abroad. Also, prof. Turliuc published more than 50 studies in ISI and BDI Journals (e.g., Journal of Happiness Studies, Journal of Family Psychology, International Journal of Stress Management, Journal of Loss and Trauma, Measurement and Evaluation in Counseling and Development, etc.).

Tetyana Vasilyeva is a Director of Oleg Balatskyi Academic and Research Institute of Finance, Economics and Management. Also she is a member of the Business Support Center in Sumy region of the European Bank for Reconstruction and Development, Editor-in-chief of the scientific journal "Business Ethics and Leadership". Research interests: banking, investment, risk management, innovation activity, social responsibility, education, academic and research integrity.

Index

G

H

I

M

N

O

P

R

S

T

U

V

W

www.ingramcontent.com/pod-product-compliance
Lightning Source LLC
LaVergne TN
LVHW081250011026
849162LV00006BA/1365